Summary of Contents

Enterprise Application Architecture

With VB, MTS and ASP

Joseph Moniz

Wrox Press Ltd. ®

Enterprise Application Architecture

wrox

Published by Wrox Press Ltd. Arden House, 1102 Warwick Rd, Birmingham, B27 6BH
Printed in Canada
2 3 4 5 TRI 00 99

ISBN 1-861002-58-0

Trademark Acknowledgements

Wrox has endeavored to provide trademark information about all the companies and products mentioned in this book by the appropriate use of capitals. However, Wrox cannot guarantee the accuracy of this information.

Credits

Author
Joseph Moniz

Managing Editor
Dominic Shakeshaft

Editors
Craig A. Berry
Kate Hall

Technical Reviewers
Richard Anderson
Rich Bonneau
Henri Cesbron
Steve Danielson
John Granade
Erik Hermansen

Technical Reviewers
Dan Maharry
Marc Simkin
Dorai Thodla
Donald Xie

Design/Layout
Frances Olesch

Cover
Andrew Guillaume
Concept by Third Wave
Photo by Bill Groethe

Index
Andrew Criddle

I dedicate this book:

To my Mom – who taught me to care

To my Dad – who taught me to see the things that weren't there… yet!

To Jenny and Laura – who I would be proud to call my daughters

And especially to Dawn – my friend, my soulmate, my Love

Acknowlegements

These are the most important pages in this book. This book was not a one-man effort. It would not have been possible without the help of some very wonderful groups of people.

The Core Object Team

When I began my last consulting assignment, I served as a mentor to some very talented individuals. They thought I could teach them some important things. They were right. But all I ever did was to teach them a few very simple concepts: break the problem down into smaller pieces, take on the pieces one step at a time, focus on that one piece, and make the solution as perfect as you possibly can. That's it. Then I asked them to do some things that anyone else would have *known* were impossible. You will find those things throughout the pages of this book. I was introduced to this bunch of wizards as their teacher. As I leave them, I do so in awe of their genius, as their student, and as their friend. Allow me to introduce in alphabetical order.

Glen Haberman – you would love this guy. His dedication and drive are the stuff that Rocky movies are made from. He may be the best VB programmer I have ever met. He writes his programs the way he lives, with integrity, loyalty, and honor.

Kenny Miller – quiet and brilliant, this guy doesn't need to think about database relationships. He is as in tune with these things as he is with the birds, trails, and mountains that he loves so dearly. What happens when Kenny and I together work is nothing short of magic. Every once in a while, you meet someone, your minds compliment each other, and great things happen.

Bill Rath – that should really read: Bill – third normal form *no problem* – Rath. One of the most important and difficult facets of engineering is identifying and isolating the problems. Bill may be one of the finest problem identifiers/isolators in the business. Our users owe this guy a big pat on the back. He is truly their champion.

Farzad Ziai – Farzad Ziai joined the core object team rather late during my assignment. Working with him was a joy. At first he was very quiet – taking in all of the information – then one day, everything clicked, and he just *knew* this stuff. Watching the light go on was really something to behold.

The Core Object Team's Manager

Monte Gloe – Monte is a programmer that moved into management. He alone was responsible for bulldozing through the financial and political impasses the team faced. He wisely insulated the members of the team from these distractions. Unfortunately, it is often too easy for us *technical* people to overlook the fact that it is people like Monte who enable us to practice our craft.

I listed the Object Team first, because I am a programmer and therefore in some ways a slave to concepts like chronological order. I met the object team before I met another team I am honored to be a part of.

The Wrox Team

One of the biggest reasons why I decided to write this book in the first place was because I had read just about everything that Wrox Press had published at the time. Every time I picked up one of their books, I stood in awe. I couldn't help but to imagine what kind of wondrous organization this Wrox Press must be, and I longed to be a part of it. Well, let me tell you that no matter how wonderful I had imagined it, the team at Wrox proved to be even better. I was fortunate enough to work very closely with two very talented and motivated editors. I can say in all honesty that the only reason that you are reading this book is because of their efforts. At times when I didn't think I could go on, these two encouraged, pushed, or **carried** me through the most difficult terrain.   Allow me to introduce:

Craig A. Berry – I thought I was the most driven person in the universe until I met Craig. There is no way for me to describe his contribution. You have to imagine a person who is capable of taking in more than 1000 pages of mostly raw code, developing an immediate understanding of both the general concepts and the finest details of that code, and then is somehow able to organize all of that information into something that actually makes sense. And, even if you can imagine someone that brilliant, you have to add to that image his writing ability. His talent is responsible for turning something as dry as my code into something that you should enjoy reading.

Kate Hall – Kate is another of Wrox's most talented editors. In addition to her technical expertise and her natural gift for writing, she also has a wonderful sense of style and art. If you find yourself grinning from time to time when you read through this book, you should think of Kate. She was quick to warn me when things were beginning to get too boring, and she was there to encourage me to when I dared what I thought might be a risky phrase here and there.

The Wrox Team Manager

Dominic Shakeshaft – The first person I got to know at Wrox was my Managing Editor Dominic Shakeshaft. He is the person who has enabled me to share my thoughts with you today. He stayed with me during the early phases, when this book was more of an idea than anything you could see or touch. It is lucky for me that he is one of those all-too-rare individuals who can actually see ideas when they are nothing more than a sparkle in someone's eye. His foresight is a wonderful thing, but if it wasn't for his ability to back that foresight up with his skill, talent, and perseverance you wouldn't be reading this book today. Dominic, I am forever in your debt.

In addition to the people I just mentioned, there are a lot of others at Wrox who worked hard to make this book a reality. I would like to thank them all. In addition to its in-house staff, Wrox uses a virtual army of very knowledgeable reviewers during its editing cycles. I am afraid that I am certain to miss some of them but I would like to thank: Richard Anderson, Rich Bonneau, Henri Cesbron, Steve Danielson, John Granade, Erik Hermansen, Dan Maharry, Marc Simkin, Dorai Thodla, and last but not least Donald Xie.

I also would like to thank some other individuals who helped to make this book possible including: Glade Slaugh, Brian Wieczorek, Tom Wempe, Pat Snow, David Bishop, Bubba Woodard, Grover Hickman, Cary Winters, Otto Doll, and Denise Luckhurst.

Person
Base Properties

ID
Last Name
First Name
Middle Name
Birth Date
Sex

Object Type Definitions

Object Typ

Superman OTD	Lower OTD	Engineer OTD	Doctor OTD	Student OTD	
Clerks	Specialty	Specialty	Specialty	Major	R
Sales	Hourly Rate	Experience	Certification	Minor	D
Property 3	Law School	Property 3	Property 3	Year	E
Property 4	Property 4	Property 4	Property 4	Property 4	P
Property 5	Property 5	Property 5	Property 5	Property 5	P
Property 6	Property 6	Property 6	Property 6	Property 6	P
Property 7	Property 7	Property 7	Property 7	Property 7	P
Property 8	Property 8	Property 8	Property 8	Property 8	P
Property 9	Property 9	Property 9	Property 9	Property 9	P
Property 10	Property 10	Property 10	Property 10	Property 10	P

Property Set Definitions

Property Set D

Table of Contents

Table of Contents

{831FDD16-0C5C-1 ...

Form frmPropNameControllers

Style = 3 'Fixed Dial

= "Properties for

eight = 4845

eft = 45

p = 330

idth = 11460

c = "Form1"

ton = 0 'False

d = -1 'True

ton = 0 'False

eight = 4845

idth = 11460

Taskbar = 0 'False

Person
Base Properties

ID
Last Name
First Name
Middle Name
Birth Date
Sex

Object Type Definitions

Object Ty

	Lawyer OTD	Engineer OTD	Doctor OTD	Student OTD
	Specialty	Specialty	Specialty	Major
	Hourly Rate	Experience	Certification	Minor
	Law School	Property 3	Property 3	Year
Property 4	Property 4	Property 4	Property 4	Property 4
Property 5	Property 5	Property 5	Property 5	Property 5
Property 6	Property 6	Property 6	Property 6	Property 6
Property 7	Property 7	Property 7	Property 7	Property 7
Property 8	Property 8	Property 8	Property 8	Property 8
Property 9	Property 9	Property 9	Property 9	Property 9
Property 10	Property 10	Property 10	Property 10	Property 10

Property Set Definitions

Property Set

Introduction

As a consultant, I move from job to job looking for new problems to solve. Over the many years I have been doing this job, I've come to notice that many of the problems I'm asked to solve, stem from the same core problems. In most cases, I find I'm teaching the developer teams practically the same solution again and again. Not that I want to write myself out of a job, but it seemed to me, if my solutions and techniques are so generically applicable, then many other developers and consultants could also benefit greatly from my experience.

This book represents the sum of my experiences distilled down into an accessible and structured form. I hope you will find the content as illuminating as many of my teams find it. I don't think enough people really realize the potential that is available to us these days for developing enterprise systems. Too many developers, consultants and managers alike, are limiting themselves with either antiquated or just plain erroneous beliefs. Yes, I said "beliefs"! You may think that we're really being limited by the technologies or our abilities, but more often than not its really our beliefs that are holding us back. For, if we don't believe that something can be done, then we won't even try. It's kind of like Schrödinger's Cat in quantum physics. The cat is neither alive nor dead until we observe it in either state. Therefore, it is illogical to believe it is either alive or dead until we know one way or the other. By the same logic, we shouldn't *believe* that we can't design or construct a system one particular way until we've tried.

You may be wondering what makes me so different, why should you pay any closer attention to what I've got to say? Well let me put it this way. I trained as a chemical engineer and not as a computer scientist. Although I might have read a few books on the subject, I've never had any formal training in OOP, data access, etc. What this means, for want of a better phrase, I don't know any better. Whereas many developers are constrained by what they think they know, or rather what they have been told to be true, I have nothing to hold me back. As far as I'm concerned there's no one looking over my shoulder telling me, "you can't do it that way." Anything is possible until you try, and if you don't try then you'll never know.

That, in essence, is what my book's all about. You won't find much of my code or my server farm design especially clever or original. Rather, I'm hoping that I will be able to change your horizons so that you no longer believe you *have* to design your system one way because that's the way its always been done. If the only thing you take away from this book is a more open mind, even if you disagree with most of what I propose, then my job will be complete. I prefer to think of this book more of a journey than a teaching opportunity, and I hope when you reach the end of the last chapter that you feel this way too.

What You Need to Use this Book

To run the code discussed in this book you'll need at least:

- ❏ Windows NT Workstation 4.0 Service Pack 4
- ❏ Windows NT Option Pack (this includes MTS, MSMQ, and IIS)
- ❏ SQL Server 6.5 - 7.0 is 10,000,000,000% better, but 6.5 will do fine for development
- ❏ Visual Basic 5.0, but of course 6.0 is much better
- ❏ Internet Explorer 4.01 Service Pack 1

What's Covered in This Book

This book is split into three major sections dealing with the infrastructure of an enterprise caliber system, what an Enterprise Caliber Data Object is and how to construct one, and how to build enterprise caliber applications.

Section I - The Infrastructure

The first section of this book is designed to give you a solid grounding in what the infrastructure of an Enterprise Caliber system should be like. I'll begin by introducing to you to the three fundamental objectives for an Enterprise Caliber system - that it is available, scalable and secure.

I'll show you that there is no need to have a mainframe to achieve these objectives and that they can be attained by having a well-designed group of servers (a cluster farm) at the heart of our enterprise.

The final chapter in this section, Chapter 4, introduces you to my extension of the n-tier architecture - the n-sphere architecture.

Section II - Enterprise Caliber Data Objects

In this section, we'll look at what I call Enterprise Caliber Data Objects. These objects are specially designed to handle all their data processing for you. What this means is you can point them at a data store and they can take care of all the data processing tasks for you. We'll see that this is because of eight key data handling processes that they expose.

We'll also see how we can divide these processes across the various physical sphere of the system so as to dramatically increase the availability and accessability of the core data.

Finally in this section, we'll see how we can extend the functionality of the data objects by allowing us to define a base object as a particular type and to easily extend the object's properties using a device called the Property Bag.

Section III - Building Enterprise Caliber Applications

Once we have both our hardware and software design, we'll look at how to put the various pieces together in such a way so as to allow us to quickly and easily throw together world-class applications. We'll see how the time and effort we spendt developing our data objects pays off, because we are now able to separate our business rules from our data - a key goal of Enterprise Architecture.

Finally in the book, we'll look at how to depoly our applications across the enterprise that we defned in Section I, by creating a web-based front end using ASP and DHTML.

Conventions Used

I've used a number of different styles of text and layout in the book to help differentiate between different kinds of information. Here are some of the styles I've used and an explanation of what they mean:

> **These boxes hold important, not-to-be forgotten, mission-critical details that are directly relevant to the surrounding text.**

Background information, asides and references appear in text like this.

- ❑ **Important Words** are in a bold font
- ❑ Words that appear on the screen, such as menu options, are in a similar font to the one used on screen, for example, the File menu
- ❑ Keys that you press on the keyboard, like *Ctrl* and *Enter*, are in italics
- ❑ All filenames, function names and other code snippets are in this style: DblTxtBx

Code that is new or important is presented like this:

```
Private Sub mobjPerson_Valid(blnIsValid As Boolean)

    cmdOK.Enabled = blnIsValid

End Sub
```

Whereas code that we've seen before or has little to do with the matter being discussed, looks like this:

```
Option Explicit

Private mstrButtonPressed As String
Private WithEvents mobjPropBag As UCPerson.clsPropBag
Private mcolPropValuHistory As UCPerson.colPropBags
Private mstrSourceControl As String
Private mcolPropItems As UCPerson.colPropItems
```

Source Code

All the projects that are given in this book can be downloaded from Wrox's web sites at:

```
http://www.wrox.com/
http://www.wrox.co.uk/
```

More information about the downloadable source code can be found in Appendix A.

Tell Us What You Think

This is my first book and I hope that you'll find it useful and enjoyable. You are the one that counts and I would really appreciate your views and comments on this book. You can contact me either by email (feedback@wrox.com) or via the Wrox web site.

{831FDD16-0C5C-1 D2 A9FC-6

Form frmPropNameControlLst

Style = 3 'Fixed Dialog

= "Properties for

eight = 4845

eft = 45

p = 330

idth = 11460

c = "Form1"

ton = 0 'False

d = -1 'True

con = 0 'False

eight = 4845

idth = 11460

Taskbar = 0 'False

Person
Base Properties

ID
Last Name
First Name
Middle Name
Birth Date
Sex

Object Type Definitions

Person OTD	Lawer OTD	Engineer OTD	Doctor OTD	Student OTD
	Specialty	Specialty	Specialty	Major
	Hourly Rate	Experience	Certification	Minor
	Law School	Property 3	Property 3	Year
Property 4	Property 4	Property 4	Property 4	Property 4
Property 5	Property 5	Property 5	Property 5	Property 5
Property 6	Property 6	Property 6	Property 6	Property 6
Property 7	Property 7	Property 7	Property 7	Property 7
Property 8	Property 8	Property 8	Property 8	Property 8
Property 9	Property 9	Property 9	Property 9	Property 9
Property 10	Property 10	Property 10	Property 10	Property 10

Property Set Definitions

1

Delivering an Enterprise

If you are anything like me, you're probably sick and tired of hearing the UNIX and Mainframe pros rattling off the reasons why our PC based systems can't handle the *tough jobs* their overpriced boxes perform. For quite a while now, we have had to bide our time, bite our tongues, and bear with their bloated senses of superiority. *That time has passed.* Our venerable PC is all grown up. It has matured into a powerful creature, more than capable of standing toe-to-toe with any of its alternatives. But be warned. This newfound prowess is really a double-edged sword. The fact that our equipment is up to the task doesn't mean that *we* are completely ready to step into the ring with the big boys yet. We still have a lot of work to do. This book is a step-by-step guide designed to give you all the tools you need to create an **Enterprise Caliber System** for your organization, no matter what size it is.

Using this Book

I want to avoid any confusion or misconceptions, so I want to make a couple of things clear at the start. First, the main focus of this book is the **design**, **development**, and **deployment** of world-class applications across a **distributed architecture**. What that really means, is that we can use as many machines as we need in order to accomplish a given task. So if we were collecting and managing information from every cash register across the globe for a major retail company, then we might need 80 or 100 machines to handle that task. But, if our task was to design and develop software, then we can accomplish that task with a single machine.

> *In other words, you can model an entire server farm and run all of the code in this book (or other code you develop using this technique) on a single Pentium class machine.*

Then you can take that code, and distribute it across 2, 3, 4 or even 100 or more machines if that is what the application calls for.

> You will not need to change a single line of code to re-deploy your application.

The reason I have emphasized the multi-machine platform in this book is so that I could give you the concepts and specific instructions you need to deploy and use your application across multi-machine platforms. Most of the books I have read go to great lengths to say that this can be done, but then they fail to give you a clue about *how* to actually do it. This book is intended as a practical guide for *delivering* an enterprise. So, it contains the real-world instructions you are likely to need.

Second, you might notice that there is a lot of code in this book. Please don't let the volume of code cause you to believe that the coding techniques in this book are difficult to accomplish. My teams use the code in this book every day to get real work accomplished quickly and efficiently. In other words, sometimes I know that the actual code itself is really more valuable than anything I might have to say about the code. I think a good programming book should be, kind of, like having a smart friend sitting next to you – one that you can count on. In other words, what you will learn in this book is not some 'pie-in-the-sky' theory of how things should be done. It's a *practical* guide that explains exactly *how* to do it.

I have presented the material in an order that I believe will give you the tools you need to be able to "read" the code more and more easily as the chapters progress. I have also provided several tools that will actually do the job of writing some of the more nasty sections of code for you. I think about it like this. If I can handle some of the coding chores for you then I have sort of paid a price for your time. I hope that price gives you the freedom you need to stop, take some time, and really consider some of the interesting ideas in this book without any unnecessary aggravation.

An Enterprise Caliber System

Distributed Architecture, ActiveX, Java Beans, OLE, DNA, ASP, XYZ, 123, blah blah blah. Right about now you are probably wondering if it will ever end. Don't worry so is everyone else. Every once in a while, just when I think I've got it all figured out, someone goes and throws another new twist at me, and I to begin to wonder if it is all worth it. How can I ever hope to build a reliable, stable system if someone keeps changing the rules? I will tell you how, take a hint from the classics. Even in these turbulent technical times, there are some timeless design principles that we can rely upon to guide us through the confusion. They are the same principles that good programmers and engineers have been using for years.

> *The designs that follow have been carefully crafted to allow us to construct a system that is powerful enough to meet the needs of today's enterprise while being flexible enough to allow an enterprise to grow and meet any future needs or programming challenges.*

The cornerstone of this design is that the entire system is constructed in a modular fashion, which divides the processing into *atomic units* that can be tuned with pinpoint accuracy. This same atomicity allows the system to be flexible enough to handle anything else Uncle Bill at Microsoft may be planning to throw at us.

The Physical System

It is not possible to buy the perfect piece or pieces of hardware that will magically give an organization an Enterprise Caliber system. This is a hard notion for many companies to swallow. In the past, it may have been a perfectly reasonable approach to buy the biggest and best mainframe (or midrange) available and depreciate the beast over the next X number of years. If a company needed more computing power, they just bought a bigger box – problem solved. Today, while I imagine it's still possible to just go out and buy the biggest and best mainframe, most companies have come to the conclusion that this monolithic approach is probably not the best way to solve an organization's long term information management problems.

I am not going to go into the cost benefit analysis between mainframe hardware and an enterprise hardware approach to a given problem. If you are reading this book, chances are that, either you or someone in your organization has looked at the numbers and come to the conclusion that the enterprise solution is the less expensive option for some of its computing needs.

Mainframes

What I do want to talk about is the problems that occur when you try to apply the mainframe (or buy a bigger box mentality) to the enterprise design problem. This image is supposed to represent a big mainframe connected to a large number of client workstations. When most people envision a physical information system this image, or one rather like it, is probably what they conjure up:

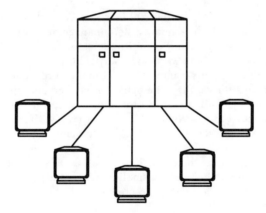

So, it is not surprising that when companies first started creating enterprise level client-server solutions that they first envisioned the client-server model as something of a scaled down mainframe. It seemed like a perfectly reasonable solution to buy a single, powerful, server and connect a bunch of clients to it. The problem with this approach is that a mainframe is really very much more than just a big box. It is really a finely tuned orchestration of **processes**. The fact that these processes are executed, more or less, in the same box made the management of these different processes an expected, understood, and vital responsibility of the system's keepers.

Enterprise Servers - The Wrong Way

When companies took their first run at designing an enterprise using servers in place of the mainframe, the structured environment that the mainframe had provided was missing. When the performance of these systems turned out to be less than anticipated everyone naturally assumed that this was due to the new server's physical lack of processing power:

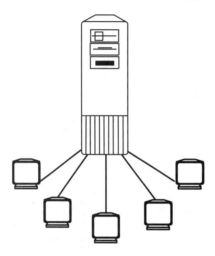

Of course the real problem was not the less powerful machine as much as it was the system's lack of structure. This was due to the fact that the overall system management functions, that the mainframe world takes for granted, were often not identified, misunderstood, or just plain overlooked. In other words, in these server-based systems, there were few if any reins placed upon the clients. There was nothing stopping any, or all of the clients from initiating 1,000,000 row queries against a database simultaneously. You can imagine the results – the machines choked and died. Of course, everyone attributed the server's inability to handle the load to its most noticeable feature – its diminutive CPU. In other words, most people failed to realize that the real reason mainframes can handle so many clients is because mainframe systems don't let their clients run amok in the system.

Anyway it seems that the industry as a whole concluded that, because of their lack of processing power, server-based systems could only handle a small number of users. What followed was an understandable, but incorrect impression of how to create an Enterprise Caliber system.

> *PC based systems are not the only ones that have fallen to this misconception; UNIX servers are also deployed in nearly the same fashion in most of the places where I have worked.*

Take a look at the next image and see if it looks familiar:

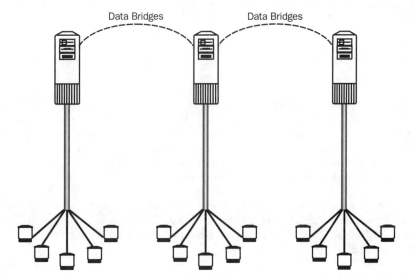

I bet your organization's infrastructure is set up something like this. Instead of having a single centralized resource, you probably have quite a few databases or servers spread throughout your organization. If you ask just about anyone why this is so, they will almost certainly answer that the smaller systems (UNIX and NT based) can only manage X number of users.

They might also argue departmental necessity or security issues, but that is really a symptom of the underlying problem...

> **It is entirely possible to divide and secure data on a single server that can be used by multiple departments.**

If you work for a large company, then you know the other discouraging facet of this design. This facet is perhaps the most expensive one – the myriad of "data bridges" most companies employ in an heroic but nearly futile attempt to make some sense from all of the different pockets of information they have collected. Unfortunately, when most people think about distributed computing, they just take it for granted that the system must be designed as shown above – several separate lines of communication between different user groups and their associated data stores. *This is so wrong!* This design is nothing more than the illegitimate child of a reasonable but incorrect delusion the industry adopted some years ago.

> **Distributed architecture does not have to mean distributed data.**

Enterprise Servers - The Correct Way

Let me make my major point clear. Although enterprise level servers are not as powerful as mainframes, the reason that mainframes seem to be able to handle so many more clients is because, inherently, the mainframe system actively *manages* the clients' access to its available resources.

At some point, this management is more important to the overall system performance than the amount of raw processing power. Think about your friends or acquaintances for a minute; I bet you know two people that earn about the same amount of money, but one of them seems to be more financially secure than the other one. For both individuals the available resource, money, is limited and essentially the same. How do you explain the difference? Like every other engineering problem, it always boils down to one thing – the management (or better, the optimization) of a limited resource.

What this means is that while it doesn't hurt to have more powerful machines, what we really need to do at the enterprise level is to hire a *smarter* machine. We need a machine (read machine to include the operating system) that can monitor the demands on the system and respond accordingly. In other words, we *do* need to do what the mainframes do. But fortunately for us, we don't need to do it the same way. While the mainframe world has essentially one option "I think I need a bigger box", we have a nearly infinite number of choices at our disposal.

> **If we do it right, we can always add processing power by exercising our option of adding *another* box. This simple concept is the essence of distributed architecture.**

The real trick here is learning how to integrate the additional resources into the system in a manner that will enhance the system as a whole. This problem cannot be solved with hardware alone. It requires the same finely tuned orchestration of processes that the mainframe world applies to the problem. In real terms, this means that when an organization purchases or deploys hardware it has to do more than the typical polite interchange that too often occurs between the hardware and development teams.

Developers really need to understand what hardware options are available and just as importantly, the hardware team really *needs* to understand the nature of distributed architecture from the system architect's perspective. The good news is that even if your organization has made every mistake in the book, this problem is really more about the deployment and management of physical resources rather than a hardware specific issue. In other words, as long as the hardware/network team has purchased basically sound equipment, it can always be re-organized into a more efficient configuration that can grow to meet the needs of *any number* of clients.

The Software Component System

A good part of this book is dedicated to designing, developing, and deploying **Data objects**. No, I don't mean business objects; I mean Data objects. Business objects are responsible for integrating an organization's skill and talent with the organization's data, while Data objects are concerned with managing an organization's data. There is a difference.

Data Objects

Think of an organization's data as raw material, maybe something like a pile of wood. If you give a carpenter a pile of wood, depending upon his skill and talent, he might build you a chair, a table, or maybe even a house. Organizations do essentially the same thing with information. If I give a top-notch sales organization a list of names and addresses, they will apply their organization's skill and talent to that list and build customers. If I give the same list to a top-notch Information

Technology Recruitment Company, that organization would apply their organization's skill and talent to the list and find products – new employees for their customers. In either case, the raw material is the same, a list of names and addresses.

What that means is that at some point, we can treat the data for both organizations exactly the same way.

Right about now, you are probably thinking that although the core of data is the same in both cases, we will actually need different information to satisfy each organization's needs. While the sales organization might be interested in information like purchasing power and customer tastes, the recruitment organization is probably more interested in things like years of experience and salary requirements.

It is possible to build a single Data object that can handle both organizations' data management needs, out of the box, without knowing *anything at all* about either company's skill and talent (their business rules). From the above requirements, it sounds like the organizations both need to manage information about people, so we would probably design a Data object that we might call a *Person* object.

The Property Bag

In order to make this Data object flexible enough to handle both organizations' data management tasks, we would divide the object's properties into two sets – a base set and an extended set. In this case, our task is to keep track of information about persons, so we might make the **base set of properties** something like ID, Last Name, First Name, Middle Name, Birth Date, etc.

Notice that I have chosen things that don't need to change whether the person is an engineer, a customer, or an employee etc.

Then in addition to the base set of properties, we give each person object a set of **extended properties**. These extended properties are not pre-defined and can be configured as needed:

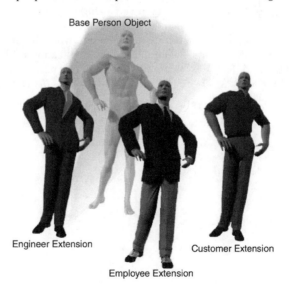

Base Person Object

Engineer Extension

Employee Extension

Customer Extension

To keep the extended properties organized, we give each *Person* object an additional base property – something we will call a **Property Bag**. You can imagine that this Property Bag allows each organization to configure the Data object to carry whatever information it needs in order to apply its business rules most effectively. We'll being going into the details of this later in the book, but for now you might like to know that all of this can happen without changing a single table, stored procedure, or line of code anywhere in the system. That means that we can build 100% **reusable** Data objects.

Using Data Objects

We can create one *Person* Data object that can be cast as *any* type of person. In other words, if we need to track employees, all we have to do to create an *Employee* object from a *Person* Data object is to define a new Property Bag for the *Person* object that contains employee specific information. And, if the problem was to track customers, then we can use exactly the same *Person* object (yes and even the same base set of data) to add a *Customer* Property Bag that contains the information we want to track for customers. Notice that I didn't call either of these extended objects a business object. I called them Data objects. I guess you could argue that the selection of what information to place in the Property Bag is a business rule and that by defining the Property Bag we were executing a business rule. I would have to agree, but that just means that the Data object is flexible enough to be able to handle any set of business rules. Changing the set of properties contained in the Property Bag doesn't change a line of code in the object. The Data object is designed to simply manage data so it doesn't need to contain a single business rule in its code.

This distinction is important because we cannot build 100% reusable business objects. Remember that business rules are akin to an organization's skill and talent. While two different carpenters might both build a chair from the same pile of wood, the chairs would be as different as the carpenters.

> *One chair might be crooked and worthless while the second chair becomes a priceless piece of art. It is important to note that in both cases, we can use exactly the same technique to plant the tree, cut the tree down, and mill the tree. We can even use the same truck to deliver the wood from the tree to the carpenters' woodpile.*

In other words, a good part of the work that we do when we deliver an application is the same for every application we build. The act of storing or retrieving the data can be handled in the same manner no matter what application happens to be using that data. That means that Data objects are completely reusable. Just like the carpenters and the wood, two different applications can use the same raw materials – the Data objects – even though the application of the business rules will make the final results very much different. We can think of Data objects as raw material for applications, and this means that it is a worthwhile endeavor to build *high-quality* Data objects.

The following image is intended to depict the relationship between Data objects and a business object. As you can see, the Data object is an integral part of every business object:

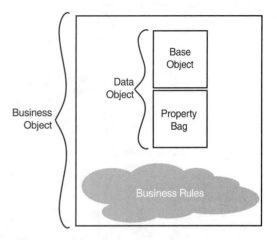

A good part of this book contains step-by-step instructions for designing and building Enterprise Caliber Data Objects. These objects' sole responsibility is to manage data. They do it in a fashion that may seem foreign to your experience. For instance, every object has the ability to maintain a complete history about the data it manages. In other words, if an application used a *Person* object and a user changed the `FirstName` property of a particular Data object from `Jane` to `Jill`, the object would make the change, record who did it, when they made the change, and keep track of the previous value. The object allows every user in the enterprise to view a list of previous values for any property. The object also gives the user the option of using the information in that list to undo any change that was made to an object. We call this history of changes to the object data over time an **audit trail**. The object's audit trail is also used for other things. Maybe instead of changing the `FirstName` property, the user accidentally deleted the entire object from the data store. The Data objects we will build in this book also have the capability to retrieve a list of currently deleted objects and restore them to their state at the time they were deleted. This may seem like a lot of functionality for a simple Data object, but remember that the Data object is the raw material from which we build our applications so the better we make our Data objects the more powerful the applications we can build.

In our initial example in this section I mentioned a list that contained both names and addresses. Then I proceeded to talk about the data as though it only contained the names of persons. I am sure many of you caught me on this one. I didn't forget or overlook the necessary connection between a particular person and the address or addresses that are related to that person. Rather I needed to give you a sense of the difference between Data objects and business objects before we tackled the concept of **Connector objects**.

Connector Objects

As the name implies, a Connector object is a special kind of Data object – one that is charged with the responsibility of managing the relationships between objects. This object is constructed with the same attention to detail as the other Data objects we talked about earlier. In other words, it has a complete audit trail and so on. That means that not only can we look at a relationship between two objects, but we can also look at the history of relationship(s) for an object. Yeah, that's right, this person used to be connected to this address etc. Powerful stuff! Anyway, look at the new image for the business object with the addition of the Connector object. Notice that the business rules are still quite separate from any of the three Data objects:

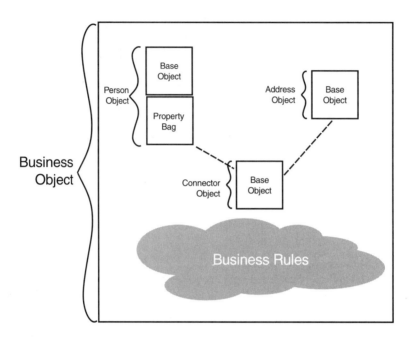

This means that we can use the business rules to control any or all of the three Data objects as required by the problem the business object is designed to solve. Now that you can see the relationship visually, let's take a closer look at the concept of Connector objects. We will use the carpenter example.

Most carpenters use more than wood as their raw material. They may use nails, screws, or glue, etc. Think about where the carpenter's skill and talent come into play when he is building a chair. Does his knowledge about what to do with nails come with the nails? No. It is part of the carpenter's skill and talent. Does his knowledge about what to do with nails come from the physical connection between the wood and nails he is using at this moment? No. It is part of the carpenter's skill and talent developed from countless experiences with the connection of two types of raw materials. In other words, the carpenter draws upon his skill and talent (business rules) to allow him to select the correct pieces of wood, the correct connector – nail, screw, or glue - to join those pieces of wood together. There is a real difference between an actual physical connection that the carpenter creates – the nail, screw, or glue, and his understanding of how to create the connection – his skill and talent. This difference is very much like the difference between the Connector Data object and the business rules in a business object. It is possible to separate the knowledge required to insert a relationship into a database from the knowledge required to determine that the relationship is important. The data insertion is very much like a mechanical device, a nail, a screw, a Connector object, while the reasoning that goes into understanding that the relationship is important is dependent upon the skill and talent of the carpenter, or of the business rules that an organization employs.

Let's reconsider our list of persons and addresses. Suppose that in one instance we needed a business object that tracked customers at their home address – maybe we are selling swimming pools. And in another instance we need a business object that tracked customers at their business address – maybe we are selling office furniture. In these cases, our different sets of business rules tell us which relationship Customer-Home Address or Customer-Business Address that we need to use, but it doesn't tell us anything about the actual physical data connection. That is the same in both cases.

The actual physical data connection is managed by a mechanical device and is not dependent upon the business rules. That means that we can solve both problems with three objects, a *Person* Object – extended into a Customer with a Property Bag, an *Address* object, and a Connector object that we use to express the relationship between the *Person* and *Address* objects. We can use exactly the same three objects (*and exactly the same data store*) in either case. The business rules *alone* make one application different from the other.

> **Separation of content and function – this is the key.**

I also let one other thing slide as we talked earlier. A couple of times now I have shown you images with one or more data objects and some business rules shown in a container called a business object. That container or business object is actually the last major concept in this book.

Veneers

When I think about the way that business rules envelope the underlying Data objects, I always imagine that a business object (or component) is kind of like an M & M® candy. You know a chocolate, or peanut, center covered by a thin coating or **Veneer** – a candy shell. This candy coating protects your hands from being covered in chocolate – the ultimate expression of encapsulation. Well just like M&Ms use a candy veneer to encapsulate the peanut or chocolate center, we use a software veneer to encapsulate the data and business rules at the center of our business object:

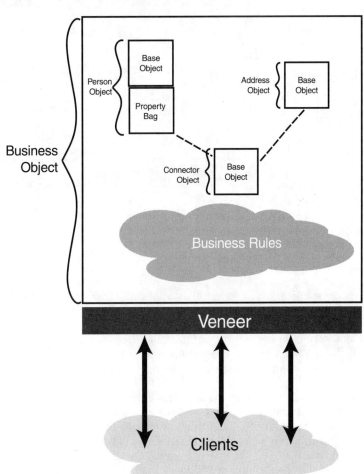

17

This gives us a way to work with several Data objects related by a set of business rules as one unit of information. As you might guess, it is possible to encapsulate several Data objects and some business rules into a business object. It is also possible to use a veneer to encapsulate several business objects into another veneer that we call an application:

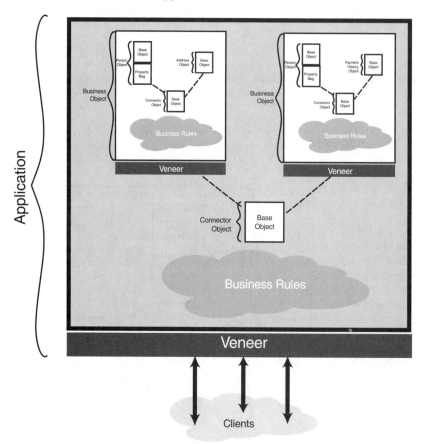

This means that our concept of an application has changed. Now we can consider applications as a collection of business objects that are glued together with a set of business rules and maybe a couple of Connector objects. This gives us the ability to do something like construct a contact management application for the sales department and then turn around and use exactly the same application – including the data, as a component in our marketing or even our billing application. I know that probably sounds like a stretch, so let me break it down for you.

Consider what a contact management application is. It manages the names, addresses, telephone numbers, and maybe email addresses for a group of people. What information do you think the marketing department needs when it executes a nationwide direct mail campaign? What information do you think the billing department needs in order to send bills out to customers? If you were a salesman, do you think that your contact management application would be enhanced if you could include things like purchase history? I am going to leave you to fathom the possibilities.

Pulling the Pieces Together

Before we begin to look at how to configure an Enterprise Caliber system, let's take a minute or two and try to get a sense of how the applications designed to run on a true distributed architecture differ from their more monolithic predecessors. There are three systems shown in the following images, a thin client system, a fat client system, and a multi-tier system:

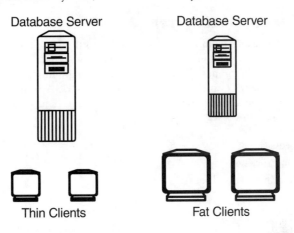

In the first two systems on, the processing is shared between the server and the client machines to varying degrees. We use the terms, thin client and fat client, in an effort to quantify how much processing occurs at the client level. This is probably how most people, including hardware/integration specialists, view a standard client-server environment. In some *very rudimentary* sense, these are *actually* examples of distributed architecture. If you view the enterprise as either one of these systems, it seems perfectly reasonable to ask questions like where is the application going to be installed – on the client or on the server. But, true distributed architecture systems really look more like this third system. Notice how the same question about where to install the application doesn't really apply:

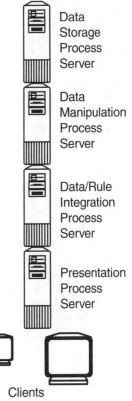

In a distributed architecture, an application isn't really installed on any one machine. It just exists throughout the entire system. This can be a disconcerting concept. Exactly how does an application exist throughout an entire system??? Like any other engineering problem, it's easier to understand the problem if we apply the divide and conquer principle. Let's break the big problem down into more manageable pieces. For our purposes, we will identify those pieces as the different sets of processes that must occur to deliver an application to a client.

The Enterprise Caliber Physical System

I know this is starting to move away from the physical and into the logical realms of design, but remember that you can't solve this problem with hardware alone. What we need to do is to integrate both the hardware and software elements of our system into a single functional unit that is capable of delivering the highest level of service to the largest number of users. Anyway, if we overlook the system management functions we spoke about earlier, we can express just about any application in terms of the following 4 minor processes:

❑ Data Storage Processes
❑ Data Manipulation Processes
❑ Data/Business Rule Integration Processes
❑ Presentation Processes

I am not going to go into a discussion about the details of each process; well be getting into that shortly. I think that for our purposes here, the names are almost self-explanatory. The more important thing to notice from a physical perspective is the relative locations of the processes. The information must pass through all four processing centers (machines) before it can be displayed to the client or consigned to the data store.

At first blush, I am sure that this multi-tier/multi-machine notion might seem like a ridiculous thing. But, remember that we can't solve this problem with hardware alone. What we are doing here is identifying hardware modules that are available for use within our physical design. This modularization of the applications across the entire system allows us to exercise a higher degree of control over the system's performance at the hardware level. We need to go a little further before all of this will fall into place, but think about this for a minute. If an application is distributed across several machines in this fashion, then we can identify processing bottlenecks as a function of CPU utilization, Disk I/O, etc...

In other words, we can learn exactly where to add the horsepower to the system to get the most bang for our buck. For example, if the techs learn through standard hardware analysis techniques that the heavy processing in the Data/Business Rule Integration machine is overtaxing that server's CPU. They can pass this information on to the development team to see if they can improve the process' design. If they can't improve the process, we still have the option of "*throwing more hardware at the problem*" but in this case, we don't simply throw hardware at an amorphous problem, we direct the hardware at the root of cause of the problem. We can add a server or two (or 3 or 4 or 5...) to the Data/Business Rule Integration processing tier of the system and address the processing shortfall directly.

When you read that last paragraph, I hoped you noticed that our distributed architecture design can grow **horizontally** as well as vertically. Don't worry I am going to explain that last sentence. Take a look at this next image:

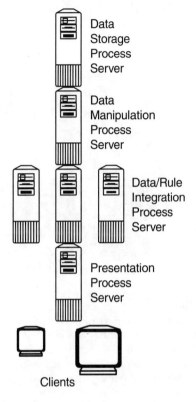

Notice that in the Data/Business Rule Integration Process server tier there are three servers rather than a single server as in the other processing tiers. This is an example of horizontal growth.

> *All it means is that we can add multiple servers to any of the processing tiers as needed.*

This is a subtle point, but notice that we are no longer limited to adding machines to just the Data Storage processing tier. Instead, when we determine that there is a need for more processing power, we can apply that power with pinpoint precision to the root cause of the processing shortfall.

This capacity for horizontal growth can also help to make a single system capable of handling requests from virtually any number of clients. We will take a look at exactly how to do that shortly but first, we need to make sure that we handle the overall system management functions that control the users' access to the system's resources. To do that we will need a way to measure the clients' real-time draw upon the system's resources.

Take a look at the next image; pay special attention to the way that the client machines are connected to the two servers. Notice that in this image all of the clients are connected to a cloud rather than to any one server:

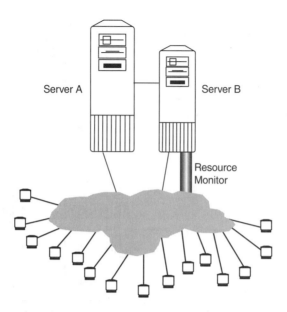

The next thing to notice is that Server A is depicted as larger than Server B. This is not intended to illustrate the relative power of each server, but rather to give us a sense of the relative availability of each server. In other words, consider that both servers are essentially equal except that Server B has the added responsibility of monitoring the available resources and dispatching the client to the least busy resource – either to Server A or to itself. This added responsibility means that Server B will be less available to the clients – that is why it is shown as being smaller.

If we combine the two concepts we just covered, we have just about all of the tools we need to construct a distributed physical system that is capable of meeting the needs of any number of users while also being flexible enough to be able to grow to meet any future needs as well.

For those of you that are still here, I am going to make some broad statements concerning the different characteristics of the different types of processing. Actually, what I am going to do is to give you some rules of thumb concerning the relative amount of processing time each minor process requires. You can always use these general rules to design a good first cut at a physical enterprise installation.

- ❑ Data Storage processes excute relatively quickly because they only have to deal with reading and writing to the data store.
- ❑ Data Manipulation processes take longer to exectue than Data Storage processes because they inherently depend upon the Data Storage process completing before they themselves are complete.
- ❑ Data/Business Rule Integration processes take longer again because they depend upon the first 2 processes finishing before they can complete their own execution.
- ❑ Presentation processes take the longest to finish because they depend upon the other 3 processes finishing before they can complete their own execution.

Think about the four broad statements above. Then take a look at the next image. Notice that the number of servers on each tier mirrors the processing time requirements outlined in the four statements.

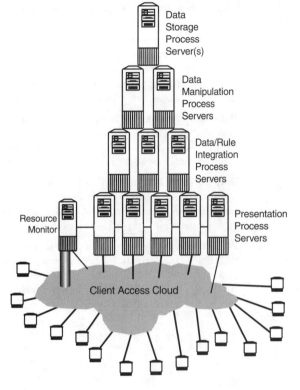

We said that Presentation processes took the longest time to complete, so we added more servers to this tier. Data/Business Rule Integration processes took the second longest time to complete so we have added less servers to this tier, and so on...

Think about the difference between this design and the one we looked at earlier with three separate database servers each serving their own pod of users. In that design, we incorrectly identified the processing bottleneck as occurring on the database server. So, to remedy that problem we added more database servers to the enterprise. The end result was that we had many pockets of data spread throughout the organization that must be bridged to give us an overall picture of our data. The best way I can think of to describe that kind of design is to say that it represents a **distributed data system**. There are multiple pockets of data each serving different pods of users. Distributed architecture does not have to mean distributed data!

> **The goal of distributed architecture is to distribute the *processing load* across as many resources as necessary NOT to distribute the data within the system.**

The Enterprise Caliber Component System

Ok, now that you have a sense of how the individual pieces that make up an object-oriented application fit together, it is time to take another look at the objects from a different perspective. Remember our overall goal, we are designing an enterprise, and for us that means that we need to be able to deploy our applications, or our objects, across a distributed architecture. As we saw in the physical section, distributed architecture requires more than just adding a couple of machines to a system. In order to get any benefit from a distributed physical architecture, we must build Data objects that are designed to take advantage of that architecture.

Generally, this means that we must design each object as several distinct set of processes. We've already defined these processes but we have yet to discuss them in any detail:

- ❑ **Data Storage Processes** – These processes are responsible for handling the physical reads and writes to the data store. To keep things simple, we will consider that these processes are under the control of an ODBC compliant Database Management System like SQL Server or Oracle. That means that for our purposes we can consider the data storage processes a collection of tables, stored procedures, and views in a relational database.

- ❑ **Data Manipulation Processes** – These processes remind me of a card catalog in a library. We use them to find out exactly where the data is, or should be, located. That means for our purposes, these cards would contain the names and parameter requirements for the stored procedures in our relational database and have the ability to execute those stored procedures.

- ❑ **Data/Business Rule Integration Processes** – These processes are used to add value to an organization's data. Remember the carpenter example. These processes are responsible for combining an organization's data with the organization's talent. That means for our purposes, these processes might perform tasks like special calculations or manage important relationships.

- ❑ **Presentation Processes** – These processes are responsible for delivering information to the user and retrieving information from the user. This is really just the typical GUI or reporting system for an application. In the physical system, these processes might exist in many different places. However, I believe that in most newly developed applications, these processes should probably be executed at a web server like IIS for instance.

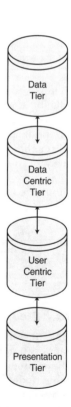

This means that each one of the objects we described earlier, like the *Person* object or the *Address* object, is really comprised of four separate sections of code or DLLs. It is a common practice in the industry to call each of these sections of code a **tier**. Anyway, just as we physically segregated the processes onto separate servers in a physical treatment, we must also segregate the different sections of code onto different tiers in a logical treatment:

This is actually what makes the physical treatment possible. It wouldn't matter if we had 1000 machines if the code is a single block that can only be run on a single machine.

The sections of code are split out as follows:

❑ The sections of code that handle the Data Storage processes are found in the **Data tier**.

❑ The sections of code that handle the Data Manipulation processes are found in the **Data Centric tier**.

❑ The sections of code that handle the Data/Business Rule Integration processes are found in the **User Centric tier**.

❑ The sections of code that handle the Presentation processes are found in the **Presentation tier**.

Using both hardware and software together, we have isolated each of the processes that an application requires onto a different machine or bank of machines. We can use this isolation to add processing power, either physical by adding another server(s), or virtual by adding another instance(s) of the process in exactly the place it will do the most good. For example, if we found that we were having a processing bottleneck on the User Centric tier and that the servers in that bank still had plenty of CPU available, then we could just start another instance of our person object's user centric processes on that machine.

This ability to pinpoint the source of processing (I/O etc.) bottlenecks and cure them with the same precision is the hallmark of good enterprise design.

Book Overview

This book is divided into three sections. If you are a programmer, then I would strongly recommend starting at the beginning and working your way through each of the chapters of the book in turn. Please don't skip the first section. Even though the first section presents materials that have to do with things like hardware and management techniques, this entire book is really all about programming. As you work through the sections on fault tolerance, parallel processing, and security you will learn the basic foundational concepts that are deeply ingrained in every facet of world-class enterprise design. In other words, in order to design programs that take full advantage of distributed architecture you really need to understand, at least logically, how a server farm works.

If you are not a programmer, then I would still suggest reading through each of the chapters of the book in turn. Although the information in the first and last section of the book is technical, most of those sections are written in plain English – and you can comfortably skip through any sections of code that are in those sections without missing a beat. When you get to the middle section of the book, I would recommend that you just read through the first 10 or 20 pages of each chapter – don't worry, if you are not a programmer, you will know where to stop. In this section, I cover the major concept and the major functionality at the beginning of each chapter. This information is really all you need to know to be able to spec-out applications using this technique, but don't be fooled. You *do* need to know it. If you're a manager or team leader, let me say that, "While it is true that you don't have to know exactly how electricity works to use the light switch, you do have to know where the light switch is and how to turn it on in order see in the dark". The first 10 or 20 pages of each chapter in this section will show you where the light switch is and tell you exactly what you should expect will happen when you turn it on or off.

Section I - The Infrastructure

The first section of this book is designed to give you a solid base of information that you can draw upon when you address the issues that will arise when you are installing an NT based Enterprise Caliber system for your organization. By the time you finish this section of the book, you will have a good sense of the infrastructure (both hardware and operating system) options that are available to you.

In the next chapter, we will take a closer look at the information we need to consider when we translate an organization's information processing requirements into the actual infrastructure. In order to do that we will consider the following three topics:

- ❑ First, we'll develop an understanding about the concept of fault tolerance.
- ❑ Second, we'll consider design techniques that we can use to create a system that is capable of true parallel processing.
- ❑ Third, we'll take a look at some of the things we need to consider when we attack the issue of enterprise security. In this book, I use a particular technique that I call inherent system security. This technique uses hardware, operating system, and application level controls to ensure that the system's users are guarded from any of the harms that typically befall them.

In the last chapter in this section, we will take a look at some real concrete measures we can take to construct a dynamic physical system that is capable of growing with our organization. To do this, we will cover four major topics:

- ❑ First, we will cover the conceptual/physical design of server farms without hardware level clustering.
- ❑ Second we will develop an understanding of hardware level clustering using the current version of Microsoft Cluster Server.
- ❑ Third, we will cover the design of server farms that can take advantage of hardware level clustering.
- ❑ Finally, we will look at techniques we can use to combine hardware clustering with MSCS and Windows Load Balancing Services (WLBS) to provide the most flexible solution with a much lower total cost of ownership.

Section II - Enterprise Caliber Data Objects

In this section of the book, we are going to learn how to construct Data objects that are truly worthy of being deployed across a world-class enterprise installation. I have employed a tried and true engineering paradigm in this section of the book. In other words, we are going to learn to build the best damn black boxes anyone has ever seen. This also means that despite some of the experts' incorrect opinions to the contrary, we will learn to build completely reusable data objects. *Count on it.*

Of course, it almost goes without saying that these objects will have the ability to manage information in the data store, which means that they can insert, update, delete, and retrieve information from the data store. But, these objects, designed to complement the Windows NT security model, also keep a complete audit history of every action that any user has ever taken against each object. This audit history is one part of the overall system security model, but it also offers some additional benefits. It will allow us to provide any user with the ability to perform unlimited undos.

You know, when you make a mistake typing a line or two of data, you press Ctrl + Z *or you select* Undo *from the* Edit *menu and the application takes you back step-by-step through time until your data is restored to its previous, correct, state.*

This functionality is inherent in every Data object. And, using the same audit history, we will also offer the user the ability to restore an object from a deleted state. Of course, we are professionals, so when we design a user interface we will ensure that any user can always perform these actions with, at most, a couple of intuitive mouse clicks. Really! I am not kidding.

The major thrust of this book is *Enterprise Architecture,* so we will do our part in this section by learning to design and build Data objects that can take full advantage of a distributed architecture. In practice, that means that we will build each object as two or more dynamic link libraries that can be installed on different machines. This is one of the key things we must understand to take full advantage of the parallel processing capabilities we have designed into our server farm.

I don't want to be a nag, but even if you hate hardware, don't forget to read through the part on server farm design. It is basic information for programmers who design code for true parallel processing systems. Yes! That is exactly what you are going to do.

Section III - Building Enterprise Caliber Applications

In this section of the book, we will begin the process of pulling together the pieces that we examined in the two previous sections. We still need to cover a couple of VB coding techniques, but we will shift our major focus here from using VB to create Data objects to using VB to create business objects and applications. In a distributed architecture, an application doesn't have to be an executable that sits on the client's desktop. It can be a lot of different things including a dynamic link library (DLL) that can exist anywhere within the enterprise. This application, or veneer DLL, contains all of the business rules that an organization applies to its data for a particular application. The veneer is designed to both apply those rules and bring together all of the different Data objects an application needs into a single point of contact that can be used for programming any type of user interface.

Once we have learned how to use Data objects, business objects, and veneers to build applications, we will take another look at some of the rewards our separation of data, business rules, and the user interfaces in the previous sections has wrought. We will look at some of our options concerning the development of interfaces. We will also take a look at some of the different options available for developing user interfaces. In this section of the book, I will focus on a particular method for application deployment – Active Server Pages.

Active Server Pages (ASP) allow us to deliver applications, literally, to any place in the world without ever touching the individual desktop machines. This means that we can develop a user interface for an application today, install it on our server farm today, and virtually any number of users can begin using that application today. That is precisely the kind of efficiency you need to deliver your enterprise's services to your organization. Of course, the term ASP is a very generic term. You can be sure that we will approach ASP with the same dedication to quality that we applied to our data objects. In this section, we will learn to combine ASP, veneers, VB Script, and DHTML to deliver world-class interfaces to the extents of our enterprise.

Summary

Phew! For a first chapter we've already covered a lot of ground. Don't worry, we'll be coming back to many of the concepts I've introduced here throughout the rest of the book, but I wanted to give you something of an idea of what's on the trail ahead.

Trying to walk in the dark is difficult enough but trying to do it with a wrong image of the route is harder still, and that's what this first chapter has really all been about. Not only did I want to you to give you some brief background to some of the key concepts that we'll be developing over the course of the following chapters. But, perhaps more importantly, I also wanted to broaden your horizons so that you can go into the rest of the book realizing that many of the design principles we will be using are indeed viable. There are many misconceptions regarding enterprise architecture and I wanted to straighten these out before we began the real work.

In the next few chapters, we'll be looking at an Enterprise Caliber infrastructure before moving onto looking at some code behind the Enterprise Caliber Data Objects.

Person
Base Properties

ID
Last Name
First Name
Middle Name
Birth Date
Sex

Object Type Definitions

Business OTD	Lawer OTD	Engineer OTD	Doctor OTD	Student OTD
	Specialty	Specialty	Specialty	Major
	Hourly Rate	Experience	Certification	Minor
Property 3	Law School	Property 3	Property 3	Year
Property 4	Property 4	Property 4	Property 4	Property 4
Property 5	Property 5	Property 5	Property 5	Property 5
Property 6	Property 6	Property 6	Property 6	Property 6
Property 7	Property 7	Property 7	Property 7	Property 7
Property 8	Property 8	Property 8	Property 8	Property 8
Property 9	Property 9	Property 9	Property 9	Property 9
Property 10	Property 10	Property 10	Property 10	Property 10

Property Set Definitions

Property Se...

2

Available, Scalable, and Secure

A good friend of mine cautioned me that the word **enterprise** was becoming a bit overused – he likened it to other marketing-speak terms like industrial-strength, new-and-improved, etc. In many ways, I have to agree with him on that point, so during this chapter, we will work to develop a common understanding of the concept of an **Enterprise Caliber System** by defining some of the things we should expect from such a system. We will lay down a few, very broad, design strokes that we will revisit again and again throughout the remainder of this book. Those strokes are **available**, **scalable**, and **secure**.

As we work through this chapter and the next, we will consider some of the design options available to us for developing an enterprise infrastructure. As we do this, we will strive to create an environment that enables us to distribute the processing load of the system across as many machines as possible. Remember that distributed architecture means that we need to distribute the processing – not that we distribute the data. The consummate system would enable true parallel processing to take place across the entire system. (If we were to use only serial processing then each process would have to wait for the one before it to complete before it could begin - even if could perform most of the task without referring to that previous process.) Of course, this is an ideal. But, each time we inch a little closer towards the ideal of true parallel processing, we will have taken a great stride towards designing a system that is more available, more scalable, and in many ways more secure.

As with any journey, we will begin this one with a single step. We will learn what things we need to do to make a single machine robust enough to handle its share of the enterprise load. First, we will pass through the perhaps foreign worlds of hardware components and network connections. We will take the time to understand how the basic elements of a single machine can be made to work together to provide fault tolerance and maybe even some slight improvements in scalability. As we do this, we may learn a thing or two about the underlying hardware, but our goal here is really to draw some parallels between the capabilities of the hardware and the demands our software will place upon it. As we come to know those capabilities, we will be better able to take advantage of all that the infrastructure has to offer.

Once we have developed a kinship with the single enterprise caliber machine, we will take another step towards the ideal of true parallel processing. We will begin a long and deliberate dissection of the monoliths that we currently refer to as applications. In order for an application to distribute its processing, that application must be designed in a way that makes this possible. We will learn to see applications as many complimentary pieces that work together rather than as a solitary monument with a singular purpose. We will learn that there are many natural processing divisions and that we only need to find these divisions to take advantage of the parallel processing opportunities they present. As we come to understand that applications, systems, and enterprises are really a harmony of processes rather than the monotony of a monolith, we will be able to take on other enterprise-wide challenges with this knowledge.

We may even begin to view something as substantial as enterprise security as a problem that is better solved in pieces. Once we have pierced through the security industry's subterfuge to find this view, we will discover that we are not alone with our vision. We will learn that Windows NT achieved its C2 security classification (from the US Department of Defense) partly because it handles security in a similar fine-grained manner. Rather than attempting to control the whole of the enterprise using a monolithic approach, Windows NT implements security at the object level. We will endeavor to emulate this world-class model by building upon and using its strengths from within. This inner strength approach will give us a system that becomes more and more difficult to breach as an intruder gets closer and closer to the data. So, rather than taking the approach of designing a thin veil over our enterprise, we will learn to think of security as something that is ingrained into every aspect of the enterprise.

I understand that it may be difficult to think about security in particular and distributed architecture in general as something that permeates a system, an enterprise or an organization. But it shouldn't be. In the last chapter we talked, at a very general level, about techniques we can use to ensure that each tiny portion of our system is capable of managing its own affairs. We talked about building data objects that could handle their own security from within. We considered how we might deploy an army of these highly capable data objects throughout our system. We realized that these objects could each take on a portion of the overall processing load that our system demanded. Through this discussion, we discovered that we could distribute processing without necessarily having to distribute data. The last chapter was a discussion. In this chapter, we will begin to assemble the foundation for our distributed processing system. One of the corner stones of that foundation has to be **fault tolerance**. The slickest parallel processing system in the world won't do an organization a bit of good if it isn't available for service.

Available

An enterprise's resources must be available. Do you remember the last time the electricity went out? I'm sure, that at first it might have seemed kind of exciting. The last time the electricity at my home went out, I spent a couple of wonderful minutes watching our dog Dakota chasing the business end of my laser pointer around the living room. This little diversion was interesting for a while, but before too long, even the sight of the deranged dog chasing that little red dot 4 feet up the wall lost its appeal. It was then that I realized how little I think about the electricity in my home or office. In fact, I really don't think about it at all; I just expect to be there. When I pick up the handset of my telephone, I am never surprised to hear a dial tone – I have come to depend on it.

Most organizations have come to expect this same level of availability from their mainframe systems and enterprise-level systems (read enterprise-level in this context as the old guard of enterprise-level systems Unix, AS-400, etc).

The information they manage is often mission-critical in nature, and great care has been taken to ensure that the resources these systems provide are available without failure. Considering the cost of the systems and the importance of the information they contain, it is not surprising that availability is such a huge concern.

It is surprising, however, that most of the organizations I have worked with do not seem to expect the same level of availability from their PC-based systems. Perhaps this is because in the past, most of the applications developed for the PC platform have not been considered real mission-critical applications. Maybe at that time, it wasn't economically prudent to consider things like RAID, hot swappable power supplies, and entirely redundant servers, etc.

That time has passed.

This book is about the new enterprise systems and although their ancestry links their hardware with the eight-oh-eighty-eight processors of old, the systems – both the hardware and the software – we will consider in this book are not mere PCs. The applications these systems are called upon to host are mission critical applications. This means that, as professionals, we have a responsibility to ensure that these systems are available; we must consider things like fault tolerance, disaster recovery plans, and more.

Although the first section of this book places special emphasis on the hardware/operating system (OS) portion of the enterprise, I must caution you that it is not possible to create an enterprise caliber system with hardware and operating system upgrades alone. Even the best hardware/OS available is not 100% immune to lightening strikes, tornadoes, and other natural or man-made disasters. We need to add several software elements into our system to ensure a reasonably high degree of availability.

In this chapter, we will begin to look at some basic techniques you can use to ensure that your enterprise's resources will be available. It makes me very proud that my teams compare our system to Federal Express – "when it absolutely positively has to be there". This type of high-availability system is really not that difficult to design these days. Microsoft, Compaq, Dell, and host of other companies are working round the clock to develop the pieces of the infrastructure that make this possible. All we really need to do is to learn how to put those pieces together. I suppose that we could approach that task in a rather dry manner. I am certain that we could develop some cost to benefit ratio equations, but I have always been the kind of engineer that deals best with practical matters. I have learned to depend upon something my father used to call common sense. In other words, we are about to take a common sense approach to the problem of fault tolerance – the expensive term for availability.

The most certain way to ensure that a resource is continuously available is to have more than the required amount of resources available at all times. It is a safe bet that you have a spare tire for your car. This spare tire gives your car a level of fault tolerance. If one of the tires goes flat, you can replace it and be on your way in a matter of minutes. When it comes to tires, fault tolerance makes sense, but most of us don't have spare engines, fenders, or bumpers for our cars, do we? No, of course not.

Fault tolerance, like everything else in this world has a price. It makes sound economic sense for us to have a spare tire for our car. It costs less (in most cases) to have a spare tire than it would cost to get our car towed to a place where we could get the flat tire repaired or replaced. This is especially true if we amortize the cost of the spare over the life expectancy of the set of tires. We cannot say the same thing (in most cases) about an automobile's engine. The benefit of having a spare engine probably doesn't justify the cost of the spare engine. If you think about it, there is something else to consider in addition to the cost. One difference between tires and engines is that (in most cases) tires will become flat more often than engines will become inoperable.

There are a couple of other things for us to ponder when we consider fault tolerant tires vs. fault tolerant engines. The first is the ease of installation. Can you imagine the difficulties of carrying a spare engine around with you? How about performing an engine replacement on the side of a busy throughway? The second thing may be a little less obvious. One of the things we do with tires is to rotate them. When we rotate our tires, we remove the spare from the trunk and replace one of the currently active tires with the spare. Then we move the tire that has become inactive into the trunk. This practice lowers the amount of wear and tear on all 5 tires by distributing the total amount of wear and tear, more or less, equally between all 5 tires including the spare. It is difficult to imagine a comparable scenario for an engine.

Yeah, I know... What the heck do tires and automobile engines have to do with designing an Enterprise Caliber System? Well, let's think about the ways we might make an enterprise system fault tolerant the same way we looked at the tires and the engine. We can do that by examining each of the pieces of the system and thinking about whether or not it makes sense to have a spare. First let's make a sample list of pieces to consider. A partial list might look something like the following (I am not trying to handle all of the things you might need to consider here. We will just go over some of the things we might consider in order to develop a common sense way to answer these types of questions in the future.):

- ❑ Data stored in the system
- ❑ Software (OS and applications) loaded onto the system
- ❑ Disks (storage areas)
- ❑ Power source (think of an outlet in the wall)
- ❑ Power supply
- ❑ Network connection
- ❑ Network card
- ❑ System chips/parts (CPUs, memory, motherboard, etc.)

Data

The first item on the list was data. You may not consider backing up data files a fault tolerant device. But if you think about it, that is exactly what it is. We don't really need to do a cost/benefit analysis on this one. Not backing up the data in the system is like driving cross-country with a flat spare tire. We can almost take it for granted that, the cost of performing regular backups of the data in the system is less than the cost of the down-time/data re-entry that we would have to perform otherwise. I have included this category just to bring the concept of fault tolerance down to earth where it belongs. One of the best things we can do to gain a level of fault tolerance is regular back-ups of all of our data.

Software

Ditto the data remarks. But, let me add that there are several different techniques that we can use to back up data, application, and system software. Some of these techniques are so inexpensive, that it may make sense to provide several levels of back-ups. Let me give you an example: On our production systems, we perform a primary backup to a disk-array on another machine. Then we back-up that disk to two different tapes. The last step we take is to remove one of the tapes completely off the site. The second disk gives us immediate access to the last backup. The on-site tape is inexpensive insurance for the on-site back-up disk. We can restore from the on-site tape almost as fast as we can restore from the on-line disk.

The final level of protection we afford our back-ups is the tape that we store 40 miles off-site. We do this to ensure continuity in case of catastrophic occurrences like fire, tornadoes, nuclear winter, etc.

This entire backup strategy is very inexpensive, and as long as both sites are not completely destroyed we have ensured nearly continuous availability of the data, application, and system software.

Disk – System Data Storage

The disk is the first real hardware we have looked at in terms of fault tolerance. The disk represents a danger because it offers a **single point of failure** for the entire system. If a system relies upon a single disk and that disk fails, the entire system fails. Whenever we are considering hardware-level fault tolerance issues, the single point of failure test is almost always an appropriate first step.

As I hinted in the last section, there are many ways to back up data. Our first and best defense is to use a **Redundant Array of Independent Disks**, **RAID**. Although this may not be a true technical backup, it gives us immediate access to, in essence, a second copy of our files (read files in this context to include data, system, and application files). Most RAID systems also offer the ability to **hot swap** (exchange disks without powering down the machine). We will take a closer look at this hardware in Chapter 3, but let me give you a quick overview of the two different levels of RAID that we will consider.

I know that this is not a programming problem, but please take the time to work through this section. The most important thing you will learn about programming in this book concerns the distribution of processes across many machines in an enterprise. The way we will accomplish this distribution of processing across machines is very much the same way that RAID uses to distribute data across several disks. In other words, most of the programming concepts we will cover in this book are modeled after some of the same basic concepts found in a RAID system.

RAID Level 1 – Mirrored Disks

Level 1 RAID requires pairs of disks – 2 disks or 4 or 8 etc. The total storage for all of the disks in the system is only equal to the total storage on half of the disks. This means that if we have two 18 Gig disks, we have 18 Gig of usable storage space available. The other half of the disk space is really used to provide a *mirror* (hence the name) of the space we actually get to use. The disk controller(s) use hardware to synchronize the data across disks. Due to this hardware intervention, these two disks perform almost the same as if we were writing to a single disk. There is little, if any, degradation in overall performance. (RAID 1 does not offer any speed or throughput improvements over a single SCSI disk.) RAID 1 is designed for fault tolerance. If one disk experiences a failure, the other one can take over immediately without missing a beat. In other words, if RAID were a spare tire, it wouldn't just sit in your trunk. It would be able to sense when a tire went flat and then it would install itself in place of its deflated associate.

In a RAID 1 system, the act of mirroring the data from the primary to the redundant disk is a hardware function that we can essentially consider a black box for the purposes of this discussion.

RAID 1 System

If we wanted to write the word DOG to a RAID Level 1 disk-array, we would only have access to a single data-transfer stream, which each letter would have to pass through in a serial fashion. That means that we can visualize the process of writing the word DOG as four distinct steps:

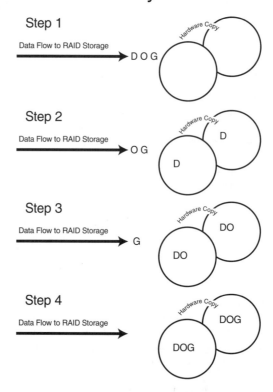

Step 1

Data Flow to RAID Storage ⟶ D O G

Hardware Copy

Step 2

Data Flow to RAID Storage ⟶ O G

Hardware Copy

D

D

Step 3

Data Flow to RAID Storage ⟶ G

Hardware Copy

DO

DO

Step 4

Data Flow to RAID Storage ⟶

Hardware Copy

DOG

DOG

1. Preparation. The data has been passed to the threshold of the disk array.

2. Write the first data block. In this example, the first block of data is the letter "D". The hardware writes a "D" to the mirror disk.

3. Write the second data block. In this example, the second block of data is the letter "O". The hardware writes an "O" to the mirror disk.

4. Write the third data block. In this example, the third block of data is the letter "G". The hardware writes a "G" to the mirror disk.

Of course in real life, these steps would use another method of data block measurement based upon an algorithm programmed into the hardware. A disk array doesn't really work with the data at the level of particular characters. To the array, all the data is simply a series of 1s and 0s. However, I am not a disk array, so you are going to have to bear with me.

RAID Level 5 – Striped Disks

Level 5 RAID requires a minimum of three disks. The total storage for all disks is equal to the sum of the total storage of each disk minus the total storage of a single disk. Oops, I said there wouldn't be any math, but trust me it is a lot easier to get this one if we take a look at some numbers.

For example, if we designed a system with six x 8 Gigabyte disks, we would end up with a total storage of 40 Gigabytes (6 x 8 - 8 = 40).

It is kind of a good thing that we took the little detour down the math road. Did you notice that when we use RAID 5, we end up with more disk space than if we used RAID 1? If we had six x 8 Gigabyte disks in a RAID 1 system we would only have three of those disks available at any one time and 3 x 8 = 24. We got 16 more Gigabytes with the RAID 5 system than we would have gotten if we used a RAID 1 system. And that is not even the cool thing about RAID 5, which is that the data is written across all of the disks simultaneously. RAID 5 uses something called parity to make this work. I am not going to talk about parity bits. Even the thought makes me dizzy, but what it all boils down to is that, somehow, the disks can use this parity bit to reconstruct data in case one of the disks fails. At first blush, this system may not seem to offer any advantages over the simpler Level 1 RAID besides the extra disk space, but it does.

The act of striping data across disks is really an example of a parallel process. When we copy identical data to a mirrored disk like in Level 1 RAID, we have only have access to the maximum throughput of a single disk. When we stripe data across several disks, we have access to the maximum throughput of all of the disks – minus the one we need for parity. Let's look at an example:

> *In a RAID 5 system, the disk controllers perform the act of determining the value of the parity block. We can essentially ignore this function for the purposes of this discussion.*

Now, if we wanted to write the word DOG to a RAID Level 5 disk-array with four disks, we would actually have access to four separate data transfer streams – one for each disk. That means that we can visualize the process of writing the word DOG using only two distinct steps:

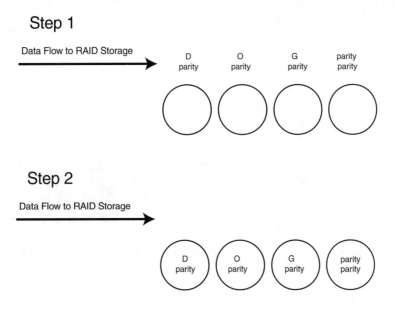

RAID 5 System

1. Preparation. The data has been passed to the threshold of the disk array. The hardware calculates the parity block and separates the data into four more or less equal blocks of data.

2. Write the data. Each block of data is written simultaneously to one of the four disks.

Of course, this is an intentional oversimplification of the process. In real life, the last disk would not have two parity blocks. In this example, it would contain something like one quarter of the word DOG and each disk would have a parity block or something like that.

Compare this with the RAID 1 system we looked at earlier. In that case we needed three steps to write the word DOG to the disks. With RAID 5, we only needed 2. This is an example of the power of parallel processing. Actually I guess that this is a case of parallel disk writing, but you get the idea. If we can take a big task and break it down into smaller tasks that can be executed in parallel, we will get finished sooner. And I bet you thought this RAID stuff was going to be hard. I am not sure exactly how RAID 5 measures up in terms of spare tires and engines, but I think we might be able to compare it to rotating the tires. Remember? When we rotated our tires, we took the spare out of the trunk and replaced one of the active tires with the spare. This made all of the tires, including the spare, wear more evenly.

I guess you could say that I've balanced the load that the tires had to bear across all 5 tires rather than letting the 4 active tires wear out sooner. It is kind of like that with RAID 5. Rather than writing all of the data to one disk, we are sharing the load across multiple disks.

Before we go on, let me give you a visual concerning RAID 5 disk failures. I don't know if it helps you, but a lot of times it is easier for me to get a handle on something if I can picture it. With RAID 5, if one of the disks fails, the remaining disks use the parity data on the remaining disks to reconstruct the information that was stored on the failed disk. In the example above, if the disk containing the letter "G" failed. The controller would use the parity data stored from each of the remaining disks to deduce that the letter "G was actually stored on the failed disk. Then it would store that information using the same technique across each of the remaining disks. The results of a failure might look like the following:

Step 2

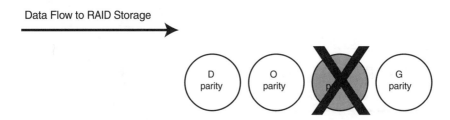

Once again these are illustrative examples, the RAID controller does not treat the data as anything like recognizable characters – just binary data.

Perhaps the most important thing we can learn from these two RAID examples is that it is possible to design systems that can improve both fault tolerance and performance. Just remember that if we use RAID 1, we can expect improvements in fault tolerance.

What we have done is to provide the system with essentially real-time data backup/restoration for system failures involving a system disk. The cost for this protection is that we must make one of our resources (the redundant disk) unavailable for storage space in anticipation of failure. With RAID 1 only half of the functioning resources are available to us at any time.

RAID 5 offers fundamentally the same level of fault tolerance with respect to disk integrity. But it also improves overall system performance. It does this by sharing the total system load across all the available resources – both primary and redundant. With RAID 5, all of the functioning resources are on-line all of the time.

> **The basic difference between the two configurations is that RAID 1 is essentially serial in nature while RAID 5 operates in a more parallel fashion.**

Generally, I would say that next to a careful backup plan, the best step to take towards system fault tolerance is the addition of a RAID storage area. RAID has the effect of providing real-time data backup/restoration in the case of disk failures. As an added bonus when RAID Level 5 is employed, our efforts to increase fault tolerance also return improvements in overall system performance as well.

Power Source

When I think about hardware and fault tolerance at the same time, I find that I only really need to ask one question. If this piece of hardware fails, will the system go down? In other words, in this case we need to ask the question of whether or not the power source is a single point of failure for the system. Let me think now, what happens when I pull out the plug?

Of course, the addition of a fault tolerant power source is another one of those no-brainers. Even most home computers are equipped with **uninterruptible power supplies** (**UPS**), which allow the user to continue working for a short time in the event of a power outage. It has been my experience that, the best possible use for these inexpensive home devices is that it allows the user to power down the computer in a controlled fashion. Most of them do not have the ability to sustain any real use for even a short period of time. Enterprise Caliber UPSs are another story. They should at minimum allow for a controlled power down, but it is not unreasonable for these devices to be used as power sources that ensure continuous availability of service. In most true enterprise installations, the UPS devices are used as bridge power sources. They ensure that the system remains available during the amount of time required for the backup generators to light up and take the place of the conventional power source.

Power Supply

The power supply for most computers is a single transformer unit. By now, when you hear the word "single" with respect to hardware, you should be wondering what will happen if the thing breaks. If I only have one power supply for a computer and it breaks will the computer continue to work? No! That means that the power supply (transformer unit) is a single point of failure for the system.

This is different than a power source. A power supply is the physical transformer unit that modifies, splits and transfers the power from the power source (electrical outlet) to the chips in the computer. If a power supply fails, the computer will shut down in an uncontrolled fashion, regardless of whether or not a UPS is present.

An Enterprise Caliber Server should have a continuously available, redundant power supply with automatic **fail over**. If the first power supply fails, then the second one can immediately take over for the first power supply. Ideally, these power supplies should also be hot swappable. In other words, we should be able to treat the power supplies about the same way we treat the disks in a RAID system. If one breaks, we should be able to rip it out and replace it without shutting the machine down.

Network Connection

The network connection is a single point of failure for a single computer. I know that if we followed the same reasoning we used earlier, we might come to the conclusion that we needed a redundant network connection for every computer. In this case, we need to think about the problem a little more. Remember when we talked about the automobile's engine? The engine was a single point of failure for an automobile, but most people don't have spare engines the way that most people have spare tires. That is because it is very expensive to keep a spare engine considering the remote possibility that you will ever need it. In other words, we need to balance the cost of the resource with the cost of the failure of the resource.

In other words when we are designing a network for an enterprise, it is not unreasonable for every workstation (client) in the network to have access to just a single network connection. After all, if the connection between the user and the hub or switch breaks, the most our organization stands to lose is the work that is normally accomplished on that particular client machine:

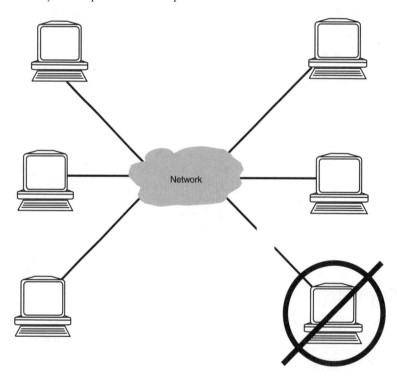

So, when we are talking about client workstations, a redundant network connection is probably not a worthwhile investment.

But, if we look at the network from a larger perspective – considering the connections that link hubs and switches, then redundant network connections might begin to make sense. We can call this type of network connection a **backbone connection**:

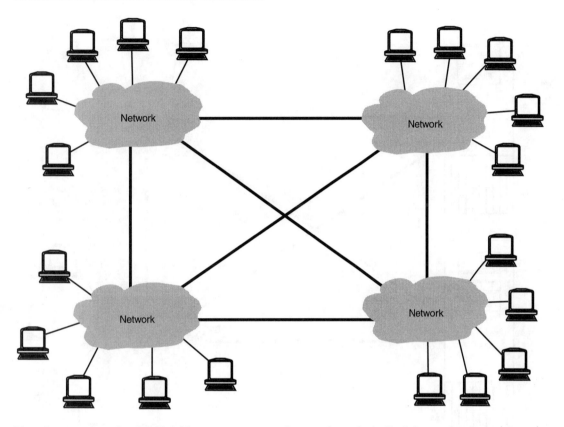

If we lose a non-redundant backbone connection, then we have lost all of the workstations (clients) connected to that particular hub. Most organizations find it economically feasible to protect against the loss of a backbone connection.

Take a minute to look at the image above. Notice that if any backbone connection is broken, the entire system can still continue to function. Most organizations have networks with this level of redundancy. They ensure a high degree of availability at a reasonable cost.

There is one other place where we need to consider redundant network connections. That place is at the level of mission-critical servers. Just so we can talk, let's develop a working definition for a mission-critical server – we'll just say that a mission-critical server is any server that is required for X numbers of users to perform their assigned duty.

Now, although these resources may be single computers, if one of these computers is unavailable due to a faulty network connection, then we have put X number of employees out of work until that network connection is returned to service.

When we are talking about mission-critical resources, even if that resource is a single server, then we should consider providing a redundant network connection to this resource:

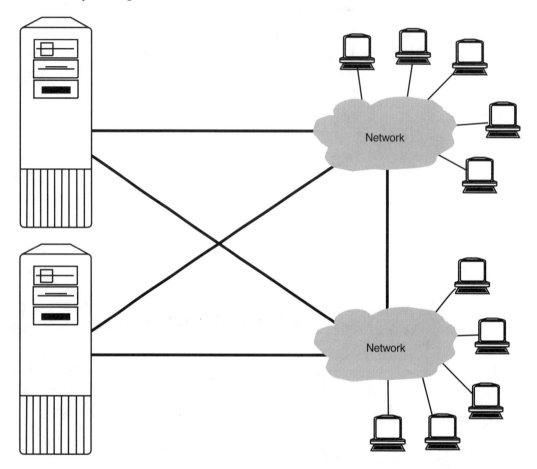

Providing an additional network connection to enterprise resources is a relatively inexpensive way to ensure a high level of availability.

Network Card

The network card is a single point of failure for the system. Of course, we should think about this problem just about the same way we worked through the network connection problem earlier. In this case, it is not so much a question of whether or not the hardware device is a single point of failure, as it is a question of how much will it cost if the hardware breaks? And, again we probably can make a rule that if the resource is a mission-critical resource (more than X users depend upon it to work) then it probably needs to be redundant. If it isn't a mission-critical resource, then it probably doesn't need to be redundant.

Although it is a good practice to have redundant, distinct network connections to a mission-critical enterprise resource, it is imperative that we have redundant network cards installed in every mission-critical server. Of course, this is not as ideal as having both redundant network connections and redundant network cards, but it does offer a higher degree of fault tolerance at a fairly small cost:

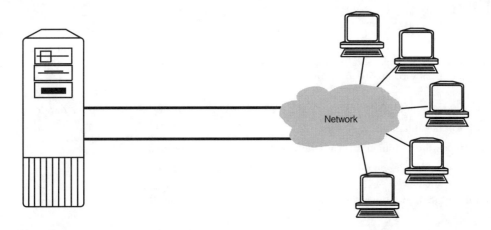

System Chips/Parts

Generally, rather than considering each of the individual chips on the motherboard or other electronic component, we consider that the component and the chips attached to it form a single point of failure for the system. By now, we would probably approach the redundancy question from the same common sense perspective, so I won't test your patience by going over it again. That's ok. Because in this case, once we determine that we need a redundant resource, we have another complex problem to solve.

The only real way to provide real-time redundancy at this level is to have a second stand-by resource. If your organization can stand a couple of hours of downtime, you might be able to get away with having a well-stocked parts department and a team of highly trained technicians. But there are many, relatively inexpensive, ways of adding even this high degree of fault tolerance to an enterprise. When we begin to add redundant resources as all-encompassing as entire servers to an enterprise, we begin working with something called a **cluster of resources**. This is such an important idea that we will talk about it in its own chapter, but for now, let's compare it to the RAID systems we talked about earlier.

With the RAID 1 system, we have essentially two resources available – a primary disk and a redundant disk. Remember that with the RAID 1 system, only one of the resources can be available for storage space at any one time. The redundant disk waits ready to take over in case of primary disk failure. We can do almost exactly the same thing with entire servers. We can create a redundant (mirrored) server that stands by passively waiting for the primary server to fail. When the primary server fails, the redundant (mirrored) server goes on-line and takes the place of the failed primary server. With RAID systems we call this disk configuration RAID 1, when we are working with entire servers, we call this server configuration **Active - Passive**. Like RAID 1, this configuration is essentially serial in nature.

Remember that with the RAID 5 system, we have a number of disks available and all of the functioning disks are on-line all of the time. All of the disks in a RAID 5 system share the entire load placed upon the system more or less equally. Of course, we can do almost exactly the same thing with entire servers. We can create an array of servers that work in parallel to handle the entire load placed upon the system. If one of the servers fails, that server is taken off-line and the entire load is redistributed more or less equally among the remaining servers. With RAID systems we called this disk configuration RAID 5, when we are working with entire servers, we can call this server configuration **Active – Active**. Like RAID 5, this configuration is essentially parallel in nature.

Fail Over

We use the words **fail over** to describe the steps that must be taken to allow the redundant resource to replace the primary resource in the system. This process can take many forms. At one level the process of restoring backed-up files is an example of a manual fail over process. If we examine the steps in detail, they probably look something like this:

❑   Preparation for failure. Perform regular backups, which create/refresh the redundant resource.

❑   At time of failure:

❑   repair the condition that caused the failure of the original resource.

❑   restore the files on the original resource to their last backed-up state.

As you might imagine, this process takes some time. Let's call the time this process takes the **recovery time**.

Of course, there is an alternative to manual fail over processes. An example is the type of fail over offered by the RAID system we talked about earlier. With a RAID system, the fail over process is automated. Whenever any disk in the array fails, the remaining disk(s) automatically assume the responsibilities of the failed resource. To the casual user, the transfer of control from one disk to the other(s) appears instantaneous. But upon closer examination, we find that there is, really, a recovery period. In well-designed RAID systems, the data flow during the recovery period is cached in local memory storage on the disk controller. The local memory storage serves to bridge the processing gap during the recovery period. This bridge is what gives the illusion of continuous operation and instantaneous fail over. Automated fail over processes are not limited to RAID controllers, we utilize automated fail over techniques in all aspects of enterprise design – including clustered servers.

Of course, the primary difference between manual and automated fail over is the length of the recovery time. In general, automated fail over processes are faster than comparable manual processes. But, it can still take several minutes for, say, a redundant server to replace its primary counterpart. One of the most interesting design problems we will work through in this book is the management of data flow during this recovery period. In a well-designed enterprise, the entire system should be able to give the illusion of continuous operation and instantaneous fail over in all but the most catastrophic circumstances.

Fault Tolerance and Load Balancing

As we saw with the Level 5 RAID system, one of the fringe benefits we can get from designing a fault tolerant system is the ability to use the redundant resources to share the load on the system. Let's go back to the spare tire example for a minute. Remember when we talked about the process of rotating tires. One of the things we did in that process was to move the spare tire from the trunk and place it on one of the axles. This allowed us to share the wear and tear more evenly among all 5 tires. The result of this process is to extend the usable life of all 5 tires – including the spare. Our fault tolerant resource, the spare tire, handled a more or less equal portion of the entire load when compared to the rest of the tires.

Let's compare this with RAID systems we talked about earlier. With the RAID 1 system, we have a primary resource and a duplicate resource – the primary disk and the mirrored disk. We utilized these resources in a serial fashion. We write to the primary disk, and through some hardware magic what we wrote on the primary disk is copied to the mirrored disk, in what appears to be real-time. In this scenario, the only benefit we get from the duplicate resource (mirrored disk) is a real-time backup/restoration for disk failures.

The duplicate resource does nothing to assist the primary resource with its everyday tasks. With RAID 1 there is no load balancing, no parallel processing, and no improvements in scalability. RAID 1 is serial in nature.

Next, let's consider the RAID 5 system. With the RAID 5 system, all of the disks in the array are all available as a primary resource (all disks are also available for redundant or backup duty as well). When we write to the disk array, we are in essence writing a little bit of data to each of the disks in parallel. We have already discussed how this increases the available bandwidth (throughput) for the entire array. With the RAID 5 model, we are utilizing parallel processing. This distributes the load across all of the available resources. RAID 5 systems are more scalable than RAID 1 systems, because RAID 5 is parallel in nature. That brings us to the next broad design stroke we need to consider when we are delivering an enterprise – **scalability**.

Scalable

Let's get this one straight at the start.

> Scalable means that a system is capable of growth. It does not mean that your enterprise must be capable of servicing the needs of tens of thousands of users the first day you turn the key. It does mean that the system should be capable of growing large enough to meet needs of any future number of users.

Historically, scalability has been the place where most PC-based development has fallen short. This was in part due to the general lack of processing power that older xx86 processor offered. But, it probably had more to do with the operating system's inability to perform real multi-user/multi-tasking processing. There is both good news and bad news on this front. The good news is that these hardware/OS shortcomings have been all but eliminated. The bad news is that we face another, more deeply entrenched barrier to scalability – antiquated development/deployment practices. These antiquated practices are the expected progeny of a system where multi-user/multi-tasking processing capability did not exist. Unfortunately, it is a lot harder to change old habits than it is to replace a motherboard or upgrade an operating system.

Developers and system integrators have grown accustomed to viewing the PC as an individual resource. This is a mistake. The real power of this class of machine is that there are hordes of them. With a little effort and a maybe a lot of imagination we can combine their capacities into a virtually unlimited amount of processing power. When we use multiple machines to handle processing, we can increase fault tolerance and optimize the performance of the entire system through load balancing.

In this chapter, we will take a look load balancing as well as a number of other techniques you can use to ensure that your enterprise caliber system is capable of growing to meet your organization's future needs. The first step in that direction is to be able to identify and separate the processing requirements.

Major Process Isolation

One of the first things we learn in engineering is that in order to solve any problem we must first define the problem. The second thing we learn is that the better we define the problem, the closer we are to the solution. For a long time now, there has been a huge, virtually undefined problem with most PC-based information system installations – the lack of major process isolation. Let's take at look now at the two major processes that should be separated.

OLTP – On Line Transaction Processing

Over the past 20 years or so, there have been great advances in the capacity of information processing systems. While it is true that we can attribute a lot of the improvement to better hardware and operating systems, there has been another quieter evolution going on. This evolution is responsible for the current techniques we use for storing and working with information at the database level. Over time, we have gradually reached the point where we have driven most of the redundancy out of our well-designed database systems. As an industry we have learned to design and optimize our systems around a unit of work we call a **transaction**. A transaction is one or more actions that are either performed as a whole or none of them are performed at all. The most optimal transaction uses the smallest possible data set that will get a particular task accomplished. This makes sense. At its core, every computer action manipulates a set of binary data. The smaller that set of binary data is, the faster we can process it. This type of processing is called **On-Line-Transaction-Processing (OLTP)**.

Of course, nothing is free. The problem with OLTP is hidden in one of the words we used to describe the process, that word is *optimize*. When we optimize any system to specialize in a particular task, we almost without exception, lessen that system's ability to perform different types of tasks. Think of a giraffe; this animal is optimized for grazing at the treetops. However, if a giraffe had to exist in grassland, devoid of trees, I am sure it would consider the experience nothing more than a big pain in the neck. Systems optimized to handle OLTP have essentially the same problem. They are finely tuned systems that thrive in a carefully balanced universe. If we disrupt the harmony of an optimized system in any way, we do more damage than we would if we did exactly the same thing to a non-optimized system. Now, the easiest way to throw an OLTP system off kilter is to ask it to process a huge multi-row, multi-table query. Remember that this system is optimized to work with the smallest possible data set. OLTP systems are not designed to handle the type of questions our users typically need to ask. Does this mean that we need to abandon everything we have learned about OLTP in the last 20 years? No!

What it means is that we have to learn to accept the OLTP system for what it is. It is as perfect as a giraffe. It offers the finest model we have for working with an incredibly huge number of very tiny, generally repetitive transactions, such as checking the balance of a bank account. What this means to the enterprise, is that we can use OLTP to handle approximately half of the work it will typically be asked to perform. What we need, now, is an equally optimized technique for handling the other half of the work.

DSS/OLAP – Decision Support Systems/On Line Analytical Processing

We call that other system, the **Decision Support Systems (DSS)**. There is also another phrase that people use to describe Decision Support System these days - **On-Line-Analytical-Processing (OLAP)** systems. I will use the two phrases interchangeably throughout this book. I have a feeling that the industry will move in the direction of accepting the OLAP moniker, but there are an awful lot of Decision Support System teams out there, so you never know.

Anyway, while the OLTP system is best characterized by its lack of redundancy, the DSS system revels in redundancy. We won't go into all of details here, but suffice it to say that in an DSS system, it wouldn't be unusual to find a particular city name stored repeatedly 100,000 or more times. While in a well-designed OLTP system, I would be surprised to see any city name stored more than once – period.

Of course, the DSS system is not designed for real-time transaction processing; it is really something of a data warehouse, i.e. it is optimized in a manner that makes it easy to get answers to questions, even complex enterprise-wide ones, in a very short time. This gives our users the type of tool they can use to find out how many Snickers candy bars were purchased from a particular store between the hours of 3:30 pm and 5:00 pm on the 5th of June 1998. The way the DSS is optimized, they could also find out how many Snickers candy bars were sold throughout the world during the same time frame with a couple of mouse clicks. In this case, we have optimized the system to make it easy to query. We do this at the cost of storage space, processing time, response time, and more. But all that really means is that this portion of our system has something of a different personality.

We expect the OLTP portion of the system to respond *immediately* to all requests, updates, etc. This system is optimized (at the database level) for speed first and then ease of use when dealing with single items (one employee, one customer, one purchase etc.). OLTP is a speed demon!

On the other hand, we expect the DSS portion of the system to provide us with easy access to answers for difficult (maybe formerly impossible) questions that span multiple (enterprise wide, all the employees, all the customers in France, etc.) items. This system is optimized (at the database level) for ease of use first and then speed when dealing with multiple items. DSS is easy to query.

Please note that when I refer to speed or ease of use, I am considering the system from a programmer's perspective. From the casual user's perspective, both systems should be easy to use and provide reasonable response times. Most users do not have trouble facing the reality that it takes slightly longer retrieve answers to enterprise-wide questions like – *How many Snickers bars were sold in Texas during the month of June?* - than it does to retrieve other answers like – *What is the suggested retail price for a Snickers bar in Texas?* Users understand this; it is common sense. But many IT departments operate as though these two questions are fundamentally the same. They are not. They utilize system resources differently. They must be handled separately.

Parallel Processing

Whenever I hear the word scalable or scalability in an enterprise design context, I immediately substitute the phrase **parallel processing**. The best way to ensure that a system is scalable (capable of growth) is to design the capacity for parallel processing into the system from the start. Parallel processing may be a foreign concept for most developers, but fear not; we have already taken a couple of huge steps towards understanding parallel processing while we looked at major process divisions and fault tolerance.

It is not difficult to understand the increases in fault tolerance and performance that parallel processing offers. But there are a number of ways to design a system that utilizes parallel processing. We need a little more information before we start making design decisions concerning parallel processing. In one of my Chemical Engineering classes, I had a Process Design professor that used to make the biggest deal out of continuums. It drove me crazy. In every one of his classes, he had to waste at least 5 precious minutes of my life talking about the difference between discrete and continuous values. I always wanted to scream, "WE GET IT!!! NOW SHUT UP AND GET ON WITH THE CLASS." I never yelled, and to this day I still don't understand his fixation with the subject, but I am going to talk about it anyway. Please bear with me.

Perhaps due to my naturally binary tendencies, I have come to realize that my professor had something of a point. While it is true that everything is not black and white, we can choose to define some gray color as the black and white boundary. In other words, if we were working with a continuous range of values of 1 to 100 representing white to black, we could set the black and white boundary at 50 and say that everything greater than 50 is a black number and everything below 50 is a white number. Therefore 14 1/3 would be a white color and 97.0004 is a black color.

This kind of generalization makes dealing with the continuous process much simpler. What we need to do in this section of the chapter is to define something of an informal parallel processing/serial-processing boundary. In other words, when we say that a system performs parallel processing, we should really say that the system kind of has parallel processing capabilities. Think about it; all computers perform some tasks in parallel. Parallelism is a kind of continuum; there are many degrees of parallelism that a system can exhibit. For instance, these days most enterprise caliber servers and many workstations have multiple processors.

Multiple Processor Servers

Multiple processor machines are everywhere these days. These give our system parallel processing capabilities, don't they? Well, yes and no. Machines with multiple processors do process some tasks in parallel. They do perform load balancing, and it has been my experience that they do this very well. However, I don't think we can truly say that a system made up of computers with multiple processors is a system with true parallel processing capabilities.

What machines with multiple processors do is to allow us to utilize more of the resources of the machine in question. Say that we have a machine with a system (bus disk I/O etc) that can transfer 100 units of data per second. Let's also say that each CPU on the machine is capable of processing 25 units of data per second. If this machine has only 1 CPU, then at best we can expect 25% utilization of the system's resources. If we add a second CPU, then we might expect to utilize 50% of the system's resources. I won't step through every possibility, but consider what happens when we add the 5th CPU. Can we transfer 125 units of data through the system? No! Is this computer scalable? Well, yes and no. If we purchased this box with 1 or 2 processors, then we can expect it to grow until it has a total of 4 processors. If we purchased this box with 4 processors, then it cannot continue to grow. In short, there is a real limit to the amount of processing that we can perform with a single machine. Most manufacturers have found that the real improvements in performance begin to decrease after 4 processors. And with present technology, anything more than 8 processors in a single computer does not significantly improve the computer's performance. What multiple CPU machines do is to move the limit from the processor to another limit in the same box. The bottom line is that there is a limit. That means that for a truly scalable (parallel) system we need another answer.

Multiple Servers

It almost goes without saying that, we should try to maximize the performance of every piece of our enterprise. So, depending upon the performance requirements of a particular component (read component in this context as one of the servers in our enterprise), multiple processors are an excellent way to ensure high utilization of the component's resources. But if we want to design a scalable system with true parallel processing capabilities, we need to do more than just add processors to individual servers. We need to add more servers.

If we can dedicate multiple machines to a particular task, then we have increased the fault tolerance of the system. If one of the machines or any part of that machine fails, we should be able to replace it with the other machine(s) designed to perform that task. The question is how do we best utilize the redundant resources.

We could do that by having a stand-by server for each server in our enterprise. This would give us something like the RAID 1 system – **Active-Passive**. It would increase the fault tolerance of our system, but it wouldn't do anything to improve the system's overall performance characteristics. It would also mean that we have at best only 50% of our enterprise's resources available at any one time.

There is another possibility. We can model our multiple server solution after the RAID 5 system instead of the RAID 1 system. This would give us an **Active-Active** server configuration. If we do that, then every server in the enterprise including the redundant servers, will be available all of the time unless one of them fails. We can then plan to utilize their resources in parallel, nearly the same way we utilize the RAID 5 system's disks. This places 100% of our enterprise's resources on-line rather than the 50% a serial solution would offer.

This is the point on the continuum where we will draw the boundary line where we consider that the system is capable of true parallel processing – when we have multiple servers dedicated to a single processing task available in an Active-Active configuration. Now that we have a common point of reference, let's take another look at process division.

Major Process Load Balancing

The first step in load balancing is to segregate the major processes that utilize the servers' resources in wildly different manners. For any but the smallest of installations, this means that we need an entirely separate database systems for OLTP and DSS portions of our enterprise (read system in this context as every piece of hardware/OS/software required to move data from the user to the storage area and back). In some installations this may mean a single server for OLTP portion and a second for DSS portion, in others it may mean tens of servers for each portion. The bottom line is that every enterprise is comprised of at least two physical systems – the OLTP and the OLAP systems:

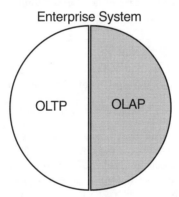

Minor Process Load Balancing

The next step in load balancing also involves processes. In this case, we are attempting to balance a finer grain of processing. To avoid any confusion let me say at the outset, that we must perform an identical minor process analysis on both the OLTP and OLAP portions of the enterprise. In this section, we will walk through each of the minor processes. We will start with the processes that occur closest to the data storage area and work outward through each of the other processes we must perform to either deliver data to or receive data from the end user. Basically, this minor processing includes four kinds of processing:

- ❑ Data storage
- ❑ Data manipulation
- ❑ Data/Business rule integration
- ❑ Presentation

Data Storage Processes

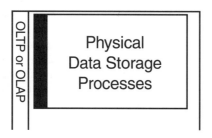

The processes that are used to store data are quite different from the other process in our enterprise. Take a second to think about the physical/mechanical actions that must take place when we work with physical data storage.

If we design our system correctly, this may be one of the few places where the system is actually performing reads and writes to an actual physical disk. If we compare this type of activity with another type of activity, say working with a dynamic link library that has been previously loaded into memory, we see that the two activities are so dissimilar that we might spec out entirely different servers to perform each action.

> **In other words, for a server that spends most of its time reading from and writing to physical disks, like a typical relational database, we would be wise to spend the lion's share of our equipment budget on the physical disk subsystem.**

We can improve overall system performance if we design this server to handle the specialized task of performing physical disk reads and writes. Of course, this means that we are building something as specialized as a giraffe. When we tune this machine's performance characteristics for improved disk I/O, we are probably making it somewhat inefficient for another task. Is this specialization the best course of action? It depends; in a pinch you *can* drive in a screw with a hammer, and I guess that you *can* pound in a nail with a screwdriver. But I don't know too many *professional* carpenters that would advocate either practice.

I always liken the data storage area of an enterprise system to a precious gem, a diamond. The bottom line of most computer activity is to either place information into the system or retrieve information from the system. Information is the most precious commodity that an organization can possess. Even if your organization mines diamonds for a living, it won't profit one whit unless it knows where the diamonds are located and can deploy its assets in an economically feasible manner to retrieve the gems. Information is what makes this possible. The organization's information **is** the data store.

Please don't take this to mean that all of the information for an organization should be stored in a single server or bank of clustered servers. This would make programming simple and life wonderful, but it ignores reality. In every organization, the data is typically stored in everything from mainframes to Excel spreadsheets. What we need to do is to strive to design a system that allows us to work with our organization's data as though it did exist on a single machine. When we make decisions about how to distribute processing across the available infrastructure, we must always remember that the goal of distributed architecture is to distribute the processing – not to distribute the data. In this book, we will focus on the data store server as a controllable device – a relational database, but the overall design of the infrastructure must give us the ability to point the entire system at a different data store without skipping a beat.

What this really means is that we have identified a second set of processes that must exist close to our data store. These processes must be able to wrap around our enterprise's data store and make it appear to be a single source. Let's call these processes **Data Manipulation processes**.

Data Manipulation Processes

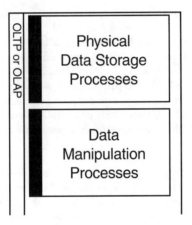

Data manipulation processes are designed to know where an organization's data is stored and know the steps that must be taken to retrieve, remove, or change that data. These processes do not typically perform tasks like disk I/O themselves. They usually invoke other processes, most of them on another physical machine, to handle the physical writes and reads. As I said above, the data manipulation processes are designed to wrap around the core of data available to our organization and give the programmers, and the users, access to the entirety of that data as though the data existed on a single machine. In reality, that data may exist on a centralized SQL Server machine, but it may also exist in legacy machines like mainframes, tired old UNIX systems, in flat files, and maybe even somewhere out on the Internet.

Once the data manipulation processes have located the correct storage area and have executed the proper commands required to invoke those storage process, they have one additional responsibility. They must package/unpackage (**marshal**) the data for transport either to or from the data storage process it has identified for the particular data set it is working with.

In many ways, it is like the data manipulation processes replace traditional database tables and flat files from the programmer's perspective. We use these specialized processes to encapsulate or hide the sometimes messy things we have to do to work with these devices – database tables, flat files, a web site on the Internet, etc. We create these specialized processes, in part, so that we can solve the data access problem once and be done with it. But we have also done something else – something far more important. We have given ourselves a way to separate out one of the processes our system needs to perform. This process is now freed from the monolith. We can work with it as a separate entity. We can move it from one machine to another, we can run the process simultaneously on several machines if we want to or need to. If we find that this particular process demands a little extra from our system, we can address its needs directly without having to make changes to every other portion of the system.

In this case, we have learned that we can think of data manipulation processes as a set of functions that cover an organization's data. They are intended give us a kind of intelligence about the underlying data that would be difficult to come by otherwise. Rather than demanding that every developer and user understand the curious and perhaps confusing design of the underlying data store, these functions are designed to provide access to that data without regard to its particular physical storage context. When you spend a lot of time identifying and working with different sets of processes, you come to find that processes have personalities or characteristics. In general, the data manipulation processes are essentially functions. Their personality is strictly business – they execute a task and return a value. They perform that task as quickly as and efficiently as possible and do not hang around for long periods of time.

It is important to segregate the data manipulation processes from the data storage processes. While the physical act of storing data is a disk-intensive process, the data manipulation processes rarely perform any disk I/O. A well-designed data manipulation server should spend most of its time making calls to a series of dynamic link libraries. Ideally, these dynamic link libraries should already be loaded into fast random access memory (RAM). The disk I/O in this process should be only that amount required by the operating system for memory swaps. Of course, there should be enough system memory and raw processing power to ensure that the disk-based memory swaps are as infrequent as possible.

The next set of minor processes we must consider are the processes that integrate the data we have stored with the business rules our organization has chosen to apply to the data. We can call that set of processes the **Data/Business Rule Integration processes**.

Data/Business Rule Integration Processes

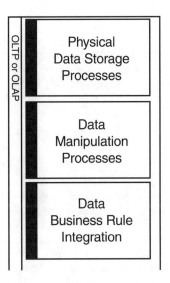

This set of processes is responsible for integrating the data the organization stores with the organization's business savvy or talent. These processes are kind of like the work a master carpenter performs when he turns six oak boards into a piece of fine furniture. For a retail company, the organization's talent (business rule integration processes) may be the carefully crafted functions that set the retail price of an item at exactly the point that maximizes sales volume while simultaneously maximizing profits.

At first, glance, the way these processes execute physically is nearly identical to the data manipulation processes we just considered. But if you look close enough you will find that there are two real differences in the way these processes perform their task.

The first difference between the two is what the processes *know*. While data manipulation processes know about the organization's data, the data/business rule integration processes know about the organization's talent. Their job is to pull together data and business rules, and by combining the two, somehow increase the value of both. Again, if data were wood, the business rules would be the carpenter's talent or skill. This difference doesn't seem to change our processing requirements at all. By the time these processes see the data, it is delivered in memory (or at least available through some cache/virtual memory facility). We do not have any disk I/O issues to contend with here. Why do these processes deserve a different category if they are so similar to the data manipulation processes?

I am sure many of you are prepared to argue that both types of processes use a series of dynamic link libraries. In both cases, the dynamic link libraries should be loaded into the host machine's random access memory for optimal performance. The division between these two sets of processes is really more of a logical (*theoretical*) difference than a physical difference. So, unless the physical proximity between the data store and the presentation sphere dictates it, there is no reason to separate these processes onto different machines.

Did I mention the second difference? No? Oops!

The second difference between these two sets of processes is found in their personality. The data manipulation processes are just-the-facts type of guys. You tell them what you need. They deliver it. They shut down. (Well actually, they cycle, but that is another story.) The data/business rule integration processes have a different personality. They might hang around for a while. Instead of being like a single function, they offer an assortment of goodies that a programmer might need to use for a while. So, although they are functionally (from a purely technical point of view) identical, they do actually take up the server's resources quite differently. To sum it up, the second difference between the two types of processes is the amount of time each one hangs around before they shut down. Generally, the data manipulation processes execute quickly and shut down, while the data/business rule integration processes tend to stick around in memory for a while.

> *If we do our jobs correctly, even this time difference will be measured in milliseconds, but those little guys add up. Our purpose here is to identify the difference so that we can choose to do something to manage it in our enterprise's design.*

Now that we have identified this set of processes, we can peel them away from the monolith that most developers see as an application. As with the data manipulation processes we discussed earlier, once we have separated them, we can address their needs specifically. In this case, we have a set of processes that generally take longer to complete than their related data manipulation processes. When these two sets of processes had to be treated as a single unit, we could not do anything to address this difference. Now that we have separated them, we can immediately see one way to make our system more scalable. Because these processes take longer to execute, we should instantiate more of these processes than the number of data manipulation processes that are running at any one time. Think about this carefully. This simple notion is one of the most powerful allies we have to make our systems more scalable. If a process takes longer to complete, then we can even up the processing load across an entire system by running more instances of the slower process than instances of the faster process. I learned this concept as something called the **critical path method**. All it really means is that we can improve system performance by identifying potential bottlenecks and doing something to cure the bottleneck. When we treat an entire system or application as a single set of processes, we have given up the ability to tune the system at this level. If we don't separate out the data manipulation processes from the data/business rule integration processes, then each data manipulation process will require the same amount of time from our system as the longer data/business rule integration process that spawned it.

If you think about it for a minute, you might come up with another place where we could do some tuning. Just like this process spawned a data manipulation process, there is another process that spawns the data/business rule integration process – exactly, the **Presentation process**.

Presentation Processes

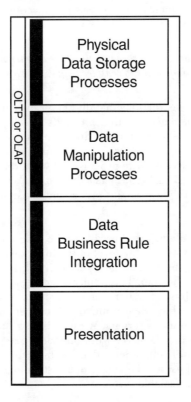

Although it may not be too intuitive, the presentation set of processes is more like the data storage set of processes than the two other intermediate processes. Think about it.

The GUI's job is to present or receive data to or from the end user. The real difference between the data storage and presentation set of processes is where we write the end result of the process. While the data storage processes primarily write to the system's disks, the presentation processes primarily write to the end users' workstation screens, files, and printers. Nevertheless, both sets of processes are concerned with changing fleeting binary data transmissions into something of a more persistent nature.

The most important thing to realize about presentation processes is that they are by definition the slowest processes in our system. They must wait until the other processes have completed before they can begin to perform their task. If you are thinking that we have identified another bottleneck in the critical path of our system, I agree with you completely. When we think about the impact of the presentation processes on our system, we need to consider where these processes really execute. If they are really executing on the clients' desktops, as long as we separate them from the other processes we have done our jobs of distributing the processing load across the entire system. But, if they execute on servers, we might need to give these guys more weight in our design considerations. In the case of the application we will be focusing on in this book, we will be using Internet Information Server to handle the presentation processes.

If we utilize an Internet Information Server (IIS) machine in our enterprise, then we are in fact performing a lot of the GUI programming at the level of the server(s). True, the IIS machine does not perform the actual screen writes, but when someone asks it a question, it must look to the disk to find the correct page, read it into memory, and execute the instructions on the page.

Notice the disk I/O issue as with the data storage process. If we do our jobs well, we should be able to limit this activity, but it is important to consider it in our design analysis.

With Active Server Pages (ASP), the instructions that the server executes at the server are, in large part, designed to cause the data to be placed on the end user's screen in a specific way. That is a lot of server-side processing dedicated to the user interface. So I think it is reasonable to place the processes that define the look of the user's screen (even if they execute on a server) in the same bunch of presentation processes as the actual screen write processes. If we add this set of processing responsibilities to the ones we covered earlier it means that, in total, we have identified four minor processing divisions that exist within the two major processing divisions we have for every enterprise system.

Now that we have taken the time to identify and break out the different processing requirements, we have gained the ability to tune our system at the level of the individual processes. This means that rather than solving every processing shortfall at the level of an entire application, we can focus our attention on the actual source of the shortfall. This ability to add resources where they are needed will allow us to design an efficient physical system that can grow to meet the needs of any number of users. In the next chapter, we will see how we can mirror the concept of logical processing divisions across a physical system composed of many servers. We will discover that this division of processes is really a lot more than just a thought problem. We will find that the steps that we have taken to divide the processes will translate into a set of components that can be distributed across as many machines as we need to handle any number of users. The ability of a system to grow to meet the needs of any number of users is the definition of a scalable system.

So far, we have covered the topics of availability and scalability. I am sure that in many readers' minds that means that we haven't even considered the third broad design stroke of security yet. I am afraid that I would have to disagree. As far as I am concerned, security is a lot more than something we can simply drape over an existing system. Security must be designed into even the tiniest element of the system at the time that element is designed.

Secure

Personally, I have a little trouble with this one. When most people think about enterprise security, their mind immediately turns to external threats. They conjure up images of some caffeine-swilling outcast spending untold hours trying to break into their system. And many really believe (perhaps with some level of justification) that their competitors have hired industrial espionage experts to break into their system and steal their company's secret designs for men's mini-skirts or something. Sadly, the same decision-makers that will cheerfully spend sinful amounts of money battling these unlikely windmills cringe at the thought of spending 1/1,000th the amount on a something as basic as a redundant server. When we say that an enterprise is secure it means a lot more than when we say that the enterprise is safe from some external threat. In real life, it doesn't matter whether the rat that brought the system down was some cracker spoofing an IP address or an actual rodent that chewed through a non-redundant power cord. In either case, the result is the same. The system is no longer available to the users.

Does this mean that we can ignore the crackers, crooks, and spies? Of course not! These can be real threats. They should be given their due. But, we do need to stop thinking about security threats solely as external menaces that break into our system from the outside. The number of real threats any enterprise system faces is huge. What we need to do is to modify our definition of a secure system. When we say that an enterprise is secure, what we should be saying is that the authorized users of that system and the organization that owns it can count on the system to protect their interests.

Let's play a little game. Imagine for a moment that we could design and implement a system that was 100% safe from external threats. Can we now say that this system is secure? Does it protect the organization's interests? Let's throw a couple of thought problems at it and see how this perfect security system fairs.

- ❑ **Problem:** A real rat decides to commit suicide by chewing through a non-redundant power cable to a non-redundant server that houses all of the organization's data.
  Outcome: The system is down. The external threat security system did not protect the organization's interests.

- ❑ **Problem:** The company's new marketing program was a stellar success. The system responsible for taking and filling the orders cannot keep up with the demand. Some orders are not being filled.
  Outcome: The organization has lost the profits from the orders that it failed to fill. The external threat security system did not protect the organization's interests.

- ❑ **Problem:** Stan in accounting decides that he will use his security privileges to transfer some of the money from the organization's savings account into his own savings account.
  Outcome: This threat comes from within. The external threat security system did not protect the organization's interests.

- ❑ **Problem:** Crumb, the criminal cracker spends 1-man year attempting to breach the enterprise's new security system.
  Outcome: Crumb is foiled. The external threat security system protected the organization's interests.

Calm down! I know that we don't typically view all of these things as security threats. That's unfortunate. I would love to do a study comparing the real cost of the first three items against the fourth item on the list. I am sure that I would find that most organizations do a pretty good job of shooting themselves in the foot without any outside help. You don't have to tell anyone else, but I want you to take a minute or two, look to your own experience, and add up all the time you have spent doing battle with ingenious crackers. Done? OK, now add up all the time you have spent doing battle with idiotic internal threats. Enough said?

When I consider the things that really pose a threat to an enterprise's users' or owners' interests, I usually end up with a roadmap that looks something like this:

- ❑ Fault tolerance
- ❑ Scalability
- ❑ Internal access control
- ❑ External access control

Throughout this book, we will revisit these four subjects time and time again. They are the cornerstones upon which we will construct a secure enterprise system. We have already taken a look at the first two concepts earlier in this chapter, so let's concentrate on last two - internal access and external access - for the remainder of this chapter.

Security means Controlling Access to Resources

Windows NT has achieved a C2 security rating from the US Department of Defense (DoD). That sounds pretty impressive, but what does it mean to a real enterprise installation. It means that the Windows NT operating system has the potential to be the basis for an extremely secure enterprise.

One of my great joys in life is creating art. So to indulge myself, every once in a while, I splurge on some ridiculously expensive graphics software. One time, a friend of mine asked me what I could do with the high-end graphics application I had just purchased. The question took me by surprise. At first I thought she was kidding, but I could see by her expression that she really wanted to know. So, I thought about it for a second or two before I gave her my reply. Then I asked her this question. "What can a carpenter do with a load of wood?" She paused, smiled knowingly and said that she "...guessed it depended upon the carpenter."

Windows NT manages security by controlling access to objects. To Windows NT, everything is an object – files are objects, users are objects, printers are objects, and so on... When an authorized user logs onto NT, the OS creates a unique instance of a user object to represent the physical user, and assigns that object an ID. We can call that ID an **access token**.

Every time the user attempts to access *any* object, the OS checks to see whether or not the particular access token has permission (in NT this is known as a **privilege**) to access the object in question. This means that NT gives us the ability to control access for any access token all the way down to the object level. Incredible! But it doesn't stop there. Controlling access at the object level offers a lot of security potential, but we can actually reduce the grain of access control further. Consider that we can also specify in the privileges exactly how this particular access token may interact with the object in question. One access token may have read-only privileges while another access token, representing the user sitting just to the right, may have write, execute, or some other combination of interaction privileges. Powerful! If you agree that this level of control is really something you may be amazed to learn that, just to tie a bow on the whole security process, NT will faithfully keep track of every interaction every user has made with every object. How's that for a load of wood?

The Windows NT security model gives us a lot of raw material to work with, but it won't do anything if we don't use it correctly. This is not a book about NT administration, so I am not going to rehash the remove the guest account, etc. stuff. If you are responsible for that type of thing, then I am sure you have several good books on the subject. Instead, I am going to touch a couple of basic topics that we will build on during the programming and application development portions of the book. I will try to approach the security topic with the same common sense approach that we applied to the fault tolerance issue earlier. In other words, we will try to identify some security issues, and then we will consider how to deal with them. Rather than trying to end up with some rigid list of do's and don'ts we should try to develop something akin to a common sense approach that we can use whenever we have to deal with a security issue.

Internal Access

Charity starts at home. So, before we venture off into the dark realm of Bastion Hosts, Belt & Suspender firewalls, Point-to-Point-Tunneling-Protocol and the like, we need to take an inventory of our efforts to control access to resources on our site. This internal examination is a must, before we even begin to consider the dangers from without.

Physical Access

It is possible to configure Windows NT so that the most potentially dangerous activities must be performed at the system console. In other words, the person who wishes to inflict harm on the system by performing these activities must be physically sitting at the computer to gain access to the objects on that computer. This means that we can exercise a high degree of control over a system's resources simply by limiting the number of individuals that have physical access to the mission-critical servers. Our first line of defense is to limit the individuals that can gain access to the equipment.

A common sense rule might state that the enterprises valuable resources are safer when they are physically out of the reach of the bad guys. Most organizations wouldn't dream of leaving 50 or 100 thousand dollars in cash lying around in a room without a lock. But, it is not unusual for the same organizations to have mission-critical servers sitting in rooms with minimal or no physical security.

> **If a resource is valuable enough to require security, lock it up.**

System Accounts

When a user attempts to log onto any Windows NT workstation, the user is prompted for a username and password. The combination of username and password are run through a *reportedly* one-way algorithm that changes the unique combination into something, let's call it an authorization string. This is more important than it sounds. It means that this authorization string is the only thing that passes through the network, not the password or username. Common sense tells us that the less exposure something as important as a username/password combination gets, translates into less chances for the bad guys to be able to steal or otherwise commandeer it. Anyway, the authorization string works like this. The string is compared against the **security accounts manager** (**SAM**) file that is stored in the `Winnt\System32\Config` directory of one of the domain (backup or primary) controllers on the network. If the authorization string is found, then the user is authenticated. If the authorization string is not found, then the user is denied all access. What this means to us is that we don't have to reinvent this wheel when we are designing applications for our enterprise. Instead, we can build upon the strong foundation Windows NT offers us.

Remember the Windows NT security model. Once a user has successfully logged onto a Windows NT system, the system believes that the user is whoever the user said he or she was. From that point on, the system vouches for the user acknowledging that the user has been verified. It says in essence, "this user's credentials are in order." It does that by assigning every user a unique token, which represents the user from that point on. Every action that the token initiates is funneled through the security reference monitor.

This system will only allow the user access to those objects that the user has privileges for. And, as we learned earlier, it can also be used to grant only specific types of access to specific users. If the object we need to provide security for is important enough, we can also track every access or attempted access of that object. In short, Windows NT allows us to control the access of every user right down to the way that user can interact with any particular object.

When we design an application to run on an enterprise, we should be able to count on Windows NT security. For the most part, we can. The only thing we really can't count on is that the original logon was honest. In other words, the Windows NT security system is powerful, but it is not omniscient. All it can do is to compare the username/password combination to see if it matches the SAM file. There is no way for the system to know whether or not the user at the console is who the user says he is.

This means that the biggest improvement we can make to the overall security of a system is to ensure that each user makes it difficult to decipher his or her password. Microsoft offers a free application that can enable the system administrator to enforce a very complex password policy. If an enterprise is serious about security, after controlling physical access to the machines, this is the next step to take.

Application Access

Once we have done our part to limit physical access to machines and our part to train, or force if necessary, our users to use strong password protection, it is almost like we have hired Microsoft to construct the foundation for our applications' security model. We can off-load a big portion of our security issues right onto Windows NT. We can safely begin to design an application security model that begins with the premise that Windows NT has authenticated the user. If we accept Windows NT's acknowledgement that the user's credentials are in order, we don't need to worry about keeping track of application-level passwords. This by itself plugs up a huge security hole. I cannot tell you how many assignments I have been on where I found tables with user logon IDs and unencrypted passwords right out in the open. Anyway, we can use NT Security to filter out the non-authenticated users. In Chapters 9 through 16, we will cover a myriad of ways that we can design our own objects to build on Windows NT's verification of credentials. We will examine ways that we can extend the security model right down to the individual properties and methods our objects are constructed from.

Audit Trails

As I have already said, we can instruct Windows NT to log every activity that an individual attempts while logged onto the system, or even while that individual is attempting to log on to the system. This is powerful stuff, but this book is really not about NT administration, so I won't bore you with ways that we can use NT's audit trails. This book is about programming. Therefore, I will tell you that when we learn to build enterprise caliber objects, we extend NT's audit trail standard right into each object we build. In other words, every time a user changes or attempts to change the data in our system, we will create an audit trail that shows who did it, when they did it, where they did it, and what they did. As an added measure of protection, we also include the ability to undo anything that anyone has done.

Windows NT offers a robust security model that we will utilize and emulate in every way possible. As you will see, this technique requires us to design security into every object in our system. Rather than attempting to plug up or cover up security holes, we will strive to eliminate them during the design phase. This will result in a security system that gets ever more difficult to breach as the intruder gets closer to the center – or data – of our system. In other words, while the occasional dedicated cracker might penetrate some of our outer defenses, that interloper should be faced with increasingly more difficult challenges as he or she attempts to further breach the system. Even though our security net is designed to get tighter as we get further into the system, we still won't make it easy for the bad guys to get through the outer layer of armor. We will control external access.

External Access

Almost everyone knows that Windows NT has earned a C2 security rating, but I don't think that most people know that it earned its C2 rating configured as a stand-alone computer without a network connection or a floppy drive. I was surprised too! I bring that up, because what it means is that as soon as we connect any two computers together, we have placed ourselves at a higher level of jeopardy. Moreover, just so we are clear as to the extent of the problem, I want to point out that what we are doing as an industry, is working feverishly to ensure that every computer in the world is connected to every other computer in the world. Now that you have a sense of the overall scope of the problem, we can begin to tackle the external side of the access equation. To most people these days, when we talk about external threats, their minds immediately shift to questions concerning the Internet and its cousins the Intranet and the Extranet.

Intranet

An Intranet is really just those portions of our LAN or WAN that are connected using the TCP/IP protocol. So, the external access risk we face here is really handled by standard NT Security in exactly the same manner we talked about earlier under the heading Internal Access.

There is one area of the WAN that we should pay special attention to though. That is the **Remote Access Services** (**RAS**). This service does use standard Windows NT security model, so it treats those users as though they were sitting at any other desk in the office. However, it may not really be safe to do this, because the users that access the system in this way do not go through any of the ordinary physical security measures most places of business employ. In other words, as long as the users are on site, we can employ physical mechanisms to keep out unauthorized individuals. We lock buildings. We place guards at the door. We just sense that if the guy sitting in John's desk is not John, that something may be awry. It is not possible to do this type of human reasoned security checking with RAS users. Other than that, we treat the Intranet proper, as just an extension of the network.

Internet

All over the world, organizations are rushing to get at least part of their resources out onto the Internet. It is great for business. It offers an excellent way for companies to deliver cost efficient 24 hour a day customer service. I can track my packages on FedEx web site without either one of us paying a dime for the long distance charges. I regularly purchase software over the Internet, and I collaborated with my editors at Wrox over the Internet. If you want the most up-to-date copy of the sample code in this book you can get it by logging onto Wrox's web site. Make no mistake about it. That is the direction, and I think its great!

But it means that organizations need to consider the external access security issues on this front. I wouldn't even want to attempt to list the external access hazards; it would take too long, and I could only be certain that I missed at least some of them. There are of course other political issues concerning what data should be open to the general public and so on… That is a job for a bureaucrat so I won't go there. As for the protection of our precious data that the politicians expose to the general public, we will cover the steps that we can take to ensure data safety when we learn to construct Enterprise Caliber Data Objects. What we will do here is to look at the best investment any organization can make when considering placing any of their resources on the Internet – the firewall.

The Firewall

The firewall works very much like the name implies. It places an impenetrable barrier (a wall of fire) around an organization's internal network assets. But it really is more like a very secure passageway rather than an impassable barrier. It picks and chooses exactly which data transmissions it will allow into and out of the network it is charged to protect. And, rather than being something like a single device, it is actually a series of devices and processes that work together to ensure that the firewall filters out the packets (a small amount of information) it is not authorized to transfer across the boundary that the firewall delineates. This means that in order to understand the concept of a firewall, we really need to understand the devices, processes, and policies that make up the firewall.

Packet Filtering

The simplest types of *firewalls* are really nothing more than a packet-filtering mechanism – this can be accomplished with just about any router capable of screening packets. It works like this: all of the external network traffic is directed to a single point of penetration that exposes the protected network. On a hardware level, this point of penetration is a device called the **screening router**.

As the name implies, the screening router is used to filter out which IP addresses are allowed to pass through the point of penetration:

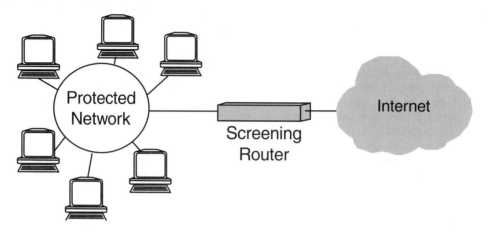

Of course, I wouldn't want the job of updating the list of IP addresses that are allowed to pass through this point of penetration. A true enterprise-level solution requires something a little more manageable. For most enterprises, the real job of managing this list of acceptable addresses falls to the next device in our firewall, the **Bastion Host**.

Bastion Hosts

A Bastion Host is really just a secure server that is placed at the protected network's point of penetration, often in front of the screening router. In most cases the screening router is still used, but in these cases it serves as a gateway to the single Bastion Host.

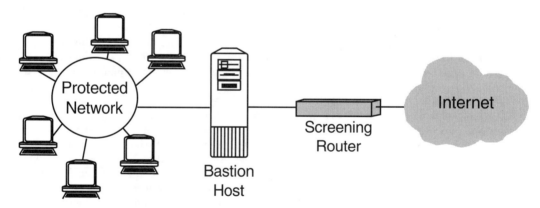

Of course, since the Bastion Host is really a server it is easier to program it, or configure it, for the job of managing the list of IP addresses than can be allowed to access the protected network. Indeed, the Bastion Host can use any set of rules that we select in order to do its acceptance and rejection of users.

Our firewall is no longer limited to simple IP address filtering. We can handle that portion of the access problem with looser controls on the screening router and apply whatever level of control we choose at the Bastion Host. Allow me to suggest that the Windows NT security model offers an excellent model for the control of authorized users and their access of resources (objects) deployed across the enterprise.

Yeah, that means that we can use a Windows NT Domain controller as a Bastion Host and that we can use exactly the same Windows NT security that we employ to protect our enterprise, to protect the outside world's access via the Internet. We can control every user's access to every object in the system. Of course, when we are talking about the Internet, we have to realize that some of the users will not members of our domain. We can use Windows NT to grant these users access to some portion of our resources, but we need to realize that this places some of our resources at risk. This realization is responsible for one of the finest examples of external security currently available – the **Belt and Suspenders firewall**.

Belt & Suspenders Firewall

Perhaps the most accepted firewall system is the Belt and Suspenders firewall. If you look at it the image, you should notice why it got its name. In case it isn't obvious, the diagonally striped section makes a convincing belt and the two lines that are made up from the screening routers to the firewall could be mistaken for suspenders. That's how I remember it anyway. I think the name actually originated as a tribute to its high level of security. If you look carefully, you will notice that it is really more like two firewalls than one, as it has a dual screening router design. This added protection makes it as safe as wearing both a belt and suspenders.

It works very much like the simpler Bastion Host/screening router solution. In fact, the first firewall is actually those two components connected to the Internet. The second firewall is given by the combination of the Bastion Host and the second screening router that connects to the protected network. The striped area that I referred to as a belt, is really called the **demilitarized zone** (**DMZ**). It is almost as though, in this section of our network between the two screening routers, we have called a truce with the external threats. We took our best shot to protect some of our assets with the first screening router. The machines that live in the demilitarized zone are almost like sacrificial lambs. We place them in somewhat of a less protected area than the rest of our network assets. It is the price we pay for access to the Internet. Notice that one of the servers in the demilitarized zone is the RAS server. Many organizations do this. I think that they have an intuitive sense of the slightly more risky nature of the RAS portion of the WAN. Personally, I don't understand this. It seems to me that if someone can logon by impersonating another user, Windows NT will allow that impersonator to fool all portions of the system, no matter if the RAS server is in the DMZ or not.

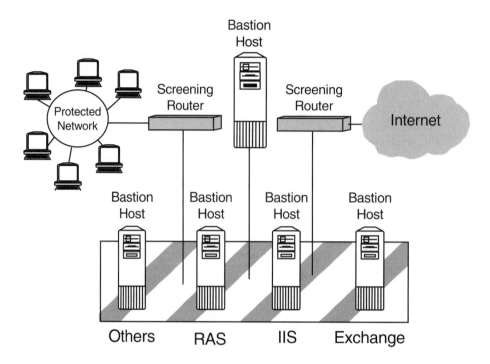

Extranet – Virtual Private Network

The term **Extranet** seems to come and go. I almost think people are beginning to get so used to the idea of the Internet – making purchases with credit cards etc. – that they forget how open and dangerous the Internet really can be. An Extranet (also known as a **Virtual Private Network**, **VPN**), is an extension, or perhaps I should say implant, that strives to make the Internet a safe place between two specific points. It uses a special protocol called **Point-to-Point-Tunneling-Protocol** (**PPTP**) to carve out a private channel between two specific nodes in the Internet:

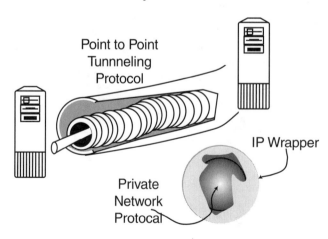

If you look at the image shown here, the outermost communication casing (the one that is cut away) represents the standard connection between the two Internet nodes. Within that casing, you should notice another section of "wire" that appears to be flexible, maybe like an accordion. This offers a something of a visual representation of what the Point-to-Point-Tunneling-Protocol does. It is almost as though PPTP pushes the accordion-like structure through the main connection – it drills a tunnel or private channel. Once this private channel has been opened, the two nodes can communicate freely within this channel safe from prying eyes.

The way PPTP actually works is really a pretty good example of good object-oriented programming. It can take a different type of network protocol NetBEUI, for instance, and encapsulate it in a standard IP packet. I think of it like an M&M candy where the IP packet is the candy coating that stops the chocolate inside from melting on your hands. Anyway, the interface just below the IP packet contains enough information to allow Windows NT to make some security decisions concerning the safety of the underlying contents. If it passes all of the NT security barriers, then the packet is opened and the information is allowed to enter the private network allowing the users to perform tasks that they might not have been able to do without the other protocol.

We can use this PPTP to create virtual private networks, but at this time, it still requires some special equipment. The client must be equipped with a Front End Processor. The Front End Processor and the PPTP-capable server transmit encrypted data over the PPTP. The combination of the encrypted data and NT security allow any authorized user a private, secure, personal link to the server using the Internet as the trunk line. This means the organization can save money on long distance telephone calls and or the expense of dedicated WAN lines.

Summary

In this chapter, we began to look at a number of different techniques you can use to ensure that whenever any of your customers needs an enterprise resource, that resource will be available. In general, we found that this type of high-availability system owes its robustness to some very basic design decisions we make concerning fault tolerance. Then we began a long and deliberate dissection of the processes that make up applications to learn how we could take advantage of those separations to design a system that was truly scalable. Finally, we took a look at some basic security concepts that we could employ to safeguard our users' interests in the enterprise. Of course, this chapter only represents the beginning of our design process.

In the next chapter, we will take some of the information that we considered in this chapter and see if we can mirror what we found about processes into an actual physical system. In the next chapter, we will work through the design of an enterprise caliber server farm.

Person
Base Properties

ID
Last Name
First Name
Middle Name
Birth Date
Sex

Object Type Definitions

Object Ty...

Employee OTD	User OTD	Engineer OTD	Doctor OTD	Student OTD
Grade	Specialty	Specialty	Specialty	Major
Status	Hourly Rate	Experience	Certification	Minor
Property 3	Law School	Property 3	Property 3	Year
Property 4	Property 4	Property 4	Property 4	Property 4
Property 5	Property 5	Property 5	Property 5	Property 5
Property 6	Property 6	Property 6	Property 6	Property 6
Property 7	Property 7	Property 7	Property 7	Property 7
Property 8	Property 8	Property 8	Property 8	Property 8
Property 9	Property 9	Property 9	Property 9	Property 9
Property 10	Property 10	Property 10	Property 10	Property 10

Property Set Definitions

Property Set

3

Clustering & Server Farm Design

We spent a good portion of the last chapter learning to dissect monolithic applications into a set of major and minor processing divisions. We did that because we instinctively realized that in order to distribute an application's processing, that application has to exist as a collection of pieces that work together rather than as a singular block of code. In that chapter we talked about the distribution of these processes without much consideration of *how* we might actually cause this symphony of processes to be executed across many different machines.

In this chapter, we'll think about some real things that we can do to divide our physical infrastructure into a set of major and minor processing resources. Fortunately for us, we don't have to do this in a vacuum. The work we did in the last chapter has given us something of a blueprint that we can follow. What we will do is design a physical system that mirrors, and therefore, enhances our efforts to develop distributed processing software. Just as we learned to think of applications as a set of complimentary processes that work together, we will learn to view the servers in our enterprise as a pool of dynamic resources that we can focus on a particular processing need.

This will allow us to create a truly scalable resource, but it also offers other benefits as well. It will give us the opportunity to design a physical system that also offers a high level of fault tolerance. Again, we will not have to perform this work in a vacuum. We can build upon the fault tolerance concepts we developed in the last chapter.

When we have finished this chapter, we will have designed a scalable and fault tolerant physical system for our enterprise. We have an advantage because from the start, we can design a system that mirrors our software design efforts. This mirroring of processing requirements and physical resources will allow us to create a formidable yet flexible reservoir of raw computing power to serve the needs of our enterprise.

Server Farms

Have you ever tried to tear a telephone book in half? It can be done, but it's really kind of difficult. A telephone book is made from hundreds of pages. Individually, each one of those pages is not too strong. But together...

We can learn a lot from the pages of a telephone book. Each of the pages, taken singly, has a nearly infinitesimal resistance to tearing. The strength of the book comes from combining all of those tiny resistances into a single pool of resistance that we work with as a telephone book. When we design a **server farm**, we are essentially using the same principle. We pool the comparatively meager resources from a number of modest computers into a single potent force.

This pool of computers does a lot more than add raw processing power to the enterprise. After all, if processing power was all we were after, it would be easier to use a single machine with more, better, and/or faster CPU(s) etc. We could also add raw processing power by using a mainframe. So why build a server farm?

Well, a server farm is made from many individual servers; these fully functioning atomic units offer us a great deal of flexibility. The units can be configured as purely redundant resources, as redundant/parallel resources, or as some combination of both. In the last chapter we learned how to increase fault tolerance through the use of redundant resources, so, I won't rehash the reasons why a single server with multiple CPUs can never be as fault tolerant as two separate servers. We also learned that with a little careful planning, we could use the available redundant resources in a parallel rather than serial fashion to increase the overall amount of resources available to the enterprise at any one time.

In the rest of this chapter, we will take a closer look at the techniques we can use to design server farms that will meet the enterprise requirements of *availability* and *scalability*. We will approach that design problem two ways, first without the benefit of a clustered server and then a second time using Microsoft Cluster Server.

A Quick Aside

Before we go on, I would like to take a minute or two to give you an assumption that you should have in mind when you work through the chapter. We are about to cover some potentially complex parallel processing issues. As you might imagine, this could get a little confusing, but I don't think it has to. It will be a lot easier to understand the important concepts if we can forget about the kind of trivial diversions that typically stop most people from getting to the core of a problem.

> In this case, I want you to try to think of each machine that we discuss as a resource that is only capable of performing a *single* task in a *serial* fashion.

I know that servers can perform many tasks in what appears to be a parallel fashion, but knowing this really doesn't help us to design a system that can work in parallel across several servers. Actually, it tends to complicate the matter and it makes it much more difficult to discuss the *parallel processing across multi-servers* concept. Making the assumption that the servers of the farm are only capable of serial processing will never hurt your server farm design. Think about it. If you design a system expecting that you only have serial processing machines available, the server farm can only benefit if those machines suddenly become capable of parallel processing. This means that it is not only safe, but it is probably advantageous, to think of the servers of the server farm as serial resources – especially during the early design phases.

Server Farms without Clusters

The server farm designs we will consider in this book are intended as an infrastructure for the deployment of Enterprise Caliber applications that are capable of performing real parallel processing. Our primary focus in the first section of this chapter will be on multiple server design techniques that we can adopt to make true parallel processing possible.

> *Please don't take the exact number of machines in the designs as a fixed value. I use the number of machines in each section of the farm for illustrative purposes only. This is to give you a sense of the relative scale of each processing segment of the server farm in relation to the other processing segments.*

Effective server farms may contain as few as 3 or 4 machines or as many as the organization's requirements dictate. And, although I wouldn't recommend it to customers with the sufficient financing, it is possible to construct any of the server designs in the first half of this chapter using "surplus" Pentium 90s or better.

> **A good general principle with regard to server placement is to use the highest-powered servers available at the center and the extremities of the server farm.**

In other words use your best servers first as database servers and then as the IIS servers. These machines have more influence over the users' perception of the performance of the overall system. The middle machines – those machines strictly running MTS or MSMQ – are also very important to the system, but in this area it may be possible to improve system performance by adding a larger number of less-powerful servers rather than adding fewer higher-powered servers.

As we learned in the last chapter, fault tolerance is another important issue. So, we will also consider some simple techniques that we can employ to provide fault tolerance without using Microsoft Cluster Server in this section. But I must warn you ahead of time, I really think that Microsoft has done a great job of handling the fault tolerance issue with Cluster Server. By that I mean that if the organization can afford it, you are probably better off using Cluster Server for the fault tolerant foundation rather than trying to reinvent the wheel.

The Design

The first step in designing a high performance server farm is to consider its general application. As far as we're concerned in this book, we will design our server farm to provide an infrastructure upon which we can deliver a host of Enterprise Caliber applications throughout the full extent of our organization's enterprise and its affiliates. This includes clients that will access these resources via web-based applications using three main access routes:

- ❑ Intranet (LAN and WAN including RAS - This means the resources owned by the organization that use TCP/IP)
- ❑ Extranet (Point-to-Point Tunneling Protocol (PPTP) over an otherwise standard Internet connection)
- ❑ Internet connections

Of course, we must also be able to deliver additional, more traditional client-server applications to the customers on the LAN or WAN.

In the last chapter, we talked a little about the different hardware requirements that different processes require. We identified two *major* processes:

- ❑ On Line Transaction Processing (OLTP)
- ❑ On Line Analytical Processing (OLAP)

We also identified four other *minor* types of system processing:

- ❑ Data Storage Processes
- ❑ Data Manipulation Processes
- ❑ Data/Business Rule Integration Processes
- ❑ Presentation Processes

In logical n-tier design, it is customary to call each of these minor-processing segments a **tier**. In our physical system we have 4 minor processing segments, so we can say that our system has 4 tiers:

- ❑ The Data Storage Processes exist within the **Data tier**
- ❑ The Data Manipulation Processes exist within a tier we shall call the **Data Centric tier**
- ❑ The Data/Business Rule Integration Processes exist within a tier we shall call the **User Centric tier**
- ❑ The Presentation Processes exist within a tier we shall the **Presentation tier**

If we could envision the logical major and minor processing divisions, they might look something like the image that follows:

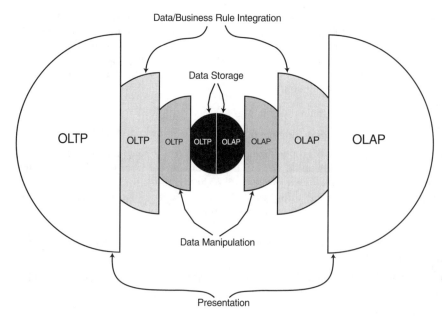

Notice that overall, the system is split into two halves – each half represents a major process – the OLTP half on the left and the OLAP half on the right. To the left of the center, we see each of the minor OLTP processes depicted as a concentric half-circle. To the right of the center, we see each of the minor OLAP processes are also depicted as concentric half circles. This image is really something of an exploded view of the system. This is to make it easier to work with the individual machines on each tier. If we viewed this system in a non-exploded form, it might look something like the image below. In case it is not apparent, the data in this system moves outward from the center of the image starting with the Data tier, passing through the Data Centric tier and the User Centric tier until it meets the user at the Presentation tier. Of course, the reverse trip, from the user back to the Data tier is also understood:

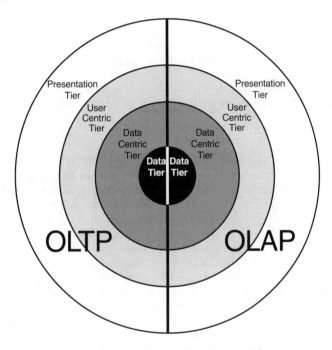

When you look at the image depicting the process divisions above, you probably see a series of concentric circles. Take another look at it. When I look at this image, I see the concentric circles too, but I also see something else – something I couldn't draw. What I see is **focus**. I am going to take a chance here. I am going to guess that if you are reading this book that you have probably spent more than a few minutes totally absorbed by some kind of challenge. You know what I mean, you sit down at your computer, wrap your mind around some delicious problem, and the next thing you know you look up to find the night janitor scratching his head trying to figure out how he is going to get at the wastebasket under your desk. FOCUS! If you *do* remember a time like that then let me ask you something; Did you win? Did you solve the problem? Did you paint the picture? Climb the mountain? Do you think you could have done as well if you allowed your attention to be scattered?

On some level organizations are like people. I don't know exactly how you might measure it, but have you ever watched a world-class sports team? Somehow, the members of the team stretch the concept of focus until it encompasses every member of the team. They confidently pass balls, pucks, or whatever into absolutely empty space because somehow they just *know* that their teammate will be there when the time comes. They can *know* this because they are acting as a team.

> *For some brief period of time they don't just act as individuals, they pull together as singular force, a unified intelligence with a single focus.*

Of course you know exactly what I am going to say next. Enterprise Caliber Information Systems are really not much different than an organization... or a person. Just like a person, an enterprise can have its energies scattered or it can have its energies focused. This is a book about distributed architecture. But it's more than that; it's also a book about *focus*.

Distributed architecture means more than executing a piece of code on this machine and another piece of code on that machine. Those pieces of code, and those machines need to work together just like the world-class sports team above.

> **The real purpose of distributed architecture is to distribute the processing load among the enterprise's resources – NOT to scatter the enterprise's resources. If we want our enterprise to *win*, we need to be able to muster all of its resources and focus the entirety of those resources with pinpoint precision.**

In the first chapter of this book, we talked about the requirements we needed to bring together in order to deliver an Enterprise Caliber System. When we talked about the physical requirements, we looked at an image that depicted the servers in our enterprise laid out in a triangular formation; they looked something like a pyramid or maybe a 'piece of pie'. We didn't have a lot of time to discuss it then, but even with the few minutes we did have, we found that we could do a lot to optimize the system by focusing its resources towards a point at its center – the organization's data store. This pie shaped version of the server farm we developed was really just a first step along the path to designing a true Enterprise Caliber System. It was an important but tiny slice of a much larger vision. Take a look at the next image. Notice that the concentric-circle vision of the enterprise is a natural evolution of the 'slice of pie' perception we developed earlier:

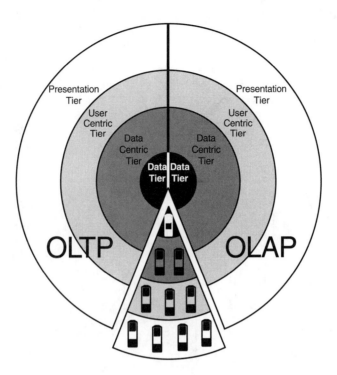

Just like the pie shaped version, this concentric circle design focuses the available resources of the system towards the data store at the center. The different sizes of the concentric circles are intended to offer a sense of the relative number of simultaneous data connections possible between processes. This increasing of available resources from a small number at the center of the system – the Data tier – to a large number at the outer reaches of the system – the Presentation tier - is made possible by drawing upon the server farm's parallel processing capabilities. We'll see exactly why this is when we discuss processor timesharing.

> *Remember that this is a purely logical view of the system we are designing. In actual practice, the distinction between the OLTP and OLAP halves of the system tend to blur as we move away from the data storage area.*

In other words, the casual user should have no sense that the OLTP and OLAP portions of the application are different. But that issue is more of a user interface design problem that we will tackle in a later chapter. For now, it is best if we keep this OLTP/OLAP division clearly in mind while we design the server farm.

Now that we have a sense of the overall problem, we can begin to translate the pieces of our logical system into the physical computers that make up our server farm. Let's start with the data storage area.

The Data Storage Processes – The Data Tier

Our first responsibility here is to ensure that we divide the major processes onto two separate servers. Remember from our discussion in the last chapter that the OLTP server must be tuned to handle many small, simple requests for service, but the OLAP server should be tuned to handle fewer, but far-more-complex, requests for service. These two processes cannot coexist on a single server in any but the smallest enterprise installations.

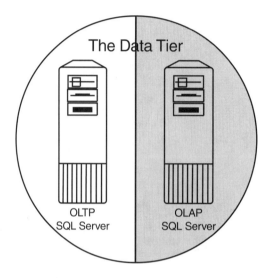

Other than the obvious split between OLTP and OLAP, there are really not many opportunities to perform multi-server-parallel-processing at the database level with the current tool set available from Microsoft. That doesn't mean that we should not expect a tremendous boost in overall performance from this simple step towards parallel processing. I would to say that it is the first place any designer should look to for performance improvements.

> *It is the simplest way to improve performance in any system that doesn't already make this distinction between OLTP and OLAP.*

Although two database servers shown are tuned to handle quite different tasks, they are also designed to compliment each other. The major function of the OLAP server is to provide the end users with an easy-to-query summary of the information that has been entered into the OLTP system. The OLAP server's adept handling of most of the data analysis tasks means that it removes a tremendous processing burden from the OLTP server. Of course, in order for this to happen, the summary information must be passed from the OLTP server to the OLAP server. The data is replicated from the OLTP to the OLAP server on a predefined recurrent basis. So, depending upon the size of the organization and the design of the OLAP system, this may mean that huge quantities of data must be passed between the two machines. That means that we must ensure that these two servers enjoy a fast, efficient, preferably private, line of communication.

Transactions

While we are considering the Data tier, I would like to define a unit of work that we will use throughout this book. We will call that unit of work a **transaction**. As you may recall, a transaction is a series of operations that must succeed or fail as a single unit. If any one of the operations in that series fails, then the entire series of operations must fail. As the name suggests, the OLTP portion of the system is built around the concept of the transaction. That's obvious. However, although it may not be so obvious, we can also identify the unit of work done in the OLAP portion of the system as a transaction.

The concept of the transaction or more accurately, the concept of the length of time a transaction occupies is central to developing an understanding of parallel processing. Of course, we all know that every transaction takes a different amount of time to complete. We understand that it takes more time to update 10 tables than it does to update 1 table. That's common sense. But as we go through this section of the book, I want you to try to forget about the differences between transactions and instead think of all transactions as though they are identical – especially when we think about the amount of time a transaction takes to complete. For the purposes of our discussion and to keep things simple, let's define the amount of time that an average transaction requires as 1 second. Once again, this simplification technique is designed to allow us to focus on core of the problem.

The Data Manipulation Processes – The Data Centric Tier

The Data Centric tier can consist of multiple servers that are designed to work in parallel to share the Data Manipulation Processing (DMP) load placed upon the system. This tier offers us our first real opportunity to perform true parallel processing/load balancing. Let's take a minute or two to review exactly what three things we can expect from the DMP:

- ❑ The processes within this tier have been designed to *know* exactly where to locate data within the enterprise, no matter where that data is located: SQL Server, other relational databases, mainframe resources, flat files, the Internet etc.

- ❑ Each process has been given the complete set of valid commands available for working with the data it is designed to manage.

- ❑ Each DMP has the ability to marshal (*package/unpackage*) the data and transport that data to either the Data tier or the User Centric tier as appropriate.

In the last chapter, we talked about process divisions. We learned that if we divided the processes an application requires into separate dynamic link libraries, that somehow we could install these DLLs on several machines to distribute the processing for an application across more than one machine. At that time, we didn't really take the time to consider what this meant in terms of the actual DLLs and machines. To keep things practical in this chapter, let's consider what we actually have to do to install the Data Manipulation Processes across the OLTP portion of our Data Centric tier.

In this image, we have designated two machines to handle the Data Manipulation Processes for the OLTP half of our system. What that means in real-terms is that we will physically install a DLL that contains a set of DMP instructions on each of the two servers in the OLTP portion of Data Centric tier.

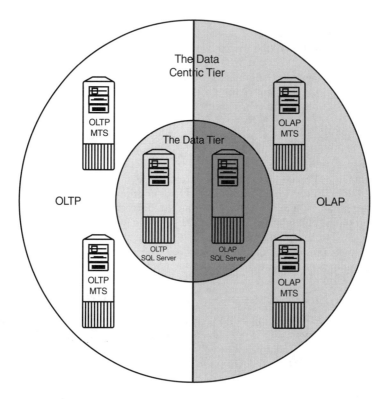

In other words, we will create two mirrored MTS servers. We will go over the details of MTS replication in Chapter 15, but for now just realize that we are installing identical copies of the same DLL on both machines.

> *Of course, we would also repeat this process using the appropriate DLLs on the OLAP section of the Data Centric tier. From now on, I will assume that all references to the OLTP section is understood to include a similar set of actions for the OLAP portion of the system. This will make it easier for both of us.*

Let's say that the Data Manipulation Processes we just installed on the servers have been programmed with a set of instructions which allows them to manage information about widgets.

Now, if we had two users that wanted to work with the data about widgets, we could direct each user to a different DMP machine. Both users would have access to an identical DLL, but both of those DLLs could execute simultaneously each on a different machine – true parallel processing. In this example we would have given each user access to 100% of the server's available resources, CPU, memory, disk, etc.

At this moment, you probably have identified a potential bottleneck. You should be thinking that although we have divided the DMPs, we only have a single OLTP SQL Server Machine and that the Data Storage Processes (DSP) must still execute serially on that server. By some measures this is true. But, if you remember from our brief discussion about the four minor processes from the last chapter, you will see why this really doesn't matter as much as you might think.

As we talked about each process, we took the time to realize that each minor process had something of a **characteristic time**. This was especially true if we compared the time of one minor process relative to other minor processes it interacted with. This characteristic time of each minor process will allow us to define some general rules that we can count on when we are designing, tuning, or modifying an Enterprise Caliber server farm. It allows us to do something that we will call **processor timesharing**.

Processor Timesharing

I will begin by making what may seem like a controversial statement:

> **Data Manipulation Processes always take longer than Data Storage Processes.**

Think about it. Data Manipulation Processes spawn Data Storage Processes. In other words, in order for a Data Storage Process to occur, something must invoke that process. That something is the Data Manipulation Process. This means that the DSPs have to take longer to execute. Take a look at the graphical representation of both processes:

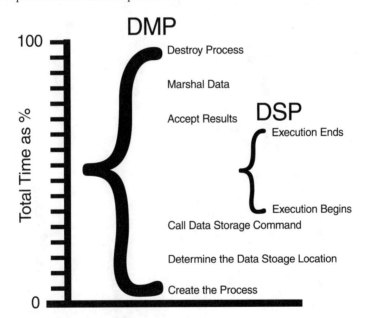

What this image shows, is that in order for a Data Storage Process to take place, we must perform all of the tasks that are required to invoke the data storage. And once the DSP has executed we still have additional tasks that must be performed by the Data Manipulation Process before the DMP is complete.

Of course, this graph is a generalization; the position of the Data Storage Process within the Data Manipulation Process may vary. And as we discussed earlier, the length of the Data Storage Processes (transactions) do vary, but I hope that you can see that no matter how quickly or slowly the Data Storage Process executes, it will always finish before the Data Manipulation Process that spawned it.

So, if we say that the length of time it takes for the Data Storage Process to execute is 1 second, then we can safely say that the time it takes for the Data Manipulation Process to complete is longer than 1 second.

To keep things simple, let's just say that all Data Manipulation Processes execute in 10 seconds. In fact, in a well-designed OLTP system the Data Storage Processes are so efficient, that the ratio of DSP over DMP is a very small number indeed. So the 1 to 10 ratio gives a good, conservative, sense of the actual times. Using these values, we find that during the time it takes to execute one DMP, we could execute ten DSPs.

It also means that we have a great deal of room for optimization. If a DMP takes 10 seconds to execute and we execute 3 DMPs one after another, then it will take a total of 30 seconds (10 +10 +10) for all of the processing to be completed. As each of our Data Manipulation Processes calls a single Data Storage Process in this case, and we have agreed that each Data Storage Process takes 1 second to complete, then this means that SQL Server was standing around with nothing to do for 27 seconds. (30 − (3 * 1) = 27)

This may be a little easier to grasp visually. The graph compares serial and parallel execution times. On the left, it shows the total time that it takes to execute three processes in a serial fashion. On the right, we see the total time it takes to execute the same three processes if we begin to execute all three simultaneously.

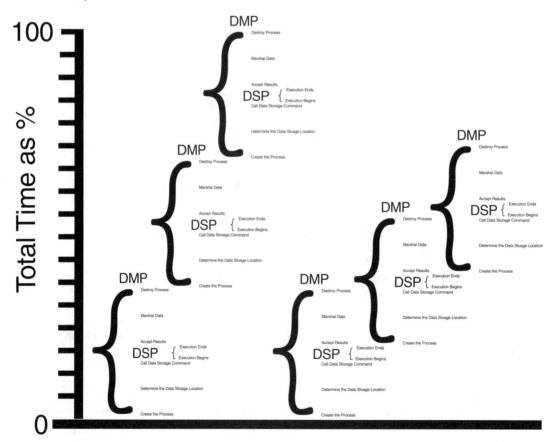

As you can see visually, the total time is significantly less. What happens is this:

1. We try to start all three processes at exactly the same time. We have two DMP servers and two DLLs, so two of the processes do start immediately. That means that both servers are busy, and that the third process cannot start. We can say that this process is queued by one of the servers and will begin as soon as one of the two others has completed. In this case that means it will start in exactly 10 seconds.

2. Next, both active processes attempt to execute the DSPs (or transactions) they have been instructed to spawn. There is only one OLTP SQL Server, so we will say that only one transaction can begin. SQL Server places the other in a queue. As soon as the first transaction has been completed, the queued transaction is started.

3. Using our figures, the first Data Storage Process starts at 4.5 seconds and is completed at 5.5 seconds (assuming that the DSP occurs half-way through the DMP, i.e. $(10 - 1)/2 = 4.5$).

4. This means that the second Data Storage Process can now start at 5.5 seconds. If we had used serial execution, we would have had to wait until the first Data Manipulation Process was completely over before we could even start the second Data Manipulation Process. That would mean that the second Data Storage Process would not have been queued and could not even begin executing until 14.5 $(10 + 4.5)$ seconds. A full 9 seconds later.

If we perform the same calculations with the remaining processes, we find that it takes 21 seconds to complete all the processes in a parallel fashion compared to the 30 seconds serially. This means that SQL Server was standing around for 18 seconds with nothing to do instead of 27 seconds. Still this represents about a 1/3 improvement.

> *Please remember not to take this example too literally, as I indicated before, SQL Server, IIS, and MTS are capable of executing parallel transactions without multiple machines. What we are doing here is learning how to use the same techniques employed by SQL Server, IIS and MTS on a macro (server-to-server) level. All we are really doing is implementing the same sound techniques across several machines that Microsoft exploits within single applications.*

The Data/Business Rule Integration Processes – The User Centric Tier

Think about it. We can take exactly the same concepts we learned about parallel processing in the Data Centric tier and apply them again to the User Centric tier. In other words, it is just as true to say that:

> *Data/Business Rule Integration Processes always take longer than Data Manipulation Processes.*

As it is to say that:

> *Data Manipulation Processes always take longer than Data Storage Processes.*

This means that when we design the User Centric tier of the server farm, we should end up with a design that looks something like this (see over page):

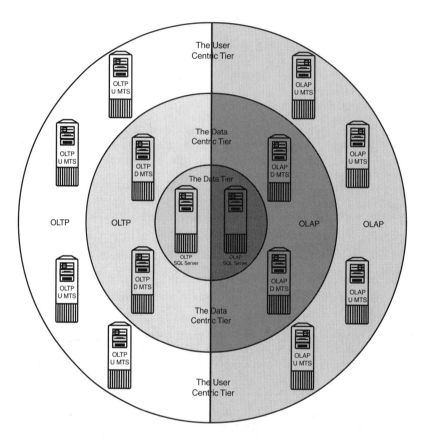

This image shows that a bank of 4 servers has been added to the OLTP and OLAP sides of the server farm. These servers are essentially the same as the ones we used for the Data Centric tier earlier. Except that, in the case of the User Centric tier these servers host a set of Data/Business Rule Integration Processes instead of a set of Data Manipulation Processes.

I want to make sure that I keep this conversation practical. So let's walk through the actual physical steps we must take to install the Data/Business Rule Integration Processes on the servers in the User Centric tier.

We would install the dynamic link library that contains the Data/Business Rule Integration Processes on all four of the servers in the OLTP half of the User Centric tier. In other words, we would create four mirrored servers. Let's see what the addition of these four extra servers does to meet our processing requirements.

In our last example on the Data Centric tier we had only two users, but our system has grown, so let's try this example with four users. If we had four users that needed to work with data about widgets, we could direct each user to a different machine on the User Centric tier. All four users would have access to identical DLLs, but those DLLs could execute simultaneously on four different machines – once again, true parallel processing. Sound familiar? Good!

I know it may seem like rehashing the issue, but it is important for us to go over the parallel /serial time comparison again. We have something additional to consider - we have 4 additional machines in the User Centric tier.

Take a look at this image:

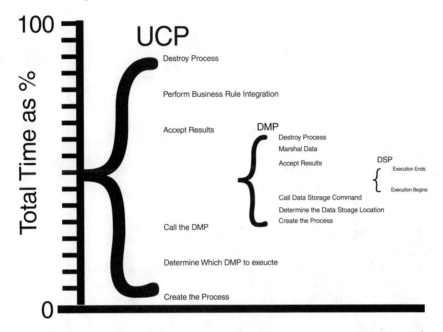

I think you can see by the size of the brackets the relative amount of time each process requires. Let's say, for the sake of argument, and to keep things simple, that it takes 100 seconds for a Data/Business Rule Integration Process to complete. If we executed the same three processes we used last time from the User Centric tier in a serial fashion, it would take 300 seconds for the processing to be completed. (100 + 100 + 100 = 300)

In order for us to determine how long this would take using parallel processing, we need to find the start times and end times for the D/BRIP and the processes it spawns. Remember that I chose the following times to make the math easier – DSP = 1 sec, DMP = 10 sec, and D/BRIP = 100 seconds. If we use those values with for a single D/BRIP, we will get the start time and end times in the following table:

	D/BRIP	DCP	DSP
Start Time	0	45	49.5
End Time	100	55	50.5

Let's consider what happens if we try to execute the processes on our server farm using parallel processing. We have four servers in the User Centric tier, so that means that we can begin all processes simultaneously. We only have two servers in the Data Centric tier, so that means we must queue one process there.

And we only have one server in the Data tier, this means that we also queue one process there. The start and end times we get from executing the processes in parallel are shown below:

		D/BRIP	DCP	DSP
User 1	Start Time	0	45	49.5
	End Time	100	55	50.5
User 2	Start Time	0	45	50.5
	End Time	101	56	51.5
User 3	Start Time	0	55	59.5
	End Time	110	65	60.5
User 4	Start Time	0	56	60.5
	End Time	111	66	61.5

Notice the difference in overall execution time between the serial and parallel techniques now! As we move out through the tiers using parallel processing, our results get better. The first layer of parallel processing only reduced the overall time by about one third. This layer reduced the overall time by about two thirds. This is not magic. It is just a directed effort designed to maximize the utilization of the database server(s). We do this by spreading the load across several servers and employing parallel processing at the server-to-server level.

The Presentation Processes – The Presentation Tier

The final step in our server farm design is the Presentation tier, and as you can probably guess by now we use the same principles to design this tier of the server farm that we used on each of the other tiers. There is one thing to note here though, it is possible, and reasonable, to collapse the Presentation and User Centric tiers into a single tier. Whether we do this or not really depends upon our final deployment strategy.

If we plan on using IIS as our primary means of delivering applications, then we may be served better by having each IIS server also function as an MTS server, effectively eliminating the physical User Centric tier.

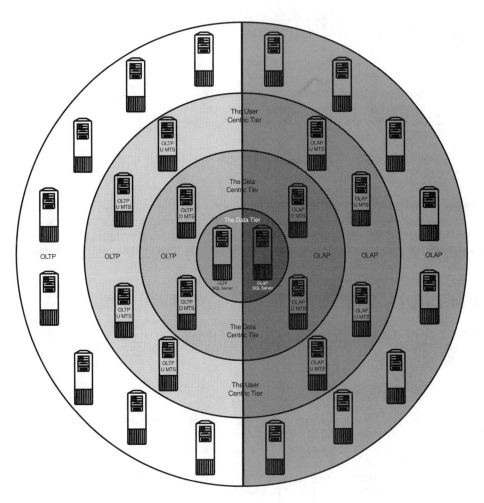

If, on the other hand, we expect that our primary deployment method will be a more traditional client-server approach, then we must provide a direct line of communication between the client machine and the application server (MTS) on the User Centric tier. In that case, the desktop client machine is actually acting as the Presentation tier. So, we don't really need the additional layer of servers in the Presentation tier. The design above shows both the User Centric and Presentation tiers as separate banks of servers in the server farm. This was done to facilitate both types of delivery. In other words, we can direct the more traditional calls directly to the User Centric tier and the web-based calls to the Presentation tier. This middle of the road approach has some advantages.

Generally, I think that with server farm design, like database design, we should err on the side of atomicity. In other words, I would prefer to have more servers dedicated to singular functions than to have fewer servers that have to be used for multiple tasks. The reason for this is simple.

> It is easier to reallocate a server that is performing a single function than it is to reallocate a server that is performing multiple functions.

We need to consider the servers in our farm as *mobile* assets. We can re-allocate them as needed to optimize the system. For instance, we can take an MTS server from the User Centric tier, install a different set of DLLs on it and cause it to become a Data Centric asset.

It is also an interesting programming problem to consider managing the shifting of assets from one tier to another in a dynamic fashion.

I won't repeat the parallel processing time study for the Presentation tier, it really depends on your final deployment strategy, but realize that when we add the Presentation tier as servers we are reaping the benefits of server-to-server parallel processing yet one more time. This is a valuable tool that we can use to give the largest possible number of users access to our most precious resource – the data store.

Load Balancing

Ok, now that we have all of the servers set up and the DLLs installed, how do we actually direct the users to the correct machine. There are several different techniques we can use to accomplish this, and again, the one we select depends upon our particular final deployment strategy.

Client-Server Deployment

If we are using a more traditional client-server deployment strategy, where the executable (even if it's a really thin executable) is actually installed on the client machine, then we need to approach the problem of load balancing on a client installation-by-client installation basis. In other words, we "tell" the client application which DLL to use. We do that when we register the remote DLL on the client machine. If we have 4 clients and 4 user centric MTS servers, then we would assign one client to each server. If we had 40 clients and 4 user centric MTS servers, then we would, of course, assign 10 clients to each machine and so on...

There is another thing to consider here too. We must perform essentially the same assignment task between the MTS machines on the User Centric and Data Centric tiers. In other words, if we had 4 user centric MTS machines and 2 data centric MTS machines, then we have to assign the DLLs on 2 of the user centric machines to one of the data centric MTS machines. Of course, we would assign the other 2 user centric machines to the remaining data centric machine.

Web-Based Deployment

If we use web-based deployment, we have a lot more options available for load balancing. We will cover some of them shortly. But, before we begin, I would like to point out one thing to consider with web-based deployment. When we used the traditional client-server deployment, we had to assign each client DLL calls to a particular MTS server. In actual practice that meant that we need to update the registry settings on the client machine. Now if one of the MTS machines goes down, (without a fail-over server standing by to take over) we'll need to change the registry settings on every client machine that is assigned to that server.

There are slick ways to automate this task, but generally I prefer the elimination option over the automation option whenever possible.

With web-based deployment, the registry setting changes are *always* limited to the servers that are part of the server farm. This makes maintenance a much simpler task to automate, and if worse came to worse, we could probably do this task by hand if we absolutely had to.

With web-based deployment, we can actually perform dynamic load balancing across several machines. This can be done using a traditional round robin technique – direct the first user to IIS machine #1 and the second user to IIS machine #2 and so on... This is probably the simplest technique, but it may not be the best. It is not always a safe assumption that the third user should be directed to the #3 server. It may be the case that the #3 server is redlining and the other IIS machines are just sitting around twiddling their silicon thumbs. I don't mean to put down round robin techniques. In lower usage applications, it may be more economical to use this pre-defined server selection rather than polling each individual server like we do with the more dynamic techniques. Anyway, this type of load balancing still shows the general principle. Direct the users' requests to as many different machines as possible. Each machine will initiate an instance of the parallel process we worked through earlier. It is really that simple.

LoadBal

There are a couple of additional options we can use for load balancing. The first one is to use the **LoadBal** object that ships with the IIS Resource Kit. This tool is just a DLL that loads on the IIS machine and polls all of instances of IIS using its resource monitor. This works as follows: In each Active Server Page that is called, we instantiate the LoadBal object and ask it to redirect us to the IIS instance that is currently doing the least work.

I'm not too sure about this approach. I have never really performed a strict test, but instinctively it seems like the work of instantiating an object on a potentially busy machine and asking it where to go next is kind of foolish. I suppose this would work well in an environment where you had an instance of IIS that you could set aside as something like a dispatcher. If this machine's sole responsibility was to read the current server poll results and redirect the users, we could probably nail down the usage patterns quite well and ensure that this machine did not itself become the bottleneck it should be preventing.

WLBS

There is another, better option – **WLBS**. It never ceases to amaze me, and it never fails! I am sitting around trying hard to solve some difficult problem; I suffer over it for countless hours, and in the meantime, Microsoft has just purchased, or partnered-with, the company that owns the answer. WLBS is short for **Windows Load Balancing Service**. And, as the name implies, it performs load balancing. The way it works is pretty similar to the way I described the LoadBal working with a dispatcher. We set aside a single machine, which is really a gateway for all of the other available machines. We direct all requests for service to this machine, or more accurately, the IP address assigned to that machine, and this machine redirects us to a particular server. We can configure WLBS to use either dynamic (resource monitor directed) or round robin techniques. At the time of writing, WLBS allowed us to stack a maximum of 32 machines in the outer ring of our server farm. That gives us 32 machines in the Presentation tier that can appear to the user base as a single machine. That's quite a bit of horsepower. In addition to giving us the ability to initiate parallel requests for service, WLBS also offers us a substantial improvement in fault tolerance. It can tell when a server is down and will not direct a user to an unavailable server.

This sounds like the answer to all of our problems until you realize that if the server that has been set aside as the dispatcher fails, the whole system will be down until we can bring this server back up. Software alone can give us a lot of fault tolerance, but to make it really effective, we need to add some hardware components to the mix as well. Let's get on to another option for building high-performance server farms that provide this hardware-level fault tolerance - clustering.

Microsoft Cluster Server

Microsoft has taken on the enterprise challenge with a fervor nearly as intense as its drive into the world of the Internet. It understands that in order to compete successfully in the enterprise arena, its enterprise operating system must have the capacity to pool the resources from several machines into something the users can view as single resource. Of course, as with almost everything else Microsoft, this is not a new concept. Companies like Tandem, and DEC have been deploying these multi-server solutions for years. The industry has a word for using multiple computers as a single resource; that word is **clustering**.

Microsoft adopted the industry's term when it renamed its multi-server-development-initiative from its original codename Wolfpack to its current name: **Microsoft Cluster Server (MSCS)**.

When it comes to fault tolerance, MSCS is definitely a step in the right direction. It allows two servers to work together as a single fault tolerant resource. If one node of the cluster fails or is taken off-line, the second node in the cluster assumes the identity of its fallen comrade and continues to perform in its stead.

> *In cluster speak; each server in a cluster is referred to as a **node**.*

With MSCS, the transfer of processes from the failed node to the redundant node is automatic and occurs in a fairly short period of time – from 9 seconds to a little over 1 minute in my tests.

Electronic Heartbeats

At its core, MSCS is really a just set of communication processes layered over the NT operating system. Each node of the cluster continually runs a process that emits something of akin to an **electronic heartbeat**. And, each node of the cluster also continually runs another process that listens for the other node's heartbeat.

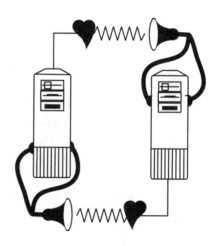

As long as each node hears the rhythmic sound from its clustered counterpart, it's business as usual for the pair. Each server just goes about its assigned tasks – whatever they may be – without even thinking about what the other server is doing for a living.

But, if either one of the nodes fails to hear its brethren's heartbeat, then it immediately goes into action. First it searches all of its available network connections in an attempt to locate its counterpart's heartbeat. It does this to eliminate the possibility that the other node is still functioning, but has lost one of its network cards or connections. If it still cannot hear the other node's heartbeat, it concludes that the other node is in trouble and begins the **automated fail over process**.

The Automated Fail Over Process

In order to we understand, the automated fail over process, we need to add a couple of concepts to our current knowledge. One of those concepts is the **Shared Disk Subsystem (SDS)**. For now just think of the SDS as a single disk that both computers in a cluster can use. We will cover the mechanics of shared disk subsystems a little later in the chapter. The next thing we need to understand is the concept of the **Quorum disk**. One way to think of a Quorum disk is as something like an INI file or a series of registry entries. In other words, it's really just a space on a disk that contains cluster-level configuration information.

The Quorum Disk

In addition to the communications processes that must run on each node of the cluster continually, MSCS demands one other resource – a Quorum disk. This is a "small" portion of the shared disk subsystem (see below) that contains the cluster's configuration information.

The Quorum disk can only be owned by one node at a time. So, even though both nodes in a cluster are theoretically equal, we'll call the node that owns the Quorum disk the **master node**. This master node manages the common cluster specific information that both nodes of the cluster use during operation.

It is important to realize that the master node can change freely from Node 1 to Node 2, and it doesn't really make any difference as to which node is the master node at a particular time.

The primary function that occurs during the automated fail-over process is the transfer of the ownership of the Quorum disk. Let's consider an example using the cluster shown in the image:

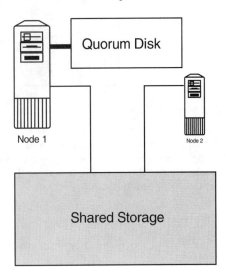

Please note that this image marks a particular point in time. And at that point in time, Node 1 is the master node. We can tell this, because in this image, Node 1 is shown as the owner of the Quorum disk. I have used the size differences between Node 1 and Node 2 just to emphasize the fact that Node 1 is in charge at this particular point in time.

Failure of the Non-Master Node

Given the set of circumstances depicted in the image above: If Node 2's heartbeat stopped, Node 1 would first search all available connections for the missing heartbeat. At the end of that search, if Node 1 concluded that Node 2 was unavailable, then Node 1 would perform the following 4 steps:

1. Read Node 2's configuration information from the Quorum disk.

2. Using the information found on the Quorum disk it will communicate with the Primary or Backup Domain Controller (PDC or BDC) and assume Node 2's identity.

3. It will take ownership of Node 2's shared resources (shared disk subsystem).

4. It will execute all of Node 2's cluster-aware processes on Node 1.

At the end of this process, we could envision the system as shown here:

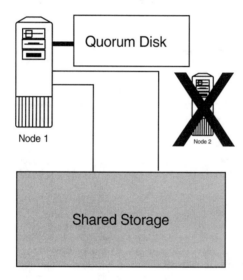

Failure of the Master Node

We can use the same initial (non-failed) image from above to consider what happens when the master node fails. This is a little more work because the remaining node must take control of the Quorum disk. If Node 1's heartbeat stopped, Node 2 would first search all available connections for the missing heartbeat. At the end of that search, if Node 2 concluded that Node 1 was unavailable, then Node 2 will perform the following 5 steps:

1. Take control of the Quorum disk

2. Read Node 1's configuration information from the Quorum disk.

3. Using the information found on the Quorum disk it will communicate with the PDC or BDC and assume Node 1's identity

4. It will take ownership of Node 1's shared resources (shared disk subsystem).

5. It will duplicate Node 1's cluster-aware processes on Node 2.

At the end of this process, we could envision the system as shown here:

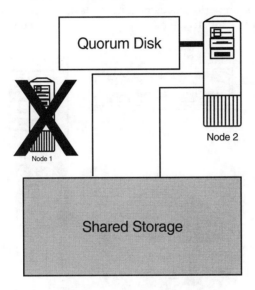

The Shared Disk Subsystem

A little earlier I introduced the concept of the shared disk subsystem without any real description of the beast. And, unless your enterprise uses some sort of Storage Area Network (SAN) you may not be familiar with shared disk subsystems. In this section of the chapter, we will develop an understanding of SANs in general, then we will take a look at a couple of common techniques that are used to construct one.

The General Concept

Basically a shared disk subsystem (SDS) allows two or more computers to share a single disk (or a single array of disks). Of course if this were all that it did, we wouldn't need to discuss it here. We can share disks, directories, and files quite easily throughout an entire enterprise without the benefit of a single SDS. The reason we use a SDS is to increase performance.

A SDS allows a disk (or an array of disks) to exist outside of a particular host computer. Any computer that has the correct hardware can use the storage space available in the SDS and expect about the same performance characteristics that we might expect from an on-board hard disk system. This is possible for two reasons:

❑ Nearly all of the processing that is required (disk read/writes) is handled by the SDS hardware

❑ The system requires specialized high-bandwidth connections between the SDS and the computer(s) that utilize its resources

There are several different ways of setting up a SDS.

The SCSI Solution

Generally, SCSI (Small Computer Systems Interface) disks offer better performance over other common types of hard disks like IDE, EIDE, etc. This is, in part, due to the design of the SCSI controller card. This type of controller has an on-board processor, which executes the disk reads and writes with virtually no assistance from the computer's main CPU(s). To anyone familiar with SCSI disks, the idea of having one or more external hard disks is not a new one. Most SCSI devices can be connected externally with little or no performance penalty. In fact, it is possible to connect several external SCSI devices together using an arrangement known as a **daisy chain**.

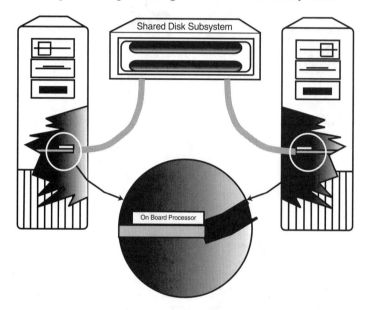

The thing that *is* unusual about a SCSI shared disk subsystem is that more than one computer can access its external disk(s) at one time. This is possible due to a special bus configuration, which offers two input ports instead of the single port we expect from a standard external SCSI disk. The SCSI SDS depends upon the processor(s) located on the controller cards in the computers to move the data onto or off from the disk(s). The SDS housing itself doesn't contain any electronic devices besides the disks and the power supply that power the disks. The current crop of off-the-shelf shared SCSI bus systems have a limit of 2 input ports, which means that at most two computers can share the resource. At present, MSCS also has the same 2-node limit, so this is not too much of a problem now. But, we should expect future MSCS releases to allow more than 2 nodes. So...

Fiber Channel Shared Disk Subsystem

There is another type of SDS available. This one uses fiber channel controllers in place of the SCSI controllers. As you can probably guess by its name, the fiber channel disk subsystems use pulses of light to transmit data through the system. Generally, fiber channel communication is faster and offers more "bandwidth" than standard electronic transmission mediums, but there are other features that make this a better choice than the SCSI system. The most important is that it requires fewer complex components. Let's examine why this is so.

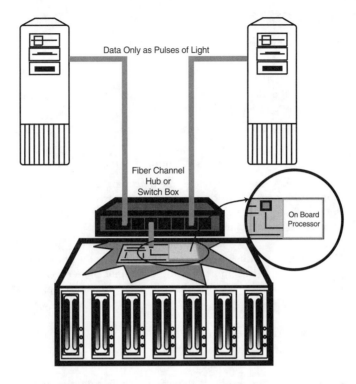

Data Only as Pulses of Light

Fiber Channel
Hub or
Switch Box

On Board
Processor

Remember that with the SCSI system, we were required to have a controller with a high-powered processor in each computer. We also learned that there were no electronics other than the disk and power supply in the SDS housing. If you think about it, this means that not only do we have to send the data to the disk, but we also have to carry on a conversation with the disk concerning its every activity. I would never want to write the code, but this conversation would include things like positioning the heads at the correct location to read/write each chunk of data.

With a fiber channel solution, the only processing that takes place at each computer is the trivial translation from electrical impulses to pulses of light. The work of controlling the disks occurs in the SDS housing, which is where the single disk controller for the entire system resides.

What all this means, is that instead of having two or more disk controllers that remotely control the disk array, we have a single controller that manages the disk array. And instead of having to transmit every single instruction required to read/write data across a relatively slow connection, we only need to ship the data along with a read/write flag. Sometimes less is more.

Due to the simplification of the data transfer, with the fiber channel we can treat all the elements in the system, computers and shared disk subsystems as though they are essentially the same. As far as the system is concerned, they are all simply devices that receive or transmit data expressed as pulses of light. This allows us to handle the data transmission with a simple hub or switch, which is essentially a light-enabled version of the standard network hub or switch. And, since it really doesn't matter whether the units that plug into the hub are computers or SDSs, we can add just about any number of either computers, SDSs or some combination of both to the system.

Cluster Configurations

Let's take a minute or two to review what we know about MSCS:

❑ MSCS allows us to connect two computers to a single shared disk resource – the SDS.

❑ A small portion (partition) of that SDS is set-aside to house cluster specific configuration information; that partition is called the Quorum disk.

❑ At any one time, only one of the two nodes in the cluster can be in-charge-of, or *own*, the Quorum disk.

❑ We can call the node that currently *owns* the Quorum disk the master node.

❑ In the case of a failure of any one of the nodes, the remaining node will take control of the Quorum disk (if that node doesn't already own it). Assume the identity of its fallen counterpart, and replace all of the cluster-aware processes that were available on the failed node with identical processes that can run on the remaining node.

That is really all that MSCS does in a nutshell. But, there are some other things to consider when designing a clustered solution. The most important is the **run-time cluster dynamics**. With an MSCS cluster, we have two nodes, or resources. We can, theoretically, choose to make these resources available in a number of different ways:

❑ We can make one of the two nodes a stand-by resource. In this case, the second node of the cluster is only used in the event of a failure of the first node. We call this an **Active–Passive** configuration.

❑ We can also set up each node of the cluster to perform a different task at the same time. With this configuration, if one node fails the second node takes-over the processes that were running on the failed node and runs both sets of processes itself. Microsoft calls this an **Active–Active** configuration.

Of course there are many intermediate configuration possibilities between the pure Active-Passive or Active-Active configurations. This configuration flexibility is where the true power of MSCS lies. But, before we can begin to design sophisticated solutions, it is probably a good idea to have a full understanding of the boundaries that the Active-Passive and Active-Active configurations represent.

Active–Passive

When we configure a process to utilize the nodes of a cluster in an Active-Passive manner, what we are doing, essentially, is making one of the nodes a back-up server for that process. Imagine for example that we have set up a SQL Server process to run in an Active-Passive manner. In that case, the active node will do all of the work. Every request or command that is directed at SQL Server will be directed to the active node. The passive node will just sit idly by waiting for the active node to fail. When that failure occurs, the node will take control of the Quorum disk, the remainder of the SDS, and the SQL Server process that was executing on the active node. As you can see, while an Active-Passive configuration does offer a measure of fault tolerance, it actually takes half of our available resources off-line all of the time. This does not make the most efficient use of the available resources.

You can compare this to the RAID 1 disk array we looked at in the last chapter.

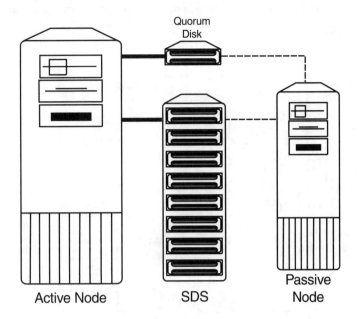

Active–Active

There is another configuration option available for the nodes of MSCS. The Active-Active configuration makes it possible to have both nodes of cluster active at the same time. This almost leads one to believe that we can perform true parallel processing with MSCS out of the box.

After all, if both nodes are active at the same time, then they can both be executing the same process at the same time. Right? If only it were true. MSCS's Active–Active configuration does allow us to utilize the resources of both servers, but it doesn't allow the servers to be running exactly the same process at the same time in the way you might hope.

Let's consider an example with SQL Server running in an Active–Active configuration:

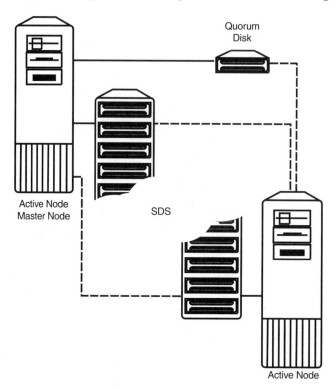

Take a moment to examine the Active–Active configuration diagram. Notice that the Quorum disk is owned by the active node on the left. The same server also owns about half of the disk space available in the SDS. The second node in the cluster is also active, but it only owns the remainder of the SDS.

> *Note that currently it is not possible for one node to access the portion of the SDS owned by the other node while both are active.*

I've used dashed-lines to show the potential connections that can or will be made upon the failure of one of the nodes of the system. We have already gone over the steps involved during a fail over, the steps are essentially the same for both Active-Passive and Active-Active configurations.

Remember that this Active-Active configuration is not what we might hope. While we can install SQL Server on both nodes of a cluster in an Active-Active configuration, currently it is not possible for both nodes to share the same portion of the SDS at the same time. This means that each instance of SQL Server is and must be, independent of the other instance. This is a subtle problem, but it means that it is not possible to have two servers running in parallel on different machines hitting the exact same set of data without complex replication or mirroring.

> *So we can, say, run a different instance of SQL Server on each node of the cluster at the same time, but we cannot run a single instance of SQL Server across both nodes at the same time.*

If we could do that, then we could build single virtual SQL Servers that used the resources of two (or more) servers at the same time. Alas, maybe in a future release.

If we ignore this one very critical shortcoming, we can still get a lot of computing power using an Active-Active configuration when compared to the Active-Passive choice. We could still run two instances of SQL Server – one on each node. While the two servers would not be able to transparently share data, without some data centric programming, they do offer twice the raw computing power that the Active-Passive option made available. Instead of one of the servers sitting by idly waiting for a catastrophe, both servers can be working full time except for during actual catastrophes. This is a much more efficient use of available resources.

Combinations

Now that we have a better understanding of the Active-Active and Active-Passive configurations, we will take a look at some techniques we can use which combine both configuration options. Let's take on some real world scenarios and see how we can solve them using MSCS.

Say that we have a well-designed, but un-clustered, 3-tier application that uses SQL Server to manage the data store on the Data tier and Microsoft Transaction Server (MTS) to manage the business objects in a middle tier. We can also assume that in this case, the clients are using a locally installed Visual Basic interface that makes calls to the business objects under MTS's control. If we were to draw a diagram of this system, we might end up with an image something like the one here. Notice that if either one of the servers fails, the system cannot continue to operate. **This system has a single point a failure.** The point of failure is either one of the servers in the system.

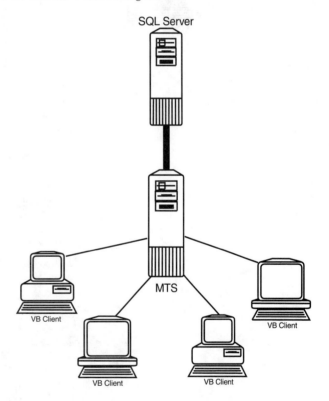

SQL Server

MTS

VB Client

VB Client

VB Client

VB Client

If we redesigned this system as a clustered system using a strict Active-Passive configuration, we might end up with a design that looks something like one of the systems shown on the right:

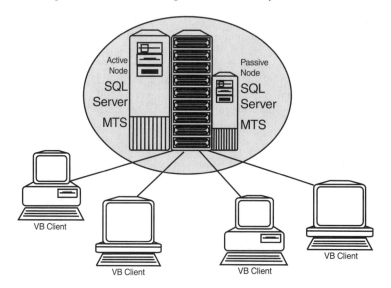

The system on the right top uses a single cluster with both SQL Server and MTS installed in an Active-Passive configuration. Notice that when we set up the system like this, we are really setting aside one of our servers as an off-line redundant device.

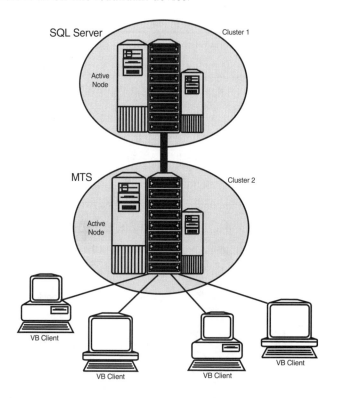

The next system also on the lower right uses two clusters with SQL Server installed in an Active-Passive configuration on one cluster and MTS installed in Active-Passive on the second cluster.

The problem with either of these clustered diagrams above is that in both cases, we have left half of the server resources unused at all times. Sure, we have done an excellent job of ensuring that our enterprise's needs are served with fault tolerant resources. We have removed the single points of failure with either design. However if we measure our design(s) effectiveness using a wider perspective than the question of fault tolerance, we will find that both designs are lacking.

If we could make real-time use of the unused redundant resource(s), we would essentially double our computing power with virtually no additional cost. A 100% increase in throughput will substantially increase the system's overall availability. We can get this increase by using the Active-Active configuration.

In other words, as shown in the image on the right, we can configure SQL Server to be Active on one node and MTS to be active on the second node. In case of failure, either node could be replaced by the other node, so we have ensured fault tolerance. But perhaps more importantly, we have also doubled the amount of raw CPU power available to the system. As I said earlier, Microsoft calls this configuration Active-Active. I think it might be better to call it a combination configuration. It really uses two Active-Passive processes deployed diametrically opposite each other.

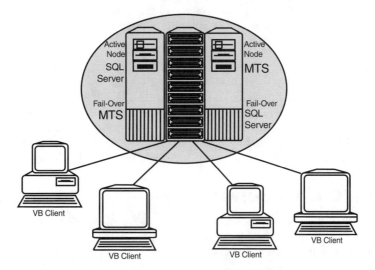

We could also design this system to make use of more servers like we saw earlier with the Active-Passive, 4-node design. But, think about it for a minute. We have achieved exactly the same amount of availability and fault-tolerance with the far less expensive design above. That doesn't mean that we should ignore the possibility of using multiple two-node clusters. In fact that is just what we are about to do next when we take a look at how we might add some of the MSCS fault tolerance capabilities to the server farm design we looked at earlier.

A Server Farm That Utilizes MSCS

As I said earlier, Microsoft didn't invent clustering. A lot of other companies have been deploying clustered solutions for years. These companies use a combination of hardware (essentially the same SCSI or fiber channel SDS we learned about earlier) and proprietary software that manages the automated fail over process. Many of these companies' products, like Tandem's for instance, do not recognize the two-node limit that MSCS imposes. Unfortunately, I think that the proprietary nature of their systems makes it unlikely that their products will supplant Microsoft's efforts in this direction. So, until Microsoft builds a system capable of clustering 3 or more servers, we need to look at other techniques to facilitate higher order clustering. While MSCS's two-node limit doesn't really hamper our efforts to develop fault tolerant systems, it does not help us in our efforts to create real parallel processing load balanced solutions.

Remember our discussion last chapter about RAID 1 and RAID 5 disk arrays. We didn't get any load balancing from the RAID 1 system. That was because it was serial in nature. When we wrote the word "DOG" to the RAID 1 array, we had to pass the letter "D" first, then pass the letter "O", then pass the letter "G". Well, presently MSCS is really a serial system. In other words, while it can perform two tasks simultaneously, it cannot separate a single task into smaller pieces or "threads" and run each one of those threads on a different server. What we need is a way to build our server farm so that it behaves more like the RAID 5 system. Remember how that worked? When we wanted to write the word "DOG" with the RAID 5 system we separated the word into smaller pieces and saved each of the pieces on a different disk at exactly the same time. We performed a true parallel write across several disks.

Fortunately, there are techniques, hardware and software, we can use to make our system capable of performing very much like a RAID 5 system. That is really what a good portion of this book is about. Just because MSCS cannot currently separate tasks into threads and execute each thread on a different server doesn't mean that our enterprise's resources cannot be pulled together to accomplish this task. We will rely upon MSCS's strong fault tolerance features to provide the building blocks for a fault tolerant, load-balanced Enterprise Caliber Server Farm, but we will rely upon our own ingenuity to handle the process isolation, parallel processing, and load balancing capabilities.

An Enterprise Caliber Server Farm

As we discussed earlier, the first step in designing a high performance server farm is to consider its general application. To recap, we need to be able to support clients that will access the enterprise via web-based applications using three main access routes.

- ❑ Intranet
- ❑ Extranet
- ❑ Internet

We must also be able to deliver additional, more traditional client-server, applications to the customers on the LAN, WAN. Earlier in this chapter, we learned to mirror our processing divisions with physical hardware. We identified two major processes and four minor processes and worked out ways to match these processing requirements with physical resources:

The Major Processes:

- ❏ On Line Transaction Processing (OLTP)
- ❏ On Line Analytical Processing (OLAP)

The Minor Processes:

- ❏ Data Storage Process
- ❏ Data Manipulation Process
- ❏ Data/Business Rule Integration Process
- ❏ Presentation Process

Now that we have a sense of the overall problem, we'll begin to translate the pieces of our un-clustered solution into a second design for a server farm that can take advantage of MSCS.

The Data Storage Processes – The Data Tier

As with the non-clustered farm we designed earlier, our first responsibility here is to ensure that we divide the major OLTP and OLAP processes onto two separate servers.

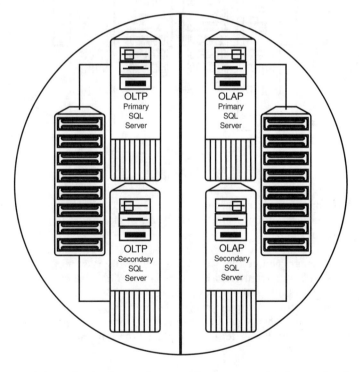

The first thing you might notice is that we have used two two-node clusters for the Data tier. By now, you probably realize that we could have used a single two-node cluster with essentially the same results. We could have used an Active-Active SQL Server configuration. Then if the OLTP node failed, it could collapse onto the OLAP node and visa versa. In fact, if we were constructing this server farm for a simpler two-tier client/server system that may have been the best way to go.

The Data Manipulation Processes – The Data Centric Tier

But in this case, we are building a server farm that is designed to deliver n-tier applications. The next image should make clear why we used an Active-Passive SQL configuration on each cluster earlier. As you can see, this configuration allowed us to use the redundant SQL Server nodes as the Active MTS nodes in the Data Centric tier. This way, all of the nodes in both clusters are used for some type of active processing as long as none of the nodes has failed. If you work through the potential fail-over scenarios for this configuration, you will see that we can take an outage of any one of the nodes and the entire system will still continue to function.

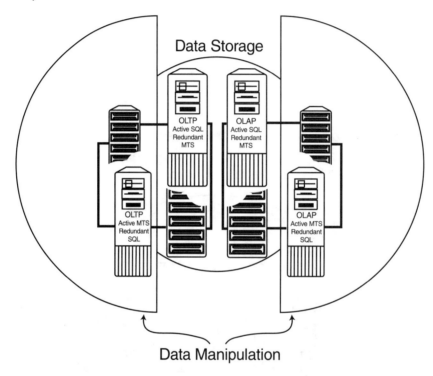

Up until now, we have handled adding servers to our system design by using MSCS. In this next step, we will add additional servers without using MSCS. We will also begin to add some true parallel processing power to the system.

Take a look at the next image. Notice that we have added two servers to the Data Centric tier. Notice also, that these servers are not currently clustered resources. They are independent servers that are connected simultaneously to both of the nodes in the cluster via standard network connection marked as an ODBC connection. Technically, these servers are mirror images of the primary MTS node in the cluster. We could use these servers as a fault tolerant resource under the dire circumstances that would make that necessary. But that is not why we placed them in the Data Centric tier.

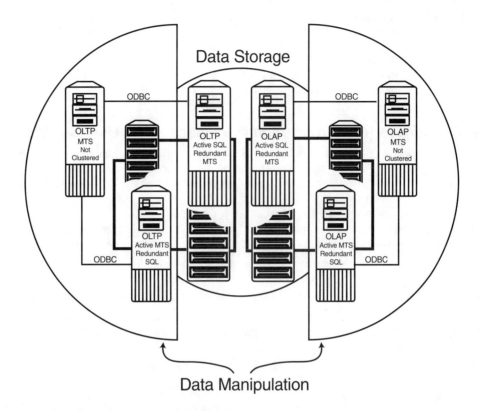

Data Storage

Data Manipulation

Load Balancing Through Parallel Processing

These servers offer the clustered system its first real opportunity to perform parallel processing/load balancing. Let's take a minute or two to review exactly what three things we expect from the Data Manipulation Processes (DMP) on the Data Centric tier:

- ❑ The processes within this tier have been designed to *know* exactly where to locate data within the enterprise, no matter where that data is located: SQL Server, other relational databases, mainframe resources, flat files, the Internet etc.

- ❑ Each process has been given the complete set of valid commands available for working with the data it is designed to manage.

- ❑ Each DMP has the ability to marshal (*package/unpackage*) the data and transport that data to either the Data tier or the User Centric tier as appropriate.

If we had to install the processes on these machines we would do the following:

Install the dynamic link library (DLL) that contains the DMPs on all of the servers that may have an opportunity to act as a DMP server. In this case, that means that the DLL must be installed on:

- ❑ The Active MTS, redundant SQL Server node
- ❑ The Active SQL Server, redundant MTS node
- ❑ The un-clustered MTS server

Think about what this means physically. If all the nodes are operable, then the DMP DLL on the Active SQL Server node will not be used. This DLL will only be used if the Active MTS node fails. So, at any time (even during a clustered node failure) we have a total of two Active DMP DLLs that can be used simultaneously on two different machines. If the DLLs managed information about widgets and we had two users that needed to work with widgets we could direct each user to a different DMP DLL on a different machine. Both processes would execute simultaneously on two different machines.

The Data/Business Rule Integration Processes – The User Centric Tier

The next tier we need to provide equipment for is the User Centric tier. Remember from the last chapter that this is where we fuse an organization's knowledge with the organization's data. Let's take a minute or two to review exactly what five things we expect from the Data/Business Rule Integration Processes on the User Centric tier:

❑   The processes within this tier need to know what data centric DLL it should use to perform data storage tasks.

❑   The processes within this tier need to know what the business rules are, or where to find them if they have been provided as dynamic values.

❑   These processes integrate the organization's business rules with the organization's data to add value to both.

❑   These processes are designed to collect and distribute information to and from the Presentation tier.

❑   These processes are designed to marshal (*package/unpackage*) data and transfer it to or from the Data tier.

Notice in the image below, that we have replaced the formerly un-clustered DMP MTS servers with clustered nodes:

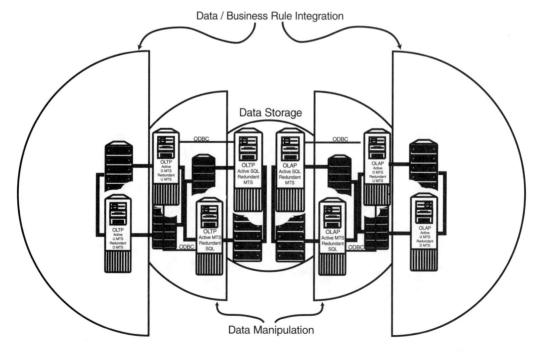

We were able to do this, because we added a new set of clusters to the system. This new cluster bridges the Data Centric tiers and the User Centric tiers. We set up the new clusters to add an active Data Centric MTS node to the Data Centric tier and a second active User Centric MTS node in the User Centric tier. Notice now that we can perform parallel processing across both MTS machines in the Data Centric tier, but that these resources are also capable of automated fail-over thanks to the addition of MSCS.

If we had to install the processes on these machines we would do the following:

Install the dynamic link library (DLL) that contains the Data/Business Rule Integration processes on all of the servers in the User Centric tier. That means they will be installed on:

- ❑ The Active User Centric MTS node
- ❑ Redundant Data Centric MTS node

Think about what this means physically. If all the nodes in this cluster are operable, then the D/BRIP DLL on the active Data Centric node will not be used. This DLL will only be used if the Active MTS node fails. This means that we have fault tolerance at the User Centric tier, but we still do not have enough resources deployed in a manner that will allow for parallel processing. I could go through the motions of adding non-clustered resources again, but I am confident you remember it from above. Instead, I would like to handle that problem by moving out onto the Presentation tier.

The Presentation Processes – Presentation Tier

The next tier we need to provide equipment for is the Presentation tier. Remember from the last chapter that this is where we draw the user interface for the client machine. If we are using web-based development, then this means that we will create an interface (web page) and deliver it to the client's workstation. If we are using more traditional client-server techniques, the Presentation tier actually includes the client's workstation. For our purposes here, designing a parallel processing server farm, we will approach the problem as though we were designing for a web-based deployment. The processes the Presentation tier MUST handle are as follows:

- ❑ The processes within this tier need to know what user centric DLL it should use to perform data manipulation tasks – this implies that the data we are working with on this tier has been run through the Data/Business Rule Integration processes.

- ❑ The processes within this tier need to know what the valid data entry possibilities are for a given object's properties.

- ❑ These processes are designed to collect and distribute information between the end user and the User Centric tier.

Notice in the image below, that we haven't added any clusters to the system – just individual servers:

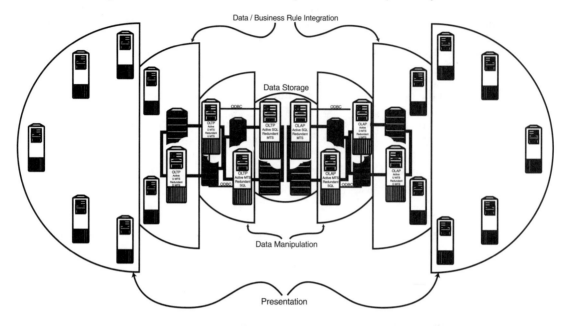

That is because we are designing for a web-based deployment. We can use WLBS to determine whether the IIS Servers are dead or alive. If one of the servers is unavailable, then the fail over at the Presentation and User Centric tiers will be handled by WLBS. It just will not direct any request to a downed resource. That means that we can gain both fault tolerance and parallel processing capabilities without the additional expense that we incur by adding clusters to the system.

If the primary use for our server farm is to distribute non-web-based client-server applications, then it would be in our best interest to beef up the Data Centric tier with at least one additional cluster for each major process. This would save us from the colossal (even if we can automate it) task of updating each client's registry setting every time a particular MTS server became unavailable.

That diagram might look something like the one below:

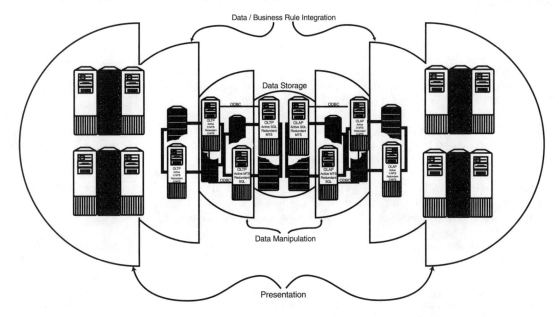

Notice that the lines that formerly separated the User Centric and Presentation tiers have been eliminated. With this type of system, we could ensure that every DLL in the User Centric tier was located on multiple sides of a clustered solution. Generally the type of application we would deploy in this manner would have a smaller audience and hopefully we could install the DLLs in a manner that ensured that we would not have to make client registry changes in cases other than major disasters. We could also use this type of clustered server farm arrangement as a sound starting point for a migration from standard client-server to a web-based deployment. As the needs of the server farm became more web-oriented, we could re-deploy more of the servers into the Presentation tier.

Summary

We can increase the overall availability of our Enterprise Caliber server farm by utilizing the concepts of fault tolerance and parallel processing at the server-to-server level. These concepts are not out of the ordinary, they are simply extensions of well-understood concepts that are used in applications everyday. Our present best use for MSCS is in a combination of clustered and un-clustered servers to maximize the return on every dollar spent, while ensuring high availability, scalability, and overall system reliability.

In the first third of this chapter, we worked through the design of a non-clustered server farm. As we did this, we focused heavily on the basic principles of parallel processing and touched lightly on the fault tolerance issue. Once we had a firm grasp on the basics of parallel processing design essentials, we took a second look at constructing a server farm in the second third of this chapter. This time, we included Microsoft Cluster Server in the design parameters. By the time we got to the third section of this chapter we were able to design the *best* (the most resources available in real-time for the money spent) server farm by using some combination of standard and clustered resources.

In the next chapter we will begin the process of looking at our enterprise more from the software design perspective. While we do this, it is important to keep the physical system we just discussed in mind. The world of PC based software development has changed. Our target audience no longer needs to be limited to a small group(s) of users. We have an Enterprise Caliber operating system in Windows NT. And, as we have seen over the last two chapters, the hardware we have available to us now can no longer be used as an excuse for a lack of fault tolerance or scalability in our applications. This means that there is only one other thing left for us to consider before we can hold our heads high in the enterprise arena. We need to take a close look at our software development practices. We will do that throughout the remainder of this book.

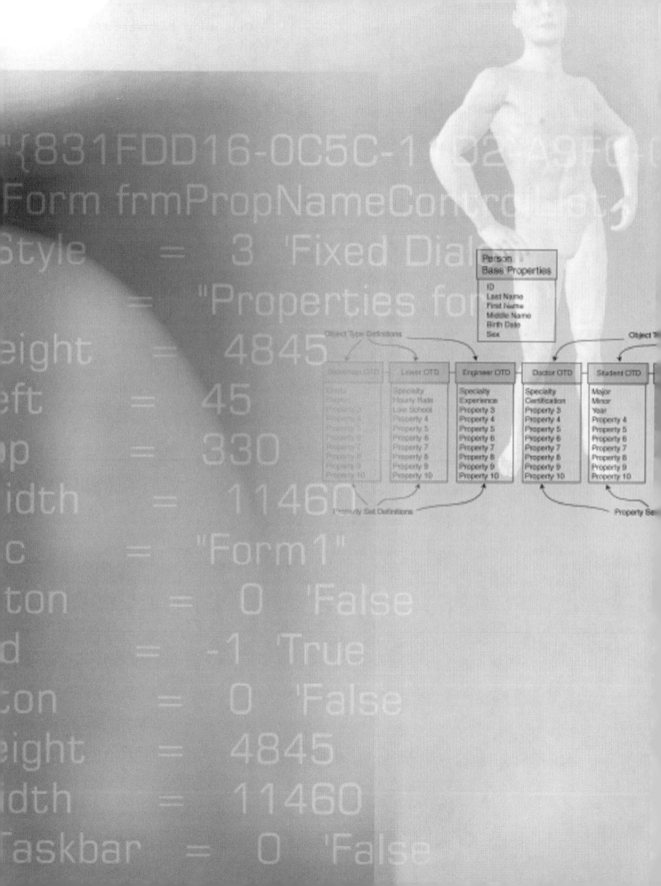

Introduction to Enterprise Caliber Data Objects

Once we believe something is possible, nothing can stop us from making it happen. Often, the most difficult part of opening new vistas is simply realizing that they exist. This chapter is designed to challenge you with some new possibilities. Prepare yourself. I'm about to raise the bar in your design universe.

In the last few chapters, I've concentrated on how we can organize our hardware to provide an available, scalable and secure infrastructure upon which we can deploy our enterprise. Although this was important information in its own right, we also learnt several important principles that we can now apply to designing the software components for our enterprise.

In this chapter, I will introduce you to a new level of excellence in systems development. The main character in this new development environment is the **Enterprise Caliber Data Object**. We will become acquainted with this object by first discovering its design objectives. Once we understand its basic qualities, we will take the steps necessary to turn those qualities into a concrete list of functional requirements.

Enterprise Design Objectives

The ActiveX components we'll design and build in this book are Enterprise Caliber Data Objects (ECDOs). In the first few chapters of this book, we took a look at enterprise level hardware and operating systems. What we found is that they were quite different from what we would normally think of as personal computer hardware or operating systems. What we'll find in this section is that the objects intended for use on an enterprise platform are different from objects we might have used on a personal computer or even on a group of networked personal computers.

Enterprise level objects must satisfy the following seven **Design Objectives**:

1. **Maintainable** – The code we write for enterprise level objects is reproducible. We use a system or methodology when we create ECDOs. The more similar we make each object, the easier they all are to develop and maintain.

2. **Reusable** – I know that you probably think reusable code is just a myth, but by the time you finish this book you will find that reusable code is really the norm. Have you used a text box or command button lately? Reusable objects are everywhere.

3. **Scalable** – Let's make sure that we understand this one. Scalable means that our system is capable of growing to meet the demands of any number of users, or, more accurately, is capable of handling any number of transactions. That doesn't mean that our objects will be called upon to do this the first day they are put into production. What it does mean is that each object we put into production, even if its initial target audience is small, must have the capacity to meet any potential demand without modification.

4. **Accessible** – This is a two-pronged objective:

   ❑ *From the user's perspective* – No matter where the user happens to be located and no matter what type of computer the customer has access to, the customer should be able to use the same object with essentially the same level of functionality.

   ❑ *From the developer's perspective* – Existing objects must be easy to find, easy to understand, and easy to reuse. This prevents us from continuously re-inventing the wheel; a plague that wastes one of the enterprise's most valuable resources, the developer's talent.

5. **Reliable** – We've already spent a great deal of time learning how to make the hardware and network portion of our system fault tolerant. Now we must shift our focus to software design. One fact we must face is that no matter how well a hardware system is designed or constructed hardware failures can, and do, happen. This means that our objects must have the ability to anticipate the inevitable hardware failures and handle those failures gracefully – *with absolutely no loss of data.*

6. **Useful** – Don't laugh. I don't know how many systems I have seen that are nothing more than separate monuments to talented DBAs, developers, and interface designers. It is true that an enterprise system is constructed from many separate components, but those components must be designed to work together to provide a *seamless* experience for the user. In many systems, this is not the case. Sure maybe the data entry portion of the application is flawless and the tables are perfectly normalized. But, when the CEO needs the answer to any thing but a pre-programmed question, they must call out the IT cavalry for the answer. An enterprise level system must be useful to the point that it allows any user with the appropriate security clearance to find the answer to even complex questions with a minimum of effort.

7. **Secure** – This is a three-pronged objective:

   ❑ The object must be designed to allow the sharing of information while still providing security at any level deemed necessary by the object's current assignment.

   ❑ Any data that passes over foreign networks must be rendered useless to any party other than the intended recipient.

   ❑ No individual without clearance should be allowed to access the network, but even if such access does occur, the intruder should not be allowed to access data through an Enterprise Caliber Data Object.

The Architecture

Now that we have a sense of the design objectives for an Enterprise Caliber Data Object, we can begin the task of designing our first system. The first step in that process is to decide on the architecture we will employ. Throughout the first section of this book, when we looked at enterprise hardware and operating systems, we examined the relative merits of different physical architectures. We found that a 4-tier physical architecture enhanced the system's ability to distribute the processing and generally resulted in more scalable system.

From the hardware perspective, we viewed the different tiers of the system as physically separate computers or perhaps as clusters of computers. But, as we move away from the hardware/operating system arena and into the realm of software design, we are going to intentionally soften this distinction between the different computers. Our first step in that direction is to look at the 4-tier architecture as a purely logical construct. In this light, we can envision our enterprise system as groups of processes that work together instead of as groups of computers that work together:

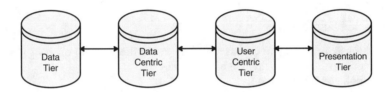

With a little effort, we find that we can logically categorize all computing processes into four distinct groups of like processes. We'll call these groups **tiers**. This division of processes into 4-tiers serves two major purposes:

From a hardware/networking perspective the division allows us to position the bulk of the processing closer to the hardware responsible for that processing. This minimizes network traffic and generally improves system performance. However, be aware that, in order to take advantage of this physical load-distributing capacity, the software we develop must be designed in a special manner.

> **Our software-architecture must also allow for a division of the processing responsibilities.**

What this means is that, when we design an object, we actually design *two halves* of an object rather than a *single* object. We design one half of the object to handle the Data Centric processes and the other half of the object to handle the User Centric processes. This software architecture offers a multitude of configuration possibilities that allows us to deploy our objects in a manner that maximizes their utilization of the systems' available resources.

From a design perspective, the logical division allows us to design databases and user interfaces that are unfettered by the business rules that too often, incorrectly, drive their design. In a logical 4-tier system, we move all the business rules into the two middle tiers of the system.

This allows us to design the data store in as pure a manner as possible. The only constraints we place on data store design are those constraints actually associated with the efficient storage and retrieval of data. We allow ourselves to forget about problems like moving money from one account to another while we are designing the data structures and data handling devices. The problems that stem from activities like moving money from one account to another are really business problems, and despite the common belief to the contrary those business problems have absolutely nothing to do with the mechanics of record locking in a database.

The user interface is also liberated when we move the business rules into the middle tiers of our logical 4-tier system. Once this is done, the interface designers can concern themselves with developing polished, attractive, and efficient data collection/dissemination devices. These new devices, freed from the weight of the business rules, can take on a lighter and more efficient persona. These interfaces can be easily modified to meet the rapidly changing conditions imposed by modern business. That is because, with this architecture, the modifications can be made without taking on the huge problems associated with reprogramming an interface that contains a great deal of business logic.

Last, and not least of all, the logical 4-tier system allows us to make changes to business rules, test the effects of the changes, and implement the changes without modifying a single database, or visiting even a single desktop. In this system, the business objects are allowed to become something of a data authority whose job is to retrieve data stored in a manner that best suits the data and repackage that data into a customized format that best suit the user.

As you can see, the logical 4-tier system goes a long way in the direction of meeting many of our enterprise design objectives. And now that we have a sense of what a logical 4-tier system is, we should take a closer look at each of the tiers.

The Data Tier

In 4-tier architecture, all of the data and data storage/retrieval processes are logically, if not physically, located on a single tier. We call that group of data storage the **Data tier**. As its name suggests, this tier is responsible for managing the storage of the data our enterprise requires for operation. As far as the objects in this book are concerned, our primary data store will be an ODBC compliant database, SQL Server.

> I'm using ODBC because it works with just about everything from SQL Server to Oracle and Informix over Unix, and we can even have an ODBC Mainframe connection.

But it is important to realize that, information in the Data tier can be stored in flat files, in a mainframe resource(s), in mini-computer(s), or anywhere on the network – which may mean anywhere on the entire Internet for some objects. Consider for example, if we recently constructed a *ZipCode* object that verifies new, or unknown, zip codes against the US Post Office's zip code database made available to the public through the Post Office's web site. We could also build another object that verifies proposed data modifications against the mainframe's data store – this object would give every user in the enterprise access to the mainframe's power with none of the hassles.

As we work through the chapters of this book, one of our main goals is to extract every ounce of performance out of each one of the four tiers. We will find that the Data tier has a huge effect on the system's performance, and we will spend a lot of time designing and coding right at the Data tier. That said, for the purposes of this discussion it is probably best to think of the Data tier just as a perfect storage medium and forget about the details.

The Data Centric Tier

The Data Centric tier is home to the object-halves that handle a group of processes we call **Data Centric processes**. They are primarily responsible for these operations:

❑ Directly requesting information from the Data tier

❑ Packaging the information for transport to the User Centric tier

❑ Transporting data packages to the User Centric tier

❑ Ensuring that object level transactions are either executed completely or ignored completely

❑ Accepting data packages from the User Centric tier

❑ Unpacking the information received from the User Centric tier

❑ Directly placing information into the Data tier

In order to carry out these operations, the object-halves on the Data Centric tier must perform a whole host of tasks that we will examine in great deal throughout the remainder of this book. For the purposes of this overview, think of the Data Centric tier as a Transaction Clearing, Data Packaging, and Data Transport machine.

The User Centric Tier

The object-halves that inhabit the User Centric tier are primarily responsible for these operations:

❑ Requesting information from the Data Centric tier

❑ Unpacking the data it receives from the Data Centric tier

❑ Transporting the data to the Presentation tier

❑ Accepting information from the Presentation tier

❑ Ensuring that the all business rules including data validation rules are observed

❑ Packaging data for transport to the Data Centric tier

❑ Transporting the data packages to the Data Centric tier

In the past, this tier was where most of the work we associate with application development was performed. *This was a mistake.* It is important that we learn to see enterprise solutions as the sum of *all* of the work on *all* of the tiers. In this book, we will learn that each tier has strengths, and for optimal performance, our objects must exploit all of the strengths of each tier. For the purposes of this overview, think of the User Centric tier as a Business Rule Clearing, Data Packaging and Data Transport machine.

The Presentation Tier

Obviously this tier is primarily responsible for presenting information to and receiving information from the user. If we design and build the other three tiers correctly, this tier should be able to take on any persona the application requires. Using this book, we could construct user interfaces that employ everything from a full blown Visual Basic interface running on a powerful workstation to a simple HTML interface that runs on a palm top PC with a 3" by 5½" screen.

User Interfaces

The objects we build do not rely upon any particular user interface or type of user interface.

> **The object is the application, not the interface.**

This is a very liberating notion. It means that we can pop out as many different versions of the interface as we need to. Throughout this book, we will construct the following types of interfaces:

Fat Client – Visual Basic

This interface most closely resembles the standard client-server model we all know. When we construct this interface, we actually make a direct reference to the User Centric object in the interface code and deliver the User Centric DLL to the desktop with the interface. In most cases, we try to stay away from this scenario, because it means we have to visit the desktop to make changes to the User Centric object. This type of interface is ideal for use with products like Microsoft's Terminal Server. We will take a look at this technique in the last section of the book.

Thin Client – Visual Basic

This interface is a little easier to manage than the fat client model. We use elementary distributed computing techniques to install the User Centric object on a server running MTS. With this solution, we still need to visit the desktop from time-to-time, but only to update those superficial things we might include in the interface. Our application really resides on the server running MTS. This solution is a good one, especially when the enterprise has access to tools like Microsoft's System Management Server (SMS) to handle the installations and hopefully infrequent updates.

Thin Client – Web-Based

This interface is phenomenal. We can create the entire interface using a combination of Active Server Pages (ASP) and Dynamic Hypertext Markup Language (DHTML). I worked with one of my teams to create entire applications that have a desktop footprint of less than 300K while still offering an excellent level of usability. This solution offers virtually zero desktop maintenance. Updates and improvements are available immediately. The only real drawback with this interface is an artificial one I'm afraid I imposed upon myself. When we first started developing them, I made a rule that a thin client web based interface should not have any ActiveX controls. Everything must be done using DHTML. This does result in a slimmer profile and offers an almost universal platform, but it is difficult to match the functionality of say a listview control using just DHTML.

Heavy Client – Web-Based

Notice that I didn't use the word fat client to describe this interface. This interface is something of a compromise. It is essentially a thin client interface that can include ActiveX controls. We loose the universal nature of the medium, but we gain something in the way of ease of coding and usability. This is an excellent choice for those enterprises that can guarantee that the only web browser that will be used is IE 4.01 or better.

A Single Tier Vision

Now that I have covered the benefits of parallel processing hardware and sung the praises of 4-tier system design. I am going to ask you to design each object as though it existed on a single tier on a single machine.

Why? Well, it's my experience that, the task of designing an object is a job best left to a directed team that owns the entire project. Sure, within that team there may be pockets of expertise that clearly exist on one or another of the tiers, but the final product is the sum of the *all* of the work on *all* of the tiers. The team members must be in close contact and have the authority to transfer anything including entire processes, from one tier to another if the final product will clearly benefit from such a transfer.

Our real mission is to provide a product – a *data component*. That product should serve to reinforce the user's view of the enterprise as a *single entity*, not as a myriad of separate pieces. This is only possible if each part of the system meshes perfectly with the rest. Again, the best way I know to ensure such a high level of harmony is to have the entire project be the responsibility of a single team.

I have said that the design and development of an individual object should be the responsibility of a single focused team. Let me add that, this doesn't have to mean that the same team that designs data objects must write the application and all of the application interfaces that use the object. In my experience this would squander a valuable resource. A team capable of designing and delivering Enterprise Caliber Data Objects should be charged with that responsibility. Once the object team has completed and tested an object, the object should be made readily available for other, maybe interface development, teams to use as they see fit. This type of specialization will maximize the performance of the entire development system.

Considering State

Unfortunately, I think that the word, **state**, is getting to be one of those overused words. We most often use the word, state, to describe an object's current property values. This is the way I prefer to use it. But, we can also use the word to describe a particular communication technique between an object and its data store. In this vein, the word, state, describes the type of connection used to facilitate that communication. If the connection is a continuous one, we say that the connection has state or is *stateful*. If the connection is intermittent, then we say that the connection is *stateless*.

For the purposes of this discussion, we will equate state with one of two types of communication techniques.

Continuous Connection – Synchronous – Stateful

With this type of connectivity, the user is working with the information in the database in real time. This makes things really simple. Every user has a real-time/full-time connection to the data store. If Sally and Bob are both working with the Acme account and Sally updates the payment field, the application on Bob's desktop can immediately reflect the update. It's great!

It's kind of like Sally and Bob are on a date and are sharing a single chocolate malted. Imagine that each has a straw and they are using the straws to drink out of the same glass at the same time. They both always have access to the treat and always have a sense of how much fluid is left in the cup. This too, is great! Well, maybe not. This scenario works fine on a date with two or maybe even three people, but what if 10 or 100 people want to share the treat? The difficulty I see here is the size of the opening in the glass. I think we would find that there is a limit to the number of straws that can fit in a single glass or perhaps more importantly the number of heads that can fit around a single glass. See the problem...

The problem with giving each user a continuous connection to the data store is almost exactly the same. Except that with data stores the limited resource isn't the size of a glass, it's the number of available database connections. These are the most precious commodities in any enterprise. Each connection requires a certain amount of system resources, memory, etc. A computer is a physical construct that has a limited amount of resources. This means that there are a fixed number of connections available for a given computer or even for a cluster of computers.

If we give each user a dedicated connection, then we must limit the number of users that can access the data store – period.

In some cases, this may be acceptable, but remember the job here. We are delivering an enterprise. Our solution must be capable of scaling to handle any number of users. We need a different tack.

Intermittent Connection – Asynchronous – Stateless

With this type of connectivity, the users work with the information in the database intermittently. Each user takes the information he or she needs to work with and immediately releases the database connection making it available for the next user. In this case, if Sally and Bob are both working with the Acme account and Sally updates the payment field, the application on Bob's desktop will not immediately reflect the update. In order for Bob to be aware of changes made to the account since he first retrieved it, he must do something that causes the data on his desktop to be refreshed.

Let's go back to Sally and Bob's date. This time, imagine that the two are feasting on a bag of potato chips. Just like with the chocolate malted, we find a limiting factor – in this case it is the size of the opening of the bag. If they both reach for a chip at the same time, the romance might be over, but the two are soul mates and with a little imagination, they overcome this limitation. Each one learns to take a turn lowering a hand into the bag and scooping out a handful of chips. With this technique Sally can munch her chips while Bob is refilling his supply, and visa versa. Ah! Organization! Bliss! And even if the same 10 or 100 intruders we met above wanted to join them, we would not have a problem – until we ran out of chips, but that's another problem…

With stateless connections, we learn to take turns like Sally and Bob did with the potato chips. Instead of each user having a continuous connection to the database, we give each user as many intermittent connections as they require.

> **This technique allows us to service a vast number of users with our limited number of database connections.**

Please notice that we haven't performed the impossible here – we haven't removed the limitation – we have just learned to work with it. Unfortunately, we have also raised a number of new issues that we'll have to deal with. But, rest assured. It is possible to deal with them.

Issues that Stem from Using Stateless Objects

It is not difficult to imagine that if 100 people are sharing a single bag of potato chips that the first person that dipped a hand into the bag may not be aware that the 99th person has taken the last chip. This is the problem with stateless connections.

We can service a virtually unlimited number of users, but at any given time, the data that each user has may no longer reflect the current condition of the data in the data store. When the information a user currently has no longer matches the current information in the data store, we can say that the user's data has become **stale**.

Freshness

Data like a potato chip is best served fresh. The minute a user receives information from the data store; its value begins to decay. Each tick of the CPU offers another opportunity for any other user to change the object's information in the data store. Let's imagine that Sally in sales, has requested the Acme account. She is working with the account at her computer and is about to enter Acme's latest order – the largest purchase our company has ever received. Meanwhile, Bob, in accounting, is also studying the Acme account at his computer. He learns that this customer has not made a single purchase from our company in the last 10 years but is still receiving its yearly Christmas card. He immediately recognizes this as a problem and reasons that he will save our company a fortune on Christmas cards by deleting the Acme account from the data store. You know the rest of the story. When Sally attempts to enter the order into the system. She is shocked to learn that Acme no longer has an account with our firm! This ridiculous example was not intended to exhaust the problems associated with stale data; it was intended to get you thinking about the potential problems. You probably can't tell, but I am pausing here for effect...

The usual response to the stale data story is "why not lock the record?" My answer, a question, is always the same – "For how long?" Which I always follow with the comment: "If Bob requested the Acme account on Monday and left it sitting on his desk until Wednesday, then Sally's attempt to enter our company's largest order on Tuesday still would have failed." This comment invariably evokes a series of responses suggesting ever-shorter periods of time during which the record could be locked.

Think about it. Record locking does not work with a stateless system! As long as the users have the appropriate security clearance, we hand out data like penny candy. That is our job – the efficient dissemination of data. We don't know what the users' intentions are every time they request information. They might want to locate a telephone number, change a contact's name, or delete an account from the data store. We cannot lock every record requested in perpetuity. Record locking is not the answer. We need another way to handle the inevitable data collisions that *will* occur in a stateless environment.

Data Collisions

A data collision occurs whenever a user makes a decision to update or delete data in the data store based upon stale information. Imagine that it is just before 12 o'clock midnight, you are ravenous from working non-stop for hours, and that the pizza deliveryman accepts delivery orders until exactly 12 o'clock midnight. You pick up the telephone and are just about to call when you remember that you still have some leftover pizza in the refrigerator. So, you don't make the call. Your mouth is watering; the clock strikes midnight just as you open the refrigerator door. At first you are simply saddened to learn that your roommate has devoured the remaining pizza, but your sadness quickly turns to dismay when you see the clock, which now reads 12:01 AM. This is a **data collision**; you made a decision not to call the pizza deliveryman because you thought there was pizza in the refrigerator. You acted based upon *stale* information and now you are going to go hungry.

Data collisions provide fertile ground for multiple-user banking account problems. You know the drill, the husband withdraws all but 5 dollars from the account at exactly the same time the wife withdraws 6 dollars from the account. Someone here is going to lose. More than likely, it will be our job to ensure that the bank is not the loser. But I think that really means that we must protect all of the bank's interests, including its interest in retaining loyal customers. We must see to it that we abide by the bank's business rules concerning money, but we can also provide the customer a detailed account of the transactions that caused the overdraft and allow the customer to recover gracefully from the data collision.

Recovery

I cannot think about data collisions or record locking without thinking about the poor souls who may have worked for hours to collect information and type it into our handsome user interface. I always think about what his or her reaction will be when that cold message pops up and reads: Could not update the record at this time, another user was modifying the record. Please try again later. "How much later?" "What has changed?" "Do I have to type all this in again?" "Stupid Computer!"

Data collisions will happen in a stateless environment. It is our job to make them as painless as possible by providing a reasonable **recovery path**. What this means, in real terms, is that we must perform collision tests on a field-by-field basis and inform the user with complete details for every collision. Then we must give the user the capability to either reattempt the action – overwriting the other user's modifications or cancel the action – accepting the other user's modifications. Right about now, I am sure you are thinking something like: "Gee, this really sounds like a lot of work. Do I have to use stateless connections?"

So, Why Use Stateless Objects?

I have seen powerful computers knuckle under the strain of just 50 users with persistent data connections. True a lot of this stress was due to some controllable factors like poor database design and the like, but even if every part of the system was perfect, how many more users do you think a stateful system could handle? Maybe an extra 150 or 250 users? In this case, just like with Bob and Sally's chocolate malted there is some, relatively small, limit to the number of users that the system can serve. Stateless objects, on the other hand, can allow a single database machine or cluster of database machines to handle thousands of simultaneous users. They can do this by using architecture best described as **n-sphere**.

N-Sphere Architecture

Whenever I am asked to describe our enterprise design, I always use a little play on words and describe our n-tier system as an n-sphere system. It may sound cute, but that's really not why I describe it as n-sphere architecture. Take a look at the image. Notice that we have depicted each of the logical 4 tiers we discussed earlier as separate spheres:

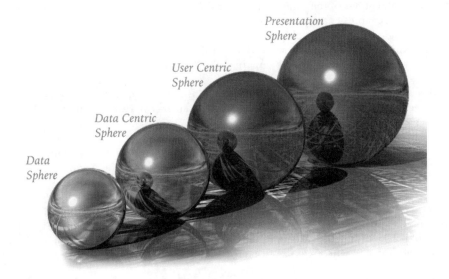

Good, now notice the relative sizes of each sphere. It should be easy to see that the Data sphere could fit into the Data Centric sphere and that the Data Centric sphere could fit into the User Centric sphere and so on. If we look at this image and consider our recent discussion on stateless connections, we should be able to develop a good mental image of how the entire system works.

Imagine that the Data sphere is really a bag of potato chips. We will also assume that it is only possible for one hand to fit into the bag of chips at a time. If we follow this line of reasoning, then the Data Centric sphere could be Bob and Sally on their date – remember? They each take turns dipping a hand into the bag. Each one withdraws enough chips to last until it is once again that person's turn at the bag.

This example is simple enough, and it shows how we can effectively increase the number of people that can eat out of a single bag of potato chips. Let's say that two other couples that join them. Can we still share the same bag of chips? Definitely! They could all take turns.

But let's suppose, for the sake of argument, that only two people can comfortably fit around the bag of chips. What do we do then? Well, how about if we put Bob and Sally to work? We can position the other couples so that they surround Bob and Sally much like Bob and Sally are surrounding the bag of potato chips.

Yes! This exactly the way the User Centric sphere surrounds the Data Centric sphere.

Then we can order (they are working now!) Bob and Sally to hand out some chips to the surrounding couples instead of eating the chips.

Now the single bag of chips is capable of feeding 4 people instead of a single person.

I bet you can guess what is going to happen next. No they do not run out of chips. Four more couples show up. Can they all eat out of the same bag of chips? Sure they can. The new couples could surround the existing couples exactly the way the Presentation sphere surrounds the User Centric sphere. Now the single bag of potato chips is feeding eight people. Can the outer ring of lovers decide to return some chips to the bag? I don't see why not. Could the outer ring of lovers deliver additional chips to the bag from some outside source? Again, I don't see why not.

If we move this example away from dates and potato chips and into data connections and objects, we find that we effectively increase the number of users that can access a single data store by using an n-sphere architecture.

Please take a minute or two to think about the choice of a *sphere* as the defining shape for each minor processing division. We could have chosen a circle – the daters around the bag of potato chips kind of formed a circle. But we didn't. We defined each processing division as a sphere. Why?

Try to think of the Data sphere inside the Data Centric sphere. If you visualize this in two dimensions, then it is possible to draw many lines that represent database connections from the outer circumference of the Data sphere to the inner circumference of the Data centric sphere. It kind of looks like a spoked-hub and wheel:

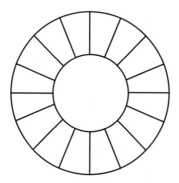

Remember our designs for the server farm in the last chapter. If we view the system like this, we are in essence equating the circumference of the Data sphere with some number of potential database connections. Of course, we could draw an outer ring, representing the user Centric sphere and draw double the number of connections from the Data Centric sphere to the User Centric sphere. Just like we did with the outer circle of daters and the potato chips.

Now visualize the system in three dimensions. If we view it like this, we can draw lines from any point on the outer surface of the Data sphere to the inner surface of the Data Centric tier:

When we consider the system in three dimensions instead of two, we are, in equating the number of connections with the surface area of each sphere instead of the circumference of each sphere. What does this give us? Exactly! The ability to share potato chips with many more couples. But it also gives us the ability to share a very limited number of database connections with a number of user orders of magnitude greater than the number of database connections.

Do you remember the assumption we made when we were designing the server farms in the last chapter? Remember that I suggested that we take on the macro (server-to-server) parallel processing case, assuming that each machine in the server farm was incapable of performing any internal parallel processing? I said that this simplification would make it easier for us to understand and solve the core problem. I also said that making this assumption could not hurt us because if the machines we expected to perform processing in a serial fashion, all of a sudden, became capable of performing parallel processing, it could only improve the system.

Well, I have really good news for you! Windows NT is a powerful operating system. As long as we design efficient minor processing units (objects or DLLs). We can expect that each machine in our server farm will be capable of executing many of our processes simultaneously on each server. What this means is that in addition to macro parallel processing capabilities that we built into the physical portion of our system, we will also have some inherent micro (*parallel processes running on a single machine)* parallel processing capabilities. I don't want to do any serious math here, but let's just think about what this means.

We designed a concentric server farm that has an increasing number of machines on each minor processing tier or server ring. In other words if we have 1 machine at the Data ring, we expect to have at least 2 on the Data Centric ring, and 4 on the User Centric ring, etc. In the last chapter, we found that we could do this because we carefully divided our processing to follow one intractable rule – the processing in the outer rings of the server farm will always take longer to execute. None of that has changed. What has changed is that we've just found out that each one of the machines on each of the rings can actually run more than one process at the same time. This means that in order to calculate the amount of processing we can initiate in parallel on the Presentation sphere we have to multiply both by the number of machines on each ring and by the number of simultaneous processes on each machine on each ring.

You can work through the math for your own system, but an easy way to visualize this software driven increase in availability of the server(s) at the center of the farm is to envision each physical ring as a logical sphere.

This type of architecture is what enables us to efficiently service thousands of users from a single data store. You might think that the driving force is economy, but you would be only partially correct. We gain so very much more. This architecture allows us to use this centralized data store to service our *entire* enterprise.

> It makes it possible for *every user* in the enterprise to *share* information in *real-time* with any other user in the enterprise.

It allows us to build true enterprise-wide OLTP solutions and establish an enterprise-wide data warehouse, OLAP, solution that can provide the users with a global view of the entire organization/enterprise.

In the last chapter we said that the goal of distributed architecture is to distribute the processing load across the enterprise's resources – NOT to distribute the enterprise's resources. In that chapter, we took it for granted that this statement meant that we needed to focus all of the enterprise's physical resources. I hope, that right about now, it is starting to become obvious that this really means a lot more. Think about it! Perhaps the most valuable resource any enterprise owns is the data that the organization has accumulated over the course of performing its business. This information represents the organization's education through experience. Maybe now is a good time to refine or add to our design goal for distributed architecture. Now we can say that:

> The goal of distributed architecture is to distribute the processing load across the enterprise's resources – NOT to distribute the enterprise's data.

Functional Requirements

Earlier in this chapter we discussed the seven design objectives for an Enterprise Caliber Data Object. And while it is really nice to have a sense of the qualities an ECDO must possess, it is imperative that we have a list of functional requirements if we are to write anything like executable code. Fortunately, I happen to have a list of the basic functional requirements for every Enterprise Caliber Data Object right here:

Each object should have the ability to:

- ❑ Produce a list of selected objects from the data store
- ❑ Add a new object to the data store
- ❑ Modify an existing object in the data store
- ❑ Delete an object from the data store
- ❑ Create its own data storage structures and stored procedures (or any other data storage/ manipulation routines it requires)
- ❑ Maintain a complete history of all changes made to the object (audit history)

- ❑ Present the object's audit history to the user on demand
- ❑ Restore an object to any previous state in the audit history (unlimited undo's)
- ❑ Maintain a list of all deleted objects
- ❑ Present the list of deleted objects to the user on demand
- ❑ Restore a deleted object back to its state at the time of deletion
- ❑ Perform the equivalent of field level collision handling and allow the user to recover from a data collision gracefully without having to re-enter the data
- ❑ Manage data validation and actively broadcast the object's current state of validation to the interested portions of the application
- ❑ Manage the complex parent-child relationships between objects internally, without programmer intervention

This may seem like a tall set of requirements for a simple object, but let your guiding principles be:

- ❑ Make each block of code, even the simple ones, perfect
- ❑ Never skimp on the foundation

Now that we have a sense of what we expect from our Enterprise Caliber Data Objects, we can begin the work of developing a set of specifications for building the objects. We can divide that list into two major categories:

- ❑ The first we shall call **Data Handling processes**. These are the processes that actually touch every tier from the Presentation tier to the Data tier. These processes have another thing in common; they all have at least one stored procedure associated with them.
- ❑ The second category of processes we shall call **Extended processes**, for lack of a better term. With one exception, these processes do not directly touch the Data tier. They handle things like data validation, general housekeeping, state management, and the complex parent-child relationships that occur between objects.

Let's take a closer look at each of the processes every Enterprise Caliber Data Object must present to the system.

The Data-Handling Processes

It's really kind of sad, but if you think about it, a lot of our work consists of just four major responsibilities:

- ❑ We add a new record to a database
- ❑ We select record(s) from the database
- ❑ We change a record in the database
- ❑ We delete a record from the database

That's it! Well the way I figure it, if that is all I have to do, I might as well do it with distinction. These four responsibilities translate into eight basic data handling processes that allow you to manage your enterprise's data with distinction.

1 – The Insert Process

As the name suggests, the *Insert* process is used to add an object's data to the data store. This process is also responsible for creating an entry in the object's audit history that marks the insertion and its current state.

2 – The Update Process

As the name suggests, the *Update* process is used to update or change an object's data in the data store. This process is also responsible for creating an entry in the object's audit history that marks the update and storing the object's last state.

3 – The DeleteProcess

The *Delete* process is used to remove an object's data from the data store. This process is also responsible for creating an entry in the object's audit history that marks the deletion and storing the object's last state.

4 – The Fetch Process

The *Fetch* process is used to fetch a single object from the data store.

5 – The Load Process

The *Load* process returns a collection of objects from the data store based upon some selection criterion.

6 – The Audit History Process

The *Audit History* process returns a collection of objects that together make up the complete history for a single object.

7 – The Show Deleted Process

The *Show Deleted* process returns a collection of objects from the data store that are currently deleted.

8 – The Restore From Deleted Process

The *Restore From Deleted* process restores an object from a deleted state back to the state it held at the time of its deletion. When an object is restored, the object's entire history must also be restored. This process is responsible for creating an entry in the object's audit history that marks the restoration.

The Extended Processes

There are four of these extended processes:

Create the Data Store

Remember our design objectives - Enterprise Caliber Data Objects are designed to be reused. What this means in real terms is that we can point a single object at several different data stores when the need arises. This also means that someone has got to build the tables and write all the stored procedures in each data store that might be used by a particular object. If we left this responsibility to any human being, we could almost guarantee one thing.

The data stores' tables and stored procedures probably would not be identical, and even if they were, we just wasted one of the enterprise's most limited resources – developer talent.

Of course, we don't leave this responsibility to a human. We delegate it to the object itself in a routine we call `EstablishDataStore`. This method examines the data store and builds or rebuilds any database entities required by the object. This technique offers an additional advantage; whenever we need to change a database entity, we use this method to perform the task for us. This ensures that every data store that is used by this object is corrected each time this method of the object is executed.

Manage State/Handle Data Collisions – Pervasive

We just spent a couple of pages, several bags of potato chips, and I believe one pizza working through the issues that arise from using stateless objects in a system. I won't belabor the point here, but realize that our data objects have to pick up the tab for all the extra users the stateless system can handle. The objects must therefore be capable of determining that data collisions have occurred, inform the user or business rule about the collision, and allow for a graceful recovery from the collision. This task requires a great deal of work on every tier of the system except for the Presentation tier. But even there we do have some minor housekeeping and communication chores to perform.

Data Validation – Property Handler Lets and Business Rules

Enterprise Caliber Data Objects provide two types of data validation. The first is handled by any object that exposes or uses a property. We call this **basic data validation**. With this type of data validation, we test the type and size of the information that is entered into any property. Our only goal here is simple stuff like making sure that Long values are not entered into Integer properties etc. We also make sure that required values that shouldn't be left null are actually filled and that we don't attempt to enter 16 characters into a database field designed to hold 15 characters. So I guess you could say that basic data validation is akin to scientific data validation. In other words, the rules that we apply here are defined by the data itself, like don't place fractions in integer fields, etc. They are just some rules enforced by the language or the database that must be upheld without question. These rules are concrete, knowable, and can be tested. All of this type of coding is written in the property handler `Let` functions.

We also program another round of data validation in our objects. We call this type of validation **business-rule data validation**. In these cases, we perform additional tests that are not necessarily scientific in nature. These tests are designed to enforce business rules that define the quality of the data that can be entered into the system. Examples of this type of data validation might include: a test that ensures that no engineer or programmer ever makes more money than the top salesperson or a test that ensures that widgets are never produced in fluorescent green.

Manage Parent-Child Relationships

One of the most potentially dangerous aspects of working with objects is their hierarchical nature. What we have achieved with our object design is to cause the normal relational database to evolve into something of an object data store with a hierarchical twist. This is not a bad thing. The relational database is, by design, a malleable device. It can become anything we need it to be.

However, this does mean that we have to pay extra attention to concepts like parent-child relationships. If you haven't read *Visual Basic 6 Business Objects* by Rockford Lhotka (also published by Wrox Press), by all means run out and get a copy immediately.

Rocky, has done a wonderful job of describing just how complicated these things can become. I won't attempt to restate his excellent discourse on the subject here. Instead, I am going to give you the two tools that we will use to manage this intricate process.

CheckOutObject

The `CheckOutObject` method encapsulates the complicated process that must be performed to manage the parent-child relationship between objects *before* any object is made editable. Essentially, it performs a series of housekeeping or record keeping chores in a very rigorous manner every time an object is made available for editing.

CheckInObject

The `CheckInObject` method is really the reverse of `CheckOutObject`. It encapsulates the complicated process that must be performed to manage the parent-child relationship between objects *after* an object has been edited. It also performs a series of housekeeping or record keeping chores in a very rigorous manner every time a user has finished working with an object.

Now that I have given you a sense of the challenges that lay ahead of you developing Enterprise Caliber Data Objects, let me give you a sense of how we are going to take on that challenge.

One Step at a Time

As you might know, I am a consultant. It might sound impressive, but all it means that I am kind of a technological hobo or maybe a technological hit-man. Basically I move around from job to job looking for new problems to solve. The way I have learned to test my success or lack of it on any assignment is to see whether or not I have worked myself out of a job. If by the time I am ready to leave the client doesn't need me to hold-together the things I worked on when I was there, then I know that I did my job well. If on the other hand, I leave and the work I did cannot stand on its own, then I have failed miserably. These days I am lucky enough that one of my primary responsibilities is to serve as a mentor to other developers. This means that, now, I have to gauge my success by those developers' ability to solve problems without my help. I do that by employing the *One Step at a Time* methodology. Here is how I use it.

I don't have to be on a job for too long before the developers I am working with begin to realize that I almost always give them just about the same answer every time they ask me a question. No matter what question someone asks me, I usually end up saying something like. Let's break the problem down into smaller pieces and then take on the problem pieces, "One Step at a Time." At first, I am sure that it this is discouraging answer to what may have been a very specific question. But, in time the best people I am working with soon realize that this, "Break the problem down into smaller pieces and take the pieces One Step at a Time" technique is really a wonderful problem solving tool. They soon understand that what I am doing when I give them that answer is showing them that they can really solve any problem without my help.

As far as I am concerned, ECDOs are a *challenge*. They are complex beasts that are bold enough to exist across an enterprise rather than being installed on any one machine. Learning about something like this is a formidable task, but you can do it. All you need to do is to "Break the problem into smaller pieces and then take on each of the pieces One Step at a Time." The way that you break ECDOs down into smaller pieces is to learn about them in increasing levels of complexity. That is how the next eight chapters of this book are arranged. The chapters expose ECDOs "Once Step at a Time" in order of increasing complexity.

We will begin with one kind of ECDO that I call a Level I Data Object. As we become comfortable with this level of complexity, we will apply what we learned about the Level I Data Object to the task of learning how to code a more complex ECDO that we will call, what else, a Level II Data Object.

The last step in this process of learning about ECDOs involves something we will just call a Level III Data Object for now. But let me warn you. When you develop a real understanding of the Level III Data Object your perceptions and understanding of programming will have been changed. Although the Level III Data Object is just a step or two away from a Level I Data object in terms of the complexity of the code, it is a *giant* leap conceptually. To mark this conceptual leap, when we take on the challenge of understanding the Level III Data Object, we will learn to call this exceptional object by a different name.

Now that the introduction is over, let's get right to work on learning to build an Enterprise Caliber project.

The Project – An Enterprise Management System

I believe the best way to learn anything is to do it, so over the next few chapters we will learn about Enterprise Caliber Data Objects by constructing a set of data objects that you can draw upon to build something you can actually use – an Enterprise Management System. This system is designed to allow an IT team to continuously monitor an enterprise's condition, analyze the data collected, identify issues, devise solutions, and track those issues through to resolution. It is a slightly scaled back version of the system my teams use to monitor the systems we are responsible for.

I call this system scaled back because, for educational purposes, I have limited the functionality of some of the objects in the system. This was done in an effort to focus your attention on the major concepts you should grasp while putting together a particular object. As your understanding of the process increases, I will suggest some modifications that you can add to the objects you have previously built. My goal is to give you the pieces (ECDOs) that you need so that you can build a real, working, system that you can deploy in your own enterprise. More importantly, you will have gained the skills you need to design any other data objects you might need for your own Enterprise Caliber system.

Let's examine the target system.

The System Requirements

❑   The system must automatically collect configuration (hardware) information from each computer linked to the enterprise (even those connecting via an external Internet connection), sense changes in any computer's configuration, record those changes, and maintain a complete history of configuration changes for every computer.

❑   The system must collect and store detailed information about each error generated in any in-house application on any computer under the enterprise umbrella.

❑   Of course, all this data collection and enterprise monitoring would serve little purpose if we didn't include convenient ways to enable the IT team to analyze the mountain of data the system collects. So, the system must make it easy to perform complex data analysis scenarios. It must help the team to identify patterns within the data and group the information from each pattern into a single entity. For the purposes of discussion, we will call that entity an **issue**.

❑ Once the information has been categorized into an issue, the system must allow the IT team to diagnose the issue, devise a solution, and track the execution of the solution through to completion.

❑ The system must allow users (Not just the IT team) to immediately determine the current status of any published issue. As an example, the system we will construct will provide real-time status information for any issue to the Help-Desk team. In addition, the system will publish extended information about each issue, like estimated completion date, temporary work-around solutions, etc.

If those requirements sound like a real challenge, Good! Actually, you can build this entire system using only 5 main objects and a single data warehouse or DSS/OLAP component. The data warehouse component is a fairly complex topic that draws upon the knowledge you will gain while we build the 5 main OLTP objects.

You can find information on the OLAP components in Appendix B.

The OLTP objects we will build are as follows:

❑ **The Application object** – This object is used to manage information about the applications deployed throughout our enterprise. We call this type of object a **Level I** object. For now, think of this object as something like a typical support table. We will use a completed version of this object in Chapter 5 to get a sense of how to work with Enterprise Caliber Data Object in general. Once we have gotten to know a little something about the characteristics of the objects, we will learn how to build any Level I object as we examine the *ErrCond* and *Computer* objects.

❑ **The ErrCond object** – This object is used to collect and manage information about errors. This object is also a Level I object. We will build this object in Chapter 6 and use it to learn about 2 of the 8 data handling processes every Enterprise Caliber Data Object exposes.

❑ **The Computer object** – This object is used to collect and manage information about computers. This object is also a Level I object. We will build this object in Chapter 7 and use it to learn about the remaining 6 data handling processes every Enterprise Caliber Data Object exposes.

❑ **The Issue object** – This object is used to categorize application, error, computer, and user information into a single manageable package, for research, diagnosis, and resolution. This object is a **Level II** object. Think of Level II objects as an object that can be classified by a **type**. For example, imagine an object that is used to manage telephone numbers. The same phone number could be both a home and business number. The distinction between the two is the *type* of phone number. Level II objects allow us to create objects that can be shared.

❑ **The Person object** – This single object can represent any type of person when it is paired with the appropriate set of properties. In this system, we will use a *Person* object *typed* as an IT customer (a user) and as an IT resource (programmer, analyst, developer, etc.) This object is a **Level III** object. A Level III object, like the Level II object can be distinguished by its type, but with the Level III object the object's type carries with it a particular set of properties and their associated values. In this case, we use the exact same *Person* object as both an IT Customer and an IT Resource. The Level III object is the most versatile object, and we will learn all about it in Chapters 9 and 10.

The diagram below is intended to offer a sense of how the objects combine to create a working system. I won't attempt to describe the entire system here. Instead, we will take a closer look at each object in the relevant chapters:

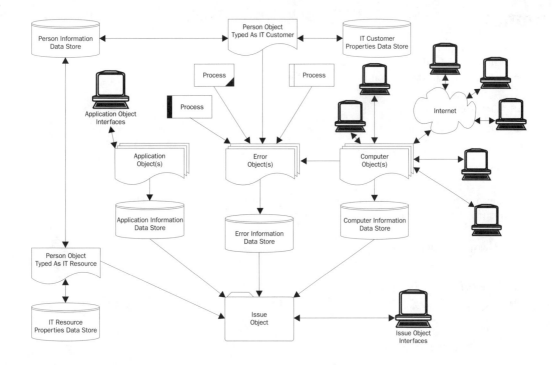

About The Object Factory

Before we go any further, I want to let you know that, there is no reason to type a single line of code in this book. First of all Wrox has a complete set of sample code for this book available at their web sit. And I have a little something extra for you as well. After spending several months trying to teach one of my teams to hand code these data objects, I learned that the hardest part of coding these objects is the infernal typing. So being the devout programmer I am, I developed an application that I call **The Object Factory**. It takes the objects' properties along with a few other tidbits of information and returns the complete set of code necessary to deliver basic Enterprise Caliber Data Objects. The code includes the SQL required to create the tables, the SQL required to create the stored procedures, the VB code for the object-halves on each middle sphere, and the code for three types of user interfaces. The interfaces include:

- ❑ A Visual Basic 6.0 user interface
- ❑ A Thin Client Dynamic HTML user interface (no ActiveX controls)
- ❑ A Heavy Dynamic HTML user interface (includes ActiveX controls)

The user interfaces may require the touch of an artist's hand before they can be put into service, but all of the controls are placed on the forms/ASPs and those controls are named using standard Microsoft naming conventions. For those of you who just can't wait, see Appendix A which is about our final source code and the Object Factory.

Summary

We've covered a lot of material in this introduction to Enterprise Caliber Data Objects. We saw how we could use the logical 4-tier design we developed in the previous chapters and develop it into an n-sphere architecture, so that we ended up with 4 spheres:

- ❑ Data sphere
- ❑ Data Centric sphere
- ❑ User Centric sphere
- ❑ Presentation sphere

We also described the functional requirements for these Enterprise Caliber Data Objects through their exposure of 8 major processes to the system:

- ❑ The *Insert* process
- ❑ The *Update* process
- ❑ The *Delete* process
- ❑ The *Fetch* process
- ❑ The *Load* process
- ❑ The *Audit History* process
- ❑ The *Show Deleted* process
- ❑ The *Restore From Deleted* process

Now, rather than just taking the list of functional requirements at its face value, we will put the Enterprise Caliber Data Object right to work in the next chapter. We will find out for ourselves if this newcomer is up to the task by employing it in the design and construction of an Enterprise Caliber application. We will come to know its capabilities first-hand. And once we believe it's possible...

Person
Base Properties

ID
Last Name
First Name
Middle Name
Birth Date
Sex

Object Type Definitions

Object Ty...

Common OTD	Lawyer OTD	Engineer OTD	Doctor OTD	Student OTD
Genre	Specialty	Specialty	Specialty	Major
Region	Hourly Rate	Experience	Certification	Minor
Property 3	Law School	Property 3	Property 3	Year
Property 4	Property 4	Property 4	Property 4	Property 4
Property 5	Property 5	Property 5	Property 5	Property 5
Property 6	Property 6	Property 6	Property 6	Property 6
Property 7	Property 7	Property 7	Property 7	Property 7
Property 8	Property 8	Property 8	Property 8	Property 8
Property 9	Property 9	Property 9	Property 9	Property 9
Property 10	Property 10	Property 10	Property 10	Property 10

Property Set Definitions

Property Set...

5

The Application Object

This chapter is designed to introduce you to the functionality of **Enterprise Caliber Data Objects (ECDO)** by allowing you to work with an existing object – the *Application* object. This will give us the perspective of our real customer – the user interface programmer. That's right, what we are really doing is building a set of reusable objects that provide a layer of abstraction over the data store. What we will do in this book is create data objects that are in many ways similar to standard Visual Basic controls like text boxes, combo boxes, and the like. But our objects won't have an interface. They are a little more abstract.

Let's take the *Application* object as an example. Its purpose is to manage information about each of the in-house applications that is deployed across our enterprise. It gives the user (the user interface programmer) access to some very complex functionality. It adds new records to the data store, it updates existing records, it keeps a complete history of every transaction, and more. Let me pose a question: Do you ever think about all of the work that is going on when you write a line of code like `Text1.Text = "Hello World"`? Probably not! Trust me, there *is* a lot work going on behind the scenes. But we don't think about all that work, we learn to accept that the control works and just use it. What Microsoft has done is to automate some highly complex, but repetitive actions so that we do not have to waste our valuable time reinventing the wheel.

The *Application* object – we will use the name `EntApp` in our code; this is short for Enterprise Application – does exactly the same thing with data handling processes that the text box control does with screen display processes. It allows the user interface programmer or application developer to add a new record to the database by writing a line of code like `EntApp.ObjectInsert` or restore a deleted record by writing a line of code like `EntApp.RestoreFromDeleted`. As I said before, in both cases a highly complex, but repetitive task has been automated so that the programmer does not have to waste valuable time reinventing the wheel. This allows us to make our data components as ubiquitous as the text box, while ensuring a level of integrity in our data and systems that is rarely considered let alone implemented. Enough talk. Let's put the *Application* object to the test and see what this thing can really do.

Overview

By the end of this chapter you will:

- ❑ Begin to learn some real-world techniques for functional analysis
- ❑ Understand the perspective of the user interface programmer or application developer
- ❑ Gain first hand experience of the functionality of Enterprise Caliber Data Objects
- ❑ Construct a complete working Visual Basic 6.0 interface using an Enterprise Caliber Data Object

The Application Object

In this book I will introduce you to the four levels of Enterprise Caliber Data Objects. Of course, this is a developer's book and according to tradition, we will start out with the "Hello World" of Enterprise Caliber Data Objects – the **Level I object**. This type of object, to use a database metaphor, takes the place of the standard support tables we use in two-tier or single-tier systems. This is the kind of object that gives us drop down lists and the like.

The *Application* object's main purpose is to manage basic information about every in-house application deployed across our enterprise. In this chapter, we will use an existing copy of the object to build a complete user interface. We will do this without thinking about how or where the data it uses is stored. One of the main thrusts of object-oriented programming is to encapsulate the complexities of conventional data access and insulate the user (or user interface programmer) from its mechanics. We accomplish that in this chapter with an object that gives the user access to data in ways you may never have thought were possible.

The Application Object Functional Analysis

The type of object we will tackle in this chapter does not require a great deal of functional analysis. Its functionality is identical to a typical support table. Let's take a look at a standard support table, one that contains basic information about the in-house applications in our enterprise – we will call this table EntApp, short for Enterprise Applications. Of course, we could make this table far more complicated, but I think that this should work for our purposes right now. As it is, the table has 5 columns or fields. And, except for the HTMLAddress field, the column names are pretty self-explanatory. ID holds an ID for the application; Name holds the name, etc. The HTMLAddress isn't all that mysterious either. This field is really just used to store the address for the HTML or ASP file that is used to deliver the application over an organization's Intranet. We will take a look at ASP a little later in the book.

ID	Name	BriefDescription	Description	HTMLAddress
1	EMS	Enterprise Management System	This application is used to …	`http://enterprise.com/Apps`
2	LASS	Licensure and Surveillance System	This application is used to …	`http://enterprise.com/Apps`

ID	Name	Brief Description	Description	HTMLAddress
3	SAS	Sales Analysis System	This application is used to …	`http://enterprise.com/Apps`
4	Another App	Another Application	This application is used to …	`http://enterprise.com/Apps`

Remember that the object we are using in this chapter is called a **data object**. From this name, we might imagine that at least in some way, this object should give us the ability to manage data. And that is exactly what it does. I find that the easiest way for me to think about this kind of object is to imagine that it represents a row in a database table. If this object represents a row in the table above, then it is not too much of a stretch for us to see that this object's properties can be very much like the columns or fields in a table. In that case, the obvious properties that this support table object should have are ID, Name, BriefDescription, Description, and HTMLAddress.

Let's take a minute to think about how we normally work with a table in a database. Let's see; we usually do things like selecting rows of data from a table. We also insert new rows of data into a table. Of course, we change or update the data stored in the rows of a table, and sometimes we remove or delete rows of data from a table. That is enough for now. I counted four things here. We select, insert, update, and delete rows of data from a table in a database.

If we want our EntApp data object to be able to do the work we normally do with a table, then it should be able to perform those four actions, and as programmers, we need a way to be able to tell it to take those actions. With VB, we normally code actions into subroutines or functions. When we are working with objects we do exactly the same thing, except that we call subroutines and functions **methods** instead of calling them subroutines and functions. That means that, in addition to the five properties that represent columns in the table, our object also needs to expose four actions or methods. The methods it exposes are:

- ❑ Load – used to select or load the objects (rows of data representing applications) from the data store into the client's local memory
- ❑ ObjectInsert – used to add a new application (row of data representing an application)
- ❑ ObjectUpdate – used to modify an existing application (row of data representing an application)
- ❑ ObjectDelete – used to remove an application (row of data representing and application) that is no longer needed

Let's recap. We have just said that when we work with the EntApp data object, we should expect to work with an object that has a set of properties that really represent the fields or columns in the EntApp table. We should be able to select or load a bunch of these objects into local memory by using a method we will call Load. When we need to add a new row of data into the EntApp table we expect to be able to do that by using another method called ObjectInsert. Of course, we might also need to update or delete the data in this table and we expect to do that using two other methods called, naturally, ObjectUpdate and ObjectDelete.

Even if our `EntApp` object just did the things that we talked about above it would still be pretty capable, but remember that we are designing Enterprise Caliber Data Objects. As we learned in the last chapter, this means that the object must also have the ability to track changes made to its data over time. A database specialist might call this kind of thing a temporal relationship. Accountants call it an audit trail. As far as we are concerned, ECDOs simply have a function or method that allows us to retrieve the history for an object and deliver that history to the user. We call this method `ObjectAuditHistory`. It is designed to return information like *what* action was performed on the object. It also tells us *when* the action was performed and *who* performed the action. If you are wondering where we will put this extra information, then you are really on the right track. It sounds like this method is going to return at least three extra pieces of data what, when, and who. We are working with an object and that means that we expect to find data in things we call properties. So, as you probably guessed, we are going to need three extra properties for the `EntApp` object.

I guess we could call these properties What, When, and Who. That's pretty descriptive, but I think we will call them `StampAction`, `StampUser`, and `StampDateTime` instead. When I hear these names, I can almost see some little guy in the database hitting each record with three rubber stamps.

- ❑ `StampAction` – used to record what action was taken - insert, update, delete, etc
- ❑ `StampUser` – used to record the identity of the person who took the action
- ❑ `StampDataTime` – used to record the date and time the action was taken

In the last chapter, we also learned that Enterprise Caliber Data Objects have the ability to retrieve a list of deleted objects and the ability to restore a deleted object. As you can probably guess by now, we have given these methods the descriptive but rather unimaginative names of `ObjectShowDeleted` and `ObjectRestoreFromDeleted`. (Of course, all Enterprise Caliber Data Objects should also expose the `ObjectFetch` method, but we don't need to use it in this chapter.) What you might not guess is that these methods need our object to keep track of one more piece of information. They require that we store an extra ID for each object. The reason why we need this extra ID is a little complicated and we will go over (and over) it later, so for now let's just imagine that the little guy in the database has to hold onto one more rubber stamp. In addition to marking each record that changes with the `StampAction`, `StampUser`, and `StampDateTime` stamps, he is also going to have to whack the records with a fourth rubber stamp that we will call `StampID`.

I don't know about you, but I think I need to recap again. According to what we have just said, when we work with the `EntApp` object we should expect to be working with an object that has something like 9 properties:

- ❑ `ID`
- ❑ `Name`
- ❑ `BriefDescription`
- ❑ `Description`
- ❑ `HTMLAddress`
- ❑ `StampAction`
- ❑ `StampUser`
- ❑ `StampDateTime`
- ❑ `StampID`

This object should also expose 8 data handling processes as methods (functions or subroutines):

- ❏ `Load`
- ❏ `ObjectInsert`
- ❏ `ObjectUpdate`
- ❏ `ObjectDelete`
- ❏ `ObjectAuditHistory`
- ❏ `ShowDeleted`
- ❏ `ObjectRestoreFromDeleted`
- ❏ `ObjectFetch`

OK, I think I got it. Now, between the properties and the methods, this object is supposed to be able to manage information about every in-house application that is currently running across our enterprise. It should allow us to select a list of information about those applications, add information about new applications, edit information about existing applications, and delete the information for unwanted applications. Just in case that isn't enough, we should also imagine that this object has a little guy in it that is keeping track of all of the changes anyone has ever made to the data that this object manages. And now, thanks to his efforts, we should be able to retrieve a history of changes for each object, retrieve a list of deleted objects, and be able to restore deleted objects back to their last state. I can almost feel the sarcasm, "Yeah *right*! And I suppose that what we just did was really Functional Analysis…" Well, yes! Of course it was. It's true that we just created a very tall list, but now we know exactly what kind of functionality to expect from the `EntApp` object. I guess you can make functional analysis complicated if you want to. But as far as I can see, that's all there really is to it.

> **Functional analysis means that: We take a few minutes to understand and write down exactly what functionality to expect from our work.**

As for our tall list of requirements, don't worry about it. As you will see shortly, you will be able to pull them off in fine style.

Our Plan of Attack

I am going to take a rather unusual approach to introduce you to Enterprise Caliber Data Objects. As you just found out, we expect quite a bit of functionality from an ECDO and right now you should be thinking that it is probably going to take us at least a couple of chapters to learn to code all that functionality. I don't know about you, but as for me, before I worked through even one of those chapters I would like to get my hands on one of those data objects. You know, just to kick it around a little bit before we get started. Well, don't worry, that is exactly what I have planned. We are going to begin by using the completed `EntApp` ECDO to build a user interface. This will allow you to discover the functionality of a well-designed data object by experience rather than by just reading about it.

Over the next few chapters, after we have used the `EntApp` object to design and build a user interface, we will work through the code that you need to write in order to build your own Enterprise Caliber Data Object. We will do this on a functional level. In other words, we will take one method at a time and learn how to write all of the code we need to make that method work. Along the way, we will also be learning how to write distributed code.

> Remember, distributed design requires that we divide the processing
> responsibilities for a single object into two or more distinct sets of processes
> that work together to move data between the user and the data store.

I hate to do it to you, but that means that sometimes I am going to call things that most people call
methods – **processes**. Don't let this throw you. When I say process in place of method, all I am doing
is acknowledging that at some level we have divided the processing for this particular method into
more than a single chunk of code.

If you haven't already done so, take a run over to Wrox's web site and download the code for this
chapter. When you unzip the code, you should have the directories and files indicated in the table
below:

Directory	FileName	Type of File
\EntApp	UIEntApp.vbp	Visual Basic Project
\EntApp\UInterface\	UImodEntApp.bas	Visual Basic Module
\EntApp\UInterface\VBForms\	frmEntAppDetail.frm	Visual Basic Form
\EntApp\UInterface\VBForms\	frmEntAppDetail.frx	Visual Basic Form Resource
\EntApp\UInterface\VBForms\	frmEntAppList.frm	Visual Basic Form
\EntApp\UInterface\VBForms\	frmEntAppList.frx	Visual Basic Form Resource
\EntApp\UCObjects\	UCEntApp.dll	Dynamic Link Library
\EntApp\DCObjects\	DCEntApp.dll	Dynamic Link Library

A Couple of Suggestions

It is really up to you how you use the information in this book. I have tried to provide enough code
in this chapter so that you should be able to work through the chapter and make this interface work
without using anything other than your own talent and the EntApp ECDO DLLs. But, I have also
provided complete sample code for the interface that I know will work. I suggest that you work
through this chapter using the sample code first and take this guy out for a test drive. Then once you
get a feel for the way that the EntApp object handles, I would try building the same interface
described in this chapter from scratch.

Once you have built one interface from scratch with an ECDO, you should take some time to exploit
the object as much as possible. Use it to create a couple of applications with different looks and feels.
The interfaces you design *do not* have to be like this one. As I said earlier, this interface is the
standard one that we deliver with each ECDO. It is good in its own way because it does exercise just
about all of the object's capabilities, but it is not perfect nor is it as creative as it could be.

I encourage you to use this object with as many different interfaces that you can think of. They don't even have to be VB interfaces. If you are comfortable with that sort of thing, you can use ECDOs in Word, Excel, Active Server Pages, etc. Over the next few chapters, our job is to learn to design and build these objects. Any experience you get working with the objects from the user interface perspective can only help you to learn to code the objects better. It will probably also give you quite a few insights that you can use to improve their designs.

About the EntApp DLLs

There are a couple of things we need to do before we begin working on this interface. The first thing we need to do is to register the ECDO. As with all ECDOs, the EntApp object is made from two halves: a user centric half – UCEntApp.dll - and a data centric half – DCEntApp.dll. Go to the Run dialog on the Windows Start menu and type the following regsvr32 command (replacing SomeDirectory with the directory you have placed the source code in):

```
regsvr32 "C:\SomeDirectory\EntApp\UCObjects\UCEntApp.dll"
```

You should see a message box that tells you that the DLL has been successfully registered. Dismiss the message box. Now enter the following command into the Run dialog:

```
regsvr32 "C:\SomeDirectory\EntApp\DCObjects\DCEntApp.dll"
```

You should see the same kind of message box again telling you that this DLL has also been registered successfully. All we did here was to introduce your workstation to the EntApp object. If you search for the names of these DLLs in your registry now, you will find several references to them.

This book assumes that you have access to SQL Server 6.5/7.0.

The last thing we need to do is to ensure that the object has some place to store the data it has been designed to manage. Create a database on SQL Server 6.5 or SQL Server 7.0 named Common. Give it at least 10 or 15 megabytes of storage space. We will be using this database throughout the remainder of the book. Once the database has been created, you need to provide an ODBC connection from your workstation to the database. The EntApp object is expecting to find an ODBC connection called Common. Create this connection now.

The User Interface

The design and construction of an Enterprise Caliber Data Object follows a system or **methodology**. This rigor is most apparent when we are doing things like delivering field-level collision handling. But it is just as important to follow a system through every step of development including designing and building user interfaces. In this section we will develop a system for designing a functional, reliable, and highly polished Enterprise Caliber Interface using Visual Basic 6.0. In a later chapter, we will develop a system for delivering comparable interfaces using Dynamic HTML as the vehicle. My teams deliver a two-form Visual Basic 6.0 user interface with every data object we create. We do not require anyone to use the interface we deliver. We take great pride in the fact that our objects are completely interface-independent. We supply this interface primarily to provide a working example of how the object should be used.

Our standard user interface for a Level I data object has two forms, a **List form** and a **Detail form**. With these two forms, the customer is able to make use of the data handling processes that the ECDO exposes. Either open up the sample VB project – UIEntApp.vbp or create a new standard EXE VB project. If you are creating a new project, add one module and two forms to the project.

Take a minute to rename the project to UIEntApp.vbp, rename one form to frmEntAppList.frm, the other form to frmEntAppDetail.frm, and the module to UImodEntApp.bas. Save the project in the EntApp directory on your workstation. When you get finished, your project explorer should look something like the image shown here:

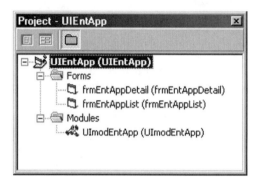

ECDO Object References within VB

Once you have created the project, you will need to create a reference to the UCEntApp.dll you registered earlier. You create this reference from within VB exactly the same way you would make a reference to ADO or DAO or any other ActiveX object. Select References from the Project menu. This brings up the References dialog box. If you scroll down the list of possible references, you will find that the UCEntApp.dll is on the list. Make sure the checkbox next to UCEntApp is checked. Remember to save the project after you do this. If you forget to do this, then the next time you open up this project you will have to redefine the references.

The reasoning may not be too obvious right now, but we *do not* need to make a reference to the DCEntApp.dll here. You might remember from the discussions in the previous chapters that we are designing applications to take advantage of a distributed architecture. What that means to us in practical terms for this chapter is that we only need to create a reference to the user centric half of the ECDO. That is because the user interface only makes calls to the user centric half of the ECDO. The user centric half of the ECDO is responsible for and capable of handling any communication with the data centric ECDO without the user interface programmer's assistance.

The List Form

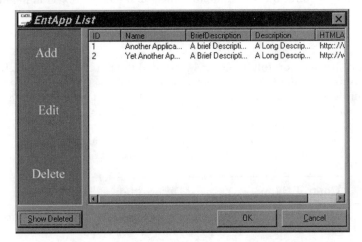

The List form, displayed in the figure, allows the user to view a list of selected objects. And, as you might expect from controls on this form, the user can add new objects to the list by pressing the Add button. The user can also edit existing objects by selecting the target object and pressing the Edit button. Of course, the user can delete an object by selecting the target object and pressing the Delete button.

What you might not expect, is that the user can also view a list of deleted objects by simply clicking the Show Deleted button:

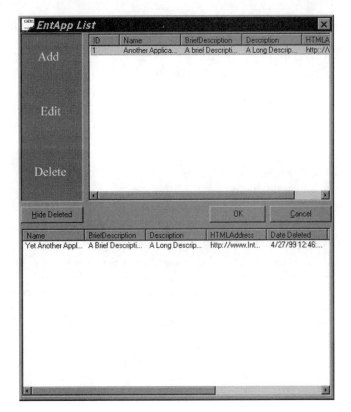

In addition, the user can also restore an object from a deleted state to the state it held at the time of deletion. This operation only requires the user to double-click on the target object in the deleted object listview.

List Form Controls

The List form requires two listview controls. One listview is used to hold the list of available objects, and the second listview is used to hold the list of deleted objects. We create a toolbar for the form by placing three image controls in a picture box container. We use three bitmaps to give the image controls their Add, Edit, and Delete faces. When we make controls like this, we use a background bitmap for the picture box control. This bitmap ensures that our toolbar matches the background color of the bitmaps in the image controls. The final step is to draw the three command buttons. The following table summarizes the controls required to build a standard list form:

Control Type	Control Name	Description
List View	lvwEntApps	Contains a collection of objects currently available for editing
List View	lvwEntAppsDeleted	Contains a collection of objects that are currently deleted
Picture Box	picToolBar	Container control used to house the image controls we use in place of command buttons
Image	imgAdd	Manage adding objects process
Image	imgEdit	Manage editing objects process
Image	imgDelete	Manage deleting objects process
Command Button	cmdDeleted	Alternatively shows or hides the collection of deleted objects stored in lvwEntAppsDeleted
Command Button	cmdOK	Sends an OK message and unloads the form
Command Button	cmdCancel	Sends a Cancel message and unloads the form

List Form Properties

We extend our forms with properties rather than using public variables. This practice allows us to exercise a high level of control over the form's local variables. The Application List form requires three properties. One property is used to house the collection of *Application* objects currently available for editing. The other is used to house the collection of deleted *Application* objects. The third property is used as a message-handling device – it allows us to pass information between forms using a standardized technique.

Property Name	Data Type	Description
EntApps	UCEntApp.colEntApps	This property houses a collection of *Application* objects that are currently not deleted and are therefore available for use.
EntAppsDeleted	UCEntApp.colEntApps	This property houses a collection of *Application* objects that are currently deleted and are therefore not available for use.
ButtonPressed	String	This property is used to pass a message between the user interface forms. The message indicates which button the user pressed to unload the form.

The List form requires three properties, so we need to create three local storage variables (note that many people call these **member variables**). We place the code for the local storage variable declarations in the declaration section of the form. Here is the complete code for the declaration section of the EntApp List form. If you are working with the sample code, you will find this block of code in the General Declarations section in the frmEntAppList.frm. If you are building this from scratch, you will have to type the following block of code into the Declarations section:

```
Option Explicit

' Dimension the local storage variables
Private mcolEntApps As UCEntApp.colEntApps
Private mcolEntAppsDeleted As UCEntApp.colEntApps
Private mstrButtonPressed As String

' Use these constants for the sizing routines
Private Const jamShowDeleted As Integer = 8760
Private Const jamHideDeleted As Integer = 4830
```

The first three declarations provide the local storage we need for our three properties. The last two lines just provide us with two form-level constants that we use to toggle the form's size to either show or hide the list of deleted objects. The numbers just give the size of form when the deleted section is visible (8760) and when it is hidden (4830). Of course, you can use different sizes for these constants depending upon the relative sizes of the two listview controls you place on the form.

> *Please don't be confused by the unorthodox constant prefix* jam. *I developed the bad habit of using my initials as the prefix for my own constants a long time ago, and I am afraid that old habits die hard.*

Most of this code should be familiar to an experienced Visual Basic programmer. But even an experienced programmer will not know exactly what type of object an UCEntApp.colEntApps object is. That is because this declaration references our custom ECDO, EntApp. The first two declaration statements show how to declare a collection of EntApp objects:

```
Private mcolEntApps As UCEntApp.colEntApps
Private mcolEntAppsDeleted As UCEntApp.colEntApps
```

We can tell a lot about an object by *reading* its declaration statement. In this case the variable is declared as a UCEntApp.colEntApps object. We can tell that this references a user centric component from the first two letters of the base name, UC. We can also tell the name of the data object by looking at the remainder of the base name – EntApp. The extended name, the portion that comes after the period tells us about the particular class of the object we are using. In this case we are using a class that defines a collection. We know that because the prefix of the extended name is col, which references a collection. We can also tell the type of objects stored in the collection by looking at the root of the extended name. In this case the objects in the collection have the same name as the data object, EntApp objects. This is not always the case.

Now that we have the local storage variables declared, we can write the code we use to manage them. Typically that code consists of a Property Get, which returns the value stored in the local variable to the programmer, and a Property Let, which allows the programmer to place a new value in the local variable. When the property handlers are used to manage objects, it is really good form to use a Property Set in place of the Property Let but there is no mechanical difference between the two. If you are working with the sample code, you will find these property handlers in the General section of the frmEntAppList.frm. If you are building this from scratch, you will have to create the properties and type the following block of code into the procedure stubs:

```
Public Property Get EntApps() As UCEntApp.colEntApps

   If mcolEntApps Is Nothing Then
      Set mcolEntApps = CreateObject ("UCEntApp.colEntApps")
   End If

   Set EntApps = mcolEntApps

End Property
```

```
Public Property Set EntApps(colEntApps As UCEntApp.colEntApps)

   Set mcolEntApps = colEntApps

End Property
```

This code is very straightforward, but it does expose one technique that we should look at. In the Property Get, we perform a test on the local storage variable. If the object the variable represents has not been instantiated, we create a new instance of the object and assign it to the variable. If it the object already exists, we just set the property value equal to the local variable. This simple technique allows us to write all the instantiation code we will ever need in a single location. Once we do this, we never have to concern ourselves with questions like where in the module do I instantiate an object. The instantiation code always executes in the Property Get that manages the object in question. The Property Set code is self-explanatory.

We need another property pair to manage the collection of deleted *Application* objects. Add another property to the List form named EntAppsDeleted and write the following property handlers:

```
Public Property Get EntAppsDeleted() As UCEntApp.colEntApps

  If mcolEntAppsDeleted Is Nothing Then
    Set mcolEntAppsDeleted = CreateObject ("UCEntApp.colEntApps")
  End If

  Set EntAppsDeleted = mcolEntAppsDeleted

End Property
```

```
Public Property Set EntAppsDeleted(colEntAppsDeleted As _
                    UCEntApp.colEntApps)

  Set mcolEntAppsDeleted = colEntAppsDeleted

End Property
```

The remaining property that we use to extend the List form is the `ButtonPressed` property. The only slightly unusual thing here is that we make the `ButtonPressed` property a read-only property. We do that by providing just the `Get` half of the property pair. Remember to delete the `Property Set` for this handler if you are writing the code from scratch:

```
Public Property Get ButtonPressed() As String

  ButtonPressed = mstrButtonPressed

End Property
```

List Form Procedures

The List form requires three independent procedures. By that I mean procedures that are not tied directly to control events. We will examine the procedures tied to control events later when we look at the data handling methods (or processes) for an Enterprise Caliber Data Object. In general, the purpose of this form's independent procedures is to provide general display-handling functionality at the form level.

Procedure Name	Description
Form_Load	This procedure configures the two listview controls and loads the collection of currently available objects into the EntApps property
LoadEntAppListView	This procedure displays each of the objects in the EntApps collection in the lvwEntApps listview control
LoadEntAppsDeletedListView	This procedure displays each of the objects in the EntAppsDeleted collection in the lvwEntAppsDeleted listview control

The `Form_Load` procedure is responsible for configuring the listviews to handle the information that each is required to display. Once this is done, it loads the collection of available objects and calls the `LoadEntAppListView` procedure, which is used to display the objects in the listview. If you are working with the sample code, you will find this block of code in the `Form_Load` routine in the `frmEntAppList.frm`. If you are building this from scratch, you will have to type the following block of code into the pre-existing `Form_Load` routine:

```
Private Sub Form_Load()

    On Error GoTo Form_LoadError
    Screen.MousePointer = vbHourGlass

    Me.Height = jamHideDeleted

    ' Construct the columnheaders for the object listview
    lvwEntApps.ColumnHeaders.Add , , "ID", 720
    lvwEntApps.ColumnHeaders.Add , , "Name", 1440
    lvwEntApps.ColumnHeaders.Add , , "Brief Description", 1440
    lvwEntApps.ColumnHeaders.Add , , "Description", 1440
    lvwEntApps.ColumnHeaders.Add , , "HTML Address", 1440
    lvwEntApps.View = lvwReport

    ' Construct the columnheaders for the
    ' Deleted object listview
    lvwEntAppsDeleted.ColumnHeaders.Add , , "Name", 1440
    lvwEntAppsDeleted.ColumnHeaders.Add , , _
                    "Brief Description", 1440
    lvwEntAppsDeleted.ColumnHeaders.Add , , "Description", 1440
    lvwEntAppsDeleted.ColumnHeaders.Add , , "HTML Address", 1440
    lvwEntAppsDeleted.ColumnHeaders.Add , , "Date Deleted", 1440
    lvwEntAppsDeleted.ColumnHeaders.Add , , _
                    "Deleted by User", 1440
    lvwEntAppsDeleted.ColumnHeaders.Add , , "Original ID", 1440
    lvwEntAppsDeleted.ColumnHeaders.Add , , "Audit ID", 1440
    lvwEntAppsDeleted.View = lvwReport

    ' Call the Load Method of the User Centric Object
    EntApps.SetDataSource mstrConnect
    EntApps.Load

    ' Load the listview
    LoadEntAppListView

    Screen.MousePointer = vbDefault

    Exit Sub

Form_LoadError:

    Screen.MousePointer = vbDefault
    MsgBox Err.Description

End Sub
```

This code should be pretty standard fare, but we will take a look at it just to make sure we are all on the same page. The first line of code just sets up an error handler for our procedure:

```
On Error GoTo Form_LoadError
```

I have skipped the error handling routine in the code for this section of the book because the error handling routines use an object you do not have yet. You will begin to build the *ErrCond* ECDO in the next chapter yourself. But, just so you'll know, the way the error handlers work in our applications is simple, they collect details about the error and use the *ErrCond* ECDO to store and manage the details about each error that is generated in any application.

The next line of code changes the cursor's shape to an hourglass. This is one of those small details people often overlook, but it is important that the interface communicate its current state to the user. We do this by changing the cursor to its hourglass shape to indicate that the application is busy and to its default state when the application is waiting for user input:

```
Screen.MousePointer = vbHourGlass
```

The next block of code is used to add column headers to the lvwEntApps listview control. We simply add one column header for each property we need this form to display. Once we have configured the lvwEntApps listview control, we configure the lvwEntAppsDeleted listview. The code is similar to the other listview configuration code, except that we place three additional columns on the deleted listview – one that displays information about who deleted the object, one that displays information about when the object was deleted, and one that contains the object's original ID:

```
' Construct the columnheaders for the Deleted object listview
   lvwEntAppsDeleted.ColumnHeaders.Add , , "Name", 1440
   lvwEntAppsDeleted.ColumnHeaders.Add , , _
                   "Brief Description", 1440
   lvwEntAppsDeleted.ColumnHeaders.Add , , "Description", 1440
   lvwEntAppsDeleted.ColumnHeaders.Add , , "HTML Address", 1440
   lvwEntAppsDeleted.ColumnHeaders.Add , , "Date Deleted", 1440
   lvwEntAppsDeleted.ColumnHeaders.Add , , _
                   "Deleted by User", 1440
   lvwEntAppsDeleted.ColumnHeaders.Add , , "Original ID", 1440
   lvwEntAppsDeleted.ColumnHeaders.Add , , "Audit ID", 1440
```

The original ID for an object in the deleted listview actually contains the StampID property we talked about earlier. Remember that I said this was a little complicated? When we are working with an object that has been deleted, we reference that deleted object by its own unique ID, which we call an audit ID. Of course we still need to keep track of the object's original ID in case we need to restore it, so we store the object's original ID in the StampID property. I bet that this is still a little confusing. Don't worry about it. We will revisit this again in this chapter, and it will be crystal clear by the time we go through a few more chapters.

The block of code that executes after the listview setup process is the first one that actually uses our EntApp data object. The first line is designed to point our object at a particular data store:

```
EntApps.SetDataSource mstrConnect
```

In this case, the mstrConnect variable should contain the value Common, which is a reference to the ODBC connection that you created earlier. The next line fills the local storage variable with a collection of *Application* objects:

```
EntApps.Load
```

These few lines of code should go a long way towards showing how easy it is to use a well-designed Enterprise Caliber Data Object. The methods we just invoked, started a complex series of actions that worked invisibly to provide the user interface programmer with a collection of objects from the data store:

```
' Call the Load Method of the User Centric Object
EntApps.SetDataSource mstrConnect
EntApps.Load

' Load the listview
LoadEntAppListView
```

The last line in this block of code calls the next procedure we need to write, the LoadEntAppListView procedure. This procedure is designed to display the collection of objects in the lvwEntApps listview. Here is the complete listing for the procedure. If you are working with the sample code, you will find this block of code in the LoadEntAppListView routine in the **General** section of the frmEntAppList.frm. If you are building this from scratch, you will have to create a new subroutine named LoadEntAppListView and type the following block of code into the stub that VB creates for you:

```
Public Sub LoadEntAppListView()

    Dim ThisObject As UCEntApp.clsEntApp
    Dim EntAppItems As ListItems
    Dim ThisItem As ListItem

    Set EntAppItems = lvwEntApps.ListItems
    EntAppItems.Clear

    For Each ThisObject In EntApps

        If Not ThisObject.IsDeleted And ThisObject.IsChild Then
            Set ThisItem = EntAppItems.Add(, ThisObject.Key, _
                               ThisObject.ID)
            ThisItem.SubItems(1) = ThisObject.Name
            ThisItem.SubItems(2) = ThisObject.BriefDescription
            ThisItem.SubItems(3) = ThisObject.Description
            ThisItem.SubItems(4) = ThisObject.HTMLAddress

        End If

    Next ThisObject

End Sub
```

Again, this code is pretty standard stuff. It just loads a listview control with data from a collection of objects. The first declaration statement should actually look somewhat familiar, it declares an object of the type UCEntApp.clsEntApp. From our previous discussions, you should recognize this as a user centric *Application* object. The only thing new in this statement is the prefix on the extended name. The cls prefix indicates that we are working with a class that represents a single object.

Once the variable declarations are complete we do a little housekeeping by clearing any existing `ListItems` from the listview control. The final block of code in this procedure is the one that really does the work. Let's take a closer look at it:

```
For Each ThisObject In EntApps

    If Not ThisObject.IsDeleted And ThisObject.IsChild Then
        Set ThisItem = EntAppItems.Add(, ThisObject.Key, _
                                ThisObject.ID)
        ThisItem.SubItems(1) = ThisObject.Name
        ThisItem.SubItems(2) = ThisObject.BriefDescription
        ThisItem.SubItems(3) = ThisObject.Description
        ThisItem.SubItems(4) = ThisObject.HTMLAddress

    End If
Next ThisObject
```

That is all there is to it. First we call the `EntApp`'s `Load` method and then we use this subroutine to display the results of that method onto the user's screen. All we need to do to load the listview with the objects from this collection is to iterate through the collection using a `For...Next` loop. There *is* one unusual thing about this code – the test we perform with the `If` statement. This is one of the few things the interface programmer *has to* consider when using an Enterprise Caliber Data Object. The tests check each object to be sure that it has not been marked for deletion and that it is currently a child. We will go into the reason why we need to perform these tests later, but for now just realize that when we are programming at the user interface level we are responsible for performing these two tests before we display an object.

The last procedure we need to write for the Application List form is the `LoadEntAppsDeletedListView` procedure. This routine is almost identical to the last one, except that it uses the second collection that houses the deleted objects. By definition, all the objects in the deleted collection are deleted. If you are working with the sample code, you will find this block of code in the `LoadEntAppsDeletedListView` routine in the **General** section of `frmEntAppList.frm`. If you are building this from scratch, you will have to create the subroutine and type the following block of code into the stub:

```
Public Sub LoadEntAppsDeletedListView()

    Dim ThisObject As UCEntApp.clsEntApp
    Dim EntAppDeletedItems As ListItems
    Dim ThisItem As ListItem

    Set EntAppDeletedItems = lvwEntAppsDeleted.ListItems
    EntAppDeletedItems.Clear

    For Each ThisObject In EntAppsDeleted
        Set ThisItem = EntAppDeletedItems.Add _
            (, ThisObject.Key, ThisObject.Name)
        ThisItem.SubItems(1) = ThisObject.BriefDescription
        ThisItem.SubItems(2) = ThisObject.Description
        ThisItem.SubItems(3) = ThisObject.HTMLAddress
        ThisItem.SubItems(4) = ThisObject.StampDateTime
        ThisItem.SubItems(5) = ThisObject.StampUser
        ' Caption reads Original ID
        ThisItem.SubItems(6) = ThisObject.StampID
        ' Caption reads Audit ID
```

```
        ThisItem.SubItems(7) = ThisObject.ID
    Next ThisObject

End Sub
```

Notice the way we use the StampID and ID properties when we load the deleted listview. The deleted object's StampID contains the original ID that the object had when it was active, and we show the deleted object's ID property in a column with the caption Audit ID. This is the same complicated problem again. Remember that we use this audit ID as a handle for the deleted object, and as you will see soon, also for audit history objects.

The Detail Form

The second form our standard user interface requires is the Detail form. This form allows the user to work with the properties of a single object:

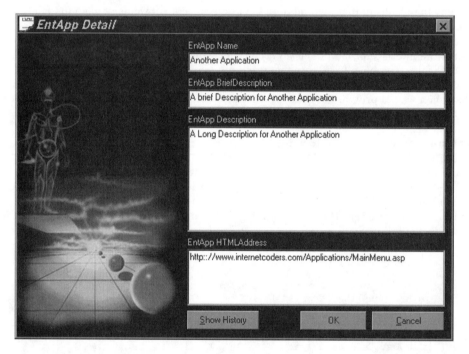

It also allows the user to retrieve a complete audit history for the current object:

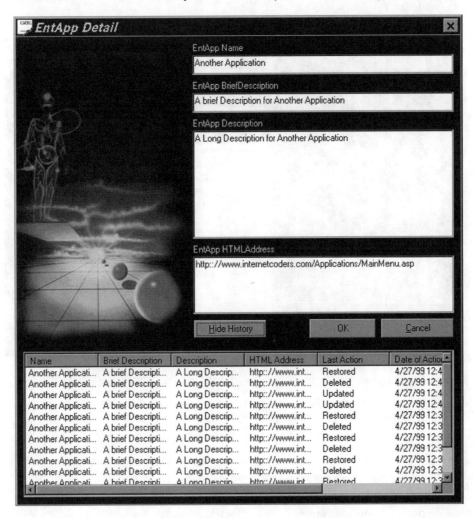

This audit history, essentially a series of snapshots of the same object over a period of time, gives the user the ability to perform unlimited undos. In other words, the user can select any of an object's previous states and copy the values from that state into the current values of the object.

The only thing it requires from the user to initiate the process is a double-click on the target state in the object's audit history listview:

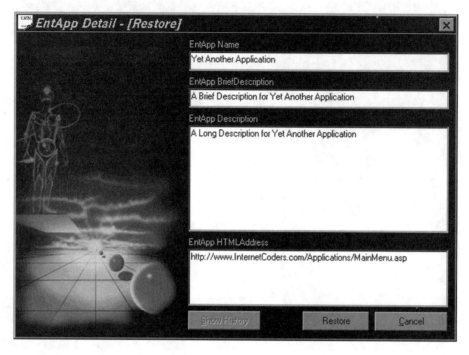

Detail Form Controls

The detail form requires one listview to display the object's audit history. It also requires an input control for each of the object's editable properties. This control may be a textbox, combobox, or any other input control capable of collecting the information required by the editable property. Additionally, the form may also require a label for each editable property depending upon the choice of control. The last step is to draw three command buttons on the `frmEntAppDetail.frm` form. The following table summarizes the required controls:

Control Type	Control Name	Description
Text Box	`txtEntAppName`	Contains or collects the application name.
Label	`lblEntAppName`	Describes to the user or prompts the user for the information in the `txtEntAppName` textbox.
Text Box	`txtEntAppBrief Description`	Contains or collects a brief description of the *Application* object.
Label	`lblEntAppBrief Description`	Describes to the user or prompts the user for the information in the `txtEntAppBriefDescription` textbox.
Text Box	`txtEntApp Description`	Contains or collects a description of the *Application* object.

Control Type	Control Name	Description
Label	`lblEntApp Description`	Describes to the user or prompts the user for the information in the `txtEntAppDescription` textbox.
Text Box	`txtEntApp HTMLAddress`	Contains or collects the HTML address for the *Application* object.
Label	`lblEntApp HTMLAddress`	Describes to the user or prompts the user for the information in the `txtEntAppHTMLAddress` textbox.
List View	`lvwEntApp History`	Contains a collection of objects that, taken together provide a complete history for the current object.
Command Button	`cmdHistory`	Alternatively shows or hides the history collection for the current object.
Command Button	`cmdOK`	Executes the method required to save the changes to the current object, sends an OK message, and unloads the form.
Command Button	`cmdCancel`	Sends a Cancel message and unloads the form.

Detail Form Properties

Property Name	Data Type	Description
`EntApp`	`UCEntApp.cls EntApp`	This property houses the *Application* object that is currently being viewed in detail.
`EntAppHistory`	`UCEntApp.col EntApps`	This property houses a collection of *Application* objects that, taken together provide a complete history for the current object.
`ButtonPressed`	String	This property is used to pass a message between user interface forms. The message indicates which button the user pressed when the form was unloaded.
`SourceControl`	String	This property is used to pass a message between user interface forms. This message is used to provide selection criterion for the `Load` method.

The Detail form requires four properties, so we need to create four local storage variables. We place the code for the variable declarations in the declaration section of the form. If you are working with the sample code, you will find this block of code in the General Declarations section of `frmEntAppDetail.frm`. If you are building this from scratch, you will have to type the following block of code into the pre-existing declarations section:

```
Option Explicit

'Dimension the local variables
Private mstrButtonPressed As String
Private WithEvents mobjEntApp As UCEntApp.clsEntApp
Private mcolEntAppHistory As UCEntApp.colEntApps
Private mstrSourceControl As String

' Use these local constants to resize the form

' History Listview Visible
Private Const jamShowHistory As Integer = 9345

' History Listview Hidden
Private Const jamHideHistory As Integer = 6360
```

The first four declarations provide the local storage we need for our four properties. The last two lines of code give us two form-level constants that we use to toggle the form size to either show or hide the object's history. Notice that we used almost exactly the same technique on both types of form. This goes towards meeting our stated design objective of maintainability. Once a programmer learns how to program one form, he or she will be able to transfer that knowledge to the other interface problems with ease.

> *Although we won't do it here, you might also think about delivering the user interface portion of an ECDO as visual ActiveX control that the user interface programmers could just draw on the form. This is the type standardization that will allow us to rise to the challenges of delivering enterprise-level applications across an organization.*

All of the declaration statements in this code, with the exception of one, should be familiar. The one that is different is the declaration for the mobjEntApp variable. This declaration includes the WithEvents clause. This clause gives us the ability to trap an event raised by the mobjEntApp. The object uses this event to signal to the host application that the object's data has been validated. We will go over exactly how this works in the form's code a little later.

The property handlers we build for the mobjEntApp object are also different from those we have seen before. That is because this is a Detail form. We use a Detail form to work with individual instances of an object. After much trial and error I have found that the best way to handle passing an object, or its state, between the List and Detail forms is just to pass the entire object. This means that our *Application* property handler must *not* create a new instance of the object if one was not passed to the form. The Get property handler checks to see if the object exists. If it doesn't the property raises an error that forcefully reminds the programmer to pass the object. If it does exist, the property just returns the object as expected. If you are working with the sample code, you will see these property handlers in the **General** section of the frmEntAppDetail.frm. If you are building this from scratch, you will have to create the property handlers and type the following blocks of code into the stubs VB that creates for you:

```
Public Property Get EntApp() As UCEntApp.clsEntApp

   If mobjEntApp Is Nothing Then
      Err.Raise vbObjectError , "frmEntAppDetail", _
            "This form requires an existing EntApp object"
   End If
```

```
    Set EntApp = mobjEntApp

  End Property

Public Property Let EntApp(objEntApp As UCEntApp.clsEntApp)

    Set mobjEntApp = objEntApp

  End Property
```

The rest of the properties are written exactly the same way we wrote the List form properties. Just so you know, we use the SourceControl property in the ObjectRestoreFromDeleted process. I won't go into all the details here as we will cover them shortly. Here is the code you need to write to create the other property handlers:

```
Public Property Get ButtonPressed() As String

  ButtonPressed = mstrButtonPressed

End Property

Public Property Get SourceControl() As String

  SourceControl = mstrSourceControl

End Property

Public Property Let SourceControl(strSourceControl As String)

  mstrSourceControl = strSourceControl

End Property

Public Property Get EntAppHistory() As UCEntApp.colEntApps

    If mcolEntAppHistory Is Nothing Then
      Set mcolEntAppHistory = CreateObject("UCEntApp.colEntApps")
    End If

    Set EntAppHistory = mcolEntAppHistory

End Property
```

Detail Form Procedures

Procedure Name	Description
Form_Load	This procedure configures the audit history listview control. Then it checks the current object to determine whether it is a new object, an existing object or an object that is being restored from a deleted state. Depending upon the results of this test, the procedure configures the form as appropriate and calls either the SetEntAppState or ClearForm procedures.

Table Continued Over the Page

Procedure Name	Description
Form_Unload	This procedure performs necessary housecleaning.
LoadEntAppHistoryListView	This procedure displays each of the objects in the *Application* object's audit history in the lvwEntAppHistory listview control.
ClearForm	This procedure clears the input controls of the form to prepare it to receive a new object.
SetEntAppState	This procedure reads the properties of the current object and transfers the properties to the input controls on the form to prepare the form for editing.

The Form_Load procedure's first responsibility is to configure the listview control to handle the object's audit history. Then it checks the value of the SourceControl property to determine whether the current object is undergoing restoration from a deleted state. If it is, the form is reconfigured to reflect the restoration process. The next test the procedure applies is designed to determine whether the current object is a new or existing object. If the object is new, then we clear the form by calling the ClearForm procedure. If the object is an existing object (and deleted objects are existing objects) then the procedure displays the object's properties by calling the SetEntAppState procedure. If you are working with the sample code, you will find this block of code in the Form_Load routine in the frmEntAppDetail.frm. If you are building this from scratch, you will have to type the following block of code into the pre-existing routine:

```
Private Sub Form_Load()

On Error GoTo Form_LoadError

Me.Height = jamHideHistory
'let the user know the application is busy
Screen.MousePointer = vbHourglass

' Set up the Object history Listview columnheaders
lvwEntAppHistory.ColumnHeaders.Add , , "Name", 1440
lvwEntAppHistory.ColumnHeaders.Add , , _
        "Brief Description", 1440
lvwEntAppHistory.ColumnHeaders.Add , , "Description", 1440
lvwEntAppHistory.ColumnHeaders.Add , , "HTML Address", 1440
lvwEntAppHistory.ColumnHeaders.Add , , "Last Action", 1440
lvwEntAppHistory.ColumnHeaders.Add , , _
        "Date of Action", 1440
lvwEntAppHistory.ColumnHeaders.Add , , _
        "Action by User", 1440
lvwEntAppHistory.ColumnHeaders.Add , , "Original ID", 720
lvwEntAppHistory.ColumnHeaders.Add , , "Audit ID", 720
lvwEntAppHistory.View = lvwReport


If Len(SourceControl) > 0 Then

    ' If this object was delivered from a deleted state
    ' then morph form
    cmdOK.Caption = "Restore"
```

```
            cmdHistory.Enabled = False
            Me.Caption = Me.Caption & " - [Restore]"

        End If

        If EntApp.IsNew Then
            ' If new object then clear the form
            cmdOK.Enabled = False
            cmdHistory.Enabled = False
            ClearForm

        Else
            ' If existing object then populate controls
            SetEntAppState

        End If

        'let the user know the application is done with its task
        Screen.MousePointer = vbDefault

        Exit Sub

    Form_LoadError:
        Screen.MousePointer = vbDefault
        MsgBox Err.Description

    End Sub
```

The `ClearForm` procedure just iterates through all of the available input controls and sets each one to its default value. In this case, all the values are string values, so we set the value to a zero length string. If any of the values were numeric, then we would set the values to zero or some other appropriate default value. If you are working with the sample code, you will find this block of code in the **General** section of the `frmEntAppDetail.frm`. If you are building this from scratch, you will have to create the routine and type the following block of code into the routine:

```
    Public Sub ClearForm()

        txtEntAppName.Text = ""
        txtEntAppBriefDescription.Text = ""
        txtEntAppDescription.Text = ""
        txtEntAppHTMLAddress.Text = ""

    End Sub
```

The `SetEntAppState` procedure essentially reverses the results of the `ClearForm` procedure. It iterates through the current object's editable properties and writes the property value to the appropriate input control. If you are working with the sample code, you will find this block of code in the **General** section of the `frmEntAppDetail.frm`. If you are building this from scratch, you will have to create the routine and type the following block of code into the routine:

```
    Public Sub SetEntAppState()

        txtEntAppName.Text = EntApp.Name
        txtEntAppBriefDescription.Text = EntApp.BriefDescription
```

```
    txtEntAppDescription.Text = EntApp.Description
    txtEntAppHTMLAddress.Text = EntApp.HTMLAddress

End Sub
```

The `LoadEntAppHistoryListView` procedure is almost identical to the procedures we used to load the listview controls on the list form. The only real difference here is the collection we get the data from. In this case, we are iterating through a collection that contains a series of previous states for the same object. If you are working with the sample code, you will find this block of code in the **General** section of the `frmEntAppDetail.frm`. If you are building this from scratch, you will have to create the routine and type the following block of code into the routine:

```
Public Sub LoadEntAppHistoryListView()

    Dim ThisObject As UCEntApp.clsEntApp
    Dim EntAppHistoryItems As ListItems
    Dim ThisItem As ListItem

    Set EntAppHistoryItems = lvwEntAppHistory.ListItems
    EntAppHistoryItems.Clear

    For Each ThisObject In EntAppHistory
        Set ThisItem = EntAppHistoryItems.Add _
            (, ThisObject.Key, ThisObject.Name)
        ThisItem.SubItems(1) = ThisObject.BriefDescription
        ThisItem.SubItems(2) = ThisObject.Description
        ThisItem.SubItems(3) = ThisObject.HTMLAddress
        ThisItem.SubItems(4) = ThisObject.StampAction
        ThisItem.SubItems(5) = ThisObject.StampDateTime
        ThisItem.SubItems(6) = ThisObject.StampUser
        ThisItem.SubItems(7) = ThisObject.StampID
        ThisItem.SubItems(8) = ThisObject.ID
    Next ThisObject

End Sub
```

The `Form_Unload` procedure is typically used to do housekeeping, like deleting any leftover objects and ensuring that the local property values are reinitialized as required. In this case, we need to make sure that the `SourceControl` property is set to a zero length string, and set both local objects to nothing. If you are working with the sample code, you will find this block of code in the `Form_Unload` routine in the `frmEntAppDetail.frm`. If you are building this from scratch, you will have to type the following block of code into the pre-existing routine:

```
Private Sub Form_Unload(Cancel As Integer)

    SourceControl = ""
    Set mcolEntAppHistory = Nothing
    Set mobjEntApp = Nothing

End Sub
```

That takes care of the basic setup requirements for both forms that we use in our standard VB 6.0 interface.

What we have done up to this point is given the forms the ability to display information to and retrieve information from the user. Now we are ready to look at the code we must write to expose the data handling methods an ECDO delivers. These functions handle all of the data storage and retrieval responsibilities for the programmer. As promised, the user interface programmer does not need to know anything about the data store except for its name.

The Functionality of an ECDO

We will now turn our attention to the following functional abilities - note that most of these map to our previously defined data handling processes:

- ❏ Load objects
- ❏ Add new object
- ❏ Edit existing object
- ❏ Delete object
- ❏ Show deleted objects
- ❏ Restore a deleted object back to its state at the time of deletion
- ❏ Show object audit history
- ❏ Restore object to a previous state (unlimited undos)

Load Selected Objects

The *Load* process is used to retrieve a collection of objects from the data store. In this, very simple, case we do not need to filter that list. We need this form to display a list of all of the in-house applications that are installed across our enterprise.

The Method Call

We have actually covered all the code we need to list selected objects using an enterprise object. The code is identical to the code we used in the `Form_Load` for the List form. Here is the actual call to the method again just to refresh your memory:

```
' Call the Load Method of the User Centric Object
EntApps.SetDataSource mstrConnect
EntApps.Load

' Load the listview
LoadEntAppListView
```

This code points the object at a particular data store given by the variable `mstrConnect`. Then once the component knows where to find the information, we give it the command to retrieve it using the statement `EntApps.Load`. In the case of the *Application* object, we need to load all the data available in the data store, so no parameters are required. If an object is designed to return some subset of the available data, the programmer is required to supply one or more parameters as necessary.

Add New Object Process

The *Add New Object* process requires us to write code in both the List form and the Detail form. The code we write in the List form displays the Detail form as a modal dialog. During the time the Detail form is displayed, the user can fill in the information required to add a new EntApp object to the data store. Once the user has completed editing the properties, the user dismisses the form. This returns control of the process to the List form where the code performs a test to see which button the user pressed to unload the Detail form. If the OK button was pressed, then the code refreshes the listview control so that it will display the new object.

The process is quite straightforward, but there are a couple of questions that do need to be answered:

❑ Exactly how do we create an object?

❑ Exactly how do we know which button the user pressed?

Let's answer the second question first.

The Detail Form's ButtonPressed Property

The Detail form is raised as a modal dialog box, and while it exists, we have given control of the *Add* process to the user. The user can edit the object's properties and press the OK button, cancel the process using the Cancel button, or simply dismiss the dialog by pressing the form's close button. This is where the Detail form's ButtonPressed property comes into play. If the OK button was pressed, we set the value of this property to "OK". If the user pressed the Cancel button, we set the value of the ButtonPressed property to "Cancel". If the form was unloaded by any other means, the ButtonPressed property will contain an empty string. We use this humble but reproducible technique to pass messages between forms. The rule is simple, if the OK button was pressed, the value of the ButtonPressed property will be "OK".

The answer to the first question is a little more involved.

The CheckOutObject and CheckInObject Methods

The usual way we expect to create a new object is to instantiate it using the New or CreateObject keyword. We do things a little differently when we are working with Enterprise Caliber Data Objects. If we need to create a new object that should be treated as a member of an existing collection, we create that object using the collection's CheckOutObject method. This method creates the new object, adds it to the existing collection, and sets the object's flags to show that it is an emancipated member of the existing collection. When we are finished working with an object and we want to place it back into the collection it came from, we use the CheckInObject method. This method really just reverses the emancipation process by setting the object's flags so that we know that it is no longer emancipated. We will go over the emancipated concept in great detail when we write the user centric code for the EntApp object, but for now you can think of it like this:

A parent might send his or her child to school for lessons. Once the parent hands the child off to the school, the parent has given up direct control of the child for some period of time. During this time, the child becomes the responsibility of the school. The child's mind is open for editing by sources other than the parent. We can say that the child has been removed or checked out from the parent's sphere of control – the child is **emancipated**. When the school day is finished, the school returns control of the child back to the parent. We can say that the child has been checked back into the parent's sphere of control – the child is no longer emancipated.

With objects, as with children, it is important to know what sphere of control an object was under when it was edited. It is a little early to go over this stuff now, but just realize that we define relationships between objects based upon things like spheres of control. The objects in this book encapsulate the complex parent/child relationships between objects in the `CheckOutObject` and `CheckInObject` methods of the user centric collection.

The List Form's imgAdd_Click Code

The code we use to initiate the *Add* process is found in the `imgAdd_Click` event on the List form. Here is a complete listing of the code that you need. If you are working with the sample code, you will find this block of code in the `imgAdd_Click` routine in the `frmEntAppList.frm`. If you are building this from scratch, you will have type the following block of code into the pre-existing routine stub:

```
Private Sub imgAdd_Click()

    Dim ThisObject As UCEntApp.clsEntApp
    Dim strButtonPressed As String

    On Error GoTo imgAdd_ClickError
    Screen.MousePointer = vbHourglass

    With frmEntAppDetail
    ' Create a new empty object in the collection and enable
    ' editing
    ' This method handles all parent/child relationships
      Set ThisObject = EntApps.CheckOutObject(0)
      .EntApp = ThisObject
    ' Replace this line with the appropriate parent type call
    ' Always pass the user logon ID for the currently logged
    ' on user
      .EntApp.StampUser = UserLogon
      .Show vbModal
    ' Simple messaging functionality which tells us which
    ' button the user pressed on the detail form
      strButtonPressed = .ButtonPressed

    End With

    If strButtonPressed = "OK" Then
    ' If the user stills wants to add the new object
    ' This places the object back into the collection, disables
    ' editing and manages all the parent/child relationships
      EntApps.CheckInObject ThisObject

    Else
    ' If the user did not press the OK button the new object
    ' is destroyed
      Set ThisObject = Nothing

    End If

  LoadEntAppListView

  Screen.MousePointer = vbDefault

    Exit Sub
```

```
imgAdd_ClickError:
   Screen.MousePointer = vbDefault
   MsgBox Err.Description

End Sub
```

Now that you understand how we pass information about which button was pressed, and how we create a new object that is an emancipated member of the collection, this code should be almost self-explanatory.

First we carve out some local memory space for the `ThisObject` and `strButtonPressed` variables. Then we let the user know the application is busy by changing the mouse's cursor into an hourglass. With the preliminaries handled, we move onto the `With` block that allows us to work with the Detail form. The first thing we do is to create a new *Application* object. We do that with the following line of code:

```
Set ThisObject = EntApps.CheckOutObject(0)
```

Notice that we passed the `CheckOutObject` method a parameter of zero, this instructs the method to create a new object in the *Applications* collection and return a reference to that object. In the next line, we pass a reference from `ThisObject` to the Detail form. We do this with the line:

```
.EntApp = ThisObject
```

Once the reference has been passed, we update one of the object's required properties, `StampUser`, with the code:

```
.EntApp.StampUser = Userlogon
```

> For your information, every Enterprise Caliber Data Object requires the identity of the user that wishes to modify an object in any way. This practice ensures a high level of integrity and accountability throughout the system.

The next line is used to show the Detail form as a modal dialog:

```
.Show vbModal
```

This effectively relinquishes control of the process to the modal dialog for as long as it takes. We'll look at the work that the Detail form does shortly, but for now let's just accept that some unknown actions have taken place which resulted in the Detail form being unloaded. We need to know what the user's intentions were when the form was unloaded. We find that information by examining the Detail form's `ButtonPressed` property:

```
strButtonPressed = .ButtonPressed
```

This value tells us exactly how the user ended the session with the Detail form. We use an `If` block to learn whether or not the OK button was pressed when the user dismissed the form. If the user dismissed the Detail form in any other manner, we simply abort the transaction and destroy the unwanted new object with the following line:

```
Set ThisObject = Nothing
```

If the user pressed the OK button, we complete the transaction by checking the new object back into the parent collection. We do that with the following line of code:

```
EntApps.CheckInObject ThisObject
```

Our last step is to refresh the form's listview by calling the procedure we created to handle that task:

```
LoadEntAppListView
```

Now that we have examined the process from the List form's perspective, we need to take a minute or two to view the process during the time that the Detail form is in control.

Data Validation

When we declared our local variable, `mobjEntApp`, for the `EntApp` property back in the declaration section of the Detail form, we declared that object `WithEvents` and I said we would go over it a little later. Well, it's a little later! An Enterprise Caliber Object is delivered with the capacity to test itself to see if it currently meets the data validation requirements that the object's developer specified. It also has the ability to broadcast a message that communicates the object's current validation state to the host application. The object does this by raising an event each time it senses that one of its property values has changed.

We can trap the event that the object raises, by adding a single line of code to our form in the `mobjEntApp_Valid` event. This line of code serves to tie the OK button's enabled state to the validity of the object. If the object is valid when the event occurs, then the command button is enabled. If the object is not valid when the event occurs the command button is disabled. If you are working with the sample code, you will find this block of code in the `mobjEntApp_Valid` routine in the `frmEntAppDetail.frm`. If you are building this from scratch, you will have type the following block of code into the pre-existing routine stub:

```
Private Sub mobjEntApp_Valid(blnIsValid As Boolean)

    cmdOK.Enabled = blnIsValid

End Sub
```

We change the object's properties on the `LostFocus` event of each input control by using code similar to the following two lines. In this case we are passing the value from a textbox to the object's property and back again:

```
Private Sub txtEntAppName_LostFocus()

  EntApp.Name = txtEntAppName.Text
  txtEntAppName.Text = EntApp.Name

End Sub
```

This has the effect of executing the data validation code that is built into the object's property handler each time the user moves from one control to the next (don't forget that this means you'll need to click away from the last text box when you've finished entering data). Of course, there are other ways of achieving the same effect, including using the Change and KeyPress event handlers, so feel free to experiment.

At work, we actually do a little additional data validation at the form level, the Object Factory adds KeyPress event handlers for date, currency, and numeric values. In these events, we limit the individual characters allowed into a control to ensure that the final result is compatible with the data type specified. The Object Factory also updates the length property for textbox controls to the maximum length specified in the property's definition. I will illustrate this point more clearly in a later chapter when we build an object that has a richer assortment of data types.

The Detail Form's cmdOK_Click Event

As soon as the object has been validated, the OK button is enabled and the user can save the changes by pressing the OK button. If you are working with the sample code, you will find this block of code in the cmdOK_Click routine in the frmEntAppDetail.frm. If you are building this from scratch, you will have type the following block of code into the routine:

```
Private Sub cmdOK_Click()

  On Error GoTo cmdOK_Click_ClickError

' let the user know that the application is busy
  Screen.MousePointer = vbHourglass
  mstrButtonPressed = "OK"
  EntApp.SetDataSource mstrConnect

  If Len(SourceControl) > 0 Then

    EntApp.ObjectRestoreFromDeleted
    cmdHistory.Enabled = True
    Unload Me
    Screen.MousePointer = vbDefault
    Exit Sub

  End If

  If EntApp.IsNew Then
    EntApp.ObjectInsert

  Else

    If Len(SourceControl) = 0 Then
      EntApp.ObjectUpdate
```

```
        End If

    End If

    Screen.MousePointer = vbDefault
    SourceControl = ""
    Unload Me
    Exit Sub

cmdOK_Click_ClickError:
    mstrButtonPressed = ""
    Screen.MousePointer = vbDefault
    MsgBox Err.Description

End Sub
```

You may notice that one of the first things we do in this routine is to set the value of the mstrButtonPressed variable with the string "OK". Take a moment to look at the procedure's error handler. If an error occurs during this procedure we send a message to the calling form by setting the value of the mstrButtonPressed variable back to a zero length string. This has the effect of nullifying the OK button press.

The next thing we do should be quite familiar by now, we tell the object where to store the data by providing it with a data store name through the mstrConnect variable.

In the first If block, we test the value of one of the Detail form's other properties, the SourceControl property. This test allows us to determine whether or not the object we are working with is in the process of being restored from a deleted state; we will take a complete look at that process a little later.

The last If block is the one we are really concerned with here. It tests the object by looking at its IsNew property. If the object is new then we execute the ObjectInsert method of the object with the following line:

```
    EntApp.ObjectInsert
```

If the object is not new, then we execute the ObjectUpdate method of the object. We will take a look at that method call when we look at the edit process. The last thing we do in the procedure is to unload the Detail form; this returns control of the process back to the calling form.

The ObjectInsert Method

The ObjectInsert method is the first object level method we have used. The methods we used previously were methods that were executed at the collection level. The ObjectInsert method takes the current property values for an object and writes those values to a persistent data store. This method, like all methods that change the data in the persistent data store, records additional information in the data store that reflects what action was taken, when the action occurred, and the identity of the person that caused the action.

The Edit Process

The *Edit* process requires us to write code in both the List form and the Detail form. The code we write in the List form locates a particular *Application* object. Then it passes the object it found to the Detail form and displays the Detail form as a modal dialog. During the time the Detail form is displayed, the user is expected to edit the object's property values. When the user is finished editing the properties, the user dismisses the form and returns control of the process back to the calling form. As soon as the List form regains control of the process, it refreshes the listview with the current values of the *Applications* collection without considering which button the user pressed to unload the Detail form.

The process is quite straightforward. We really covered the most difficult aspects when we looked at the *Add* process. The only thing we haven't covered yet is exactly how do we find the selected existing object?

Well, we perform that task in the imgEdit_Click event of the List form, but we actually laid the groundwork for the search when we populated the listview. When we populated the listview, we used a property every Enterprise Caliber Data Object contains, the Key property.

The ThisObject.Key Property

When we wrote the procedures we used to load the listviews, I allowed a small item to pass by without comment. When we load a treeview or listview, we have the option of assigning a key value to each item the control should display. In the procedures we wrote earlier, I quietly filled the key with the value found in ThisObject.Key. If you noticed this assignment, you may have wondered where the Key property came from in the first place. We didn't set the value, but we were able to use it to load the ListItems collection. What gives? Well every Enterprise Caliber Data Object has an internally maintained Key property that is managed by the collection. We use this value when we are populating controls like listviews and treeviews. It allows us to reference the object by a value that the controls can use, unchanged, as a key value. We will take a closer look at the Key property in the next chapter when we look at the internals of the object's code.

The CheckOutObject and CheckInObject Methods Revisited

In the *Edit* process, we use the exact same method to emancipate the object from the parent collection that we used in the *Add* process. However when we are performing the CheckOutObject for an existing object, we pass the object's ID as a parameter instead of passing a zero. This CheckOutObject method evaluates the parameter, and if the parameter is a non-zero value, the method searches the collection until it finds an object with an ID that matches the parameter passed into the method. If the ID is not found in the collection, the CheckOutObject doesn't set the function's return value. This has the effect of creating a trappable error.

The List Form's imgEdit_Click Code

Now that we have a sense of where Enterprise Caliber Objects get their Key value from and how we can use the CheckOutObject to emancipate an existing object, the code in the imgEdit_Click event should be pretty self-explanatory. If you are working with the sample code, you will find this block of code in the imgEdit_Click routine in the frmEntAppList.frm. If you are building this from scratch, you will have type the following block of code into the routine:

```
Private Sub imgEdit_Click()

  Dim ThisObject As UCEntApp.clsEntApp

  On Error GoTo imgEdit_ClickError

' If nothing is selected then exit now
  If lvwEntApps.SelectedItem Is Nothing Then Exit Sub

' Let the user know the application is busy
  Screen.MousePointer = vbHourglass

' Find the object in the collection the user needs to be
' edited

  For Each ThisObject In EntApps

    If ThisObject.Key = lvwEntApps.SelectedItem.Key Then
    ' Remove the selected object from the collection and
    ' enable editing
    ' This method handles all of the parent-child
    ' relationships
      Set ThisObject = EntApps.CheckOutObject(ThisObject.ID)
      Exit For

    End If

  Next ThisObject

' Redundant but, if the object still has not been set
' then exit sub
  If ThisObject Is Nothing Then Exit Sub

' Place the object on the detail form
  With frmEntAppDetail
    .EntApp = ThisObject
    ' Always pass the logon ID for the current user.
    .EntApp.StampUser = UserLogon
    .Show vbModal
  End With

' This places the object back into the collection disables
' editing and manages all the parent-child relationships
  EntApps.CheckInObject ThisObject
  LoadEntAppListView

' Let the user know the application is done
  Screen.MousePointer = vbDefault
  Exit Sub

imgEdit_ClickError:

  Screen.MousePointer = vbDefault
  MsgBox Err.Description

End Sub
```

The `imgEdit_Click` code first checks to ensure that something has actually been selected from the listview control. If nothing was selected, we just exit the subroutine. The line that does this is:

```
If lvwEntApps.SelectedItem Is Nothing Then Exit Sub
```

If something was selected, then we iterate through the *Applications* collection and compare the `Key` of the listview's selected item with the `Key` of each object in the collection. We do this using a `For...Next` loop that contains an `If` block. Here is the code:

```
' Find the object in the collection the user needs to be
' edited

For Each ThisObject In EntApps

If ThisObject.Key = lvwEntApps.SelectedItem.Key Then
    ' Remove the Selected Object from the collection and
    ' enable editing
    ' This method handles all of the parent-child
    ' relationships
    Set ThisObject = EntApps.CheckOutObject(ThisObject.ID)
    Exit For

End If

Next ThisObject
```

This works exactly as you expect. The only unusual thing is the test we perform with the `If` block. In this block we reuse the internally maintained `Key` property of the *Application* object to locate the specific object the user selected from the listview control. Now you know that this works because we originally set the `Key` value for each item in the listview equal to the `Key` of the object it represents. Once we find the target object, we emancipate it by calling the `CheckOutObject` using the selected object's ID as the parameter:

```
Set ThisObject = EntApps.CheckOutObject(ThisObject.ID)
```

If an object with a matching ID is found, the `CheckOutMethod` returns a reference to that object. If no matching ID is found, the `CheckOutMethod` returns nothing. We test the return value from the method to ensure that it contains a valid object. If it doesn't we exit the procedure. Here is the line of code that does that:

```
If ThisObject Is Nothing Then Exit Sub
```

Assuming the method returned an object, we pass that object, along with the user's identity, to the Detail form in a `With` block. Then we show the Detail form as a modal dialog, and patiently wait for that form to complete its portion of the process:

```
' Place the object on the detail form
With frmEntAppDetail
    .EntApp = ThisObject
    ' Always pass the logon ID for the current user.
    .EntApp.StampUser = UserLogon
```

```
    .Show vbModal
End With

Set frmEntAppDetail = Nothing
```

When the List form regains control of the process, it checks the object back into the local collection using the `CheckInObject` method. Notice that we don't bother to check which button the user pressed in this instance. If you think about it, you'll realize that it really doesn't matter. When we are editing an existing object, we don't have to deal with the possibility of adding a new empty object to our collection – the problem we handled in the *Add* process. We just check the object back into the collection. If it was changed, we'll know. If it wasn't changed, we still need to place it back into the collection's sphere of control. This line of code checks the object back in:

```
' This places the object back into the collection disables
' editing and manages all the parent child relationships
EntApps.CheckInObject ThisObject
```

Once our object is safely back in the collection, we simply execute the `LoadEntAppListView` procedure to refresh user display:

```
LoadEntAppListView
```

We need to take another look at the Detail form's `cmdOK_Click` event because we use the same code in the *Edit* process that we use in the *Add* process. We already looked at the complete listing of code, so for this discussion I will just show the section of code that is applicable to the *Edit* process. The *Edit* specific code is really just the `If` block that tests the object to find out whether the object is a new object or an existing object:

```
If EntApp.IsNew Then
   EntApp.ObjectInsert

Else

   If Len(SourceControl) = 0 Then
     EntApp.ObjectUpdate

   End If

End If
```

This code first determines whether the object is a new or an existing object. If it finds an existing object, it tests the form's `SourceControl` property to determine whether the object is a deleted object undergoing restoration. In this case, we are not restoring an object from a deleted state, so the `EntApp.ObjectUpdate` line is executed.

The ObjectUpdate Method

The `ObjectUpdate` method is another object-level method. This object-level method only operates on emancipated objects. This means that before we can use the `ObjectUpdate` method we must call the `CheckOutObject` method to emancipate the object we want to update. The `ObjectUpdate` method basically replaces the values in the persistent data store with the current property values in an object.

This method, like all methods that change the data in the persistent data store, records additional information in the data store that reflects what action was taken, when the action occurred, and the identity of the person that caused the action.

The Delete Process

The code for the *Delete* process is all contained on the List form. In fact, all of the user interface code required to delete an object can be found in the Click event of the imgDelete control. The beginning of the *Delete* process works exactly like the beginning of the *Edit* process we just covered. There are no new concepts in this block of code. However, there is one thing we do handle differently when we delete an object. When we are finished, we don't check the emancipated object back into the collection. We also have an additional user interface issue to deal with when we delete an object. It is possible that the user has the List form sized so that the deleted object listview is visible. If this is true, we must refresh the deleted collection and redisplay it so that the user is presented with the most accurate representation of the data. If the deleted object listview is not visible, we don't need to refresh it, because the user will do this when, and if, the Show Deleted command button is pressed.

The CheckOutObject and CheckInObject Revisited Again

In this case, we use the CheckOutObject method exactly like we did for the *Edit* process. The real difference in this process shows up in the CheckInObject method. If we delete the object we don't use the CheckInObject method. Think about it. If we delete the object, there is really no object to check in. Right about now you are probably thinking that the original object is still in the collection and that it is bound to cause us some trouble before too long. Well you are half-right. The original object is still in the collection, but it exists in the collection as an emancipated object. Remember that when we used the CheckOutObject method we emancipated the object. That means the collection has given up control of the object and the collection cannot do anything with the object until it is checked back into the collection (if it is ever checked back into the collection). In this case, the user has deleted the object and will never check it back into the collection. So, while it is true that the object still exists in the collection, it exists as merely a ghost of an object. When this instance of the collection goes out of scope, even the ghost will be destroyed. If the collection is recreated from the persistent data store, the deleted object will not be a member of that collection.

If you are working with the sample code, you will find this block of code in the imgDelete_Click routine in the frmEntAppList.frm. If you are building this from scratch, you will have type the following block of code into the routine:

```
Private Sub imgDelete_Click()

  Dim ThisObject As UCEntApp.clsEntApp

  On Error GoTo imgDelete_ClickError

' If nothing is selected then there is nothing to delete
  If lvwEntApps.SelectedItem Is Nothing Then Exit Sub

' Let the user know the application is busy
  Screen.MousePointer = vbHourglass

' Find the selected object in the collection

  For Each ThisObject In EntApps
```

```
        If ThisObject.Key = lvwEntApps.SelectedItem.Key Then
        ' Remove the selected object from the collection and
        ' enable editing
        ' This method handles all of the parent-child
        ' relationships
          Set ThisObject = EntApps.CheckOutObject(ThisObject.ID)
        ' Always pass the logon ID for the current user.
          ThisObject.StampUser = UserLogon
          ThisObject.SetDataSource mstrConnect
        ' This method deletes the object and creates an audit
        ' record
          ThisObject.ObjectDelete
          Exit For

        End If

    Next ThisObject

    LoadEntAppListView
  ' If the deleted listview is visible then refresh it
  ' If it is not visible, the showdeleted button will
  ' do this so there is no need to refresh it here.

    If Me.Height = jamShowDeleted Then
    ' This clears the local storage variable
      Set mcolEntAppsDeleted = Nothing
    ' This call to the property creates a new deleted object
    ' collection and loads it with the deleted but unrestored
    ' objects
      EntAppsDeleted.SetDataSource mstrConnect
      EntAppsDeleted.ShowDeleted
      LoadEntAppsDeletedListView

    End If


  ' Let the user know the application is done
    Screen.MousePointer = vbDefault

Exit Sub
imgDelete_ClickError:
Screen.MousePointer = vbDefault
MsgBox Err.Description
End Sub
```

Most of the code in this procedure is identical to code we have looked at in the other processes. The first section of the *Delete* process is just like the first section of the *Edit* process. Our task is to identify the target object and obtain a reference to it. We identify the object by iterating through the collection until we find an object with a key that matches the target that the user selected. Once we have identified the object, we obtain a reference to the object by checking it out of the collection. Once we have found the object, we point at a particular data store and give the object the identity of the person that will perform an action against the object. The next line of code is new. It deletes the object by calling the object's `ObjectDelete` method:

```
ThisObject.ObjectDelete
```

That is all there is to it. The object has been deleted. Once the deletion has taken place, we exit the loop, and refresh the object listview. We do this to remove the deleted object from the user's list of available objects. The code is a simply a call to the `LoadEntAppListView` procedure that we created earlier:

```
LoadEntAppListView
```

The remainder of the code is concerned with ensuring that the user is presented with an accurate representation of the data in the data store. We test the size of the form to determine whether the deleted object listview is visible:

```
If Me.Height = jamShowDeleted Then
```

This line uses the form-level constant we defined in the declaration section of the form. We just compare the form's current height with the height we use to display the deleted listview. If the values are different, we can just exit the sub. But, if they are the same then we know that we have some additional work to do. We must reload the collection of deleted objects and refresh the deleted object listview. The result will be to add the object we just deleted to the deleted object listview:

```
' This clears the local storage variable
Set mcolEntAppsDeleted = Nothing
' This call to the property creates a new deleted object collection
' and loads it with the deleted but unrestored objects
EntAppsDeleted.SetDataSource mstrConnect
EntAppsDeleted.ShowDeleted
LoadEntAppsDeletedListView
```

The first line of code destroys any preexisting collection. This ensures us that the data we display to the user is clean. The next executable line just points the `EntAppsDeleted` collection at the appropriate data store. This should be old hat by now. This line introduces a new collection-level method – `ShowDeleted`:

```
EntAppsDeleted.ShowDeleted
```

This method is almost identical to the `Load` procedure we used at the beginning of this section. Both methods return a collection of *Application* objects. The only difference between the two methods is that the `ShowDeleted` method returns a collection of *Application* objects that are deleted. We should actually say that the objects it returns are currently deleted. With Enterprise Caliber Data Objects, an object can be deleted and restored from its deleted state any number of times. This means that any list of deleted object is really a list of currently deleted objects. Too much? Don't worry about it right now. The final result of this statement is that the collection we created to contain a list of deleted objects, now contains at least one object. Our next task is to display the list to the user. We do this by using the load procedure we created when we first roughed out the List form, the `LoadEntAppsDeletedListView` procedure:

```
LoadEntAppsDeletedListView
```

The ObjectDelete Method

The `ObjectDelete` method is another object-level method. This object-level method only operates on emancipated objects. This means that before we can use the `ObjectDelete` method we must call the `CheckOutObject` method to emancipate the object we want to delete.

The `ObjectDelete` method as its name suggests, deletes an object from the persistent data store. This method, like all methods that change the data in the persistent data store, records additional information in the data store that reflects what action was taken, when the action occurred, and the identity of the person that caused the action.

Show Deleted Objects

This process retrieves the list of deleted objects from the data store and presents that list to the user. Once the list of objects has been retrieved, we display the collection by calling the display procedure we created earlier, `LoadEntAppsDeletedListView`. The main difficulty we face in this process is to determine the current display state of the List form and resize it if necessary. All of the code for *the Show Deleted Object* process is located in the List form.

The ShowDeleted Method

The `ShowDeleted` method is a collection-level method. This method returns a collection of objects that have been deleted. The deleted objects it returns are identical in all respects to active objects, except that they contain information that allows us to determine when they were deleted, who deleted them, and what their original ID numbers were when they were deleted.

If you are working with the sample code, you will find this block of code in the `cmdDeleted_Click` routine in the `frmEntAppList.frm`. If you are building this from scratch, you will have type the following block of code into the routine:

```
Private Sub cmdDeleted_Click()

  On Error GoTo cmdDeletedError


  Select Case cmdDeleted.Caption

    Case "&Show Deleted"
    ' Let the user know the application is busy
      Screen.MousePointer = vbHourglass

      cmdDeleted.Caption = "&Hide Deleted"

    ' Clear the local storage variable
      Set mcolEntAppsDeleted = Nothing

    ' This call to the property creates a new
    ' user centric collection to hold the deleted objects
      EntAppsDeleted.SetDataSource mstrConnect

    ' This method loads the deleted/unrestored objects
    ' for viewing
      EntAppsDeleted.ShowDeleted

    ' Load the listview
      DoEvents
      LoadEntAppsDeletedListView
      DoEvents

      Me.Height = jamShowDeleted
```

```
        ' Let the user know the application's task is completed
        Screen.MousePointer = vbDefault

    Case "&Hide Deleted"
        cmdDeleted.Caption = "&Show Deleted"
        Me.Height = jamHideDeleted

  End Select

  Exit Sub

cmdDeletedError:
   Screen.MousePointer = vbDefault
   MsgBox Err.Description

End Sub
```

This code is really standard stuff. And I'm afraid I have to admit that I kind of used a cheap trick here; I use the Caption of one of the buttons to determine the procedure's actions.

It would be much better to create another form-level property to serve as a flag rather than using the Caption of the cmdDeleted command button to determine the procedure's actions.

If the Caption indicates that the objects are currently visible, we just resize the form to hide the deleted objects and toggle the caption on the cmdDeleted command button. If the Caption indicates that deleted objects are currently hidden, we retrieve the collection of deleted objects with the following lines of code:

```
' Clear the local storage variable
Set mcolEntAppsDeleted = Nothing
' This call to the property creates a new
' user centric collection to hold the deleted objects
EntAppsDeleted.SetDataSource mstrConnect
' This method loads the deleted/unrestored objects for viewing
EntAppsDeleted.ShowDeleted
' Load the listview
DoEvents
LoadEntAppsDeletedListView
DoEvents
Me.Height = jamShowDeleted
```

The first line of code here ensures that any pre-existing collection of deleted objects is destroyed before we retrieve the current collection. When we are sure the local collection is empty, we point the object at the correct data store by using the SetDataSource method. The line that actually retrieves the collection is:

```
EntAppsDeleted.ShowDeleted
```

This method places a collection of deleted objects into our EntAppsDeleted property. The last thing we do in this method is to display the list of deleted objects the ShowDeleted method returned. We do this by calling the procedure we wrote earlier:

```
LoadEntAppsDeletedListView
```

We surround this call with `DoEvents` statements to ensure that the operating system has enough time to repaint the screen without flickering. You might need to relinquish control to the OS in some other places as well depending on the client machines you have available. It has been my experience that anything over a 166 MHz Pentium seems to be able to handle most of the screen paints we demand without the `DoEvents`. The only place I have noticed any flickering is in the *ShowDeleted* process, so I used it here.

Restore a Deleted Object

OK, now that we have tempted the user with a list of deleted objects, we must follow through and give the user the ability to restore a deleted object back to its state at the time of deletion. This process requires code in both the List and Detail forms. The code in the List form is found in the `DblClick` event of the `lvwEntAppsDeleted` listview control. The first part of the code works very much like the *Edit* and *Delete* processes that we examined earlier. The only real difference is that, in this case, we iterate through a collection of deleted objects instead of a collection of active objects. We compare the `Key` values until we find the target object that the user needs to restore. Once we find the target object, we call the Detail form, reconfigure it to handle the restoration process and pass the object we need restored into its `EntApp` property. In the case of a restoration, the button the user presses when the Detail form is dismissed does matter, so when we regain control of the process, we test the `ButtonPressed` property of the Detail form and proceed accordingly. If the user pressed the **OK** button we restore the object and refresh both listviews on the List form. If the user dismisses the form in any other manner, we exit the sub and leave everything as we found it.

If you are working with the sample code, you will find this block of code in the `lvwEntAppsDeleted_DblClick` routine in the `frmEntAppList.frm`. If you are building this from scratch, you will have type the following block of code into the routine:

```
Private Sub lvwEntAppsDeleted_DblClick()

  Dim ThisObject As UCEntApp.clsEntApp
  Dim strButtonPressed As String

' If nothing is selected then exit now
  If lvwEntAppsDeleted.SelectedItem Is Nothing Then Exit Sub

' Find the selected object in the deleted object collection

  For Each ThisObject In EntAppsDeleted

    If ThisObject.Key = lvwEntAppsDeleted.SelectedItem.Key Then
    ' Remove the Selected Object from the collection and
    ' enable editing
    ' This method handles all of the parent-child
    ' relationships
      Set ThisObject = EntAppsDeleted.CheckOutObject _
        (ThisObject.ID)
      Exit For

    End If

  Next ThisObject

' Redundant test, but if we still haven't found it then
' exit now
  If ThisObject Is Nothing Then Exit Sub
```

```
' Call the Detail form and set its properties that indicate
' that this call is for a restore - not an edit or add
  With frmEntAppDetail
     .SourceControl = "lvwEntAppsDeleted"
     .EntApp = ThisObject
     .EntApp.StampUser = UserLogon
     .Show vbModal
     strButtonPressed = .ButtonPressed
  End With

' Ensure that the user pressed the OK button
  If strButtonPressed = "OK" Then
   ' This places the object back into the collection disables
   ' editing and manages all the parent-child relationships
     EntApps.CheckInObject ThisObject

  Else
   ' If the OK button was not pressed, then discard the object
     Set ThisObject = Nothing

  End If


' Clear the deleted object collection local storage variable
  Set mcolEntAppsDeleted = Nothing

' Load the current deleted objects' collection with
' the latest unrestored values
  EntAppsDeleted.SetDataSource mstrConnect
  EntAppsDeleted.ShowDeleted

' Show the current values to the user
  LoadEntAppListView
  LoadEntAppsDeletedListView

End Sub
```

Although this code appears very similar to the *Edit* or `Delete` processes we looked at earlier, there are three steps being performed here. They are really quite simple, but I will spell them out to avoid confusion:

❑ We emancipate an object from the collection of *deleted* objects and pass that object to the Detail form for restoration

❑ The object restoration is performed in the Detail form

❑ If the Detail form performed the restoration, then the restored object is checked into the collection of *active* objects

Remember these steps as we look at the detail of the code, it will give you a better big picture perspective of the *Restore* process.

The first part of the code is identical to the *Edit* or *Delete* processes we looked at earlier. Our goal is to locate the user's target object. In this case, the only difference is that the target object exists in the collection of deleted objects instead of the collection of active objects.

Once we locate the target, we emancipate the object by calling the `CheckOutObject` method of the collection. In this case that collection is the deleted collection so the code looks like this:

```
Set ThisObject = EntAppsDeleted.CheckOutObject(ThisObject.ID)
```

Once we have a reference to the object, we pass it to the Detail form for further processing. We use a `With` block like we have in the past, the only difference is that in addition to setting the `UserLogon` property, we pass the name of the control that the object was selected from. The Detail form tests this property during its `Load` procedure. If the length of the property is greater than zero, then the form configures itself to perform an object restore instead of an object add or update. Here is the code from the `With` block to keep it fresh in you mind:

```
With frmEntAppDetail
   .SourceControl = "lvwEntAppsDeleted"
   .EntApp = ThisObject
   .EntApp.StampUser = UserLogon
   .Show vbModal
   strButtonPressed = .ButtonPressed
End With
```

Once the `With` block has finished executing, we will be able to test the value of the `ButtonPressed` property passed to us from the Detail form. If the user did not press the OK button, we end the transaction, destroy the local copy of the object, and leave everything like it was when we started. If the user did press the OK button, we check the object into the active collection. Here is the code that does that work:

```
' Ensure that the user pressed the OK button

If strButtonPressed = "OK" Then
' This places the object back into the collection disables
' editing and manages all the parent-child relationships
  EntApps.CheckInObject ThisObject

Else
' If the OK button was not pressed, then discard the object
  Set ThisObject = Nothing

End If
```

The last part of this procedure reloads the deleted collection and re-displays both collections in their respective listviews. Here is the code that performs that task:

```
' Clear the deleted object collection local storage variable
Set mcolEntAppsDeleted = Nothing

' Load the current deleted objects' collection with
' the latest unrestored values
EntAppsDeleted.SetDataSource mstrConnect
EntAppsDeleted.ShowDeleted

' Show the current values to the user
LoadEntAppListView
LoadEntAppsDeletedListView
```

We have seen all of this code before. In the first line, we ensure that the collection we want to reload with deleted objects is presently empty. Then we point the collection at a data store and call the ShowDeleted method. Remember; that method returns a list of currently deleted objects. The last two lines of code just re-display both collections. You will notice that we did not have to reload the active object collection. That is because when we checked the newly-restored object into that collection, it became a non-emancipated member of the collection.

Here are the pertinent parts of the Detail Form_Load and Detail cmdOK_Click procedures to refresh your memory:

```
If Len(SourceControl) > 0 Then
' If this object was delivered from a deleted state then
' morph form
   cmdOK.Caption = "Restore"
   cmdHistory.Enabled = False
   Me.Caption = Me.Caption & " - [Restore]"

End If

If EntApp.IsNew Then
' If new object then clear the form
   cmdOK.Enabled = False
   cmdHistory.Enabled = False
   ClearForm

Else
' If existing object then populate controls
   SetEntAppState

End If
```

This code fragment from the Form_Load of the Detail form shows how we reconfigure the Detail form to handle its restoration responsibilities. Remember; in the case of an object undergoing restoration, the object is not new, so the SetEntAppState procedure executes.

```
mstrButtonPressed = "OK"
EntApp.SetDataSource mstrConnect

If Len(SourceControl) > 0 Then
   EntApp.ObjectRestoreFromDeleted
   cmdHistory.Enabled = True
   Unload Me
   Screen.MousePointer = vbDefault
   Exit Sub

End If
```

This code fragment from the cmdOK_Click procedure in the Detail form shows that when the SourceControl property has been set, we call the ObjectRestoreFromDeleted method in place of the ObjectInsert or ObjectUpdate methods.

ObjectRestoreFromDeleted

The `ObjectRestoreFromDeleted` method, like most object-level methods, only operates on emancipated objects. This means that before we can use the `ObjectRestoreFromDeleted` method we must first call the `CheckOutObject` method of the `EntAppsDeleted` collection to emancipate the object we want to restore. This method takes the values from the currently deleted object and, essentially, re-inserts them into the persistent data store. This method, like all methods that change the data in the persistent data store, records additional information in the data store that reflects what action was taken, when the action occurred, and the identity of the person that caused the action.

> *One additional point of concern, in order to have a restored object show up in the active object collection, we must check the restored object into the active object collection.*

Show Object Audit History

The `ObjectAuditHistory` method returns a collection of objects that are essentially snapshots of the current object taken each time the object's state was changed. The method we use to retrieve this collection is really just a modified `Load` method. In this case, we pass the ID of the object that we want an audit history for as the selection criterion. The majority of the work in this process actually revolves around resizing the form to either hide or display the audit history listview. I am sure you will find the code self-explanatory.

The ObjectAuditHistory Method

The `ObjectAuditHistory` method is one of the few object-level methods that do not require that the object calling the method be an emancipated object. The `ObjectAuditHistory` method returns a collection of objects that are essentially snapshots of the object taken each time the object's state was changed. The history for every object begins when it was first inserted into the persistent data store. From that point in time on, the history creates an object that represents each update, deletion, or restoration applied to an object until the present time.

If you are working with the sample code, you will find this block of code in the `cmdHistory_Click` routine in the `frmEntAppDetail.frm`. If you are building this from scratch, you will have type the following block of code into the routine:

```
Private Sub cmdHistory_Click()

  On Error GoTo cmdHistory_ClickError

  Select Case cmdHistory.Caption

    Case "&Show History"
    ' let the user know the application is busy
      Screen.MousePointer = vbHourglass
      cmdHistory.Caption = "&Hide History"
    ' Clear the local audit history variable

      If EntAppHistory.Count = 0 Then
        Set mcolEntAppHistory = Nothing
    ' load the audit history for the current object
        EntApp.SetDataSource mstrConnect
        Set mcolEntAppHistory = EntApp.ObjectAuditHistory
```

```
            DoEvents
            LoadEntAppHistoryListView
            DoEvents

        End If

        Me.Height = jamShowHistory
        Screen.MousePointer = vbDefault

      Case "&Hide History"
        cmdHistory.Caption = "&Show History"
        Me.Height = jamHideHistory

    End Select

    Screen.MousePointer = vbDefault
    Exit Sub

cmdHistory_ClickError:

    Screen.MousePointer = vbDefault
    MsgBox Err.Description

End Sub
```

The bulk of the code in this procedure is used to test the current state of the form and resize it if necessary. The only really important lines as far as we are concerned are these:

```
Set mcolEntAppHistory = Nothing
' load the audit history for the current object
EntApp.SetDataSource mstrConnect
Set mcolEntAppHistory = EntApp.ObjectAuditHistory
DoEvents
LoadEntAppHistoryListView
DoEvents
```

By now you are familiar with the simple technique we use to ensure that the local collection is empty. We just destroy any existing collection by setting the variable to nothing. Then we perform another task you are familiar with when we point the object at a particular data store. The only unfamiliar line is the next one. This line loads the object's audit history from the persistent data store and passes the collection into our local variable:

```
Set mcolEntAppHistory = EntApp.ObjectAuditHistory
```

Once the history has been placed into the local variable, all we have to do is display it. We do this using the LoadEntAppHistoryListView procedure that we built when we first set up the Detail form. The last step in the process is the line that resizes the form so that the user can view the listview containing the object's audit history.

Restore Object to a Previous State (Unlimited Undos)

Once again, we have tempted the user with a list of objects; in this case, the objects represent snapshots of the current object's previous values. This list of objects offers the user the potential to undo any action taken at any time by any user. Our job is to make that potential a reality. We do that by writing a simple procedure that locates the snapshot the user has selected and copies the property values from the snapshot into the current object.

All of the code for the *Restore Object to a Previous State* process can be found in the Detail form. By now the code should look very familiar. We use essentially the same technique as we used for the *Edit* and *Delete* processes. First, we iterate through a collection to find the object the user has selected. Once we find the target object, we use it to perform some task. In this case we iterate through a list of objects that represent the previous states the current object had at some earlier time. When we identify the object that contains the values we want to reuse, we just copy those values to the current object. From that point on, the process is identical to the *Edit* process. If the user presses the OK button then we update object's values to one of its previous states. If the user doesn't press the OK button, the original property values remain unchanged.

If you are working with the sample code, you will find this block of code in the lvwEntAppHistory_DblClick routine in the frmEntAppDetail.frm. If you are building this from scratch, you will have type the following block of code into the routine:

```
Private Sub lvwEntAppHistory_DblClick()

   Dim ThisObject As UCEntApp.clsEntApp

   On Error GoTo lvwDataTypeHistory_DblClickError

' Find the object the user wants to restore

   For Each ThisObject In EntAppHistory

      If ThisObject.Key = lvwEntAppHistory.SelectedItem.Key Then
         EntApp.StampUser = ThisObject.StampUser
         EntApp.StampDateTime = ThisObject.StampDateTime
         EntApp.StampAction = ThisObject.StampAction
         EntApp.StampID = ThisObject.StampID
         EntApp.ID = ThisObject.StampID
         EntApp.Name = ThisObject.Name
         EntApp.BriefDescription = ThisObject.BriefDescription
         EntApp.Description = ThisObject.Description
         EntApp.HTMLAddress = ThisObject.HTMLAddress
         SetEntAppState

      End If

   Next ThisObject

   Exit Sub

lvwDataTypeHistory_DblClickError:
   Screen.MousePointer = vbDefault
   MsgBox Err.Description
End Sub
```

Summary

In this chapter, we were introduced to the design objectives for Enterprise Caliber Data Objects and performed a functional analysis of the *Application* object. We determined that it should have nine properties:

- ❏ ID
- ❏ Name
- ❏ BriefDescription
- ❏ Description
- ❏ HTMLAddress
- ❏ StampAction
- ❏ StampUser
- ❏ StampDateTime
- ❏ StampID

and eight data handling processes exposed as methods:

- ❏ Load
- ❏ ObjectInsert
- ❏ ObjectUpdate
- ❏ ObjectDelete
- ❏ ObjectAuditHistory
- ❏ ShowDeleted
- ❏ ObjectRestoreFromDeleted
- ❏ ObjectFetch

We familiarized ourselves with the functionality of an Enterprise Caliber Data Object, by using the EntApp object to construct a user interface using Visual Basic 6.0. We learned that we can provide the user of the ECDO with what should be ordinary abilities such as:

- ❏ Loading objects
- ❏ Adding new objects
- ❏ Editing existing objects
- ❏ Deleting objects
- ❏ Showing deleted objects
- ❏ Restoring deleted objects
- ❏ Showing a deleted object's audit history
- ❏ Restoring an object to a previous state (unlimited undos)

More importantly, we found that we can deliver this without knowing anything about where or how the data is stored. The *Application* object successfully insulated us from the powerful data-handling machine it contains.

Now that we have seen what it possible, we are well on our way to delivering this level of functionality in every application we develop.

{831FDD16-0C5C-1...

Form frmPropNameCont...

Style = 3 'Fixed Dial...

= "Properties for...

eight = 4845

ft = 45

p = 330

dth = 11460

s = "Form1"

ton = 0 'False

d = -1 'True

on = 0 'False

ight = 4845

dth = 11460

askbar = 0 'False

Person
Base Properties

ID
Last Name
First Name
Middle Name
Birth Date
Sex

Object Type Definitions

Object Typ...

Lawyer OTD	Lawyer OTD	Engineer OTD	Doctor OTD	Student OTD	
	Specialty	Specialty	Specialty	Major	S
	Hourly Rate	Experience	Certification	Minor	D
	Law School	Property 3	Property 3	Year	E
	Property 4	Property 4	Property 4	Property 4	P
	Property 5	Property 5	Property 5	Property 5	P
	Property 6	Property 6	Property 6	Property 6	P
	Property 7	Property 7	Property 7	Property 7	P
	Property 8	Property 8	Property 8	Property 8	P
	Property 9	Property 9	Property 9	Property 9	P
	Property 10	Property 10	Property 10	Property 10	P

Property Set Definitions

Property Set

6

The ErrCond Object

In the last chapter we constructed an application that had a quite a bit of functionality. As anyone might expect, the application had the ability to add, edit, delete, and browse the information it was designed to manage. But that was not all it did. It also kept a history of all of the changes that were made to the object. This allowed us to give the user the ability to not only view the history of changes but also the ability to undo any of those changes – including deletions. Considering that we did this without ever touching a database, I would say that this was pretty impressive.

Of course, the reason we were able to deliver all of this functionality so quickly was due to the object that you used to provide the data for the application – the **Enterprise Caliber Data Object**. As you learned in the last chapter, Enterprise Caliber Data Objects expose eight data handling capabilities:

- ❑ *Insert* – Adds a new object to the data store
- ❑ *Edit* – Changes the object's state in the data store
- ❑ *Delete* – Removes the object from the active data store
- ❑ *Fetch* – Retrieves a single object from the data store
- ❑ *Load* – Retrieves a list of like objects from the data store
- ❑ *Show Deleted* – Retrieves a list of currently deleted objects
- ❑ *Restore From Deleted* – Restores an object to its state at the time it was deleted
- ❑ *Audit History* – Retrieves the history of changes to an object over time

What we did in the last chapter was to use the eight data handling capabilities to build an exceptional application. What we'll do in this, and the next few chapters, is learn *how* to code these capabilities. We'll learn to write this code as we build several objects that we need for our Enterprise Management System. In this chapter, we'll concentrate on just two of the above process as we build the **ErrCond Data Object**.

The purpose of the Error Condition (*ErrCond*) Data Object is to automatically collect and manage information about the errors that occur in any in-house application deployed across the enterprise. The reason we are going to tackle this object first is because it can be quite functional, even with only two of the standard eight data handling capabilities that we expect from an Enterprise Caliber Data Object.

> *Please keep in mind that, although we will be working on a particular object in this chapter, the coding techniques we cover can be used for any object you design.*

Our major focus in this chapter will be to learn how to code the following two data handling processes:

- ❏ The *Insert* process
- ❏ The *Load* process

Let me warn you ahead of time that this is will involve a lot of work. In addition to the work required to develop the data handling processes, we'll also need to take the time to cover some general concepts concerning coding for distributed architecture. Remember, distributed design requires that we divide the processing responsibilities for a single object into two or more distinct sets of processes that work together to move data between the user and the data store. In the beginning of this chapter we'll pay special attention to the processes that execute on the Data Centric sphere, and the User Centric sphere. This is designed to give you a familiarity with the User Centric and the Data Centric objects' characteristics.

While characteristics and general concepts are important, they won't do us any good if we don't back them up with some practical knowledge. When it comes to developing distributed applications, practical knowledge includes things like the ability to work with multiple projects simultaneously in Visual Basic and the ability to define references to dynamic link libraries that might exist on a computer halfway around the world. In this chapter, you will begin to develop that practical knowledge in a hands-on manner as you put together the *ErrCond* Data Object.

As the name *ErrCond* Data Object implies, we're learning to build a **Data** object. That means that in addition to covering VB code, we'll also spend a bit of time building tables and working with SQL. I have chosen to err on the side of caution with respect to the SQL code in this book. In other words, I am going to cover some basic material to ensure that everyone is on the same page. As you work through these SQL coding tasks, you will be developing a foundation for the more advanced topics that we will cover in later chapters.

N-Sphere Thinking

When we talk about an object that has been designed to take advantage of distributed architecture, we may really be talking about 2, 3 or more DLLs, which work together to perform a particular task. These DLLs can, and as we saw in Chapter 3, often should, exist on different machines.

> **This division of processing across several machines is the essence of distributed architecture.**

Unfortunately, this division can also make it hard to define exactly what we mean when we are talking about an object or a component etc. Is an object a single class? Is an object a DLL that runs on a particular machine? Or is an object the sum of all the DLLs that work together on several machines to perform a task? There may be as many answers to this as there are questions. We really need to get to work, so I am just going to define a few of the things that we'll be working with in this chapter. Although I will give them names so that we can discuss them, please don't allow the names to get in the way of the ideas.

> In this book, we will refer to the DLL that is responsible for the data centric processing as the Data Centric object or DC object. We will call the DLL that is responsible for the user centric processing as the User Centric object or UC object. When we use the term *data object,* we will be talking about both the Data Centric and User Centric objects working together to manage a common set of data. We will reserve the name Enterprise Caliber Data Object to refer to a data object *(data and user centric objects working together)* that has the ability to perform all of the eight data handling processes that we used in the last chapter.

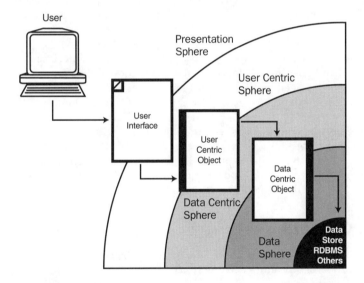

Even though, by definition, Enterprise Caliber Data Objects (**ECDOs**) consist of at least two DLLs, we will learn about ECDOs by viewing them as a collection of processes that just happen to be executed across several DLLs – *maybe even DLLs that exist on several machines*. This is because we need to foster an understanding and appreciation for the whole.

We need to think of the User Centric objects and Data Centric objects as extensions of one another; specialized tools we can use to make our job easier. The following two sections on User Centric objects and Data Centric objects are designed to give you a feel for the characteristics or personality of the Data Centric and User Centric objects.

Think of the User Centric object as a trusted friend or aide. Always there, ready, willing, and able to meet the user interface programmer's every need. Conversely, think of the Data Centric object as more of a cold, calculating, but dependable business associate. A 'just the facts' kind of guy – not good at making small talk, but when you need something it's there, unfailingly.

User Centric Objects

We can make some generalizations about User Centric objects. User Centric objects have properties – lots of them – and those properties are **rich**. That is, user centric properties are superbly capable devices that can contain data validation routines, perform internal data translations, and be used as short-term local storage devices.

The primary purpose of the User Centric object is to cater to the user interface programmer. It handles the repetitive, and often messy, tasks like data validation and data transmission. It *knows* when the data the user has placed into it is correct and acceptable for storage, and it *knows* how to manage the transmission of information to and from its Data Centric counterpart.

To the user interface programmer, blessed with the IntelliSense feature found in Visual Basic or Interdev, the User Centric object is a godsend. Once a new object has been declared, the programmer can get a list of the available properties, methods, and events, with the press of a key. And if the objects' developer has done his or her job properly, detailed information about every facet of the object can be found in the Object Browser.

Data Centric Objects

We can also make some generalizations about Data Centric objects. For the most part, Data Centric objects do *not* have properties, or more accurately; Data Centric objects do not have properties that are designed to be accessed by the object's user. Most of the properties in a Data Centric object are used internally to facilitate the transmission of data from point A to point B. The things we view as properties in a User Centric object are treated as parameters in Data Centric objects.

Consider the nature of a Data Centric object. Its primary purpose is to move information to or from the Data sphere to the User Centric sphere. It *knows* everything it needs to know to swiftly and efficiently move information into and out of its target datastore(s). It *knows* how to construct every data structure and data-handling device it requires for its operation. To meet its responsibilities it must move data through itself as quickly as possible. This serves to:

❑ Minimize the number of connections to the data store, the most limited resource in the enterprise

❑ Promote its own reuse without requiring re-creation/re-instantiation

Therefore, if we optimize the system correctly the data object will be the second most limited resource in the enterprise.

It owes its effectiveness to the efficient way it passes information. While the User Centric object relies upon properties to store and communicate information, the Data Centric object uses parameters as its primary means of data transmission.

A Bit on Passing Parameters

For many of you, this section is probably somewhere between unnecessary and ridiculous. Feel free to skip this section, but it has been my experience that many programmers are quietly baffled by some basic parameter passing techniques. C programmers and Visual Basic programmers who regularly utilize the Win32 API are used to passing data via parameters in ways that most Visual Basic programmer don't normally use. Many VB programmers are comfortable passing parameters into a procedure, but few seem to realize that they can get useful information, very quickly, by re-examining the same parameters after the procedure has executed.

For example:

```
Public Sub SomeSub(lngID As Long, strWord As String, strWord2 As String)

   Select Case lngID

     Case 1
        strWord = "One"
        strWord2 = "Uno"

     Case 2
        strWord = "Two"
        strWord2 = "Dos"

     Case 3
        strWord = "Three"
        strWord2 = "Tres"

   End Select

End Sub
```

```
Public Sub DisplayWord(lngID)

   Dim strWord As String

   strWord = ""
   strOtherWord = ""
   SomeSub lngID, strWord, strTranslateWord
   Debug.Print strWord, strTranslateWord

End Sub
```

Of course, if we call `DisplayWord` passing a value of 2, the words "Two" and "Dos" would be printed as output in the Immediate window. But what if we need to return 17 output values from a single input value? Yes, we can design a subroutine that requires 18 parameters. We could test one of the values and fill the remaining 17 with some information. Then the calling routine could extract the answers from the 17 variables we changed within the subroutine.

The reason this works is because the default mechanism that VB employs in passing parameters is By Reference.

We will use this technique extensively throughout this book to pass information between the User and Data Centric objects. Passing data between DC and UC objects is just one of the issues we need to resolve when we are working in a distributed architecture. In fact, we need to resolve a couple of issues before we can even begin to develop and test an Enterprise Caliber Data Object. The first is the issue of working with more than one Visual Basic project file at a time.

The Visual Basic Project and Group Files

If you haven't taken the time to download the sample code for this object, I suggest that you do that now. You can find instructions on this in Appendix A.

Since Visual Basic 5.0, Microsoft has given us the ability to work with multiple projects as a single project group. Thank you Microsoft! Still, there is an equalizing force in the universe. So while we do get a little more functionality, it can also get a little more complicated.

Using the source code, I'm going to give you instructions on how to put together the *ErrCond* object across the various spheres using 3 Visual Basic projects.

When you get finished with this section, the Project Explorer in your VB IDE should look like the one here:

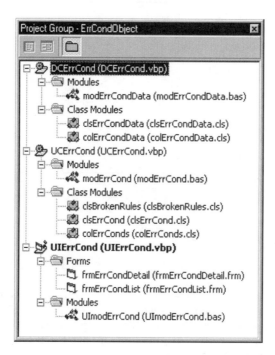

Follow the steps below to set up all three projects:

1. Create a new Standard EXE project in VB.

2. Rename the project to `UIErrCond`. This project will be used to manage the user interface elements.

3. Add a new ActiveX DLL project to the project group.

4. Rename this project `UCErrCond`. This project will form the User Centric object.

5. Add a second ActiveX DLL project to the project group.

6. Rename this project `DCErrCond`. This project will form the Data Centric object.

7. Remove all of the default classes and forms from the projects.

8. Using the table below to find the files, and insert these modules into the relevant project:

System Sphere	Directory	Source File Name
Presentation (UIErrCond.vbp)	\..\Ch06\UInterface\	UImodErrCond.bas
	\..\Ch06\UInterface\	frmErrCondDetail.frm
	\..\Ch06\UInterface\	frmErrCondList.frm
User Centric (UCErrCond.vbp)	\..\Ch06\UCObject\	modErrCond.bas
	\..\Ch06\UCObject\	clsBrokenRules.cls
	\..\Ch06\UCObject\	clsErrCond.cls
	\..\Ch06\UCObject\	colErrConds.cls
Data Centric (DCErrCond.vbp)	\..\Ch06\DCObject\	modErrCondData.bas
	\..\Ch06\DCObject\	clsErrCondData.cls
	\..\Ch06\DCObject\	colErrCondData.cls

9. Make sure that the `UIErrCond` project is set as Start Up.

10. Save the project files.

11. Save the project group file. For consistency, I make it a habit to use the suffix `Object` for the group files. In this case, I would save the *ErrCond* group as `ErrCondObject.vbg`.

Now we have the put the *ErrCond* object together, let's take a minute or two to go over the different files and types of files that are working with here.

The Data Centric Project

Take a look at all of the files that we've used to build the DCErrCond project. You should see one file called modErrCondData.bas. As you might expect, this is just a standard VB module. It contains the common information and routines that are used by the Data Centric *ErrCond* object. There are also two files with the extension cls. Although we can tell by the extension that these files are VB class files, that really doesn't tell us much about their purpose. To learn anything about these files you need to take a look at the file prefixes. Notice that one of them has the prefix cls and the other one has the prefix col. Now this tells us something. The cls prefix is used to indicate that the file contains the code for a single class. As we learned in the last chapter, we can envision a single data object as a proxy for a row in a table. The other prefix, col is used to indicate that this file contains the code used to define a collection. As you know, in VB we use a special kind of class called a collection to manage multiple objects in a single package. In this case our collection will be charged with managing those objects that we can view as proxies for rows in a table. In other words, it is reasonable to view a collection of these objects as a proxy for a database table. Together these three files contain all of the code that we need to create one Data Centric *ErrCond* ActiveX DLL.

The User Centric Project

Let's make sure we are thorough here. Check out the files we added to the UCErrCond project. You should find three files with the extension cls and one with the extension bas. Once again, the file with the bas extension is really just a standard VB module. It contains the common information and routines that are used by the User Centric *ErrCond* object. Of course, you can identify the other three files as VB class files by their cls extension. And, now you should also be able to tell by their prefixes that these class files can be divided into two types of classes. There are two classes that define a single object – clsBrokenRules.cls and clsErrCond.cls. And there is one class file that defines a collection used to manage multiple objects – colErrCond.cls. The clsBrokenRules.cls defines a simple object that is used to manage data validation rules. Even though this project is used to manage user centric objects, we can still think of the object as a proxy for a row in a table. Likewise, we can also think of the colErrCond.cls as a proxy for a database table. These four files contain all of the code that we need to create one User Centric *ErrCond* ActiveX DLL.

The User Interface Project

Finally, let's drop in on the user interface files. You should be familiar with these modules from the last chapter. As we found out in the last chapter, these two forms really kind of mirror the single object and the collection. For the most part, the frmErrCondDetail form is used to work with a single data object and the frmErrCondList form is used to work with a collection of data objects.

Now that we have our projects, we need to facilitate communication between them. We do that by creating references.

Creating References to DLLs and Projects

We are not quite finished setting up our project. We still have a couple of housekeeping chores to perform. The first one is that we need to set the references for each project.

First we will set the references for the Data Centric *ErrCond* object. Highlight the DCErrCond.vbp in VB's Project Explorer window and open the References dialog.

The default project in Visual Basic contains references to the first four items in the Available References listview, shown here. We are working with the DC project, so we need to create two additional references – one for ActiveX Data Objects 2.1 Library and another one for Microsoft Transaction Server Type Library:

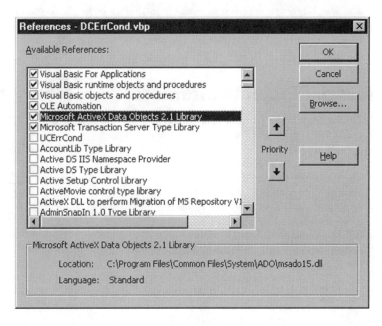

If you haven't installed MTS on your development box, now is a good time to do that. MTS is available from Microsoft in the Windows NT 4.0 Option Pack. At the time of this writing, MTS was available in Version 2.0.

Once you have made the ADO and MTS reference, you are done with the references for the DC object. We need to move on to the UC object next.

We also need to give the UC object two references. One to the ADO Recordset Library and one to the DC object. As a tribute to the design of the VB interface, notice that it is smart enough to move the most likely choices up to the top of the Available References list:

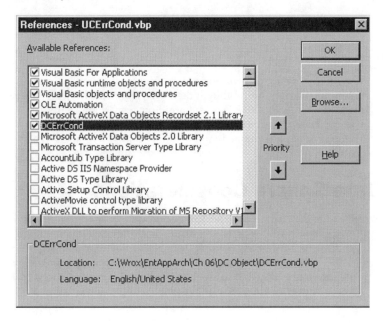

The last reference we need to make is in the UI project. The only reference we need to give the UI project is a reference to the UC project. Once you have made this reference, save the project group. If you forget to do this you will have to redefine your references.

How the Projects Interact

Take a look at the image below. It gives us a graphical representation of the way each project is connected (referenced) by the other projects. Keep this image in mind. It illustrates the flow of data throughout the system. Notice that when a user makes a request to the data store, that request is passed onto the UC object. Then the UC object passes the request on to the DC object, which finally makes the request to the data store:

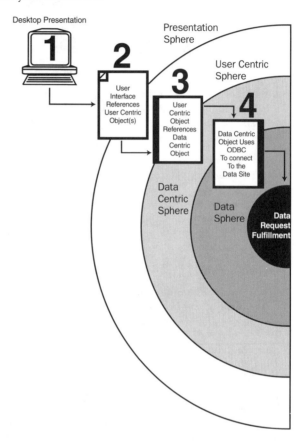

It shouldn't be too difficult to get a handle on the connection between the VB projects. After all we just went through the trouble of defining references between the projects. So, it's kind of obvious that they are connected. The Data sphere, however, is another story. It is as much a part of an Enterprise Caliber Data Object as any of the VB files you just worked with, but it is common to think of the Data sphere as a completely independent entity. We need to take some time and think about this.

Data Sphere Considerations

All of the distributed architecture design we are covering in this book has a single purpose.

> **That purpose is to position the entirety of the enterprise's resources in a manner that will allow the largest number of users to access the smallest number of database servers.**

Remember that our goal is to design systems that can distribute the processing that the system requires – not distribute the data that the system stores. A good part of the work we need to do to reach this goal can be handled by shifting the processing load away from the Data sphere and onto one of the other spheres. But, some work must be performed, and is best handled by the Data sphere. This means that we have an obligation to ensure that the processes that *must* execute on the Data sphere execute as quickly and efficiently as possible. In other words, before you are finished with this book, you are going to have learnt a bunch of SQL.

SQL Server – Visual Basic Datatype Mapping

Before we get into the details of how to code in SQL, we need to get a sense of the relationship between Visual Basic datatypes and SQL Server's datatypes. There are some differences between the ways that the two refer to datatypes. This fact could cause us trouble if we are not aware of differences.

Char, Varchar = String

These two datatypes are used to store character data. The SQL Server **char** datatype refers to a fixed number of characters, while the SQL Server **varchar** datatype refers to a variable number of characters. Both SQL Server datatypes map directly to the Visual Basic String datatype. The varchar datatype allows SQL Server to store a variable number of characters in a field up to some predefined maximum. The char datatype always stores the maximum number of characters in the field, padding the actual value with empty characters.

At first blush, it may seem like a good idea to define all fields that store strings as varchar fields, but this would be a mistake. Any field that is less than about 50 characters, or so, is better suited to the char datatype. The mechanics behind this statement has to do with SQL Server's memory page size, and are really out of the scope of this book. Rather than discuss this further, just let me say that it is our practice to define all fields less than 51 characters as char and those greater than 50 as varchar.

Datetime, Timestamp = Date

As the names suggest, these datatypes contain date/time values. Both SQL Server datatypes map directly to the Visual Basic Date datatype.

Decimal, Numeric = Single, Double

Decimal and numeric datatypes are used to store precise representations of numeric values. The decimal and numeric datatypes map to Visual Basic's Single and Double precision datatypes respectively.

Integer = Long

This datatype is often a source of confusion. The SQL Server integer value maps to the Visual Basic Long datatype. The SQL Server integer datatype can hold values up to 32 bits (± 2,147,483,647) while the Visual Basic Integer datatype can only hold values up to 16 bits (± 32,763). SQL Server also has the sub-types smallint and tinyint.

Money = Currency

This datatype is used to store currency and maps directly to the Visual Basic Currency datatype.

Text/Image

These two datatypes are sometimes referred to as BLOBS or Binary Large OBjects. They can contain binary information like text blocks longer than 255 characters for SQL Server 6.5 (8,000 for SQL Server 7.0) or image information. Most 'experts' warn against using BLOBS. Often they use the performance argument, but I think the real reason most people stay away from BLOBS is that they require special handling procedures. These handling procedures are really quite simple, and once they are mastered and encapsulated into an object, BLOBS offer many benefits that outweigh the slight degradation in performance they might cause.

The Data Tables

Conventional wisdom has it that the major shortcoming of the relational database is its inability to express temporal relationships. In other words, we are not supposed to be able to track changes to an individual piece of data across the time dimension. *Conventional wisdom is wrong.* One of the most important things we will discover in this chapter is exactly how to design objects (and data stores) that naturally exhibit temporal, or time-based, relationships.

The *ErrCond* object requires two tables:

❑ The base table - a standard table designed to contain the objects' current states

❑ The audit table - a table that allows us to preserve temporal information. It contains data that, essentially, amounts to a series of snapshots of an object over a period of time. Each of these snapshots represents the state of an object just prior to the change that caused the entry into the audit table.

For the most part, the two tables have exactly the same fields. Every field in the base table, except the `ConcurrencyID` field is duplicated in the audit table. The `ConcurrencyID` field is used internally by the Data Centric object to manage the inevitable data collisions stateless objects give rise to and is not required in the audit table. We'll see how this works later.

The audit table has four fields that do not exist in the base table. They are:

❑ `StampAction` – stores the action taken that caused the snapshot: Insert, Update, Delete, or Restore

❑ `StampDateTime` – stores the date and time the snapshot was taken

❑ `StampUser` – stores the identity of the user who caused the change in the data store

❑ `StampID` – stores the original ID of the record that was changed

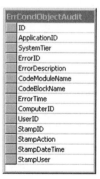

Now that we know what the tables look like, we need to spend a little time thinking about the scope of the tables. Yeah, I know that is a strange concept. We don't normally associate database tables with scope. *That is a mistake.* Just like we have modules in VB that house common subroutines and information that can be used across a VB project, every enterprise also has common data that should be available throughout the enterprise. The *ErrCond* object tables are an example of tables that should have a global scope.

Think about what this object does. It is designed to record the errors that occur in any in-house application that is deployed across the enterprise. If we hope to use this information to draw enterprise-wide conclusions about the shortcomings in the system, we need to base that information on all of the machines and all of the applications deployed across the entire enterprise. That means that these tables need to be in a database that is common to all departments, agencies, or divisions, etc. in the organization.

> *I make it a practice of keeping tables that need this kind of scope in a database called* Common. *This database hosts all of the tables that contain information that I actively try to share across an enterprise.*

The CREATE TABLE Statement

In this section we are going to cover the SQL syntax we use to create new tables. In this book we'll be using a special technique to deliver these SQL statements to the data store. We will go over where to actually write this code when we develop the EstablishDataStore procedure below.

Now that we are familiar with the most common datatype translations and we have a description for the tables we need, we're ready to learn the **CREATE TABLE** syntax. The first line in any CREATE TABLE statement must include the CREATE TABLE command followed by the table owner, table name, and an opening parenthesis:

```
CREATE TABLE dbo.ErrCondObject (
```

Once you have typed that line, then all you need to do is to describe each of the fields in the table by providing it a name, defining its datatype, and giving an indication as to whether or not the field can contain null values:

```
        ErrorDescription varchar (255) NOT NULL ,
```

We can call each of these, comma delimited, lines a **field definition**. You create a table by defining each of the fields it contains. A final closing parenthesis indicates that all of the fields have been defined. Here is the complete CREATE TABLE statement for the ErrCondObject table:

```
CREATE TABLE dbo.ErrCondObject (
        ID int IDENTITY (1, 1) NOT NULL ,
        ApplicationID int NULL ,
        SystemTier char (25) NOT NULL ,
        ErrorID int NULL ,
        ErrorDescription varchar (255) NOT NULL ,
        CodeModuleName varchar (255) NOT NULL ,
        CodeBlockName varchar (255) NOT NULL ,
        ErrorTime datetime NULL ,
```

```
        ComputerID char (25) NOT NULL ,
        UserID char (25) NOT NULL ,
        ConcurrencyID int NOT NULL
        )
```

As you might have guessed, there are quite a few additional things that can be accomplished with the CREATE TABLE command including defining indexes, default field values, referential integrity relationships, and more. We'll take a look at how to code these in a later chapter. For now, we only need one more bit of information. We want our ErrCondObject table to have a field that automatically generates a unique ID for each object represented in the table. We can accomplish that with the CREATE TABLE command by configuring one of our fields as an **identity field**. To do this, we just insert the keyword IDENTITY after the datatype definition as shown in the line below:

```
        ID int IDENTITY (1, 1) NOT NULL ,
```

The two numbers that follow the IDENTITY keyword give SQL Server a starting, or **seed value**, and an increment-by value. The sample above tells SQL server that this field should start out with the value of 1 for the first record inserted into the table then increment the value of this field by 1 for each successive record added to the table.

Here is the complete SQL Statement used to create the ErrorObjectAudit table:

```
CREATE TABLE dbo.ErrCondObjectAudit (
    ID int IDENTITY (1, 1) NOT NULL ,
    ApplicationID int NULL ,
    SystemTier char (25) NOT NULL ,
    ErrorID int NULL ,
    ErrorDescription varchar (255) NOT NULL ,
    CodeModuleName varchar (255) NOT NULL ,
    CodeBlockName varchar (255) NOT NULL ,
    ErrorTime datetime NULL ,
    ComputerID char (25) NOT NULL ,
    UserID char (25) NOT NULL ,
    StampID int NOT NULL ,
    StampAction char (1) NOT NULL ,
    StampDateTime datetime NOT NULL ,
    StampUser char (15) NOT NULL
    )
```

Once you have written these CREATE TABLE statements, you can build the tables by running the code in SQL Server's Enterprise Manager, in Interdev, or in Visual Data Tools if you prefer. Don't do this now; we are going to do something special with this SQL shortly.

The EstablishDataStore Method

We are working with an Enterprise Caliber Data Object, so the SQL required to create all of the database objects – the tables, views and stored procedures – will become an integral part of the object itself. The method that is houses all of this information is called the EstablishDataStore method.

Let's take a look at how we can use the CREATE TABLE statements we learned about above in the EstablishDataStore method of the Data Centric clsErrCondData object. In the Project Explorer window in VB, expand the DCErrCond project so that all of the files under it are visible.

Look in the Class Modules folder. Find and open the clsErrCondData.cls module. Locate the EstablishDataStore routine. If you are in the right place, the first line in the edit window should read:

```
Public Sub EstablishDataStore()
```

In this book, Enterprise objects use ActiveX Data Objects 2.1 (ADO) for database access, so our first task is to create a Connection object and a Recordset object in the VB code:

```
Dim ThisConnection As ADODB.Connection
Dim ThisRecordset As ADODB.Recordset

Set ThisConnection = New ADODB.Connection
Set ThisRecordset = New ADODB.Recordset
```

Once they have been created, we can open a connection by employing the Connection object's Open method. The Open method takes one parameter that amounts to an ODBC connection name, a second parameter that contains a valid SQL Server user account, and a third parameter that contains a valid password for the account specified:

```
ThisConnection.Open mstrConnect, GetLogon(mstrConnect), GetPassword(mstrConnect)
```

We use the GetLogon and GetPassword function calls to return valid strings for these arguments that are stored in the data centric machine's registry. This allows us to point the same object at many different data stores.

Once the connection has been opened, we run a query against the sysobjects table in SQL Server. The sysobjects table contains information about all of the objects that comprise the database. In this case, what we need to do is to ask the sysobjects table if it has a table named ErrCondObject in the target database. After all, we don't want to create a new table if one already exists. If SQL Server finds the table, it will return the numeric value that it uses internally to identify the table. If it doesn't find the table, it will return an empty recordset. We run the query by using the Open method of the Recordset object as shown in the code below:

```
strSQL = "SELECT * FROM sysobjects WHERE id = object_id" & _
         "('dbo.ErrCondObject')"
ThisRecordset.Open strSQL, ThisConnection
```

Next, we check the results of the query by testing to see if any records were returned. If both the EOF and the BOF method of the recordset return True, then we need to create the table. We do this by simply using the Execute method of the Connection object to run the CREATE TABLE command as shown in the code block below. If the table was found, then the EOF method would have evaluated to False and the Execute statement would not be run:

```
If ThisRecordset.BOF And ThisRecordset.EOF Then
    strSQL= "CREATE TABLE dbo.ErrCondObject (" & _
         "   ID int IDENTITY (1, 1) NOT NULL ," & _
         "   ErrorID int ," & _
         "   ErrorDescription varchar(255) NOT NULL ," & _
         "   SystemTier char(25) NOT NULL ," & _
         "   ApplicationID int ," & _
         "   ModuleName varchar(80) NOT NULL ," & _
```

199

```
     "     CodeBlockName varchar(80) NOT NULL ," & _
     "     UserIdentity char(25) NOT NULL ," & _
     "     ComputerName char(25) NOT NULL ," & _
     "     EventTime datetime ," & _
     "     ConcurrencyID int NOT NULL" & _
     "     )"
  ThisConnection.Execute strSQL
  strSQL = "CREATE UNIQUE INDEX IX_ErrCondObject ON dbo.ErrCondObject(ID)
  ThisConnection.Execute strSQL
End If

ThisRecordset.Close
```

We construct the audit table, views, and other database objects using exactly the same technique. I won't describe the process for the audit table here. Take a minute or two and scroll down through the EstablishDataStore subroutine in your edit window. Find the section of code that is used to create the audit table for the *ErrCond* object. Read through this section of code and try to draw some similarities to the code above. What you should find is that we can define the steps necessary to create an object (table, view, stored procedure) in the database as follows:

1. Query the sysobjects table to determine whether or not the object already exists

2. If the object (table, view, stored procedure) does not exist, then write the SQL that is needed to create the object and (optionally) stuff that SQL into a variable

3. Run the ADO Connection object's Execute method passing the SQL as a parameter

These three steps give us a simple model that we can use to modify the data store to suit the needs of our object. We can choose to run this code from just about anywhere. It is never destructive, because it will never overwrite a pre-existing database object. Many people are confused about exactly when and where to call this subroutine. There are basically two choices:

❑ We can cause this routine to run every time we run across an error that indicates that an object is missing from a data store

❑ We can control when this subroutine is executed via some object management interface that we construct for each object

In this book I have opted for an automatic approach. We trap the missing database object error in the Load method and fire off the EstablishDataStore method from within that Load method's error handler. This is to allow anyone who uses the sample code to have the data store built as soon as they start up the project. Remember that we set the list form as the start up form in the UIErrCond project. Also remember from the last chapter that the list form calls the *Load* process during the Form_Load subroutine. This means that all you need to do to build the entire data store for this object is to provide a valid ODBC source and press the run button.

In a production setting, I would opt for a more controlled method. In other words, I would proactively call this subroutine from an object management interface. We will look at object management interfaces in Chapters 8 and 9.

The Basics of SQL Stored Procedures and Views

The `EstablishDataStore` method does more than just create tables in the data store. It is also used to create **stored procedures** and **views**.

Stored Procedures

Stored procedures are really nothing more than SQL statements that are stored in the database. It's fine to think of them as subroutines or maybe as functions. Once we write a stored procedure and give it a name, we can just type the name instead of the entire SQL statement to execute that SQL statement. The advantages this offers are the same as we expect from modular coding in general.

For example, imagine that we have 6 different programs that use the same SQL statement and we code that SQL statement in each program. What happens when we need to change the SQL statement? Exactly, we have to re-write the code in 6 different programs. I can think of better things to do with my time! Now imagine that instead of writing the SQL statement in each program we just wrote the name of a stored procedure that contained the SQL statement in each of the 6 programs. What happens then if we need to change the SQL statement? Exactly, we change the SQL stored in the database once and all 6 programs are updated at one time. Even if this was the only advantage, it would be more than enough to make me use stored procedures, but there are other advantages.

The database server pre-compiles stored procedures. This means, among other things, that SQL Server doesn't need to take the time to design and optimize the query plan every time the SQL statement is executed. It does this one time and stores the query plan for future reference. What this means is that stored procedures allow us to create modular SQL code that we can use, more or less, like we use other subroutines or functions.

Views

I like to think of views as just a special kind of stored procedure. A view offers us another way to reference a SQL statement by typing a single word. The only real differences I can see between views and other stored procedures is that views cannot accept parameters, and a view always returns a set of rows. Other kinds of stored procedures can perform action queries (insert, update, delete, etc), whereas views cannot perform these action queries. What this really means is that a view is kind of like a shorthand way of typing a predefined SELECT statement.

It offers the same advantages that we expect from other modular coding techniques. If we must repeat a SELECT statement in several places, it may make sense to create one view to represent all of these SELECT statements. This allows us to use pre-compiled query plans and update all instances of a SELECT statement from one place – the code that is used to create the view.

> *The* `EstablishDataStore` *method is responsible for creating the stored procedures and views in the data store.*

Take a minute or two to look over the remainder of the code in the `EstablishDataStore` method. Press *Ctrl + F* to bring up the Find dialog box in VB. Type in the word spErrCondObjectList and press the Find Next button. What you are trying to find here is the stored procedure that is used to select a list of *ErrCond* records. You will always be able to identify the stored procedures in this book by their prefix - sp. Keep searching until you find a line that looks something like the following:

```
strSQL = "CREATE PROCEDURE spErrCondObjectList " & _
```

We are not going to go over the syntax of this stored procedure here. I just wanted you to be able to locate the stored procedure within the code. Look at the code in this part of the routine and notice that the technique we use to create the stored procedure is exactly the same as the technique we use to create the tables. If you search for the word vErrCondObjectDelete you will locate another small section of code that is used to create a view in the data store. You will always be able to identify the views in this book by their prefix. I will always use the prefix v to identify a view.

Don't worry; we are going to go over the exact syntax for each and every type of stored procedure and view that you need to write in order to be able to build an Enterprise Caliber Data Object. But, rather than give you all of the stored procedures here, I will introduce you to them one at a time as the need arises.

The First Two Data-Handling Processes

As I said at the beginning of this chapter, we are going to cover two of the eight data handling processes that an Enterprise Caliber Data Object requires. Remember that we are designing a distributed processing system, so in order to write these processes we will have to code on several spheres.

The Load Process

The *Load* process provides the user interface programmer with a collection of objects that meet some specific selection criteria. In the case of the *ErrCond* object, we will return a collection of *ErrCond* objects that all originated from the same application. This process requires programming on all four tiers or as I prefer to call them spheres. In this chapter, we will take a close look at the programming we need to write for the User Centric sphere, the Data Centric sphere, and the Data sphere.

We'll touch briefly on some Presentation sphere programming, but our primary focus is to learn how all of the spheres work together to move information from the user to the data store and from the data store to the user. We covered the Visual Basic interface programming in the last chapter, and that is really all there is to the user interface portion of it. The main thrust of n-sphere application development is to move the majority of the logic (and the work) away from the Presentation sphere.

Perhaps the most confusing aspect of n-sphere development is the inter-sphere communication. In typical client/server applications, the user interface programmer just asks the database for some information and displays it onto the screen. With n-sphere development, this requires several steps. I want to avoid any confusion, so I am just going to write down each of the steps that we have to take for the *Load* process and point out where each step occurs before we begin. Refer to the diagram shown here as necessary:

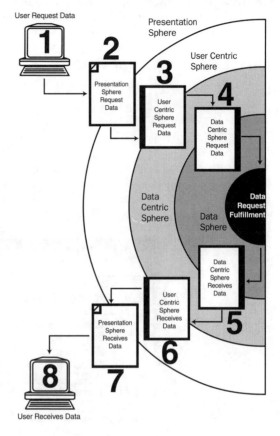

1. The User requests a set of data representing one or more objects from the data store.

2. The Presentation sphere accepts this request, instantiates a User Centric object, and passes the request to the UC object.

3. The UC object accepts the request from the Presentation sphere, instantiates a Data Centric object, and passes the request to the DC object.

4. The DC object accepts the request form the User Centric sphere, acquires a connection to the Data sphere and passes the request to the Data sphere where it is processed.

5. The Data sphere fulfills the request and passes the data to the DC object. The DC object releases the connection to the Data sphere and passes the data to the UC object.

6. The UC object accepts the data from the Data Centric sphere and destroys the DC object.

7. The Presentation sphere accepts the data from the User Centric sphere and destroys the UC object.

8. The User receives the data requested in Step 1.

Ideally, we'd walk through the above 8 steps and the code required, but that would involve jumping back and forth between the spheres. So instead I'm going to break down into the processing required for each sphere. We covered Steps 1, 2, 7 and 8 in the previous chapter so we need to start at Step 3.

The User Centric Object Code

The *Load* process in the User Centric object involves two main routines:

- ❑ The Load subroutine
- ❑ The Add function

Go to the Project Explorer window in the VB IDE. Select the UCErrCond project from the treeview and expand the project as shown in the image shown here. Drop down into the Class Modules folder and find the colErrConds file. Double-click on filename to bring this section of code into the VB edit window:

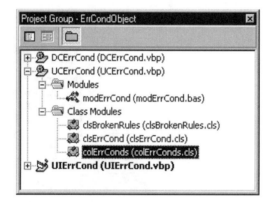

Select General from the left combo box in the edit window. Then click on the right combo box to display the list of general subroutines and functions. Scroll down the list until you find the Load subroutine.

The Load Subroutine

The first step we have to perform in the User Centric collection object's Load method is to dimension and instantiate a Data Centric object. This is done in the first two lines of code:

```
Public Sub Load(Optional strSelectStatement As String)

    Dim objData As DCErrCond.colErrCondData
    Set objData = CreateObject("DCErrCond.colErrCondData")
```

Now we need to declare the recordset that will be used to hold the collection of returned objects. This is why we needed a reference to the ADO Recordset Library in the User Centric object:

```
    Dim TheAnswer As ADOR.Recordset
```

Now I would like to direct your attention to the With block, as this is really where the work takes place:

```
    With objData

        .SetDataSource mstrConnect
        Set TheAnswer = .Fetch(strSelectStatement)
```

Remember from the last chapter that we always passed the name of a valid ODBC connection to the UC object before we invoked any method that made a call to the data store. We did this by using the `SetDataSource` method of the UC object. That method is used to stuff the name of the ODBC connection into the local storage variable `mstrConnect`. The first line of code in this `With` block uses exactly the same technique to pass that information to the DC object:

```
        .SetDataSource mstrConnect
```

The next line of code in the `With` block is used to call the `Fetch` method from the DC object, passing in any optional selection parameters:

```
        Set TheAnswer = .Fetch(strSelectStatement)
```

While we are still in the `With` block, we will move the information the Data Centric object sent to us into a local collection using the `Add` method. We're building a reusable object, so we are going to take the time, now, to be sure that we give it the ability to recover from any errors that may happen on any of the spheres. It works like this. If an error occurred in the Data or Data Centric spheres, the Data Centric object will pass us a recordset that contains a single record. That record will have a field called `DataMessage` that contains a message that indicates the cause of the problem. Because we know this, we onlly have to test for this condition when the number of records returned by the Data Centric object is one:

```
        If TheAnswer.RecordCount = 1 Then
          If Len(TheAnswer.Fields("DataMessage").Value) > 0 Then
            Err.Raise vbObjectError, "ErrCond Load", _
                      TheAnswer.Fields("DataMessage").Value
```

But, just because the recordset only contains a single record does not mean that an error occurred. It may be that there is only one object that meets the selection criterion. In that case, we add that one record to the collection as follows:

```
        Else
          With TheAnswer
            Add 0, !ID, !ApplicationID, !ErrorID, "", FixNulls(!EventTime), 2, _
                "", "", "", "",FixNulls(!SystemTier), _
                FixNulls(!ErrorDescription), FixNulls(!CodeModuleName), _
                FixNulls(!CodeBlockName), FixNulls(!ComputerID), _
                FixNulls(!UserID)
          End With
        End If
```

The next block of code is used to extract the information from the recordset the DC Object's `Fetch` method returned and add the values found in that recordset into the local collection:

```
        Else

            Do While Not TheAnswer.EOF

                With TheAnswer
                    Add 0, !ID, !ApplicationID, !ErrorID, "", FixNulls(!EventTime), 2, _
                        "", "", "", "",FixNulls(!SystemTier), _
                        FixNulls(!ErrorDescription), FixNulls(!CodeModuleName), _
                        FixNulls(!CodeBlockName), FixNulls(!ComputerID), _
                        FixNulls(!UserID)
                    .MoveNext
                End With

            Loop

        End If

    End With

    Set objData = Nothing
    Set TheAnswer = Nothing

End Sub
```

The Load routine contains two calls to the Add function so we'd better cover that before we move onto the next sphere.

The Add Function

The Add function is scoped as a Friend rather than as Public. This is because we use the Add function to help manage the parent-child relationship between the collection and the objects in the collection. Remember the emancipation discussion in the previous chapter? We used two methods of the User Centric object to handle the emancipation issues, the CheckInObject method and the CheckOutObject method:

```
Friend Function Add(lngStampID As Long, lngID As Long, _
        lngErrorID As Long, lngApplicationID As Long, _
        dtmStampDateTime As Variant, dtmEventTime As Variant, _
        intDataLocking As Integer, strStampUser As String, _
        strChangeAll As String, strStampAction As String, _
        strDataMessage As String, strErrorDescription As String, _
        strSystemTier As String, strModuleName As String, _
        strCodeBlockName As String, strUserIdentity As String, _
        strComputerName As String, Optional sKey as String) As _
        clsErrCond
```

The first thing we do in the Add function is to create a new clsErrCond object. Then we set the three flags of the object that allow it to be an un-emancipated member of the collection. The flags are set by invoking three Friend methods of the object - the EditObject method, the ObjectIsAChild method and the ObjectIsNew method:

```
' Create a new object
Dim objNewMember As clsErrCond
Set objNewMember = New clsErrCond
```

```
objNewMember.EditObject True
objNewMember.ObjectIsAChild True
objNewMember.ObjectIsNew False
```

Once the flags have been set, we update the properties of the new object with the values passed into the `Add` method as parameters:

```
' set the properties passed into the method
objNewMember.StampID = lngStampID
objNewMember.SaveStampID = lngStampID
objNewMember.ID = lngID
objNewMember.SaveID = lngID
objNewMember.ErrorID = lngErrorID
objNewMember.SaveErrorID = lngErrorID
objNewMember.ApplicationID = lngApplicationID
objNewMember.SaveApplicationID = lngApplicationID
objNewMember.StampDateTime = dtmStampDateTime
objNewMember.SaveStampDateTime = dtmStampDateTime
objNewMember.EventTime = dtmEventTime
objNewMember.SaveEventTime = dtmEventTime
objNewMember.DataLocking = intDataLocking
objNewMember.StampUser = strStampUser
objNewMember.SaveStampUser = strStampUser
objNewMember.ChangeAll = strChangeAll
objNewMember.SaveChangeAll = strChangeAll
objNewMember.StampAction = strStampAction
objNewMember.SaveStampAction = strStampAction
objNewMember.DataMessage = strDataMessage
objNewMember.ErrorDescription = strErrorDescription
objNewMember.SaveErrorDescription = strErrorDescription
objNewMember.SystemTier = strSystemTier
objNewMember.SaveSystemTier = strSystemTier
objNewMember.ModuleName = strModuleName
objNewMember.SaveModuleName = strModuleName
objNewMember.CodeBlockName = strCodeBlockName
objNewMember.SaveCodeBlockName = strCodeBlockName
objNewMember.UserIdentity = strUserIdentity
objNewMember.SaveUserIdentity = strUserIdentity
objNewMember.ComputerName = strComputerName
objNewMember.SaveComputerName = strComputerName
```

Notice that for almost every parameter passed into the method we actually set two object properties. The first one is the one we might expect to set; the second one prefixed with `Save` may not be familiar. Remember that Enterprise Caliber Data Objects are stateless. This means that while we are using an object, it is possible that it may become *stale*. In other words, someone may have changed the value in the database from what it was when we first loaded the object. We have to check for this possibility, so when we move the value from the data store into the corresponding property of an object, we store a copy of the original value that we received from the data store. We will not go into it here, but we will use this `Save` property to check the freshness of our object before we update the data store or delete an object from the data store.

Once all of the properties and the `Save` properties of the object have been set, we create an `Index` value and a `Key` for the object. Remember the `Key` value we used in the last chapter to locate objects in the listview control? This is where that value is created and maintained. The `Index` property is a transient value that can allow us to move to a particular object within a collection by using the `Previous` and `Next` methods:

```
    objNewMember.Index = mCol.Count + 1

    If Len(sKey) = 0 Then
        objNewMember.Key = "Key" & lngID
        objNewMember.EditObject False
        mCol.Add objNewMember
    Else
        objNewMember.Key = sKey
        objNewMember.EditObject False
        mCol.Add objNewMember, sKey
    End If
```

Finally, all we need to do is return the new object to the `Load` routine:

```
    'Return the object created
    Set Add = objNewMember
    Set objNewMember = Nothing

End Function
```

So, between the User Centric object's `Load` and `Add` function, we can retrieve information stored in the data store and present it to the user interface programmer as a simple collection of objects.

The Data Centric Object Code

As we saw in the UC object's code, all we need to do to return a recordset from the DC object is to make a single call to the Data Centric object's `Fetch` function.

But before we look at the data centric code we need to take a quick look at programming for MTS.

Coding For MTS

In our data centric routines you will see particular lines of code that allows our objects to make use of MTS's transactional abilities. I don't want to digress too far with a large MTS discussion so I'm just going to give you the basics on how to code for MTS.

> If you want to learn more then I suggest you read Professional MTS and MSMQ with VB and ASP also by Wrox Press.

Fortunately, coding for MTS is very easy and simply requires us to instantiate another object in our data centric routines. This object is the **Context object** that is provided by the MTS Type Library. The Context object basically hangs in the background behind our real object and manages our object's execution environment, including its transactions. To use this object we simply use a special method call provided by MTS called `GetObjectContext`. Once we have a reference to our object's context we can use methods exposed by the Context object to manage transactions. We are only really interested in two of these methods:

❑ `SetComplete` - Indicates that the transaction was successful and should be committed

❑ `SetAbort` - Indicated that there was a problem and that any changes should be rolled back

We'll see how and when to use these method calls in the code below.

Back to the Data Centric Object Code

This function use ADO to run a stored procedure in the database, which returns a recordset that includes the information we requested from the User Centric object. Once this recordset has been filled, the function releases its connection to the database. Do you remember the discussion we had on distributed processes and parallel processing. Notice that we are using those principles here. Even though the UC object still has a lot of work to do with the information we received from the database, the connection to the database and the DC object have both been freed up so that they can be recycled.

In the VB Project Explorer window expand the DCErrCond project and open the colErrCondData module in the VB Edit window:

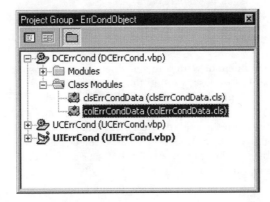

The Fetch Function

The Fetch function is the only portion of the *Load* process that actually touches the Data sphere. It can accept an optional, very generic, SELECT statement parameter that enables us to provide a customized solution without reprogramming the object. Even though we provide this flexibility as the default every time we create a new object, you will find that we probably don't use this parameter the way you might expect. Rather than typing customized SQL statements willy-nilly throughout an application, we actually use a special object to manage and deliver the customized SQL statements to the routines, like this one, that can make use of them. This object is called a Connector object which we will learn about in Chapter 13.

```
Public Function Fetch(Optional strSelectStatement) As ADODB.Recordset
```

The first few lines of code in the Fetch subroutine are used to dimension the local variables we will use in the subroutine, set the error-handling device and get a reference to the Context object:

```
Dim strSQL As String

Dim ctxObject As ObjectContext
Set ctxObject = GetObjectContext

On Error Goto FetchErrorOut
```

As you can see, all we needed to do to get a reference to the Context object was dimension a local variable as ObjectContext and then call GetObjectContext. Now we can use the ctxObject variable to handle our transactions under MTS.

Then we create the ADO Connection and Recordset objects that we will use to retrieve the information from the data store. The technique we use here is identical to the one we used in the EstablishDataStore method we looked at earlier in the chapter. Once the variables have been created, we call the Open method of the Connection object, passing it the name of an ODBC connection in the mstrConnect variable:

```
Dim ThisConnection As ADODB.Connection
Dim ThisRecordset As ADODB.Recordset

Set ThisConnection = New ADODB.Connection
Set ThisRecordset = New ADODB.Recordset

ThisConnection.Open mstrConnect, GetLogon(mstrConnect), _
    GetPassword(mstrConnect)
```

Once the connection has been opened, we test to see whether or not a special SQL statement has been passed into this routine. In this case, we find that we haven't passed one so we construct a simple SQL statement, which simply consists of the name of a stored procedure spErrCondObjectList. (We'll examine this stored procedure once we've been over the main code for this object.) Then we open the recordset by using the recordset's Open method. This method requires two parameters, the first tells SQL Server what to select, and the second tells the Recordset object which Connection object it should use. Also note that we've changed how we want to handle errors. We'll see why this is in a moment:

```
If Len(strSelectStatement) = 0 Then
    strSQL = "spComputerObjectList "
Else
    strSQL = strSelectStatement
End If

On Error Resume Next

ThisRecordset.Open strSQL, ThisConnection
```

In the last portion of the Fetch function, we check the ADO Connection object for errors. If we find any, then we build a special Recordset with a single field and stuff the description of that error into the field. Now you can see why we needed to change the way we handled errors. If we jumped into the error handler then we wouldn't be able to return the special recordset that indicates an error with the insert:

```
If ThisConnection.Errors.Count > 0 Then
    Set ThisRecordset = New ADODB.Recordset
    ThisRecordset.Fields.Append "DataMessage", adChar, 255
    ThisRecordset.AddNew
    ThisRecordset.Fields("DataMessage").Value = _
        ThisConnection.Errors(0).Description
    ThisRecordset.Update
    Set Fetch = ThisRecordset
    'Free up the object in MTS and set the Transaction Aborted flag
    ctxObject.SetAbort
```

If we didn't find any errors then our recordset is OK so we can just return it to the calling routine and call `SetComplete` to indicate the transaction was successful:

```
Else
    Set Fetch = ThisRecordset
    ' Free up the object in MTS and set the Transaction Completed flag
    ctxObject.SetComplete

End If
```

The last step we take before cleaning the house is to set the value of the `Fetch` function equal to the Recordset we received from SQL Server:

```
ThisConnection.Close

Set ThisRecordset = Nothing
Set ThisConnection = Nothing
Set ctxObject = Nothing

Exit Function

FetchErrorOut:

    ErrorHandler

End Function
```

Now we need to look at the stored procedure.

The Stored Procedure

The stored procedure `spErrCondObjectList` accepts a single parameter, an ApplicationID, and returns a list of errors that have been collected for the application.

Some Stored Procedure Basics

Stored procedures are created with the `CREATE PROCEDURE` command. This command takes a single argument, the name of the stored procedure that will be created:

```
CREATE PROCEDURE spErrCondObjectList
```

Stored procedures can accept parameters, which can be used within the stored procedure almost exactly the way variables are used in a Visual Basic subroutine. All parameters for a stored procedure are defined after the `CREATE` statement and before the `AS` keyword. Parameters must be prefaced with the @ symbol and must be followed by a valid SQL Server datatype. Of course, if multiple parameters are used, a comma must separate them:

```
@ApplicationID int, @ErrorID int
AS
```

Stored procedures can also create and use local variables. These variables, like parameters, can be used almost exactly the way variables are used in a Visual Basic subroutine. All local variables used in a stored procedure must be defined after the `AS` keyword.

According to tradition and sound programming practices we make it a practice to declare all variables immediately following the AS keyword at the start of the stored procedure. This is not an enforced limitation; we could declare variables anywhere within a stored procedure:

```
DECLARE @SomeNumber int
```

The only real difference in the treatment with variables used in stored procedures is the quirky technique we use to assign values to them. For an example: if we declared a variable named @SomeNumber and wanted to assign this variable the value 28 we would use the following statement:

```
DECLARE @SomeNumber int
SELECT   @SomeNumber = 28
```

And although it seems like it should work, the same SELECT statement that is used to assign a value to a variable cannot be made to do double-duty and return the value that was assigned. This requires a separate SELECT statement. In other words if we wanted to assign @SomeNumber the value 28 and return the value we stored in @SomeNumber, then we would have to write the following:

```
DECLARE @SomeNumber int
SELECT   @SomeNumber = 28
SELECT   @SomeNumber
```

There is a lot more to learn about stored procedures, but that is enough to get us through this section. We will revisit this topic many times throughout the remainder of this book.

The spErrCondObjectList Stored Procedure

Now may be a good time to take another look at the EstablishDataStore procedure in the clsErrCondData.cls file in the DCErrCond.vbp project. Locate and open the EstablishDataStore routine in the VB Edit Window. Scroll down or search for spErrCondObjectList. Notice that this subroutine assigns the entire stored procedure listed below to the strSQL variable. Remember that we can use the ADO Connection object's Execute method to build stored procedures in the same way we used it to build tables earlier.

Remember this three-step process:

1. Query the sysobjects table to determine whether or not the object already exists

2. If the object (table, view, stored procedure) does not exist, then write the SQL that is needed to create the object and (optionally) stuff that SQL into a variable

3. Run the ADO Connection object's Execute method passing the SQL as a parameter

Here is the complete listing of the spErrCondObjectList stored procedure. This stored procedure is really nothing more that an ordinary SELECT statement. I have not shown you the actual VB code, as it is a lot harder to read and consequently understand because of the lard amount of string concatenation going on:

```
CREATE PROCEDURE spErrCondObjectList

AS
```

```
SELECT ID,
       ApplicationID,
       SystemTier,
       ErrorID,
       ErrorDescription,
       CodeModuleName,
       CodeBlockName,
       ErrorTime,
       ComputerID,
       UserID,
       ConcurrencyID AS ConcurrencyID1

FROM   ErrCondObject

RETURN (0)

GO
```

The GO command is used to tell SQL Server to insert this stored procedure into the data store.

The Insert Process

The *Insert* process provides the user interface programmer with a method to insert new objects into the data store. Normally, we would expect this to require a typical user interface with screens and text boxes, but the *ErrCond* object is really designed to be used without user intervention. Rather it's designed to be called by the error handling routines of every enterprise application. Our primary focus here is to learn how all of the spheres work together to move information from the user to the data store and back. That means we can take it for granted that each of the properties that need to be filled have been filled via some type of user interface programming. Remember, one of the main thrust of n-sphere application development is to move the majority of the logic (and the work) away from the Presentation sphere.

The steps involved with the *Insert* process are very similar to that of the *Load* process:

1. The User supplies a set of data representing a new object that must be inserted into the data store.

2. The Presentation sphere accepts this information, instantiates a User Centric object, and passes the data to the UC object.

3. The UC object accepts the insertion command and data from the Presentation sphere, instantiates a data centric object, and passes the command and the data to the DC Object.

4. The DC object accepts the command and information from the User Centric sphere, acquires a connection to the Data sphere and executes the Insert stored procedure in the Data sphere.

5. The Data sphere inserts the data and confirms the insertion. Then it passes the confirmation data to the DC object. The DC object releases the connection to the Data sphere and passes the confirmation data to the UC object.

6. The UC object accepts the confirmation data from the Data Centric sphere and destroys the DC object.

7. The Presentation sphere accepts the confirmation data from the User Centric sphere and destroys the UC object

8. The User receives a confirmation of the insertion requested in Step 1 above.

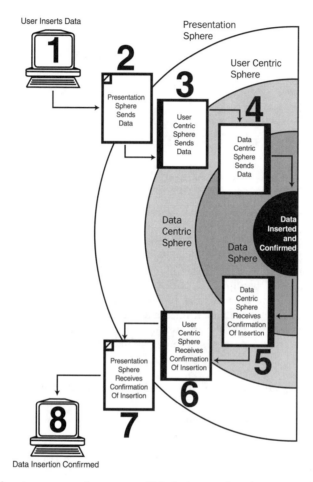

Now we know the steps we need to accomplish, let's see what the principal code looks like.

The User Centric Code

This time there is only the one main routine we need to consider - ObjectInsert.

Go to the Project Explorer window in the VB IDE. Select the UCErrCond project from the treeview and expand the project as shown in the image shown here. Drop down into the Class Modules folder and find the clsErrConds file.

Double-click on filename to bring this section of code into the VB edit window:

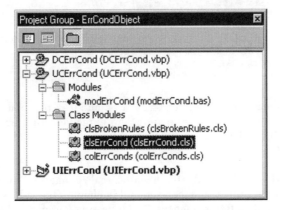

The User Centric ObjectInsert Subroutine

Search or scroll through the code until you find the ObjectInsert routine.

The user centric code first checks to ensure that the object is emancipated. If not, then an error is raised. The error we raise here is rarely, if ever, encountered. And when it is encountered it is really designed to serve as a forceful reminder to the user interface programmer that objects need to be emancipated before they can be changed. We raise the error here to ensure that there is no way for the user interface programmer to successfully execute the ObjectInsert method without first emancipating object by using the CheckOutObject method found in the colErrCond.cls file:

```
Public Sub ObjectInsert()

    If IsChild Then Err.Raise 445
```

Once we have done our bit to keep the UI team honest, we immediately instantiate the data centric mate to this object - the DCErrCond.clsErrorData object:

```
' Instantiate the remote object
Dim ThisDataObject As DCErrCond.clsErrCondData
Set ThisDataObject = CreateObject("DCErrCond.clsErrCondData")
```

Once the data object has been instantiated, we point it at a particular data store by passing it a connect string that points to a particular ODBC connection. Remember from the previous chapter, that we set this property each time we needed to access a data store. This allows us to utilize several different data stores for a single object – even from within a single application if necessary. After the object knows where to perform the action, we tell it to insert this object's data into the data store by calling the ObjectInsert method:

```
' Update the Data In the Remote Object
With ThisDataObject
    .SetDataSource mstrConnect
```

Once we have set the data source, we immediately tell the DC object to insert the information about this particular object into the data store:

```
        .ObjectInsert mlngStampID, mlngID, mlngErrorID, mlngApplicationID, _
                mdtmStampDateTime, mdtmEventTime, mintDataLocking, _
                mstrStampUser, mstrChangeAll, mstrStampAction, _
                mstrDataMessage, mstrErrorDescription, mstrSystemTier, _
                mstrModuleName, mstrCodeBlockName, mstrUserIdentity, _
                mstrComputerName
    End With
```

What we are doing here is circumventing the `Property Let` and `Get` procedures. It is fine to do this from within the object. We designed the `Lets` and `Gets` to manage information transfer with the world that exists outside the object. There is no reason to tolerate the overhead these functions impose from within the object itself.

We will go over the data centric details shortly, but for now, realize that the Data Centric object's `ObjectInsert` method is a subroutine that accepts, possibly changes the values in, and returns all of the parameters in its argument list. Remember the Bit on Passing Parameters? In this case we are passing the `mlngID` parameter, which has not yet been assigned a value. The Data Centric object's `ObjectInsert` method inserts a record into the database, determines the new ID the data store assigned the object, and fills the `mlngID` value with that new value. And, because the value we *Get* from the ID property is really the value stored in the `mlngID` storage variable, as soon as this single line has executed, the value of the ID property – and all of the others as well – is changed immediately.

After the data has been inserted into the data store, we test the `mstrDataMessage` variable to see whether the Data Centric or Data spheres have encountered any problems while inserting the object into the data store. If everything is alright, then the length of this variable will be zero. If the length of this variable is greater than zero, then we raise a trappable error and pass the error message we received in the `mstrDataMessage` variable onto the user interface programmer to handle:

```
If Len(Trim(mstrDataMessage)) > 0 Then
    'Some Data Centric Problem Has Occured
    'Inform user with mstrDataMessage
    Err.Raise vbObjectError + 1234, "ErrCond Insert", mstrDataMessage
```

If no error message is found, then we execute the code on the other leg of the `If` statement:

```
Else
    ' Reset the local object's Save State
    mlngSaveID = mlngID
    mlngSaveErrorID = mlngErrorID
    mlngSaveApplicationID = mlngApplicationID
    mdtmSaveEventTime = mdtmEventTime
    mstrSaveErrorDescription = mstrErrorDescription
    mstrSaveSystemTier = mstrSystemTier
    mstrSaveModuleName = mstrModuleName
    mstrSaveCodeBlockName = mstrCodeBlockName
    mstrSaveUserIdentity = mstrUserIdentity
    mstrSaveComputerName = mstrComputerName
    ObjectIsNew False
    ObjectIsDirty False
End If
```

```
      Set ThisDataObject = Nothing

   End Sub
```

What we are doing here is giving a second set of variables the exact values the data store returned when our object was inserted into the data store. We will use these values later to check the *freshness* of our object during the *Update* and *Delete* processes. Let's just call these guys with the word save in their names **Collision Test** variables and forget about them for now. We will cover them in the `ObjectDelete` process in the next chapter. The last two lines of code, before the `End If`, set a couple of the object's internal flags using the two Friend methods `ObjectIsNew` and `ObjectIsDirty`. These methods are used internally to manage the object's data handling operations.

> *If we want to develop professional data objects, we must encapsulate the setting of as many data handling flags as possible. I have seen too many instances where the object developer relies upon the user interface programmer to know about and set all of these flags. This is a poor practice at best.*

The Data Centric Code

In VB's Project Explorer window, select the **DCErrCond** project. The code for the DC object's `ObjectInsert` method is found in the `DCErrCond` project's `clsErrCondData.cls` file. This method carries out the Data Centric portion of the *Insert* Process.

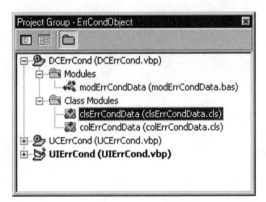

The Data Centric ObjectInsert Subroutine

The Data Centric `ObjectInsert` subroutine is the only portion of the *Insert* process that actually touches the Data sphere. The first thing programmers notice about this subroutine is the large number of parameters it requires. We could have passed a recordset, as in the *Load* process, but I've used parameters for speed. It maybe more of a pain to type but it's quicker in the long run. This subroutine expects a parameter for each property including those information-only properties like `StampUser`, which must contain the identity of the person who caused the record to be inserted into the data store:

```
   Public Sub ObjectInsert(lngStampID As Long, lngID As Long, lngErrorID As Long, _
                  lngApplicationID As Long, dtmStampDateTime As Variant, _
                  dtmEventTime As Variant, intDataLocking As Integer, _
```

```
                strStampUser As String, strChangeAll As String, _
                strStampAction As String, strDataMessage As String, _
                strErrorDescription As String, strSystemTier As String, _
                strModuleName As String, strCodeBlockName As String, _
                strUserIdentity As String, strComputerName As String)
```

The next few lines of code in this subroutine are just the declarations section and error handling:

```
Dim strSQL As String

Dim ctxObject As ObjectContext
Set ctxObject = GetObjectContext()

On Error Goto ObjectInsertError
```

We also instantiate the Context object again - we will do this in all our data centric code. You may notice that this transaction control is really unnecessary in this context because our well-designed stored procedure manages the transaction for this simple Insert procedure. This is true, but in other cases, where we are, say, storing related information in two or more databases, we *must* exercise transaction control at the Data Centric object level. We have standardized on using the transaction control on all Data Centric objects that change data. At the very least, this ensures that the object is recycled as quickly as possible.

Then we set up the usual ADO Connection and Recordset objects:

```
Dim ThisConnection As ADODB.Connection
Dim ThisRecordset As ADODB.Recordset

Set ThisConnection = New ADODB.Connection
Set ThisRecordset = New ADODB.Recordset

ThisConnection.Open mstrConnect, GetLogon(mstrConnect), GetPassword(mstrConnect)
```

Next, the SQL statement that calls the stored procedure (spErrCondObjectInsert) is prepared by constructing the command from the parameters passed into the subroutine. The jamQuote and jamComma words are just constants that have been set as a single quote and comma:

```
strSQL = "spErrCondObjectInsert " & _
        jamQuote & strStampUser & jamQuote & jamComma & _
        lngApplicationID & jamComma & _
        lngErrorID & jamComma & _
        jamQuote & strErrorDescription & jamQuote & jamComma & _
        jamQuote & strSourceModuleName & jamQuote & jamComma & _
        jamQuote & strSourceCodeBlockName & jamQuote & jamComma & _
        jamQuote & strUserIdentity & jamQuote & jamComma & _
        jamQuote & strComputerIdentity & jamQuote & jamComma & _
        jamQuote & dtmEventTime & jamQuote

On Error Resume Next

ThisRecordset.Open strSQL, ThisConnection
```

We could use the Parameters collection and its `Refresh` method available through ADO, but this involves an extra trip to the server and really doesn't offer us any benefit in this instance. We could also use the Parameters collection without using the `Refresh` method. But this really amounts to the same thing we have done here. We still need to type in each of the parameters and its name.

We will make use of the Parameters collection in the Data Warehouse object because the stored procedure parameters in the OLAP data store can change from day to day. In that case, the Parameters `Refresh` method is the most efficient technique we can use.

Notice that the technique we have used here opens a recordset rather than executing a query. It probably seems odd to invoke an action query by opening a recordset rather than using the `Execute` method from the Connection object, but remember that every stored procedure we use returns the data that exists in the database *after* the action is taken against the database. Because of this, the `Open` method is actually faster. It only involves a single trip to the data store and gives the information we need in an easy to manage Recordset object.

Once the `ThisRecordset.Open` method has been used, we check the Connection object to see if it ran into any system level errors. If it did, we can locate the primary cause of the error by looking at the value found in `ThisConnection.Errors(0).Description`. Just a reminder, the **zeroth** object in the Errors collection contains the actual cause of the error.

Many programmers mistakenly access the `Errors.Description` value, which unfortunately contains a message for the last event in a series of events that started with the initial error. Usually this `Description` contains the enlightening message "ODBC Error " or something equally useless.

Anyway, if a system level error has occurred, we take the description of the zero[th] error and pass it back to the User Centric object through our parameter list. Also note that we use `SetAbort` to cancel the transaction:

```
If ThisConnection.Errors.Count > 0 Then
    strDataMessage = ThisConnection.Errors(0).Description
' Roll back the transaction
    ctxObject.SetAbort
```

There is also another thing to consider here. Even if a system level error did not occur, we still may have encountered an error condition according to the data handling rules outlined in the stored procedure. We perform two more tests for those conditions in the second leg of the `If` block. The first is a simple test to determine whether or not our stored procedure ran to completion. If it did, then the `ThisRecordset.EOF` test will evaluate to False, because we will always have a single record. We test the name of the first field in that recordset. If it evaluates to `"ErrorCondition"` then we know that we have run across a logical error in the stored procedure. In that case we set the `strDataMessage` variable to contain the description of the error:

```
Else

    If Not ThisRecordset.EOF Then

        If ThisRecordset.Fields(0).name = "ErrorCondition" Then
            strDataMessage = ThisRecordset.Fields(0).Value
```

```
                  'Free up the object in MTS and set the Transaction Aborted flag
                  ctxObject.SetAbort

            Else
              ' This Resets the Starting Values with the current values in the UC
              'Object
              lngID = ThisRecordset.Fields("ID").Value
              lngApplicationID = ThisRecordset.Fields("ApplicationID").Value
              lngErrorID = ThisRecordset.Fields("ErrorID").Value
              dtmEventTime = ThisRecordset.Fields("EventTime").Value
              strDataMessage = ""
              strErrorDescription = _
                     FixNull(ThisRecordset.Fields("ErrorDescription").Value)
              strSourceModuleName = _
                     FixNull(ThisRecordset.Fields("SourceModuleName").Value)
              strSourceCodeBlockName = _
                     FixNull(ThisRecordset.Fields("SourceCodeBlockName").Value)
              strUserIdentity = FixNull(ThisRecordset.Fields("UserIdentity").Value)
              strComputerIdentity = _
                     FixNull(ThisRecordset.Fields("ComputerIdentity").Value)
              'Free up the object in MTS and set the Transaction Completed flag
              ctxObject.SetComplete
            End If

         Else
            strDataMessage = "Unable to Insert Record"
            'Free up the object in MTS and set the Transaction Aborted flag
            ctxObject.SetAbort

         End If

      End If
```

FixNull is just a simple function that converts null values into a zero length string to allow for an accurate comparison.

Of course if all went well and the record was inserted successfully, then we just stuff the values from the recordset into the corresponding parameter variables and pass them back as a confirmation to the User Centric object:

```
   ThisConnection.Close
   Set ThisConnection = Nothing
   Set ctxObject = Nothing

   Exit Sub

ObjectInsertError:

   ErrorHandler

End Sub
```

The Stored Procedure

As with the other Data Centric subroutines we have seen in this chapter, the `ObjectInsert` subroutine invokes a special stored procedure. That stored procedure accomplishes three things:

- ❑ It inserts a record into the database that represents the object's current state
- ❑ It inserts a record into the audit table that marks the insertion
- ❑ It returns a single record that represents the actual data as it currently exists in the data store

Once the stored procedure has executed, the Data Centric object packages that information for transport to the User Centric object.

Some More Stored Procedure Basics

In order to understand this stored procedure, we have to add a little more to our basic SQL toolbox. To many programmers, this stored procedure demonstrates six potentially new concepts:

- ❑ Accessing SQL Server global variables
- ❑ Conditional branching using an `IF` statement
- ❑ Managing transaction control at the stored procedure level
- ❑ Error handling at the stored procedure level
- ❑ Inserting data into one table as the result of a `SELECT` statement run against another table
- ❑ Getting the current time by using the `GetDate` function

The first few lines of code in this stored procedure are similar to the one we used earlier to retrieve a collection of objects from the data store. In this case, several parameters and variables are defined rather than a single parameter and variable. The first line following the declaration section sets the value of the `@ErrorNumber` variable to -1 using the same technique we covered earlier:

```
SELECT @ErrorNumber = -1
```

Then we test the SQL Server global variable `@@trancount`. Just a note, I don't think it is really correct to call this variable a global variable in the true sense of the word. Its scope is better described as a **connection level** variable. It's called a global variable because it's available throughout the entire scope of a single connection. This means that it isn't available to operations that are being carried out in another connection that is executing simultaneously.

This variable is incremented whenever SQL Server encounters another level of a nested transaction within the same connection. We store the current value of the `@@trancount` global variable in a locally defined integer variable, `@trncnt` at the start of the procedure. This ensures that the value we are testing is the same value that existed when we entered the stored procedure. Remember that `@@trancount` is something of a global variable and we don't need to take the chance that its value might be effected by other actions taken against the database. We use `@@trancount` like this: If the value of `@@trancount` was 0 when we entered the stored procedure, then we have not entered an existing transaction, so we start a new one, named T1, by issuing the `BEGIN TRANSACTION T1` command. If the `@@trancount` value is greater than 0 then this means that we have entered a *pre-existing* transaction, so we issue a `SAVE TRANSACTION T1` command. This has the effect of placing a **Savepoint** in the transaction. Once a Savepoint has been identified, we can fail to commit the part of the transaction that comes after the Savepoint while still allowing the process that issued the original `BEGIN TRANSLATION` to control its own affairs independent of what we do at the current level.

This practice allows the same stored procedure to be used with or without a controlling MTS transaction. If MTS starts a transaction the value of @@trancount will be at least 1, if not then the value of @@trancount may be 0. In either case, the stored procedure level transaction processing is handled the same way:

```
IF @trncnt = 0
    BEGIN TRANSACTION T1
ELSE
    SAVE TRANSACTION T1
```

Let's take this opportunity to find out a little about conditional branching within a stored procedure. In this case, we have used an IF...ELSE block. Notice the differences between SQL and Visual Basic? The Then and End If statements are not used. There is actually more to it than this, but we will go over branching again later.

The INSERT statement is used to insert the parameter values into the ErrCondObject table. It is exactly the same as any other INSERT statement except that most of the values in this stored procedure have been given by parameters. The INSERT statement is broken into two sections. The first identifies the fields that should be updated. The second section, the part that comes after the VALUES keyword, provides the data that should be inserted into each field defined in the first portion of the statement. The most important thing here is to be sure that the mapping between columns and the values that will be inserted into the columns is perfect. As a point of interest that will come in handy in the future, notice that we are using a literal to provide the initial value for the ConcurrencyID field:

```
INSERT ErrCondObject
    (
    ApplicationID,
    ErrorID,
    ErrorDescription,
    SourceModuleName,
    SourceCodeBlockName,
    UserIdentity,
    ComputerIdentity,
    EventTime,
    ConcurrencyID)
VALUES
    (
    @ApplicationID,
    @ErrorID,
    @ErrorDescription,
    @SourceModuleName,
    @SourceCodeBlockName,
    @UserIdentity,
    @ComputerIdentity,
    @EventTime,
    1)
```

The next section of code uses another IF statement, another global variable @@Error, and another branching device the GOTO statement. All we are doing here is checking to see whether our INSERT statement caused an error. If it did, then we will jump to the ErrorHandler. If it didn't then the @@Error variable will contain the value 0 and we will continue to execute the stored procedure:

```
IF @@Error <> 0 GOTO ErrorHandler
```

Next we determine the new value of the ID Field for the record we just inserted by checking another global variable @@Identity. This variable contains the last identity value, which is the new ID for our ErrorObject:

```
SELECT @ID = @@Identity
```

Once we have the new ID value for our object, we will place a record into the audit table that marks the insertion we just performed. To do this we will use the INSERT statement in combination with a SELECT statement. This has the effect of inserting the values we selected from one table into a second table. We also provide a timestamp by using the GetDate function provided by SQL Server and the literal value 'I' which we use to represent a record insertion:

```
INSERT ErrorObjectAudit
    (StampUser,
     StampDateTime,
     StampAction,
     StampID,
     ApplicationID,
     ErrorID,
     ErrorDescription,
     SourceModuleName,
     SourceCodeBlockName,
     UserIdentity,
     ComputerIdentity,
     EventTime)

SELECT @StampUser,
     GetDate() ,
     'I',
     ID,
     ApplicationID,
     ErrorID,
     ErrorDescription,
     SourceModuleName,
     SourceCodeBlockName,
     UserIdentity,
     ComputerIdentity,
     EventTime

FROM ErrorObject

WHERE ID = @ID
```

We perform the exact same error check again to ensure that the audit table insert was successful. If it was then we commit the transaction to its Savepoint, which may or may not be the entire transaction. Then we complete the procedure by re-selecting the values we just inserted into the data store. This may seem redundant, and it is, but we make a rule of always mirroring changed values back to the user. This provides real-time feedback and allows the user to immediately note any discrepancies between the values entered and the values stored.

The last portion of the stored procedure is an error handler designed to both ensure transaction integrity and to provide meaningful errors to the user interface programmer. This is accomplished by rolling back the transaction to the Savepoint using the ROLLBACK TRANSACTION command and selecting a descriptive message from the ErrorMessage table to return to the programmer:

```
ErrorHandler:
  ROLLBACK TRANSACTION T1
  SELECT    ErrorCondition
  FROM      ErrorMessage
  WHERE     ErrorNumber = @ErrorNumber
  RETURN  (100)
```

Now that we have covered some more basic SQL, the stored procedure below should not look too confusing. I have included it so that you could read it in its entirety. As long as we are still going over "new" SQL concepts, I will try to provide complete listings in addition to the detailed looks at the new concepts.

Remember that you can also find this code in the EstablishDataStore *procedure, but all of the delimiters, quote marks, and continuation characters required by that routine make it a lot harder to read.*

The spErrObjectInsert Stored Procedure

The forward slash followed by an asterisks, /*, denotes the beginning of a comment and an asterisks followed by a forward slash, */ ends the comment line:

```
CREATE PROCEDURE spErrCondObjectInsert
@StampUser varchar(10),
@ApplicationID int,
@ErrorID int,
@ErrorDescription varchar(255),
@SourceModuleName varchar(255),
@SourceCodeBlockName varchar(255),
@UserIdentity char(15),
@ComputerIdentity char(15),
@EventTime datetime

AS

DECLARE @trncnt int,
        @ErrorNumber int,
        @ID int

SELECT @ErrorNumber = -1

/* Save transaction count value */
SELECT @trncnt = @@trancount

/* issue begin or save transaction based on transaction count */
IF @trncnt = 0
   BEGIN TRANSACTION T1
ELSE
   SAVE TRANSACTION T1

/* Insert ErrCondObject record     */
INSERT ErrCondObject
     (
       ApplicationID,
       ErrorID,
       ErrorDescription,
```

```
            SourceModuleName,
            SourceCodeBlockName,
            UserIdentity,
            ComputerIdentity,
            EventTime,
            ConcurrencyID)
VALUES
            (
            @ApplicationID,
            @ErrorID,
            @ErrorDescription,
            @SourceModuleName,
            @SourceCodeBlockName,
            @UserIdentity,
            @ComputerIdentity,
            @EventTime,
            1)

IF @@Error <> 0 GOTO ErrorHandler

SELECT @ID = @@Identity

/* add audit record  */
INSERT ErrCondObjectAudit
            (StampUser,
            StampDateTime,
            StampAction,
            StampID,
            ApplicationID,
            ErrorID,
            ErrorDescription,
            SourceModuleName,
            SourceCodeBlockName,
            UserIdentity,
            ComputerIdentity,
            EventTime)

SELECT @StampUser,
            GetDate(),
            'I',
            ID,
            ApplicationID,
            ErrorID,
            ErrorDescription,
            SourceModuleName,
            SourceCodeBlockName,
            UserIdentity,
            ComputerIdentity,
            EventTime

FROM ErrCondObject

WHERE   ID = @ID

IF @@Error <> 0 GOTO ErrorHandler

/* commit transaction only if this proc issued begin */
IF @trncnt = 0
  COMMIT TRANSACTION T1
```

```
/* return inserted record for verification */
SELECT ID,
       ApplicationID,
       ErrorID,
       ErrorDescription,
       SourceModuleName,
       SourceCodeBlockName,
       UserIdentity,
       ComputerIdentity,
       EventTime,
       ConcurrencyID As ConcurrencyID1

FROM ErrCondObject

WHERE   ID = @ID

RETURN (0)

ErrorHandler:
    ROLLBACK TRANSACTION T1
    SELECT    ErrorCondition
    FROM      ErrorMessage
    WHERE     ErrorNumber = @ErrorNumber
    RETURN    (100)

GO
```

Summary

In this chapter we covered two of the eight data handling processes every Enterprise Caliber Data Object exposes:

- ❏ The *Load* process
- ❏ The *Insert* process

These two processes alone go a long way towards meeting our stated design objectives. But we did a lot more than learn two Data Handling Processes in this chapter. We developed a technique for defining Visual Basic projects on three spheres and combining those projects into a single group for ease of use. We covered some fairly complex SQL – including stored procedures, transaction handling, and conditional branching. We also learned how to design objects that can build and manage their own data stores by using a routine that we called the `EstablishDataStore` method.

As an exercise, let me suggest that you go back and try to create a portion of the Enterprise Application (EntApp) object we looked at in the last chapter. In that chapter, we worked with the object as though it were nothing more than a black box. Now that you understand a lot of the WHY behind the functionality, you should be able to work through at least a portion of the code required to deliver that functionality. I know we haven't covered everything you need to know just yet, but if you can apply the concepts from this chapter to the task of creating that object, you will own those concepts. You can find the sample code for the EntApp that contains the *Load* and *Insert* processes for the EntApp object in the `Additional Exercises` sub directory of this chapter's sample code.

In the next chapter we will take on the task of learning the remaining six of the eight data handling processes as we design and build the *Computer* object we need for our Enterprise Management System.

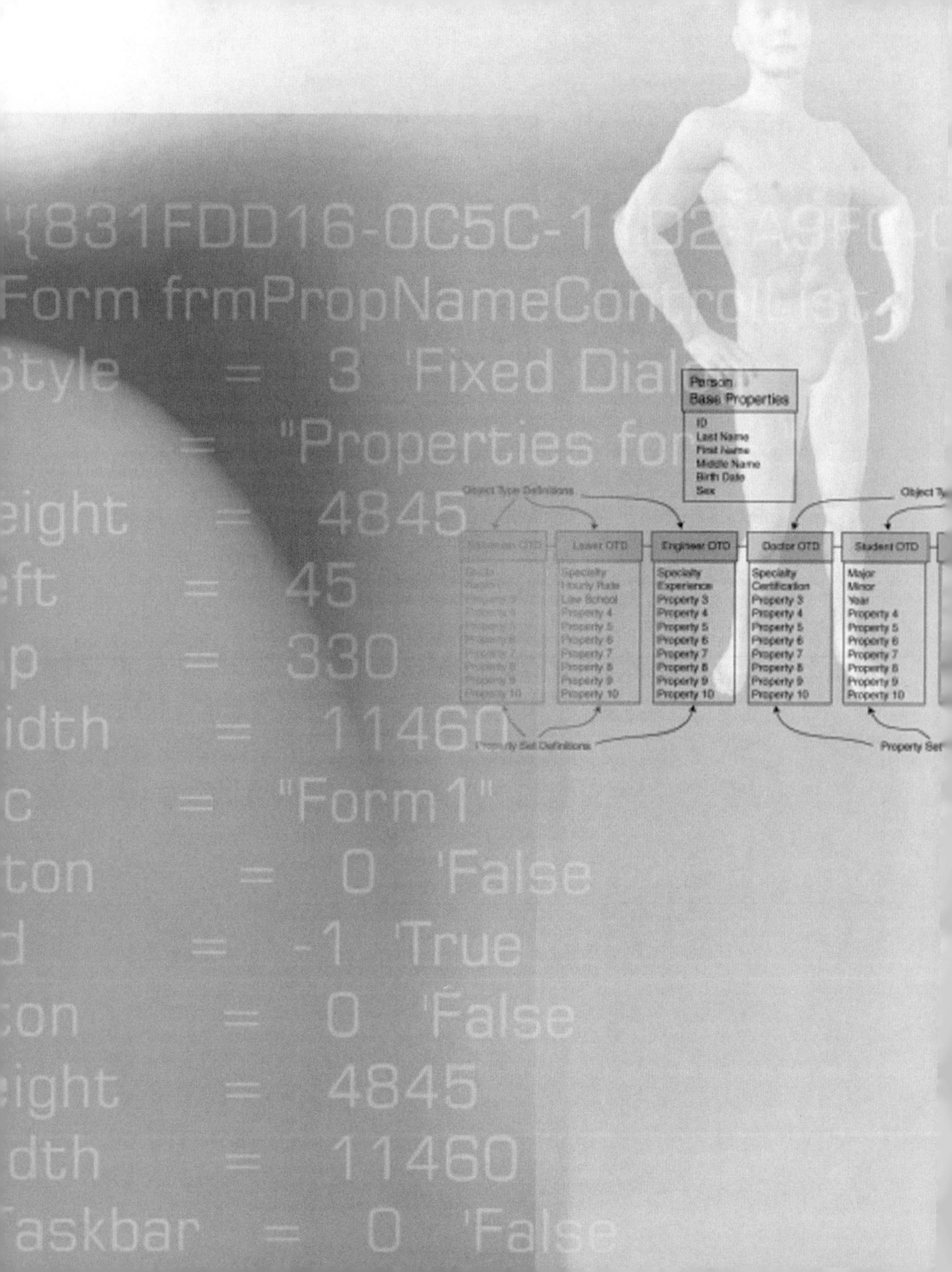

{831FDD16-0C5C-1
Form frmPropNameCon
Style = 3 'Fixed Dial
= "Properties fo
eight = 4845
eft = 45
p = 330
idth = 11460
c = "Form1"
ton = 0 'False
d = -1 'True
on = 0 'False
ight = 4845
dth = 11460
Taskbar = 0 'False
Person
Base Properties
ID
Last Name
First Name
Middle Name
Birth Date
Sex
Object Type Definitions
Lawyer OTD
Engineer OTD
Doctor OTD
Student OTD
Specialty
Hourly Rate
Law School
Specialty
Experience
Specialty
Certification
Major
Minor
Year
Property 3
Property 4
Property 5
Property 6
Property 7
Property 8
Property 9
Property 10
Property Set Definitions

7

The Computer Object

In the last chapter we began to build our first Enterprise Caliber Data Object, the *ErrCond* object. Over the course of that chapter, we spent some time talking about the four minor processing divisions or spheres in our system. We also went over the eight basic data handling processes that every ECDO exposes. These two topics, the spheres and the eight data handling processes, provide the foundation for everything else that we'll do in this book. No matter what data object we're building, no matter how simple or complex that object happens to be, it will rest upon that foundation.

Using the *ErrCond* object as a vehicle, we learned to write code for two of the eight basic data handling processes. We found out exactly what it means to write code that can actually be distributed and executed across several spheres. Now we'll tackle the remaining six data handling processes.

I guess that we could do this by adding the remaining six processes to the *ErrCond* object we started in the last chapter, but we are going to take a different tack. I need to show you that for the most part, these eight data handling processes are *always* the same. It really doesn't matter if we are working on an *ErrCond* object, a *Computer* object, or any other object you dream up. The essence, and in large part, the code that we need to write for the eight data handling processes stays the same.

Anybody can say this kind of stuff – "make reusable code", "don't reinvent the wheel", "blah, blah, blah", but we're not going to simply talk about it. We are going to do it. What that means, right now, is that we need to understand the eight data handling processes for themselves, without tying them to any one object. The best way I know to generalize knowledge is to apply it to as many different situations as possible. Thus in this chapter, we're going to use the *Computer* object to learn how to write the remaining six processes. When we are finished, you will be able to take the knowledge you have learned in this chapter and apply it directly to the *ErrCond* object without any help from me.

The Computer Object

The data object we will tackle in this chapter is a standard Level I ECDO called the **Computer object**. This object is important. It is a **reusable** data object. We'll use this very object again in another chapter when we learn how to make business objects with ECDOs using something I call a **veneer**. Once we encapsulate this data object with the veneer, the resulting business object will have some pretty amazing capabilities. It will be able to query the computer it exists on, learn about that computer, and store the information it found in the data store.

As a standard ECDO the Computer object exposes the eight data handling processes that we've been discussing. We've already learned how the *Load* and *Insert* processes function so we'll be focusing on learning to code the remaining six data handling processes:

- ❑ The *Fetch* process – Retrieves a single object from the data store
- ❑ The *Update* process – Changes the object's state in the data store
- ❑ The *Delete* process – Removes the object from the active data store
- ❑ The *Audit History* process – Retrieves the history of changes to an object over time
- ❑ The *Show Deleted* process – Retrieves a list of currently deleted objects
- ❑ The *Restore From Deleted* process – Restores an object to its state at the time it was deleted

In this chapter, we will only be concerned with giving the underlying data object the ability to manage its information in the data store and not its full functionality. It will need to store information like processor type, amount of physical memory, size of local disks, operating system, etc. In order to store this information, we are going to need two data tables.

The Data Tables

The *Computer* object, just like the *ErrCond* object, requires two tables:

ComputerObject	ComputerObjectAudit
ID	ID
Name	Name
OperatingSystem	OperatingSystem
ProcessorType	ProcessorType
TotalPhysMemory	TotalPhysMemory
AvailPhysMemory	AvailPhysMemory
TotalVirtualMemory	TotalVirtualMemory
AvailVirtualMemory	AvailVirtualMemory
DriveCSizeMeg	DriveCSizeMeg
DriveCSpaceMeg	DriveCSpaceMeg
ConcurrencyID	StampID
	StampAction
	StampDateTime
	StampUser

The base Object table is just a standard table designed to contain the objects' current state. Again we don't need to worry about creating the table manually as our *Computer* object will contatin all that functionality on our behalf. Here is the CREATE TABLE statement for that table from the `Computer` object's `EstablishDataStore` procedure:

```
CREATE TABLE dbo.ComputerObject
  (
  ID int Not Null Identity (1, 1),
  Name char(50) Not Null,
  OperatingSystem char(50) Not Null,
  ProcessorType char(50) Not Null,
  TotalPhysMemory decimal(18, 4) Not Null,
  AvailPhysMemory decimal(18, 4) Not Null,
  TotalVirtualMemory decimal(18, 4) Not Null,
  AvailVirtualMemory decimal(18, 4) Not Null,
  DriveCSizeMeg decimal(18, 4) Not Null,
  DriveCSpaceMeg decimal(18, 4) Not Null,
  ConcurrencyID int Not Null
  )
GO
```

The second table is the one that allows us to preserve temporal information; remember that it is called an Audit table. It contains data that, essentially, amounts to a series of snapshots taken over some period of time. Each snapshot represents the state of an object just prior to the change that caused the entry. Here is the CREATE TABLE SQL that you need to build the Audit Table:

```
CREATE TABLE dbo.ComputerObjectAudit
  (
  ID int Not Null Identity (1, 1),
  Name char(50) Not Null,
  OperatingSystem char(50) Not Null,
  ProcessorType char(50) Not Null,
  TotalPhysMemory decimal(18, 4) Not Null,
  AvailPhysMemory decimal(18, 4) Not Null,
  TotalVirtualMemory decimal(18, 4) Not Null,
  AvailVirtualMemory decimal(18, 4) Not Null,
  DriveCSizeMeg decimal(18, 4) Not Null,
  DriveCSpaceMeg decimal(18, 4) Not Null,
  StampID int Not Null,
  StampAction char(1) Not Null,
  StampDateTime datetime Not Null,
  StampUser char(15) Not Null
  )
GO
```

For the most part, the two tables have exactly the same fields. As you can see, every field in the base table, except the `ConcurrencyID` field is duplicated in the Audit table. As you should recall the `ConcurrencyID` field is used internally by the Data Centric object to manage data collisions. We will go over this when we look at the *Update* and *Delete* processes below.

The Visual Basic Projects

If you haven't taken the time to download the sample code for this object, I suggest that you do that now. You can find instructions on this in Appendix A.

When you get finished with this section, the Project Explorer in your VB IDE should look like the one here:

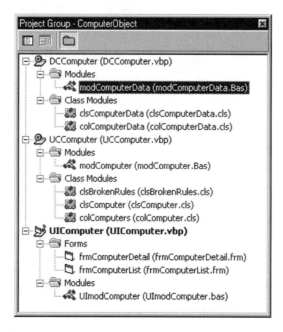

Follow the steps below to set up all three projects:

1. Create a new Standard EXE project in VB.

2. Rename the project to UIComputer. This project will be used to manage the user interface elements.

3. Add a new ActiveX DLL project to the project group.

4. Rename this project UCComputer. This project will form the User Centric object.

5. Add a second ActiveX DLL project to the project group.

6. Rename this project DCComputer. This project will form the Data Centric object.

7. Remove all of the default classes and forms from the projects.

8. Using the table below to find the files, and insert these modules into the relevant project.

System Sphere	Directory	Source File Name
Presentation (UIComputer.vbp)	\..\Ch07\UInterface	UImodComputer.bas
	\..\Ch07\UInterface	frmComputerDetail.frm
	\..\Ch07\UInterface	frmComputerList.frm

System Sphere	Directory	Source File Name
User Centric (UCComputer.vbp)	\..\Ch07\UCObject	modComputer.bas
	\..\Ch07\UCObject	clsBrokenRules.cls
	\..\Ch07\UCObject	clsComputer.cls
	\..\Ch07\UCObject	colComputer s.cls
Data Centric (DCComputer.vbp)	\..\Ch07\DCObject	modComputerData.bas
	\..\Ch07\DCObject	clsComputer Data.cls
	\..\Ch07\DCObject	colComputer Data.cls

9. Make sure that the UIComputer project is set as Start Up.

10. Save the project files.

11. Save the project group file. For consistency, I make it a habit to use the suffix Object for the group files. In this case, I would save the *Computer* group as ComputerObject.vbg.

Now we have the put the *Computer* object together, you will need to add the references to the projects. The instructions for doing this are essentially the same as last chapter. Refer to the section named "Creating References to DLLs and Projects" in the last chapter if you need a refresher.

The User Interface

The Visual Basic interface is a little subdued. Although the VB interface is completely functional and can, itself, be deployed as a viable thin client solution, we will be constructing a DHTML interface later in the book, which we'll consider our primary interface. It allows us to deploy applications immediately across the entire enterprise by dropping a file into the correct directory on the IIS machine.

Talk about savings... Anyway here are the Visual Basic forms sans the artistic flare that we could provide using a DHTML page:

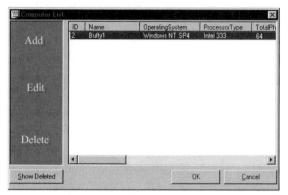
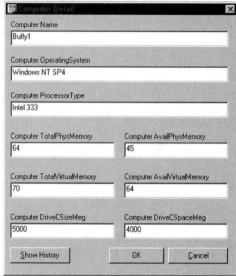

Both interfaces in this case are really intended only for the IT team to view. Remember that the *Computer* object exists on the host computer without a typical user interface. It's simply an ActiveX object that exposes its functionality to the programmer rather than to the end user directly.

We already went over the techniques you needed to create a VB interface for a Level I data object in Chapter 5, so I am not going to spend any time in this chapter going through that information again. I have provided you with a decent working interface in the sample code, so I suggest that you use that interface as it is and concentrate on the real challenge in this chapter – learning to code the remaining six data handling processes. The first process we will look at is the *Fetch* process.

The Fetch Process

The *Fetch* process is used to return a single object from the data store. As far as we are concerned in this section of the book, the *Fetch* process accepts the ID of the object as a parameter and returns the object with its state from the data store.

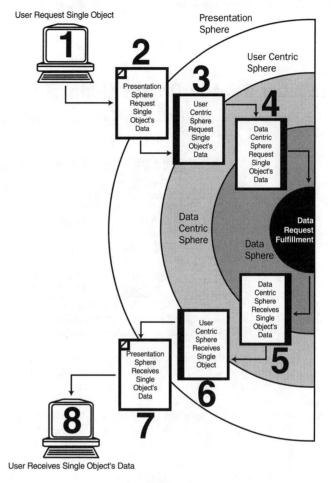

Again, coding this process requires work on all spheres of the object. Fortunately, for this process, and indeed all of the eight processes, the flow of data is practically identical. Witness the following diagram:

This diagram should be familiar from the previous chapter, and you're going to be even more familiar with it before this chapter is out. I'll go through the eight steps again to refresh your memory:

1. The User requests a set of data representing a particular object from the data store.

2. The Presentation sphere accepts this request, instantiates a User Centric object, and passed the request to the UC object.

3. The UC object accepts the request from the Presentation sphere, instantiates a Data Centric object, and passes the request to the DC object.

4. The DC object accepts the request from the User Centric sphere, acquires a connection to the Data sphere, and executes a stored procedure against data store.

5. The Data sphere fulfills the request and passes the object's data from data store to the DC object.

6. The DC object accepts the object's data from the Data Centric sphere, fills UC object's parameters with the object's data, and destroys the DC object.

7. The Presentation sphere accepts the object's data from the User Centric sphere and destroys the UC object.

8. User receives the object requested in Step 1.

The User Centric Object Code

The *Fetch* process in the User Centric object is contained in the `ObjectFetch` routine of the `clsComputer.cls` module:

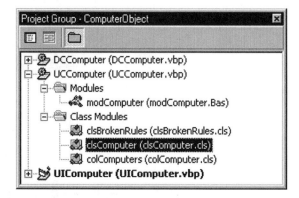

The main purpose of this method is to intercept the request for an object by the object's ID. To create its data centric counterpart and pass the request and ID on to the next sphere, and finally to receive the object's data back from its DC counterpart:

This method is really quite simple. First we instantiate the Data Centric object by using the `CreateObject` statement, and set the member variable `mlngID` (currently empty) to the ID passed in:

```
Public Sub ObjectFetch(lngID As Long)

    Dim ThisDataObject As DCComputer.clsComputerData
    Set ThisDataObject = CreateObject("DCComputer.clsComputerData")

    mlngID = lngID
```

Then we use a `With` block to perform two tasks. First, we point the Data Centric object at a particular data store by calling its `SetDataSource` method and passing our chosen data source name in the process. You should be starting to notice a similarity in the code. That's good. Remember that one of our goals was to write code that was easy to maintain:

```
With ThisDataObject
    .SetDataSource mstrConnect
```

Then we invoke the Data Centric object's `ObjectFetch` method passing the local storage variable for every property in the process.

I know that it is a little tough to type all of these parameters. I have seen people use User Defined Types and other techniques to pass the multiple parameters here. So far it has been my experience that while this works great on a single machine, from time to time it fails when we make the call across the network. I am not really sure why this happens. Anyway, I have opted for this technique that passes the parameters individually. It does require a little extra typing, but other than that this technique works great and as you might imagine it's about as fast as it can be.

Think about what we are doing. It's like we're handing the DC object a bunch of buckets and asking the DC object fill them with the data we need. The Data Centric object's `ObjectFetch` method will fill these variables with the object's state:

```
    .ObjectFetch mlngStampID, mlngID, mlngTypeID, mdtmStampDateTime, _
            mintDataLocking, mstrStampUser, mstrChangeAll, mstrStampAction, _
            mstrDataMessage, mstrName, mstrBriefDescription, _
            mstrOperatingSystem, mstrMemory, mstrDisk1Name, mstrDisk1Size, _
            mstrDisk1Space, mstrTypeName
End With
```

Notice that we are taking the same approach we took with the `ObjectInsert` in the last chapter. In other words we pass the local storage variables rather than use the properties. The reasoning is the same. The property handlers are designed to provide a controlled way to transfer information into an out of the object. We can really think of the communication that goes on between the UC and DC object as internal data transmission. That means that we can take a shortcut here. It may not seem like much, but if we can save a couple of lines of code from executing for each property every time we perform an `ObjectInsert` or `ObjectFetch`, that time will add up.

Next we check to see if any errors have occurred on the Data Centric sphere and if we find any we raise an error that the user interface programmer can trap. Think about what we are doing here. If we run into any problems in the Data or Data Centric spheres, we can use the technique below to send a message to the User Centric sphere. I have seen a lot of multi-tier books that recommended doing things like writing out error messages to the Data Centric or User Centric server. This is fine, but just because we are programming across several tiers doesn't mean that we can shirk our responsibilities. If something goes wrong, we have to do our part to handle the problem:

```
    If Len(Trim(mstrDataMessage)) > 0 Then
        'Some Data Centric Problem Has Occured
        Err.Raise vbObjectError + 1234, "Computer Fetch", mstrDataMessage
    Else
```

If no errors have occurred, we copy the new values we have received from the Data Centric object into our object's `Save` values. We touched on the concept of `Save` values lightly in the last chapter. They are used to give the users a way to recover from data collisions. I am going to ask you not to worry about them right now. We will really give this concept a thorough workout in a few pages when we take a look at the `ObjectDelete` and `ObjectUpdate` methods. Those are the only two places where collisions are actually possible. All the rest of the work we do with `Save` values is really just preparation for one of those two processes;

```
    ' Reset the local object's Save State
    mlngSaveStampID = mlngStampID
    mlngSaveID = mlngID
    mlngSaveTypeID = mlngTypeID
```

```
        msngSaveTotalPhysMemory = msngTotalPhysMemory
        msngSaveTotalPhysMemory = msngTotalPhysMemory
        msngSaveAvailPhysMemory = msngAvailPhysMemory
        msngSaveTotalVirtualMemory = msngTotalVirtualMemory
        msngSaveAvailVirtualMemory = msngAvailVirtualMemory
        msngSaveDriveCSizeMeg = mngDriveCSizeMeg
        msngSaveDriveCSpaceMeg = msngDriveCSpaceMeg
        mdtmSaveStampDateTime = mdtmStampDateTime
        mintSaveDataLocking = mintDataLocking
        mstrSaveChangeAll = mstrChangeAll
        mstrSaveStampAction = strStampAction
        mstrDataMessage = mstrDataMessage
        mstrSaveName = mstrName
        mstrSaveOperatingSystem = mstrOperatingSystem
        mstrSaveProcessorType = mstrProcessorType
        mstrSaveStampUser = mstrStampUser
```

Once you have synchronized the current and the Save values, we have one more small task that we need to do. We are going to set a couple of flags that tell us something about the object's condition. We handle this little problem from within the object. This allows us to be sure that the flags are being handled responsibly. In this case, we have just retrieved an existing object from the data store. That means we can set the following two flags as follows:

```
        ObjectIsNew False
        ObjectIsDirty False
    End If

    Set ThisDataObject = Nothing

End Sub
```

The Data Centric Object Code

As we saw with the user centric code above, the UC object passed the Fetch request onto the DC object's ObjectFetch method. The Data Centric ObjectFetch code is found in the clsComputerData.cls file in the DCComputer.vbp project:

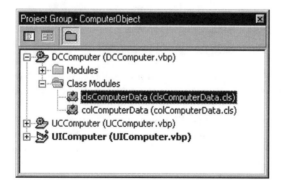

The main purpose of this method is to retrieve information from the Data sphere and transport that information into the parameters passed into the method from the User Centric object:

```
    Public Sub ObjectFetch(lngStampID As Long, lngID As Long, lngTypeID As Long, _
                           dtmStampDateTime As Variant, intDataLocking As Integer, _
                           strStampUser As String, strChangeAll As String, _
                           strStampAction As String, strDataMessage As String, _
                           strName As String, strBriefDescription As String, _
                           strOperatingSystem As String, strMemory As String, _
                           strDisk1Name As String, strDisk1Size As String, _
                           strDisk1Space As String, strTypeName As String)

    Dim strSQL As String

    Dim ctxObject As ObjectContext
    Set ctxObject = GetObjectContext()
```

Again, this portion of the process is quite simple. First we set the error handler. Then we create the
necessary ADO objects using the following statements exactly like we did in the previous chapter,
using the name of the ODBC connection in the `mstrConnect` variable:

```
    On Error GoTo ObjectFetchError

    Dim ThisConnection As ADODB.Connection
    Dim ThisRecordset As ADODB.Recordset

    Set ThisConnection = New ADODB.Connection
    Set ThisRecordset = New ADODB.Recordset

    ThisConnection.Open mstrConnect, GetLogon(mstrConnect), GetPassword(mstrConnect)
```

Next, we create a SQL statement by appending the ID value to the stored procedure
`spComputerObjectGet`:

```
    strSQL = "spComputerObjectGet " & lngID
```

We open the single record recordset by using the `Open` method of the Recordset object as follows:

```
    On Error Resume Next

    ThisRecordset.Open strSQL, ThisConnection
```

We test for an empty recordset and if one is found we send back a data message that lets the User
Centric object know that the requested object was not found in the data store. If the recordset is not
empty, that doesn't mean that everything is alright. We need to perform a test to see whether a Data
sphere error occurred. Just as we had a responsibility to pass an error from the Data Centric sphere to
the User centric sphere, we also have a responsibility to handle errors that occur within our stored
procedures whilst at the Data sphere. This means that we need a way to send a message from the
Data sphere to the Data Centric sphere.

If we trap a logical error in the stored procedure, the stored procedure handles this by sending back a
recordset with a single column. The name of that column is always the same, `ErrorCondition`.

We can think of this column as an error flag that the stored procedure manages for us. Thanks to this
flag, we can always know if the stored procedure ran into some kind of internal trouble. If we find
that this is the case, we can do our part in this chain of events across all spheres.

In other words, we send the User Centric object a message that something has gone awry. We stuff that message into the `mstrDataMessage` parameter that the User Centric object has passed into this routine.

If the name of the first column is not `ErrorCondition`, then the recordset will have a single record, and all we need to do is to move the values from that record into the parameter values the User Centric object has passed into the routine:

```
If Not ThisRecordset.EOF Then
    If ThisRecordset.Fields(0).Name = "ErrorCondition" Then
        mstrDataMessage = ThisRecordset.Fields(0).Value
        'Free up the object in MTS and set the Transaction Aborted flag
        ctxObject.SetAbort

    Else
        mlngID = ThisRecordset.Fields("ID").Value
        mstrName = ThisRecordset.Fields("Name").Value
```

And so on ...

```
        'Free up the object in MTS and set the Transaction Completed flag
        ctxObject.SetComplete

    End If
```

Of course, there is one other thing that could have happened. It is possible that we sent in an ID that does not exist in the data store. If that is the case, then we would end up on the other leg of the `If` statement. In this instance we still stuff a value into the `mstrDataMessage` parameter; but we let the User Centric object know that we didn't find the record the user requested:

```
Else
    mstrDataMessage = "Unable to find the Requested Object in the Data Store"
    'Free up the object in MTS and set the Transaction Aborted flag
    ctxObject.SetAbort
End If
```

You might be thinking that this happens quite a bit, but it really doesn't. We usually give the user some kind of a pick or select list prior to using the `ObjectFetch` process. That means two things:

❑ Unless someone has deleted the record since the pick list was filled, the record will be there

❑ This method is lightning fast because we always locate the target object by its ID – a long value stored in a clustered index field.

The only thing left to do in this subroutine is to provide an additional error handler for non-logical error conditions. For now I'll just put in the call to a routine called `ErrorHandler`. We'll cover the specifics of this routine later when we begin to pull the various parts of the Enterprise Management System together as it involves using the *ErrCond* object:

```
ThisConnection.Close
Set ThisConnection = Nothing
Set ctxObject = Nothing

Exit Sub
```

```
ObjectFetchError:

   ErrorHandler

End Sub
```

That's all there is too the data centric code, so now we need to move on an examine the stored procedure that we run in the Data sphere to return the object.

The Stored Procedure

The stored procedure used for the `ObjectFetch` process is one of the simplest we will see. It is really just a standard `Select` statement that accepts a single parameter. We went over SQL parameters in the last chapter, so I won't belabor the point here. This stored procedure code should be self-explanatory:

> *You can find this stored procedure, with all the others, in the `EstablishDataStore` method of the `colComputerData.cls` module.*

```
CREATE PROCEDURE spComputerObjectGet
/***************************************************************/
/* ComputerObject Get                                      */
/*                                                         */
/* This stored procedure returns one computer object       */
/***************************************************************/

@ID int

AS

SELECT ID,
       Name,
       OperatingSystem,
       ProcessorType,
       TotalPhysMemory,
       AvailPhysMemory,
       TotalVirtualMemory,
       AvailVirtualMemory,
       DriveCSizeMeg,
       DriveCSpaceMeg,
       ConcurrencyID As ConcurrencyID1

FROM   ComputerObject

WHERE  ID = @ID
```

The Delete Process

The primary objective of the *Delete* process is to remove an object's data from the database. But because this is an Enterprise Caliber Data Object, we have a second mandate that is to track changes to all objects and provide a technique for undoing any of those changes.

To accomplish this when we delete an object from the database, we are really just moving the object's data from the Object table to the Object Audit table. This process is almost the same as the technique we used previously to copy an inserted object's current state to the Audit table to mark the object's insertion. The most complex task in this process is the collision checking that must be performed.

Think about it. We are using stateless objects, so it's possible that an object we're attempting to delete has been changed since we loaded it into our local machine's memory. Perhaps we would no longer wish to delete the object if we knew what changes had taken place. This means that before we delete an object, we must select it from the database and compare the current values in the database with the original values that the object had when we loaded it into our local machine's memory. If any of those values are different, then we must inform the user of the changes and ask whether or not we should still delete the object. If the values are the same, then we can just go ahead and delete the object and write a record into the Audit table.

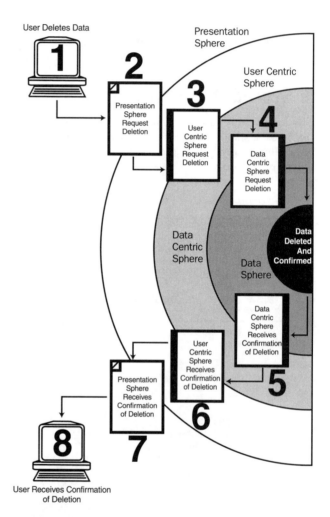

1. The User requests that an object be deleted. This requires that the user provide a list of the current values of the object that will be deleted.

2. The Presentation sphere accepts this information, instantiates a User Centric object, and passes the data to the UC object as parameters of the `ObjectDelete` method.

3. The UC object accepts the deletion command and data from the Presentation sphere, instantiates a Data Centric object, and passes the command and the object's current state to the DC object.

4. The DC object accepts the command and information from the User Centric sphere, acquires a connection to the Data sphere and calls the delete stored procedure on Data sphere where it is processed.

5. The Data sphere deletes the data and confirms the deletion. Then it passes the confirmation data to the DC object. The DC object releases the connection to the Data sphere and passes the confirmation data to the UC object.

6. The UC object accepts the confirmation of deletion from the Data Centric sphere and destroys the DC object.

7. The Presentation sphere accepts the deletion confirmation data from the User Centric sphere and destroys the UC object

8. The User Interface application receives a confirmation of the deletion requested in Step 1 above.

The User Centric Object Code

The User Centric `ObjectDelete` code is contained in the `clsComputer.cls` file in the `UCComputer.vbp` project:

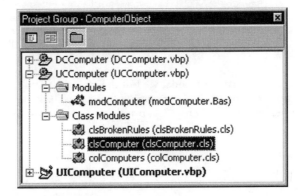

The purpose of this method is to update information from the data store, while ensuring that the data in the object has not become stale.

The VB code for the user centric `ObjectDelete` routine is quite simple. First, we perform a test to determine whether the object is emancipated. If it isn't emancipated, we raise an error directed at the user interface programmer. If the object is emancipated then we can continue with the subroutine:

```
Public Sub ObjectDelete()

    If IsChild Then Err.Raise 445
```

As you have come to expect, the next thing we do in the User Centric object is to instantiate the Data Centric object that we use to invoke the action against the data store:

```
Dim ThisDataObject As DCComputer.clsComputerData
Set ThisDataObject = CreateObject("DCComputer.clsComputerData")
```

Then we delete the object by instantiating the Data Centric object and calling its `ObjectDelete` subroutine, passing the parameters in the process. The most important thing to note here is that the parameter list includes the collision test variables we first met in the *Insert* process. Remember that they represent the exact state of the object at the time it was retrieved from the data store. This means that we can use them to test whether or not someone has changed the values in the data store since we retrieved this object. This gives us a chance to inform the user that the data has changed and offers the user an *informed* option of choosing not to delete the object:

```
'  Execute the Delete Method In the Remote Object
  With ThisDataObject
    .SetDataSource mstrConnect
    .ObjectDelete mlngStampID, mlngSaveStampID, mlngID, mlngSaveID, _
            msngTotalPhysMemory, msngSaveTotalPhysMemory, _
            msngAvailPhysMemory, msngSaveAvailPhysMemory, _
            msngTotalVirtualMemory, msngSaveTotalVirtualMemory, _
            msngAvailVirtualMemory, msngSaveAvailVirtualMemory, _
            msngDriveCSizeMeg, msngSaveDriveCSizeMeg, msngDriveCSpaceMeg, _
            msngSaveDriveCSpaceMeg, mdtmStampDateTime, _
            mdtmSaveStampDateTime, mintDataLocking, mstrChangeAll, _
            mstrSaveChangeAll, mstrStampAction, mstrSaveStampAction, _
            mstrDataMessage, mstrName, mstrSaveName, mstrOperatingSystem, _
            mstrSaveOperatingSystem, mstrProcessorType, _
            mstrSaveProcessorType, mstrStampUser, mstrSaveStampUser
  End With
```

Just as we did in the UC `ObjectInsert` code, we test the `mstrDataMessage` to determine whether the DC object ran into any trouble performing the task we asked it to do. If not, we don't really need to do anything here, but if there was a problem we need to something to inform the user about the error:

```
If Len(Trim(mstrDataMessage)) > 0 Then
    'Some Data Centric Problem Has Occured
    'Inform User with mstrDataMessage
    Err.Raise vbObjectError + 1234, "Computer ObjectDelete", mstrDataMessage

  End If

  Set ThisDataObject = Nothing

End Sub
```

When we inform the user, we need to handle the possibility that the object that we were trying to delete has not been deleted because it was changed by another user since we first got the object. It is also possible that the object we were trying to delete has already been deleted. Remember that we are working with a stateless system here. We will look at the techniques we can use to handle these possibilities when we look at the `ObjectUpdate` process shortly. For now, let's examine the work we have to do behind the scenes – in the Data Centric object – to prepare the User Centric object to be able to handle the data collision issues that arise when we are using a stateless system.

The Data Centric Object Code

The Data Centric `ObjectDelete` code is found in the `clsComputerData.cls` file in the `DCComputer.vbp` project:

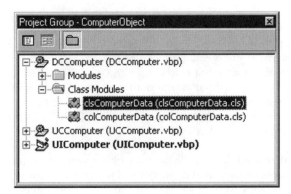

The purpose of this method is to update the data in the data store with changed information. It is also responsible for managing data collisions and ensuring that the updates are only performed on fresh data.

Surprisingly, `ObjectDelete` is a little more complex than the `ObjectInsert` method. This is because we want to perform field-level collision checking before we update or delete a record from the data store. What this means in real terms is this method requires two trips to SQL Server.

First, we retrieve the current values from the database for the object we wish to delete. Once we have those values, we compare them to the starting values we had when we first retrieved this object. Remember the collision test variables we sent to this method from the user centric code above. Those are the variables with the word `Save` in their names. We use these variables to check to see if the object we are about to delete has changed since we first had it delivered to our desk. From now on, we will say that a stateless object that has changed during the time we were working with is **stale**. If we determine that the object's data is stale then instead of deleting the object, we inform the user of the changes and ask for confirmation before we delete. If the object is not stale, then we just proceed with the deletion.

Confused, that's OK, this is really a little tricky. Maybe an example will help.

Say that we retrieve a simple object from the data store that has just two properties `ID` and `Message`. When we first get that object from the data store, we store a copy of the `Message` value in a second variable named `SaveMessage`. For the sake of argument, let's say that the after we have copied the value the phrase in both `Message` and `SaveMessage` reads "NO RAISES THIS YEAR".

The objects work as follows. The `SaveMessage` property always contains the original value that was stored in the `Message` property. So even if someone changes the data stored in the `Message` property, we always have access to the original value in the `SaveMessages` value. OK so far? Good.

Now imagine that we think that we want to delete this object. No Raises? Indeed! But what we don't know is that the CEO has changed the value of the `Message` field to "RAISES FOR EVERYONE".

We begin the *Delete* process by calling the User Centric object's `ObjectDelete` method. It passes the `ID`, `Message`, and `SaveMessage` values to the Data Centric object. The first thing the Data Centric object does it to retrieve the record that has the same `ID` number from the table. Then it stores the information it found in the `Message` field in the database into a variable called `CurrentMessage`.

The test for stale data just got very easy. If the values in `SaveMessage` and `CurrentMessage` are the same, then our object is not stale – we can say that it is **fresh**. We can delete it without worry because we are deleting exactly what the user thought he or she was deleting. But, if the values of `SaveMessage` and `CurrentMessage` do not match, then the data in our object is stale. Now instead of deleting the record, we must tell the user about the collision and give the user enough information to make an informed decision about whether or not to delete the record. In our example, maybe now that we know that the `Message` is "RAISES FOR EVERYONE" instead of "NO RAISES THIS YEAR" we may no longer wish to delete this record.

This is a little more complex than the typical collision tests I have seen in too many places – time stamping the records etc. That works fine for stateful systems where collisions are the exception rather than the norm, but in a stateless system we need to learn to expect collisions and provide the users with a graceful way to handle them. I bet that this is still pretty fuzzy. That is OK, we'll be going over this concept again in the section below and many more times throughout the book. Just keep it in mind; it will make sense in time.

The beginning of this routine is fairly familiar, but note that we've had to declared a few extra variable to handle the collisions:

```
Public Sub ObjectDelete(lngStampID As Long, lngSaveStampID As Long, lngID _
                As Long, lngSaveID As Long, sngTotalPhysMemory As Single, _
                sngSaveTotalPhysMemory As Single, sngAvailPhysMemory As _
                Single, sngSaveAvailPhysMemory As Single, _
                sngTotalVirtualMemory As Single, _
                sngSaveTotalVirtualMemory As Single, _
                sngAvailVirtualMemory As Single, _
                sngSaveAvailVirtualMemory As Single, sngDriveCSizeMeg As _
                Single, sngSaveDriveCSizeMeg As Single, _
                sngDriveCSpaceMeg As Single, sngSaveDriveCSpaceMeg As _
                Single, dtmStampDateTime As Variant, dtmSaveStampDateTime _
                As Variant, intDataLocking As Integer, strChangeAll As _
                String, strSaveChangeAll As String, strStampAction As _
                String, strSaveStampAction As String, strDataMessage As _
                String, strName As String, strSaveName As String, _
                strOperatingSystem As String, strSaveOperatingSystem As _
                String, strProcessorType As String, strSaveProcessorType _
                As String, strStampUser As String, strSaveStampUser As _
                String)

    Dim strSQL As String
    Dim lngConcurrencyID1 As Long
    Dim strCollision As String

    Dim ctxObject As ObjectContext
    Set ctxObject = GetObjectContext()

    On Error GoTo ObjectDeleteError
```

```
    Dim ThisConnection As ADODB.Connection
    Dim ThisRecordset As ADODB.Recordset

    Set ThisConnection = New ADODB.Connection
    Set ThisRecordset = New ADODB.Recordset

    ThisConnection.Open mstrConnect, GetLogon(mstrConnect), _
                    GetPassword(mstrConnect)

    On Error Resume Next
```

It's not until we get to the following line that things begin to get interesting:

```
' Select the Record to be deleted
```

In the Data Centric object's `ObjectDelete` code we use two stored procedures. The first is just a simple `SELECT` statement designed to return a single object given that Object's ID:

```
' Select the Record to be deleted
strSQL = "spComputerObjectGet " & lngID
ThisRecordset.Open strSQL, ThisConnection
```

Next, take the results from this stored procedure and populate some local variables with the current values from the database. Note the data locking test that is performed right after the record has been selected. Although we never do this, we can set the `DataLocking` property of an object to `0`, which will make it to skip the collision tests. The reason we never do this is that the only benefit we can expect from not performing the collision test is a slight decrease in execution time. And of course the only tables that don't require collision checking are the ones that are accessed so infrequently that the slight speed improvement is not worth taking the, even remote, chance that a collision might occur:

```
If DataLocking > 0 Then
  If Not ThisRecordset.EOF Then
    lngConcurrencyID1 = ThisRecordset.Fields("ConcurrencyID1").Value
    CurrentID = ThisRecordset.Fields("ID").Value
    CurrentTotalPhysMemory = ThisRecordset.Fields("TotalPhysMemory").Value
    CurrentAvailPhysMemory = ThisRecordset.Fields("AvailPhysMemory").Value
    CurrentTotalVirtualMemory = ThisRecordset.Fields("TotalVirtualMemory").Value
    CurrentAvailVirtualMemory = ThisRecordset.Fields("AvailVirtualMemory").Value
    CurrentDriveCSizeMeg = ThisRecordset.Fields("DriveCSizeMeg").Value
    CurrentDriveCSpaceMeg = ThisRecordset.Fields("DriveCSpaceMeg").Value
    CurrentName = FixNulls(ThisRecordset.Fields("Name").Value)
    CurrentOperatingSystem = _
              FixNulls(ThisRecordset.Fields("OperatingSystem").Value)
    CurrentProcessorType = FixNulls(ThisRecordset.Fields("ProcessorType").Value)
    ThisRecordset.Close

  Else
    strDataMessage = "The Requested Delete did not occur because the Record " _
                  & "was not found."
    'Free up the object in MTS and set the Transaction Aborted flag
    ctxObject.SetAbort
    ThisConnection.Close
    Set ThisConnection = Nothing
```

```
            Set ctxObject = Nothing
            Exit Sub

        End If

    End If
```

Once we have the current values from the data store in the local variables, we perform a field-by-field test to determine whether or not the data in our object is stale:

```
If NzNumber(CurrentTotalPhysMemory) <> NzNumber(sngSaveTotalPhysMemory) Then
    If Len(strCollision) > 0 Then
        strCollision = strCollision & "*" & TotalPhysMemory & "|" & _
                    CurrentTotalPhysMemory
    Else
        strCollision = TotalPhysMemory & "|" & CurrentTotalPhysMemory
    End If
End If
```

As you can see, the collision test is really quite straightforward. If the two variables are identical then we just skip this block of code. If they are not the same we either begin or continue building the strCollision value to return to the user.

At the end of this section of code, we just measure the length of the strCollision variable. If its length is zero, then no collisions have occurred. If its length is greater than 0 then that means that at least one collision has occurred:

```
If Len(strCollision) > 0 Then
```

There are three types of data locking available to Enterprise Caliber Data Objects. If we set the DataLocking property to zero then we do not perform any collision testing at all. This can be done, but is not recommended. The second level of data locking where the value of the DataLocking property is set to 1 gives us standard record locking capabilities. If any collisions have occurred, we fail the delete and send a message to the user informing the user that another person was using the target object.

```
If DataLocking = 1 Then ' DataLocking = 1 is similar to full record locking
                        ' with no recourse the user is not given detail info
                        ' about the collisions that occurred.
    strDataMessage = "Unable to Delete the object because it was being " & _
                    "edited by another user."
    'Free up the object in MTS and set the Transaction Aborted flag
    ctxObject.SetAbort
    ThisConnection.Close
    Set ThisConnection = Nothing
    Set ctxObject = Nothing
    Exit Sub
```

The third level of data locking, the default, performs a field-by-field comparison and allows the user the ability to recover from a collision gracefully:

```
      ElseIf DataLocking = 2 Then ' DataLocking = 2 Field by Field analysis the user
                                  '                    the user is given a blow by blow
                                  '                    account of the collision
          strDataMessage = "The Following Collisions have occured * " & —
                          strCollision
          'Free up the object in MTS and set the Transaction Aborted flag
          ctxObject.SetAbort
          ThisConnection.Close
          Set ThisConnection = Nothing
          Set ctxObject = Nothing
          Exit Sub
      Else
          strDataMessage = ""
      End If

   End If
```

If collision handling was used, in other words if the value of the object's DataLocking property is greater than zero, then we test the length of the strCollision variable. If it has a length of 0 then we run the second stored procedure, which creates an audit record in the audit table and deletes the target record from the object table.

But, if the field-by-field test determines that the data in the object is stale, the length of strCollision will be greater than zero, and we don't perform a delete. Instead, we pass the information about the changes via the strCollision variable to the user along with the current values. This allows the user to decide what action to take. If the user still wants to delete the record the user is armed with the new current values stored in the object's Save properties. This means the next time the delete is issued, it will work without re-confirmation from the user because the new Save value should match the new Current values unless someone has changed the data during that brief time. That unlikely possibility does exist but, in the rare instances that data is continuously changing in an object the user is trying to delete the user can continue to call the ObjectDelete process as many times as necessary to delete the object. Each time the ObjectDelete method will refresh the User Centric object's Save values with the most current information in the database.

This takes care of the macro case, but there is another thing to consider, the micro case. It is possible that during the instant we were performing the field-by-field test for collisions the data in the database has been changed. Without an additional safeguard, it is possible that we could delete a record that has been changed during the instant we were performing the item-by-item comparison. Granted, this may seem like programming for the improbable, but especially in an enterprise environment with thousands of users, it could happen. We take care of the micro case by using adding a single field to each Object table. We call it the ConcurrencyID field. It contains a SQL integer datatype. The technique is simple, when we originally enter the routine we select the object's values from the table. At this time we also select the value from the ConcurrencyID field:

```
      strSQL = "spComputerObjectDelete " & _
              jamQuote & strStampUser & jamQuote & jamComma & _
              lngID & jamComma & _
              lngConcurrencyID1
```

The data in our database record cannot be changed, under normal circumstances, without the ConcurrencyID also changing. This means that when we attempt to delete the record with the second stored procedure, we can pass the ConcurrencyID we received from the first stored procedure as a parameter. If the ConcurrencyID we pass into the stored procedure is not the same as the one currently in the table, we abort the deletion and force the user to reselect the object before deleting it. This programming handles micro case and makes the system all but bulletproof:

```
ThisRecordset.Open strSQL, ThisConnection

If ThisConnection.Errors.Count > 0 Then
    strDataMessage = ThisConnection.Errors(0).Description
    ' Roll Back the Transaction
    ctxObject.SetAbort

Else

    If ThisRecordset.Fields(0).name = "ErrorCondition" Then
        strDataMessage = ThisRecordset.Fields(0).Value
        'Free up the object in MTS and set the Transaction Aborted flag
        ctxObject.SetAbort
    Else
        strDataMessage = ""
        'Free up the object in MTS and set the Transaction Completed flag
        ctxObject.SetComplete
    End If

End If

ThisConnection.Close
Set ThisConnection = Nothing
Set ctxObject = Nothing

Exit Sub

ObjectDeleteError:

    ErrorHandler

End Sub
```

The Stored Procedure

The spComputerObjectDelete stored procedure takes 3 parameters, the identity of the person requesting to delete, the ID of the record that is targeted for deletion, and the object's most recent ConcurrencyID value. This stored procedure is almost identical to the ObjectInsert stored procedure. It uses the same transaction handling and error handling techniques. The most important thing to note here is that we add the audit record first, before we have deleted the record from the object table. This makes sense of course. If we deleted the record before we inserted the audit record, we wouldn't be able to select the information from the object table for insertion into the audit table. We would have had to select the information into local variable and then insert the values in the variables into the audit table. This is a round about approach at best, and because both actions are executed within a single transaction, the order we choose to perform the transactions doesn't really matter.

```
CREATE PROCEDURE spComputerObjectDelete
/**********************************************************/
/* ComputerObject Delete                                  */
/*                                                        */
/* Add any additional comments here                       */
/**********************************************************/

@StampUser varchar(10),
@ID int,
@ConcurrencyID1 int

AS

DECLARE @trncnt int,
        @ErrorNumber int,
        @rows int,
        @err int,
        @ConcurrencyID int

SELECT  @ErrorNumber = -1
SELECT  @ConcurrencyID = @ConcurrencyID1

/* save transaction count value */
SELECT @trncnt = @@trancount

/* issue begin or save transaction based on transaction count */
IF @trncnt = 0
   BEGIN TRANSACTION T1
ELSE
   SAVE TRANSACTION T1

/* add audit record prior to deleting  */
INSERT ComputerObjectAudit
      (StampUser,
       StampDateTime,
       StampAction,
       StampID,
       Name,
       OperatingSystem,
       ProcessorType,
       TotalPhysMemory,
       AvailPhysMemory,
       TotalVirtualMemory,
       AvailVirtualMemory,
       DriveCSizeMeg,
       DriveCSpaceMeg)
```

```
SELECT @StampUser,
       GetDate() ,
       'D',
       ID,
       Name,
       OperatingSystem,
       ProcessorType,
       TotalPhysMemory,
       AvailPhysMemory,
       TotalVirtualMemory,
       AvailVirtualMemory,
       DriveCSizeMeg,
       DriveCSpaceMeg

FROM ComputerObject

WHERE  ID = @ID

IF @@Error <> 0 GOTO ErrorHandler

/* delete ComputerObject  */
DELETE ComputerObject

WHERE  ID = @ID AND
       ConcurrencyID = @ConcurrencyID

SELECT @err = @@error, @rows = @@RowCount
IF @err <> 0 GOTO ErrorHandler
IF @rows = 0
   /* concurrency error */
   BEGIN
      SELECT @ErrorNumber = 100
      GOTO ErrorHandler
   END

/* commit transaction only if this proc issued begin */
IF @trncnt = 0
   COMMIT TRANSACTION T1

/* return count of number of deleted rows */
SELECT 'RowCount' = @rows

RETURN (0)

ErrorHandler:
   ROLLBACK TRANSACTION T1
   SELECT   ErrorCondition
   FROM     Common..ErrorMessage
   WHERE    ErrorNumber = @ErrorNumber
   RETURN   (100)

GO
```

The Update Process

The *Update* process allows the user to change an object's data in the data store. It is also responsible for inserting a record into the audit table to mark the changes caused by the update.

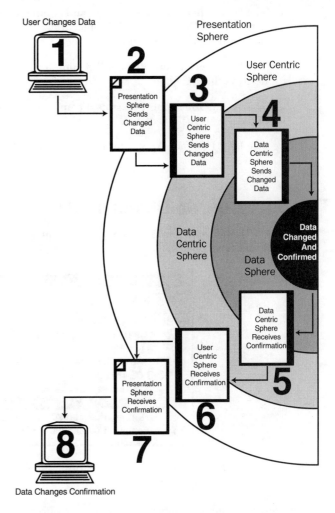

1. The User requests that an object be updated. This requires that the user provide the new set of data for the object.

2. The Presentation sphere accepts this information, instantiates a User Centric object, and passes the data to the UC object.

3. The UC object accepts the data from the Presentation sphere, instantiates a Data Centric object, and passes the data to the DC object.

4. The DC object accepts the command and information from the User Centric sphere, acquires a connection to the Data sphere and calls the Update stored procedure on Data sphere where it is processed.

5. The Data sphere updates the data and confirms the deletion. Then it passes the confirmation data to the DC object. The DC object releases the connection to the Data sphere and passes the confirmation data to the UC object.

6. The UC object accepts the confirmation of the update from the Data Centric sphere and destroys the DC object.

7. The Presentation sphere accepts the update confirmation data from the User Centric sphere and destroys the UC object.

8. The User Interface Application receives a confirmation of the update requested in Step 1 above.

The User Centric Object Code

The User Centric `ObjectUpdate` code is contained in the `clsComputer.cls` file in the `UCComputer.vbp` project:

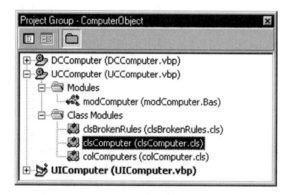

The purpose of this method is to update information from the data store, while ensuring that the data in the object has not become stale.

Considering all the work this method does, it is surprising there is not more code, but that is all there is to it. The first thing we do is check for emancipation and then instantiate a Data Centric object by using the `CreateObject` line:

```
Public Sub ObjectUpdate()

    If IsChild Then Err.Raise 445

    Dim ThisDataObject As DCComputer.clsComputerData
    Set ThisDataObject = CreateObject("DCComputer.clsComputerData")
```

Then as before we perform two tasks in the `With` block. First, we point the Data Centric object at a particular data store by evoking its `SetDataSource` method:

```
    With ThisDataObject
        .SetDataSource mstrConnect
```

Then we call the `ObjectUpdate` method of the Data Centric object passing both the object's original and changed values in the process:

```
    .ObjectUpdate mlngStampID, mlngSaveStampID, mlngID, mlngSaveID, _
            mdtmStampDateTime, mdtmSaveStampDateTime, _
            mintDataLocking, mstrStampUser, mstrSaveStampUser, _
            mstrChangeAll,  mstrSaveChangeAll, mstrStampAction, _
            mstrSaveStampAction, mstrDataMessage, mstrName, mstrSaveName, _
            mstrBriefDescription, mstrSaveBriefDescription, _
            mstrOperatingSystem, mstrSaveOperatingSystem, mstrMemory, _
            mstrSaveMemory, mstrDisk1Name, mstrSaveDisk1Name, mstrDisk1Size, _
            mstrSaveDisk1Size, mstrDisk1Space, mstrSaveDisk1Space, _
            mstrTypeName, mstrSaveTypeName
End With
```

The Data Centric object then does the dirty work of comparing the save values with the current values in the data store. All we have to do here is to test for errors or other collision messages:

```
If Len(Trim(mstrDataMessage)) > 0 Then
    'Some Data Centric Problem Has Occured
    If InStr(mstrDataMessage, "The Following Collisions have occured *") > 0 Then
        CollisionMessages = ParseCollisions(Trim(mstrDataMessage))
        Err.Raise vbObjectError + 1111, "Computer Update",_
                "Data Collisions at the field level have occured "
    Else
        ' An Data Error Other than a collision has occured.
        Err.Raise vbObjectError + 1234, "Computer Update", mstrDataMessage
    End If
```

The first thing we check is the length of the data message the Data Centric object has worked with. If it is greater than zero, then something has happened. Our task at that point is to check to see whether the problem stemmed from a collision message or some other error. We test this by looking for the message header `"The Following Collisions have occurred *"`. If we find this header, then we know at least one pair of field values has collided, and we translate the message for the user interface programmer by calling the `ParseCollisions` function. This function fills the `CollisionMessages` collection with details about each collision. If the problem given in the Data Message does not stem from a data collision then we just raise an error for the user interface programmer to trap.

If, on the other hand, the length of the data message was 0 then that means that the update completed correctly, so we just reset the object's `IsDirty` and `IsNew` properties:

```
    Else
        ' Reset the local object's State
        ObjectIsDirty False
        ObjectIsNew False
    End If

    Set ThisDataObject = Nothing

End Sub
```

We went over the concept of stale data before, but let's review it here. We are using stateless objects. The crux of the problem is that while we are working with an object, someone else may be changing the object's data in the data store without our knowledge.

This means that we need a way to test to see whether or not the data in the data store is exactly the same as it was when we first received the object. We accomplish this by storing a duplicate value of each property when we first receive an object in a second property we call a `Save` property. We allow the user to change the value in the exposed property, but we do not give the user access to the `Save` properties. This means that when the time comes to update an object's state in the data store we have access to a copy of the original values in the data store at the time we first received the object.

When we perform an update, we send both the new values we want to place in the database and the original or `Save` values. This allows the Data Centric object to perform field level tests on the data to ensure that it is not stale.

The Data Centric Object Code

Like with the *Fetch* process we just covered, the user centric `ObjectUpdate` method calls a direct data centric equivalent. This data centric `ObjectUpdate` code is found in the `clsComputerData.cls` file in the `DCComputer.vbp` project:

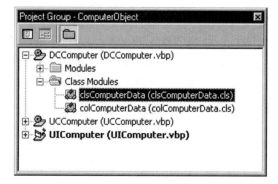

The purpose of this method is to update the data in the data store with changed information. It is also responsible for managing data collisions and ensuring that the updates are only performed on fresh data.

I have to warn you ahead of time that this is a long one. Let's break it down into bite-size pieces:

```
Public Sub ObjectUpdate(lngStampID As Long, lngSaveStampID As Long, _
                lngID As Long, lngSaveID As Long, _
                dtmStampDateTime As Variant, _
                dtmSaveStampDateTime As Variant, _
                intDataLocking As Integer, strStampUser As String, _
                strSaveStampUser As String, strChangeAll As String, _
                strSaveChangeAll As String, strStampAction As String, _
                strSaveStampAction As String, strDataMessage As String, _
                strName As String, strSaveName As String, _
                strBriefDescription As String, _
                strSaveBriefDescription As String, _
                strOperatingSystem As String, _
                strSaveOperatingSystem As String, strMemory As String, _
                strSaveMemory As String, strDisk1Name As String, _
                strSaveDisk1Name As String, strDisk1Size As String, _
                strSaveDisk1Size As String, strDisk1Space As String, _
```

```
                    strSaveDisk1Space As String, strTypeName As String, _
                    strSaveTypeName As String)

     Dim strSQL As String
  Dim lngConcurrencyID1 As Long

     Dim ctxObject As ObjectContext
     Set ctxObject = GetObjectContext()

     On Error Goto ObjectUpdateError
```

First we create an error handler and some ADO objects; we have seen this several times before:

```
     Dim ThisConnection As ADODB.Connection
     Dim ThisRecordset As ADODB.Recordset

     Set ThisConnection = New ADODB.Connection
     Set ThisRecordset = New ADODB.Recordset

     Dim strCollision As String
     strCollision = ""

     ThisConnection.Open mstrConnect

     On Error Resume Next
```

After we have instantiated the tools we need, we check the object's `DataLocking` property. We used this property earlier in the chapter in the `ObjectDelete` method, but let's go over it again just in case:

Data locking can be set to:

- ❑ Indicates no data collision handling – update without checking current values
- ❑ Indicates record-level collision handling – fail update if the record has changed
- ❑ Indicates field-level collision handling – perform a field-by-field test and allow graceful recovery without re-entering any data at the user interface.

If `DataLocking` is greater than zero, then we execute the same stored procedure we used in the `ObjectFetch` process to determine the current values in the data store. If the call returns an object, then we store those values in the Data Centric object's variables set aside for this purpose. If it does not return an object, we build a data message and roll back the transaction using the `ctxObject.SetAbort` method exactly like we did in the `ObjectDelete` process:

```
     If DataLocking > 0 Then
       'Select the record to update using the fetch stored procedure
       strSQL = "spComputerObjectGet " & lngID
       ThisRecordset.Open strSQL, ThisConnection

       If Not ThisRecordset.EOF Then
         lngConcurrencyID1 = ThisRecordset.Fields("ConcurrencyID1").Value
         CurrentID = ThisRecordset.Fields("ID").Value
```

And so on ...

```
      Else
         strDataMessage = "Unable to find the record to update in the datastore"
         'Free up the object in MTS and set the Transaction Aborted flag
         ctxObject.SetAbort
         ThisConnection.Close
         Set ThisConnection = Nothing
         Set ctxObject = Nothing
         Exit Sub
      End If
```

Assuming the object was found, the Data Centric properties with the prefix `Current` now contain the same data that is currently stored in the database. We perform a field-by-field test on these values comparing them to the `Save` parameters that the User Centric object passed into this method. The code for this is simple, but long. I will describe a single example, but you must repeat the process for any field that could potentially be stale. The code is as follows:

```
   If NzString(CurrentName) <> NzString(strSaveName) Then
      If Len(strCollision) > 0 Then
         strCollision = strCollision & "*" & Name & "|" & CurrentName
      Else
         strCollision = Name & "|" & CurrentName
      End If
   End If
```

All we are doing here is comparing the current values in the database with the original values sent to the User Centric object. If the values are the same, nothing is done, if they are different, then we build a string that contains the name of the property and the current value in the database.

At the end of this potentially long section of code, we check the length of the `strCollision` variable. If any collisions have occurred, then the length of the string will be greater than zero. If no collisions have occurred, then the length of the string will be equal to zero.

If any collisions have occurred, then we test the `DataLocking` property value again. If it is set to 1 - record locking, then we just roll back the transaction and send a simple message to the User Centric object using the `DataMessage` property. If it is set to 2 – field-level collision handling, then we create the header the User Centric object is expecting, append the collision string, and roll back the current transaction:

```
   If Len(strCollision) > 0 Then

      If DataLocking = 1 Then
         strDataMessage = "Unable to save changes, the record was being " & _
                     "edited by another user."
         'Free up the object in MTS and set the Transaction Aborted flag
         ctxObject.SetAbort
         ThisConnection.Close
         Set ThisConnection = Nothing
         Set ctxObject = Nothing
         Exit Sub
      ElseIf DataLocking = 2 Then
         strDataMessage = "The Following Collisions have occurred * " & _
                     strCollision
         'Free up the object in MTS and set the Transaction Aborted flag
         ctxObject.SetAbort
```

```
        ThisConnection.Close
        Set ThisConnection = Nothing
        Set ctxObject = Nothing
        Exit Sub
    Else
        strDataMessage = ""
    End If

End If
```

If we are still in the method, then that means that no collisions have occurred and it is OK to perform the update. We do this by executing the `spComputerObjectUpdate` stored procedure with the following code:

```
strSQL = "spComputerObjectUpdate " & _
        jamQuote & strStampUser & jamQuote & jamComma & _
        lngID & jamComma & _
        jamQuote & strName & jamQuote & jamComma & _
        jamQuote & strBriefDescription & jamQuote & jamComma & _
        jamQuote & strOperatingSystem & jamQuote & jamComma & _
        jamQuote & strMemory & jamQuote & jamComma & _
        jamQuote & strDisk1Name & jamQuote & jamComma & _
        jamQuote & strDisk1Size & jamQuote & jamComma & _
        jamQuote & strDisk1Space & jamQuote & jamComma & _
        lngTypeID & jamComma & _
        lngConcurrencyID1

ThisRecordset.Open strSQL, ThisConnection
```

You should remember the `lngConcurrencyID` from the `ObjectDelete` method, but let's review its purpose anyway. We got the current `ConcurrencyID` from the database at the start of this procedure when we executed the `spComputerObjectGet` stored procedure. This field is incremented every time someone changes the record in the database. That fact allows us to test whether or not someone has changed the data during the infinitesimal fraction of time it takes to perform the field-by-field comparison. If someone had updated the same record we were updating and their update completed during our comparisons, the value in the `ConcurrencyID` field would be different than the value we are passing into the update stored procedure. The stored procedure uses the `ConcurrencyID` as the final tiebreaker. If the value we pass into the stored procedure is not the same as the value currently in the database, the update fails.

This may border on the ridiculous, but remember that we are delivering an *enterprise*. This system must be capable of handling thousands of users. Data collisions *will* occur – even during the infinitesimal fraction of time it takes to perform the field-by-field comparison – Enterprise Caliber Data Objects must be capable of handling any collision without failure.

Of course we have to check for errors. If we find any in the Connection object, then we simply send them to the User Centric object via the `DataMessage` property, roll back the transaction, and close the connection. Remember, we also need to check the return value from the stored procedure to see if the stored procedure raised any errors of its own. If it did, then we will find that message in the first field of the recordset – `ErrorCondition`.

If no errors are found, then we simply reset the values passed into the method to the current values in the data store. This must include the Save values, or else next time the user attempts an update, collisions will seem to have occurred:

```
If ThisConnection.Errors.Count > 0 Then
    strDataMessage = ThisConnection.Errors(0).Description
    ' Roll back the transaction
    ctxObject.SetAbort
Else
    If ThisRecordset.Fields(0).Name = "ErrorCondition" Then
        strDataMessage = ThisRecordset.Fields(0).Value
        'Free up the object in MTS and set the Transaction Aborted flag
        ctxObject.SetAbort
    Else
        ' This Resets the Starting Values with the current values in the Database
        lngID = ThisRecordset.Fields("ID").Value
        lngSaveID = lngID
        lngTypeID = ThisRecordset.Fields("TypeID").Value
        lngSaveTypeID = lngTypeID
```

And so on ...

```
        'Free up the object in MTS and set the Transaction Completed flag
        ctxObject.SetComplete

    End If
End If

Set ThisConnection = Nothing
Set ThisConnection = Nothing
Set ctxObject = Nothing

Exit Sub

ObjectUpdateError:

    ErrorHandler

End Sub
```

The Stored Procedure

This process actually uses two stored procedures. It uses the spComputerObjectGet and it uses the following update stored spComputerObjectUpdate procedure: This may be the most complex stored procedure in this section of the book, but it is not too had to understand if we break it down into smaller chunks. First we define the parameters and variables that we need in the stored procedure. We went over this in great detail in the previous chapter, so I won 't bore you with it again here:

```
CREATE PROCEDURE spComputerObjectUpdate
/**********************************************************/
/* ComputerObject Update                                  */
/**********************************************************/

@StampUser varchar(10),
@ID int,
@Name char (50),
```

```
@OperatingSystem char (50),
@ProcessorType char (50),
@TotalPhysMemory decimal,
@AvailPhysMemory decimal,
@TotalVirtualMemory decimal,
@AvailVirtualMemory decimal,
@DriveCSizeMeg decimal,
@DriveCSpaceMeg decimal,
@ConcurrencyID1 int

AS

DECLARE @trncnt int,
        @ErrorNumber int,
        @rows int,
        @ConcurrencyID int,
        @err int
```

Then we set up the transaction and error handling using the same technique we used in the last chapter:

```
SELECT @ErrorNumber = -1
SELECT @ConcurrencyID = @ConcurrencyID1

/* save transaction count value */
SELECT @trncnt = @@trancount

/* issue begin or save transaction based on transaction count */
IF @trncnt = 0
   BEGIN TRANSACTION T1
ELSE
   SAVE TRANSACTION T1
```

Once the preliminaries are out of the way, we insert a record into the audit table that contains the current (pre-update) values in the database. We have seen this technique before:

```
/* add audit record prior to updating */
INSERT ComputerObjectAudit
     (StampUser,
      StampDateTime,
      StampAction,
      StampID,
      Name,
      OperatingSystem,
      ProcessorType,
      TotalPhysMemory,
      AvailPhysMemory,
      TotalVirtualMemory,
      AvailVirtualMemory,
      DriveCSizeMeg,
      DriveCSpaceMeg)

SELECT @StampUser,
       GetDate() ,
       'U',
       ID,
       Name,
```

```
            OperatingSystem,
            ProcessorType,
            TotalPhysMemory,
            AvailPhysMemory,
            TotalVirtualMemory,
            AvailVirtualMemory,
            DriveCSizeMeg,
            DriveCSpaceMeg

    FROM ComputerObject

    WHERE  ID = @ID

    IF @@Error <> 0 GOTO ErrorHandler
```

Next we update the values in the `ComputerObject` table using another standard SQL call. The only thing you might find unusual here is the technique used to update the `ConcurrencyID field`. It is really quite simple:

```
ConcurrencyID = ConcurrencyID +1
```

Also notice that we are using the `@ConcurrencyID` parameter as part of the `WHERE` clause. This ensures that the update will only occur if the `@ConcurrencyID` value is identical to the current `ConcurrencyID` value.

```
/* update ComputerObject type record */
UPDATE ComputerObject

SET
        Name = @Name,
        OperatingSystem = @OperatingSystem,
        ProcessorType = @ProcessorType,
        TotalPhysMemory = @TotalPhysMemory,
        AvailPhysMemory = @AvailPhysMemory,
        TotalVirtualMemory = @TotalVirtualMemory,
        AvailVirtualMemory = @AvailVirtualMemory,
        DriveCSizeMeg = @DriveCSizeMeg,
        DriveCSpaceMeg = @DriveCSpaceMeg,
        ConcurrencyID = ConcurrencyID +1

WHERE ID = @ID AND
        ConcurrencyID = @ConcurrencyID
```

The last section of code handles errors and reflects to the User Centric object the actual values currently in the data store at the end of the *Update* process. This may seem like overkill, but we make it a rule that Enterprise Caliber Data Objects always reflect back to the user the actual values entered into the database. It is kind of like psychology class – remember the reflection exercise – I heard you say... Well we do the same thing with the database. We take this extra step to give the user immediate feedback, which should allow them to reconcile any inconsistencies at once:

```
SELECT @err = @@error, @rows = @@RowCount
IF @err <> 0 GOTO ErrorHandler
IF @rows = 0
   /* concurrency error */
   BEGIN
```

```
        SELECT @ErrorNumber = 100
        GOTO ErrorHandler
    END

/* commit transaction only if this proc issued begin */
IF @trncnt = 0
    COMMIT TRANSACTION T1

/* return updated record for verification */
SELECT ID,
        Name,
        OperatingSystem,
        ProcessorType,
        TotalPhysMemory,
        AvailPhysMemory,
        TotalVirtualMemory,
        AvailVirtualMemory,
        DriveCSizeMeg,
        DriveCSpaceMeg,
        ConcurrencyID As ConcurrencyID1

FROM ComputerObject

WHERE  ID = @ID

RETURN (0)

ErrorHandler:
    ROLLBACK TRANSACTION T1
    SELECT   ErrorCondition
    FROM     Common..ErrorMessage
    WHERE    ErrorNumber = @ErrorNumber
    RETURN   (100)

GO
```

The Show Deleted Process

The next process we need to tackle in this chapter is the *Show Deleted* process. You will be comfortable with the VB programming right away. It is virtually identical to the *Load* process we covered in the last chapter. Both deliver a collection of objects that meet some selection criteria to the user. In this case the selection criteria just happens to be that all of the objects delivered must currently be deleted. The real difference between the two processes lives at the data store. First, we select these objects from the Object Audit table instead of the Object table, and second we use a **view**, or **virtual table** to help us to select the correct collection of objects. If you are thinking that we really don't need another method, you are right! We could have accomplished exactly the same thing by using the existing `Load` method. I chose to expose this process as a separate method because I felt that it would make it easier to understand.

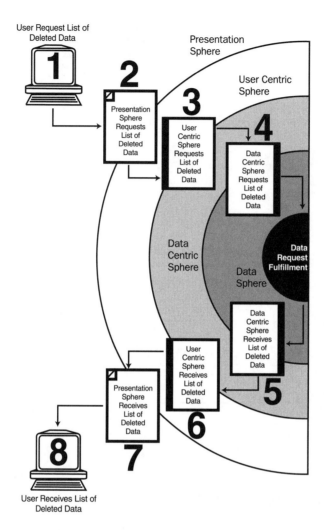

1. The User requests data representing one or more deleted objects from the data store.

2. The Presentation sphere accepts this request, instantiates a User Centric object, and passes the request to the UC object.

3. The UC object accepts the request from the Presentation sphere, instantiates a Data Centric object, and passes the request to the DC object.

4. The DC object accepts the request form the User Centric sphere, acquires a connection to the Data sphere and passes the request to the Data sphere where it is processed.

5. The Data sphere fulfills the request and passes the list of deleted objects to the DC object. The DC object releases the connection to the Data sphere and passes the data to the UC object.

6. The UC object accepts the list of deleted objects from the Data Centric sphere and destroys the DC object.

7. The Presentation sphere accepts the list of deleted objects from the User Centric sphere and destroys the UC object.

8. The User receives the list of deleted objects requested in Step 1 above.

The User Centric Object Code

The User Centric `ShowDeleted` code is contained in the `colComputer.cls` file in the `UCComputer.vbp` project:

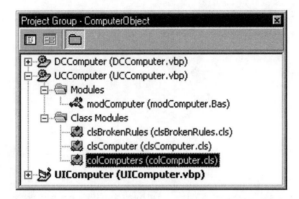

The purpose of this method is to return a list of currently deleted objects to the user. As this code is basically identical to the *Load* process I'm just going to give the complete listing with the key lines highlighted. You can refer back to the discussion in Chapter 6 if you want to refresh what's going on:

```
Public Sub ShowDeleted(Optional strSelectStatement As String)

    Dim objData As DCComputer.colComputerData
    Set objData = CreateObject("DCComputer.colComputerData")
    Dim TheAnswer As ADODB.Recordset

    On Error GoTo ShowDeletedError

    With objData
      .SetDataSource mstrConnect
      Set TheAnswer = .FetchDeleted(strSelectStatement)

    If TheAnswer.RecordCount = 1 Then

      If Len(TheAnswer.Fields("DataMessage").Value) > 0 Then
        Err.Raise vbObjectError, "Computer", TheAnswer.Fields("DataMessage").Value
      Else
        With TheAnswer

          Add !StampID, !ID, !TotalPhysMemory, !AvailPhysMemory, _
              !TotalVirtualMemory, !AvailVirtualMemory, !DriveCSizeMeg, _
              !DriveCSpaceMeg, FixNulls(!StampDateTime), 2, "", _
              FixNulls(!StampAction), "", FixNulls(!Name), _
              FixNulls(!OperatingSystem), FixNulls(!ProcessorType), _
              FixNulls(!StampUser)

        End With
```

header note

```
        End If

    Else

      Do While Not TheAnswer.EOF
         With TheAnswer
            Add !StampID, !ID, !TotalPhysMemory, !AvailPhysMemory, _
                !TotalVirtualMemory, !AvailVirtualMemory, !DriveCSizeMeg, _
                !DriveCSpaceMeg, FixNulls(!StampDateTime), 2, "", _
                FixNulls(!StampAction), "", FixNulls(!Name), _
                FixNulls(!OperatingSystem), _
                FixNulls(!ProcessorType), FixNulls(!StampUser)
            .MoveNext
         End With
      Loop

    End If

  End With

  Set TheAnswer = Nothing
  Set objData = Nothing

End Sub
```

As you can no doubt see, we call `FetchDeleted` rather than `Fetch` but we are using the same Add routine as before (of course the exact parameters we pass for the *Computer* object are different from those in the *ErrCond* object but the rest is the same).

The Data Centric Object Code

Although the `ShowDeleted` and `Load` methods we're almost identical they both call a version of the Fetch method, but in this case it's `FetchDeleted`. The Data Centric `FetchDeleted` code is found in the `colComputerData.cls` file in the `DCComputer.vbp` project:

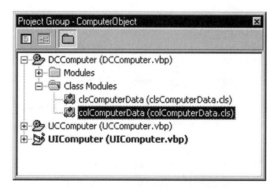

The purpose of this method is to deliver a list of deleted objects to the User Centric object:

```
Public Function FetchDeleted(Optional strSelectStatement As String) As Recordset

  Dim strSQL As String
```

```
Dim ctxObject As ObjectContext
Set ctxObject = GetObjectContext

On Error Goto FetchDeletedError
```

After we have considered the error handler we create the necessary ADO objects; we have seen this several times before:

```
Dim ThisConnection As ADODB.Connection
Dim ThisRecordset As ADODB.Recordset

Set ThisConnection = New ADODB.Connection
Set ThisRecordset = New ADODB.Recordset

ThisConnection.Open mstrConnect, GetLogon(mstrConnect), GetPassword(mstrConnect)
```

The first thing we need to do here is to determine what selection criterion to use. One of the possibilities is that we have been given a SQL command from another object (we'll cover this in Chapter 13). So, although it may not make too much sense right now, we check to see if there is an overriding SQL command that we should be using. If not, then we proceed to select the records using the default SQL command that invokes the spComputerObjectAuditDeletes that is paired with this process, and open the recordset:

```
If Len(strSelectStatement) = 0 Then
    strSQL = "spComputerObjectAuditDeletes "
Else
    strSQL = strSelectStatement
End If

On Error Resume Next

ThisRecordset.Open strSQL, ThisConnection
```

Then our first task is to check the ThisConnection object for errors as shown. If we find any, then we create a new recordset with a single field called DataMessage. Then we take the error message from the connection object and stuff it into the field as shown:

```
If ThisConnection.Errors.Count > 0 Then
    Set ThisRecordset = New ADODB.Recordset
    ThisRecordset.Fields.Append "DataMessage", adChar, 255
    ThisRecordset.Open
    ThisRecordset.AddNew
    ThisRecordset.Fields(0).Value = ThisConnection.Errors(0).Description
    ThisRecordset.Update
    'Free up the object in MTS and set the Transaction Aborted flag
    ctxObject.SetAbort
    Set FetchDeleted = ThisRecordset
Else
    'Free up the object in MTS and set the Transaction Completed flag
    ctxObject.SetComplete
    Set FetchDeleted = ThisRecordset
End If
```

Notice no matter what happened, we will have a recordset – either the one that was returned from the Data sphere or one that we just created above. We set the value of this function equal to that recordset:

```
Set FetchDeleted = ThisRecordset
```

As always, we finish up the routine by performing the necessary housekeeping chores:

```
    ThisConnection.Close
    Set ThisConnection = Nothing
    Set ctxObject = Nothing

    Exit Function

FetchDeletedError:

    ErrorHandler

End Function
```

The Stored Procedure

The stored procedure we use for this process is a little unusual. We need to take a few minutes to go over some more basic SQL. In this case, we are going to take a look at something called a **view**.

Enterprise Caliber Data Objects have the capacity to deliver to the user a list of deleted objects and allow the user to restore an object from a deleted state. This means that a single object can be deleted and restored an infinite number of times. Each successive deletion removes the record from the Object table and places a record in the Object Audit table that marks the deletion. As you might imagine, this presents a small problem when we need to retrieve a list of deleted objects. We need that list to contain only a single entry for each object, no matter how many times it has been deleted. And more, we need that list to contain only the last deletion record for each object. There are many ways to accomplish this, but the technique we use involves creating a view for each object. Lets take a moment or two to review exactly what a view is and how we can use it for the task at hand.

A view is very much like a table in SQL Server. It contains columns and records like any other table, and as long as certain requirements have been met, we can insert records into a view, update records in a view, and delete records from a view. *Views are different from tables, though.* A view does not actually *contain* any data.

> *Think of a view as a virtual table where each column maps to a column of another table or a column in a resultset.*

In our case, we will create a view from a single table, the Audit table. Remember, that table contains records that are snapshots of action taken against objects at some time in history. If an object was deleted six times and restored five times, then there would be six records indicating deletion and five records indicating restoration. When we need to show the user a list of deleted objects, we should show the user only a single record for each currently deleted object – the last deletion that has not yet been restored.

Let's use the table below for an example and step through, logically, what we have to do to get this list of objects returned:

ID	StampID	SomeValue	StampAction
1	1	135	I
2	1	135	D
3	1	135	R
4	1	135	D
5	2	177	I
6	2	177	D
7	2	177	R
8	2	177	D

First, we need to select only those records that have a D in StampAction. This would return the set of records that have been deleted. Those are the records that have been shaded in the above table:

ID	StampID	SomeValue	StampAction
2	1	135	D
4	1	135	D
6	2	177	D
8	2	177	D

Then we need to further refine that query to return just the last deletion for each distinct StampID. We do that by grouping the records and selecting only the ones in each group with the maximum ID value. This would further limit our resultset and would return just 2 records–the records with IDs 4 and 8:

ID	StampID	SomeValue	StampAction
4	1	135	D
8	2	177	D

A SELECT statement that would give us this result set is:

```
SELECT StampID, 'ID'=Max(ID)
     FROM ComputerObjectAudit
     WHERE StampAction = 'D'
     GROUP BY StampID
```

We can make this query into view by using the `CREATE VIEW` command in SQL Server. Once the view has been created, we can use it exactly like we would any other table. But in this case our view gives us a virtual table that contains only 2 records – the records for the IDs 4 and 8. Now, we don't need to worry about dealing with duplicate values or complex SQL. We can encapsulate the logic we just worked through into a view and use that view like any other table. The syntax we use to create the view consists of a single line that names the view followed by the SQL statement that defines the view:

```
CREATE VIEW vComputerObjectDelete AS

/* This view lists the most recent deletions by ID        */
SELECT StampID, 'ID'=Max(ID)
FROM    ComputerObjectAudit
WHERE   StampAction = 'D'
GROUP   BY StampID


GO
```

In the `EstablishDataStore` method, we first test for existence of the view and if we need to create it, we use the `Execute` method of the Connection object as shown below:

```
    strSQL = "SELECT * FROM sysobjects WHERE id = " _
             object_id('dbo.vComputerObjectDelete ')"

    ThisRecordset.Open strSQL, ThisConnection
    If ThisRecordset.EOF Then
        strSQL = "CREATE VIEW vComputerObjectDelete AS " & _
                "    SELECT StampID, 'ID'=Max(ID) " & _
                "    FROM    ComputerObjectAudit " & _
                "    WHERE   StampAction = 'D' " & _
                "    GROUP   BY StampID"
        ThisConnection.Execute strSQL
    End If
```

The stored `spComputerObjectAuditDeletes` is almost identical to the `spComputerObjectList` stored procedure. The only unusual thing about this stored procedure is the join to the view. Let's work our way through this portion of the stored procedure and see how it works:

```
INNER JOIN       vComputerObjectDelete On ComputerObjectAudit.ID =
                 vComputerObjectDelete.ID
LEFT OUTER JOIN ComputerObject ON ComputerObjectAudit.StampID = ComputerObject.ID
WHERE            ComputerObjectAudit.StampAction = 'D' AND
                 ComputerObject.ID IS NULL
```

We are selecting something, either a `COUNT(*)` or series of columns, from the `ComputerObjectAudit` table. We refine this list by telling SQL to join the `ComputerObjectAudit` table with the view we just created, `vComputerObjectDelete` using the ID column to match the records. Step through this logically. We end up with the same information we asked for in our view, the Original ID and the Audit ID, but now we also have the additional fields from the `ComputerObjectAudit` table available to perform the required joins and comparisons.

Then we ask SQL server to give us only those records that exist in the view but do not exist in the
Object Table:

```
CREATE PROCEDURE spComputerObjectAuditDeletes
/***********************************************************/
/* ComputerObject AuditDeletes                           */
/*                                                       */
/* Add any additional comments here                     */
/***********************************************************/

AS

DECLARE @CountOfRows int

/* Determine number of rows which will be returned */
SELECT @CountOfRows =
   (
   SELECT          Count(ComputerObjectAudit.StampID)
   FROM            ComputerObjectAudit
   INNER JOIN      vComputerObjectDelete ON ComputerObjectAudit.ID =
                   vComputerObjectDelete.ID
   LEFT OUTER JOIN ComputerObject ON ComputerObjectAudit.StampID =
                   ComputerObject.ID
   WHERE           ComputerObjectAudit.StampAction = 'D' AND
                   ComputerObject.ID IS NULL
   )

/* Return row count as first field followed by ComputerObject fields */
SELECT          'RowCount' = @CountOfRows,
                ComputerObjectAudit.StampID,
                ComputerObjectAudit.StampUser,
                ComputerObjectAudit.StampDateTime,
                ComputerObjectAudit.StampAction,
                ComputerObjectAudit.ID,
                ComputerObjectAudit.Name,
                ComputerObjectAudit.OperatingSystem,
                ComputerObjectAudit.ProcessorType,
                ComputerObjectAudit.TotalPhysMemory,
                ComputerObjectAudit.AvailPhysMemory,
                ComputerObjectAudit.TotalVirtualMemory,
                ComputerObjectAudit.AvailVirtualMemory,
                ComputerObjectAudit.DriveCSizeMeg,
                ComputerObjectAudit.DriveCSpaceMeg

FROM            ComputerObjectAudit

INNER JOIN      vComputerObjectDelete ON ComputerObjectAudit.ID =
                vComputerObjectDelete.ID
LEFT OUTER JOIN ComputerObject ON ComputerObjectAudit.StampID =
                ComputerObject.ID
WHERE           ComputerObjectAudit.StampAction = 'D' AND
                ComputerObject.ID IS NULL

ORDER BY StampDateTime DESC

RETURN (0)
```

271

The Audit History Process

The *Audit History* process provides the user interface programmer with a collection of objects that represent the history of a single object over some period of time. Although this process should seem very easy because it is like the *Load* and *Show Deleted* processes we have seen before, there is one little thing you need to look out for.

In this process we use a single object on the User Centric sphere to instantiate a collection of User Centric objects. These objects represent a series of snapshots of the User Centric object that taken together represent a history for a single object.

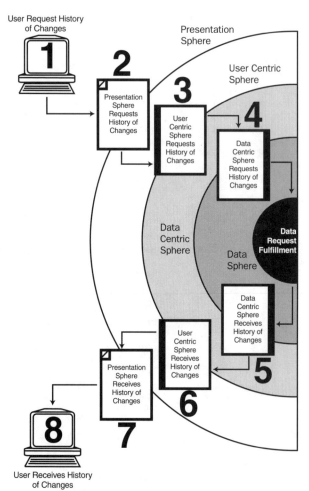

1. The User requests a set of data representing the history for an object from the data store.

2. The Presentation sphere accepts this request, instantiates a User Centric object, and passes the request to the UC object.

3. The UC object accepts the request from the Presentation sphere, instantiates a Data Centric object, and passes the request to the DC object.

4. The DC object accepts the request form the User Centric sphere, acquires a connection to the Data sphere and passes the request to the Data sphere where it is processed.

5. The Data sphere fulfills the request and passes a list of the history for the object to the DC object. The DC object releases the connection to the Data sphere and passes a collection representing the history of the object to the UC object.

6. The UC object accepts a collection representing the history for the object from the Data Centric sphere and destroys the DC object.

7. The Presentation sphere accepts the collection of objects representing the history from the User Centric sphere and destroys the UC object.

8. The User receives the list that represents the history for an object requested in Step 1 above.

The User Centric Object Code

The User Centric `ObjectAuditHistory` code is contained in the `colComputer.cls` file in the `UCComputer.vbp` project:

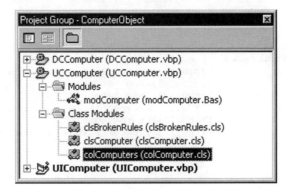

The purpose of this method is to retrieve a collection that consists of all of the previous states for a particular object.

The majority of this function is the same as the `ShowDeleted` subroutine we looked at earlier, so I am not going to walk you through every line. Instead I will try to point out the places where this routine is different from the `ShowDeleted` method. The first difference that you should notice is that this routine is a `Function` instead of a subroutine. It is a little curious, but this function returns a collection that is identical to the collection it might normally be a part of – it returns a `colComputers` collection:

```
Public Function ObjectAuditHistory(Optional strSelectStatement As String) _
       As colComputers
```

This section is identical to the `ShowDeleted` and `Load` routines. We just create a local recordset to hold the information from the Data Centric object:

```
Dim objData As DCCOmputer.colComputerData
Set objData = CreateObject("DCComputer.colComputerData")

Dim TheAnswer As ADODB.Recordset
```

The next step is quite different. What we are doing here is creating an empty collection of `colComputer` objects. We will use this collection to hold the history of the object that is making this call:

```
Dim colAuditHistory As UCComputer.colComputers
Set colAuditHistory = CreateObject("UCComputer.colComputers")
```

Now the only difference between this and the `ShowDeleted` routine is that we call a special routine on the Data Centric object – the `ObjectHistory` routine. This routine returns the same type of recordset we saw earlier in the `ShowDeleted` routine. We perform identical error handling:

```
With objData
  .SetDataSource mstrConnect
  Set TheAnswer = .ObjectHistory(mlngID, strSelectStatement)

  If TheAnswer.RecordCount = 1 Then

    If Len(TheAnswer.Fields("DataMessage").Value) > 0 Then
      Err.Raise vbObjectError, "Computer", _
                TheAnswer.Fields("DataMessage").Value
    Else
      With TheAnswer
        colAuditHistory.Add !StampID, !ID, !TotalPhysMemory, !AvailPhysMemory, _
                            !TotalVirtualMemory, !AvailVirtualMemory, _
                            !DriveCSizeMeg, !DriveCSpaceMeg, _
                            FixNulls(!StampDateTime), 2, "", _
                            FixNulls(!StampAction), "", FixNulls(!Name), _
                            FixNulls(!OperatingSystem), _
                            FixNulls(!ProcessorType), FixNulls(!StampUser)
        .MoveNext
      End With
    End If

  Else

    Do While Not TheAnswer.EOF
      With TheAnswer
        colAuditHistory.Add !StampID, !ID, !TotalPhysMemory, !AvailPhysMemory, _
                            !TotalVirtualMemory, !AvailVirtualMemory, _
                            !DriveCSizeMeg, !DriveCSpaceMeg, _
                            FixNulls(!StampDateTime), 2, "", _
                            FixNulls(!StampAction), "", FixNulls(!Name), _
                            FixNulls(!OperatingSystem), _
                            FixNulls(!ProcessorType), FixNulls(!StampUser)
        .MoveNext
      End With
    Loop

  End If

End With

' Clean House
Set TheAnswer = Nothing
Set objData = Nothing
```

Remember that this routine is function rather than a subroutine. It returns the collection of snapshots about our object to the user interface programmer:

```
' Return the Collection
   Set ObjectAuditHistory = colAuditHistory

End Function
```

The Data Centric Object Code

As we just saw one of the few differences with the `ObjectAuditHistory` routine was that it called the `ObjectHistory` function in its data centric counterpart. The Data Centric `ObjectHistory` code is found in the `colComputerData.cls` file in the `DCComputer.vbp` project:

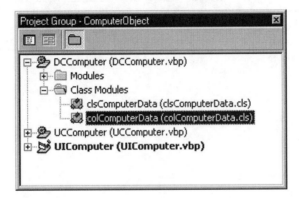

The purpose of this method is to return a collection of objects that represent the previous states for a particular object. This code is virtually identical to the `ShowDeleted` process we covered earlier, so I am not going to go over the details again here:

```
Public Function ObjectHistory(Optional lngID As Long, _
                      Optional strSelectStatement As String) As Recordset

    Dim strSQL As String

    Dim ctxObject As ObjectContext
    Set ctxObject = GetObjectContext

    On Error GoTo ObjectHistoryError

    Dim ThisConnection As ADODB.Connection
    Dim ThisRecordset As ADODB.Recordset

    Set ThisConnection = New ADODB.Connection
    Set ThisRecordset = New ADODB.Recordset

    ThisConnection.Open mstrConnect, GetLogon(mstrConnect), GetPassword(mstrConnect)

    If Len(strSelectStatement) = 0 Then
        strSQL = "spComputerObjectAuditList " & lngID
    Else
```

```
        strSQL = strSelectStatement
    End If

    On Error Resume Next

    ThisRecordset.Open strSQL, ThisConnection

    If ThisConnection.Errors.Count > 0 Then
        Set ThisRecordset = New ADODB.Recordset
        ThisRecordset.Fields.Append "DataMessage", adChar, 255
        ThisRecordset.Open
        ThisRecordset.AddNew
        ThisRecordset.Fields(0).Value = ThisConnection.Errors(0).Description
        ThisRecordset.Update
        'Free up the object in MTS and set the Transaction Aborted flag
        ctxObject.SetAbort
        Set ObjectHistory = ThisRecordset
    Else
        'Free up the object in MTS and set the Transaction Completed flag
        ctxObject.SetComplete
        Set ObjectHistory = ThisRecordset
    End If

    ThisConnection.Close
    Set ThisConnection = Nothing
    Set ctxObject = Nothing

    Exit Function

ObjectHistoryError

    ErrorHandler

End Function
```

The only significant difference with the above function is the stored procedure used.

The Stored Procedure

The spComputerObjectAuditList stored procedure is virtually identical to the spComputerObjectList stored procedure we went over earlier. It is really just a simple SELECT statement that accepts a single parameter. There are two things you need to be aware of here:

❑   This stored procedure selects its data from the Object Audit table rather than from the standard Object table.

❑   The parameter that is passed into this stored procedure is the StampID rather than the ID that we have bee using previously. Remember that when we displayed the StampID in the user interface we called it the OriginalID. We perform the SELECT statement here using an object's StampID or OriginalID. This will return us a recordset from the Audit table that are snapshots of the same object as given by its StampID.

```
CREATE PROCEDURE spComputerObjectAuditList
/**********************************************************/
/* ComputerObject AuditList                             */
/**********************************************************/

@StampID int

AS

SELECT  StampID,
        StampUser,
        StampDateTime,
        StampAction,
        ID,
        Name,
        OperatingSystem,
        ProcessorType,
        TotalPhysMemory,
        AvailPhysMemory,
        TotalVirtualMemory,
        AvailVirtualMemory,
        DriveCSizeMeg,
        DriveCSpaceMeg

FROM    ComputerObjectAudit

WHERE   StampID = @StampID

ORDER BY StampDateTime DESC

RETURN (0)
```

The Restore From Deleted Process

In the last chapter we looked at the process we use to retrieve a list of deleted objects from the data store. Now, it's nice to be able to retrieve a list of deleted objects, but I am sure you would agree that it would be far better if we could retrieve the deleted object from the list as well. Well we can. As far as the Visual Basic code goes, this process is almost identical to the *Fetch* process.

The only real difference is that in this case we are returning an object that has been deleted instead of an object that is currently active.

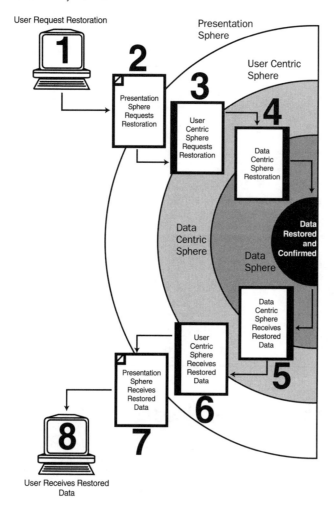

1. The User requests an object to be restored.

2. The Presentation sphere accepts the request, instantiates a User Centric object, and passes the request to the UC object.

3. The UC object accepts the request from the Presentation sphere, instantiates a Data Centric object, and passes the request to the DC object.

4. The DC object accepts the request form the User Centric sphere, acquires a connection to the Data sphere and passes the request to the Data sphere where it is processed.

5. The Data sphere fulfills the request and passes the data for the restored object to the DC object. The DC object releases the connection to the Data sphere and passes the data to the UC object.

6. The UC object accepts the data for the restored object from the Data Centric sphere and destroys the DC object.

7. The Presentation sphere accepts the data for the restored object from the User Centric sphere and destroys the UC object.

8. The User receives the restored object requested in Step 1 above.

The User Centric Object Code

The User Centric `ObjectRestoreFromDeleted` code is contained in the `clsComputer.cls` file in the `UCComputer.vbp` project:

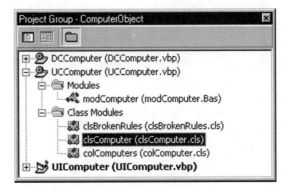

The purpose of this method is to restore an object from a currently deleted state to its state at the time of deletion. This process works in conjunction with the *Show Deleted* process we covered earlier.

Here is the complete listing of the `ObjectRestoreFromDeleted` code. You should notice the similarities to the `ObjectFetch` routine we created earlier in the chapter. The two routines are virtually identical. We could have used the same routine for both processes, but I felt that it was easier to understand if we kept the two procedures separate:

```
Public Sub ObjectRestoreFromDeleted()

    'Instantiate the remote object
    Dim ThisDataObject As DCComputer.clsComputerData
    Set ThisDataObject = CreateObject("DCComputer.clsComputerData")

    'Get the Data From the Remote Object
    With ThisDataObject
        .SetDataSource mstrConnect
```

The only real difference between the two processes is found in the call to the Data Centric object. In this case we call the `ObjectRestoreFromDeleted` method of the Data Centric object rather than `ObjectFetch`:

```
        .ObjectRestoreFromDeleted mlngStampID, mlngID, msngTotalPhysMemory, _
                            msngAvailPhysMemory, msngTotalVirtualMemory, _
                            msngAvailVirtualMemory, msngDriveCSizeMeg, _
                            msngDriveCSpaceMeg, mdtmStampDateTime, _
```

```
                              mintDataLocking, mstrChangeAll, mstrStampAction, _
                              mstrDataMessage, mstrName, mstrOperatingSystem, _
                              mstrProcessorType, mstrStampUser
    End With

    If Len(Trim(mstrDataMessage)) > 0 Then
        'Some Data Centric Problem Has Occured
        'Raise a Error that can be trapped by the programmer
        Err.Raise vbObjectError + 1234, "Computer Restore From Deleted", _
                mstrDataMessage
    Else
        'Reset the local object's State
        mlngSaveStampID = mlngStampID
        mlngSaveID = mlngID
        msngSaveTotalPhysMemory = msngTotalPhysMemory
        msngSaveAvailPhysMemory = msngAvailPhysMemory
        msngSaveTotalVirtualMemory = msngTotalVirtualMemory
        msngSaveAvailVirtualMemory = msngAvailVirtualMemory
        msngSaveDriveCSizeMeg = msngDriveCSizeMeg
        msngSaveDriveCSpaceMeg = msngDriveCSpaceMeg
        mdtmSaveStampDateTime = mdtmStampDateTime
        mintSaveDataLocking = mintDataLocking
        mstrSaveChangeAll = mstrChangeAll
        mstrSaveStampAction = mstrStampAction
        mstrDataMessage = mstrDataMessage
        mstrSaveName = mstrName
        mstrSaveOperatingSystem = mstrOperatingSystem
        mstrSaveProcessorType = mstrProcessorType
        mstrSaveStampUser = mstrStampUser
        ObjectIsNew False
        ObjectIsDirty False
    End If

    Set ThisDataObject = Nothing

End Sub
```

The Data Centric Object Code

The Data Centric ObjectRestoreFromDeleted code is found in the clsComputerData.cls file in the DCComputer.vbp project:

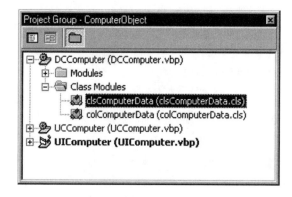

The purpose of this method is to restore an object from a deleted state to an active state. This code is identical to the object `ObjectFetch` code we looked at in the earlier except for the name of the stored procedure:

```
Public Sub ObjectRestoreFromDeleted(lngStampID As Long, lngID As Long, _
            sngTotalPhysMemory As Single, sngAvailPhysMemory As Single, _
            sngTotalVirtualMemory As Single, sngAvailVirtualMemory As Single, _
            sngDriveCSizeMeg As Single, sngDriveCSpaceMeg As Single, _
            dtmStampDateTime As Variant, intDataLocking As Integer, _
            strChangeAll As String, strStampAction As String, strDataMessage _
            As String, strName As String, strOperatingSystem As String, _
            strProcessorType As String, strStampUser As String)
```

```
    Dim strSQL As String
    Dim ctxObject As ObjectContext
    Set ctxObject = GetObjectContext()

    On Error GoTo ObjectRestoreFromDeletedError

    Dim ThisConnection As ADODB.Connection
    Dim ThisRecordset As ADODB.Recordset

    Set ThisConnection = New ADODB.Connection
    Set ThisRecordset = New ADODB.Recordset

    ThisConnection.Open mstrConnect, GetLogon(mstrConnect), GetPassword(mstrConnect)

    strSQL = "spComputerObjectRestore '" & strStampUser & "', " & lngID
    ThisRecordset.Open strSQL, ThisConnection

    If Not ThisRecordset.EOF Then
        If ThisRecordset.Fields(0).name = "ErrorCondition" Then
            strDataMessage = ThisRecordset.Fields(0).Value
            'Free up the object in MTS and set the Transaction Aborted flag
            ctxObject.SetAbort
        Else
            lngID = ThisRecordset.Fields("ID").Value
            sngTotalPhysMemory = ThisRecordset.Fields("TotalPhysMemory").Value
            sngAvailPhysMemory = ThisRecordset.Fields("AvailPhysMemory").Value
            sngTotalVirtualMemory = ThisRecordset.Fields("TotalVirtualMemory").Value
            sngAvailVirtualMemory = ThisRecordset.Fields("AvailVirtualMemory").Value
            sngDriveCSizeMeg = ThisRecordset.Fields("DriveCSizeMeg").Value
            sngDriveCSpaceMeg = ThisRecordset.Fields("DriveCSpaceMeg").Value
            strDataMessage = ""
            strName = FixNulls(ThisRecordset.Fields("Name").Value)
            strOperatingSystem = _
                    FixNulls(ThisRecordset.Fields("OperatingSystem").Value)
            strProcessorType = FixNulls(ThisRecordset.Fields("ProcessorType").Value)
            'Free up the object in MTS and set the Transaction Completed flag
            ctxObject.SetComplete
        End If
    Else
        strDataMessage = "Unable to find the Requested Record in the Persistant " & _
                    "Data Source"
        'Free up the object in MTS and set the Transaction Aborted flag
        ctxObject.SetAbort
    End If
```

```
    ThisConnection.Close
    Set ThisConnection = Nothing
    Set ctxObject = Nothing

    Exit Sub

ObjectRestoreFromDeletedError:

    ErrorHandler

End Sub
```

The Stored Procedure

The real trick to this process is the table design, the Enterprise Caliber methodology, and the stored procedure. We have seen all of this SQL before. The only new thing here is the way we put it together.

The first thing we do is to define the parameters and the local variables:

```
CREATE PROCEDURE spComputerObjectRestore
/***********************************************************/
/* ComputerObject Restore                                  */
/***********************************************************/

@StampUser varchar(10),
@RestoreID int

AS

DECLARE @trncnt int,
        @ErrorNumber int,
        @ID int,
        @Name char (50),
        @OperatingSystem char (50),
        @ProcessorType char (50),
        @TotalPhysMemory decimal,
        @AvailPhysMemory decimal,
        @TotalVirtualMemory decimal,
        @AvailVirtualMemory decimal,
        @DriveCSizeMeg decimal,
        @DriveCSpaceMeg decimal
```

Then we set the value of the @ErrorNumber variable to -1 and test for existing transactions:

```
SELECT @ErrorNumber = -1

/* save transaction count value */
SELECT @trncnt = @@trancount

/* issue begin or save transaction based on transaction count */
IF @trncnt = 0
    BEGIN TRANSACTION T1
ELSE
    SAVE TRANSACTION T1
```

Once the preliminaries have been handled, we select the object we want to restore from the audit table with the following SELECT statement:

```
/* retrieve audit record to be restored */
SELECT @ID = StampID,
       @Name = Name,
       @OperatingSystem = OperatingSystem,
       @ProcessorType = ProcessorType,
       @TotalPhysMemory = TotalPhysMemory,
       @AvailPhysMemory = AvailPhysMemory,
       @TotalVirtualMemory = TotalVirtualMemory,
       @AvailVirtualMemory = AvailVirtualMemory,
       @DriveCSizeMeg = DriveCSizeMeg,
       @DriveCSpaceMeg = DriveCSpaceMeg

FROM ComputerObjectAudit

WHERE ID = @RestoreID
```

Now that we have the values our object had when it was deleted, we need to re-insert the record back into the base table. There is one problem here though. We used an identity field for the ID in the base table. This means that SQL Server is expecting to tell us what the ID number should be. In this case we need to tell SQL Server what the ID value should be. This means that we have to stop the identity field from incrementing and allow us to supply a value for the ID. We do that by using the following line:

```
SET Identity_Insert ComputerObject ON
```

This stops SQL Server from forcing a value into the ID field and allows us to supply our own value. Once we have inserted the values into the table, we need to remember to tell SQL server that we expect it to supply ID values from this point on. We do that with the following line:

```
SET Identity_Insert ComputerObject OFF
```

If we combine those two lines with an INSERT statement we get the code that follows. This effectively places a previously deleted record back into the base table:

```
/* re-add ComputerObject record */
SET Identity_Insert ComputerObject ON
INSERT ComputerObject
    (
     ID,
    Name,
    OperatingSystem,
    ProcessorType,
    TotalPhysMemory,
    AvailPhysMemory,
    TotalVirtualMemory,
    AvailVirtualMemory,
    DriveCSizeMeg,
    DriveCSpaceMeg,
    ConcurrencyID
    )
```

```
        VALUES
            (
            @ID,
            @Name,
            @OperatingSystem,
            @ProcessorType,
            @TotalPhysMemory,
            @AvailPhysMemory,
            @TotalVirtualMemory,
            @AvailVirtualMemory,
            @DriveCSizeMeg,
            @DriveCSpaceMeg,
            1
            )
    IF @@Error <> 0 GOTO ErrorHandler

    SET Identity_Insert ComputerObject OFF
```

The next thing we need to do is to insert a new record into the audit table that marks the restoration. We have seen this block of SQL several times before:

```
/* add audit record */
INSERT ComputerObjectAudit
        (StampUser,
         StampDateTime,
         StampAction,
         StampID,
         Name,
         OperatingSystem,
         ProcessorType,
         TotalPhysMemory,
         AvailPhysMemory,
         TotalVirtualMemory,
         AvailVirtualMemory,
         DriveCSizeMeg,
         DriveCSpaceMeg)

SELECT  @StampUser,
        GetDate() ,
        'R',
        ID,
        Name,
        OperatingSystem,
        ProcessorType,
        TotalPhysMemory,
        AvailPhysMemory,
        TotalVirtualMemory,
        AvailVirtualMemory,
        DriveCSizeMeg,
        DriveCSpaceMeg

FROM ComputerObject

WHERE  ID = @ID

IF @@Error <> 0 GOTO ErrorHandler
```

Once we have done the housekeeping, we test for errors and commit the transaction if we were the ones that began the transaction. We have seen this code before as well:

```
IF @@Error <> 0 GOTO ErrorHandler
/* commit transaction only if this proc issued begin */
IF @trncnt = 0
  COMMIT TRANSACTION T1
```

The last step in the process is to return the object back to the user. Again, we always perform this step to ensure that the user's perception of what is currently in the data store is in sync with the actual values in the data store:

```
/* return restored record for verification */
SELECT ID,
       Name,
       OperatingSystem,
       ProcessorType,
       TotalPhysMemory,
       AvailPhysMemory,
       TotalVirtualMemory,
       AvailVirtualMemory,
       DriveCSizeMeg,
       DriveCSpaceMeg,
       ConcurrencyID As ConcurrencyID1

FROM ComputerObject

WHERE  ID = @ID

RETURN(0)

ErrorHandler:
   ROLLBACK TRANSACTION T1
   SELECT   ErrorCondition
   FROM     ErrorMessage
   WHERE    ErrorNumber = @ErrorNumber
   RETURN   (100)

GO
```

Summary

In the last chapter we learned to code two of the eight basic data handling processes that Enterprise Caliber Data Objects expose:

- ❏ *Insert* – Adds a new object to the data store
- ❏ *Load* – Retrieves a list of like objects from the data store

In this chapter we went over the remaining six processes:

- ❏ *Fetch* – Retrieves a single object from the data store
- ❏ *Edit* – Changes the object's state in the data store
- ❏ *Delete* – Removes the object from the active data store
- ❏ *Audit History* – Retrieves the history of changes to an object over time
- ❏ *Show Deleted* – Retrieves a list of currently deleted objects
- ❏ *Restore From Deleted* – Restores an object to its state at the time it was deleted

Now that you have gone through all of the code necessary to write these processes for a Level I object, it would be a good idea for you to go back and add these processes to your *ErrCond* object from the last chapter. You can do this by writing the code from scratch if you want to. But if you look in the additional exercises directory for the sample code in this chapter, you will see that I have provided the entire code for the *ErrCond* object there. Please take the time to become intimate with these processes before you go on with this book.

In the next chapter we will begin a very exciting journey into the world of 4-Dimensional Data Objects. You will need to have a solid understanding of the eight basic data handling processes before we proceed. 4-Dimensional Data Objects are constructed by combining these same processes in some curious ways.

{831FDD16-0C5C-1...D2-A9F0-0

Form frmPropNameControl...st

Style = 3 'Fixed Dial...

= "Properties fo...

...eight = 4845

...ft = 45

...p = 330

...dth = 11460

...c = "Form1"

...ton = 0 'False

...d = -1 'True

...con = 0 'False

...ight = 4845

...dth = 11460

...askbar = 0 'False

Person
Base Properties

ID
Last Name
First Name
Middle Name
Birth Date
Sex

Object Type Definitions

Object Ty...

Employee OTD	Lawyer OTD	Engineer OTD	Doctor OTD	Student OTD	
Duty	Specialty	Specialty	Specialty	Major	
Hours	Hourly Rate	Experience	Certification	Minor	
Property 3	Law School	Property 3	Property 3	Year	
Property 4	Property 4	Property 4	Property 4	Property 4	
Property 5	Property 5	Property 5	Property 5	Property 5	
Property 6	Property 6	Property 6	Property 6	Property 6	
Property 7	Property 7	Property 7	Property 7	Property 7	
Property 8	Property 8	Property 8	Property 8	Property 8	
Property 9	Property 9	Property 9	Property 9	Property 9	
Property 10	Property 10	Property 10	Property 10	Property 10	

Property Set Definitions

Property Set

Introduction to the 4-Dimensional Data Object

In the last three chapters we have learned how to create a type of Enterprise Caliber Data Object called a **Level I Data Object**. By now you probably realize that a Level I Data Object is actually just an amazingly good object model for an everyday list or standard database table. A Level I Data Object manages information that would typically be stored in a flat-file, a single database table, or perhaps in a spreadsheet, etc. Historically, the information managed by a Level I Data Object has been viewed as two-dimensional data.

In our treatment of Level I Data Objects we learned to add another dimension to this data – the dimension of time. We did this by recording the changes to the data over time using audit tables, specialized stored-procedures, and carefully crafted object methods. In this chapter, we begin the process of adding a fourth dimension to our data objects.

We will learn how to use 4-Dimensional Data Objects in the same top-down approach we have used in previous chapters. We will begin by looking at two user interfaces exposed by these objects and learning how to use them to maintain our 4-Dimensional Data Objects. Then in later chapters, we will study how we actually build these objects.

What is a 4-Dimensional Data Object?

When we add a fourth dimension to our data objects, we give them something of a chameleon-like quality. They become highly malleable devices that we can mold into just about anything. I find the easiest way to think about **4-Dimensional Data Objects** is to envision them as a cube of data. This cube of data gives me a solid three-dimensional object that I can physically place somewhere in time and space. If we take this concept of the data cube and pair it with a representation of time, even a simple time line, we have a model for a 4-Dimensional Data Object.

I am sure this is getting a little hard to grasp. So, let's start off examining the simple data cube. Once we have gained a better understanding of how a three-dimensional data object behaves, we will be well on our way to a solid understanding of multidimensional data. With that understanding, we can venture off into the higher dimensions – the 4th and beyond.

In the following image, I have a drawn a simple data cube. The data in this particular cube represents the *Person* object we will build over the next few chapters. At the front of the cube, we see information about a group of people in the manner we are accustomed to viewing it – in two dimensions – much like a spreadsheet.

This data constitutes the core set of information for our object – the object's base set of properties. In this case we have three columns or base properties, Last Name, First Name, and Middle Name.

If you look to the rear of the data cube, you notice that the remainder of the cube is broken up into several slices. On top of each of these slices is a descriptive name – Patient, Employee, or Customer etc.

Each one of these slices represents a different aspect, or view, of our *Person* object. This way, our software *Person* object, just like a real person, can be an Employee, a Patient, or both. Let's call the name on top of each one of these slices an **Object Type Definition** (**OTD**).

In real life, we need more information than we find in the name Employee, Patient etc. We need to be able to manage additional, sometimes highly specific data that really defines each person as an Employee, a Patient, or a Customer. To do this we use another conceptual tool – the **Property Set Definition** (**PSD**). A PSD contains a collection of properties that we use to manage detailed information about an OTD.

Now look at the following image. Notice that the Customer slice OTD and its associated PSD have been moved into a position, which allows us to work with the Customer data in a two-dimensional format:

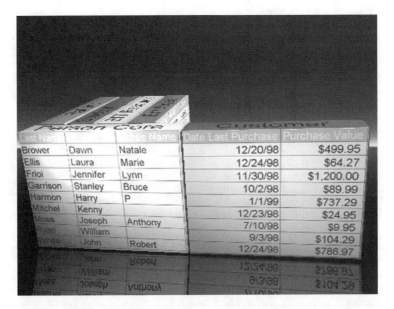

If you are thinking that we could also replace the Customer OTD with the Patient OTD you're on the right track. This would give us another two-dimensional view of the *Person* object, but this time we would find information that helped to describe the *Person* object as a patient instead of a customer. This idea should not be too much of a stretch for anyone who has worked with a properly designed relational database.

In fact, if you are familiar with relational databases, then you are probably thinking, "I could do that by adding a Customer and Patient table and linking the rows in those tables to the rows in a common Person table." Well, you could do that, but that is not what we have done here.

> The way our data store is designed and managed, we can create new OTDs, and their associated PSDs without changing anything but the data in the data store.

I am not going to attempt to explain exactly how this works in this chapter. It is one of the most important concepts in this book, and we will work on it for 5 chapters. Please don't let the thought of a 5-chapter concept throw you. If you have read and understood the previous chapters, you already know most of the information that you need to build 4-Dimensional Data Objects. What we will do over the course of the 5 chapters is to take what you have learned about designing and building Level I objects and use that knowledge to construct the pieces that comprise a 4-Dimensional Data Object. Once we have built all of the pieces, we will work through the task of assembling our target object, the *Person* object.

Before we go on I want to take a minute and give you a table that clarifies what I mean when I talk about dimensions. I had hoped that the visual images would convey this information, but some of Wrox's excellent reviewers helped me to understand that it is beneficial to have these things spelled out in words to give us a common vocabulary that everyone agrees on. This eliminates confusion and makes it easier for us to talk about the ideas.

Dimension	Database Equivalent	Description
First dimension	Columns of data	Description of information in rows
Second dimension	Rows of data	Information/data
Third dimension	Audit table	Time
Fourth Dimension	Set of properties	Set of information that contains its own description – name/value property pair.

Let's take a minute or two here to plan what we are going to do over the next 5 chapters:

1. In this chapter, we will start with an overview of the **Administrative User Interface**. This is the user interface that we use to configure the Object Type Definitions, Property Set Definitions, and individual **Property Definitions** (a number of which make up each PSD) that make up a 4-Dimensional Data Object. It allows programmers and developers to perform the data entry tasks that are required to create, edit, delete, or otherwise manage the objects. We will not write the code for this interface until the next chapter, we are just going to attempt to understand the administrative capabilities of the object by examining the tasks that are required to administer it. Once we have developed a sense of the administrative side of the object, we will begin to tackle the real objective of this chapter, the **Production User Interface**. This is the user interface that the customers see. We will step through every line of code that we need to know to build standard forms using 4-Dimensional Data Objects. As we do that, we will start to become familiar with the production capabilities of the object. We will be introduced to concepts such as the **Property Bag** and **Item List**.

2. In the next chapter, we will focus on the administrative functionality of the 4-Dimensional Data Object. We will develop a deeper understanding of its capabilities by using the object to construct the Administrative User Interface. We will step through, just about, every line of code that we need to create the Administrative User Interface. As we build the interface, we will be introduced to concepts like **Object Types**, the **Property Names** (Property Definition), and the **Property Items**.

3. In Chapter 10, we will construct an intermediate object, a **Level II object**. This chapter will give us the tools we need to take two Level I objects and glue them together into a higher-level object. We will create a Level I *Person* object and a Level I *Type* object. Then we will combine both objects into a Level II *Person* object. What we will end up with is a *Person* object that can be classified as a particular type of person, e.g. doctor, lawyer, patient, client. But this object will not have the ability to manage extended information about any of the types. This chapter is focused on the code we need to write to manage Object Type Definitions. I have presented and commented on the entire listing of the code for the *Type* object, because you can re-use this code exactly as printed for every 4-Dimensional Data Object you ever build.

4. In the next chapter, we will begin to build the most challenging object, the Property Bag. This object is used to manage the extended information about types. In other words, if we had a *Person* object that we cast as a type Patient object, the property bag would allow us to manage patient specific information like perhaps, height, weight, etc. The Property Bag object is actually a composite of three Level I objects – the PropName (Property Definition) object, the PropValu (property value) object, and the PropItem (property item) object. This chapter focuses on building that portion of the Property Bag that is used for administrative purposes. In other words, that portion of the Property Bag that allows us to work with OTDs, PSDs, and the individual Property Definitions. This is the portion of the object that would allow us to create a patient OTD and assign it individual Property Definitions like Height, Weight, etc.

5. The last thing we need to do is finish the Property Bag object by looking at it from the Production User Interface perspective. This will give us insight to that portion of the Property Bag that communicates with the end user. This is the portion of the object that would allow the user working with the Patient OTD to input the values 6' 2" for Height and 200 lbs for Weight.

By the time you finish this section of the book, you will have the tools and the code you need to design and build fully functioning 4-Dimensional Data Objects. As you might imagine, this is going to take a bit of work. I don't know about you, but it's easier for me to work through the task of writing a lot of code if I have an idea of exactly what it is that I am working towards. In the next section, we will take a look at exactly what functionality we should expect from a 4-Dimensional Data Object. We will do that by examining what these data objects look like to their users. This is quite a bit of work, because each object actually exposes two interfaces:

❑ An administrative interface that developers use to manage the object (i.e. create new OTDs and PSDs)
❑ A production interface that the object exposes to the typical end user

When I think of these interfaces, I really think of the programmable interface that the object exposes to the developer. However, I think that it is easier to gain a sense of them both, and 4-Dimensional Data Objects, if we take a look at a couple of actual user interfaces that expose this programmable interface.

The Working Example

If you haven't already done so, now is a great time to download the sample code for this chapter. In addition to the source code, the samples include a couple of DLLs and an executable file that you will need to work through the first part of this chapter.

As I said earlier, I think that it is a lot easier for us to understand the functionality we are after from a data object by working with the object from the user's perspective. This is especially true with 4-Dimensional Data Objects because they expose two interfaces. In many ways, the administrative interface the object exposes is very much a programming tool. It allows developers to extend an existing data object by defining types (OTDs) and adding properties (PSDs) to the object. It is a little difficult to describe how to use this interface to a person that has never worked with one like it. So I hope you can imagine how very difficult it would be for me to give you instructions on how you should go about building the thing when you have never even seen one.

In other words before we take on the task of building the interface, we will work with one that I have provided to introduce you to its functionality.

You will need to have an ODBC source defined on your workstation that points to the same Common database you created back in Chapter 5. If you skipped this section, you will not be able to run the examples in this chapter.

Once you have downloaded the code, open up the Person directory. There are a couple of DLLs that you will need to register in order to run the examples.

Registering the Person DLLs

There are a couple of things we need to do before we can use the *Person* examples. The first thing we need to do is to register the ECDO. As with all ECDOs, the *Person* object is made from two halves: A user centric half (UCPerson.dll) and a data centric half (DCPerson.dll). Type the following regsvr32 command into the Run dialog and hit *Enter*:

```
regsvr32 "\..\Ch08\UCPerson.dll"
```

You should see a message box that tells you that the DLL has been successfully registered. Dismiss the message box. Now type the following command into the Run dialog, and hit *Enter*:

```
regsvr32 "\..\Ch08\DCPerson.dll"
```

You should see the same kind of message box again telling you that this DLL has also been registered successfully. All we did here was to introduce your workstation to the *Person* object. If you search for the names of these DLLs in your registry, now you will find several references to them.

Running the Example Person Data Object Interface

Once you have created the Common ODBC source and have registered the DLLs you will be able to run the executable UIPerson.exe on your workstation. It is a good idea to have this beast in running in front of you as we go through the next section.

Administrative User Interface Overview

We will step through every detail required to build every form later in this chapter. For now, let's just use the sample data object to learn about the functionality that we require from each form. This will help us to understand what we should expect from a 4-Dimensional Data Object. Suppose that we have a 4-Dimensional *Person* Data Object and we need to extend this *Person* object to manage information about a person who is an IT Resource (an analyst, programmer, developer, etc). How would we do that using this interface?

Begin by selecting Create Data Store from the Work With menu of the Person Object Maintenance Application form. This is an artificial step that I have included to check for (and add if necessary) some stored procedures and views in your Common database; we will discuss all of these in detail later in the book.

Introduction to the 4-Dimensional Data Object

The first real step in the process is to add an Object Type Definition. Let's create one called IT Resource. We can do that by using the **Person Type List** form. To bring up this form select **Person Types** from the **Work With** option on the menu:

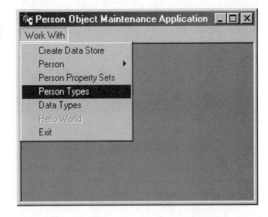

The form that comes up should look quite familiar; you learned how to construct this form and the Level I Data Object it exposes in the last 3 chapters.

Click on the **Add** image control. This will bring up the Detail form for the *Person* object. Notice that this form is very much like the Detail forms you have been building over the past few chapters. We use this one to create the new Object Type Definition, IT Resource for the *Person* data object. Take a moment to notice that our **Person Type List** allows us to view deleted *Person* types. The OTD object has the same functionality as any other Enterprise Caliber Object.

Use the Detail form to enter the information that describes our new Object Type Definition. First enter the words IT Resource into the **Type Name** field, then type the value ITR into the **Key Prefix** field. Finally enter an appropriate brief description and description into the fields provided. Notice that these two forms offer exactly the same functionality (show/restore from deleted, show/restore from history) that we provided earlier. We demand this functionality from every object. Dismiss both forms.

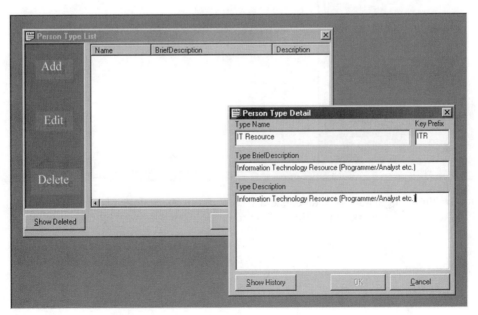

295

You have just created an Object Type Definition called IT Resource. The next thing you need to do is to specify the detailed information you want to manage for this the IT Resource OTD. To do that, select Person Property Sets from the main form's Work With menu. That brings up the modal dialog called Person Type Select List, which allows us to select the particular OTD we want to work with:

In this case, select the IT Resource you just created. The modal dialog is designed to unload itself as soon as you make a selection. It also calls the next form you will use - the Property Set Control List form:

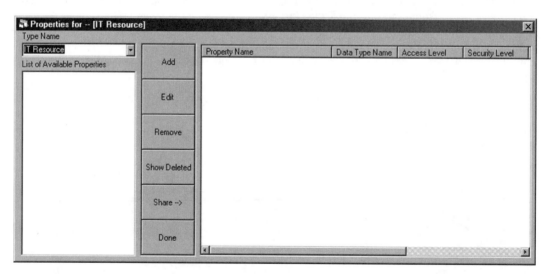

You will use this form to add, edit, delete, and *share* Property Definitions. Let's add a new Property Definition to see how it works. Press the Add button.

You will be presented with a modal dialog that you can use to create and edit Property Definitions:

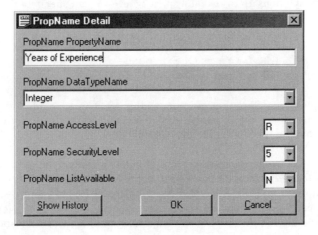

Type Years of Experience or the name of some other suitable property for an IT Resource. Next, select a data type from the combo box called DataTypeName. I used an Integer data type to hold the value Years of Experience.

Property Definitions allow us to specify other information besides the name and data type. For instance, we can also specify the access level. I haven't done anything fancy here. I have the possible values for AccessLevel as R for read-only access and W for write access. When you build this form, you might spell out words to make it easier for the user. This flag is used when we share properties between different OTDs. If we give a property write access then all the OTDs that share the property can edit the value for the property. If we give a property read-only access then the OTDs that share the property can only read the value. They cannot change the value. I wouldn't worry about this one right now, pick whatever you like. The next thing we need to do is to specify the SecurityLevel. All we do here is to select an integer value from 0 to 99. Let's say for the sake of argument that 99 means no security and 0 is something like ultimate security. Then when you design your application you can use this value to make decisions about which users can access, write to, etc. this particular property. What you do is to assign our user objects a security level. If the user object's security level is less than the value stored in this field, then we allow the user to view the property. If the value is greater than the stored value, the user will not even be allowed to view this particular property. Let's consider an example:

Say that we have an OTD called Employee and one of the Property Definitions assigned to the Employee Property Set is Salary. Now, it may be alright for certain information about an employee to be shared freely throughout an enterprise, but most organizations would want to keep tight reigns on the users that can gain access to an employee's salary information. One way we can manage access to this property is to set the security level for the Salary property to a value of 10. Then, the only individuals that will even be able to see the Salary property will be those individuals with a security level of 9 or less. It is still a little early to get into all of the details, but notice how we have addressed only a part of the security issue at the object level. If we attempted to handle all of the security at the object level that would minimize the amount of reuse we could expect from the object. Instead, we use a combination of objects and administration functions to produce a finely grained security net. If this sounds strikingly familiar to NT's security model that's because it is! Through careful administration (business rules), we can provide field-level security on a user-by-user basis. In other words, we can make it possible for Sally to work with Joe's salary information, while Jack who sits next to Sally may not even know that Salary is even a property of the Employee data set.

I think you are going to like the next field, the ListAvailable flag. Select Y for this value and watch what happens. The dialog opens up to reveal a space where we can specify a list of valid entries for this particular property.

If you are working along with my examples then you will agree that it really doesn't make much sense to use a list of valid entries for Years Of Experience. Change the ListAvailable box back to N for now and press OK. You will be returned to the Property Set Control List form.

Now click the Add button to add another property to this set. This time add a definition called Job Title with the String data type and a SecurityLevel of 5. You can do that exactly the same way you made the Years of Experience Property Definition.

Once you have created the property, select Y from the ListAvailable combo box. The form morphs and we can add items to the list of valid entries for the Job Title property. Let's say that the valid entries for this definition are System Analyst, Programmer, Developer, and Database Administrator. All you need to do to use this is to type a job title, say System Analyst, in the text box above the List Item listview. When you are happy with the wording (and spelling) press the Add button. This will add the item to the list of valid entries for this property:

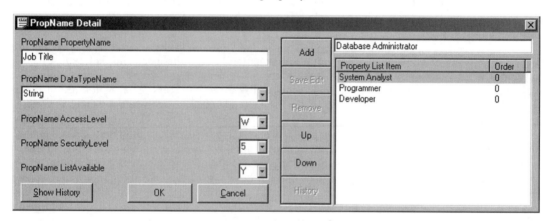

Let's review what we have done up until this point. If you are using my examples, we started with a basic 4-Dimensional Data Object, the *Person* object. Then we extended that *Person* object into an IT Resource object. We did that by creating an Object Type Definition (OTD) called IT Resource. After we defined the object's type, we assigned that type two new Property Definitions:

❑ Years of Experience – this property has the data type integer, is read-only to anyone not using the Employee OTD, has a security level of 5, and does not have a list of valid entries available.

❑ Job Title – this property has the data type string, can be written to by other OTDs, has a security level of 5, and does have a list of valid entries available. The list contains four items System Analyst, Programmer, Developer, and Database Administrator.

If we take another look at the Property Set Control List form for the IT Resource type we see that now it contains the properties we added to our Object Type Definition. There are some other things we should notice about this screen. On the left, there is a combo box called Type Name that contains the entry IT Resource. There is also a listbox under this combo box.

That listbox always contains a list of available properties for the Object Type Definition currently displayed in the combo box:

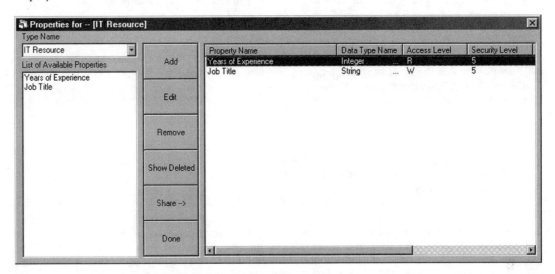

If you want to continue to work through the examples with me, you will need to create another OTD called IT Customer. Add three properties to this type using the same techniques you used for the IT Resource OTD. Make the properties User Logon ID (give it a string data type), Position (give it a string data type), and Training Level (make it a string data type with a list available). Now close down the Property Set Control List form.

Reopen the Person Type Select List form and select IT Resource once more. Now select IT Customer from the combo box, the list of available properties changes as shown in the next image:

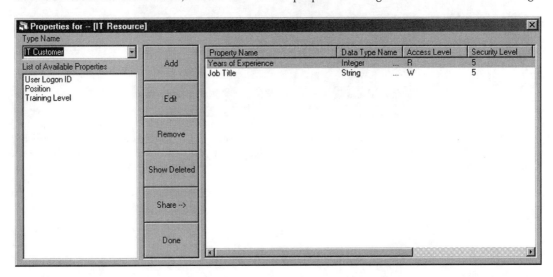

In this screen shot, the Object Type Definition visible in the combo box is IT Customer. Notice that the title of the form still displays Properties for – [IT Resource]. Also notice that the list of properties in the listview on the right is the same as it was earlier. This form only allows you to add edit or delete properties for the Object Type Definition listed in the form's title bar.

> If you are following along with me what you have done up to here is to
> make the Property Set Definition of IT Customer available to the IT
> Resource Object Type Definition.

Now that we know what properties are available for IT Customer, we can decide whether or not we
wish to *share* any of the IT Customer's available properties with our new Object Type Definition - IT
Resource. In this case, the Property Definition User Logon ID seems like a good candidate for
sharing. If we share this property, every IT Resource will have the Property Definition User Logon
ID.

> More importantly for every person who is both an IT Resource and an IT
> Customer, both objects will share the same property value as well as the
> Property Definition.

Let's go through the rest of the steps we must perform to share a property between OTDs. After we
have found a suitable candidate, in this case User Logon ID, all you need to do to is to select that
item from the left-hand listbox and press the Share --> button. This brings up the same Detail screen
we used earlier to add a new Property Definition to the PSD:

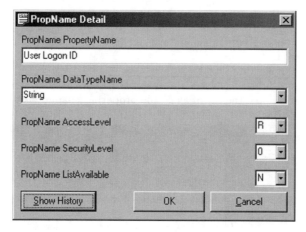

This time all the Detail screen wants to know from you is that you confirm that you do want to share
the property. Press OK, the Detail form will be dismissed and you will be returned to the Property Set
Control List form as shown in the following figure.

From this form, we see that our PSD for IT Resource now contains the new property definition User Logon ID:

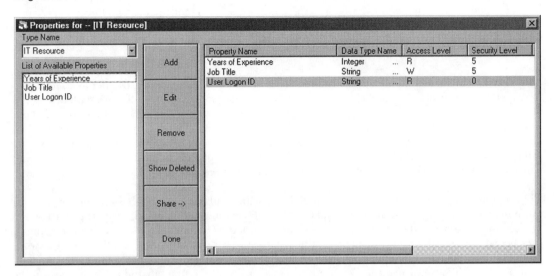

Notice that the new shared property is visible in the listview and the listbox. From this point on, the User Logon ID property is an element of the IT Resource Property Set Definition and we can use it (within the bounds of the original OTD's security definition) as though it was added to the IT Resource PSD from scratch.

What we have just done is to work with one interface that 4-Dimensional Data Objects expose – the administrative interface. We use this interface to extend and maintain 4-Dimensional Data Objects. This interface, in many ways is used to program our objects. Instead of creating new tables, adding fields to existing tables, or otherwise changing our database structure, we simply make a few entries via this interface to meet our customers' needs.

Think about what this means. If a department decides that it needs to track some additional information, we just add a new Property Definition to that object's PSD. For example: If accounting all of a sudden wants to start tracking Mother's Maiden Name, we can accommodate them with a few mouse clicks. We don't need to change a single table or stored procedure in the database. All we need to do is to add the Mother's Maiden Name Property Definition to the PSD. All of our object code will continue to work without modification. Even our Production User Interface will keep working without modification. That is because on every screen we provide a listview that contains all of the properties defined for a particular object type. We load the properties listview with the most current set of properties available for that object type. For example, say that at 9:00 AM the Accounting PSD contained two properties, Gross Income and Net Income. We add the Property Definition for Mother's Maiden Name, using the steps above, and finish that task by 9:01 AM. Immediately after 9:01 AM all users would find the Mother's Maiden Name property in their property listview. That doesn't mean that we wouldn't make changes to the Production User Interface (screens) to accommodate our users' needs. Of course we would. But it does mean that we can make the changes necessary to track the data within seconds. Then even if it takes us a week or two to modify the user interface, making them nicer to look at and easier to use, it won't stop the Accounting department from tracking the new property for this particular object. We will learn exactly how this works in the next chapter, when we will take a look at designing the default Production User Interface for a 4-Dimensional Data Object.

Production User Interface Overview

Earlier, we looked at the administrative interface that we use to manage objects, Object Type Definitions, Property Set Definitions, and individual Property Definitions. That interface's purpose is to allow developers to configure objects for a particular application. You just used it above to create an IT Resource object from a *Person* object.

Now that we have taken a look at the administrative side of a 4-Dimensional Data Object, let's see how this object can be presented to the casual user. The user interface we will work with in this chapter is the default VB interface that the Object Factory delivers with every 4-Dimensional Data Object. The Object Factory also creates several ASP/DHTML interfaces that we will cover in a later chapter. Just like the Level I interfaces we have been working with over the past three chapters, this interface is intended as a starting point. We use it to test data objects to make sure that they do the work they were designed to do (those eight data handling processes) correctly.

This Detail form has quite a task to do. It is charged with displaying a set of base properties that are more or less fixed. But it also must be capable of displaying a set of extended properties for extended types. You just found out how easy it is to add new properties to an OTD, so as you can imagine that means that our Detail form needs to be flexible. It must be able to give the users the ability to work with a set of properties that may be very fluid and change frequently. To handle this task, I used a form with a tab control. I present the base set of properties on the first tab and use a listview on the second tab which is used to present the current set of properties to the user for viewing/editing.

This technique for delivering properties is one of the things that gives us so much flexibility. If we need to add a new property to an object's PSD, we can make it available immediately to all of our users via the property listview. This means that our development team can make a new "field" functionally available to our users in minutes. How's that for turn around time?

Of course, our users expect a lot more from our interfaces than mere functionality. They expect the interface to conform to their wants and wishes as well as to manage their data effectively. What this means in terms of 4-Dimensional Data Objects is that we typically modify the default screen so that one or more properties in the PSD show up in places other than the additional properties listview. This is a fairly trivial task that we will cover in detail in a later chapter. What we will focus on in this chapter, however, is the default Production User Interface of a 4-Dimensional Data Object. It is functionally effective and makes an excellent starting point for designing some pretty impressive user interfaces. Of course, the best thing about ECDOs, and 4-Dimensional ECDOs especially, is that you can use them with any interface. There is absolutely nothing stopping you from delivering these objects via Word, Excel, ASP, and so on... Before you do that though, how about working with the default Production User Interface to see how it handles. Working with it should give you some ideas of how you can improve it.

The starting point for the Production User Interface should look familiar. It follows the same approach that we used with the Level I Data Objects. The first screen the user typically encounters is the List screen as shown:

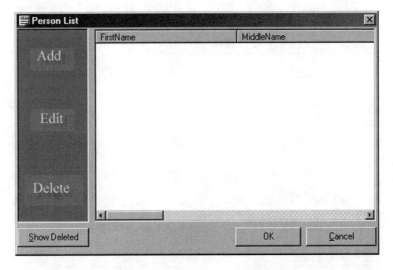

There is one caveat here. For the most part, we don't ever expose an object in its base configuration. In other words, most users don't expect to work with persons. They expect to work with employees or patients etc. What this means is that our List screen should be modified to reflect what type of person (or other 4-Dimensional Data Object) is currently being worked with.

This means the caption in the title bar should read something like IT Resource List, or Customer List rather than Person List as shown. We will go over the mechanical things we need to do to work with a particular type of object when we look at the code behind the VB forms. For now, let's aim for a broader understanding of the overall process.

You can bring up this form by selecting Person | Add New Person from the Work With menu of the MDI form. Click the Add button. It will bring up a Detail form that allows us to work with detailed information about the extended *Person* object. Just to clarify, if the List form displayed a list of IT Resources, the Detail form will display details about an individual *Person* object extended into an IT Resource. If the List form displayed a list of patients, the Detail form would display information about a patient, etc. Each of these extended objects is still a *Person* at its core.

In this case, our List form was set to work with the new OTD we just created – IT Resource. That means that the list of persons that we viewed in the listview would all be IT Resources. It also means that the Property Set Definition loaded for this person on the Detail form is the IT Resource PSD. Fill in some information for the required fields and press OK. When you do that, the Properties tab and the Show History button will become enabled. If you think about it, this makes sense.

Before we have saved the object it doesn't have a history and we couldn't have assigned any addition properties to it.

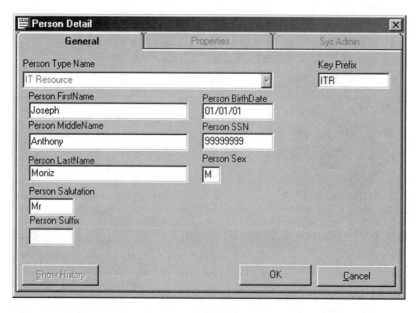

Notice the way that this form is laid out. By default, the base properties for the object are located on the first tab and the extended properties are located on the second tab. We typically reserve the third tab for administrative functions.

If we take a look at the Properties tab for our IT Resource now, we find the list of the properties we assigned to the Property Set Definition for this Object Type Definition. The ones on your screen will not display any values yet. We will get to that in a minute. I hope that it is obvious that if we added a new Property Definition to the Property Set Definition then that property would be functionally available to every user that has permission to access it via this listview. If it isn't obvious, go back and add a new property to the IT Resource OTD. The next time you bring up this form it will be there.

Over the next 4 or 5 chapters we will go over each and every line of code you need to understand to make this work!

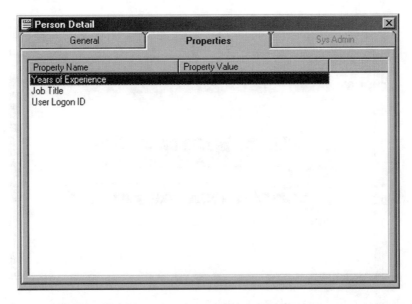

At this point, I must remind you again not to get too carried away with the particulars concerning the user interface. The user interface is a place where we can have a lot of fun. I love designing them myself, but I find that it is a lot more fun to work on user interfaces when I can concentrate on them without the additional programming load that comes from dealing with database functionality and business rule concerns. That is the freedom ECDOs can give you.

As you may or may not expect from the image of the Properties tab above, if you double-click on a particular property, a modal dialog box will be presented that will allow you to edit the value of the property.

If that Property Definition does not specify that a list is available, then the modal dialog box displays a text box for input. This is because it is not possible to have a list of valid entries available for every property. A property can hold just about any kind of information. But, if a list is available, then the modal dialog displays a combo box with the available items.

To get an idea how this works, double-click on the Job Title property and you will be able to select a job title from the list you created earlier:

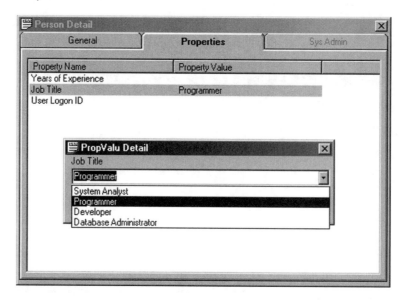

That is really all there is to the default Production User Interface. It was designed with flexibility as the foremost concern. No matter how we have chosen to extend a Person object, this interface will handle the task. The base properties will be displayed on the General tab and the extended properties will be displayed on the Properties tab.

The remainder of this chapter gives you all of the code you need to write to create the Production User Interface. You should find that with very few exceptions it is as easy to work with a 4-Dimensional Data Object as it was to work with a Level I Data Object.

Building the Production User Interface

The Person Object Base Properties

We have been talking about a *Person* object as though we all had exactly the same concept of what information it contained. That is probably not the case. We should treat the development of a 4-Dimensional Data Object just the same way we treat the development of a Level I Data Object, so let's define a base set of properties for a *Person* object. This is not a complete laundry list analysis, but I think it will suffice for our purposes here:

Property Name	Data Type	Length
ID	Long	
LastName	String	30
FirstName	String	30

Property Name	Data Type	Length
MiddleName	String	30
Salutation	String	10
Suffix	String	10
Sex	String	1
BirthDate	Date	
Social Security Number	String	9

Notice that the properties we have chosen as base properties are those things that are common to most people. (Social Security Number is a specific USA contrivance; please ignore or substitute some other base property as appropriate). There is nothing here to suggest that the person is a patient or a doctor etc. We could construct this object using exactly the same techniques we learned earlier for Level I Data Objects.

The Person Object Sample Source Code

When you get finished with this section, the Project Explorer in your VB IDE should look like the one here:

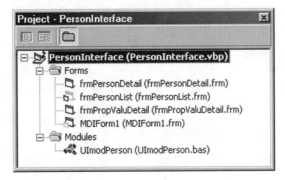

To set up the sample interface project either open the PersonInterface.vbp in the Person directory, or if you wish to create this project from scratch follow these steps:

1. Open a new standard EXE project and rename it PersonInterface.vbp.

2. Add three standard forms and one MDI form to the project. Name the standard forms frmPersonList.frm, frmPersonDetail.frm, frmPropertyValuDetail.frm.

3. Add one module to the project and rename it to UImodPerson.bas.

4. Make a reference to the UCPerson.dll from within the project.

5. Save the project.

The Person Object Production User Interface Screens

The Person Object List Screen

This form, whose file name is `frmPersonList.frm`, is virtually identical to the List forms that we have been using for the last three chapters. The only real difference here is that when we work with higher-level objects we need to specify the type of object that we want a list for. In other words, if we wanted to fill this screen with a list of patients, we would need to specify that we wanted a list of patients by providing the `TypeID` that we use to distinguish patient persons from say doctor persons.

Other than that small difference, you will find that building a List form for a 4-Dimensional Data Object is nearly identical to the steps we took to build a Level I Data Object List form. Because of this similarity, I am just going to point out each of the routines you need to write. You can use the sample code or the code in a previous chapter if you need to refresh your memory. If there are any glaring differences, I will point them out.

Declaration Section

The declaration section of the form is used to provide the form-level local storage variables that we need to work with on this form. If you are working with the sample code, you will find this block of code in the General Declarations section of the `frmPersonList.frm`. If you are building this from scratch, you will have to type the block of declaration code below into the Declarations section.

The first two variables appear to be identical to their Level I counterparts. For the most part, they are. They give us access to two collections – the collection of currently active *Person* objects and a collection of currently deleted *Person* objects. This is exactly the same as the Level I treatment.

The next collection object introduces the new concept we need to talk about here:

```
Private mcolTypes As UCPerson.colTypes
```

This collection contains all of the available Object Type Definitions for the *Person* object. In other words, this collection might read like: Engineer, Doctor, Lawyer, Patient, Customer, Student, etc. We work with it exactly like we worked with other Level I Data Objects in the previous chapters. The next line in the code that might look unfamiliar is the following:

```
Private mlngParentTypeID As Long
```

This local storage variable is provided to hold the `TypeID` for our target objects. In other words, if the `TypeID` for Doctor was 7, then this variable would contain the value 7. The rest of this section should be self-explanatory as everything about it is the same as the Level I treatment:

```
Option Explicit

' Dimension the local storage variables
Private mcolPersons As UCPerson.colPersons
Private mcolPersonsDeleted As UCPerson.colPersons
Private mcolTypes As UCPerson.colTypes
Private mstrButtonPressed As String

' Use these constants for the sizing routines
```

```
Private Const jamShowDeleted As Integer = 8760
Private Const jamHideDeleted As Integer = 4830

Private mlngParentTypeID As Long
```

Form-Level Properties

We use property handlers as the sole means of access to the local storage variables in a form or other module of code. This allows us to manage the housekeeping tasks in a single location and also provides us with a measure of control over the information that flows into or out of a given module. In this case, we need five pairs of property handlers, one for each form-level storage variable.

Persons

```
Public Property Get Persons() As UCPerson.colPersons

    If mcolPersons Is Nothing Then
        Set mcolPersons = New UCPerson.colPersons
    End If
    Set Persons = mcolPersons

End Property
```

```
Public Property Let Persons(colPersons As UCPerson.colPersons)

    Set mcolPersons = colPersons

End Property
```

Deleted Persons

```
Public Property Get PersonsDeleted() As UCPerson.colPersons

    If mcolPersonsDeleted Is Nothing Then
        Set mcolPersonsDeleted = New UCPerson.colPersons
    End If
    Set PersonsDeleted = mcolPersonsDeleted

End Property
```

```
Public Property Let PersonsDeleted(colPersonsDeleted As _
                          UCPerson.colPersons)

    Set mcolPersonsDeleted = colPersonsDeleted

End Property
```

Types

```
Public Property Get Types() As UCPerson.colTypes

    If mcolTypes Is Nothing Then
        Set mcolTypes = New UCPerson.colTypes
    End If
```

```
      Types = mcolTypes

  End Property
```

```
  Public Property Let Types(colTypes As UCPerson.colTypes)

      Set mcolTypes = colTypes

  End Property
```

Parent Type ID

```
  Public Property Get ParentTypeID() As Long

      ParentTypeID = mlngParentTypeID

  End Property
```

```
  Public Property Let ParentTypeID(lngParentTypeID As Long)

      mlngParentTypeID = lngParentTypeID

  End Property
```

Button Pressed Message

```
  Public Property Get ButtonPressed() As String

      ButtonPressed = mstrButtonPressed

  End Property
```

Form_Load - frmPersonList.frm

The next section of code you need to write is the Form_Load routine. This is just about the same as the Level I treatment, so I won't reprint it here. The things we need to accomplish in this routine are to:

- ❑ Prepare the active listview
- ❑ Configure the deleted listview
- ❑ Load a collection of *Person* objects from the data store
- ❑ Display the collection on the active listview

The only difference we will find between this routine and a Level I Form_Load routine is the line that loads the collection of objects:

```
      Persons.Load ParentTypeID
```

Notice here that we are passing a parameter to the Load method. This parameter is used to identify the type of *Person* objects we want to load onto this form. Again, if Doctors were identified by a TypeID of 7, then this form-level property, ParentTypeID, would contain the value 7.

LoadPersonListView – frmPersonList.frm

Once again, this code is virtually identical to the Level I treatment. The purpose of this routine is to load the active listview with the *Person* objects in the local collection. The only thing you need to be sure to do here to use the correct declaration as shown:

```
Dim ThisObject As UCPerson.clsPerson
```

imgAdd_Click

This subroutine is used to add a new member to the collection. The only real difference between this code and its Level I counterpart is that in addition to passing the new empty *Person* object to the Detail form, we also pass the *Person* `TypeID` information to the Detail form:

```
.PersonTypeID = ParentTypeID
.Person = ThisObject
```

imgEdit_Click

This subroutine is used to allow the user to work with an individual object. First, it determines which object from the collection the user wants to work with. Then it passes the selected object to the Detail form and displays the Detail form modally. Notice that except for passing the `TypeID`, there is *no* difference between the Level I and 4-Dimensional Data Object treatment:

```
.PersonTypeID = ParentTypeID
.Person = ThisObject
```

imgDelete_Click – frmPersonList.frm

This subroutine is used to delete an existing element from a collection. There is one slight difference between the Level I and 4-dimensional treatment. We must remember that we are working with a collection of *Person* objects that have been cast as, say, patient objects. This means that if the deleted listview is visible and must be updated, we must remember that when we ask to see a list of the deleted members, that what we are really asking for is to see a collection of deleted members of a particular type. In other words, if we are working with patients, we only want to see deleted patients – not deleted doctors, nurses. This requirement may sound rather daunting, but it is not difficult to handle. Actually, all we need to do at the user interface level to handle this task is to specify which deleted objects we want to view. We do that by, I bet you guessed it, passing the `TypeID` into the `ShowDeleted` method.

In other words, the only difference between this treatment and the Level I treatment is the following line where we, in essence, ask for a response filtered by `TypeID`:

```
PersonsDeleted.ShowDeleted ParentTypeID
```

cmdDeleted_Click – frmPersonList.frm

This subroutine is used to display members of the collection that are currently deleted. As with the `imgDelete_Click` routine, there is one slight difference between the Level I and 4-dimensional treatment. We must remember to ask for a response that has been filtered by `TypeID`:

```
PersonsDeleted.ShowDeleted ParentTypeID
```

cmdOK_Click

The `cmdOK_Click` is used to send a message to the calling form (if there is one) and unload the listview form:

```
Private Sub cmdOK_Click()

    mstrButtonPressed = "OK"
    Unload Me

End Sub
```

cmdCancel_Click

The `cmdCancel_Click` is used to send a message to the calling form (if there is one) and unload the listview form:

```
Private Sub cmdCancel_Click()

    mstrButtonPressed = "Cancel"
    Unload Me

End Sub
```

lvwPersons_DblClick

The `lvwPersons_DblClick` event should be tied to the Edit control. This allows the user to select and call the Detail form with a single action:

```
Private Sub lvwPersons_DblClick()

    imgEdit_Click

End Sub
```

LoadPersonsDeletedListView

Once again, this code is virtually identical to the Level I treatment. The purpose of this routine is to load the deleted listview with the *Person* objects in the deleted collection.

lvwPersonsDeleted_DblClick

This subroutine is used to work with members of the collection that are currently deleted. This code is really kind of a modified edit subroutine. The major difference between the two is that we pass a string that indicates that this object is currently deleted in the `SourceControl` property as shown.

```
.SourceControl = "lvwPersonsDeleted"
```

Remember from the Level I treatment that if the length of this property is greater than 0, that means that the object we are working with on the detail form is currently deleted. This is not the only similarity. Overall, this code is identical to the Level I treatment with the following exception:

```
PersonsDeleted.ShowDeleted ParentTypeID
```

This line is used to refresh the local collection to reflect the changes that have been made to the data store. We must treat it exactly the same way we treated it when we initially loaded this collection. That means that when we ask to see a list of the deleted members, that what we are really asking for is to see a collection of deleted members of a particular type. In other words, if we are working with patients, we only want to see deleted patients – not deleted doctors, nurses. Actually, all we need to do at the user interface level to handle this task is to specify which deleted objects we want to view.

lvwPersons_ColumnClick

This routine allows the user to sort the listview by any column by simply clicking on the column header.

lvwPersonsDeleted_ColumnClick

This routine allows the user to sort the deleted listview by any column by simply clicking on the column header.

Form_Unload

As with all good development, we are careful to perform housekeeping chores whenever we complete a task. In this case, we ensure that each of the local object variables is destroyed. The errors that stem from failing to perform this simple task are countless, confounding, and unnecessary:

```
Private Sub Form_Unload(Cancel As Integer)

    Set mcolPersons = Nothing
    Set mcolPersonsDeleted = Nothing
    Set mcolTypes = Nothing

End Sub
```

The Person Object Detail Screen

The next screen we need to design and build to work with a 4-Dimensional Data Object should not look familiar. It is not the same as its Level I counterpart. But, fortunately the differences between the two are slight. The first difference is that this screen contains not just an instance of an object, but an extended instance of an object. In other words, this screen is for working with *Person* objects expressed as doctors, patients, lawyers, clients, etc. That means that each object is delivered to this screen with an associated `TypeID`.

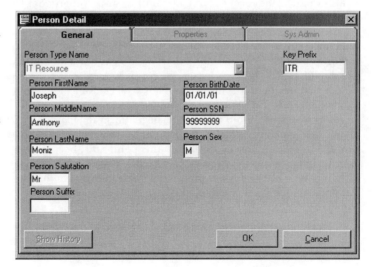

The second difference is that this screen contains a list of properties and associated values that define the *Person* as the extended object:

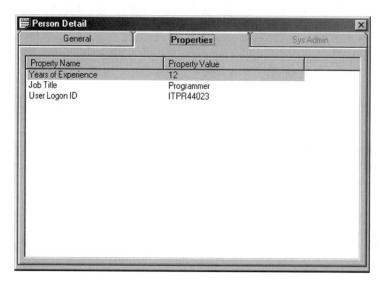

In this case, we are working with a *Person* object extended into an IT Resource. That means that we have 3 additional pieces of information to manage. In this case:

❑   Years of Experience
❑   Job Title
❑   User Logon ID

We do not need to be concerned with the contents of this list at all when we design this form. Our goal is to make the form capable of handling any Property Set Definition. This is an expression of what allows us to reuse most of our code. I say expression, because the user interface is one area where code reuse is *not* really a priority. (Surprised?) Our ultimate goal when we deliver an enterprise is to make the users' experience better. That means that we create custom forms for applications at the drop of a hat. What we don't do is create custom data objects at the drop of a hat. I hope you can see the difference. It is less expensive for us to display the three properties above in separate controls on the first tab, than it is for us to create a special object just to handle IT Resource information.

In other words, we could redesign a special form for handling IT Resources information without changing the underlying objects that manage the data. This would be easy, cheap, and win us a lot of points from the end users. I bring up this point now, because we will handle the forms in this chapter from a very generic perspective. Our goal in this chapter is to design a single form that is capable of handling type of a particular object. The person form can handle doctors, lawyers, programmers, etc. An organization form could handle corporations, partnerships, sole proprietorships, etc.

> *Please do not misinterpret the goals of this book. We are designing reusable data objects, not reusable interfaces. Reusable data objects are cost effective and enhance the overall perception of quality of the system, while reusable boilerplate interfaces tend to lessen the users esteem for the system. Certainly, reusable interfaces are easy to design and cheap to implement.*

But, I would not say that they are cost effective or that they enhance the overall quality of the enterprise. Imagine if everyone in the world had to drive the exactly the same car, or wear exactly the same clothes. The beauty of reusable data objects is that we can reuse the underlying mechanics (the critical part the users and most managers really don't care about) while still offering each different group of users an individual expression.

Declaration Section

When we look through the declaration section of the Detail form, we find that we are familiar with almost all of the local storage variable definitions except for three. The first one that should look foreign is the `mcolTypes` variable. The second one that should look foreign is the `mcolPropBag` declaration. This is that portion of the 4-Dimensional Data Object that contains the extended properties collection. The third is the `mblnSysAdmin` variable. This flag is used to enable or disable the system administration tab. It may not be clear yet, but we test the user's security level and if it is sufficiently high enough, then we allow the system administration tab to be accessed:

```
Option Explicit

'Dimension the local variables
Private mstrButtonPressed As String
Private mlngPersonTypeID As Long
Private WithEvents mobjPerson As UCPerson.clsPerson
Private mcolPersonHistory As UCPerson.colPersons
Private mcolTypes As UCPerson.colTypes
Private mcolPropBag As UCPerson.colPropBags
Private mstrSourceControl As String
Private mblnSysAdmin As Boolean


' Use these local constants to resize the form
' History Listview Visible
Private Const jamShowHistory As Integer = 8520

' History Listview Hidden
Private Const jamHideHistory As Integer = 5115
```

Form-Level Properties

We use property handlers as the sole means of access to the local storage variables in a form or other module of code. This allows us to manage the housekeeping tasks in a single location and also provides us with a measure of control over the information that flows into or out of a given module. In this case, we need eight property handlers, one for each form-level storage variable.

Person

```
Public Property Get Person() As UCPerson.clsPerson

    If mobjPerson Is Nothing Then
        Err.Raise vbObjectError, _
          "This form requires an existing Person object"
    End If
    Set Person = mobjPerson

End Property
```

```
Public Property Let Person(objPerson As UCPerson.clsPerson)

    Set mobjPerson = objPerson

End Property
```

Person Property Bag

```
Public Property Get PropBag() As UCPerson.colPropBags

    If mcolPropBag Is Nothing Then
        Set mcolPropBag = New UCPerson.colPropBags
    End If
    Set PropBag = mcolPropBag

End Property
```

Person History Collection

```
Public Property Get PersonHistory() As UCPerson.colPersons

    If mcolPersonHistory Is Nothing Then
        Set mcolPersonHistory = New UCPerson.colPersons
    End If
    Set PersonHistory = mcolPersonHistory

End Property
```

Person Type ID

```
Public Property Get PersonTypeID() As Long

    PersonTypeID = mlngPersonTypeID

End Property
```

```
Public Property Let PersonTypeID(lngPersonTypeID As Long)

    mlngPersonTypeID = lngPersonTypeID

End Property
```

Types

```
Public Property Get Types() As UCPerson.colTypes

    If mcolTypes Is Nothing Then
        Set mcolTypes = New UCPerson.colTypes
    End If
    Set Types = mcolTypes

End Property
```

```
Public Property Let Types(colTypes As UCPerson.colTypes)

    Set mcolTypes = colTypes

End Property
```

System Administration Flag

```
Public Property Get SysAdmin() As Boolean

    SysAdmin = mblnSysAdmin

End Property
```

```
Public Property Let SysAdmin(blnSysAdmin As Boolean)

    mblnSysAdmin = blnSysAdmin

End Property
```

Button Pressed Message

```
Public Property Get ButtonPressed() As String

    ButtonPressed = mstrButtonPressed

End Property
```

Source Control

```
Public Property Get SourceControl() As String

    SourceControl = mstrSourceControl

End Property
```

```
Public Property Let SourceControl(strSourceControl As String)

    mstrSourceControl = strSourceControl

End Property
```

Form_Load

Our next task is to perform the `Form_Load`. This code should also look familiar, but it really diverges from the Level I code in several areas. You can find the sample code in the `frmPersonDetail.frm`.

The first thing we need to do is to configure the tabs on the form. That is done with the following code:

```
SSTab1.TabEnabled(2) = SysAdmin
SSTab1.Tab = 0
```

This is really straightforward; if the user has sufficient privileges, then the SysAdmin property will contain the value True. If the user doesn't have sufficient privileges, then it will contain the value False. This sets the enabled state for the **Sys Admin** tab. The next line just ensures that the currently active tab is tab zero - in this case the **General** tab.

After this section of code, we are just concerned with configuring the listviews that we need to use to hold the property pairs and the object's history. We are familiar with this code.

Once the listviews have been configured, the next step is to check the object we are working with to determine whether or not the user is attempting to restore it from a deleted state:

```
If Len(SourceControl) > 0 Then
    ' If this object was delivered from a deleted state then
    ' morph form
    cmdOK.Caption = "Restore"
    cmdHistory.Enabled = False
    Me.Caption = Me.Caption & " - [Restore]"
End If
```

We have seen this code before with the standard Level I Detail Form. Once we know where the object came from, we can perform another step towards configuring this form for use:

```
'Initially disable properties tab if this is an add or restore
If Person.IsNew Or Len(SourceControl) Then
  SSTab1.TabEnabled(1) = False
End If
```

If the object is a new one then it will not have a property bag, so in that case we disable the second or **Properties** tab. If the object is currently deleted then it will not have a connection to its property bag (which is also deleted) so we need to disable the second tab in this case as well.

This next set of code is really more important for our purposes here, which is to understand how 4-Dimensional Data Objects work. In actual production code, I would eliminate the following step, which loads a list of available types for the base object. We use this so that we can test many different extended objects with a single set of forms. As we covered earlier, for production environments, we would add forms as necessary. That means that by the time we got to a particular Detail form we would already know what type of extended object we were working with.

```
If mcolTypes Is Nothing Then
    Types.SetDataSource strConnect
    Types.Load
End If

For Each ThisType In Types
    cboTypeName.AddItem ThisType.Name
    If ThisType.ID = PersonTypeID Then
        cboTypeName.Text = ThisType.Name
        Person.TypeID = PersonTypeID
    End If
Next ThisType
```

The next step is used to test whether or not the object is new. If it is, then we clear the form and allow the load to continue. If it is not new, then we test to see if the user is attempting to restore the object.

If this object is not currently deleted then "length of source control = 0" and we load the extended property information for this object using the `PropBag.Load` method:

```
If Person.IsNew Then
    ' If new object then clear the form
        cmdOK.Enabled = False
        cmdHistory.Enabled = False
        ClearForm
        cboTypeName_Click
Else
    If Len(SourceControl) = 0 Then
        PropBag.SetDataSource strConnect
        PropBag.Load Person.ID, PersonTypeID, UserLogon
    End If
    ' Populate controls
    SetPersonState
End If
```

Notice that the technique we use to load the property bag is very similar to the technique we use to load all other collections. We simply type the name of the method and pass the required parameters. In this case, the parameters are the base object's ID, the `TypeID`, and the `UserLogon`. We won't go into the details here, but the `UserLogon` is required because it is possible that during a `PropBag` load the data store might be changed to reflect changes in the Property Set Definition. For instance, suppose someone deleted a Property Definition or someone added a Property Definition since the last time this object's Property Bag was loaded. The Property Bag load routine tests for these possibilities and synchronizes the object's current Property Set Definition with this type's current Property Set Definition.

mobjPerson_Valid

We have seen this code before; it uses the `Valid` event of the *Person* object to reflect the object's current validation state. This routine synchronizes the OK button with that state:

```
Private Sub mobjPerson_Valid(blnIsValid As Boolean)

    cmdOK.Enabled = blnIsValid

End Sub
```

lvwProperties_DblClick

In addition to giving the user a way to view the extended properties for an object, we also need to give the user a way to edit the extended properties. This is handled in the `lvwProperties_DblClick` event. Now, even though we are working with a new object, the `PropBag` object, you should notice a similarity between this subroutine and all of the other listview double click routines that we have written before. Think about it, they are the same. In both cases, we are just selecting a particular object from a collection, checking that object out from the collection and working with that object. We work with the object on a Detail form that we raise from this routine. In both cases, when we are finished working with the object, we just check it back into the collection. If you read through the code, you will also see that not only is this code exactly like all other listview double click routines, but that we can also reuse this code for any 4-Dimensional Object's Property Bag. To use this code with any *Widget* object, all we have to do is to perform a search and replace on this section of code and replace the word `Person` with the word `Widget`:

```
Private Sub lvwProperties_DblClick()

    Dim ThisObject As UCPerson.clsPropBag

    On Error GoTo lvwProperties_DblClickError

    ' Let the user know the application is busy
    Screen.MousePointer = vbHourglass

    ' Find the Object in the collection the user needs to edited
    For Each ThisObject In PropBag
        If ThisObject.Key = lvwProperties.SelectedItem.Key Then
            ' Remove the Selected Object from the collection and
            ' enable editing
            ' This method handles all of the parent-child
            ' relationships
            Set ThisObject = PropBag.CheckOutObject(ThisObject.ID)
            Exit For
        End If
    Next ThisObject

    ' Redundant but, if the object still has not been set then
    ' exit sub
    If ThisObject Is Nothing Then Exit Sub
```

We need to give the user a way to edit property values. We use the Property Value Detail form for this purpose. As we will see below, that form handles all of the updating tasks so all we really need to do here is to pass the property that needs to be edited and show the form modally:

```
    ' Place the object on the detail form
    With frmPropValuDetail
        .PropBag = ThisObject
        ' Always pass the Logon ID for the current User.
        .PropBag.StampUser = UserLogon
        .Show vbModal
    End With
    Set frmPropValuDetail = Nothing

    ' This places the object back into the collection disables
    ' editing and manages all the parent child relationships
    PropBag.CheckInObject ThisObject
    LoadPersonProperties

    ' Let the user know the application is done
    Screen.MousePointer = vbDefault

    Exit Sub

lvwProperties_DblClickError:

    ErrorHandler

End Sub
```

Note the call to ErrorHandler - this is a routine which instantiates an instance of the ErrCond object, which we'll discuss in a later chapter.

cmdHistory_Click

This routine is used to show the history of changes over time for the object currently loaded onto the Detail form. Although there are quite a few differences between this Detail form and the Level I treatment, you can handle showing the object history in exactly the same fashion.

LoadPersonHistoryListView

This routine loads the individual snapshots of an object's history into the history listview. We have seen this routine many times before. The only difference from object to object is the name of the properties we display in the listview. It is identical to the Level I treatment.

cmdOK_Click

The OK button click raises a couple of new problems that we haven't faced before. So I will ask you to look at the code now and try to identify the changes. Then we will step through each of the new coding requirements below.

```
Private Sub cmdOK_Click()

    On Error GoTo cmdOK_Click_ClickError

    ' let the user know that the application is busy
    Screen.MousePointer = vbHourglass
    mstrButtonPressed = "OK"
    Person.SetDataSource strConnect

    If Len(SourceControl) > 0 Then
        Person.ObjectRestoreFromDeleted
        Unload Me
        Screen.MousePointer = vbDefault
        Exit Sub
    End If

    If Person.IsNew Then
        Person.ObjectInsert
        SSTab1.TabEnabled(1) = True
        PropBag.SetDataSource strConnect
        PropBag.Load Person.ID, Person.TypeID, UserLogon
        LoadPersonProperties
        Screen.MousePointer = vbDefault
    Else
        If Len(SourceControl) = 0 Then
            Person.ObjectUpdate
            PropBag.BatchSave
            Screen.MousePointer = vbDefault
            SourceControl = ""
            Unload Me
        End If
    End If

    Exit Sub

cmdOK_Click_ClickError:

    ErrorHandler

End Sub
```

The first thing you might have noticed is the test to see whether or not the currently loaded object is being restored from a deleted state. If so, we need to invoke the object's `RestoreFromDeleted` method. This is not new; we do exactly the same thing with Level I objects:

```
If Len(SourceControl) > 0 Then
    Person.ObjectRestoreFromDeleted
    Unload Me
    Screen.MousePointer = vbDefault
    Exit Sub
End If
```

The portion of the code that is new is in the next section where we test to see if the object is new. If it is, then we insert the object. This causes a Property Bag of the correct type to be built for the object. Then we need to enable the second (**Properties**) tab on the tab control and load the properties. This is handled in exactly the same way we handled it in the `Form_Load` routine. Once the Property Bag has been loaded, we display the objects in the properties listview by calling the `LoadPersonProperties` routine:

```
If Person.IsNew Then
    Person.ObjectInsert
    SSTab1.TabEnabled(1) = True
    PropBag.SetDataSource strConnect
    PropBag.Load Person.ID, Person.TypeID, UserLogon
    LoadPersonProperties
    Screen.MousePointer = vbDefault
Else
    If Len(SourceControl) = 0 Then
        Person.ObjectUpdate
        PropBag.BatchSave
        Screen.MousePointer = vbDefault
        SourceControl = ""
        Unload Me
    End If
End If
```

If the object is not new, and the object is not being restored from deleted, then we use the code above to save the changes to the data store. The `Person.ObjectUpdate` line updates the object's base properties and the `PropBag.BatchSave` line causes any changes in the Property Bag that have not been sent to the database to be saved at this time.

Before we move onto the next command button we ought to just quickly visit the `LoadPersonProperties` routine:

LoadPersonProperties

This routine basically just cycles through the Property Bag and loads the properties into the listview control:

```
Public Sub LoadPersonPropeties()

    Dim ThisProperty As UCPerson.clsPropBag
    Dim Items As ListItems
    Dim ThisItem As ListItem

    Set Items = lvwProperties.ListItems
    Items.Clear
```

```
      For Each ThisProperty In PropBag
         Set ThisItem = Items.Add(, ThisProperty.Key, ThisProperty.PropertyName)
         ThisItem.SubItems(1) = ThisProperty.Value
      Next ThisProperty

   End Sub
```

cmdCancel_Click

If the user clicks the <u>C</u>ancel button, we need to do three things:

- ❏ Send a message to the calling form
- ❏ Call the object's `CancelEdit` method (this sets the object's state back to what it was before the user performed any editing)
- ❏ Unload the form.

```
   Private Sub cmdCancel_Click()

      If mstrButtonPressed <> "OK" Then
         mstrButtonPressed = "Cancel"
      End If
      Person.CancelEdit
      Unload Me

   End Sub
```

ClearForm

The `ClearForm` subroutine is really about the same as the Level I treatment:

```
   Public Sub ClearForm()

      txtPersonFirstName.Text = ""
      txtPersonMiddleName.Text = ""
      txtPersonLastName.Text = ""
      txtPersonSalutation.Text = ""
      txtPersonSuffix.Text = ""
      txtPersonBirthDate.Text = ""
      txtPersonSSN.Text = ""
      txtPersonSex.Text = ""
      txtCertificationNumber.Text = ""
      txtCertificationDate.Text = ""

   End Sub
```

SetPersonState

You might think that the `SetPersonState` routine would be very similar to the Level I treatment, but there is one very big difference. When we are working with 4-Dimensional Data Objects, we have to manage the added responsibility of managing the Property Bag. Of course, we do that with a single routine called `LoadPersonProperties` so that we don't have to duplicate the code. But it is important to remember to call that routine, otherwise the values in the Property Bag will not be displayed on the screen:

```
Public Sub SetPersonState()

    txtPersonFirstName.Text = Person.FirstName
    txtPersonMiddleName.Text = Person.MiddleName
    txtPersonLastName.Text = Person.LastName
    txtPersonSalutation.Text = Person.Salutation
    txtPersonSuffix.Text = Person.Suffix
    txtPersonBirthDate.Text = Person.BirthDate
    txtPersonSSN.Text = Person.SSN
    txtPersonSex.Text = Person.Sex
    cboTypeName.Text = Person.TypeName
    LoadPersonProperties

End Sub
```

lvwPersonHistory_DblClick

This routine allows the user to select a set of previous values for an object and enter those values into the input controls with a mouse double click. It is important to note that we are not saving the changes when the user double clicks this listview. We are merely copying the previous values to the current object. The user still has to actively save the changes to cause the old values to replace the current values in the data store. This functionality offers the user the ability to undo any changes that have been made to an object. This is necessary in an environment where an entire organization is sharing the same data store.

```
Private Sub lvwPersonHistory_DblClick()

   Dim ThisObject As UCPerson.clsPerson

   On Error GoTo lvwDataTypeHistory_DblClickError

' find the object the user wants to restore
   For Each ThisObject In PersonHistory
     If ThisObject.Key = lvwPersonHistory.SelectedItem.Key Then
        Person.IsValid = ThisObject.IsValid
        Person.StampUser = ThisObject.StampUser
        Person.ChangeAll = ThisObject.ChangeAll
        Person.StampDateTime = ThisObject.StampDateTime
        Person.StampAction = ThisObject.StampAction
        Person.StampID = ThisObject.StampID
        Person.DataMessage = ThisObject.DataMessage
        Person.CollisionMessages = ThisObject.CollisionMessages
        Person.DataLocking = ThisObject.DataLocking
        Person.ID = ThisObject.StampID
        Person.FirstName = ThisObject.FirstName
        Person.MiddleName = ThisObject.MiddleName
        Person.LastName = ThisObject.LastName
        Person.Salutation = ThisObject.Salutation
        Person.Suffix = ThisObject.Suffix
        Person.BirthDate = ThisObject.BirthDate
        Person.SSN = ThisObject.SSN
        Person.Sex = ThisObject.Sex
        Person.TypeID = ThisObject.TypeID
        Person.TypeName = ThisObject.TypeName
        SetPersonState
        Exit For
```

```
      End If
   Next ThisObject

   Exit Sub

 lvwDataTypeHistory_DblClickError:

   ErrorHandler

End Sub
```

Local Data Validation Handling

The following routines have been provided to give you an idea of how we handle some very general data validation issues right on the user interface. In other words, we try to take advantage of the things we *can* know – numeric fields should not accept alphabetical characters, date fields must have a value that evaluates to a date etc. The headings are designed to identify data types rather than any particular property.

txtNON-DATE_BASE_PROPERTY_LostFocus

The following code has been provided to illustrate the fact that we must actively copy the values from the input controls into the form's current object. This can be done on the LostFocus or the Change events. There are advantages and drawbacks to both methods. I have settled on the LostFocus event as the lessor of two evils. It allows us to perform high quality data validation at the object level. Sometimes, as with dates for example, we need the user's complete input in order to make these kinds of decisions. The Change event executes on every keystroke. We use the KeyPress event to perform data validation at that level. See below:

```
Private Sub txtPersonFirstName_LostFocus()

   Person.FirstName = txtPersonFirstName.Text
   txtPersonFirstName.Text = Person.FirstName

End Sub
```

```
Private Sub txtPersonMiddleName_LostFocus()

   Person.MiddleName = txtPersonMiddleName.Text
   txtPersonMiddleName.Text = Person.MiddleName

End Sub
```

txtDATE_PROPERTY_LostFocus

If the property that our input control is handling is a date then we add the following line of code to the LostFocus event. Although data validation is handled in the business object, we try to catch the most obvious rule-breakers at the source in the name of efficiency. The following code does that nicely:

```
Private Sub txtPersonBirthDate_LostFocus()

   If Len(txtPersonBirthDate.Text) > 0 Then
      If Not IsDate(Trim(txtPersonBirthDate)) Then
         MsgBox "A Valid Date is required for this field"
```

```
            txtPersonBirthDate.SetFocus
            Exit Sub
        End If
    End If

    Person.BirthDate = txtPersonBirthDate.Text
    txtPersonBirthDate.Text = Person.BirthDate

End Sub
```

txtPersonBirthDate_KeyPress

The KeyPress is another place where we can do some data validation. In the example below, we use the KeyPress event to ensure that all of the values that get entered into a textbox are either a value from 0 to 9, a backspace, or a forward slash – in other words, valid date characters:

```
Private Sub txtPersonBirthDate_KeyPress(KeyAscii As Integer)

    ' Integer and Long Keypress Test Includes 0123456789/
    Select Case KeyAscii
        Case 47 To 57, 8
        Case Else
            KeyAscii = 0
    End Select

End Sub
```

cboTypeName_KeyPress

In the case of a combo box, we might not wish to accept any keystrokes as user input. Most likely the reason we use a combo box is to limit the possible data entry values to the items in the combo box. The following code illustrates how to negate any keystrokes the user enters:

```
Private Sub cboTypeName_KeyPress(KeyAscii As Integer)

    KeyAscii = 0

End Sub
```

This doesn't handle the very real possibility that the user will attempt to enter a keystroke combination (*Ctrl* + *V* to paste data into a control) or press the *Delete* key or something. To handle those occurrences we need to use the following little piece of code:

```
Private Sub cboTypeName_KeyDown(KeyCode As Integer)

    KeyCode = 0

End Sub
```

cboTypeName_Click

This code is provided in the standard output from the Object Factory. It is provided to give us a form that will allow us to switch between different OTDs. I cannot recommend this practice in production. This code has been provided to illustrate a technique:

```
Private Sub cboTypeName_Click()

  Dim strTypeName As String
  Dim ThisType As UCPerson.clsType
  strTypeName = cboTypeName.Text

  For Each ThisType In Types
     If ThisType.Name = strTypeName Then
        Person.TypeID = ThisType.ID
        Exit For
     End If
  Next ThisType

  Set ThisType = Nothing

End Sub
```

IvwPersonHistory_ColumnClick

As always we add a little bit of code to the listview to allow the user to sort the data by clicking on the column headers. You can find an example of this code in any sample List or Detail form.

Form_Unload

As with all good development, we are careful to perform housekeeping chores whenever we complete a task. In this case, we ensure that each of the local object variables is destroyed. The errors that stem from failing to perform this simple task are countless, confounding, and unnecessary:

```
Private Sub Form_Unload(Cancel As Integer)

   SourceControl = ""
   Set mcolPersonHistory = Nothing
   Set mobjPerson = Nothing
   Set mcolTypes = Nothing

End Sub
```

The Person Object Property Value Detail Screen

The Property Value Detail screen does not have a corollary in the Level I object screen set. It is unique to the 4-Dimensional Data Object. Still, you should find that we use nearly the same techniques to work with data on this screen as we used in all of the previous screens:

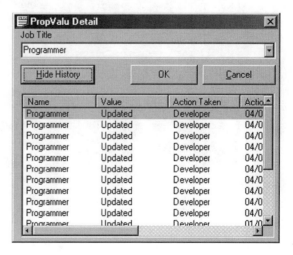

The Property Value Detail screen has a single purpose. It is designed to collect a valid response from a user for a particular Property Definition. In order for it to perform this simple task, it first needs to be able to determine whether or not the property it is editing has a list of valid responses or not. It also needs to be able to identify what data types are valid responses for a particular Property Definition.

Declaration Section

When we look through the declaration section of the Property Value Detail form, we find that we are familiar with almost all of the local storage variable definitions except for one. The only one that should look foreign is the `colPropItems` declaration. This local storage variable is used to handle the property definitions that offer a specific list of available responses:

```
Option Explicit

'Dimension the local variables
Private mstrButtonPressed As String
Private WithEvents mobjPropBag As UCPerson.clsPropBag
Private mcolPropValuHistory As UCPerson.colPropBags
Private mstrSourceControl As String
Private mcolPropItems As UCPerson.colPropItems

' Use these local constants to resize the form
' History Listview Visible
Private Const jamShowHistory As Integer = 4395

' History Listview Hidden
Private Const jamHideHistory As Integer = 1455
```

Form-Level Properties

We use property handlers as the sole means of access to the local storage variables in a form or other module of code. This allows us to manage the housekeeping tasks in a single location and also provides us a measure of control over the information that flows into or out of a given module. In this case, we need five property handlers, one for each form level storage variable.

Property Bag

```
Public Property Get PropBag() As UCPerson.clsPropBag

    If mobjPropBag Is Nothing Then
        Err.Raise vbObjectError, _
        "This form requires an existing PropValu object"
    End If
    Set PropBag = mobjPropBag

End Property

Public Property Let PropBag(objPropBag As UCPerson.clsPropBag)

    Set mobjPropBag = objPropBag

End Property
```

Property Item List

This is a property that is unfamiliar to us. It is really quite simple. If a Property Definition has a list of valid responses, we use the `colPropItems` collection to manage those responses:

```
Public Property Get PropItems() As UCPerson.colPropItems

    If mcolPropItems Is Nothing Then
        Set mcolPropItems = New UCPerson.colPropItems
    End If
    Set PropItems = mcolPropItems

End Property
```

Property Value History

Because 4-Dimensional Data Objects are constructed from Level I ECDOs every sub-object exhibits the same 8 data handling processes. That means that we can always expect to find an audit history, even for the property values:

```
Public Property Get PropValuHistory() As UCPerson.colPropBags

    If mcolPropValuHistory Is Nothing Then
        Set mcolPropValuHistory = New UCPerson.colPropBags
    End If
    Set PropValuHistory = mcolPropValuHistory

End Property
```

Button Pressed Message

```
Public Property Get ButtonPressed() As String

    ButtonPressed = mstrButtonPressed

End Property
```

Source Control

```
Public Property Get SourceControl() As String

    SourceControl = mstrSourceControl

End Property
```

```
Public Property Let SourceControl(strSourceControl As String)

    mstrSourceControl = strSourceControl

End Property
```

Form_Load

Our next task is to perform the `Form_Load`. This code should also look familiar. And although it diverges from the standard Level I treatment, we have already covered the concepts you need to know to understand this code. Read through the listing, we will examine the details below:

```
Private Sub Form_Load()

   On Error GoTo Form_LoadError

   Me.Height = jamHideHistory
   'let the user know the application is busy
   Screen.MousePointer = vbHourglass

   ' Set up the Object history Listview columnheaders
   ' lvwPropValuHistory.ColumnHeaders.Add , , "Name", 1440
   lvwPropValuHistory.ColumnHeaders.Add , , "Value", 1440
   lvwPropValuHistory.ColumnHeaders.Add , , _
                     "Action Taken", 1440
   lvwPropValuHistory.ColumnHeaders.Add , , _
                     "Action By User", 1440
   lvwPropValuHistory.ColumnHeaders.Add , , _
                     "Date of Action", 1440
   lvwPropValuHistory.ColumnHeaders.Add , , "Original ID", 720
   lvwPropValuHistory.ColumnHeaders.Add , , "Audit ID", 720
   lvwPropValuHistory.ColumnHeaders.Add , , "Owner ID", 720
   lvwPropValuHistory.ColumnHeaders.Add , , "Property ID", 720
   lvwPropValuHistory.View = lvwReport

   If Len(SourceControl) > 0 Then
   ' If this object was delivered from a deleted state then
   ' morph form
      cmdOK.Caption = "Restore"
      cmdHistory.Enabled = False
      Me.Caption = Me.Caption & " - [Restore]"
   End If


   If mobjPropBag Is Nothing Then Exit Sub

   If PropBag.IsNew Then
      ' If New object then Clear the form
      cmdOK.Enabled = False
      cmdHistory.Enabled = False
      ClearForm
   Else
      If Len(Trim(PropBag.Value)) = 0 Then cmdOK.Enabled = False
   ' If existing object then populate controls
   ' display a text box or a combo box depending upon whether
   ' a list is available for this property
      If PropBag.ListAvailable = "Y" Then
         cboPropValuValue.Visible = True
         txtPropValuValue.Visible = False
         PropItems.SetDataSource strConnect
         PropItems.Load PropBag.PropertyID
         LoadValueComboBox
         SetPropValuState
      Else
         cboPropValuValue.Visible = False
         txtPropValuValue.Visible = True
         SetPropValuState
      End If
   End If

   'let the user know the application is done with its task
   Screen.MousePointer = vbDefault
```

```
    Exit Sub

Form_LoadError:

    ErrorHandler

End Sub
```

First the test to determine whether or not the current object is being restored from deleted. We have seen this before:

```
If Len(SourceControl) > 0 Then
    ' If this object was delivered from a deleted state then
    ' morph form
    cmdOK.Caption = "Restore"
    cmdHistory.Enabled = False
    Me.Caption = Me.Caption & " - [Restore]"
End If
```

The next test is not really necessary. I have placed it on the form, mostly to be thorough, as you will see; it is not possible to have Property Bag object that is new at the Production User Interface. The creation of all of these objects occurs at the Data Centric sphere of the system:

```
If PropBag.IsNew Then
    ' If New object then Clear the form
    cmdOK.Enabled = False
    cmdHistory.Enabled = False
    ClearForm
Else
```

This next section of code tests to see whether or not a list is available for this particular property. If one is available, then we load the `PropItem` collection by calling the `Load` method and passing the property's ID. Once the collection has been filled, we use it to load a combo box. Then we set the current value using the `SetPropValuState` subroutine:

```
If PropBag.ListAvailable = "Y" Then
        cboPropValuValue.Visible = True
        txtPropValuValue.Visible = False
        PropItems.SetDataSource strConnect
        PropItems.Load PropBag.PropertyID
        LoadValueComboBox
        SetPropValuState
    Else
        cboPropValuValue.Visible = False
        txtPropValuValue.Visible = True
        SetPropValuState
    End If
End If
```

If a list is not available, then we skip over the section of the code that loads the list collection and just display the value on the screen using the `SetPropValuState` routine.

mobjPropValu_Valid

We have seen this code before; it uses the `Valid` event of the Property Value object to perform data validation exactly the way that we used it in every other object we have built so far:

```
Private Sub mobjPropValu_Valid(blnIsValid As Boolean)

   cmdOK.Enabled = blnIsValid

End Sub
```

mobjPropBag_Valid

This is not a misprint. In addition to the testing the Property Value object to see if it has been validated, we also need to test the Property Bag object to ensure that it is also valid:

```
Private Sub mobjPropBag_Valid(blnIsValid As Boolean)

   cmdOK.Enabled = blnIsValid

End Sub
```

LoadValueComboBox

This routine simply iterates through the collection of available Property Items and fills the combo box with items in the collection. The code is self-explanatory:

```
Private Sub LoadValueComboBox()

   Dim objPropItem As UCPerson.clsPropItem

   For Each objPropItem In PropItems
     cboPropValuValue.AddItem objPropItem.DisplayValue
   Next objPropItem

   Set objPropItem = Nothing

End Sub
```

cboPropValuValue_KeyPress

In the case of a combo box, we might not wish to accept any keystrokes as user input. Most likely the reason we use a combo box is to limit the possible data entry values to the items in the combo box. The following code illustrates how to negate any keystrokes the user enters:

```
Private Sub cboPropValuValue_KeyPress(KeyAscii As Integer)

   KeyAscii = 0

End Sub
```

This doesn't handle the very real possibility that the user will attempt to enter a keystroke combination (*Ctrl* + *V* to paste data into a control) or press the *Delete* key. To handle those occurrences we need to use the following little piece of code:

```
Private Sub cboPropValuValue_KeyDown(KeyCode As Integer)

    KeyCode = 0

End Sub
```

cboPropValuValue_LostFocus

The following code has been provided to illustrate the fact that we must actively copy the values from the input controls into the form's current object. This can be done on the LostFocus or the Change events. There are advantages and drawbacks to both methods. I have settled on the LostFocus event as the lessor of two evils. It allows us to perform high quality data validation at the object level. Sometimes, as with dates for example, we need the user's complete input in order to make these kinds of decisions. The Change event executes on every keystroke. We use the KeyPress event to perform data validation at that level:

```
Private Sub cboPropValuValue_LostFocus()

    PropBag.Value = cboPropValuValue.Text
    cboPropValuValue.Text = PropBag.Value

End Sub
```

cmdCancel_Click

```
Private Sub cmdCancel_Click()

    mstrButtonPressed = "Cancel"
    Unload Me

End Sub
```

cmdHistory_Click

This routine, like every other Show History button routine we have seen so far, loads a series of snapshots of an object's values over time into a collection on the form. The code here is identical to any Level I object. But, this code can be used without modification for any 4-Dimensional Data Object:

```
Private Sub cmdHistory_Click()

    On Error GoTo cmdHistory_ClickError

    Select Case cmdHistory.Caption
        Case "&Show History"
            ' let the user know the application is busy
            Screen.MousePointer = vbHourglass
            cmdHistory.Caption = "&Hide History"
            'km - added if statement to prevent loading
            'collection if it has already been loaded
            If PropValuHistory.Count = 0 Then
                ' Clear the local audit history variable
                Set mcolPropValuHistory = Nothing
                ' load the audit history for the current object
                PropBag.SetDataSource strConnect
```

```
                Set mcolPropValuHistory = PropBag. _
                        ObjectAuditHistory()
                DoEvents
                LoadPropValuHistoryListView
                DoEvents
            End If
            Me.Height = jamShowHistory
            Screen.MousePointer = vbDefault
        Case "&Hide History"
            cmdHistory.Caption = "&Show History"
            Me.Height = jamHideHistory
    End Select

    Screen.MousePointer = vbDefault

    Exit Sub

cmdHistory_ClickError:

    ErrorHandler

End Sub
```

LoadPropValuHistoryListView

This routine is loads the individual snapshots of an object's history into the history listview. We have seen this routine many times before. This block of code is somewhat special though, because we can use this code for any 4-Dimensional Data Object by changing a single line as follows.

To use this code with any *Widget* object change this line:

```
Dim ThisObject As UCPerson.clsPropBag
```

To read:

```
Dim ThisObject As UCWidget.clsPropBag
```

```
Public Sub LoadPropValuHistoryListView()

    Dim ThisObject As UCPerson.clsPropBag
    Dim PropValuHistoryItems As ListItems
    Dim ThisItem As ListItem

    Set PropValuHistoryItems = lvwPropValuHistory.ListItems
    PropValuHistoryItems.Clear

    For Each ThisObject In PropValuHistory
            Set ThisItem = PropValuHistoryItems.Add _
                (, ThisObject.Key, ThisObject.Value)
        ThisItem.SubItems(1) = ThisObject.StampAction
        ThisItem.SubItems(2) = ThisObject.StampUser
        ThisItem.SubItems(3) = ThisObject.StampDateTime
        ThisItem.SubItems(4) = ThisObject.StampID
        ThisItem.SubItems(5) = ThisObject.ID
```

```
                ThisItem.SubItems(6) = ThisObject.OwnerID
                ThisItem.SubItems(7) = ThisObject.PropertyID
          Next ThisObject

     End Sub
```

lvwPropValuHistory_DblClick

This routine allows the user to select a set of previous values for an object and enter those values into the input controls with a mouse double click. The code is identical to the Level I treatment. It is important to note that we are not saving the changes when the user double clicks this listview. We are merely copying the previous values to the current object. The user still has to actively save the changes to cause the old values to replace the current values in the data store. This functionality offers the user the ability to undo any changes that have made to an object. This is necessary in an environment where an entire organization is sharing the same data store. This code can be used with any 4-Dimensional Data Object by changing just two lines as follows.

To use this code with any *Widget* object, change these two lines:

```
     Dim ThisObject As UCPerson.clsPropBag
     Dim ThisItem As UCPerson.clsPropItem
```

To read:

```
     Dim ThisObject As UCWidget.clsPropBag
     Dim ThisItem As UCWidget.clsPropItem
```

```
     Private Sub lvwPropValuHistory_DblClick()

        Dim ThisObject As UCPerson.clsPropBag
        Dim ThisItem As UCPerson.clsPropItem

        On Error GoTo lvwDataTypeHistory_DblClickError

        ' find the object the user wants to restore
        For Each ThisObject In PropValuHistory
           If ThisObject.Key = lvwPropValuHistory.SelectedItem.Key Then
              PropBag.IsValid = ThisObject.IsValid
              PropBag.ChangeAll = ThisObject.ChangeAll
              PropBag.StampDateTime = ThisObject.StampDateTime
              PropBag.StampAction = ThisObject.StampAction
              PropBag.StampID = ThisObject.StampID
              PropBag.DataMessage = ThisObject.DataMessage
              PropBag.CollisionMessages = ThisObject.CollisionMessages
              PropBag.DataLocking = ThisObject.DataLocking
              PropBag.ID = ThisObject.StampID
              PropBag.OwnerID = ThisObject.OwnerID
              PropBag.PropertyID = ThisObject.PropertyID
              PropBag.PropertyName = ThisObject.PropertyName
              PropBag.Value = ThisObject.Value
              SetPropValuState
           End If
```

```
    Next ThisObject

    Exit Sub

lvwDataTypeHistory_DblClickError:

    ErrorHandler

End Sub
```

cmdOK_Click

The code for the OK button click is identical to any other Level I object. We perform a test to see whether or not the object is being restored from a deleted state. If it is, the length of the `SourceControl` property will be greater than zero. In that case, we invoke the `ObjectRestoreFromDeleted` method and unload the form. If not, then we perform an ordinary update using the `ObjectUpdate` method:

```
Private Sub cmdOK_Click()

    On Error GoTo cmdOK_Click_ClickError

    ' let the user know that the application is busy
    Screen.MousePointer = vbHourglass
    mstrButtonPressed = "OK"
    PropBag.SetDataSource strConnect
    If Len(SourceControl) > 0 Then
        PropBag.ObjectRestoreFromDeleted
        cmdHistory.Enabled = True
        Unload Me
        Screen.MousePointer = vbDefault
        Exit Sub
    Else
        PropBag.ObjectUpdate
    End If
    Screen.MousePointer = vbDefault
    SourceControl = ""
    Unload Me
    Exit Sub

cmdOK_Click_ClickError:

    ErrorHandler

End Sub
```

ClearForm

The only trick here it to check for the existence of an item list. If one exists, then we just set the combo box to the first value in the list. If a list doesn't exist, then we set the value of the text box to a zero length string:

```
Public Sub ClearForm()

    If PropBag.ListAvailable = "Y" Then
        cboPropValuValue.Text = cboPropValuValue.List(0)
```

```
      Else
          txtPropValuValue.Text = ""
      End If

  End Sub
```

SetPropValuState

There are actually two things to notice here. The first one is that the `PropBag.PropertyName` is used for the label that identifies the input control. And the second is that, once again, we must test for the existence of an item list. If one exists, then we get the value for the object from the combo box. If a list doesn't exist, we take the value from the text box.

```
  Public Sub SetPropValuState()

      lblPropValuName.Caption = PropBag.PropertyName
      If PropBag.ListAvailable = "Y" Then
          cboPropValuValue.Text = PropBag.Value
      Else
          txtPropValuValue.Text = PropBag.Value
      End If

  End Sub
```

txtPropValuValue_KeyPress

This is a pretty long subroutine for a simple textbox, but it enables us to test that each `KeyPress` is a valid entry for the particular data type that the current Property Definition expects. Although the code is lengthy, it uses exactly the same technique we used earlier in the `KeyPress` events. The only difference is the addition of the `Case` statement that determines the data type that the Property Definition demands:

```
  Private Sub txtPropValuValue_KeyPress(KeyAscii As Integer)

      Select Case PropBag.DataTypeName

          Case "Date"
              Select Case KeyAscii
                  Case 47 To 57, 8
                  Case Else
                      KeyAscii = 0
              End Select

          Case "Integer", "Long"
              Select Case KeyAscii
                  Case 48 To 57, 8, 45
                  Case Else
                      KeyAscii = 0
              End Select

          Case "Single", "Double"
              Select Case KeyAscii
                  Case 48 To 57, 8, 45, 46
                  Case Else
                      KeyAscii = 0
              End Select
```

```
      Case "Currency"
         Select Case KeyAscii
            Case 48 To 57, 8, 45, 46, 36
            Case Else
               KeyAscii = 0
         End Select

      Case Else

   End Select

End Sub
```

txtPropValuValue_LostFocus

Once again, this is a pretty long block of code for a single input control LostFocus event, but it enables this form to handle any possible type of property value. It uses the same data-validation techniques we saw earlier. The only difference is that it uses a Case statement to determine which data validation rule to employ:

```
Private Sub txtPropValuValue_LostFocus()

   Select Case PropBag.DataTypeName

   Case "Date"
      If Len(txtPropValuValue) > 0 Then
         If Not IsDate(txtPropValuValue) Then
            MsgBox "A Valid Date is required for this Property"
            txtPropValuValue.SelStart = 1
            txtPropValuValue.SelLength = Len _
                (txtPropValuValue.Text)
            txtPropValuValue.SetFocus
         Else
            PropBag.Value = txtPropValuValue.Text
            txtPropValuValue.Text = PropBag.Value
         End If
      Else
         PropBag.Value = txtPropValuValue.Text
         txtPropValuValue.Text = PropBag.Value
      End If

   Case "Integer", "Long", "Single", "Double", "Currency"
      If Len(txtPropValuValue.Text) > 0 Then
         If Not IsNumeric(txtPropValuValue) Then
            MsgBox "A Numeric value is requred for this Property"
            txtPropValuValue.SelStart = 1
            txtPropValuValue.SelLength = Len _
                (txtPropValuValue.Text)
            txtPropValuValue.SetFocus
         Else
            PropBag.Value = txtPropValuValue.Text
            txtPropValuValue.Text = PropBag.Value
         End If
      Else
         PropBag.Value = txtPropValuValue.Text
         txtPropValuValue.Text = PropBag.Value
      End If
```

```
      Case Else
        PropBag.Value = txtPropValuValue.Text
        txtPropValuValue.Text = PropBag.Value

  End Select

End Sub
```

lvwPropValuHistory_ColumnClick

As always, we add a routine to the `ColumnClick` event, which allows the user to sort the listview by clicking on the column.

Form_Unload

As with all good development, we are careful to perform housekeeping chores whenever we complete a task. In this case, we ensure that each of the local object variables is destroyed. The errors that stem from failing to perform this simple task are countless, confounding, and unnecessary:

```
Private Sub Form_Unload(Cancel As Integer)

    SourceControl = ""
    Set mcolPropValuHistory = Nothing

End Sub
```

Summary

In this chapter, we were introduced to a new kind of Enterprise Caliber Data Object, the 4-Dimensional Data Object. The most distinguishing feature of this object is that we can use it to represent different types of the underlying object. For example, a *Person* object can be cast as a doctor, a patient, a customer, or an employee. Each of these different person types carry a complete set of properties in something we call a Property Bag. This object exposes two programmable interfaces:

❑ An administrative interface, that we use to create, edit, or delete Object Type Definitions and their associated Property Set Definitions.

❑ A production interface that we use exactly like we would use any other object. This interface exposes the characteristic set of eight data handling processes we have come to expect from an Enterprise Caliber Data Object.

We also took a little tour through two different user interfaces that we use to expose the data object's programmable interface. These were user interfaces were aptly named administrative and production. Finally we worked through the code that we needed to write to build the Production User Interface.

In the next chapter, we will take little more time to get to know the administrative interface. We will do that by writing a complete Administrative User Interface that exposes the programmable administrative interface.

Person
Base Properties

ID
Last Name
First Name
Middle Name
Birth Date
Sex

Object Type Definitions

Object Ty...

Lawyer OTD	Engineer OTD	Doctor OTD	Student OTD
Specialty	Specialty	Specialty	Major
Hourly Rate	Experience	Certification	Minor
Law School	Property 3	Property 3	Year
Property 4	Property 4	Property 4	Property 4
Property 5	Property 5	Property 5	Property 5
Property 6	Property 6	Property 6	Property 6
Property 7	Property 7	Property 7	Property 7
Property 8	Property 8	Property 8	Property 8
Property 9	Property 9	Property 9	Property 9
Property 10	Property 10	Property 10	Property 10

Property Set Definitions

Property Set...

9

The Administrative Interface

In the last chapter, we learned how to build a Production User Interface for a 4-Dimensional Data Object. In this chapter, we will work through all of the code that we need to write to build an Administrative User Interface for a 4-Dimensional Data Object. This interface gives us the tools we need to manage Object Type Definitions, Property Set Definitions, and individual Property Definitions. It automates a portion of our development task.

It is rather an unusual undertaking for a developer or development team to spend a great deal of time on an interface that not a single casual end user is even likely to see, let alone work with. But, generally I think that this is something of an oversight on our (the development community) part. Often we spend years of development time automating incredibly simple tasks for users. But unfortunately it is a rare company indeed that allows the developers to spend even a small fraction of time developing tools to make the task of software development easier. How many companies have a real library of reusable code? Or more importantly, how many companies have a real library of reusable code that the developers actually use? Perhaps this has something to do with the, sometimes, incorrect notion that software development requires something more akin to art than science. But I think there is something more evil lurking here. Software development is a business. We perform a service for a customer. Sadly, management is often so bombarded with user requests for immediate service that they cannot imagine taking the time to stop and do things right the first time. In the world of business, the manager who panders to the users' near-term happiness in the shortest amount of time wins. It doesn't seem to matter if that happiness is short lived or results in an eternal maintenance problem. Unfortunately, this business-induced short sightedness doesn't allow most managers to conceive that there might be a better way to serve the customer and the business.

I have a great friend named Glade who told me a supposedly true story about a programmer. It goes like this:

> *A programmer is sitting back in his chair with his feet up on the desk thinking about a problem. He is busy crafting the mental picture of the processes and data flow. His manager walks into the office, sees the programmer entranced in thought and in a fit of anger asks the programmer, "Just exactly what the #@!# are you doing?" The programmer replied, "Why sir, I am thinking". To this the manager responded, "Stop wasting my time thinking! I am paying you to write programs! So TYPE! TYPE! TYPE!"*

This chapter is for programmers. We will spend it designing and building a tool that will allow us to make our job easier. It allows us to automate some difficult tasks that are mechanical in nature and would require very many hours of work to code by hand (*TYPE! TYPE! TYPE!*). I realize that it may be a foreign concept to believe that a developer's time is well spent building tools that make his or her job easier. I am sure that it is even more foreign to think that this practice might actually be good for the customer, but I don't really care. I *know* that I can apply the same techniques I use for customers to make my job easier. And despite many managers' beliefs to the contrary, I *know* that our job *is to think*. I always tell the members of my teams that I would rather that they code less and think more.

This chapter is all about developing software that will make your team's, or your own, day a little more imaginative and a little less tedious. We are going to spend a little time creating a tool just for us developers – an administrative interface for our 4-Dimensional Data Object. My fondest wish is that this chapter will inspire you to automate some of your other tasks, so put your feet up on your desk, and THINK! THINK! THINK!

Overview

Before we get on with the job of writing the code for this interface, I want to take a few minutes and go over the general concepts. We are going to be using phrases like Object Type Definition, Property Set Definition, and Property Definitions. If that isn't bad enough, I am probably going to start abbreviating these things with the acronyms OTD and PSD. This means that if I am not careful, you might have to read sentences like: "Create a new property called Specialization; add it to the PSD for the Engineering OTD." Ugh! Don't worry; it really isn't as bad as I make it out to be.

In fact I think once you get a sense of how this whole thing works, you will enjoy the concept enough to enable you to put up with the ugly sentences like that one that might slip by from time to time.

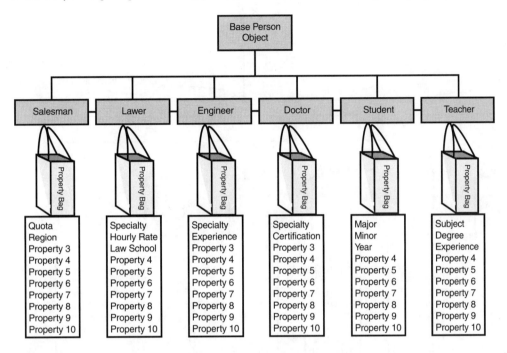

Take a look at the image above. Notice that at the top center of the image, I have placed something called a Base Person Object. If you look below this Base Person, you will see six different words - Salesman, Lawyer, Engineer, Doctor, Student and Teacher. We can say that these words help us to describe different types of people. In other words, it is true that a Salesman, an Engineer, and a Doctor are all different expressions of a Person.

I guess, if you think about it, maybe rather than saying that these words are different expressions of a person it is probably better for us to say that these words describe different extensions of a person. The fact that a person is a student or a teacher doesn't make him or her any less of a person. You are a person. Think about the other ways that you can describe your self – as a programmer, analyst, developer, husband, wife, father, son, consumer... All these words have one thing in common. They **add** something to the base person. **They never** (I had to put a lawyer in there right?) **take away from the base person**. In the real world, using everyday language, we might say that these words categorize different types of people.

> In this book we are working with people, or virtual people, as data objects.
> So we will say those words that categorize different types of *Person* objects
> can be called an Object Type, or to be more precise, an Object Type
> Definition – a definition that describes an object's type (OTD).

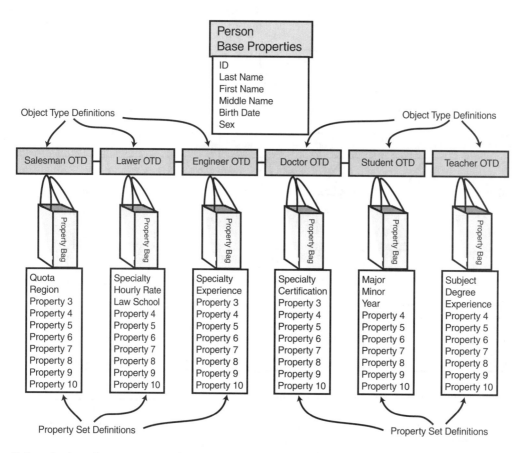

Take a look at the next image shown above. Notice that this image is not really that much different than the one we looked at earlier. This image does as good a job as the one above of describing the base person and the different OTDs. You might notice that while I removed the pictures of the different OTDs, I left the little bags that were in front of them in this image. These little bags are the next thing we need to talk about.

When we talked about the OTDs, we said that these things always **added** something to the base person. In the real world, that something might be a degree, position, or a title. In the virtual world, the something that is added is always some kind of data or property. So, in the virtual world, we will need a place to put that additional data or properties. That is what the bags are for. They give our OTDs a place to store the extra properties that they require. I always see OTDs as the people in the earlier image, carrying around this bag of properties wherever they go. So, now we have an OTD that describes an extension of a person and a Property Bag that the OTD carries around to store the extra information that extension requires. The next question is. How do we know what information each OTD needs?

We need a way to define the additional information each OTD should have in its Property Bag.

Person Base Properties
ID
Last Name
First Name
Middle Name
Birth Date
Sex

Object Type Definitions → ← Object Type Definitions

Salesman OTD	Lawer OTD	Engineer OTD	Doctor OTD	Student OTD	Teacher OTD
Quota	Specialty	Specialty	Specialty	Major	Subject
Region	Hourly Rate	Experience	Certification	Minor	Degree
Property 3	Law School	Property 3	Property 3	Year	Experience
Property 4	Property 4	Property 4	Property 4	Property 4	Property 4
Property 5	Property 5	Property 5	Property 5	Property 5	Property 5
Property 6	Property 6	Property 6	Property 6	Property 6	Property 6
Property 7	Property 7	Property 7	Property 7	Property 7	Property 7
Property 8	Property 8	Property 8	Property 8	Property 8	Property 8
Property 9	Property 9	Property 9	Property 9	Property 9	Property 9
Property 10	Property 10	Property 10	Property 10	Property 10	Property 10

Property Set Definitions — Property Set Definitions

Notice that in the image above, I have eliminated the graphic of the Property Bag. I hope you also notice that the concept of the Property Bag is still there. When I look at this image, I still see the definition of the base person. I also still see the different OTDs. And I can tell that there must be a Property Bag there because each OTD has a number of properties connected to or associated with it. What I don't see is the information that tells me what properties should be in each bag. Sure, I see the phrase Property Set Definitions. I am fairly certain that is supposed to indicate that there is something here that defines what properties go into which Property Bag. But I can't see it. The reason I can't see this thing is because a Property Set Definition (PSD) is really more of a set of rules than it is something that we can see or touch. Somewhere, somehow, somebody *knows* that a salesman OTD's Property Bag should be filled with a particular set properties. I think that this is really the first time in this book that we have come face-to-face with a business rule.

In every organization, there will be rules that will help us to define a set of properties that describe each different type of person. In every enterprise, there are business rules that define a PSD for a particular OTD. The administrative interface we will construct in this chapter is designed to allow us to implement those business rules without changing the functionality of our underlying data objects.

> **Separation of content and function – this is key.**

If we take the images we have looked at over the last few pages and distill the information into a simpler, more generalized form, we might get an image that looks something like the one shown here. From now on, we will use this image to represent the relationship between the base object, an OTD, and its Property Bag:

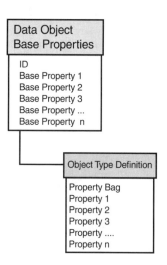

Notice that it has all of the elements of any of the three images we looked at earlier. It has a base object with a set of base properties. It has an Object Type Definition or OTD, and it has a Property Bag which it uses to carry around the extended set of properties that some business rule has determined are necessary for the OTD. We call this set of rules a Property Set Definition or PSD for short. When we look at this image, we can't see the PSD the way we might be able to see the base person, or the Property Bag, or even the properties in the Property Bag. That is because a PSD is really a business rule and we **never** put business rules in data objects. Instead, we make our data objects smart enough to have the ability to manage and store the business rules in the enterprise's data store.

This means that when somebody, somewhere, somehow decides to change his or her perception of the information a salesman's OTD should have (and they **will**) we can make those changes without changing the code in the underlying object. The interface you will build in this chapter exposes the functionality in 4-Dimensional Data Objects that makes this possible.

The 4-Dimensional Data Object Administrative User Interface

The Administrative User Interface allows the developer to manage the task of extending base 4-Dimensional Data Objects into specialized programming tools. The job of extending objects requires up to 4 distinct steps

1. Create a new Object Type Definition (OTD) – this is essentially a type name, i.e. Doctor, etc.

2. Create a new Property Set Definition (PSD) for the OTD

3. Create and add the individual Property Definitions to the PSD

4. If necessary, add each of the individual items to the list of available items for an individual Property Definition

OK, now that we have a sense of what we want to be able to accomplish with a 4-Dimensional Data Object's Administrative User Interface, we can begin the process of learning how to construct it. If you have read the previous chapters, this should be a piece of cake. One of the best things about the objects in this book is that they are all designed to work in essentially the same way. We will have to add a couple of new concepts to handle the higher dimensions, but even the new concepts are built upon the same solid design principles we covered in the earlier chapters.

Registering the Person DLLs

If you haven't already registered the two DLLs that make up the *Person* object you should do so now. To register the user centric half of the *Person* object, type the following command into the <u>R</u>un dialog (located off the Start menu) and press *Enter*:

```
regsvr32 "\..\Ch08\UCPerson.dll"
```

You should see a message box that tells you that the DLL has been successfully registered. Dismiss the message box.

To register the data centric half of the *Person* object, type the following command into the <u>R</u>un dialog, and hit *Enter*:

```
regsvr32 "\..\Ch08\DCPerson.dll"
```

You should see the same kind of message box again telling you that this DLL has also been registered successfully. If you search for the names of these DLLs in your registry, now you will find several references to them.

The PersonInterface Project

When you get finished with this section, the Project Explorer in your VB IDE should look like the one shown here:

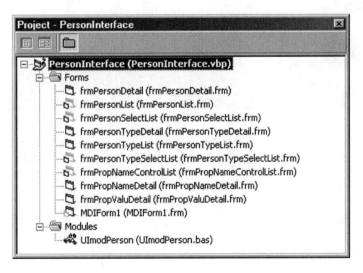

In this chapter, we will continue working with the `PersonInterface.vbp` project that we were using in Chapter 8. If you are building this project yourself, follow the steps below:

1. Open the `PersonAdministration.vbp` project

2. Add six new standard forms called `frmPersonTypeList.frm`, `frmPersonTypeDetail.frm`, `frmPersonSelectList.frm`, `frmPersonTypeSelectList`, `frmPropNameControlList`, and `frmPropNameDetail.frm`

3. Save the project

The PersonObject Type Administrative Screens

The four forms used in the set of PersonObject Type Administrative Screens all allow the user to work with an OTD. They allow you to create, edit, delete and select OTDs. They are also used to add, edit and delete Property Definitions and share them between OTDs.

frmPersonTypeList.frm

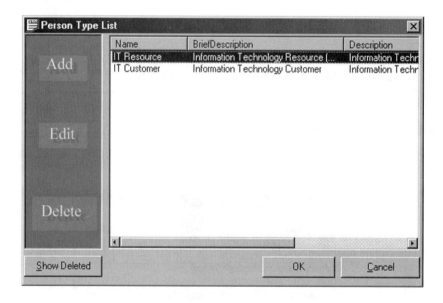

If you are building this from scratch, the instructions for building this type of form can be found in Chapter 5. If you are working through the sample code with me, double-click on the `frmPersonTypeList.frm` in the Project Explorer.

The first thing we need to do when we extend any base object, like a *Person* object, into an extended object, say an IT Resource is to add a new Object Type Definition (OTD). The **Person Type List** form is the starting point in that process for the *Person* object. It displays a list of the different Object Type Definitions that are currently available in the data store. From this screen, we can add a new OTD, edit an existing OTD, delete an existing OTD, or get a list of currently deleted OTDs.

This form's code should be familiar to you. It is functionally identical to the code we wrote when we created the Level I List form. The only difference here is the set of properties that the OTD object contains.

Fortunately, every Object Type Definition object has exactly the same set of five properties: ID, Name, Brief Description, Description, and Key Prefix. That means that the only real difference between an Object Type List form for a *Person* object and any *Widget* object is the project name we reference on the form. For example, if we look at the code for a 4-Dimensional Person Object Type List form, we will find the following variables dimensioned in the general declarations section of the form:

```
Private mcolTypes As UCPerson.colTypes
Private mcolTypesDeleted As UCPerson.colTypes
```

If this object were a *Widget* object, then we would have the following two lines of code:

```
Private mcolTypes As UCWidget.colTypes
Private mcolTypesDeleted As UCWidget.colTypes
```

Notice that the only difference is in the name of the project. While the *Person* object pointed to a `UCPerson` project, the *Widget* object points to a `UCWidget` project. The extensions are identical – `colTypes`. There are several techniques that you can use to make this project name information available to the form at run time. In other words, it is a perfectly reasonable goal to have a single Object Type List form that will manage ODT information for *Person*, *Widget*, *Organization*, *Animal* objects, and so on... You can use any of the sample code for any Object Type List form and turn that form into an all-purpose Object Type List form. The instructions for building this type of form can be found in Chapters 5 and 8. Once again, it is really just a specialized Level I Data Object with the properties ID, Name, Brief Description, Description, and Key Prefix. You already know how to do this!

frmPersonTypeDetail.frm

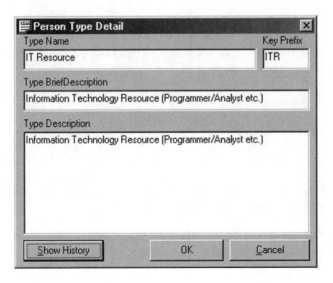

349

If you are building this from scratch, the instructions for building this type of form can be found in Chapter 5. If you are working through the sample code with me, double-click on the frmPersonTypeDetail.frm *in the Project Explorer.*

When we add or edit an Object Type Definition, we use the Type Detail form to edit the OTD's properties. From this form we can edit and save changes to an OTD. We can also view a complete history of any changes made to the OTD over time. Of course, because this is an Enterprise Caliber Data Object, we can also undo any of those changes. You already know exactly how to build this form. It is functionally identical to the code we wrote when we created the Level I Detail form. The only difference here is the set of properties the Object Type Definition object contains – ID, Name, Brief Description, Description, and Key Prefix. I have not included a complete listing for this form because the general instructions for building one are in Chapters 5 and 8. You can also take any one of the sample Object Type Detail forms and turn it into a generic Object Type Detail form with minimal changes.

frmPersonTypeSelectList.frm

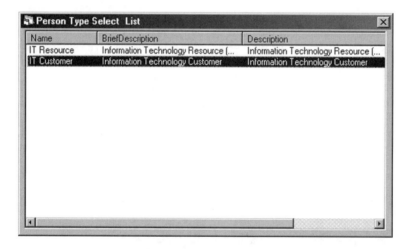

If you are building this from scratch, all of the code you need is presented in this chapter. If you are working through the sample code with me, double-click on the frmPersonTypeSelectList.frm *in the project explorer.*

The next form we need to build doesn't really have a corollary in the Level I Data Object. So, I will provide the entire code listing for this form. The form has a narrowly defined purpose in our administrative user interface. It is designed to do just one thing. It provides the developer with a list of OTDs that are currently available for a given 4-Dimensional Data Object. Once the developer selects (double-clicks) on a particular OTD, this form is unloaded and the developer is sent to the next form in the process – the Property Set Control List. From that form, the developer can add, edit or delete Property Definitions from the Property Set Definition.

Even though this form is different than any of the other forms we have built until this point, its code will still be familiar to you. This form is actually a slimmed down standard List form. Internally, it works almost the same way. The major difference is more procedural than technical. Usually when we call a Detail form from a List form, the List form is not dismissed.

We raise the Detail form modally. The user does some work, and we send the user back to the original List form that initiated the process. The user makes the decision what to do next from that point. With the Selection form, we don't expect to return to this form. This form represents a single step in a multi-step process. From this form, the user selects a particular object to work with and will be sent on a one-way trip to a Detail form that will allow the user to complete the task. If they want to work with another object at the Detail level, they need to initiate the process over again from the start.

Declaration Section

In the declaration section of this form, we need to create a private storage variable for a collection of types:

```
Option Explicit
Private mcolTypes As UCPerson.colTypes
```

If we wanted to use this form with another 4-Dimensional Object, we could take two different approaches when we dimension this variable. We could use early binding and explicitly declare the variable like we did above. This means that if we were working with a *Widget* object we would write the line:

```
Private mcolTypes As UCWidget.colTypes
```

We could also use late binding and declare the variable as a generic object. In that case, we would write the line as follows:

```
Private mcolTypes as Object
```

Each technique has advantages and drawbacks. The first approach (early binding) is likely to produce slightly faster code. It also offers all of the advantages that come with IntelliSense. But, it also means that the form is always expecting a particular type of object – *Person*, *Widget*, etc. This means that we may need to create many forms that are essentially identical. If we use the second approach (late binding), the code will execute a little slower, and we would have to work without IntelliSense. But with a few minor changes, we would be able to pass any 4-Dimensional Data Object onto the form and it will work for all of them without modification. I have used an early binding example in this book, but I think that it is a great idea to experiment with late binding principles for this form.

Form-Level Properties

This form's lineage to our standard Level I Object List form should be apparent here. We create exactly the same form-level property that we used for the standard List form. The difference between the two forms is really the absence of the deleted objects' collection in this form. This form is transient in nature. We don't expect to be able to show deleted objects from this form. We also don't need a `ButtonPressed` property. There are no controls. This form performs a single task – it identifies the selection and sends the user on to the next form.

Types

```
Public Property Get Types() As UCPerson.colTypes
    If mcolTypes Is Nothing Then
        Set mcolTypes = CreateObject("UCPerson.colTypes")
    End If
```

```
    Set Types = mcolTypes
End Property
```

```
Public Property Let Types(colTypes As UCPerson.colTypes)
    Set mcolTypes = colTypes
End Property
```

Form_Load Subroutine

This is pretty standard stuff. All we do here is configure the listview to display the information we
need to show the user, call the `Types` collection's `Load` method, and call the subroutine that loads
the listview. We have seen this functionality before. Consider, for a moment, that every OTD has
exactly the same set of properties. That means that we can use this routine without modification for
every Level II or Level III Data Object:

```
Private Sub Form_Load()

    On Error GoTo Form_LoadError
    ' Construct the columnheaders for the object listview
    lvwTypes.ColumnHeaders.Add , , "Name", 1440
    lvwTypes.ColumnHeaders.Add , , "BriefDescription", 2880
    lvwTypes.ColumnHeaders.Add , , "Description", 2880
    lvwTypes.ColumnHeaders.Add , , "KeyPrefix", 1440
    lvwTypes.ColumnHeaders.Add , , "ID", 720
    lvwTypes.View = lvwReport

    ' Call the Load Method of the User Centric Object
    Types.SetDataSource strConnect
    Types.Load

' Load the listview
    LoadTypeListView

    Exit Sub
Form_LoadError:
    ErrorHandler
End Sub
```

LoadTypeListView

This next routine just loads the listview with the information in the `Types` collection. We have seen
this functionality before. The only difference between the routine here and one that we might have
constructed for a Level I listview object is the property names. Fortunately, every OTD uses the same
property names, so that means that the only line of code we need to consider to make this form
completely portable is the following:

```
Dim ThisObject As UCPerson.clsType
```

Everything else is completely reusable:

```
Public Sub LoadTypeListView()
    Dim ThisObject As UCPerson.clsType
    Dim TypeItems As ListItems
    Dim ThisItem As ListItem
```

```
    Set TypeItems = lvwTypes.ListItems
    TypeItems.Clear

    For Each ThisObject In Types
        If Not ThisObject.IsDeleted And ThisObject.IsChild Then
            Set ThisItem = TypeItems.Add _
                        (, ThisObject.Key, ThisObject.Name)
            ThisItem.SubItems(1) = ThisObject.BriefDescription
            ThisItem.SubItems(2) = ThisObject.Description
            ThisItem.SubItems(3) = ThisObject.KeyPrefix
            ThisItem.SubItems(4) = ThisObject.ID
        End If
    Next ThisObject

End Sub
```

lvwTypes_ColumnClick

Once again, this routine is really standard fare on any form that contains a listview. It allows the user to sort on any column by clicking on a column header. We have seen this code before. I have included it here because this functionality is vitally important to the user and I wanted to ensure that we have included it in this general model for all transient Selection forms:

```
Private Sub lvwTypes_ColumnClick(ByVal ColumnHeader As _
                                 MSComctlLib.ColumnHeader)
    lvwTypes.SortKey = ColumnHeader.Index - 1
    lvwTypes.Sorted = True
    If lvwTypes.SortOrder = lvwDescending Then
        lvwTypes.SortOrder = lvwAscending
    Else
        lvwTypes.SortOrder = lvwDescending
    End If
    lvwTypes.Refresh
End Sub
```

lvwTypes_DblClick

This routine is the one place where our Selection form differs from a standard List form. Remember that this form is used as a step in a process. Once it has completed its task, it is dismissed. Compare that to what we do when we use a standard List form. When we raise a Detail form from a standard List form, we normally raise the Detail form as a modal child to the List form. Once the modal dialog has completed its task, it returns control to its parent the List form.

What we need to do with the Selection form is to pass control to the next form as an equal. There is no parent-child relationship between the forms. So, from the Selection form, we load the next form in the process, pass it the information it needs to do its job, and unload the Selection form.

If you read through the code, you should notice a similarity to the code that is under the `imgEdit` control on a standard List form. The first thing we do is to ensure that something has been selected. If nothing is selected, then we just exit the sub with the following line:

```
If lvwTypes.SelectedItem Is Nothing Then Exit Sub
```

Our next step is to determine which object the user has selected. We do that by iterating through the collection of objects. We compare every object's Key with the Key that the user selected. When we find the keys that match, we check the selected object out of the collection. Then we exit the For loop:

```
' Find the Object in the collection the user needs to be
' edited
For Each ThisObject In Types
    If ThisObject.Key = lvwTypes.SelectedItem.Key Then
        ' Remove the Selected Object from the collection
        ' and enable editing
        ' This method handles all of the parent-child
        ' relationships
        Set ThisObject = Types.CheckOutObject(ThisObject.ID)
        Exit For
    End If
Next ThisObject
```

The last step we take is to pass the Object Type Definition ID to the next form in the process, the Property Control List form. We do this within the same With block that we use to pass some display parameters and show the form. After the With block has finished executing, we simply unload the Selection form:

```
' Place the object on the detail form
    With frmPropNameControlList
        .ParentTypeID = ThisObject.ID
        .Top = 0
        .Left = 0
        .Height = 5265
        .Width = 11550
        Screen.MousePointer = vbDefault
        .Show
    End With
Unload Me
```

Form_Unload

The final block of code for the Selection form is the Form_Unload code. It performs a little housekeeping to ensure that there are no ghost objects running around taking up memory and otherwise wreaking havoc with our application:

```
Private Sub Form_Unload(Cancel As Integer)
    Set mcolTypes = Nothing
End Sub
```

frmPropNameControlList.frm

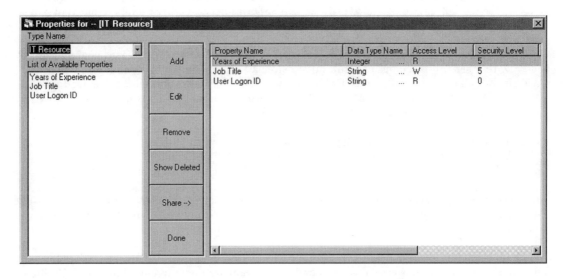

If you are building this from scratch, all of the code you need is presented in this chapter. If you are working through the sample code with me, double-click on the frmPropNameControlList.frm *in the Project Explorer.*

Before we go over the code for the Property Set Control List form, I want to take some time to go over what information this form has been designed to manage. Take a look at this image:

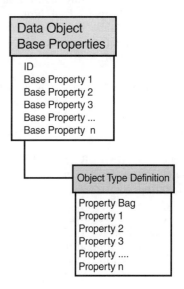

It should look familiar. It is the general image we arrived at earlier in this chapter when we took some time to consider things like OTDs and PSDs. Remember that we said that somehow, even though we couldn't see it, this image depicted the Property Set Definition for a particular OTD. We said that the reason that we couldn't really see the PSD was because it isn't really as much of a data element as it is a business rule.

Well, even though we cannot see the PSD itself, we could use an image like this to see the results of the PSD. In other words the business rules that define a Property Set Definition may be kind of invisible, but we can see the Property Definitions that those business rules tell use we need for a particular OTD. If we look at the image on the right, we see that this OTD is specifying that we place Property 1 to Property n inclusive into the Property Bag.

In other words, we can use an image like this to allow us to view the Property Definitions that the PSD tells us we need for a particular OTD. The form we will build in this section is designed to manage the list of Property Definitions that the PSD tells us we need for a particular OTD.

This form, like the Selection form above, does not really have corollary in the set of forms we use to manage Level I Data Objects. We have not written code for a form of this type. So in this section, we will step through every line of code you need to know to create this form.

This form is kind of like a standard List form. The listbox on the left is really just a standard list of the items in a collection. In this case, the items in the collection are the individual Property Definitions that make up the Property Set Definition.

Just like the List forms we made earlier, we can add new Property Definitions to the collection of Property Definitions by using the Add button. We can edit a Property Definition by clicking the Edit button or delete a Property Definition by clicking the Remove button. And, because this is an Enterprise Caliber Data Object, we can also view a list of deleted Property Definitions and restore any of the deleted definitions back to their state at the time they were deleted. No problem here! We already know this stuff.

The thing that makes this form unique is that it also functions as an assignment form. This assignment function is only really apparent when we share Property Definitions between PSDs. Let's go over the process we used to share the User Logon ID between the IT Customer and IT Resource PSDs again to see how this works.

When we created the IT Resource PSD, we created two new properties from scratch – Years of Experience and Job Title. Then we added a third property to the PSD, User Logon ID, but we didn't create this property. Instead we shared a preexisting Property Definition from another PSD.

The User Logon ID was originally created as a new property for the IT Customer PSD. When we wanted to add a User Logon ID property to our IT Resource PSD, we looked at the other *Person* object PSDs and found that the IT Customer already had a User Logon ID. So, rather than creating a new one we decided to share this property between both PSDs. This means that if we have a person who is both a IT Resource (like you and me) and an IT Customer (also like you and me), we only need to keep one copy of that person's User Logon ID in the data store. That means that if we need to change it for any reason, we only need to do it once and both the IT Customer and IT Resource User Logon ID values will be updated simultaneously.

This doesn't mean that we cannot have two PSDs with a User Logon ID property that is not shared. If we didn't want to share the User Logon ID data between the IT Customer and IT Resource PSDs, we could have just added a new User Logon ID to the IT Resource PSD. In other words, just because both PSDs have a Property Definition with the same name, it does not mean that they are necessarily sharing the property values. If we want to share the values, we must consciously perform the steps that link the information in the data store. I know that sounds ominous, but don't worry. As far as we are concerned right now, we only need to learn how to write the code under the Share --> command button. We will learn how to perform the actual linking at the database level in another chapter. You will see there that it is not all that difficult at that level either.

In order for the user to be able to share Property Definitions from another PSD, the user needs to know what Property Definitions the other PSDs have. That is what the combo box and listbox on the left of the form are for. When this form is first loaded, the combo box on the left displays the same name as the form's caption. For example if this form's caption said IT Resource, then the combo box would display IT Resource when it was first loaded. The listbox directly below the combo box always displays the current list of available properties for the PSD displayed in the combo box.

For example in the following image, the combo box displays the OTD IT Customer and below those words are the Property Definitions assigned to IT Customer:

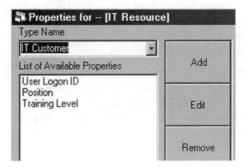

When we decided to share the User Logon ID from the IT Customer OTD, we just selected that property from the left hand listbox and pressed the Share --> button. This brought up the Detail form and we confirmed the sharing assignment when we pressed OK. I think that is enough background for now; let's go over the code behind this form.

Declaration Section

We always use the declarations section of the form to create all of the form-level storage variables we need. As you can see from the code below, in this case, we need quite a few:

```
Option Explicit
' Use these constants for the sizing routines
Private Const jamHideDeleted As Integer = 5265
Private Const jamShowDeleted As Integer = 8235

' Dimension the local storage variables
Private mcolPropNames As UCPerson.colPropNames
Private mcolAvailablePropNames As UCPerson.colPropNames
Private mcolPropNamesDeleted As UCPerson.colPropNames
Private mcolTypes As UCPerson.colTypes
Private mstrButtonPressed As String
Private mlngParentTypeID As Long
```

The first two lines are just constants used to size the form. These are self-explanatory. The next few lines are the ones we really need to look at. Let's take one storage variable at a time, find out what it contains, and how we are planning to use it:

- ❏ `mcolPropNames` is a collection of Property Definitions. For IT Resource, it would contain three objects: Years of Experience, Job Title, and User Logon ID. This collection is always used to fill the right-hand listview control. This form does not allow us to change the target Property Set Definition. That means that if we want to work with a PSD for another OTD, we need to close this form and go through the Selection form. That would reload this form with the correct target OTD.

- ❏ `mcolAvailablePropNames` is another collection of Property Definitions. This collection is always used to fill the left-hand listbox control. When we first load the form, this collection is filled with the same information as the `mcolPropNames` collection. This collection is cleared and re-loaded each time the value in the combo box changes. For example, if I was working on the IT Resource PSD, when the form first loaded this collection would contain the same information as the `mcolPropNames` collection. As soon as I selected another PSD name from the combo box, this collection would be cleared. Then it would be refreshed with the correct Property Definitions for the PSD name in the combo box.

- ❏ `mcolPropNamesDeleted` is a collection of Property Definitions that were once members of the target PSD but are currently deleted. This is standard functionality; we will not pay too much attention to this collection at this time. Treat it exactly the same way we did for the Level I Data Object.

- ❏ `mcolTypes` is the collection of OTDs defined for this particular 4-Dimensional Data Object. For a person it might contain IT Resource, IT Customer, Doctor, Patient etc.

- ❏ `mstrButtonPressed` is used the same way we always used it.

- ❏ `mlngParentTypeID` is a long value that identifies the target type definition we are working with. For example, if the ID we use for IT Resource is 7, then this value would contain the value 7. This value does not change during the lifetime of the form. It is just used to configure the form to work with a particular target PSD.

Form-Level Properties

By now, you should be able to determine which local storage variables are handled by which pair of property handlers. This type of code should be familiar. The way we write the property handler doesn't change too much from form to form. Notice that we have not created a form-level property handler for the list of available properties. That is essentially a scope issue; we destroy and recreate that collection every time a user changes the combo box. The information we handle with properties is a little less volatile in nature. That doesn't mean that we couldn't have used a property handler pair for this list. It just recognizes the different personality of the collection of property names.

Types

```
Public Property Get Types() As UCPerson.colTypes
    If mcolTypes Is Nothing Then
        Set mcolTypes = CreateObject("UCPerson.colTypes")
    End If
    Set Types = mcolTypes
End Property

Public Property Let Types(colTypes As UCPerson.colTypes)
    Set mcolTypes = colTypes
End Property
```

Parent Type ID

```
Public Property Get ParentTypeID() As Long
    ParentTypeID = mlngParentTypeID
End Property
```

```
Public Property Let ParentTypeID(lngParentTypeID As Long)
    mlngParentTypeID = lngParentTypeID
End Property
```

Property Names (Property Definitions)

```
Public Property Get PropNames() As UCPerson.colPropNames
    If mcolPropNames Is Nothing Then
      Set mcolPropNames = CreateObject("UCPerson.colPropNames")
    End If
    Set PropNames = mcolPropNames
End Property
```

```
Public Property Let PropNames(colPropNames As _
                             UCPerson.colPropNames)
    Set mcolPropNames = colPropNames
End Property
```

Deleted Property Names (Property Definitions)

```
Public Property Get PropNamesDeleted() As UCPerson.colPropNames
    If mcolPropNamesDeleted Is Nothing Then
      Set mcolPropNamesDeleted = CreateObject _
                            ("UCPerson.colPropNames")
    End If
    Set PropNamesDeleted = mcolPropNamesDeleted
End Property
```

```
Public Property Let PropNamesDeleted(colPropNamesDeleted As _
                                UCPerson.colPropNames)
    Set mcolPropNamesDeleted = colPropNamesDeleted
End Property
```

Button Pressed

```
Public Property Get ButtonPressed() As String
    ButtonPressed = mstrButtonPressed
End Property
```

Form_Load

Of course, we have a little extra work to do in this Form_Load than we are used to. We need to configure two listviews. Then we need to load two different collections with information from the data store. Once that information has been loaded, we need to fill one combo box, one listbox, and one listview with the information in the collections.

Please note that the property names for the Property Definition object never change. This means that we can reuse this code for every 4-Dimensional Data Object. It doesn't matter whether we are working with a *Person* object or any *Widget* object. When we are working with a Property Definition, we always need to manage the same set of 7 base properties:

- ❑ ID   Long
- ❑ Property Name   String
- ❑ Data Type Name   String
- ❑ Access Level   Long
- ❑ Security Level   String
- ❑ List Available   String
- ❑ Display Order   Long

One of the things that we are doing a little differently here is loading a combo box with the elements of a collection. Remember that the `Types` property manages the information in the `mcolTypes` storage variable. This variable is designed to hold a list of the different Object Type Definitions available for the *Person* object. We load this collection in just about the same way we have loaded every other collection up to this point. We first point it at a data store by invoking the `SetDataSource` method and passing it the name of our target data store in the `strConnect` string. Once the collection knows where to look for the data, we call the `Load` method. This fills up the collection with the information from the data store.

Once the collection has been filled, we just iterate through the collection and add a new item to the combo box for every item in the collection. As we iterate through the collection we test each value to determine whether or not the object in the collection represents our target PSD. If it does, then we set the form's `Caption` and the `Text` value for the combo box in addition to adding the item to the combo box. If not, we just add the item to the combo box:

```
' Call the Load Method of the User Centric Object
    Types.SetDataSource strConnect
    Types.Load

    ' Load the ComboBox
    For Each ThisType In Types
        If ThisType.ID = ParentTypeID Then
            cboObjectTypes.Text = ThisType.Name
            Me.Caption = Me.Caption & "[" & ThisType.Name & "]"
        End If
        cboObjectTypes.AddItem ThisType.Name
    Next ThisType
```

The next step is identical to the step we take when we load a standard List form's collection object. We point the object at a particular data store by invoking the `SetDataSource` method, and then we call the object's `Load` method. Notice that in this case we are passing a parameter to the `Load` method. This is a little different. Let's think about why we need to do this.

```
' Call the Load Method of the User Centric Object
    PropNames.SetDataSource strConnect
    PropNames.Load ParentTypeID
```

When we loaded the `Types` collection above, we just called the `Load` method without any parameters. That is because we wanted the data store to return a collection of every possible `Type` for the *Person* object – IT Customer, IT Resource, Doctor, etc. But, when we loaded the `PropNames` collection, we passed a parameter `ParentTypeID`. This value is used to tell the data store which Property Set Definition we want to work with.

For example, say that the Object Type Definition IT Resource has an ID of 7. When we pass the value 7 into the `PropNames.Load` method, it returns the collection of Property Definitions that are assigned to IT Resource. It is that simple.

Notice that in the next line of code we make the collection of available properties and the target collection of properties the same. We do that with the following line:

```
Set mcolAvailablePropNames = mcolPropNames
```

Once this has been done, we call a simple routine that loads the available properties list box control and then we call the `LoadPropNameListView` method we became familiar with in the last three chapters:

```
LoadAvailablePropNameListBox
' Load the listview
LoadPropNameListView
```

LoadAvailablePropNameListBox

This routine is just used to load the left-hand list box with the information in the `mcolAvailablePropNames` collection. This routine is called every time the value in the combo box changes:

```
Public Sub LoadAvailablePropNameListBox()
    Dim ThisProperty As UCPerson.clsPropName

    lstAvailableProperties.Clear

    For Each ThisProperty In mcolAvailablePropNames
      lstAvailableProperties.AddItem ThisProperty.PropertyName
    Next ThisProperty

End Sub
```

LoadPropNameListView

This routine is essentially the same as we use on all standard List forms. The only difference in this case is that the object that we are loading is a collection of extended properties for our 4-Dimensional Data Object instead of a something like a list of customer names or a list of books.

Remember that the Property Definition (`PropName`) object always uses the same set of properties. This allows us to reuse essentially the same code for every 4-Dimensional Data Object. The only change that must be made according to the practice I have adopted for this book is that we must refer to the correct project in the `clsPropName` dimension statement:

```
Public Sub LoadPropNameListView()
    Dim ThisObject As UCPerson.clsPropName
    Dim PropNameItems As ListItems
    Dim ThisItem As ListItem

    Set PropNameItems = lvwPropNames.ListItems
    PropNameItems.Clear

    For Each ThisObject In PropNames
```

```
        If Not ThisObject.IsDeleted And ThisObject.IsChild Then
            Set ThisItem = PropNameItems.Add _
                (, ThisObject.Key, ThisObject.PropertyName)
            ThisItem.SubItems(1) = ThisObject.DataTypeName
            ThisItem.SubItems(2) = ThisObject.AccessLevel
            ThisItem.SubItems(3) = ThisObject.SecurityLevel
            ThisItem.SubItems(4) = ThisObject.ListAvailable
            ThisItem.SubItems(5) = ThisObject.DisplayOrder
            ThisItem.SubItems(6) = ThisObject.ID
        End If
    Next ThisObject

End Sub
```

cboObjectTypes_KeyPress

This routine merely prevents the user from entering a value into the combo box:

```
Private Sub cboObjectTypes_KeyPress(KeyAscii As Integer)
    KeyAscii = 0
End Sub
```

cboObjectTypes_Click

This routine is called every time the combo box is clicked. It performs a couple of validation tests, then it destroys the current collection of available Property Definitions stored in the `mcolAvailablePropNames` variable. Lastly it fills the list box with the collection of available Property Definitions assigned to the PSD displayed in the combo box.

The first thing we do in this routine is to make sure that we have a valid PSD name. Remember that we loaded the combo box with the names of all of the OTDs available for our object. That means that every possibility in the combo box is a valid entry. We don't let the user enter a single keystroke into the combo box, so that means that as long as the length of `cboObjectTypes.Text` is greater than zero, we have a valid entry:

```
If Len(cboObjectTypes.Text) = 0 Then Exit Sub
```

Next we iterate through the collection of OTDs that we loaded when we loaded the form. When we find a match, we exit the `For` loop:

```
For Each ThisType In Types
    If cboObjectTypes.Text = ThisType.Name Then
        Exit For
    End If
Next ThisType
```

Then we test to see whether or not `mcolAvailablePropNames` has been instantiated. If it has, then we destroy it by setting it to `Nothing`. We could skip this step and just instantiate a new `mcolAvailablePropNames`, but I prefer to take the extra step and illustrate the concept whenever possible:

```
      If Not mcolAvailablePropNames Is Nothing Then
         Set mcolAvailablePropNames = Nothing
      End If
```

Then we instantiate a new `mcolAvailablePropNames` object. Once the object has been created, we point it at a particular data store by using the `SetDataSource` method and passing it the name of our target data store in the variable `strConnect`:

```
      Set mcolAvailablePropNames = CreateObject _
                            ("UCPerson.colPropNames")
      mcolAvailablePropNames.SetDataSource strConnect
```

Then we load the `mcolAvailablePropNames` collection by calling the `Load` method and passing it the ID of the OTD that we selected from the combo box. Realize that this `Load` is the same one we used earlier during the `Form_Load`. The `mcolAvailablePropNames` and `mcolPropNames` objects are identical. But even though the two collections are identical, it is possible for them to contain different sets of data.

Think of it like this: I can have two recordsets that have been filled with information from a single table. Maybe recordset A contains a list of all of the data where the ID is less than 10. And maybe the second recordset, B, contains a list of all of the data where the ID is greater than 10. The structure of the recordsets is identical in both cases, but they contain different data.

In this case, we are loading the `mcolAvailablePropNames` collection with a list of available Property Definitions for the PSD that was indicated by the combo box selection. We do that by passing the ID of the OTD as a parameter. If the ID in this case was the ID that pointed to IT Customer OTD, then we would return a list of Property Definitions assigned to the IT Customer OTD. If it pointed to Doctor, then we would return a list of Property Definitions assigned to the Doctor OTD:

```
      mcolAvailablePropNames.Load ThisType.ID
      LoadAvailablePropNameListBox
```

The last thing we do is to call the load list box routine we looked at above.

cmdAdd_Click

The `cmdAdd_Click` routine is used to add a new object to the collection of objects we are working with on the form. It creates a new object by checking out an object from the existing collection. It does that with the line:

```
   Set ThisObject = PropNames.CheckOutObject(0)
```

Once this object has been created, it is passed to the Detail form and its `TypeID` is set using the following line:

```
   .PropName.TypeID = ParentTypeID
```

The remainder of the code is essentially identical to the Level I treatment. This code can be used for any 4-Dimensional Data Object and is self-explanatory:

```
Private Sub cmdAdd_Click()
  Dim ThisObject As UCPerson.clsPropName
  Dim strButtonPressed As String

  On Error GoTo cmdAdd_ClickError

    With frmPropNameDetail
        ' Create a new empty object in the collection and
        ' enable editing
        ' This method handles all parent child relationships
        Set ThisObject = PropNames.CheckOutObject(0)
        .PropName = ThisObject
        ' Replace this line with the appropriate parent type
        ' call
        .PropName.TypeID = ParentTypeID
        ' Always pass the User Logon ID for the currently logged
        ' on user
        .PropName.StampUser = UserLogon
        .Show vbModal
        ' Simple messaging functionality which tells us which
        ' button the user pressed on the Detail form
        strButtonPressed = .ButtonPressed
    End With

    If strButtonPressed = "OK" Then
        ' If the user stills wants to add the new object
        ' This places the object back into the collection,
        ' disables editing and manages all the parent child
        ' relationships
        PropNames.CheckInObject ThisObject
    Else
        ' If the user did not press the OK button the new
        ' object is destroyed
        Set ThisObject = Nothing
    End If
    LoadPropNameListView
    cboObjectTypes_Click
  Exit Sub
cmdAdd_ClickError:
    ErrorHandler
End Sub
```

cmdEdit_Click

The cmdEdit_Click routine identifies the currently selected PropName object, emancipates it from the collection of PropName objects by using the CheckOutObject method, and passes the emancipated object to a Detail form so that it can be edited. Once the modal Detail form has been dismissed, this routine checks the object back into the parent collection's control:

```
Private Sub cmdEdit_Click()
  Dim ThisObject As UCPerson.clsPropName

  On Error GoTo cmdEdit_ClickError

  ' If nothing is selected then exit now
  If lvwPropNames.SelectedItem Is Nothing Then Exit Sub

  ' Let the user know the application is busy
```

```
        Screen.MousePointer = vbHourglass

        ' Find the object in the collection the user needs to edit
        For Each ThisObject In PropNames
            If ThisObject.Key = lvwPropNames.SelectedItem.Key Then
                ' Remove the selected object from the collection and
                ' enable editing
                ' This method handles all of the parent-child
                ' relationships
                Set ThisObject = PropNames.CheckOutObject(ThisObject.ID)
                Exit For
            End If
        Next ThisObject

        If ThisObject Is Nothing Then Exit Sub

        ' Place the object on the detail form
        With frmPropNameDetail
            .PropName = ThisObject
            ' Always pass the Logon ID for the current User
            .PropName.StampUser = UserLogon
            .Show vbModal
        End With

        ' This places the object back into the collection,
        ' disables editing and manages all the parent child
        ' relationships
        PropNames.CheckInObject ThisObject
        LoadPropNameListView
        cboObjectTypes_Click

        ' Let the user know the application is done
        Screen.MousePointer = vbDefault

    Exit Sub
cmdEdit_ClickError:
    ErrorHandler
End Sub
```

lvwPropNames_DblClick

This just allows a double-click to cause the same response as pressing the cmdEdit button:

```
Private Sub lvwPropNames_DblClick()
    cmdEdit_Click
End Sub
```

cmdRemove_Click

The first portion of the cmdRemove_Click routine works a lot like the cmdEdit_Click routine. Both routines perform a Key comparison to determine which object the user wants to work with:

```
Private Sub cmdRemove_Click()
    Dim ThisObject As UCPerson.clsPropName

    On Error GoTo cmdRemove_ClickError

    ' If nothing is selected then there is nothing to delete
    If lvwPropNames.SelectedItem Is Nothing Then Exit Sub
```

```
         ' Let the user know the application is busy
         Screen.MousePointer = vbHourglass

         ' Find the selected object in the collection
         For Each ThisObject In PropNames
            If ThisObject.Key = lvwPropNames.SelectedItem.Key Then
               ' Remove the selected object from the collection and
               ' enable editing
               ' This method handles all of the parent-child
               ' relationships
```

In the next section of code in this routine, the selected object is emancipated from the parent collection by using the CheckOutObject method. Once the object is no longer under the control of the parent collection, it is deleted by calling its ObjectDelete method:

```
               Set ThisObject = PropNames.CheckOutObject(ThisObject.ID)
               ' Always pass the Logon ID for the current User.
               ThisObject.StampUser = UserLogon
               ThisObject.SetDataSource strConnect
               ' This method deletes the object and creates an audit
               ' record
               ThisObject.ObjectDelete
               Exit For
            End If
         Next ThisObject

         LoadPropNameListView
         cboObjectTypes_Click
         Screen.MousePointer = vbHourglass
```

The last section of code in this routine performs a test to determine whether or not the form has been configured to show deleted objects. In this case, the deleted listview would be visible. If this is the case, then the deleted object collection is refreshed and the deleted listview is reloaded. If the deleted listview is hidden, then there is no reason to reload it until the user asks to see it:

```
         ' If the deleted listview is visible then refresh it
         ' If it is not visible, the showdeleted button will do this
         ' so there is no need to refresh it here.
         If Me.Height = jamShowDeleted Then
            ' This clears the local storage variable
            Set mcolPropNamesDeleted = Nothing
            ' This call to the property creates a new deleted object
            ' collection and loads it with the deleted but
            ' unrestored objects
            PropNamesDeleted.SetDataSource strConnect
            PropNamesDeleted.ShowDeleted ParentTypeID
            LoadPropNamesDeletedListView
         End If

         ' Let the user know the application is done
         Screen.MousePointer = vbDefault

      Exit Sub
   cmdRemove_ClickError:
      ErrorHandler
   End Sub
```

cmdShare_Click

You might think that sharing properties between objects is a difficult job. From the user interface programmer's perspective, it isn't. In fact, this code is very similar to the `cmdEdit_Click` code. There are a couple of differences between the routines, but they are minor. The real work involved in sharing property values takes place at the database. There is absolutely no reason to let that difficulty permeate throughout an application. In general it is easier to manage difficult sections of code if they are localized. I think you will agree that from this, the user interface developer's perspective, it is fairly easy to share property values between multiple Property Set Definitions.

The first thing we do in the routine is to determine what Property Definition the user wants to share with the target Property Set Definition. We do that by finding the selected item in the listbox using the following line:

```
strPropertyName = lstAvailableProperties.List _
                        (lstAvailableProperties.ListIndex)
```

Once we know what to look for, we iterate through the available properties until we find a match:

```
For Each SelectedObject In mcolAvailablePropNames
    If SelectedObject.TypeID = ParentTypeID Then Exit Sub
    If SelectedObject.PropertyName = strPropertyName Then
        Exit For
    End If
Next SelectedObject
```

Of course, it is ridiculous to share properties with the same PSD, so if the selected item is already a member of our target type we just exit the sub using the following line:

```
If SelectedObject.TypeID = ParentTypeID Then Exit Sub
```

If the `PropertyName` matches the property name that the user selected, we exit the `For` loop using this line:

```
If SelectedObject.PropertyName = strPropertyName Then
```

Now the `SelectedObject` is the one the person chose. We take that object and load it onto the Detail form in the following `With` block:

```
With frmPropNameDetail
    ' Create a new empty object in the collection and
    ' enable editing
    ' This method handles all parent-child relationships
    Set ThisObject = PropNames.CheckOutObject(0)
    ThisObject.ID = SelectedObject.ID
    ThisObject.PropertyName = SelectedObject.PropertyName
    ThisObject.DataTypeID = SelectedObject.DataTypeID
    ThisObject.DataTypeName = SelectedObject.DataTypeName
    ThisObject.ListAvailable = SelectedObject.ListAvailable
    ThisObject.AccessLevel = SelectedObject.AccessLevel
    ThisObject.ControllingTypeID = _
                    SelectedObject.ControllingTypeID
    ThisObject.DisplayOrder = 0
```

```
        ThisObject.TypeID = ParentTypeID
        .SourceControl = "ShareThis"
        .PropName = ThisObject
        ' Replace this line with the appropriate parent
        ' type call
        ' Always pass the User Logon ID for the currently
        ' logged on user
        .PropName.StampUser = UserLogon
        .Show vbModal
        ' Simple messaging functionality which tells us which
        ' button the user pressed on the detail form
        strButtonPressed = .ButtonPressed
    End With
```

This routine looks a little more complex than the cmdEdit_Click routine. That is because we are actually adding a new object to the PropNames collection, and copying the properties from the selected object into the new object. The new object is created with the following line:

```
    Set ThisObject = PropNames.CheckOutObject(0)
```

Remember that when we want to add a new item to an existing collection we always check out object number zero. This has the same effect as creating a new object, but it also manages the parent-child relationship between the object and its parent collection. Once we have created the new object, we just copy the values from the selected object into the new object and call the Detail form. The only other thing we have to do here to share the object is to let the Detail form know our intentions. We do that with the following line:

```
    .SourceControl = "ShareThis"
```

This line is just used to configure the Detail form to share properties. It is not required for the actual sharing processes. That happens at the database level and is invisible to the user interface programmer. We will cover this process in detail in an upcoming chapter.

cmdClose_Click

```
    Private Sub cmdClose_Click()
        Unload Me
    End Sub
```

lvwPropNamesDeleted_DblClick

This routine is nearly identical to the Level I treatment. Even though we have gone over this kind of code before, there are a couple of little twists that bear repeating. The first section of code is almost identical to the imgEdit_Click and imgRemove_Click routines we looked at earlier. It is just used to identify the user's target PropName object. Once that has been done, the object is emancipated from the deleted objects collection. There is no reason to step through this code. If you need to review this material, see the comments on either of those sections above.

What is different in this routine is what happens after the object as been identified and emancipated. It is passed to a modal Detail form. However, notice that when we pass the object, we also pass the name of its control of origin as shown in the following line:

```
    .SourceControl = "lvwPropNamesDeleted"
```

This tells the Detail form that the object it has been passed is currently deleted and allows that form to morph itself to handle the restoration task.

Once the Detail form has returned control to this form, we determine whether or not the object was restored by testing the Detail form's `ButtonPressed` property. If the OK button was pressed, then the object was restored, so we check it into the collection of *undeleted* `PropNames` and refresh the listviews:

```
If strButtonPressed = "OK" Then
    ' This places the object back into the collection,
    ' disables editing and manages all the parent-child
    ' relationships
    PropNames.CheckInObject ThisObject
Else
```

Please look carefully at the section of code above. Be sure you realize that we are not checking the object back into the same collection it came from.

> We are checking the object into the undeleted **PropNames** collection. We never check it back into the **PropNamesDeleted** collection. This is a subtle point.

Also note that a failure to do this doesn't in any way effect the restoration process at the database level. The restoration has taken place at the Detail form. The only real danger here is that the user's interface may not accurately reflect the current condition of the data store unless this routine is executed as shown.

Form_Unload

This routine, like all `Form_Unload` routines performs the necessary housekeeping chores:

```
Private Sub Form_Unload(Cancel As Integer)
    On Error Resume Next
    Set mcolPropNames = Nothing
    Set mcolAvailablePropNames = Nothing
    Set mcolPropNamesDeleted = Nothing
    Set mcolTypes = Nothing
End Sub
```

Review Routines

I am not going to go over the code in the following routines. It is virtually identical to the code with the same name that we used in the Level I Object List form. If you need a refresher you can always look back to Chapter 5:

- ❏ cmdDeleted_Click
- ❏ LoadPropNamesDeletedListView
- ❏ lvwPropNamesDeleted_ColumnClick

The PersonObject Property Name Administrative Screen

The Property Definition Detail form is accessed via the Property Set Control Panel. This form allows you to work with the actual Property Definitions themselves.

frmPropNameDetail.frm

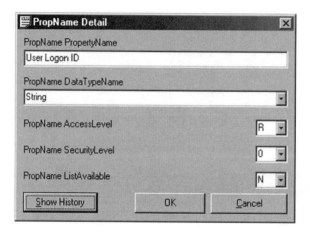

At first glance, the Property Definition Detail form looks quite unassuming. But there is a lot of design under the hood of this little form.

❑ Notice the DataTypeName combo box. It allows us to create Property Definitions that contain strings, long values, dates, and even other 4-Dimensional Data Objects.

❑ The AccessLevel property allows this property definition to be marked as (R) read only or (W) read/write enabled.

❑ The SecurityLevel property allows us to set a numeric value as the security level for this property definition.

We can use this security level in conjunction with individual user security levels to create individual user to individual field level security. Let's consider an example:

Say that our PSD contains three property definitions: Property 1, Property 2, and Property 3. Now let's assign each of these properties a different security level:

❑ Property 1 = 10
❑ Property 2 = 20
❑ Property 3 = 27

If we used that PSD, and a user with a security level of 30 accessed the extended 4-Dimensional Data Object, that user would not be able to see any of the object's extended properties. That user would only have access to the base set of properties. This user would not even know that an extended property existed for this object.

If another user had a security level of 25, then that user would be able to see Property 3 only. The user would not even be aware that the other properties existed. Think about the different ways you might combine the security level property with the access level property to manage an object's security right down to the individual user – individual field (property) level.

I don't want to belabor the point, but if another user had a security level of 15, then that user would be able to see Property 2 and Property 3. And if a different user had a security level of 8 then that user would be able to use all of the extended properties. Remember our discussion about Windows NT security? Its finest attribute was that it allows an administrator to enforce a level of control equal to the value of the data when compared to the possible threat. That is exactly what we have here. We can have properties locked up so tight that only one person in the organization can work with them, and others configured so that everyone can work with them. We can exercise pinpoint control in the circumstances that warrant it without effecting the rest of the data in the system. Best of all, you can ignore all of it if you want to. You can build your application first, and then determine anytime what level of security each piece of it requires.

There is one property on the Detail form that we haven't discussed yet. It is the ListAvailable property. If a Property Definition has the ListAvailable flag set to Y (yes), then the Detail form changes to accommodate the Property Definition. It opens up and displays an area that can be used to manage list items. In the image below, we are working with the Job Title Property Definition. Notice that there is a list of valid entries available for this Property Definition. We can add new items, edit existing items, and remove items from this list by using the controls on the form:

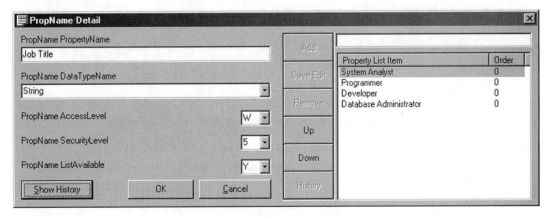

As you might imagine, there is a bit of work required to build this form. But, you will find that the techniques we employ here are essentially identical to the ones we have been using all along.

Declarations Section

The declarations section of the form shows that we need to create quite a few form-level storage variables. We will actually be working with three Level I Data Objects on this form. First, take a look at the code; it should be self-explanatory:

```
Option Explicit

'Dimension the local variables
Private mstrButtonPressed As String
Private mobjPropName As UCPerson.clsPropName
Private mcolPropNameHistory As UCPerson.colPropNames
```

```
Private mcolItemList As UCPerson.colPropItems
Private mcolItemListDeleted As UCPerson.colPropItems
Private mobjPropItem As UCPerson.clsPropItem
Private mcolItemAuditHistory As UCPerson.colPropItems

Private mcolDataTypes As UCPerson.colDataTypes
Private mstrSourceControl As String

' Use these local constants to resize the form
' History Listview Visible
Private Const jamShowHistory As Integer = 6735
' History Listview Hidden
Private Const jamHideHistory As Integer = 3855

' Item List Visible
Private Const jamListAvailable As Integer = 10695
' Item List Hidden
Private Const jamNoListAvailable As Integer = 5370
```

Now let's make a list of the different objects we will work with on this form.

❑ UCPerson.colDataTypes collection. This collection is used to manage information about all of the different data types available to our enterprise. Generally this is a small list, but it can grow. Any Level I Data Object or 4-Dimensional Data Object can be a data type. We will see how this works in Chapters 14 and 15:

```
Private mcolDataTypes As UCPerson.colDataTypes
```

❑ UCPerson.PropName object. This object is used to manage information about the Property Definition:

```
Private mobjPropName As UCPerson.clsPropName
Private mcolPropNameHistory As UCPerson.colPropNames
```

❑ UCPerson.PropItem object. This object is used to manage the list of available items if one exists for the particular Property Definition:

```
Private mcolItemList As UCPerson.colPropItems
Private mcolItemListDeleted As UCPerson.colPropItems
Private mobjPropItem As UCPerson.clsPropItem
Private mcolItemAuditHistory As UCPerson.colPropItems
```

Note that it is possible to reuse this form for any 4-Dimensional Data Object with a minimum of coding. The only thing that really changes from object to object is the project references.

Form-Level Properties

We have already spent a little time looking at each of the three types of objects we will use on this form. We have also spent a lot of time going over the whys and why nots concerning property handlers. So I am just going to give you a complete listing of the property handlers you need for this form. And, instead of going over each one individually, we will just use them in each of the routines as we need them.

Data Type Object Property Handlers

```
Public Property Get DataTypes() As UCPerson.colDataTypes
    If mcolDataTypes Is Nothing Then
        Set mcolDataTypes = New UCPerson.colDataTypes
    End If
    Set DataTypes = mcolDataTypes
End Property
```

```
Public Property Let DataTypes(colDataTypes As UCPerson.colDataTypes)
    Set mcolDataTypes = colDataTypes
End Property
```

Property Definition Property Handlers

```
Public Property Get PropName() As UCPerson.clsPropName
    If mobjPropName Is Nothing Then
        Err.Raise vbObjectError, _
        "This form requires an existing PropName object"
    End If
    Set PropName = mobjPropName
End Property
```

```
Public Property Let PropName(objPropName As UCPerson.clsPropName)
    Set mobjPropName = objPropName
End Property
```

```
Public Property Get PropNameHistory() As UCPerson.colPropNames
    If mcolPropNameHistory Is Nothing Then
        Set mcolPropNameHistory = New UCPerson.colPropNames
    End If
    Set PropNameHistory = mcolPropNameHistory
End Property
```

List Item Property Handlers

```
Public Property Get ListItem() As UCPerson.clsPropItem
    If mobjPropItem Is Nothing Then
        Set mobjPropItem = New UCPerson.clsPropItem
    End If
    Set ListItem = mobjPropItem
End Property
```

```
Public Property Let ListItem(objPropItem As UCPerson.clsPropItem)
    Set mobjPropItem = objPropItem
End Property
```

```
Public Property Get ListItemHistory() As UCPerson.colPropItems
    If mcolItemAuditHistory Is Nothing Then
        Set mcolItemAuditHistory = New UCPerson.colPropItems
    End If
    Set ListItemHistory = mcolItemAuditHistory
End Property
```

```
Public Property Let ListItemHistory(colItemAuditHistory As _
                                    UCPerson.colPropItems)
```

```
        Set mcolItemAuditHistory = colItemAuditHistory
    End Property
```

Item List Property Handlers

```
Public Property Get ItemListDeleted() As UCPerson.colPropItems
    If mcolItemListDeleted Is Nothing Then
        Set mcolItemListDeleted = New UCPerson.colPropItems
    End If
    Set ItemListDeleted = mcolItemListDeleted
End Property
```

```
Public Property Let ItemListDeleted(colItemListDeleted As _
                                    UCPerson.colPropItems)
    Set mcolItemListDeleted = colItemListDeleted
End Property
```

```
Public Property Get ItemList() As UCPerson.colPropItems
    If mcolItemList Is Nothing Then
        Set mcolItemList = New UCPerson.colPropItems
    End If
    Set ItemList = mcolItemList
End Property
```

```
Public Property Let ItemList(colItemlist As UCPerson.colPropItems)
    Set mcolItemList = colItemlist
End Property
```

Miscellaneous Property Handlers

```
Public Property Get ButtonPressed() As String
    ButtonPressed = mstrButtonPressed
End Property
```

```
Public Property Get SourceControl() As String
    SourceControl = mstrSourceControl
End Property
```

```
Public Property Let SourceControl(strSourceControl As String)
    mstrSourceControl = strSourceControl
End Property
```

Form_Load

The bad new is, as you might guess, this Form_Load routine requires a lot of work. And, as I hope you have come to expect by now, the good news is that you already know how to do it. We do have a few extra things to consider when we work with a form this complex, but each of those things is really just a different flavor of similar problems that we have solved earlier in this book.

The first section of code is old hat. It just configures 4 listviews to display the data to the user. We have done this many times before.

The next few lines of code are also pretty standard stuff, but I want to touch on them just to make sure we cover all the bases:

```
    cboPropNameAccessLevel.AddItem "R"
    cboPropNameAccessLevel.AddItem "W"

    cboPropNameListAvailable.AddItem "Y"
    cboPropNameListAvailable.AddItem "N"

    For i = 0 To 99
        cboPropNameSecurityLevel.AddItem i
    Next I
```

In the lines of code above we prepare all of the combo boxes with the values they need. In the `AccessLevel` combo box we add the possible values `"R"` and `"W"`, for read and write. In the `ListAvailable` combo box, we add the possible values `"Y"` and `"N"` for yes and no. And in the `SecurityLevel` combo box we add the values from 0 to 99 for the possible security levels. There is very little reason to store these values in the data store because the nature of this interface is administrative (intended to be used by developers etc). But it is possible to create simple objects to manage the data if we wished to store it in the data store. The next block of code illustrates an example of that technique:

```
    DataTypes.SetDataSource strConnect
    DataTypes.Load
    For Each ThisDataType In DataTypes
        cboPropNameDataTypeName.AddItem ThisDataType.Name
    Next ThisDataType
    cboPropNameDataTypeName.Text = cboPropNameDataTypeName.List(0)
```

In this case, we have a list of possible data types in the data store and we use that list to fill this combo box via the `DataType` object. This allows us to use a centrally controlled list that is dynamic in nature. If we add a new data type to the list (create another 4-Dimensional Data Object) then it is immediately available for reuse. The `For` loop etc, is self-explanatory:

```
If PropName.IsNew Then
    ' If new object then clear the form
    If Len(SourceControl) > 0 Then
        SourceControl = ""
        SetPropNameState
    Else
        ClearForm
    End If
Else
    ' If existing object then populate controls
    SetPropNameState
End If
```

This code is not new; we have seen it before. The only thing to note here is that in this case we may pass a `SourceControl` string that says `"ShareThis"`. If we do, then the form operates as though we had sent it an existing object and goes through the motions required to share the Property Definition between the PSDs:

```
If Len(SourceControl) > 0 Then
    ' If this object was delivered from a deleted state then
    ' morph form
```

```
    cmdOK.Caption = "Restore"
    cmdHistory.Enabled = False
    Me.Caption = Me.Caption & " - [Restore]"
End If
```

We have seen this code before as well. It is used to indicate that the process the Detail form is managing is the *Restore From Deleted* process.

cboANYCOMBOBOX_KeyPress

Remember from above that I said that we don't allow the user to type into the combo box. We do that by setting the `KeyAscii` value of all of the keystrokes sent into the combo box to zero. We have seen this code before many times and there are a number of different techniques we could use to accomplish the same thing.

cboPropNameAccessLevel_LostFocus

We have gone over this before; all we are doing here is setting the property value in the object each time an input control loses focus. Then we copy the value from the object back into the input control. This ensures that the data validation routines in the object's property handlers are invoked:

```
Private Sub cboPropNameAccessLevel_LostFocus()
    PropName.AccessLevel = cboPropNameAccessLevel.Text
    cboPropNameAccessLevel.Text = PropName.AccessLevel
End Sub
```

cboPropNameDataTypeName_LostFocus

This section of code is similar to the text box example above. In this case, we are also performing a translation. We are accepting a string value and updating both a string and long value. We do that by iterating through a local collection of objects to determine the correct ID value for a given `DataTypeName`:

```
Private Sub cboPropNameDataTypeName_LostFocus()
    Dim ThisDataType As UCPerson.clsDataType

    PropName.DataTypeName = cboPropNameDataTypeName.Text
    cboPropNameDataTypeName.Text = PropName.DataTypeName

    For Each ThisDataType In DataTypes
      If ThisDataType.Name = PropName.DataTypeName Then
         PropName.DataTypeID = ThisDataType.ID
         Exit For
      End If
    Next ThisDataType

End Sub
```

This example shows one way to accomplish that, but you should seriously consider moving this logic from the user interface into the user centric object's property handler. Think about how you would do that. It is really quite simple. Logically, all we need to do is to copy the `For...Next` loop into the `DataTypeName` property `Let`. That way, we could perform the translation inside the object itself and relieve the user interface programmer of this responsibility. The resulting code on the form would then look like this:

```
Private Sub cboPropNameDataTypeName_LostFocus()
    PropName.DataTypeName = cboPropNameDataTypeName.Text
    cboPropNameDataTypeName.Text = PropName.DataTypeName
End Sub
```

Obviously there is a lot less chance of making a mistake here…

The resulting code in the property handler might look something like this. Notice what we have done here, we may have complicated a single property handler, but we have simplified every call to that property handler:

```
Public Property Let DataTypeName(strDataTypeName As String)
    Dim DataTypes As colDataTypes
    Dim ThisDataType as clsDataType
    Dim lngID as Long

    If Len(strDataTypeName) = 0 Then Exit Property

    Set DataTypes = CreateObject("UCDataType.colDataTypes")
    DataTypes.SetDataSource mstrConnect
    DataTypes.Load

    For Each ThisDataType In DataTypes
        If ThisDataType.Name = strDataTypeName Then
            ID = ThisDataType.ID
            MstrDataTypeName = strDataTypeName
            Exit For
        End If
    Next ThisDataType

End Property
```

cboPropNameListAvailable_Click

This routine is used to set the width of the form to accommodate a list of available items for the property if neessary:

```
Private Sub cboPropNameListAvailable_Click()
    If cboPropNameListAvailable.Text = "Y" Then
        Me.Width = jamListAvailable
    Else
        Me.Width = jamNoListAvailable
    End If
End Sub
```

cboPropNameListAvailable_LostFocus

This code is almost identical to that for cboPropNameAccessLevel_LostFocus. Every time the cboPropNameListAvailable control loses focus, we set the property value in the object. Then we copy the value from the object back into the combo box control, ensuring that data validation is performed:

```
Private Sub cboPropNameListAvailable_LostFocus()
    PropName.ListAvailable = cboPropNameListAvailable.Text
    cboPropNameListAvailable.Text = PropName.ListAvailable
End Sub
```

cboPropNameSecurityLevel_LostFocus

As with the `cboPropNameListAvailable_LostFocus` routine,
`cboPropNameSecurityLevel_LostFocus` effectively invokes data validation routines:

```
Private Sub cboPropNameSecurityLevel_LostFocus()
    PropName.SecurityLevel = cboPropNameSecurityLevel.Text
    cboPropNameSecurityLevel.Text = PropName.SecurityLevel
End Sub
```

lvwPropertyItems_DblClick

This tiny block of code is quite different than the listview double-click code we have been using.
Normally when we double-click on the listview, we know that we want to edit the object we have
selected. In this case, we are performing the detail tasks on the same form, so we check out the object
and place it into the input control for editing. We also copy the same value to both the `Text` and `Tag`
properties of the input control. This allows us to apply a simple (has this value been edited) test. If
the `Tag` and `Text` values do not match, then the value has changed:

```
Private Sub lvwPropertyItems_DblClick()
    Dim ThisObject As UCPerson.clsPropItem
    For Each ThisObject In ItemList
        If ThisObject.Key = lvwPropertyItems.SelectedItem.Key Then
            Set mobjPropItem = ItemList.CheckOutObject(ThisObject.ID)
            txtPropertyItem.Text = ThisObject.DisplayValue
            txtPropertyItem.Tag = ThisObject.DisplayValue
            Exit For
        End If
    Next ThisObject
End Sub
```

txtPropertyItem_Change

This routine performs several tasks. First, it performs a simple data validation test to ensure that some
value has been entered into the input control:

```
If Len(txtPropertyItem.Text) > 0 Then
```

Then it ensures that the current Property Definition (`PropName` object) has been saved previously. If
it hasn't been saved, then the user is sent a message which instructs him or her that the Property
Definition must be saved before any items can be added to the PSD. If the Property Definition has
been saved, the command buttons are reconfigured to either allow an item to be added to the
Property Definition or enable an item selected from the list to be edited, removed or have its history
shown:

```
    If PropName.ID > 0 Then
        If mobjPropItem Is Nothing Then
            cmdAdd.Enabled = True
        Else
            cmdEdit.Enabled = True
            cmdItemHistory.Enabled = True
            cmdRemove.Enabled = True
        End If
    Else
        MsgBox "This property must be saved before items can" & _
```

```
          " be added." & vbCrLf & "Press the OK button to save" & _
          " the Property Definition."
```

If the value entered into the textbox failed the data validation test, the controls are reconfigured as follows:

```
    Else
        Set mobjPropItem = Nothing
        cmdAdd.Enabled = False
        cmdEdit.Enabled = False
        cmdRemove.Enabled = False
        cmdItemHistory.Enabled = False
        lblAuditTrailView.Caption = "List of Deleted Items"
        lvwDeletedItems.Visible = True
        lvwPropItemHistory.Visible = False
    End If
```

cmdAdd_Click

The `cmdAdd_Click` routine is used to add a new object to the collection of objects we are working with on the form. Generally, this process calls a second modal form, but in this case we complete the entire process with a single form. This makes the code slightly different than a typical Level I treatment. The first thing we do is to perform some data validation with the following line. It just makes sure that there is actually a value for us to insert:

```
    If Len(txtPropertyItem.Text) = 0 Then Exit Sub
```

Then we perform a simple test to ensure that we are not attempting to insert the save item more than once. We do that by simply iterating through the collection of available items as shown below:

```
    For Each ThisObject In ItemList
        If ThisObject.DisplayValue = Trim(txtPropertyItem.Text) _
            Then Exit Sub
    Next ThisObject
```

If the data validation tests passed, then we create a new item object. In this case, we create the new item object by checking out object number 0 from the existing collection. Remember that checking out object 0 creates a new object:

```
        Set ThisObject = ItemList.CheckOutObject(0)
```

Once this object has been created, its properties are read from the item's parent object, `PropName`, the system variables, `UserLogon` and `strConnect`, and the input controls on the form as follows:

```
        ThisObject.DisplayValue = txtPropertyItem.Text
        ThisObject.StampUser = UserLogon
        ThisObject.SetDataSource strConnect
        ThisObject.PropertyID = PropName.ID
```

As we observed earlier, we are accomplishing this task with a single form, so rather than raising a modal dialog, we just save the new object by calling the `ObjectInsert` method as follows:

```
        ThisObject.ObjectInsert
```

cmdEdit_Click

This code should look familiar; it combines the standard Level I treatment onto a single form like the routine above. First, we perform a simple test to ensure that something is selected:

```
If Len(txtPropertyItem.Text) = 0 Then Exit Sub
```

Notice that we perform this test by checking the textbox instead of the listview. That is because we use the same double-click event on the listview for both the `Edit` and `Remove` routines. This means that all the double-click event does is to copy the value to the textbox and emancipate the object. In other words, as long as the textbox has some value, we can proceed.

The next thing we do is to ensure that the value has been edited. We use an old trick for this one. When we copy a value to the textbox from the listview, we also copy the value to the `Tag` property of the textbox. Then, instead of performing all kinds of gyrations to determine whether or not the value has changed, we just do a direct comparison between the starting and present values. Simple is good!

```
If txtPropertyItem.Text <> txtPropertyItem.Tag Then
```

Assuming we need to update the value, we simply copy the values into the correct properties as follows:

```
        ListItem.DisplayValue = txtPropertyItem.Text
        ListItem.SetDataSource strConnect
        ListItem.StampUser = UserLogon
```

Once the values have been copied, we update the object, and check it back into the collection. Remember that we checked it out in the `lvwPropertyItems_Dblclick` event:

```
        ListItem.ObjectUpdate
        ItemList.CheckInObject ListItem
```

After the object has been checked back into the collection, we refresh the collection and reload the listview:

```
        Set mcolItemList = Nothing
        Set mcolItemList = New UCPerson.colPropItems
        mcolItemList.SetDataSource strConnect
        mcolItemList.Load PropName.ID
        LoadPropItemListView
```

The last step is to clear both the textbox `Text` and `Tag` properties for reuse:

```
        txtPropertyItem.Text = ""
        txtPropertyItem.Tag = ""
```

cmdRemove_Click

Again, this code is similar but not identical to the Level I treatment. We have to do some things differently here because we are working on a single form. However, the differences are not as pronounced as the `cmdEdit_Click` routine. Remember that when we delete an object using a Level I treatment, we only use a single form.

As always, our first responsibility is to ensure that something has been selected:

```
' If nothing is selected then there is nothing to delete
If Len(txtPropertyItem.Text) = 0 Then Exit Sub
```

When we do this on a standard list form, we test to see whether something has been selected from the listview. However, when we perform the same test on this form, we check the length of the value of the textbox instead. That is because we use the double-click event of the listview to emancipate an object and copy it to the textbox so that the user can work with the value.

Once we are sure that we have something to work with, we iterate through the list to locate the object in the collection of items. If we find a match, we delete it using the code below. If we don't find it, then there is nothing to delete and we just let the routine run its course:

```
For Each ThisObject In ItemList
    If ThisObject.Key = lvwPropertyItems.SelectedItem.Key Then
        ' Always pass the Logon ID for the current User.
        ThisObject.StampUser = UserLogon
        ThisObject.SetDataSource strConnect
        ' This method deletes the object and creates an audit
        ' record
        ThisObject.ObjectDelete
        Exit For
    End If
Next ThisObject
Set mobjPropItem = Nothing
txtPropertyItem.Text = ""
```

The remainder of the routine is handled exactly the same way we handle any Level I delete routine. We test to find out whether or not the `lvwDeletedItems` listview is displayed. If it is, then we refresh all of the listviews. If it is hidden, then we only refresh the active listview.

cmdUp_Click

The original intention for the `DisplayOrder` property in the `PropItem` object was to allow us to define an order that we could use when we delivered a list of items to the user. This stub has been provided for that purpose. What we need to do here is to change the display order values for each of the property items in the current list relative to the others and then batch save the whole lot of them. Have fun!

```
Private Sub cmdUp_Click()
    If lvwPropertyItems.SelectedItem Is Nothing Then Exit Sub
        ' Future Enhancement
End Sub
```

cmdDown_Click

Of course, this goes with the one above:

```
Private Sub cmdDown_Click()
    If lvwPropertyItems.SelectedItem Is Nothing Then Exit Sub
        ' Future Enhancement
End Sub
```

ClearForm

The only unusual thing about the ClearForm routine is that we need to remember to set the width of the form according to the current value in the cboPropNameListAvailable combo box:

```
Public Sub ClearForm()

    txtPropNamePropertyName.Text = ""
    cboPropNameDataTypeName.Text = _
                        cboPropNameDataTypeName.List(0)
    cboPropNameDataTypeName_LostFocus
    cboPropNameAccessLevel.Text = _
                        cboPropNameAccessLevel.List(0)
    cboPropNameAccessLevel_LostFocus
    cboPropNameSecurityLevel.Text = _
                        cboPropNameSecurityLevel.List(0)
    cboPropNameSecurityLevel_LostFocus
    cboPropNameListAvailable.Text = _
                        cboPropNameListAvailable.List(0)
    cboPropNameListAvailable_LostFocus
    txtPropertyItem.Text = ""

    If cboPropNameListAvailable.Text = "Y" Then
        Me.Width = jamListAvailable
    Else
        Me.Width = jamNoListAvailable
    End If

End Sub
```

Review Routines

I am not going to go over the code in the following routines. It is virtually identical to the code with the same name that we used in the Level I Object List form. If you need a refresher, you can always look back to Chapter 5:

- ❑ cmdHistory_Click
- ❑ cmdItemHistory_Click
- ❑ cmdOK_Click
- ❑ cmdCancel_Click
- ❑ LoadPropItemListView
- ❑ SetPropNameState
- ❑ lvwDeletedItems_ColumnClick
- ❑ lvwDeletedItems_DblClick
- ❑ lvwPropertyItems_ColumnClick
- ❑ lvwPropItemHistory_DblClick
- ❑ lvwPropNameHistory_DblClick
- ❑ txtPropNamePropertyName_LostFocus
- ❑ LoadPropNameHistoryListView
- ❑ lvwPropNameHistory_ColumnClick
- ❑ LoadItemListDeletedListView
- ❑ LoadPropItemHistoryListView
- ❑ Form_Unload

Summary

In this chapter, we've continued our look at the user interface of the *Person* object by studying the Administrative User Interface. This interface is only available to the programmers, it is not seen by any customers. Its purpose is to simplify the process of creating and working with OTDs and their associated Property Definitions; freeing the programmer's time up for more important, complex and less tedious activities.

To put the Administrative User Interface into perspective, we've reviewed:

- ❏ Base objects
- ❏ Object Type Definitions (OTDs)
- ❏ Property Bags
- ❏ Property Set Definitions (PSDs)
- ❏ Property Definitions

In the next chapter, we'll discover how to create a Level II object as the first step towards building a 4-Dimensional Data Object.

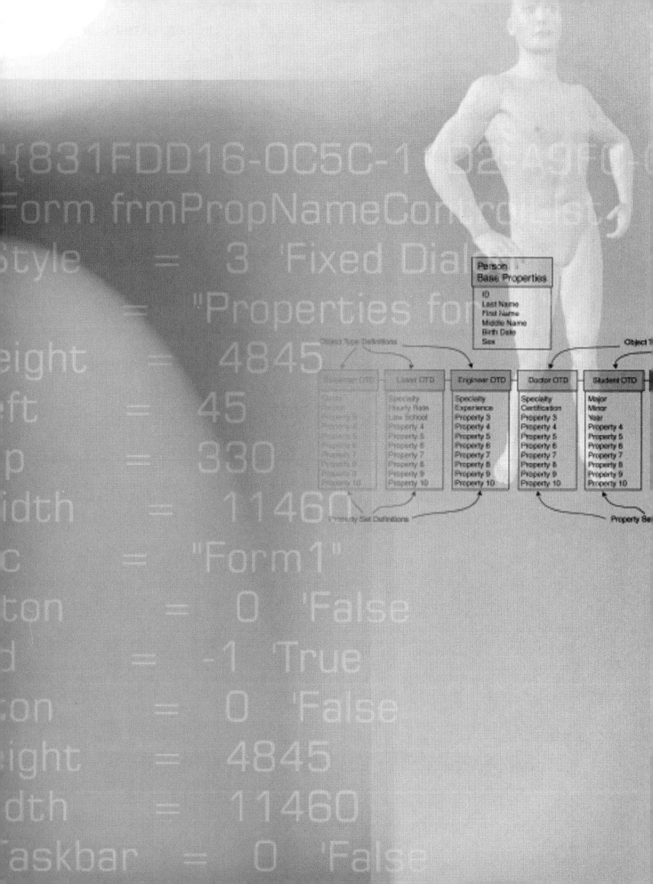

10

Level II Objects

Over the last two chapters, we designed an interface for a 4-Dimensional Data Object, the *Person* object. I introduced you to the twin concepts of Object Type Definitions and Property Set Definitions. We learned that we could design a single piece of software that could model both a doctor and a patient with absolutely no changes to the object code, the table structures, or the stored procedures. In this chapter, we will begin the process of learning how to turn that 'pie-in-the-sky' design into a real world entity.

As you might imagine, building a 4-Dimensional Data Object requires a bit of coding. Fortunately, you have already been given almost all the tools you'll need to build this object. As we learned when we used the *Person* object in the last chapters, Level III objects are constructed by creating and combining several modified Level I Data Objects. By now, you already know how to build Level I Data Objects.

In this chapter we will construct an intermediate object that I call a Level II object.

> *I must warn you ahead of time that Level II objects don't seem to exist in the real world. Without exception every object that might be modeled as a Level II object can, and probably should, be modeled as a Level III object.*

We will use the Level II object as a stepping-stone in order to learn some of the mechanics required for building Level III objects. Specifically, we will use the Level II object to learn how to manage information about Object Type Definitions.

The Three Different Levels of Data Objects

Way back in Chapter 4, we spent a little time going over the different levels of data objects we would talk about in this book. Chapter 4 was really something of an overview, so we didn't really take much time going into all of the details about each different object level. I think that was OK during that portion of the book. In Chapters 5, 6, and 7, we worked with objects that we called Level I objects. We learned to think about these objects as something that served as a proxy for a single table in the database. During that time, we didn't work with any higher-level objects, so there really wasn't much reason to worry about the difference between the different levels.

Over the last two chapters, you worked with something I call a 4-Dimensional Data Object. Again, we didn't take a lot of time to find out where this object fits into the scheme of things. Rather than filling your head with a bunch of theory about levels of objects, I thought it would be better for both of us if I introduced you to the 4-Dimensional Data Object by working with it. I wanted you to get a real feel for what made the thing tick. In the last chapter, you created an Administrative User Interface that allowed you to create Object Type Definitions (OTD) for 4-Dimensional Data Objects. I said that this user interface allowed us to "manage" the business rules that really define things like OTDs and the Property Set Definitions (PSD) assigned to these OTDs. Of course, what I really should have said is that the user interface allows us to access the functionality of the 4-Dimensional Data Object that is used to manage those business rules. The user interface doesn't do the work. The objects that the user interface exposes are independent of the user interface. To prove that point, when we get to Chapter 16, we'll learn how to construct a different user interface to handle the administration of a 4-Dimensional Data Object over the web using Active Server Pages. We don't have to change the underlying object to do this. The object stays the same. We only change the interface.

This means that now we need to learn how to provide the administration capability in the object itself rather than in the user interface. It also means that we need to take a little time to think about the different levels of objects in a little more detail.

Level I Objects

Level I Objects are objects that serve as proxies for a single table in the database. They are ECDOs so they expose the 8 basic data handling processes, and physically we know that this means that there are really two tables in the database for this object. We work with this object just about the same way we work with a single table in the database.

Level I Object

These objects give us things like pick lists and the like. If we look at a Level I object the same way we looked at the OTDs and PSDs in the last chapter, we would find that we could view this level of object in much the same way we viewed any base object without any OTDs or PSDs:

Data Object
Base Properties

ID
Base Property 1
Base Property 2
Base Property 3
Base Property ...
Base Property n

Notice that this object does not have any internal references to any other objects or non-audit tables in the database. Level I objects represent single tables without dependent relationships. But of course you already know about Level I objects because you have worked with them and learned how to build them.

Level II Objects

We haven't really talked about Level II objects at all until this point. That is because I really consider Level II objects something of a *concept bridge* more than anything we might actually build. In the last chapter, we took time to understand something we called an Object Type Definition (OTD). We kind of discovered that we have been using OTDs all of our lives; like when we say that a person is a doctor or an engineer etc. We came to the conclusion that an OTD is really just a way of talking about something we add to a *Person* object (or any other data object) which allows us to categorize extensions of that object.

If we look at a Level II object the same way we looked at the OTDs and PSDs in the last chapter, we would find that we could view this level of object as a base object with an Object Type Definition attached to it.

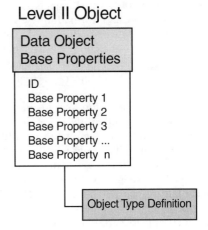

I think this image does a fair job of describing a Level II object. Notice that it doesn't show any extended properties, like the 4-Dimensional *Person* Data Object we worked with the last two chapters. This object just consists of a base object and an OTD that allows us to categorize that base object.

This means that we could use Level II Objects to say that a person is a doctor, or an engineer, or a teacher. But it also means that we wouldn't have any way to carry around the extra properties that we might need to be able to describe this person as a doctor, or an engineer, or a teacher. As you might imagine, there are times when just knowing how to categorize an object is a very good thing. But I think that most of the time Level II objects would leave us wandering around looking for a place to put that extra information that we need to know about the doctor, or the engineer, or the teacher. In practice, this means that most of the time when we think we can use a Level II object to model something in the real world, we can probably do a better job of modeling that thing with a Level III or 4-Dimensional Data Object.

That doesn't mean that Level II objects are not useful. I can't think of a better way to develop the skills we need to learn in this chapter. Level II objects do something that Level I objects don't. They manage a relationship in the database for us. They provide the link and all the mechanics used to link, the object's base set of properties with the OTD that we can use to categorize that object. I think that this alone would be a good enough reason for us to take some time to learn to build them, but there is more.

Every 4-Dimensional Data Object, like the *Person* object, has an OTD. That means that we have to write this code *on the way* to developing a fully functioning 4-Dimensional Data Object anyway. While we are doing this, we will think of the object that we are building as a Level II object so that we can talk about it in its own right. This object can teach us a lot about Object Type Definitions, and we need to know about them before we get on to our next task – developing a Level III or full fledged 4-Dimensional Data Object.

Level III Objects

Right about now, I am sure that you are saying "OK Joe, what is it? Do you want to call these things 4-Dimensional Data Objects, or do you want to call them Level III objects. Let's get this straight. My head is starting to spin." Please accept my apology, and allow me to give you a little background.

When I work with teams in person, I always start off with Level I objects just like we did in this book. We take a lot of time learning to build them without even thinking about things like 4 Dimensions. Then we work through Level II objects so that we learn the things that we will learn in this chapter. Once we understand that information, we move on in a logical progression to something called a Level III object. While we are building Level III objects, we learn to call them 4-Dimensional Data Objects. We also learn that although we can use the lessons we learned during the Level II development that there are not too many cases where we would select a Level II object over a Level III or 4-Dimensional Data Object in actual practice.

I can organize the information like this in person because, in person, I can release the information in a specific order. It is a little different with a book. If you wanted to, you could start someplace in the middle, or at the end. This fact makes it a little difficult for me to work through the Levels and get to the Ah Ha! that normally comes with the realization that we are building 4-Dimensional Data Objects. Anyway, the levels are really a way for us to think about the relative complexity of each object. As we have seen, Level I objects are the simplest kind of data objects. They serve as proxies for a single table in the database. Level II Objects are more complex, they serve as proxies for two tables in the database – the base table and another table that's used to describe the OTD. This brings us to Level III objects and in a logical progression, these objects are the most complex objects. Level III objects *are* 4-Dimensional Data Objects.

Level III Object

Level III Objects have the same things that Level I and Level II objects have, but they also have one other thing. Level III objects have a **Property Bag** that they use to carry around a set of properties. If we look at a Level II object the same way we looked at the OTDs and PSDs in the last chapter, we would find that we could view this object as a base object with an Object Type Definition, with additional properties, attached to it:

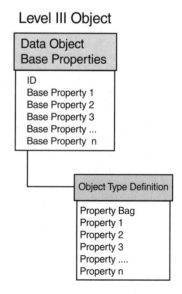

Data Object
Base Properties

ID
Base Property 1
Base Property 2
Base Property 3
Base Property ...
Base Property n

Object Type Definition

Property Bag
Property 1
Property 2
Property 3
Property ....
Property n

I think this image does a pretty good job of describing a Level III or 4-Dimensional Data Object. A Level III object consists of a base object (yes a Level I object) and an Object Type Definition. It also has several sub-objects that work together to give us something we have come to know as a Property Bag. The Property Bag is a **data device** that is used to manage the information that is defined by some set of business rules.

> *This separation of data and business rules allows us to build 'pure' data objects – objects uncluttered by the confusing mess of constantly changing business rules.*

We learned in the last chapter that we can enter these business rules the way that we enter any other data into our system. We can manage these business rules using the Administrative User Interface we constructed in the last chapter.

I hope I straightened that out. Let's get back to the job of building a Level II Data Object.

Level II Objects - A Closer Look

Level III Objects have Object Type Definitions and Property Set Definitions. Level II Objects only have Object Type Definitions. Let me use the following table to illustrate. On the left we have a Level II *Person* object that we have extended by creating three different OTDs. The three OTDs are:

- ❑ Engineering Student
- ❑ Law Student
- ❑ Math Student

On the right side of the table we have done exactly the same thing, but we have also added some extended properties to the Object Type Definitions.

> *Of course, we wouldn't use a Person object as a vehicle for managing students' grades or schedules; that would be incredibly poor design. This example is only to give you a sense of our target for this chapter.*

Level II Object		Level III Object		
Base Object	**Type**	**Base Object**	**Type**	**Extended Property Set**
Person	Engineering Student	Person	Engineering Student	
				Thermodynamics Grade
				Statistics Grade
Person	Law Student	Person	Law Student	

Table Continued on Following Page

Level II Object		Level III Object		
Base Object	Type	Base Object	Type	Extended Property Set
Person	Math Student	Person	Math Student	Property Law Grade
				Torts Grade
				Contracts Grade
				Calculus III Grade
				Knot Theory Grade

In this chapter, we will step through building a Level II object. That will give us the skills necessary to create and manage Object Type Definitions for any object. Once we have mastered the Level II object, we will be prepared to take on Level III objects.

The Tables and Views

As far as the database is concerned, what we really do when we build a Level II object instead of a Level I object is to create 3 additional tables, 8 additional stored procedures, and 1 additional view. In other words, It is like we are adding another Level I object. That means that we have an additional 8 stored procedures, and 1 additional view. Two of the tables we add are virtually identical to the tables we visited in the previous chapters.

There is one table for the *Person* OTD object and another to track the audit trail for that object. To keep things simple and maintainable, every OTD object has exactly the same set of base properties.

The Base Tables For A Level II Person Object

PersonObject
- ID
- FirstName
- MiddleName
- LastName
- Salutation
- Suffix
- BirthDate
- SSN
- Sex
- ConcurrencyID

PersonObjectAudit
- ID
- FirstName
- MiddleName
- LastName
- Salutation
- Suffix
- BirthDate
- SSN
- Sex
- StampID
- StampAction
- StampDateTime
- StampUser
- TypeID
- TypeName
- KeyPrefix

These tables are exactly the same as the tables we have designed in the previous chapters for Level I objects. I am not going to include the `EstablishDataStore` routine code here, because it is identical to the routine we use earlier to create the data store for our Level I objects in the previous chapters.

I have, however included the `CREATE TABLE` SQL to give you a second look at the syntax and to give you a head start on building the Level II object.

PersonObject CREATE TABLE SQL

```
CREATE TABLE dbo.PersonObject
  (
  ID int IDENTITY (1, 1) NOT NULL ,
  FirstName varchar (60) NOT NULL ,
  MiddleName varchar (60) NOT NULL ,
  LastName varchar (60) NOT NULL ,
  Salutation char (10) NOT NULL ,
  Suffix char (10) NOT NULL ,
  BirthDate datetime] NULL ,
  SSN char (9) NOT NULL ,
  Sex char (1) NOT NULL ,
  ConcurrencyID int NOT NULL
  )
```

PersonObjectAudit CREATE TABLE SQL

```
CREATE TABLE dbo.PersonObjectAudit
  (
  ID int IDENTITY (1, 1) NOT NULL ,
  FirstName varchar (60) NOT NULL ,
  MiddleName varchar (60) NOT NULL ,
  LastName varchar (60) NOT NULL ,
  Salutation char (10) NOT NULL ,
  Suffix char (10) NOT NULL ,
  BirthDate datetime NULL ,
  SSN char (9) NOT NULL ,
  Sex char (1) NOT NULL ,
  StampID int NOT NULL ,
  StampAction char (1) NOT NULL ,
  StampDateTime datetime NOT NULL ,
  StampUser char (15) NOT NULL ,
  TypeID int NOT NULL ,
  TypeName varchar (80) NOT NULL ,
  KeyPrefix char(10) NOT NULL
  )
```

The Person Object Type Pair of Tables

Once again, the Person Object Type pair of tables are no different than any other Level I pair of tables. The only thing to note here is that we use exactly the same fields for every Object Type Pair. The only thing that ever changes from object to object is the name of the table. This standardization allows us to reuse all of our OTD handling code for every level II or Level III object. It eases maintenance and promotes a higher level of understanding of the structure of the database.

PersonObjType CREATE TABLE SQL

Because the fields for the OTD are always the same, you can use the same CREATE TABLE SQL for every OTD that you ever build. The only thing that should change from object to object is the first line. For instance, if we wanted to use the PersonObjType CREATE TABLE SQL to create the IssueObjType table we would change the first line from this:

```
CREATE TABLE dbo.PersonObjType
```

To this:

```
CREATE TABLE dbo.IssueObjType
```

Everything else stays exactly the same! This makes our data store predictable, easy to understand and easy to manage. Remember that one of our stated goals for Enterprise Caliber Data Objects was that they be easy to maintain.

This brings up another point I haven't mentioned previously. We need to ensure that the base name for our objects is less than 9 characters in length. It may not seem obvious yet, but you should begin to notice that we use a rigorous naming convention for all stored tables, views, and stored procedures. SQL Server 6.5 imposes a limit of 30 characters on the name of stored procedures. As long as we keep the name of our base object under 9 characters in length, we will not go over this limit using the naming convention in this book. The table below gives the names we use to create the 8 stored procedures for a base object:

Prefix	ObjectName	Base Object	Suffix -- Action
sp	Person	Object	AuditDeletes
sp	Person	Object	AuditList
sp	Person	Object	Delete
sp	Person	Object	Get
sp	Person	Object	Insert
sp	Person	Object	List
sp	Person	Object	Restore
sp	Person	Object	Update

```
CREATE TABLE dbo.PersonObjType
   (
   ID int IDENTITY (1, 1) NOT NULL ,
   Name varchar (80) NOT NULL ,
   BriefDescription varchar (80) NOT NULL ,
   Description varchar (255) NOT NULL ,
   KeyPrefix char (10) NOT NULL ,
   ConcurrencyID int NOT NULL
   )
```

PersonObjTypeAudit CREATE TABLE SQL

Of course, the Object Type Definition Audit table follows the same conventions as we observed for the Object Type Definition table. This table is the one that allows us to maintain a complete history of every Object Type Definition. At first this may seem a little like overkill, but think of how much trouble it would be if someone accidentally deleted an Object Type Definition. We can compare the results directly to what would happen if someone deleted a Patient or Doctor table in a standard system. The Audit table is like an insurance policy. We already paid the premium for this insurance policy when we learned how to create and work with them in the last 5 chapters. Now we can begin to reap the benefits of all of our work.

```
CREATE TABLE dbo.PersonObjTypeAudit
   (
   ID int IDENTITY (1, 1) NOT NULL ,
   StampUser char (15) NOT NULL ,
   StampDateTime datetime NOT NULL ,
   StampAction char (1) NOT NULL ,
   StampID int NOT NULL ,
   Name varchar (80) NOT NULL ,
   BriefDescription varchar (80) NOT NULL ,
   Description varchar (255) NOT NULL ,
   KeyPrefix char (10) NOT NULL
   )
```

Just like we used a special naming convention for our base set of stored procedures, we also use a special naming convention for our OTD stored procedures. We use this naming convention to organize the stored procedures in SQL Server. When SQL Server lists things like stored procedures, tables, and views it does so by alphabetical order. The naming convention we are using here groups all of the stored procedure together because they all start off with spPerson. Then it groups all of the stored procedures for the base object together because, as we saw earlier, the base stored procedures all start off with spPersonObject. When we write the stored procedures to manage the OTD, we start off the name with spPersonObjType. This always places the OTD stored procedures directly under the base object stored procedures. The following table illustrates the naming convention for the OTD stored procedures:

Prefix	ObjectName	OTD Object	Suffix -- Action
sp	Person	ObjType	AuditDeletes
sp	Person	ObjType	AuditList
sp	Person	ObjType	Delete
sp	Person	ObjType	Get
sp	Person	ObjType	Insert
sp	Person	ObjType	List
sp	Person	ObjType	Restore
sp	Person	ObjType	Update

The PersonTypeBridge Table

The relational model for a Level II object supports many-to-many relationships. The only table we need to construct to manage the many-to-many relationship is something I call a **Bridge table**. It is a simple table that just lists each Person ObjectID and its corresponding TypeID:

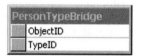

Notice the naming convention we use for the fields. Rather than calling the first field PersonID, we use the name ObjectID. This allows us to use exactly the same stored procedure syntax for every object. The only thing that changes here is the name of the table. It works just like the OTD tables we looked at earlier. In order to re-use the Create Bridge table SQL we only need to change the first line of code.

The PersonTypeBridge CREATE TABLE SQL

```
CREATE TABLE dbo.PersonTypeBridge
   (
   ObjectID int NOT NULL ,
   TypeID int NOT NULL
   )
```

The Relational Model

Now we have all of the tables we need to create a many-to-many relationship between our base objects and their Object Type Definitions. The next step in understanding the model is to gain a sense of how those tables work together to support the many-to-many relationship. We can represent the relationship visually as shown here:

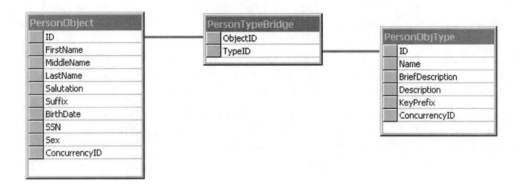

Let's see what this many-to-many relationship gives us in real life. Imagine that we have six different OTDs available:

- ❑ Salesman - ID 1
- ❑ Lawyer - ID 2
- ❑ Engineer - ID 3
- ❑ Doctor - ID 4
- ❑ Student - ID 5
- ❑ Teacher - ID 6

Now, let's also imagine that we have two different persons in our data store:

- ❑ Alexander - ID 1
- ❑ Willow - ID 2

Maybe Alexander (`ObjectID 1`) is a Doctor (`TypeID 4`) and Willow (`ObjectID 2`) is an Engineer (`TypeID 3`). If that were the case then it is easy to see that the Bridge table would look like the one here. This is not at all complex. It represents a one-to-one relationship between the object and its OTD. (Of course, our real table would only have the numbers in it. I added to text to make it easier to follow.)

ObjectID	TypeID
1 (Alexander)	4 (Doctor)
2 (Willow)	3 (Engineer)

But now let us suppose that Alexander also teaches a couple of classes at the Medical School. And to complicate things a little more, let's also say that Willow is Alexander's student. How would we represent the data then? It could look exactly like this second table:

ObjectID	TypeID
1 (Alexander)	4 (Doctor)
2 (Willow)	3 (Engineer)
2 (Alexander)	6 (Teacher)
1 (Willow)	5 (Student)

At this point, the relationship is one-to-many. Each `TypeID` is only listed once, but the `ObjectIDs` are listed twice. `ObjectID` 2 is both `TypeID` 3 (Engineer) and `TypeID` 5 (Student), and `ObjectID` 1 is both `TypeID` 4 (Doctor) and `TypeID` 7 (Teacher).

Now if we wanted to get really evil, we might imagine that Alexander and Willow are also both Lawyers (`TypeID` 2). Notice here that now we have some TypeIDs listed twice. We need to manage that information by using a many-to-many relationship:

ObjectID	TypeID
1 (Alexander)	4 (Doctor)
2 (Willow)	3 (Engineer)
2 (Willow)	5 (Student)
1 (Alexander)	6 (Teacher)
1 (Alexander)	2 (Lawyer)
2 (Willow)	2 (Lawyer)

With this table, it would be a cinch to get a list of all of the `LawyerObjectIDs` or all the `EngineerObjectIDs`. In other words, with a single `SELECT` statement, we can learn that we have two Lawyers in our data store:

1) Alexander
2) Willow

We could also return a list of `TypeIDs` for a particular *Person* object. In other words, with a single `SELECT` statement, we can learn that Willow (`ObjectID` 2) is:

1) An Engineer
2) A Student
3) A Lawyer

Notice that we were able to make the people in our example become different types of people without adding any records to the base table. All we needed to do to express the different relationships was to add a record to the bridge table.

I think you can begin to see that many-to-many relationships are powerful stuff.

Take a moment to consider the implications. Say that we have 3 applications using the same base *Person* object. In one case we are tracking customers using the *Person* object with the OTD Customer. In another we are tracking patients using the *Person* object with the OTD Patient. And in the third, we are tracking employees using the *Person* object with the OTD Employee. If Willow gets married and her Last Name changes from Rosenberg to Summers, all three applications are updated simultaneously. And because we are using 4-Dimensional Data Objects, which also track changes across time, we have a record of when her Last Name changed, who changed it, and what its previous value was.

> **Four dimensions are better than two.**

This also brings up the issues concerning the requirement for a good set of business rules. If something as important as Willow's Last Name changes, we might have a little additional housekeeping to perform. We perform this type of programming at the User Centric sphere when we connect objects together into an application (we'll see how to do this in the last section of the book).

Coding Level II Objects

When we look at the *Person* object as a Level II object, we find three additional properties:

- ❑ TypeID – A Long value that identifies the object's type
- ❑ TypeName – A String value that identifies the object's type
- ❑ KeyPrefix – A String value that can be appended to an object's key

Let's take a closer look at each of these properties.

The TypeID Property

The TypeID property provides a *numeric* link between the PersonObject table and the PersonObjType table.

The TypeName Property

The TypeName property provides a *textual* link between the PersonObject table and the PersonObjType table.

The KeyPrefix Property

The KeyPrefix property is kind of like a shorthand way to identify a particular type. We call it a KeyPrefix because in practice we append a prefix to an object's ID to create a unique key for each object.

Say we were going to load a treeview with all of the persons in a school. Further, let's suppose that we have previously created the OTDs for Administrators, Instructors, and Students. We might use the treeview to show the relationship between each administrator and the instructors that report to her. We could also use the same treeview to display a list of all of the students that report to each instructor.

Remember from an earlier chapter that our objects have a Key property. We used it when we populated the listviews. Remember too, that for Level I object's the key is constructed from the word "Key" and the object's ID. When we work with higher-level objects, we need an additional technique to distinguish between objects. With a Level I object, each object can only be represented in one way. With Level II and Level III objects, the same object may be defined as several different types.

Consider the test case we just outlined, suppose an Administrator or Instructor is also a Student in a class. If we didn't have a way to distinguish between types using the Key property we would have two problems. First we would have duplicate node-key values, which causes an error. Second, we would have given up a very powerful filtering tool, the node's key. The KeyPrefix property gives a simple way to handle this type of problem.

In this example we might assign the string Adm to the KeyPrefix property for the Administrator type, the string Ins to the KeyPrefix property for the Instructor type, and the string Stu to the KeyPrefix for the student type. Then when we populated a treeview with the list of different types of *Person* objects, if might look like this:

```
Adm1 –
        Ins2 –
                Stu3
                Stu4
                Stu5
                Stu1
        Ins3 –
                Stu2
                Stu4
                Stu5
```

Notice that the person who is the Administrator for the school has the ID 1. We can tell this because we can see that the number 1 has been appended onto the Administrator's KeyPrefix. Adm. From this treeview, we can see that the Administrator is also a student. Notice that the ID 1 is also associated with the KeyPrefix for Student Stu. This technique alone doesn't handle all problems associated with loading treeviews and the like. In fact, we would have to do something like append the parent node's key to each successive key to ensure that the treeview didn't break when we loaded it. Still, the object's Key giving us the KeyPrefix and the ID in a single package allows us to determine both the object and the object's type from a single property.

Notice that on each branch of the tree, we never repeat a key. If the same person is listed 3 times as three different Object Type Definitions, then that person will have three different key prefixes. This doesn't handle cases where the same ObjectID is repeated on different branches. We see this problem with Stu3 and Stu4. There are several coding techniques we can user to handle this type of problem, but the KeyPrefix field is a powerful tool for handling a single branch of a tree. We will go over some techniques for handling the other problems in Chapters 14 – 16.

The Level II Person Object Code

You can use the pieces of the interface you built over the last chapters to test the objects we will build in this chapter. As we work through this chapter, it is really more important for you to think about the object code rather than the user interface code that uses the object. Please take a little extra time to be sure that your interface is fully functional using the sample DLLs before you work through this chapter. I don't want you to have to deal with any bugs or problems that do not come directly from the data object. If you would like to, it might be a good idea to use the sample user interface that I have provided especially for this chapter.

About the DLLs

There are a couple of things we need to do before we can use the Person examples. The first thing we need to do is to *unregister* the ECDOs that we used over the last few chapters. I know that you can get away without doing this, but it has been my experience that, if I let this simple action slide, I end up with several DLLs registered on my machine that all have the same name. I just consider this a good housekeeping chore and do it without thinking about it. Here is how you unregister the Person ECDO. It's basically the same procedure we used to register them in the first place except this time we use the /u switch:

```
regsvr32 \..\Ch08\UCPerson.dll /u
```

You should see a message box that tells you that the DLL has been successfully unregistered. Dismiss the message box. Do the same for the DC object:

```
regsvr32 \..\Ch08\DCPerson.dll /u
```

You should see the same kind of message box again telling you that this DLL has also been unregistered successfully. Close the command window. We don't need these DLLs registered now, because you are going to create your own objects.

The Level II Person Project Group

We're going to take the user interface that we put together in the last two chapters and give it the objects it needs. When you get through the following steps your Project Explorer should look something like this:

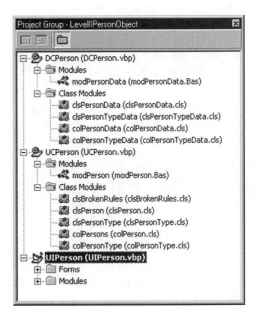

1. Open the `PersonInterface.vbp` project in VB from the previous chapter.

2. Add a new ActiveX DLL project to the project group.

3. Rename this project `UCPerson`. This project will form the User Centric object.

4. Add a second ActiveX DLL project to the project group.

5. Rename this project `DCPerson`. This project will form the Data Centric object.

6. Remove the default classes from the two DLL projects.

7. Using the table below, find the files, and insert these modules into the relevant project.

System Sphere	Directory	Source File Name
User Centric	`\..\Ch10\UCObject\`	`modPerson.bas`
(UCPerson.vbp)	`\..\Ch10\UCObject\`	`clsBrokenRules.cls`
	`\..\Ch10\UCObject\`	`clsPerson.cls`
	`\..\Ch10\UCObject\`	`colPersons.cls`
	`\..\Ch10\UCObject\`	`clsPersonType.cls`
	`\..\Ch10\UCObject\`	`colPersonType.cls`
Data Centric	`\..\Ch10\DCObject\`	`modPersonData.bas`
(DCPerson.vbp)	`\..\Ch10\DCObject\`	`clsPersonData.cls`
	`\..\Ch10\DCObject\`	`colPersonData.cls`
	`\..\Ch11\DCObject\`	`clsPersonTypeData.cls`
	`\..\Ch10\DCObject\`	`colPersonTypeData.cls`

8. Save the project files.

9. Save the project group file. I've called it `LevelIIPersonObject.vbg`.

Level II objects, just like their Level I counterparts have 8 fundamental capabilities. In fact, the coding for the *PersonType* object is almost identical to coding for any Level I object right down to the table design and the stored procedures.

> **The only difference between an OTD object and a Level I object is that the base property set for an OTD object is predefined.**

Because of this similarity, I won't bother reproducing the code for the *Person* OTD object here. Instead, I will give you a brief description of the basic processes and their fundamental purpose. The real meat of this chapter is found with the changes we need to make to the Level I object's base code in order to support the many-to-many relationship between the base objects and their Object Type Definitions.

The Person Object Type Definition Object

Constructing an OTD object, compared to Level I objects we've built so far, is very straightforward. There is practically no difference to we're on solid ground.

The Predefined Base Property Set

As we just stated a Object Type Definition, unlike Level I objects, has a predefined base set of properties. These are:

ID – Long (4)

The unique ID for each Object Type Definition.

Name – String (80)

The name for each Object Type Definition, e.g. Doctor, Lawyer, Engineer etc.

BriefDescription – String (80)

A brief description for each Object Type Definition, e.g. Engineers generally like math

Description – String (255)

The description for each Object Type Definition, e.g. Engineers generally like math a lot

KeyPrefix – String (10)

This property gives us a shorthand way to refer to the OTD without using numeric values. We do this to make it easy to use common controls like the listview and the treeview, e.g. Eng

The Eight Data Handling Processes

We don't need to go through all of the code for the eight data handling processes for the *Person* OTD object. You already know how to write this code. It is identical, in every way save one, to the code you created for the *ErrCond,* and *Computer* objects in the earlier chapters. The only difference between this code and that code is the names of the properties. That means that you can either use the sample code or follow the code found in the sections indicated under each of the 8 data handling processes.

The Fetch Process

The purpose of the *Fetch* process is to return a single object from the data store. This process for the *Person* OTD object is virtually identical to its Level I counterpart. The only difference is that we identify the stored procedure using the name `spPersonObjTypeGet` to indicate that we working with an OTD, but the stored procedure code is identical. It is designed to accept a single long parameter, the target object's ID. This code was discussed in Chapter 7.

The Insert Process

The purpose of the *Insert* process is to add a new object's data to the data store. It also makes a record that indicates that the new data was inserted, and returns the most current information about the target object back to the user. This process for the *Person* OTD object is virtually identical to its Level I counterpart. The only difference is that we identify the stored procedure using the name `spPersonObjTypeInsert` to indicate that we working with an OTD, but the stored procedure code is identical. This code was discussed in Chapter 6.

The Update Process

The purpose of the *Update* process is to change the information in the data store. It also makes a record that indicates the update took place, and returns the most current information about the target object in the data store back to the user. This process for the *Person* OTD object is virtually identical to its Level I counterpart. The only difference is that we identify the stored procedure using the name `spPersonObjTypeUpdate` to indicate that we working with an OTD, but the stored procedure code is identical. This code was discussed in Chapter 7.

The Delete Process

The purpose of the *Delete* process is to delete the information for a particular object from the data store. It also makes a record that indicates that the deletion took place, and returns the most current information about the target object in the data store back to the user. This process for the *Person* OTD object is virtually identical to its Level I counterpart. The only difference is that we identify the stored procedure using the name `spPersonObjTypeDelete` to indicate that we working with an OTD, but the stored procedure code is identical. This code was discussed in Chapter 7.

The Restore From Deleted Process

The purpose of the *Restore From Deleted* process is to restore an object from a deleted state back to its state at the time of its deletion. It also makes a record that indicates that the restoration took place, and returns the most current information about the target object in the data store back to the user. This process for the *Person* OTD object is identical is virtually its Level I counterpart. The only difference is that we identify the stored procedure using the name `spPersonObjTypeRestore` to indicate that we working with an OTD, but the stored procedure code is identical. This code was discussed in Chapter 7.

The Show Deleted Process

The purpose of the *Show Deleted* process is to return to the user a list of the deleted objects that are available for restoration from the data store. This process for the *Person* OTD object is virtually identical to its Level I counterpart. The only difference is that we identify the stored procedure using the name `spPersonObjTypeAuditDeletes` to indicate that we working with an OTD, but the stored procedure code is identical. This code was discussed in Chapter 7.

The Audit History Process

The purpose of the *Audit History* process is to return a complete history for a particular object. This history is in essence a series of snapshots of the object taken every time the data in the data store was changed for any reason. This process for the *Person* OTD object is virtually identical to its Level I counterpart. The only difference is that we identify the stored procedure using the name `spPersonObjTypeAuditList` to indicate that we working with an OTD, but the stored procedure code is identical. This code was discussed in Chapter 7.

The Load Process

The purpose of the *Load* process is to return a collection of objects that meet some criterion. This process also accepts a SQL string as a parameter. We use this parameter in conjunction with Connector objects. We will go over the specific techniques we use to employ this additional parameter in great detail in Chapter 13. This process for the *Person* OTD object is virtually identical to its Level I counterpart. The only difference is that we identify the stored procedure using the name `spPersonObjTypeList` to indicate that we working with an OTD, but the stored procedure code is identical. This code was discussed in Chapter 6.

The Base Person Object

Level II Objects, just like their Level I counterparts have 8 data handling processes, but there are some differences between coding a Level II Object and a Level I Object. The major difference between the two revolves around the additional code that is required to manage the many-to-many relationship that can occur when we re-cast a particular object as an object with another OTD. Fortunately, these differences exist close to the database. That means that we will find most of the differences in coding in the Data Centric and Data spheres. Therefore, even though we are delving into some very complex database concepts, you should find the code in this chapter quite familiar.

The Fetch Process

The major difference between a Level I and a higher-level `ObjectFetch` method is the addition of the `lngTypeID` parameter. It's not possible to retrieve the base properties for a single higher-level object without using the `TypeID` parameter. Even though the base properties for a patient and a doctor are identical we need the `TypeID` information to be able to relate the extended property information with each type of object. The addition of the `TypeID` in this call is really a preparation for retrieving the object's extended properties. We will not be returning extended property sets in this chapter, because we are using Level II objects.

The User Centric Object Code

The User Centric `ObjectFetch` code is contained in the `clsPerson.cls` file in the `UCPerson.vbp` project. The main purpose of this method is to retrieve information from the data store and place it into the local object's properties so that the user interface programmer can work with the information easily:

```
Public Sub ObjectFetch(lngID As Long, lngTypeID As Long)

    'Instantiate the remote object
    Dim ThisDataObject As DCPerson.clsPersonData
    Set ThisDataObject = CreateObject("DCPerson.clsPersonData")
    mlngID = lngID
    mlngTypeID = lngTypeID

    'Get the Data From the Remote Object
    With ThisDataObject
        .SetDataSource mstrConnect
        .ObjectFetch mlngID, mlngTypeID, mlngStampID, mdtmStampDateTime, _
                    mdtmBirthDate, mintDataLocking, mblnChangeAll, mstrStampUser, _
                    mstrStampAction, mstrDataMessage, mstrFirstName, _
                    mstrMiddleName, mstrLastName, mstrSalutation, mstrSuffix, _
                    mstrSSN, mstrSex, mstrTypeName, mstrKeyPrefix
    End With

    If Len(Trim(mstrDataMessage)) > 0 Then
    ' Some Data Centric Problem Has Occured
        Err.Raise vbObjectError + 1234, "Person", "A Data Error Has Occured"
    Else
    ' Reset the local object's State
        mlngSaveID = mlngID
        mlngSaveTypeID = mlngTypeID

    And so on...

        ObjectIsNew False
```

```
      ObjectIsDirty False
    End If

  Set ThisDataObject = Nothing

End Sub
```

At the user centric level, the `ObjectFetch` routine for a Level II Object (or third for that matter) is virtually the same as the `ObjectFetch` routine we used for a Level I Object. The only real differences between the two are the additional properties that a Level II or Level III Object requires – `TypeID`, `TypeName` and `KeyPrefix`.

The Data Centric Object Code

The Data Centric `ObjectFetch` code is found in the `clsPersonData.cls` file in the `DCPerson.vbp` project. The main purpose of this method is to retrieve information from the Data sphere and transport that information into the parameters passed into the method from the User Centric object:

```
Public Sub ObjectFetch(lngID As Long, lngTypeID As Long, lngStampID As Long, _
                dtmStampDateTime As Variant, dtmBirthDate As Variant, _
                intDataLocking As Integer, blnChangeAll As Boolean, _
                strStampUser As String, strStampAction As String, _
                strDataMessage As String, strFirstName As String, _
                strMiddleName As String, strLastName As String, _
                strSalutation As String, strSuffix As String, _
                strSSN As String, strSex As String, _
                strTypeName As String, _
                strKeyPrefix As String)

  Dim strSQL As String

  Dim ctxObject As ObjectContext
  Set ctxObject = GetObjectContext()

  On Error GoTo ObjectFetchError

  Dim ThisConnection As ADODB.Connection
  Dim ThisRecordset As ADODB.Recordset

  Set ThisConnection = New ADODB.Connection
  Set ThisRecordset = New ADODB.Recordset

  ThisConnection.Open mstrConnect, GetLogon(mstrConnect), GetPassword(mstrConnect)
```

As we will see below, the OTD stored procedures require an extra parameter. This parameter is used to return a specific object type:

```
  strSQL = "spPersonObjectGet " & lngID & ", " & lngTypeID
  ThisRecordset.Open strSQL, ThisConnection

  If Not ThisRecordset.EOF Then
    If ThisRecordset.Fields(0).Name = "ErrorCondition" Then
      strDataMessage = ThisRecordset.Fields(0).Value
      'Free up the object in MTS and set the Transaction Aborted flag
      ctxObject.SetAbort
```

```
        Else
            lngID = ThisRecordset.Fields("ID").Value
            lngTypeID = ThisRecordset.Fields("TypeID").Value
```

And so on...

```
            strKeyPrefix = FixNulls(ThisRecordset.Fields("KeyPrefix").Value)
            'Free up the object in MTS and set the Transaction Completed flag
            ctxObject.SetComplete
        End If
    Else
        strDataMessage = "Unable to find the Requested Record in the " & _
                         "Persistant Data Source"
        'Free up the object in MTS and set the Transaction Aborted flag
        ctxObject.SetAbort
    End If

    ThisConnection.Close
    Set ThisRecordset = Nothing
    Set ThisConnection = Nothing
    Set ctxObject = Nothing
    Exit Sub

ObjectFetchError:

    Error Handler

End Sub
```

The data centric code for the `ObjectFetch` is, once again, almost identical to the Level I treatment. The only real difference we find here is the way we construct the SQL command. We provide the `TypeID` as an additional parameter.

The Stored Procedure

This is where we really start to see the difference between Level I and higher Level objects. With higher level objects, we need to actively manage the relationship between the Object and Object Type tables. The first difference we notice between this stored procedure and its Level I cousin is the addition of the `@TypeID` parameter. Remember our objective; we need our *Person* object to be able to be cast many different ways. The same individual may be both a doctor and a patient. What this means technically, is that in order to return the correct set of extended properties, we are required to specify the Person's TypeID:

From this point forward in the book, I will format the stored procedures with multiple columns on a single line. I do not support this practice for production code. It is 1000% easier to read and debug the SQL if each column is written on a separate line. When you look at the sample files, you will see that all of the stored procedures are written that way. I am using multiple columns on a single line in the book to save a couple of pages of space while still giving you a handy reference for all of the stored procedures. Also, instead of commenting at the beginning and end of the code, I will give you a list at the beginning of each stored procedure. That list will contain an ordered list of the major operations we will accomplish with the stored procedure. If I need to illustrate a special handling technique, I will provide those comments in line with the source of the stored procedure.

```
CREATE PROCEDURE spPersonObjectGet
@ID int,
@TypeID int
AS

SELECT
    PersonObjType.ID As TypeID, PersonObjType.Name As TypeName,
    PersonObjType.KeyPrefix As KeyPrefix, PersonObject.ID,
    PersonObject.FirstName, PersonObject.MiddleName, PersonObject.LastName,
    PersonObject.Salutation, PersonObject.Suffix, PersonObject.BirthDate,
    PersonObject.SSN, PersonObject.Sex, PersonObject.ConcurrencyID As
ConcurrencyID1

FROM        PersonObject

INNER JOIN  PersonTypeBridge ON
            PersonObject.ID = PersonTypeBridge.ObjectID

INNER JOIN  PersonObjType ON
            PersonObjType.ID = PersonTypeBridge.TypeID

WHERE       PersonTypeBridge.ObjectID = @ID AND
            PersonTypeBridge.TypeID = @TypeID

RETURN (0)
```

The second place we notice the difference in the stored procedure is with the two INNER JOINS. This is the first time our stored procedure has had to join tables. This is pretty basic stuff, but lets take a look at how we create a three-table join using 92+ SQL.

The first line in the FROM clause identifies the first table – PersonObject. Then we connect the second table – PersonTypeBridge – by specifying the field to join the tables ON:

```
FROM        PersonObject

INNER JOIN  PersonTypeBridge ON
            PersonObject.ID = PersonTypeBridge.ObjectID

INNER JOIN  PersonObjType ON
            PersonObjType.ID = PersonTypeBridge.TypeID
```

For the "old" timers, this is equivalent to the following statement:

```
FROM     PersonObject PO,
         PersonTypeBridge PTB,
         PersonObjType PT

WHERE    PO.ID = PTB.ObjectID
AND      PT.ID = PTB.TypeID
```

The 92+ SQL syntax really just moves the relationship between the tables to the FROM clause. In 92-SQL, the WHERE clause was responsible for specifying the relationship between tables. Conceptually, the 92+ SQL is more accurate and allows us to construct more "modular" SQL. The code that defines the relationships is confined to the FROM clause and the code that defines the specific selection criteria is confined to the WHERE clause. Maybe this will become more apparent if we compare the remainder of the statement using 92+ and 92- SQL versions:

92+ SQL Version:

```
FROM        PersonObject

INNER JOIN  PersonTypeBridge ON
            PersonObject.ID = PersonTypeBridge.ObjectID

INNER JOIN  PersonObjType ON
            PersonObjType.ID = PersonTypeBridge.TypeID

WHERE       PersonTypeBridge.ObjectID = @ID AND
            PersonTypeBridge.TypeID = @TypeID
```

92- SQL Version:

```
FROM    PersonObject PO,
        PersonTypeBridge PTB,
        PersonObjType PT

WHERE   PO.ID = PTB.ObjectID
AND     PT.ID = PTB.TypeID
AND     PTB.ObjectID = @ID
AND     PTB.TypeID = @TypeID
```

The Insert Process

Again there is very little difference between this code for Level I and higher-level objects, beside the addition of the extra properties.

The User Centric Object Code

The User Centric ObjectInsert code is found in the clsPerson class file in the UCPerson project. At the user centric level, the only real difference between Level I and Level II (or III) objects is the additional property that a Level II or Level III object requires – TypeID:

```
Public Sub ObjectInsert()

  If IsChild Then Err.Raise 445

' Instantiate the remote object
  Dim ThisDataObject As DCPerson.clsPersonData
  Set ThisDataObject = CreateObject("DCPerson.clsPersonData")

' Update the Data In the Remote Object
  With ThisDataObject
    .SetDataSource mstrConnect
    .ObjectInsert mlngStampID, mlngID, mlngTypeID, mdtmStampDateTime, _
                  mdtmBirthDate, mintDataLocking, mblnChangeAll, mstrStampUser, _
                  mstrStampAction, mstrDataMessage, mstrFirstName, _
                  mstrMiddleName, mstrLastName, mstrSalutation, mstrSuffix, _
                  mstrSSN, mstrSex, mstrTypeName, mstrKeyPrefix
  End With

  If Len(Trim(mstrDataMessage)) > 0 Then
' Some Data Centric Problem Has Occured
' Inform User with mstrDataMessage
    Err.Raise vbObjectError + 1234, "Person Insert", mstrDataMessage
```

```
    Else
      ' Reset the local object's Save State
      mlngSaveID = mlngID
      mlngSaveTypeID = mlngTypeID
```

And so on...

```
      ObjectIsNew False
      ObjectIsDirty False
    End If

End Sub
```

The Data Centric Object Code

The Data Centric ObjectInsert code is found in the clsPersonData.cls file in the DCPerson.vbp project. Once again, it is almost identical to the user centric code. The only real difference we find here is the construction of the SQL command. We provide the TypeID as an additional parameter:

```
Public Sub ObjectInsert(lngStampID As Long, lngID As Long, lngTypeID As Long, _
               dtmStampDateTime As Variant, dtmBirthDate As Variant, _
               intDataLocking As Integer, blnChangeAll As Boolean, _
               strStampUser As String, strStampAction As String, _
               strDataMessage As String, strFirstName As String, _
               strMiddleName As String, strLastName As _
               String, strSalutation As String, strSuffix As String, _
               strSSN As String, strSex As String, _
               strTypeName As String, strKeyPrefix As String)
```

```
    Dim strSQL As String
    Dim lngRows As Long

    Dim ctxObject As ObjectContext
    Set ctxObject = GetObjectContext()

    On Error Goto ObjectInsertError

    Dim ThisConnection As ADODB.Connection
    Dim ThisRecordset As ADODB.Recordset

    Set ThisConnection = New ADODB.Connection
    Set ThisRecordset = New ADODB.Recordset

    ThisConnection.Open mstrConnect, GetLogon(mstrConnect), GetPassword(mstrConnect)
```

```
    strSQL = "spPersonObjectInsert " & _
            jamQuote & strStampUser & jamQuote & jamComma & _
            lngID & jamComma & _
            jamQuote & strFirstName & jamQuote & jamComma & _
            jamQuote & strMiddleName & jamQuote & jamComma & _
            jamQuote & strLastName & jamQuote & jamComma & _
            jamQuote & strSalutation & jamQuote & jamComma & _
            jamQuote & strSuffix & jamQuote & jamComma & _
            jamQuote & dtmBirthDate & jamQuote & jamComma & _
            jamQuote & strSSN & jamQuote & jamComma & _
```

```
              jamQuote & strSex & jamQuote & jamComma & _
              lngTypeID

   On Error Resume Next

   ThisRecordset.Open strSQL, ThisConnection

   If ThisConnection.Errors.Count > 0 Then
       strDataMessage = ThisConnection.Errors(0).Description
       ' Roll back the transaction
       ThisConnection.Close
       ctxObject.SetAbort

   Else
       If Not ThisRecordset.EOF Then
           If ThisRecordset.Fields(0).Name = "ErrorCondition" Then
               strDataMessage = ThisRecordset.Fields(0).Value
               'Free up the object in MTS and set the Transaction Aborted flag
               ctxObject.SetAbort

           Else
           ' This Resets the Starting Values with the current values in the UC Object
               lngID = ThisRecordset.Fields("ID").Value
               lngTypeID = ThisRecordset.Fields("TypeID").Value
               dtmBirthDate = ThisRecordset.Fields("BirthDate").Value
               strDataMessage = ""
               strFirstName = FixNulls(ThisRecordset.Fields("FirstName").Value)
               strMiddleName = FixNulls(ThisRecordset.Fields("MiddleName").Value)
               strLastName = FixNulls(ThisRecordset.Fields("LastName").Value)
               strSalutation = FixNulls(ThisRecordset.Fields("Salutation").Value)
               strSuffix = FixNulls(ThisRecordset.Fields("Suffix").Value)
               strSSN = FixNulls(ThisRecordset.Fields("SSN").Value)
               strSex = FixNulls(ThisRecordset.Fields("Sex").Value)
               strTypeName = FixNulls(ThisRecordset.Fields("TypeName").Value)
               strKeyPrefix = FixNulls(ThisRecordset.Fields("KeyPrefix").Value)
               'Free up the object in MTS and set the Transaction Completed flag
               ctxObject.SetComplete
           End If
       Else
           strDataMessage = "Unable to Insert Record"
           'Free up the object in MTS and set the Transaction Aborted flag
           ctxObject.SetAbort
       End If
   End If

   ThisConnection.Close
   Set ThisRecordset = Nothing
   Set ThisConnection = Nothing
   Set ctxObject = Nothing

   Exit Sub

ObjectInsertError:

   ErrorHandler

End Sub
```

The Stored Procedure

Once again, the real difference between Level I and higher-level objects coding is found at the Data sphere. In the `ObjectInsert` stored procedure we have to accomplish 4 things:

- ❑ Insert a new record in the Object table
- ❑ Insert a new record in the ObjectTypeBridge table that relates the new object to an existing type
- ❑ Make an entry in the ObjectAudit table that records the insertion
- ❑ Mirror the results of the transaction to the user

```
CREATE PROCEDURE spPersonObjectInsert
@StampUser varchar(10), @ID int, @FirstName varchar (60), @MiddleName varchar
(60),
@LastName varchar (60), @Salutation char (10), @Suffix char (10),
@BirthDate datetime, @SSN char (9), @Sex char (1), @TypeID int

AS

DECLARE @trncnt int, @ErrorNumber int

SELECT @ErrorNumber = -1

/* save transaction count value */
SELECT @trncnt = @@trancount

/* issue begin or save transaction based on transaction count */
IF @trncnt = 0
   BEGIN TRANSACTION T1
ELSE
   SAVE TRANSACTION T1
```

If the ID parameter that was sent into the stored procedure is 0 that means that this is a new person and we need to perform an insert:

```
If @ID = 0
   /* add a new PersonObject record */
   BEGIN
      /* Insert PersonObject record */
      INSERT PersonObject
               (FirstName, MiddleName, LastName, Salutation, Suffix, BirthDate,
               SSN, Sex, ConcurrencyID )

      VALUES
               (@FirstName, @MiddleName,@LastName, @Salutation, @Suffix,
               @BirthDate, @SSN, @Sex, 1 )

      IF @@error <> 0 GOTO ErrorHandler

      SELECT @ID = @@Identity
   END
```

The next major operation is to insert a record into the bridge table that connects the person to a particular OTD:

```
/* Add link record for this PersonObject and type */
INSERT PersonTypeBridge
        (ObjectID, TypeID)

VALUES
        (@ID, @TypeID)

IF @@error <> 0 GOTO ErrorHandler
```

Assuming that no errors were raised, we add an audit record by copying the fields from the Object table into the Audit table as follows:

```
/* Add audit record */
INSERT PersonObjectAudit
   (StampUser, StampDateTime, StampAction, StampID, FirstName, MiddleName,
LastName,
    Salutation, Suffix, BirthDate, SSN, Sex, TypeID, TypeName, KeyPrefix)

SELECT    @StampUser, GetDate(), 'I', PersonObject.ID, PersonObject.FirstName,
          PersonObject.MiddleName, PersonObject.LastName, PersonObject.Salutation,
          PersonObject.Suffix, PersonObject.BirthDate, PersonObject.SSN,
          PersonObject.Sex, PersonObjType.ID, PersonObjType.Name,
          PersonObjType.KeyPrefix

FROM      PersonObject

INNER JOIN PersonTypeBridge ON
          PersonObject.ID = PersonTypeBridge.ObjectID

INNER JOIN PersonObjType ON
          PersonObjType.ID = PersonTypeBridge.TypeID

WHERE     PersonTypeBridge.ObjectID = @ID AND
          PersonTypeBridge.TypeID = @TypeID

IF @@error <> 0 GOTO ErrorHandler
```

If another transaction is in control of this procedure, then we allow that transaction to issue the COMMIT TRANSACTION command. If not, then we perform the commit ourselves.

```
/* commit transaction only if this proc issued begin */
IF @trncnt = 0 COMMIT TRANSACTION T1
```

We mirror the results of the procedure to the user:

```
/* Return PersonObject fields for confirmation */
SELECT
    PersonObjType.ID As TypeID, PersonObjType.Name As TypeName,
    PersonObjType.KeyPrefix As KeyPrefix, PersonObject.ID,
    PersonObject.FirstName, PersonObject.MiddleName, PersonObject.LastName,
    PersonObject.Salutation, PersonObject.Suffix, PersonObject.BirthDate,
    PersonObject.SSN, PersonObject.Sex,
    PersonObject.ConcurrencyID As ConcurrencyID1

FROM  PersonObject
```

```
INNER JOIN   PersonTypeBridge ON
             PersonObject.ID = PersonTypeBridge.ObjectID

INNER JOIN   PersonObjType ON
             PersonObjType.ID = PersonTypeBridge.TypeID

WHERE        PersonTypeBridge.ObjectID = @ID AND
             PersonTypeBridge.TypeID = @TypeID

RETURN (0)
```

If any errors occurred, we would have been sent to the error handler, which rolls back any uncommitted portions of the transaction and selects an appropriate error message from the Common database's Error Message table. Note that we keep the error messages in a special database called Common. This ensures that everyone in the organization will be using the same set of error messages:

```
ErrorHandler:
    ROLLBACK TRANSACTION T1
    SELECT    ErrorCondition
    FROM      Common..ErrorMessage
    WHERE     ErrorNumber = @ErrorNumber
    RETURN    (100)
```

The Update Process

The purpose of the *Update* process is to update the information in the data store; record that the update took place, and to return the most current information in the data store back to the user.

The User Centric Object Code

The User Centric `ObjectUpdate` code is found in the `clsPerson.cls` file in the `UCPerson.vbp` project. The `ObjectUpdate` method for the *Person* OTD object is almost identical to its Level I counterpart apart from the additional properties:

```
Public Sub ObjectUpdate()

  If IsChild Then Err.Raise 445

  Dim ThisDataObject As DCPerson.clsPersonData
  Set ThisDataObject = CreateObject("DCPerson.clsPersonData")

' Update the Data In the Remote Object
  With ThisDataObject
     .SetDataSource mstrConnect
     .ObjectUpdate mlngStampID, mlngSaveStampID, mlngID, mlngSaveID, mlngTypeID, _
                mlngSaveTypeID, mdtmStampDateTime, mdtmSaveStampDateTime, _
                mdtmBirthDate, mdtmSaveBirthDate, mintDataLocking, _
                mblnChangeAll, mblnSaveChangeAll, mstrStampUser, _
                mstrSaveStampUser, mstrStampAction, mstrSaveStampAction, _
                mstrDataMessage, mstrFirstName, mstrSaveFirstName, _
                mstrMiddleName, mstrSaveMiddleName, mstrLastName, _
                mstrSaveLastName, mstrSalutation, mstrSaveSalutation, _
                mstrSuffix, mstrSaveSuffix, mstrSSN, mstrSaveSSN, mstrSex, _
                mstrSaveSex, mstrTypeName, mstrSaveTypeName, mstrKeyPrefix
  End With
```

```
    If Len(Trim(mstrDataMessage)) > 0 Then
    ' Some Data Centric Problem Has Occured
        If InStr(mstrDataMessage, "The Following Collisions have occured *") > 0 Then
            CollisionMessages = ParseCollisions(Trim(mstrDataMessage))
            Err.Raise vbObjectError + 1111, "Person Update", _
                    "Data Collisions at the field level have occured "
        Else
        ' An Data Error Other than a collision has occured.
            Err.Raise vbObjectError + 1234, "Person Update", mstrDataMessage
        End If
    Else
    ' Reset the local object's State
        ObjectIsDirty False
        ObjectIsNew False
    End If

End Sub
```

The Data Centric Object Code

The Data Centric code for the ObjectUpdate method is found in the clsPersonData.cls file in the DCPerson.vbp project. The code for a higher-level object is almost identical to the code we used for a Level I object. The major differences revolve around the three additional fields, TypeID, TypeName, and KeyPrefix. The stored procedure call also requires an additional parameter lngTypeID.

```
Public Sub ObjectUpdate(lngStampID As Long, lngSaveStampID As Long, _
                    lngID As Long, lngSaveID As Long, lngTypeID As Long, _
                    lngSaveTypeID As Long, dtmStampDateTime As Variant, _
                    dtmSaveStampDateTime As Variant, _
                    dtmBirthDate As Variant, _
                    dtmSaveBirthDate As Variant, intDataLocking As Interger, _
                    blnChangeAll As Boolean, blnSaveChangeAll As Boolean, _
                    strStampUser As String, strSaveStampUser As String, _
                    strStampAction As String, strSaveStampAction As String, _
                    strDataMessage As String, strFirstName As String, _
                    strSaveFirstName As String, strMiddleName As String, _
                    strSaveMiddleName As String, strLastName As String, _
                    strSaveLastName As String, strSalutation As String, _
                    strSaveSalutation As String, strSuffix As String, _
                    strSaveSuffix As String, strSSN As String, _
                    strSaveSSN As String, strSex As String, _
                    strSaveSex As String, strTypeName As String, _
                    strSaveTypeName As String, strKeyPrefix As String)

    Dim strSQL As String
    Dim lngRows As Long
    Dim lngConcurrencyID1 As Long

    Dim ctxObject As ObjectContext
    Set ctxObject = GetObjectContext()

    On Error Goto ObjectUpdateError

    Dim ThisConnection As ADODB.Connection
    Dim ThisRecordset As ADODB.Recordset

    Set ThisConnection = New ADODB.Connection
    Set ThisRecordset = New ADODB.Recordset
```

413

```
    Dim strCollision As String
    strCollision = ""

    ThisConnection.Open mstrConnect
    If DataLocking > 0 Then
     'Select the record to update using the fetch stored procedure
       strSQL = "spPersonObjectGet " & lngID & ", " & lngTypeID
       ThisRecordset.Open strSQL, ThisConnection

       If Not ThisRecordset.EOF Then
         lngConcurrencyID1 = ThisRecordset.Fields("ConcurrencyID1").Value
         CurrentID = ThisRecordset.Fields("ID").Value
         CurrentTypeID = ThisRecordset.Fields("TypeID").Value
```

And so on ...

```
       Else
         strDataMessage = "Unable to find the record to update in the datastore"
         'Free up the object in MTS and set the Transaction Aborted flag
         ctxObject.SetAbort
         ThisConnection.Close
         Set ThisRecordset = Nothing
         Set ThisConnection = Nothing
         Set ctxObject = Nothing
         Exit Sub
    End If

    If NzNumber(CurrentTypeID) <> NzNumber(lngSaveTypeID) Then
        If Len(strCollision) > 0 Then
           strCollision = strCollision & "*" & TypeID & "|" & CurrentTypeID
        Else
           strCollision = TypeID & "|" & CurrentTypeID
        End If
    End If

    If NzString(CurrentBirthDate) <> NzString(dtmSaveBirthDate) Then
        If Len(strCollision) > 0 Then
           strCollision = strCollision & "*" & BirthDate & "|" & CurrentBirthDate
        Else
           strCollision = BirthDate & "|" & CurrentBirthDate
        End If
    End If
```

And so on...

```
    If Len(strCollision) > 0 Then

        If DataLocking = 1 Then
           strDataMessage = "Unable to save changes, the record was being " & _
                           "edited by another user."
           ThisConnection.Close
           'Free up the object in MTS and set the Transaction Aborted flag
           ctxObject.SetAbort
           ThisConnection.Close
           Set ThisRecordset = Nothing
           Set ThisConnection = Nothing
           Set ctxObject = Nothing
           Exit Sub
```

```
        ElseIf DataLocking = 2 Then
            strDataMessage = "The Following Collisions have occurred * " & _
                        strCollision
            'Free up the object in MTS and set the Transaction Aborted flag
            ctxObject.SetAbort
            ThisConnection.Close
            Set ThisRecordset = Nothing
            Set ThisConnection = Nothing
            Set ctxObject = Nothing
            Exit Sub
        Else
            strDataMessage = ""
        End If

    End If

    strSQL = "spPersonObjectDelete " & _
            jamQuote & strStampUser & jamQuote & jamComma & _
            lngID & jamComma & _
            lngTypeID & jamComma & _
            lngConcurrencyID1

    On Error Resume Next

    ThisRecordset.Open strSQL, ThisConnection
    If ThisConnection.Errors.Count > 0 Then
        strDataMessage = ThisConnection.Errors(0).Description
        ' Roll back the transaction
        ctxObject.SetAbort
    Else
        If ThisRecordset.Fields(0).Name = "ErrorCondition" Then
            strDataMessage = ThisRecordset.Fields(0).Value
            'Free up the object in MTS and set the Transaction Aborted flag
            ctxObject.SetAbort

        Else
            ' This Resets the Starting Values with the current values in the Database
            lngID = ThisRecordset.Fields("ID").Value
            lngSaveID = lngID
            lngTypeID = ThisRecordset.Fields("TypeID").Value
            lngSaveTypeID = lngTypeID
```

And so on ...

```
            'Free up the object in MTS and set the Transaction Completed flag
            ctxObject.SetComplete
        End If
    End If

    ThisConnection.Close
    Set ThisRecordset = Nothing
    Set ThisConnection = Nothing
    Set ctxObject = Nothing

    Exit Sub

ObjectUpdateError:

    ErrorHandler

End Sub
```

The Stored Procedure

The order of the main objectives for this stored procedure is as follows:

❏ Insert a record in the Audit table to fix the object's current state
❏ Update the record in the Object table with the new values
❏ Mirror the results to the user

```
CREATE PROCEDURE spPersonObjectUpdate
@StampUser varchar(10), @ID int, @FirstName varchar (60), @MiddleName varchar
(60),
@LastName varchar (60), @Salutation char (10), @Suffix char (10),
@BirthDate datetime, @SSN char (9), @Sex char (1), @TypeID int, @Concurrency1 int

AS

DECLARE @trncnt int, @ConcurrencyID int, @ErrorNumber int, @rows int, @err int

SELECT @ConcurrencyID = @Concurrency1
SELECT @ErrorNumber = -1
```

The standard issue transaction code:

```
/* save transaction count value */
SELECT @trncnt = @@trancount

/* issue begin or save transaction based on transaction count */
IF @trncnt = 0
    BEGIN TRANSACTION T1
ELSE
    SAVE TRANSACTION T1
```

Inset a record into the Audit table to fix the object's current state:

```
/* add audit record prior to updating  */
INSERT PersonObjectAudit
  (StampUser, StampDateTime, StampAction, StampID, FirstName, _
    MiddleName, LastName, Salutation, Suffix, BirthDate, SSN, _
    Sex, TypeID, TypeName, KeyPrefix)

SELECT    @StampUser, GetDate(), 'U', PersonObject.ID, PersonObject.FirstName,
          PersonObject.MiddleName, PersonObject.LastName, PersonObject.Salutation,
          PersonObject.Suffix, PersonObject.BirthDate, PersonObject.SSN,
          PersonObject.Sex, PersonObjType.ID, PersonObjType.Name,
          PersonObjType.KeyPrefix

FROM      PersonObject

INNER JOIN  PersonTypeBridge ON
            PersonObject.ID = PersonTypeBridge.ObjectID

INNER JOIN  PersonObjType ON
            PersonObjType.ID = PersonTypeBridge.TypeID

WHERE     PersonTypeBridge.ObjectID = @ID AND
```

```
                PersonTypeBridge.TypeID = @TypeID

IF @@error <> 0 GOTO ErrorHandler
```

Assuming that we have not raised any errors, we simply insert the record into the Object table:

```
/* Update PersonObject */
UPDATE PersonObject

SET
   FirstName = @FirstName, MiddleName = @MiddleName, LastName = @LastName,
   Salutation = @Salutation, Suffix = @Suffix, BirthDate = @BirthDate, SSN = @SSN,
   Sex = @Sex, ConcurrencyID = ConcurrencyID + 1

WHERE ID = @ID AND ConcurrencyID = @ConcurrencyID

SELECT @err = @@error, @rows = @@RowCount

IF @err <> 0 GOTO ErrorHandler
```

We have seen this test before. It makes the assumption that if no errors were raised, then the reason no records were effected is due to the additional concurrency criterion. All we are doing here is flagging the event with a known value @ErrorNumber = 100, and branching the routine to the error handler:

```
IF @rows = 0
   /* concurrency error */
   BEGIN
      SELECT @ErrorNumber = 100
      GOTO ErrorHandler
   END
```

Standard COMMIT TRANSACTION code as before:

```
/* commit transaction only if this proc issued begin */
IF @trncnt = 0    COMMIT TRANSACTION T1
```

Mirror the results to the user:

```
/* Return PersonObject fields for confirmation */
SELECT
   PersonObjType.ID As TypeID, PersonObjType.Name As TypeName,
   PersonObjType.KeyPrefix  As KeyPrefix, PersonObject.ID, PersonObject.FirstName,
   PersonObject.MiddleName, PersonObject.LastName, PersonObject.Salutation,
   PersonObject.Suffix, PersonObject.BirthDate,
   PersonObject.SSN, PersonObject.Sex,
   PersonObject.ConcurrencyID As ConcurrencyID1

FROM        PersonObject

INNER JOIN  PersonTypeBridge ON
            PersonObject.ID = PersonTypeBridge.ObjectID

INNER JOIN  PersonObjType ON
```

```
                    PersonObjType.ID = PersonTypeBridge.TypeID

    WHERE           PersonTypeBridge.ObjectID = @ID AND
                    PersonTypeBridge.TypeID = @TypeID

    RETURN (0)
```

Standard error handler treatment:

```
ErrorHandler:
   ROLLBACK TRANSACTION T1
   SELECT   ErrorCondition
   FROM     Common..ErrorMessage
   WHERE    ErrorNumber = @ErrorNumber
   RETURN   (100)
```

The Delete Process

The purpose of the *Delete* process is to delete the information for a particular object from the data store. It also makes a record that indicates that the deletion took place, and returns the most current information about the target object in the data store back to the user.

The User Centric Object Code

The User Centric `ObjectDelete` method is found in the `clsPerson.cls` file in the `UCPerson.vbp` project. The only difference between this code and the Level I treatment is the addition of the three additional properties `TypeID`, `TypeName`, and `KeyPrefix`:

```
Public Sub ObjectDelete()

   If IsChild Then Err.Raise 445

' Instantiate the remote object
   Dim ThisDataObject As DCPerson.clsPersonData
   Set ThisDataObject = CreateObject("DCPerson.clsPersonData")

' Execute the Delete Method In the Remote Object
   With ThisDataObject
      .SetDataSource mstrConnect
      .ObjectDelete mlngStampID, mlngSaveStampID, mlngID, mlngSaveID, mlngTypeID, _
                    mlngSaveTypeID, mdtmStampDateTime, _
                    mdtmSaveStampDateTime, _
                    mdtmBirthDate, mdtmSaveBirthDate, mintDataLocking, _
                    mblnChangeAll, mblnSaveChangeAll, mstrStampUser, _
                    mstrSaveStampUser, mstrStampAction, mstrSaveStampAction, _
                    mstrDataMessage, mstrFirstName, mstrSaveFirstName, _
                    mstrMiddleName, mstrSaveMiddleName, mstrLastName, _
                    mstrSaveLastName, mstrSalutation, mstrSaveSalutation, _
                    mstrSuffix, mstrSaveSuffix, mstrSSN, mstrSaveSSN, mstrSex, _
                    mstrSaveSex, mstrTypeName, mstrSaveTypeName, mstrKeyPrefix
   End With

   DataMessage = mstrDataMessage
   If Len(Trim(mstrDataMessage)) > 0 Then
      'Some Data Centric Problem Has Occured
      'Inform User with strDataMessage
```

```
      Err.Raise vbObjectError + 1234, "Person Delete", mstrDataMessage
    End If

  Set ThisDateObject = Nothing

End Sub
```

The Data Centric Object Code

The Data Centric `ObjectDelete` method is found in the `clsPersonData.cls` file in the `DCPerson.vbp` project. This code is essentially identical to its Level I counterpart. The only real difference here, is the addition of the `lngTypeID` parameter for the stored procedures:

```
Public Sub ObjectDelete(lngStampID As Long, lngSaveStampID As Long, _
                        lngID As Long, lngSaveID As Long, lngTypeID As Long, _
                        lngSaveTypeID As Long, dtmStampDateTime As Variant, _
                        dtmSaveStampDateTime As Variant, _
                        dtmBirthDate As Variant, _
                        dtmSaveBirthDate As Variant, intDataLocking, _
                        blnChangeAll As Boolean, blnSaveChangeAll As Boolean, _
                        strStampUser As String, strSaveStampUser As String, _
                        strStampAction As String, strSaveStampAction As String, _
                        strDataMessage, strFirstName As String, _
                        strSaveFirstName As String, strMiddleName As String, _
                        strSaveMiddleName As String, strLastName As String, _
                        strSaveLastName As String, strSalutation As String, _
                        strSaveSalutation As String, strSuffix As String, _
                        strSaveSuffix As String, strSSN As String, _
                        strSaveSSN As String, strSex As String, _
                        strSaveSex As String, strTypeName As String, _
                        strSaveTypeName As String, strKeyPrefix As String)
```

```
    Dim strSQL As String
    Dim lngConcurrencyID1 As Long
    Dim strCollision As String

    Dim ctxObject As ObjectContext
    Set ctxObject = GetObjectContext()

    On Error GoTo ObjectDeleteError

    Dim ThisConnection As ADODB.Connection
    Dim ThisRecordset As ADODB.Recordset

    Set ThisConnection = New ADODB.Connection
    Set ThisRecordset = New ADODB.Recordset

    ThisConnection.Open mstrConnect, GetLogon(mstrConnect), GetPassword(mstrConnect)

    'Select the Record to be deleted
    strSQL = "spPersonObjectGet " & lngID & ", " & lngTypeID
    ThisRecordset.Open strSQL, ThisConnection

    If DataLocking > 0 Then
      If Not ThisRecordset.EOF Then
        lngConcurrencyID1 = ThisRecordset.Fields("ConcurrencyID1").Value
        CurrentID = ThisRecordset.Fields("ID").Value
```

```
                  CurrentTypeID = ThisRecordset.Fields("TypeID").Value
```

And so on....

```
         ThisRecordset.Close
      Else
        strDataMessage = "The Requested Delete did not occur because the " & _
                     "Record was not found."
        'Free up the object in MTS and set the Transaction Aborted flag
        ctxObject.SetAbort
        ThisConnection.Close
        Set ThisConnection = Nothing
        Set ctxObject = Nothing
        Exit Sub
      End If
   End If

' This Code checks the values of each field and builds a collision string which is
' passed to the user centric object for further processing

   If NzNumber(CurrentTypeID) <> NzNumber(lngSaveTypeID) Then
      If Len(strCollision) > 0 Then
         strCollision = strCollision & "*" & TypeID & "|" & CurrentTypeID
      Else
         strCollision = TypeID & "|" & CurrentTypeID
      End If
   End If

   If NzString(CurrentBirthDate) <> NzString(dtmSaveBirthDate) Then
      If Len(strCollision) > 0 Then
         strCollision = strCollision & "*" & BirthDate & "|" & CurrentBirthDate
      Else
         strCollision = BirthDate & "|" & CurrentBirthDate
      End If
   End If
```

And so on...

```
   If Len(strCollision) > 0 Then
     If DataLocking = 1 Then ' DataLocking = 1 is similar to full record locking
                              ' with no recourse the user is not given detail info
                              ' about the collisions that occurred.
        strDataMessage = "Unable to Delete the object because it was being " & _
                     "edited by another user."
       'Free up the object in MTS and set the Transaction Aborted flag
        ctxObject.SetAbort
        ThisConnection.Close
        Set ThisRecordset = Nothing
        Set ThisConnection = Nothing
        Set ctxObject = Nothing
        Exit Sub
     ElseIf DataLocking = 2 Then ' DataLocking = 2 Field by Field analysis the user
                                  '                 the user is given a blow by blow
                                  '                 account of the collision
        strDataMessage = "The Following Collisions have occured * " & strCollision
         'Free up the object in MTS and set the Transaction Aborted flag
         ctxObject.SetAbort
```

```
            ThisConnection.Close
            Set ThisRecordset =Nothing
            Set ThisConnection = Nothing
            Set ctxObject = Nothing
            Exit Sub
      Else
            strDataMessage = ""

      End If

   End If
```

```
   strSQL = "spPersonObjectDelete " & _
            jamQuote & strStampUser & jamQuote & jamComma & _
            lngID & jamComma & _
            lngTypeID & jamComma & _
            lngConcurrencyID1
```

```
   On Error Resume Next

   ThisRecordset.Open strSQL, ThisConnection

   If ThisConnection.Errors.Count > 0 Then
       strDataMessage = ThisConnection.Errors(0).Description
       ' Roll Back the Transaction
       ctxObject.SetAbort
   Else
       If ThisRecordset.Fields(0).name = "ErrorCondition" Then
           strDataMessage = ThisRecordset.Fields(0).Value
           'Free up the object in MTS and set the Transaction Aborted flag
           ctxObject.SetAbort
       Else
           strDataMessage = ""
           'Free up the object in MTS and set the Transaction Completed flag
           ctxObject.SetComplete
       End If
   End If

   ThisConnection.Close
   Set ThisRecordset = Nothing
   Set ThisConnection = Nothing
   Set ctxObject = Nothing

   Exit Sub

ObjectDeleteError:

   ErrorHandler

End Sub
```

The Stored Procedure

We've already covered the spPersonObjectGet stored procedure so here are the details for spPersonObjectDelete. The order of the major objectives for this stored procedure is as follows:

❑ Add a record to the Audit table to fix the object's current state
❑ Delete the record from the Bridge table

❑ Test to see whether or not other OTDs are using this object.

❑ Delete the object record if appropriate after Step 3

```
CREATE PROCEDURE spPersonObjectDelete
@StampUser varchar(15), @ID int, @TypeID int, @Concurrency1 int

AS

DECLARE @trncnt int, @ConcurrencyID int, @ErrorNumber int, @DeletedRows int,
        @rows int, @err int

SELECT @ConcurrencyID = @Concurrency1
SELECT @ErrorNumber = -1
```

Standard transaction treatment:

```
/* save transaction count value */
SELECT @trncnt = @@trancount

/* issue begin or save transaction based on transaction count */
IF @trncnt = 0
   BEGIN TRANSACTION T1
ELSE
   SAVE TRANSACTION T1
```

Add a record to the Audit table to fix the object's current state:

```
/* add audit record prior to deleting  */
INSERT PersonObjectAudit
   (StampUser, StampDateTime, StampAction, StampID, FirstName,
   MiddleName, LastName,
   Salutation, Suffix, BirthDate, SSN, Sex, TypeID, TypeName, KeyPrefix)

SELECT @StampUser, GetDate(), 'D', PersonObject.ID, PersonObject.FirstName,
       PersonObject.MiddleName, PersonObject.LastName, PersonObject.Salutation,
       PersonObject.Suffix, PersonObject.BirthDate, PersonObject.SSN,
       PersonObject.Sex, PersonObjType.ID, PersonObjType.Name,
       PersonObjType.KeyPrefix

FROM       PersonObject

INNER JOIN PersonTypeBridge ON
           PersonObject.ID = PersonTypeBridge.ObjectID

INNER JOIN PersonObjType ON
           PersonObjType.ID = PersonTypeBridge.TypeID

WHERE      PersonTypeBridge.ObjectID = @ID AND
           PersonTypeBridge.TypeID = @TypeID

IF @@error <> 0 GOTO ErrorHandler
```

Delete the record that links this person to an OTD:

```
/* delete link record */
DELETE PersonTypeBridge
```

```
   WHERE  ObjectID = @ID AND TypeID = @TypeID

   SELECT @err = @@error, @DeletedRows = @@RowCount

   IF @err <> 0 GOTO ErrorHandler
```

If this object is using any other OTDs, then that means all we want to do is to delete the Bridge record. In other words, maybe our *Person* object is both an Employee and a Customer. If this employee is fired, maybe we do want to delete the link between this *Person* object and the Employee table, but we do not want to delete the *Person* object if it is also a Customer. So, before we delete the *Person* object we need to test whether the object is still in use as another OTD. All we do to test for that occurrence is to count the number of instances of this *Person* object's ID in the PersonTypeBridge table. If there are no instances, then we can safely delete the *Person* object. If there are any instances, then we cannot delete the *Person* object:

```
/* Determine whether any other PersonObject types */
/* are linked to this PersonObject.              */
IF (SELECT  Count(*)
    FROM PersonTypeBridge WHERE ObjectID = @ID) = 0

    BEGIN
```

If the number of OTDs currently using this object is 0, then we can delete the person. Also note that the same concurrency treatment is used here as above:

```
        /* delete PersonObject if there are no other links */
        DELETE PersonObject

        WHERE ID = @ID AND ConcurrencyID = @ConcurrencyID

        SELECT @err = @@error, @rows = @@RowCount

        IF @err <> 0 GOTO ErrorHandler

        IF @rows = 0
           /* concurrency error */
           BEGIN
               SELECT @ErrorNumber = 100
               GOTO ErrorHandler
           END
    END
```

Standard commit-transaction code:

```
/* commit transaction only if this proc issued begin */
IF @trncnt = 0 COMMIT TRANSACTION T1
```

Mirror the results to the user:

```
/* return count of number deleted links */
SELECT 'RowCount' = @DeletedRows

RETURN (0)
```

Standard error handling code:

```
ErrorHandler:
    ROLLBACK TRANSACTION T1
    SELECT    ErrorCondition
    FROM      Common..ErrorMessage
    WHERE     ErrorNumber = @ErrorNumber
    RETURN    (100)
```

The Restore From Deleted Process

The purpose of the *Restore From Deleted* process is to restore an object from a deleted state back to its state at the time of its deletion. It also makes a record that indicates that the restoration took place, and returns the most current information about the target object in the data store back to the user.

The User Centric Object Code

The User Centric `ObjectRestoreFromDeleted` code is found in the `clsPerson.cls` file in the `UCPerson.vbp` project. This code is essentially identical to its Level I counterpart. The only real difference between the two treatments is the addition of the extra three parameters `TypeID`, `TypeName`, and `KeyPrefix`.

```
Public Sub ObjectRestoreFromDeleted()

  'Instantiate the remote object
  Dim ThisDataObject As DCComputer.clsComputerData
  Set ThisDataObject = CreateObject("DCComputer.clsComputerData")

  'Get the Data From the Remote Object
  With ThisDataObject
     .SetDataSource mstrConnect
     .ObjectRestoreFromDeleted mlngStampID, mlngID, mlngTypeID, _
                               mdtmStampDateTime, mdtmBirthDate, _
                               mintDataLocking, mblnChangeAll, mstrStampUser, _
                               mstrStampAction, mstrDataMessage, _
                               mstrFirstName, mstrMiddleName, mstrLastName, _
                               mstrSalutation, mstrSuffix, mstrSSN, mstrSex, _
                               mstrTypeName, mstrKeyPrefix
  End With

  If Len(Trim(mstrDataMessage)) > 0 Then
     'Some Data Centric Problem Has Occured
     'Raise a Error that can be trapped by the programmer
     Err.Raise vbObjectError + 1234, "Person Restore From Deleted", _
              mstrDataMessage
  Else
     'Reset the local object's State
     mlngSaveStampID = mlngStampID
     mlngSaveID = mlngID
     mlngSaveTypeID = mlngTypeID
     mdtmSaveStampDateTime = mlngStampDateTime
     mdtmSaveBirthDate = mdtmBirthDate
     mintSaveDataLocking = mintDataLocking
     mblnSaveChangeAll = mblnChangeAll
     mstrSaveStampUser = mstrStampUser
     mstrSaveStampAction = mstrStampAction
     mstrSaveDataMessage = mstrDataMessage
     mstrSaveFirstName = mstrFirstName
```

```
            mstrSaveMiddleName = mstrMiddleName
            mstrSaveLastName = mstrLastName
            mstrSaveSalutation = mstrSalutation
            mstrSaveSuffix = mstrSuffix
            mstrSaveSSN = mstrSSN
            mstrSaveSex = mstrSex
            mstrSaveTypeName = mstrTypeName
            ObjectIsNew False
            ObjectIsDirty False
        End If

        Set ThisDataObject = Nothing

    End Sub
```

The Data Centric Object Code

The Data Centric `ObjectRestoreFromDeleted` code is found in the `clsPersonData.cls` file in the `DCPerson.vbp` project. This code is essentially identical to its Level I counterpart. One rather curious thing to notice is that we do not have to pass the `TypeID` into the stored procedure. This is really quite different than what we have been doing. The reasoning should become clear when we go through the stored procedure below.

```
Public Sub ObjectRestoreFromDeleted(lngStampID As Long, lngID As Long, lngTypeID _
            As Long, dtmStampDateTime As Variant, dtmBirthDate As Variant, _
            intDataLocking As Integer, blnChangeAll As Boolean, _
            strStampUser As String, strStampAction As String, _
            strDataMessage As String, strFirstName As String, _
            strMiddleName As String, strLastName As _
            String, strSalutation As String, strSuffix As String, strSSN As _
            String, strSex As String, strTypeName As String, mstrKeyPrefix _
            As String)
```

```
    Dim strSQL As String

    Dim ctxObject As ObjectContext
    Set ctxObject = GetObjectContext()

    On Error GoTo ObjectFetchError

    Dim ThisConnection As ADODB.Connection
    Dim ThisRecordset As ADODB.Recordset

    Set ThisConnection = New ADODB.Connection
    Set ThisRecordset = New ADODB.Recordset

    ThisConnection.Open mstrConnect, GetLogon(mstrConnect), GetPassword(mstrConnect)

    strSQL = "spPersonObjectRestore '" & strStampUser & "', " & lngID

    ThisRecordset.Open strSQL, ThisConnection

    If Not ThisRecordset.EOF Then
        If ThisRecordset.Fields(0).Name = "ErrorCondition" Then
            strDataMessage = ThisRecordset.Fields(0).Value
            'Free up the object in MTS and set the Transaction Aborted flag
            ctxObject.SetAbort
```

```
      Else
        lngStampID = FixNulls(ThisRecordset.Fields("StampID").Value)
        lngID = ThisRecordset.Fields("ID").Value
        lngTypeID = ThisRecordset.Fields("TypeID").Value
        dtmStampDateTime = FixNulls(ThisRecordset.Fields("StampDateTime").Value)
        dtmBirthDate = ThisRecordset.Fields("BirthDate").Value
        blnChangeAll = FixNulls (ThisRecordset.Fields("ChangeAll").Value)
        strStampUser = FixNulls (ThisRecordset.Fields("StampUser").Value))
        strStampAction = FixNulls (ThisRecordset.Fields("StampAction").Value)
        strDataMessage = ""
        strFirstName = FixNulls (ThisRecordset.Fields("FirstName").Value)
        strMiddleName = FixNulls (ThisRecordset.Fields("MiddleName").Value)
        strLastName = FixNulls (ThisRecordset.Fields("LastName").Value)
        strSalutation = FixNulls (ThisRecordset.Fields("Salutation").Value)
        strSuffix = FixNulls (ThisRecordset.Fields("Suffix").Value)
        strSSN = FixNulls l(ThisRecordset.Fields("SSN").Value)
        strSex = FixNulls (ThisRecordset.Fields("Sex").Value)
        strTypeName = FixNulls (ThisRecordset.Fields("TypeName").Value)
         'Free up the object in MTS and set the Transaction Completed flag
          ctxObject.SetComplete
      End If
  Else
      strDataMessage = "Unable to find the Requested Record in the Persistant " & _
                   "Data Source"
    'Free up the object in MTS and set the Transaction Aborted flag
      ctxObject.SetAbort
  End If

  ThisConnection.Close
  Set ThisRecordset = Nothing
  Set ThisConnection = Nothing
  Set ctxObject = Nothing

  Exit Sub

ObjectFetchError:

  ErrorHandler

End Sub
```

The Stored Procedure

The order of the major objectives of this stored procedure is as follows:

❑ Select the record to be restored from the Audit table
❑ Check to see whether or not an existing record is in the Object table. (Remember that the record in the Audit table may record that a patient was deleted, but may be a doctor record still exists in the Object table.)
❑ If no existing record was found (this means that the last deletion was the also the last remaining OTD assigned to this object) then re-insert the record into the Object table.
❑ Re-insert the record back into the bridge table that links this object to an OTD.
❑ Add an audit record to mark the restoration
❑ Mirror the results to the user

```
CREATE PROCEDURE spPersonObjectRestore
@StampUser varchar(10), @RestoreID int

AS

DECLARE @trncnt int, @ErrorNumber int, @ID int, @FirstName varchar (60),
        @MiddleName varchar (60), @LastName varchar (60), @Salutation char (10),
        @Suffix char (10), @BirthDate datetime, @SSN char (9), @Sex char (1),
        @TypeID int

SELECT @ErrorNumber = -1
```

Standard transaction treatment:

```
/* save transaction count value */
SELECT @trncnt = @@trancount

/* issue begin or save transaction based on transaction count */
IF @trncnt = 0
   BEGIN TRANSACTION T1
ELSE
   SAVE TRANSACTION T1
```

Retrieve the record to be restored from the Audit table. Note that the ID that was passed into this stored procedure is the row ID for the Audit table record, not the ID for the object. This difference is a subtle one, but it is what allows us to reuse the same logic throughout the entire system. Notice that the StampID that is returned from the Audit table is stuffed into the object's ID:

```
/* retrieve audit record to be restored */
SELECT @ID = StampID, @FirstName = FirstName, @MiddleName = MiddleName,
       @LastName = LastName, @Salutation = Salutation, @Suffix = Suffix,
       @BirthDate = BirthDate, @SSN = SSN, @Sex = Sex, @TypeID = TypeID

FROM    PersonObjectAudit

WHERE   ID = @RestoreID
```

Next, we check to see whether or not the object we are supposed to be restoring is really deleted. Remember that our end user may be working with this particular *Person* object cast as a doctor. That means that the person's link to the doctor OTD may be deleted, but the person may still exist as a patient, employee, customer, etc.

```
IF (SELECT Count(*) FROM PersonObject WHERE ID = @ID) = 0
```

If the person doesn't exist in the Object table, then we must re-insert the record. This requires a little Transact SQL Trickery. We need to turn off SQL Server's AutoNumber or Identity function when we re-insert the record. This allows us to re-use the same ID for the object. This syntax is bizarre, but we turn the autonumbering off by using the SET Identity_Insert PersonObject ON command, and we turn it on by using the SET Identity_Insert PersonObject OFF command. Oh Well...

```
/* PersonObject record no longer exists and must be readded */
BEGIN
```

```
      SET Identity_Insert PersonObject ON

        INSERT PersonObject
          (ID, FirstName, MiddleName, LastName, Salutation, Suffix, BirthDate, SSN,
          Sex, ConcurrencyID)

        VALUES
          (@ID, @FirstName, @MiddleName, @LastName, @Salutation, @Suffix,
          @BirthDate,
          @SSN, @Sex, 1)

        IF @@error <> 0 GOTO ErrorHandler

        SET Identity_Insert PersonObject OFF

    END
```

Then we insert the record that links this person to a particular OTD. Notice that we don't have to use an Audit table for this part of the procedure. The required information was passed into the procedure in the original list of parameters:

```
/* Re-Add link record for this PersonObject and type */
INSERT PersonTypeBridge
        (ObjectID, TypeID)

VALUES (@ID, @TypeID)

IF @@error <> 0 GOTO ErrorHandler
```

As usual, we add an audit record. This one records the fact that we restored this object:

```
/* Add audit record */
INSERT PersonObjectAudit
  (StampUser, StampDateTime, StampAction, StampID, FirstName, MiddleName,
  LastName,
  Salutation, Suffix, BirthDate, SSN, Sex, TypeID, TypeName, KeyPrefix)

SELECT
    @StampUser, GetDate(), 'R', PersonObject.ID, PersonObject.FirstName,
    PersonObject.MiddleName, PersonObject.LastName, PersonObject.Salutation,
    PersonObject.Suffix, PersonObject.BirthDate, PersonObject.SSN,
    PersonObject.Sex, PersonObjType.ID, PersonObjType.Name, PersonObjType.KeyPrefix

FROM        PersonObject

INNER JOIN  PersonTypeBridge ON
            PersonObject.ID = PersonTypeBridge.ObjectID

INNER JOIN  PersonObjType ON
            PersonObjType.ID = PersonTypeBridge.TypeID

WHERE       PersonTypeBridge.ObjectID = @ID AND
            PersonTypeBridge.TypeID = @TypeID

IF @@error <> 0 GOTO ErrorHandler
```

Standard commit-transaction code:

```
/* commit transaction only if this proc issued begin */
IF @trncnt = 0 COMMIT TRANSACTION T1
```

Mirror the results of this procedure back to the user:

```
/* Return PersonObject fields for confirmation */
SELECT PersonObjType.ID As TypeID, PersonObjType.Name As TypeName,
       PersonObjType.KeyPrefix  As KeyPrefix, PersonObject.ID,
       PersonObject.FirstName, PersonObject.MiddleName, PersonObject.LastName,
       PersonObject.Salutation, PersonObject.Suffix, PersonObject.BirthDate,
       PersonObject.SSN, PersonObject.Sex,
       PersonObject.ConcurrencyID As ConcurrencyID1

FROM        PersonObject

INNER JOIN  PersonTypeBridge ON
            PersonObject.ID = PersonTypeBridge.ObjectID

INNER JOIN  PersonObjType ON
            PersonObjType.ID = PersonTypeBridge.TypeID

WHERE       PersonTypeBridge.ObjectID = @ID AND
            PersonTypeBridge.TypeID = @TypeID

RETURN (0)
```

Standard error handler:

```
ErrorHandler:
    ROLLBACK TRANSACTION T1
    SELECT   ErrorCondition
    FROM     Common..ErrorMessage
    WHERE    ErrorNumber = @ErrorNumber
    RETURN   (100)
```

The Show Deleted Process

The purpose of the *Show Deleted* process is to return to the user a list of the deleted objects that are available for restoration from the data store. With higher level objects, this method requires the lngTypeID parameter. This ensures that the user looking for say a deleted patient record does not have to wade through all of the deleted doctor or programmer records as well.

The User Centric Object Code

The ShowDeleted method is found in the colPersons.cls file in the UCPerson.vbp project. This code is essentially identical to its Level I counterpart apart from the additional TypeID property handling.

```
Public Sub ShowDeleted(Optional lngTypeID As Long, _
                       Optional strSelectStatement As String)

    Dim objData As DCPerson.colPersonData
    Set objData = CreateObject("DCPerson.colPersonData")
```

```
    Dim TheAnswer As ADODB.Recordset

    With objData
      .SetDataSource mstrConnect
      Set TheAnswer = .FetchDeleted(lngTypeID, strSelectStatement)

      If TheAnswer.RecordCount = 1 Then

        If Len(TheAnswer.Fields("DataMessage").Value) > 0 Then
          Err.Raise vbObjectError, "Person", TheAnswer.Fields("DataMessage").Value
        Else
          With TheAnswer
            Add !StampID, !ID, !TypeID, !StampDateTime, !BirthDate, 2, _
                "", !StampUser, !StampAction, "", !FirstName, _
                !MiddleName, !LastName, !Salutation, !Suffix, !SSN, !Sex, _
                !TypeName, !KeyPrefix
          End With
        End If

      Else

        Do While Not TheAnswer.EOF
          With TheAnswer
            Add !StampID, !ID, !TypeID, !StampDateTime, !BirthDate, 2, _
                "", !StampUser, !StampAction, "", !FirstName, _
                !MiddleName, !LastName, !Salutation, !Suffix, !SSN, !Sex, _
                !TypeName, !KeyPrefix
            .MoveNext
          End With
        Loop

      End If

    End With

    Set TheAnswer = Nothing
    Set objData = Nothing

  End Sub
```

The Data Centric Object Code

The Data Centric FetchDeleted code is found in the colPersonsData.cls file in the DCPerson.vbp project. This code is essentially identical to its Level I counterpart but this time we pass the TypeID to the stored procedure:

```
Public Function FetchDeleted(Optional lngTypeID As Long, _
                        Optional strSelectStatement As String) As Recordset

  Dim strSQL As String

  Dim ctxObject As ObjectContext
  Set ctxObject = GetObjectContext

  On Error Goto FetchDeletedError

  Dim ThisConnection As ADODB.Connection
  Dim ThisRecordset As ADODB.Recordset
```

```
Set ThisConnection = New ADODB.Connection
Set ThisRecordset = New ADODB.Recordset

ThisConnection.Open mstrConnect, GetLogon(mstrConnect), GetPassword(mstrConnect)

If Len(strSelectStatement) = 0 Then
    strSQL = "spPersonObjectAuditDeletes " & lngTypeID
Else
    strSQL = strSelectStatement
End If

On Error Resume Next

ThisRecordset.Open strSQL, ThisConnection

If ThisConnection.Errors.Count > 0 Then
    Set ThisRecordset = New ADODB.Recordset
    ThisRecordset.Fields.Append "DataMessage", adChar, 255
    ThisRecordset.Open
    ThisRecordset.AddNew
    ThisRecordset.Fields(0).Value = ThisConnection.Errors(0).Description
    ThisRecordset.Update
    'Free up the object in MTS and set the Transaction Aborted flag
    ctxObject.SetAbort
    Set FetchDeleted = ThisRecordset
Else
    'Free up the object in MTS and set the Transaction Completed flag
    ctxObject.SetComplete
    Set FetchDeleted = ThisRecordset
End If

    ThisConnection.Close
    Set ThisRecordset = Nothing
    Set ThisConnection = Nothing
    Set ctxObject = Nothing

FetchDeletedError

    ErrorHandler

End Function
```

The Stored Procedure

The only main objective for this stored procedure is to mirror the results to the user:

```
CREATE PROCEDURE spPersonObjectAuditDeletes
@TypeID int

AS

SELECT  PersonObjectAudit.StampID,
        PersonObjectAudit.StampUser, PersonObjectAudit.StampDateTime,
        PersonObjectAudit.StampAction, PersonObjectAudit.TypeID,
        PersonObjectAudit.TypeName, PersonObjectAudit.KeyPrefix,
        PersonObjectAudit.ID, PersonObjectAudit.FirstName,
        PersonObjectAudit.MiddleName, PersonObjectAudit.LastName,
        PersonObjectAudit.Salutation, PersonObjectAudit.Suffix,
```

```
            PersonObjectAudit.BirthDate, PersonObjectAudit.SSN, PersonObjectAudit.Sex

FROM        PersonObjectAudit

INNER JOIN  vPersonObjectDelete ON
            PersonObjectAudit.ID = vPersonObjectDelete.ID
LEFT OUTER JOIN PersonTypeBridge ON
            PersonObjectAudit.StampID = PersonTypeBridge.ObjectID AND
            PersonObjectAudit.TypeID = PersonTypeBridge.TypeID

WHERE       PersonObjectAudit.StampAction = 'D' AND
            PersonObjectAudit.TypeID = @TypeID AND
            PersonTypeBridge.ObjectID IS NULL

ORDER BY    StampDateTime DESC

RETURN (0)
```

The Audit History Process

The purpose of the *Audit History* process is to return a complete history for a particular object. This history is in essence a series of snapshots of the object taken every time the data in the data store was changed for any reason.

The User Centric Object Code

The ObjectAuditHistory method is found in the clsPerson.cls file in the UCPerson.vbp project. This code is essentially identical to its Level I counterpart, except for...you guessed it!

```
Public Function ObjectAuditHistory(Optional strSelectStatement As String) _
     As colPersons

  Dim objData As DCPerson.colPersonData
  Set objData = CreateObject("DCPerson.colPersonData")

  Dim TheAnswer As ADODB.Recordset

  Dim colAuditHistory As DCPerson.colPersons
  Set colAuditHistory = CreateObject("DCPerson.colPersons")

  With objData
     .SetDataSource mstrConnect
     Set TheAnswer = .ObjectHistory(mlngID, mlngTypeID, strSelectStatement)

     If TheAnswer.RecordCount = 1 Then

       If Len(TheAnswer.Fields("DataMessage").Value) > 0 Then
         Err.Raise vbObjectError, "Person", TheAnswer.Fields("DataMessage").Value
       Else
         With TheAnswer
            colAuditHistory.Add !StampID, !ID, !TypeID, !StampDateTime, _
                        !BirthDate, 2, "", !StampUser, _
                        !StampAction, "", !FirstName, _
                        !MiddleName, !LastName, !Salutation, _
                        !Suffix, !SSN, !Sex, !TypeName, !KeyPrefix
            .MoveNext
         End With
```

```
            End If

        Else

            Do While Not TheAnswer.EOF
                With TheAnswer
                    colAuditHistory.Add !StampID, !ID, !TypeID, !StampDateTime, _
                                        !BirthDate, 2, "", !StampUser, _
                                        !StampAction, "", !FirstName, _
                                        !MiddleName, !LastName, !Salutation, _
                                        !Suffix, !SSN, !Sex, !TypeName
                    .MoveNext
                End With
            Loop

        End If

    End With

' Clean House
    Set TheAnswer = Nothing
    Set objData = Nothing

' Return the Collection
    Set ObjectAuditHistory = colPersons

End Function
```

The Data Centric Object Code

The Data Centric `ObjectHistory` code is found in the `colPersonData.cls` file in the `DCPerson.vbp` project. This code is essentially identical to its Level I counterpart, but...

```
Public Function ObjectHistory(Optional lngID As Long, _
              Optional lngTypeID As Long, _
              Optional strSelectStatement As String) As Recordset

    Dim strSQL As String

    Dim ctxObject As ObjectContext
    Set ctxObject = GetObjectContext

    On Error Goto ObjectHistoryError

    Dim ThisConnection As ADODB.Connection
    Dim ThisRecordset As ADODB.Recordset

    Set ThisConnection = New ADODB.Connection
    Set ThisRecordset = New ADODB.Recordset

    ThisConnection.Open mstrConnect, GetLogon(mstrConnect), GetPassword(mstrConnect)

    If Len(strSelectStatement) = 0 Then
        strSQL = "spPersonObjectAuditList " & lngID & ", " & lngTypeID
    Else
        strSQL = strSelectStatement
```

```
    End If

    On Error Resume Next

    ThisRecordset.Open strSQL, ThisConnection

    If ThisConnection.Errors.Count > 0 Then
        Set ThisRecordset = New ADODB.Recordset
        ThisRecordset.Fields.Append "DataMessage", adChar, 255
        ThisRecordset.Open
        ThisRecordset.AddNew
        ThisRecordset.Fields(0).Value = ThisConnection.Errors(0).Description
        ThisRecordset.Update
        'Free up the object in MTS and set the Transaction Aborted flag
        ctxObject.SetAbort
        Set ObjectHistory = ThisRecordset
    Else
        'Free up the object in MTS and set the Transaction Completed flag
        ctxObject.SetComplete
        Set ObjectHistory = ThisRecordset
    End If

    Set ThisRecordset = Nothing
    ThisConnection.Close
    Set ThisConnection = Nothing
    Set ctxObject = Nothing

    Exit Function

ObjectHistoryError

    ErrorHandler

End Function
```

The Stored Procedure

Again the only real purpose of this stored procedure is mirror the results to the user:

```
CREATE PROCEDURE spPersonObjectAuditList
@ID int, @TypeID int

AS

SELECT StampID, StampUser, StampDateTime, StampAction,
       TypeID, TypeName, KeyPrefix, ID, FirstName, MiddleName, LastName,
       Salutation, Suffix, BirthDate, SSN, Sex

FROM  PersonObjectAudit

WHERE StampID = @ID AND TypeID = @TypeID OR
      StampID = @ID AND StampAction = 'U'

ORDER BY    StampDateTime Desc

RETURN (0)
```

The Load Process

This method returns a collection of objects that meet some criterion. For higher-level objects, the criterion may be one or several of the objects property values.

The User Centric Object Code

The User Centric `Load` method is found in the `colPersons.cls` file in the `UCPerson.vbp` project. Notice the addition of the `strSelectStatement`. I let this pass by without comment in earlier chapters. This `SELECT` statement parameter overrides any of the other selection criteria. In other words, if it exists, it will be executed. It might seem like we are opening the floodgates for a great deal of SQL in our application code. That is not the intention. The source for these `SELECT` statements is from another object, a Connector object that we use to manage the relationship between objects. We will go over Connector objects in great detail in Chapter 13.

```
Public Sub Load(Optional lngTypeID As Long, Optional strLastName As String, _
                Optional strSelectStatement As String)

    Dim objData As DCPerson.colPersonData
    Set objData = CreateObject("DCPerson.colPersonData")

    Dim TheAnswer As ADOR.Recordset

    With objData
        .SetDataSource mstrConnec
        Set TheAnswer = Fetch(strSelectStatement, lngTypeID, strLastName)

    If TheAnswer.RecordCount = 1 Then
        If Len(TheAnswer.Fields("DataMessage").Value) > 0 Then
            Err.Raise vbObjectError, "Person", TheAnswer.Fields("DataMessage").Value
        Else
            With TheAnswer
                Add 0, !ID, !TypeID, "", !BirthDate, _
                    2, "", !StampUser, !StampAction, _
                    "", !FirstName, !MiddleName, !LastName, _
                    !Salutation, !Suffix, !SSN, !Sex, !TypeName, !KeyPrefix
            End With
        End If

    Else

        Do While Not TheAnswer.EOF

            With TheAnswer
                Add 0, !ID, !TypeID, !StampDateTime, !BirthDate, _
                    2, "", !StampUser, !StampAction, _
                    "", !FirstName, !MiddleName, !LastName, _
                    !Salutation, !Suffix, !SSN, !Sex, !TypeName
                .MoveNext
            End With

        Loop

    End If

    Set objData = Nothing
    Set TheAnswer = Nothing

End Sub
```

The Data Centric Object Code

The Data Centric `Fetch` code is found in the `colPersonData.cls` file in the `DCPerson.vbp` project. Notice the `If...ElseIf` block of code in this method. What we are doing here is testing for the existence of an overriding `SELECT` Statement. If one is found, `Len(strSelectStatement) > 0 = True`, then we use that `SELECT` statement to filter the collection we will return to the user:

```
Public Function Fetch(Optional strSelectStatement As String, Optional lngTypeID _
                    As Long, Optional strLastName As String) As ADODB.Recordset

    Dim strSQL As String

    Dim ctxObject As ObjectContext
    Set ctxObject = GetObjectContext

    On Error GoTo PersonFetchError

    Dim ThisConnection As ADODB.Connection
    Dim ThisRecordset As ADODB.Recordset

    Set ThisConnection = New ADODB.Connection
    Set ThisRecordset = New ADODB.Recordset

    ThisConnection.Open mstrConnect, GetLogon(mstrConnect), GetPassword(mstrConnect)

    If Len(strSelectStatement) > 0 Then
        strSQL = strSelectStatement
    ElseIf Len(strLastName) > 0 Then
        strSQL = "spPersonObjectListByName '" & Trim(strLastName) & "%'"
    Else
        strSQL = "spPersonObjectList " & lngTypeID
    End If

    On Error Resume Next

    ThisRecordset.Open strSQL, ThisConnection

    If ThisConnection.Errors.Count > 0 Then
        Set ThisRecordset = New ADODB.Recordset
        ThisRecordset.Fields.Append "DataMessage", adChar, 255
        ThisRecordset.AddNew
        ThisRecordset.Fields("DataMessage".Value _
            ThisConnection.Errors(0).Description
        ThisRecordset.Update
        Set Fetch = ThisRecordset
        'Free up the object in MTS and set the Transaction Aborted flag
        ctxObject.SetAbort

    Else
     Set Fetch = ThisRecordset
     'Free up the object in MTS and set the Transaction Completed flag
     ctxObject.SetComplete
    End If

    ThisConnection.Close

    Set ThisRecordset = Nothing
    Set ThisConnection = Nothing
    Set ctxObject = Nothing
```

```
     Exit Function

PersonFetchError:

     ErrorHandler

End Function
```

The Stored Procedures

This process actually makes use of two stored procedures. The first simply mirrors the results to the user:

```
CREATE Procedure spPersonObjectList
@TypeID int

AS

SELECT PersonObjType.ID As TypeID,
       PersonObjType.Name As TypeName, PersonObjType.KeyPrefix As KeyPrefix,
       PersonObject.ID, PersonObject.FirstName, PersonObject.MiddleName,
       PersonObject.LastName, PersonObject.Salutation, PersonObject.Suffix,
       PersonObject.BirthDate, PersonObject.SSN, PersonObject.Sex,
       PersonObject.ConcurrencyID As ConcurrencyID1

FROM        PersonObject

INNER JOIN  PersonTypeBridge ON
            PersonObject.ID = PersonTypeBridge.ObjectID

INNER JOIN  PersonObjType ON
            PersonTypeBridge.TypeID = PersonObjType.ID

WHERE       PersonTypeBridge.TypeID = @TypeID

RETURN (0)
```

The second stored procedure offers a second way to load *Person* objects. In this case, we send in the parameter that is actually a portion of a person's last name. Then we filter our list by this name. This exact same stored procedure can be modified to accept any single parameter as an argument. We could also use it as a template for multi-parameter queries.

```
CREATE Procedure spPersonObjectListByName
@Name varchar (80)

AS

SELECT PersonObjType.ID As TypeID,
       PersonObjType.Name As TypeName, PersonObjType.KeyPrefix As KeyPrefix,
       PersonObject.ID, PersonObject.FirstName, PersonObject.MiddleName,
       PersonObject.LastName, PersonObject.Salutation, PersonObject.Suffix,
       PersonObject.BirthDate, PersonObject.SSN, PersonObject.Sex,
       PersonObject.ConcurrencyID As ConcurrencyID1

FROM        PersonObject
```

```
INNER JOIN   PersonTypeBridge ON
             PersonObject.ID = PersonTypeBridge.ObjectID

INNER JOIN   PersonObjType ON
             PersonTypeBridge.TypeID = PersonObjType.ID

WHERE        PersonObject.LastName Like @Name

RETURN (0)
```

Summary

Over the last two chapters, we used something called an Object Type Definition in a Standard User Interface and an Administrative User Interface. We learned that this OTD gave us the ability to categorize objects into different types. For example, we found that we could extend a *Person* object using OTDs so that we could use the *Person* object to represent a Doctor, a Lawyer, or an Engineer etc. In this chapter, we worked through the code we needed to write to actually build an OTD for our *Person* object. What we found is that, with the exception of a few minor changes in the object's code and the complimentary changes in our stored procedure format, that the code we need to write to manage an OTD is really not very much different than the code we used to create Level I objects.

In the next chapter, we will build on the information we learned in this chapter. Now that we know how to add an OTD to our base object, we are ready to take on the challenge of finishing up the administrative functionality of the *Person* object.

```
{831FDD16-0C5C-1...2A9F...
Form frmPropNameControl...
Style    =    3  'Fixed Dial...
         =    "Properties fo...
eight    =    4845
ft       =    45
p        =    330
idth     =    11460
c        =    "Form1"
ton      =    0  'False
d        =    -1  'True
on       =    0  'False
ight     =    4845
dth      =    11460
askbar   =    0  'False
```

Person
Base Properties

ID
Last Name
First Name
Middle Name
Birth Date
Sex

Object Type Definitions

Object Ty...

Supervisor OTD	Lawyer OTD	Engineer OTD	Doctor OTD	Student OTD	
Staff	Specialty	Specialty	Specialty	Major	S...
Report	Hourly Rate	Experience	Certification	Minor	E...
Property 4	Law School	Property 4	Property 3	Year	F...
Property 5	Property 4	Property 5	Property 4	Property 4	F...
Property 6	Property 5	Property 6	Property 5	Property 5	F...
Property 7	Property 6	Property 7	Property 6	Property 6	F...
Property 8	Property 7	Property 8	Property 7	Property 7	F...
Property 9	Property 8	Property 9	Property 8	Property 8	F...
Property 10	Property 9	Property 9	Property 9	Property 9	F...
	Property 10	Property 10	Property 10	Property 10	

Property Set Definitions

Property Set...

11

Administrating Properties

In the last two chapters, we've been working with the two types of user interface for a 4-Dimensional *Person* Data object. I also introduced you to the concept of a Property Bag.

The **Property Bag** is what gives 4-Dimensional Data Objects their chameleon-like quality. It enables us to define and re-define a set of properties for each permutation of our base object without ever changing a line of code in the object, the structure of a single table, or a single stored procedure in our database. Creating the code for the Property Bag is no small task. It requires some highly complex programming on the Data sphere, the Data Centric sphere, and, to a lesser extent, the User Centric sphere of our system. It also requires a high level of integration between these spheres.

On the bright side, once you have written the Property Bag code, there is a way to use the exact same code for every 4-Dimensional Data Object you ever build. The only thing that changes from object to object is the names of the tables and the references to those tables in the stored procedures. Fortunately, the structure of the tables and the stored procedures is constant for every 4-Dimensional Data Object.

You see this as we work through the code behind the Property Bag in these next two chapters. In this chapter, we'll concern ourselves with the objects behind the Property Bag that allow us to work with Property Definitions. Then in Chapter 12, we'll look at the objects behind Property Values.

The Property Bag

The Property Bag is actually a set of extended properties for our base object. As an example, let's try a little thought experiment to think about how we might design a Library system.

In a Library system it makes sense for us to design and build a *Book* object. Its base properties could include things like Title, Abstract, Publisher, Author, etc. There is no doubt that this would work, but there is a problem. These days most libraries allow you to borrow more than just books. It's not uncommon to also be able to borrow magazines. What would we do in this case? There are two obvious choices available to us.

Firstly, we could elect to save ourselves much bother and to simply use the *Book* object to also represent magazines. It doesn't seem that bad an idea, after all a magazine isn't that far removed from a book.

> *This doesn't have to be just a thought experiment. Go get a magazine and compare it to this book.*

However, if we use the *Book* object then we run into problems when we have to actually create a *Book* object to represent a magazine. A magazine will have properties like Title and Publisher but what about Number Of Chapters? Well I suppose we could use the number of articles instead, but what about properties such as Cover Material? Who ever heard of a magazine with a hardback cover? OK, you can put your hands down now, but let's put a spin on it and consider the properties that a magazine might have but a book wouldn't. An obvious example would be Volume or Issue number. They're not terribly relevant to a book but they're very important to a magazine.

This fact alone might cause us to decide that a better solution would be to create an entirely new *Magazine* object. This gets us around all the difficulties in trying to fit a magazine into a *Book* object, so we're happy right? Well yes, but just as we're putting the finishing touches to our *Magazine* object, the library decides the way forward is to also lend audio cassettes. What do we do now?

> *At this point you may want to go get an audio cassette to compare with the book and magazine.*

Well it should be obvious that trying to use a *Book* object or a *Magazine* object to model an audio cassette is going to be awkward at best. So we put on our programmer's hat and go and build a *Cassette* object. But then we realize a curious thing. As this is a library, one of the principal forms of cassette that the library is loaning is an audio book. Now we have something of a dilemma. Under our current design we might have two different objects (a *Book* and *Cassette*) which both represent the same piece of literature. This means we'll have the same data replicated in different places in our database. It seems a shame but what can you do? But as we are designing our *Cassette* object we begin to get a strange sense of déjà vu. Let's take a look at the properties that define a *Book* object, a *Magazine* object and a *Cassette* object:

Book object	Magazine object	Cassette object
ID	ID	ID
Title	Title	Title
Abstract	Subject Category	Author/Artist
Authors	Volume	Abstract
Number Of Chapters	Issue	Category
Number Of Pages	Number Of Pages	KeyWords
Cover Material	Author/Editor	CheckOut
Category	KeyWords	DateCheckedOut
KeyWords	CheckedOut	DueDate
CheckedOut	DateCheckOut	Publisher
DateCheckOut	DueDate	PublisherID
DueDate	Publisher	DatePublished
PublisherID	PublisherID	DateAcquired
DatePublished	DateAcquired	
DateAcquired		

When put side-by-side like this it becomes pretty clear that there are certain properties that all three objects share. Wouldn't it be great if there was some way we could use these same common properties for all objects and then just add those properties particular to each individual type of media?

Well it should have occurred to you that there is. Although we've spend the last few chapters using a *Person* object rather than this library example the principle is *exactly* the same. We use a common base object, in this case we'll create a *Media* object, and then simply cast that base object as a particular type. So instead of wasting valuable time and resources creating new object for each type of media the library acquires we only ever need to create this one *Media* object.

Using the previous table we can design a *Media* object that would look like this:

Media Object
ID
Title
Subject
Authors
KeyWords
CheckedOut
DateCheckedOut
DueDate
PublisherID
DatePublished
DateAcquired

If we use this *Media* object instead of the *Book, Magazine* and *Cassette* objects, we could extend the *Media* object with Object Type Definitions like we did in the last chapter. That means that we could track books, magazines and cassettes with the *same* object.

What if we wanted to know things like the number of pages or chapters in a book? Those properties are missing from the *Media* object. How do we track them and how can we track things like the number of disks in a software program or the length in time of a video or audiotape with such a generic object?

One answer is to use a *different* set of extended properties for each *different type* of *Media* object. If we could relate a different set of properties to each Object Type Definition, we could decide exactly what information to track for each different OTD. This would allow us to track pages for a book and the number of disks for a software program. If you think this sounds like it requires a great deal of planning and complex coding; you're right. It does! Fortunately, it is also exactly the functionality the Property Bag offers. It allows us to assign a different set of properties to each Object Type Definition. It also allows us to share properties and Property Values between different object types. But I am starting to get ahead of myself. For now, let's try to gain an understanding about the basics of property sets by looking at some examples.

Let's consider the following table of possible Object Type Definition/Property Sets for our *Media* object:

Book		Magazine		Video		Audio		Software	
Number of Pages		Volume		Video Media Type		Audio Media Type		Media Type	
Number of Chapters		Issue		Item 1	VHS	Item 1	8 Track	Item 1	Floppy
Cover Material		Number of Pages		Item 2	Beta	Item 2	Cassette	Item 2	CD ROM
Item 1	Hard	Subject Category		Item 3	DVD	Item 3	Rebel	Operating System	
Item 2	Paperback	Item 1	Law	Number of Items		Number of Items		Item 1	PC
		Item 2	Medicine	Total Length Minutes		Total Length Minutes		Item 2	Mac
		Item 3	Business			Music Type			
						Item 1	Rock		
						Item 2	Blues		
						Item 3	Jazz		
						Item 4	Alternative		

In this table, we have defined 5 different media types and have added a different set of properties (represented by the dark gray and white boxes) for each type. The properties that are displayed with a dark gray background are properties that have a list of valid entries for the property (represented by the light gray boxes). This means that for the *Media* Type, Book, we have a set of 3 properties:

- ❑ Number of Pages
- ❑ Number of Chapters
- ❑ Cover Material

In the case of the third property, Cover Material, has two valid values:

- ❑ Hard
- ❑ Paperback

We want to limit the property to being either one of the two valid values, it would make no sense to allow anyone to enter a value such as water in this property. We'll see how to achieve this later.

This sampling of properties is not intended to be exhaustive; I am sure that you could think of many more *Media* types Paintings, Drawings, Artifacts, etc. I am also certain that we could increase the number of properties in each list. But let's leave that for another time and take another look at designing our library system using our new *Media* object.

With our *Media* object and these Object Type Definitions/Property Set combinations we can track books, magazines, video, audio, and software. Our base properties contain information that is common to all library media. That means we can perform a search by Title, Author, Subject, Keyword, Publisher, etc that crosses all types of media. We can also filter the list by the current CheckedOut status etc. Finally, when we find the item(s) we are looking for, we can get detailed information about the item(s) that is tailored to the type of media we have located. If it is a software application, we can find out if it will work on our PC or if we need to buy a Macintosh to use the media. If it is a book, we can find out whether it is a hardcover or a paperback.

> Note, because this is a 4-Dimensional Data Object we also track every change to the data across time; this means that we can without additional effort bring up a complete history of use for the object. With the press of a single button, we can find out how many times this particular piece of media was checked out, who checked it out, etc.

Now let's suppose that the library inherits a collection of sculptures that it has decided to loan to its patrons. Do we have to change our application? No! We just add a new Object Type Definition and create a new Property Set Definition for that new OTD. How's that for a maintainable application? OK, now that I have, hopefully, convinced you of how powerful a Property Bag object can be, let's get to the task of building one.

Working with the Property Bag

In Chapter 8 we created something called a Production User Interface for the *Person* object. This user interface's target audience was the typical end user. It allowed the user to do things like add, edit, and delete information (the values within the properties) about `Person` objects. In Chapter 9 we created something called an Administrative User Interface for the *Person* object. That user interface's target audience was developers or maybe system administrators. We used that interface to do things like create properties and assign them to particular Property Set Definitions.

What I hoped you realized is that although these interfaces both use the Property Bag they are using it in completely different ways. With the Administrative Interface we were actually concerned with managing the Property Set Definition. In other words, we were only interested in *defining* properties. If you think about it, what we're actually doing is defining fields in a database table. Therefore, what we actually doing is defining the properties that make up the Property Bag - so we're really only using the Property Bag as a concept not as an actual entity.

Conversely, when we use the Production Interface we are simply *using* the properties we defined with the Administrative Interface and placing *values* into the properties. This is akin to entering data into the fields of a table in a database. In this case, we're actually working with the Property Bag rather than the properties themselves.

This distinction I'm trying to make is quite subtle but I want to make sure we get it absolutely straight in our heads before we move onto looking at how to support these interfaces.

> **Administrative tasks are those that involve defining the objects and properties, i.e. we define what the Property Bag contains. Production tasks are those that involve using those definitions to manage data, i.e. we insert values into the Property Bag.**

Now we're, hopefully, straight on this issue, we need to think what this all means in terms of coding the Property Bag.

The Property Bag Interfaces

It may not be apparent but we can also say that the Property Bag has an Administrative and Production Interface. Before we go on to discuss the difference between these two interfaces, I think we should clear up some confusion regarding the term "interface".

COM Interfaces

When most people think of the word **interface**, they probably conjure up visions of a screen or series of screens that a user works with to perform some task. I would like to introduce you to another type of interface – the programmer's interface. This interface does not have screens. It is comprised of that set of properties, methods, and events that our objects expose to the programmer. This is our object's **COM interface**.

> *I don't really want to get sidetracked into a big discussion about COM so I'm just going to give the base essentials. If you would like to learn more I recommend reading* VB COM: A Visual Basic Programmer's Introduction to COM, *also published by Wrox Press.*

If you think about it, we work with interfaces that we can't see all of the time. When you create a `Connection` or `Recordset` with ADO, you are using the interface that Microsoft has created to give developers access to the functionality of ADO. Although we might not think about it like this most of the time, ADO is really a very sophisticated application – in many ways no different than Excel or Word. When it comes right down to it, the biggest differences between say Word and ADO is really the application's purpose and target audience. Word is a word processor and it has an interface that is designed to serve that purpose for the business people who are its target audience. ADO is a data transport/management application so it has an interface that is designed to serve that purpose and the developers who are its target audience. So, when we develop Enterprise Caliber Data Objects, we are really developing highly capable applications that other programmers can use as the primary building blocks for their applications.

When we built the user interface with the `EntApp` object way back in Chapter 5, we used the `UCEntApp` interface that I designed for developers to work with. In Chapters 6 and 7 we developed our own objects. When we developed these objects we also developed an interface for each object. This interface is merely a list of the Public methods, variables and events that the object exposed. An easy way to see this interface is to use the Object Browser or even IntelliSense.

When we compile our objects into a DLL, there is actually a lot going on behind the scenes. COM (Component Object Model) builds a binary construct, the interface, which contains a list of all the exposed code plus a few other bits and pieces, which allow you to query this interface etc.

There's a hell of a lot more that we could discuss but we don't really need to. Visual Basic hides away a lot of the additional COM processing for us. I just wanted to make sure that when I start discussing the Property Bag in terms of programmable interfaces that we are both on the same page.

The Property Bag Programmable Interfaces

> From this point on, I will use the words "user interface" to mean those things that we normally think of as interfaces with forms or screens. I will use the words "programmable interface" when I am referring to a COM interface.

As we've seen, *defining* the Property Bag and *using* the Property Bag are two very different kettles of fish. The difference is even more apparent when we look at the code behind the two user interfaces.

In terms of the programmable interface for the Property Bag, we need to expose those functions that will allow the user (either as an Administrator or Production user) to manipulate the OTDs and PSDs for our objects:

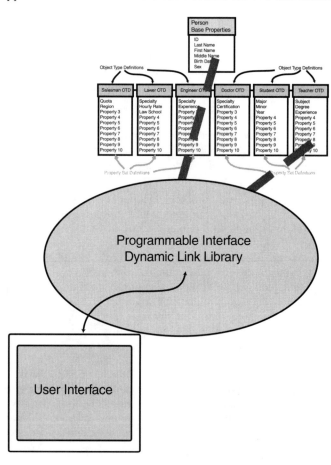

As both types of user interface accomplish different tasks the programmable interface that needs to be exposed will be different. Fortunately for us, both programmable interfaces are created from Enterprise Caliber Data Objects. This means that, for the most part, we are already familiar with the functionality that we need to expose in our programmable interfaces.

We shall spend this chapter looking at the programmable Administrative Interface and move onto the programmable Production Interface in the next chapter.

The Property Bag's Programmable Administrative Interface

In order to construct the programmable interface we need to review the functions that this interface allows the user (Administrator) to do. We must be able to:

- ❑ Create an Object Type Definition
- ❑ Assign a Property Set Definition to the Object Type Definition
- ❑ Add individual Property Definitions to the type
- ❑ If appropriate, assign a list of items to the particular property

In the last chapter, we saw how to construct an Object Type Definition object so that it takes care of the first requirement now what about the others. This chapter will give us the tools we need to meet the last three challenges in the list. One of the reasons I dragged you through the user interface chapters before we built the underlying objects was so that you would have some hands-on experience with the functionality we were after. Now that you have had the chance to work through the discussion and work in a hands-on fashion with the interface, you might think that we are going to write something like a Property Set Definition object. However if you think about it, that would actually limit the flexibility of our Property Bag. In Chapter 9, we saw that we could share properties across several Property Sets, so in a way, it really makes more sense for us handle the properties from the bottom up. In other words, just like we did with all of the objects in the previous chapters, and even the physical servers in the first section of this book, we are going to err on the side of *atomicity*. Rather than creating some big beast of a Property Set Definition Object that contains a collection of individual Property Definitions, we will focus our energies and talents on building the individual Property Definition objects. The reason for this is simple. It is almost always possible to add two things together to get something with more value than either had originally, but it is not always possible to divide something large into its original elemental pieces.

The word we need to use here is **atomicity**, but I like to think about this problem the same way that I might think about adding sugar to a cup of coffee or tea. It is always possible for me to add more sugar to the drink to make it sweeter. It quite another problem to get the sugar out of the mix once I have made the mistake of putting too much in. If we build *atomic* things, like Property Definitions, we can always grab a bunch of them and call the collection a Property Set Definition. As long as they are individual objects, it is possible to do things like share the Property Definitions. It is quite another problem to share some portion of an entire Property Set Definition.

If we err on the side of atomicity and work on the level of the individual Property Definitions, it is also possible to do things like *share* Property Definitions. But that is not all. It is also a lot easier to imagine doing things like building a relationship between a single Property Definition and a list of valid responses for that Property Definition. I don't know about you, but if I try to think about doing something like that from the perspective of the entire Property Set Definition, it gets so confusing that my head starts to spin. As always, when I break the problem down into manageable pieces, take the pieces "One Step at a Time", and think about the much smaller problems these pieces present I find that I can solve just about any problem.

That's good. Because the other thing we are going to do in this chapter is to learn how to build a PropItem object that we will be able to use to provide a list of valid responses for each Property Definition that can benefit from such a list.

What I am trying to say here is that, our programmable Administrative Interface exposes the following objects:

- ❏   OTD object
- ❏   Property Definition object
- ❏   Property Item object

And, as I said, we know how to build OTD objects so let's move onto the Property Definition object.

The Property Definition Object (PropName)

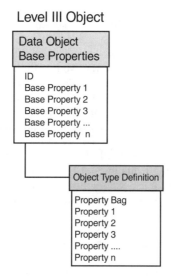

As the name suggests, the Property Definition object manages the Individual Property Definition information for our Property Bag.

> *When I first created the Property Bag object, I used the term* PropName *in place of the more accurate term Property Definition. I've stuck with this name in the book because I felt it would be less confusing if there wasn't another definition term flying around.*

Let's take a look at how to use the PropName object.

Once we have created an Object Type Definition, we can assign a set of properties to this particular OTD. We call that collection of properties a Property Set Definition. When we are working with the programmable Administrative Interface, we actually define the PSD by defining the individual Property Definitions. When we create a Property Definition, we are really creating the Property Name half of a Property Value pair.

In practice, this separation of Name and Values gives us a world of freedom. It means that we can do things like change the extended property for our *Media* object from "Number of Chapters" to read "Number of Chapters including Indexes". Remember from our work with the Administrative User Interface that in order to do this we would go to the Property Set Control List form and select Number of Chapters from the listview. We would then double-click on it or press the Edit button. This would raise the Detail screen, which would expose base properties of the PropName object. We could then edit the value of the name from Number of Chapters to read Number of Chapters including Indexes and press the OK button. From that instant on, our Property Bag would return Number of Pages, Number of Chapters including Indexes, and Cover Material whenever we loaded the properties for the Book Media Type. This means that all of our users can have the benefits from the changed code *now*.

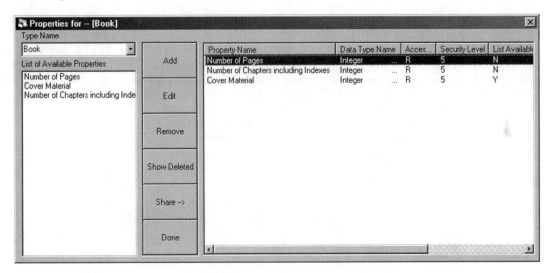

As I mentioned earlier, the object's name in code, PropName, is a little misleading. The PropName object is also responsible for a number of other things like:

- ❑ Defining the data type for the property
- ❑ Indicating whether or not there is a list of valid options available for the property
- ❑ Indicating whether or not the property is a read-only or write-enabled property
- ❑ Indicating the security level required for access to the property

The PropName object is really a specialized Level I Data object. It has exactly the same functionality as any other Level I Data object. That means that it offers a complete audit history, the ability to perform unlimited undo's, and the ability to restore an object from deleted. It also means that you already know exactly how to code the PropName object.

The Tables and Views

As with all Enterprise Caliber Data Objects we need to construct two tables for this object. These tables are generic for the Property Bag, so although we've used Person in their name, you can use them for any PropName object you create. We are also going to construct an additional view, which allows us to view the deleted objects.

This table is holds the information that we use to define the Property Name half of the Property Name/value pair that our Property Bag object exposes to the casual users. As with every other ECDO, it has an ID value that gives a unique handle for this particular Property Name object. The next field has the ominous name `ControllingTypeID`. Don't let this throw you. For our purposes, we just need to realize that this field contains the name of the *original* Object Type Definition that this property was assigned to when it was created. The `ControllingType` portion of the word was chosen to make it easier to sort out the TypeID names in the stored procedures when we are dealing with shared Property Values. The next field contains the Property Name that the end user sees on the screen. One of the great things about this separation is that it really doesn't matter what we call the Property Names. If somebody in accounting or production or sales disagrees with the name of some property, you don't need to worry about it. If some silly committee decides that we should start calling 'chapters of a book' the 'leaves of a book' or something equally ridiculous, no problem. They can call any Property Name whatever they like - *it doesn't change the relationships in the data store.* The names are really superficial; all of the relationships in the database are created using the ID and TypeID values. The next two fields are almost self explanatory. Of course, the `DataTypeID` gives us a sense of what kind of data this property should hold. We use this data type information to build data validation devices at the user interface. The `ListAvailable` field is just a flag that lets us know whether or not this particular Property Definition is associated with a list of valid responses. We have already talked about `ConcurrencyIDs`, so I won't go through that again. Of course this Audit table does the same thing as all of the rest. It gives us a way to store temporal information about Property Names. The view is also something you know about now. This one is used like the rest; it allows us to retrieve a list of deleted Property Names.

The PersonPropName Table

```
CREATE TABLE dbo.PersonPropName
    (
    ID int IDENTITY (1, 1) NOT NULL ,
    ControllingTypeID int NOT NULL ,
    PropertyName varchar (60) NOT NULL ,
    DataTypeID int NOT NULL ,
    ListAvailable char (1) NOT NULL ,
    ConcurrencyID int NOT NULL
    )
```

The PersonPropNameAudit Table

```
CREATE TABLE dbo.PersonPropNameAudit
    (
    ID int IDENTITY (1, 1) NOT NULL ,
    StampUser char (15) NOT NULL ,
    StampDateTime datetime NOT NULL ,
    StampAction char (1) NOT NULL ,
    StampID int NOT NULL ,
    ControllingTypeID int NOT NULL ,
    TypeID int NOT NULL ,
    DisplayOrder int NOT NULL ,
    SecurityLevel int NOT NULL ,
    DataTypeName varchar (60) NOT NULL ,
    DataTypeID int NOT NULL ,
    PropertyName varchar (60) NOT NULL ,
    AccessLevel char (1) NOT NULL ,
    ListAvailable char (1) NOT NULL
    )
```

The vPersonPropNameDelete View

```
CREATE VIEW vPersonPropNameDelete AS
/* This view lists the most recent deletions by ID        */
SELECT StampID, 'ID'=Max(ID)
FROM    PersonPropNameAudit
WHERE   StampAction = 'D'
GROUP   BY StampID
```

The Eight Data Handling Processes

We'll extend the Person object group from the last chapter to include the Property Bag. Open the `LevelIIPersonObject.vbg` file and add the following modules:

System Sphere	Directory	Source File Name
User Centric	\..\Ch11\UCObject\	clsPropName.cls
(UCPerson.vbp)	\..\Ch11\UCObject\	colPropName.cls
	\..\Ch11\UCObject\	clsPropItem.cls
	\..\Ch11\UCObject\	colPropItem.cls
	\..\Ch11\UCObject\	colPersonType.cls
Data Centric	\..\Ch11\DCObject\	clsPropNameData.cls
(DCPerson.vbp)	\..\Ch11\DCObject\	colPropNameData.cls
	\..\Ch11\DCObject\	clsPropItemData.cls
	\..\Ch11\DCObject\	clsPropItemData.cls

Save the Project group as `PersonObjectPropBag.vbg`.

The Fetch Process

The purpose of the *Fetch* process is to retrieve a single object from the data store. The end result of this process is that the User Centric object is populated with a copy of the most current information concerning the object that exists in the data store.

The User Centric Object Code – clsPropName.cls

The user centric `ObjectFetch` code is contained in the `clsPropName.cls` file in the `UCPerson.vbp` project. The main purpose of this method is to retrieve information from the data store and place it into the local object's properties so that the user interface programmer can work with the information easily. Because the properties don't change, the sample code provided can be used almost exactly as it is for the Property Bag of any 4-Dimensional Data Object. The only difference between the code from object to object would the name of the project. In other words, to use this code for any *Widget* object, use the code as printed with the following exception:

Replace this line:

```
Set ThisDataObject = CreateObject("DCPerson.clsPropNameData")
```

With this line:

```
Set ThisDataObject = CreateObject("DCWidget.clsPropNameData")
```

The user centric `ObjectFetch` code accomplishes three things:

- ❑ It instantiates the Data Centric object
- ❑ It calls the `ObjectFetch` method of the Data Centric object
- ❑ It resets the object's local state

As with every other `ObjectFetch`, this one takes the ID of the object as a parameter, but notice that we also pass a parameter called `lngControllingTypeID` into this `ObjectFetch` routine:

```
Public Sub ObjectFetch(lngID As Long, lngControllingTypeID As Long)
```

This is one of the slight differences between this code and a standard Level I treatment. The ControllingTypeID is used to determine which PSD originally created the Property Definition in cases where the Property Definition is shared between different PSDs. We will take a closer look at this concept when we look at the data centric code and the stored procedure below. Other than this minor difference, this code was discussed in Chapter 7.

The Data Centric Object Code

The data centric `ObjectFetch` code is found in the `clsPropNameData.cls` file in the `DCPerson.vbp` project. The main purpose of this method is to retrieve information from the Data sphere and transport that information into the parameters passed into the method from the User Centric object.

The data centric `ObjectFetch` code accomplishes four things:

- ❑ It accepts parameters that it will use for search criteria
- ❑ It creates a call to a stored procedure
- ❑ It executes the stored procedure
- ❑ It returns the results of the stored procedure to the User Centric object

The main reason this code is different than the Level I treatment is due to the extra parameter, `lngControllingTypeID`. Because the properties don't change, the sample code provided can be used almost exactly as it is for the Property Bag of any 4-Dimensional Data Object. The only thing that needs to be changed to use this code with another object is to change the name of the stored procedure. For example, to use this routine with any *Widget* object, we would change the following line:

```
strSQL = "spPersonPropNameGet " & lngID & ", " & lngControllingTypeID
```

to read:

```
strSQL = "spWidgetPropNameGet " & lngID & ", " & lngControllingTypeID
```

Of course, that means that we could make this section of code 100% reusable, as printed, if we just added a parameter that allows us to pass the syntax for the stored procedure into the routine. Well as you might expect, that is exactly what we do in a production installation. I am purposefully ignoring this possibility at this point in the book, because we have a special technique that we use to house, manage, and pass stored procedures between objects. This technique will be illustrated in the Chapter 13 when we talk about Connector objects. For now, just realize that we have addressed this problem. The `ObjectFetch` method for the PropName object is identical to its Level I counterpart. This code was discussed in Chapter 7.

The Stored Procedure

The `spPersonPropNameGet` stored procedure selects a single object from the database and sends the results to the Data Centric object.

The order of the main objectives for this stored procedure is as follows:

- ❑   Select the record from the data store
- ❑   Mirror the results to the user

Stored procedures cannot be reused as easily as compiled VB code. While it is reasonable to pass things like stored procedure syntax into a precompiled DLL, it is not as good of an idea to pass parameters like table names into stored procedures. Let's think about this for a minute.

If we wanted to make any of our stored procedures more generic, we could do things like passing the object name into a stored procedure. This might look something like the following:

```
CREATE PROCEDURE spObjectPropNameGet
@ObjectName, varchar(8), @ID int, @TypeID int
```

We could use the object name that we passed into the stored procedure to identify which tables to use. Then we could use that information to build the stored procedures we need to use dynamically. It might look something like the following where `@ObjectName = Person`:

```
SELECT strSelect = "SELECT " + @ObjectName + "PropName.ID,"
```

Of course, you can see that we can use this technique to build a very generic stored procedure that we could use with every object. This is not a new idea; programmers have been using variations on this technique for years. We do not use this approach, because while it may not require an actual re-compile of the stored procedure, it causes SQL Server to make an optimization plan that is different than the one it makes when it knows which tables it will be working with. We want this portion of our system to be highly efficient, so we assign a set of stored procedures to each object. This does increase the maintenance problem because we do end up with more stored procedures. But once the team learns the stored procedures for one 4-Dimensional Data Object it knows exactly how the stored procedures for every other object work. In fact, if we find that we need to change a concept in a stored procedure, we can work out the logic on a single instance of that stored procedure and then update all of them automatically with a simple VB program. The fact that they are all nearly identical is one of their best features. This approach allows us to increase efficiency while keeping the maintenance headaches to a minimum. The instructions for changing each stored procedure to handle any other object are given at the start of each stored procedure.

To use this code for another object, all instances of the word `Person` in this stored procedure must be replaced with the appropriate object name. This includes the name of the stored procedure as follows:

```
CREATE PROCEDURE spPersonPropNameGet
```

There is another thing I want to bring to your attention. With Property Bag information, we need to manage two Concurrency IDs instead of one as before. That is because we need to keep track of the records in the Object table and the records in the Bridge table during each transaction. If either one of the Concurrency IDs changes, we must roll back the transaction:

```
CREATE PROCEDURE spPersonPropNameGet
@ID int, @TypeID int

AS

SELECT      PersonPropName.ID, PersonPropName.ControllingTypeID,
            PersonTypePropertyBridge.TypeID, PersonPropName.PropertyName,
            PersonPropName.DataTypeID, Common..DataTypeObject.DataTypeName,
            PersonPropName.ListAvailable, PersonTypePropertyBridge.DisplayOrder,
            PersonTypePropertyBridge.AccessLevel,
            PersonTypePropertyBridge.SecurityLevel,
            PersonPropName.ConcurrencyID AS ConcurrencyID1,
            PersonTypePropertyBridge.ConcurrencyID AS ConcurrencyID2

FROM        PersonTypePropertyBridge

INNER JOIN PersonPropName ON
            PersonTypePropertyBridge.PropertyID = PersonPropName.ID

INNER JOIN Common..DataTypeObject ON
            PersonPropName.DataTypeID = Common..DataTypeObject.ID

WHERE       PersonTypePropertyBridge.PropertyID = @ID AND
            PersonTypePropertyBridge.TypeID = @TypeID

RETURN      (0)
```

The Insert Process

The purpose of the *Insert* process is to insert a new object into the data store. During this process, a record is added to an Audit table that indicates that the insertion took place. The end result of this process is that the User Centric object is populated with the most current information concerning this object that exists in the data store.

The User Centric Object Code

The user centric `ObjectInsert` code is contained in the `clsPropName.cls` file in the `UCPerson.vbp` project. The main purpose of this method is to insert the information about a new object in the data store. Because the properties don't change, the sample code provided can be used almost exactly as it is for the Property Bag of any 4-Dimensional Data Object. The *Insert* process for the *Person* PropName is identical to its Level I counterpart. This code was discussed in Chapter 6.

The user centric `ObjectInsert` code accomplishes four things:

❑   Checks the object to see if it is emancipated
❑   It instantiates the Data Centric object
❑   It calls the `ObjectInsert` method of the Data Centric object
❑   It resets the object's local state

The Data Centric Object Code

The `ObjectInsert` procedure of the Data Centric object carries out the data centric portion of the *Insert* process. It calls SQL Server and executes a stored procedure, which inserts the information into the data store. Because the properties don't change, the sample code provided can be used almost exactly as it is for the Property Bag of any 4-Dimensional Data Object. The *Insert* process for the *Person* PropName is identical to its Level I counterpart. This code was discussed in Chapter 6.

The data centric `ObjectInsert` code accomplishes four things:

❑   It opens a connection to the data store
❑   It creates a call to a stored procedure
❑   It executes a stored procedure
❑   It returns the results of that stored procedure to the User Centric object

The Stored Procedure

The `spPersonPropNameInsert` stored procedure adds a new record to the Object table, adds a history record to the Audit table, and returns the current representation of the object from the data store to the Data Centric object.

The order of the main objectives for this stored procedure is as follows:

❑   Insert a new property record if this one is new and not shared
❑   Assign this property definition to the PSD indicated by the TypeID
❑   Insert an audit record that marks the insertion
❑   Mirror the results of the procedure back to the user

```
CREATE PROCEDURE spPersonPropNameInsert
@StampUser varchar(10), @ID int, @TypeID int, @PropertyName varchar(60),
@DataTypeID int, @ListAvailable char(1), @DisplayOrder int, @AccessLevel char(1),
@SecurityLevel int

AS

DECLARE @trncnt int, @ErrorNumber int

SELECT @ErrorNumber = -1
```

Standard transaction handling:

```
SELECT @trncnt = @@trancount

/* issue begin or save transaction based on transaction count */
IF @trncnt = 0
```

```
      BEGIN TRANSACTION T1
   ELSE
      SAVE TRANSACTION T1
```

Insert a new Property Definition record if the one is new and not shared. If this ID was shared, then its value could not be 0. It would have a particular long value:

```
IF @ID = 0
   BEGIN
    INSERT PersonPropName
            (ControllingTypeID, PropertyName, DataTypeID, ListAvailable,
            ConcurrencyID)

    VALUES (@TypeID, @PropertyName, @DataTypeID, @ListAvailable, 1)

    IF @@error <> 0 GOTO ErrorHandler

    SELECT @ID = @@Identity

   END
```

Assign this Property Definition to the PSD indicated by the `TypeID`:

```
INSERT PersonTypePropertyBridge
    (TypeID, PropertyID, DisplayOrder, AccessLevel, SecurityLevel, ConcurrencyID)

VALUES (@TypeID, @ID, @DisplayOrder, @AccessLevel, @SecurityLevel, 1)

IF @@error <> 0 GOTO ErrorHandler
```

Insert an audit record that marks the insertion:

```
INSERT PersonPropNameAudit
        (StampUser, StampAction, StampDateTime, StampID, ControllingTypeID,
        TypeID, PropertyName, DataTypeID, DataTypeName, ListAvailable,
        DisplayOrder, AccessLevel, SecurityLevel)

SELECT @StampUser,'I', GetDate(), PersonPropName.ID,
        PersonPropName.ControllingTypeID, PersonTypePropertyBridge.TypeID,
        PersonPropName.PropertyName, PersonPropName.DataTypeID,
        Common..DataTypeObject.DataTypeName, PersonPropName.ListAvailable,
        PersonTypePropertyBridge.DisplayOrder,
        PersonTypePropertyBridge.AccessLevel,
        PersonTypePropertyBridge.SecurityLevel

FROM        PersonTypePropertyBridge

INNER JOIN  PersonPropName ON
            PersonTypePropertyBridge.PropertyID = PersonPropName.ID

INNER JOIN  Common..DataTypeObject ON
            PersonPropName.DataTypeID = Common..DataTypeObject.ID

WHERE       PersonTypePropertyBridge.PropertyID = @ID AND
            PersonTypePropertyBridge.TypeID = @TypeID

IF @@error <> 0 GOTO ErrorHandler
```

Standard commit transaction code:

```
IF @trncnt = 0 COMMIT TRANSACTION T1
```

Mirror the results of the procedure back to the user:

```
SELECT PersonPropName.ID, PersonPropName.ControllingTypeID,
       PersonTypePropertyBridge.TypeID, PersonPropName.PropertyName,
       PersonPropName.DataTypeID, Common..DataTypeObject.DataTypeName,
       PersonPropName.ListAvailable, PersonTypePropertyBridge.DisplayOrder,
       PersonTypePropertyBridge.AccessLevel,
       PersonTypePropertyBridge.SecurityLevel,
       PersonPropName.ConcurrencyID AS ConcurrencyID1,
       PersonTypePropertyBridge.ConcurrencyID AS ConcurrencyID2

FROM       PersonTypePropertyBridge

INNER JOIN PersonPropName ON
           PersonTypePropertyBridge.PropertyID = PersonPropName.ID

INNER JOIN Common..DataTypeObject ON
           PersonPropName.DataTypeID = Common..DataTypeObject.ID

WHERE      PersonTypePropertyBridge.PropertyID = @ID AND
           PersonTypePropertyBridge.TypeID = @TypeID

RETURN     (0)
```

Standard error handler:

```
ErrorHandler:
   ROLLBACK TRANSACTION T1
   SELECT   ErrorCondition
   FROM     Common..ErrorMessage
   WHERE    ErrorNumber = @ErrorNumber
   RETURN   (100)
```

The Update Process

The purpose of the *Update* process is to change existing information in the data store. During this process, a record is added to an Audit table that indicates that the update took place. The end result of this process is that the User Centric object is populated with the most current information concerning this object that exists in the data store.

The User Centric Object Code

The user centric `ObjectUpdate` code is contained in the `clsPropName.cls` file in the `UCPerson.vbp` project. The purpose of this method is to update information from the data store, while ensuring that the data in the object has not become stale. The `ObjectUpdate` method for the *Person* PropName is identical to its Level I counterpart. This code was discussed in Chapter 7.

The user centric `ObjectUpdate` code accomplishes four things:

- ❑ Checks the object to see if it is emancipated
- ❑ It instantiates the Data Centric object

- ❏ It calls the `ObjectUpdate` method of the Data Centric object
- ❏ It resets the object's local state

The Data Centric Object Code

The data centric `ObjectUpdate` code is found in the `clsPropNameData.cls` file in the `DCPerson.vbp` project. The purpose of this method is to update the data in the data store with changed information. It is also responsible for managing data collisions and ensuring that the updates are only performed on fresh data.

The data centric `ObjectUpdate` code accomplishes six things:

- ❏ It opens a connection to the data store
- ❏ It requests the current state for the target object from the data store including the Concurrency ID
- ❏ It performs a macro data collision test on a field-by-field basis, comparing the parameter starting values with the current information in the data store
- ❏ It creates an Update stored procedure call using the information passed into the routine via the parameters
- ❏ It executes the stored procedure call, which executes a micro data collision test using the Concurrency ID as its criterion for collisions
- ❏ It returns the results of that stored procedure to the User Centric object

There is one unusual thing to note in this block of code. It is subtle and it would be easy to miss. Notice that we are using two Concurrency IDs in this procedure. That is because we have to actively monitor two tables during the time that this routine is executing. This is not really any more difficult than the task we performed for a Level I object. In both cases, we are just ensuring that during the millisecond or so that passes while we are performing the update that the original data in the data store has not changed. If it does, then we must tell MTS that we aborted the transaction and send the user the information that will allow the user to re-attempt or cancel the update as appropriate:

```
Public Sub ObjectUpdate(lngStampID As Long, lngSaveStampID As Long, lngID As _
                Long, lngSaveID As Long, lngControllingTypeID As Long, _
                lngSaveControllingTypeID As Long, lngDataTypeID As _
                Long, lngSaveDataTypeID As Long, lngSecurityLevel _
                As Long, lngSaveSecurityLevel As Long, _
                lngDisplayOrder As Long, lngSaveDisplayOrder As _
                Long, lngTypeID As Long, lngSaveTypeID As Long, _
                dtmStampDateTime As Variant, dtmSaveStampDateTime As _
                Variant, intDataLocking, blnChangeAll As Boolean, _
                blnSaveChangeAll As Boolean, strStampUser As String, _
                strSaveStampUser As String, strStampAction As String, _
                strSaveStampAction As String, strDataMessage, _
                strPropertyName As String, strSavePropertyName As _
                String, strDataTypeName As String, _
                strSaveDataTypeName As String, strAccessLevel As _
                String, strSaveAccessLevel As String, strListAvailable _
                As String, strSaveListAvailable As String)

    Dim strSQL As String
    Dim lngRows As Long
```

Notice that in this case we are dimensioning two Concurrency IDs:

```
Dim lngConcurrencyID1 As Long, lngConcurrencyID2 As Long

Dim ctxObject As ObjectContext
Set ctxObject = GetObjectContext()

On Error GoTo ObjectUpdateError

Dim ThisConnection As ADODB.Connection
Dim ThisRecordset As ADODB.Recordset

Set ThisConnection = New ADODB.Connection
Set ThisRecordset = New ADODB.Recordset

Dim strCollision As String
strCollision = ""

ThisConnection.Open mstrConnect, GetLogon(mstrConnect), GetPassword(mstrConnect)

If DataLocking > 0 Then
   'Select the record to update using the fetch stored procedure
   strSQL = "spPersonPropNameGet " & lngID & ", " & lngTypeID
   ThisRecordset.Open strSQL, ThisConnection

   If Not ThisRecordset.EOF Then
```

Note that the recordset returns both Concurrency IDs:

```
      lngConcurrencyID1 = ThisRecordset.Fields("ConcurrencyID1").Value
      lngConcurrencyID2 = ThisRecordset.Fields("ConcurrencyID2").Value
      CurrentID = ThisRecordset.Fields("ID").Value
      CurrentControllingTypeID = ThisRecordset.Fields("ControllingTypeID").Value
      CurrentDataTypeID = ThisRecordset.Fields("DataTypeID").Value
      CurrentSecurityLevel = ThisRecordset.Fields("SecurityLevel").Value
      CurrentDisplayOrder = ThisRecordset.Fields("DisplayOrder").Value
      CurrentTypeID = ThisRecordset.Fields("TypeID").Value
      CurrentPropertyName = FixNulls(ThisRecordset.Fields("PropertyName").Value)
      CurrentDataTypeName = FixNulls(ThisRecordset.Fields("DataTypeName").Value)
      CurrentAccessLevel = FixNulls(ThisRecordset.Fields("AccessLevel").Value)
      CurrentListAvailable = _
            FixNulls(ThisRecordset.Fields("ListAvailable").Value)
      ThisRecordset.Close
   Else
      strDataMessage = "Unable to find the record to update in the datastore"
      'Free up the object in MTS and set the Transaction Aborted flag
      ctxObject.SetAbort
      ThisConnection.Close
      Set ThisRecordset = Nothing
      Set ThisConnection = Nothing
      Set ctxObject = Nothing
      Exit Sub
   End If

   If NzString(CurrentPropertyName) <> NzString(strSavePropertyName) Then
      If Len(strCollision) > 0 Then
         strCollision = strCollision & "*" & PropertyName & "|" & _
                     CurrentPropertyName
      Else
```

```
            strCollision = PropertyName & "|" & CurrentPropertyName
        End If
    End If
```

And so on...

```
    End If

    If Len(strCollision) > 0 Then
        If DataLocking = 1 Then
            strDataMessage = "Unable to save changes, the record was being " & _
                             "edited by another user."
        'Free up the object in MTS and set the Transaction Aborted flag
        ctxObject.SetAbort
        ThisConnection.Close
        Set ThisRecordset = Nothing
        Set ThisConnection = Nothing
        Set ctxObject = Nothing
        Exit Sub
        ElseIf DataLocking = 2 Then
            strDataMessage = "The Following Collisions have occured * " & _
                             strCollision
        'Free up the object in MTS and set the Transaction Aborted flag
        ctxObject.SetAbort
        ThisConnection.Close
        Set ThisRecordset = Nothing
        Set ThisConnection = Nothing
        Set ctxObject = Nothing
        Exit Sub
        Else
            strDataMessage = ""
        End If
    End If

    strSQL = "spPersonPropNameUpdate " & _
             jamQuote & strStampUser & jamQuote & jamComma & _
             lngID & jamComma & _
             lngTypeID & jamComma & _
             lngControllingTypeID & jamComma & _
             jamQuote & strPropertyName & jamQuote & jamComma & _
             lngDataTypeID & jamComma & _
             jamQuote & strListAvailable & jamQuote & jamComma & _
             lngDisplayOrder & jamComma & _
             jamQuote & strAccessLevel & jamQuote & jamComma & _
             lngSecurityLevel & jamComma & _
```

We pass both Concurrency IDs back into the stored procedure:

```
             lngConcurrencyID1 & jamComma & _
             lngConcurrencyID2
```

```
    On Error Resume Next

    ThisRecordset.Open strSQL, ThisConnection
```

We handle the standard errors that SQL or ADO would raise in this branch of the `If` statement:

```
If ThisConnection.Errors.Count > 0 Then
    strDataMessage = ThisConnection.Errors(0).Description
  'Roll back the transaction
    ctxObject.SetAbort
Else
```

We handle internal errors (i.e., concurrency errors) in this branch of the `If` statement. As long as no concurrency errors have occurred then we mirror the data to the user:

```
If ThisRecordset.Fields(0).Name = "ErrorCondition" Then
    strDataMessage = ThisRecordset.Fields(0).Value
  'Free up the object in MTS and set the Transaction Aborted flag
    ctxObject.SetAbort
Else
' This Resets the Starting Values with the current values in the Database
    lngID = ThisRecordset.Fields("ID").Value
    lngSaveID = ThisRecordset.Fields("ID").Value
    lngControllingTypeID = ThisRecordset.Fields("ControllingTypeID").Value
    lngSaveControllingTypeID = ThisRecordset.Fields("ControllingTypeID").Value
    lngDataTypeID = ThisRecordset.Fields("DataTypeID").Value
    lngSaveDataTypeID = ThisRecordset.Fields("DataTypeID").Value
    lngSecurityLevel = ThisRecordset.Fields("SecurityLevel").Value
    lngSaveSecurityLevel = ThisRecordset.Fields("SecurityLevel").Value
    lngDisplayOrder = ThisRecordset.Fields("DisplayOrder").Value
    lngSaveDisplayOrder = ThisRecordset.Fields("DisplayOrder").Value
    lngTypeID = ThisRecordset.Fields("TypeID").Value
    lngSaveTypeID = ThisRecordset.Fields("TypeID").Value
    strDataMessage = ""
    strPropertyName = FixNulls(ThisRecordset.Fields("PropertyName").Value)
    strSavePropertyName = FixNulls(ThisRecordset.Fields("PropertyName").Value)
    strDataTypeName = FixNulls(ThisRecordset.Fields("DataTypeName").Value)
    strSaveDataTypeName = FixNulls(ThisRecordset.Fields("DataTypeName").Value)
    strAccessLevel = FixNulls(ThisRecordset.Fields("AccessLevel").Value)
    strSaveAccessLevel = FixNulls(ThisRecordset.Fields("AccessLevel").Value)
    strListAvailable = FixNulls(ThisRecordset.Fields("ListAvailable").Value)
    strSaveListAvailable = _
        FixNulls(ThisRecordset.Fields("ListAvailable").Value)
  'Free up the object in MTS and set the Transaction Complete flag
    ctxObject.SetComplete
    End If
End If

ThisConnection.Close
Set ThisConnection = Nothing
Set ctxObject = Nothing

Exit Sub

ObjectUpdateError:

HandleError

End Sub
```

The Stored Procedure

The spPersonPropNameUpdate stored procedure changes a record in the Object table, adds a history record to the Audit table, and returns the current representation of the object from the data store to the Data Centric object.

The order of the main objectives for this stored procedure is as follows:

- ❑ Add an audit record to mark the update
- ❑ Update the Property Definition
- ❑ Update the PSD assignment which is stored in the Bridge table
- ❑ Mirror the results of the procedure back to the user

```
CREATE PROCEDURE spPersonPropNameUpdate
@StampUser varchar(10), @ID int, @TypeID int, @ControllingTypeID int,
@PropertyName varchar(60), @DataTypeID int, @ListAvailable char(1),
@DisplayOrder int, @AccessLevel char(1), @SecurityLevel int, @Concurrency1 int,
@Concurrency2 int

AS

DECLARE @trncnt int, @PropertyConcurrency int, @BridgeConcurrency int,
        @ErrorNumber int, @rows int, @err int

SELECT @PropertyConcurrency = @Concurrency1
SELECT @BridgeConcurrency = @Concurrency2
SELECT @ErrorNumber = -1
```

Standard transaction handling:

```
SELECT @trncnt = @@trancount
/* issue begin or save transaction based on transaction count */
IF @trncnt = 0
   BEGIN TRANSACTION T1
ELSE
   SAVE TRANSACTION T1
```

Add audit record to mark the update:

```
INSERT PersonPropNameAudit
      (StampUser, StampAction, StampDateTime, StampID, ControllingTypeID,
      TypeID, PropertyName, DataTypeID, DataTypeName, ListAvailable,
      DisplayOrder, AccessLevel, SecurityLevel)

SELECT @StampUser, 'U', GetDate(), PersonPropName.ID,
      PersonPropName.ControllingTypeID, PersonTypePropertyBridge.TypeID,
      PersonPropName.PropertyName, PersonPropName.DataTypeID,
      Common..DataTypeObject.DataTypeName, PersonPropName.ListAvailable,
      PersonTypePropertyBridge.DisplayOrder,
      PersonTypePropertyBridge.AccessLevel,
      PersonTypePropertyBridge.SecurityLevel

FROM          PersonTypePropertyBridge

INNER JOIN    PersonPropName ON
```

```
                    PersonTypePropertyBridge.PropertyID = PersonPropName.ID

INNER JOIN          Common..DataTypeObject ON
                    PersonPropName.DataTypeID = Common..DataTypeObject.ID

WHERE               PersonTypePropertyBridge.PropertyID = @ID AND
                    PersonTypePropertyBridge.TypeID = @TypeID

IF @@error <> 0 GOTO ErrorHandler
```

Update the Property Definition:

```
UPDATE PersonPropName

SET     PropertyName = @PropertyName, DataTypeID = @DataTypeID,
        ControllingTypeID = @ControllingTypeID, ListAvailable = @ListAvailable,
        ConcurrencyID = ConcurrencyID + 1

WHERE   ID = @ID AND ConcurrencyID = @PropertyConcurrency

SELECT @err = @@error, @rows = @@RowCount

IF @err <> 0 GOTO ErrorHandler
```

Standard concurrency error handling – Object table:

```
IF @rows = 0
   BEGIN
      SELECT @ErrorNumber = 100
      GOTO ErrorHandler
   END
```

Update the PSD assignment:

```
UPDATE PersonTypePropertyBridge

SET     DisplayOrder = @DisplayOrder, AccessLevel = @AccessLevel,
        SecurityLevel = @SecurityLevel, ConcurrencyID = ConcurrencyID + 1

WHERE   TypeID = @TypeID AND PropertyID = @ID AND
        ConcurrencyID = @BridgeConcurrency

SELECT @err = @@error, @rows = @@RowCount

IF @err <> 0 GOTO ErrorHandler
```

Standard concurrency error handling – Bridge table:

```
IF @rows = 0
   BEGIN
      SELECT @ErrorNumber = 100
      GOTO ErrorHandler
   END
```

Standard commit transaction handling:

```
IF @trncnt = 0 COMMIT TRANSACTION t1
```

Mirror the results to the user:

```
SELECT  PersonPropName.ID, PersonPropName.ControllingTypeID,
        PersonTypePropertyBridge.TypeID, PersonPropName.PropertyName,
        PersonPropName.DataTypeID, Common..DataTypeObject.DataTypeName,
        PersonPropName.ListAvailable, PersonTypePropertyBridge.DisplayOrder,
        PersonTypePropertyBridge.AccessLevel,
        PersonTypePropertyBridge.SecurityLevel,
        PersonPropName.ConcurrencyID AS ConcurrencyID1,
        PersonTypePropertyBridge.ConcurrencyID AS ConcurrencyID2

FROM        PersonTypePropertyBridge

INNER JOIN PersonPropName ON
        PersonTypePropertyBridge.PropertyID = PersonPropName.ID

INNER JOIN Common..DataTypeObject ON
        PersonPropName.DataTypeID = Common..DataTypeObject.ID

WHERE       PersonTypePropertyBridge.PropertyID = @ID AND
        PersonTypePropertyBridge.TypeID = @TypeID

RETURN (0)
```

Standard error handling:

```
ErrorHandler:
    ROLLBACK TRANSACTION T1
    SELECT   ErrorCondition
    FROM     Common..ErrorMessage
    WHERE    ErrorNumber = @ErrorNumber
    RETURN   (100)
```

The Delete Process

The primary objective of the *Delete* process is to remove an object's data from the database. However, because this is an enterprise-level object, we have a second mandate that is to track changes to all objects and provide a technique for undoing any of those changes. To accomplish this when we delete an object from the database, we really just move the object's data from the Object table to the Audit table. This process is almost the same as the technique we used previously to copy an inserted object's current state to the Audit table to mark the object's insertion. The most complex task in this process is the collision checking that must be performed.

The User Centric Object Code

The user centric `ObjectDelete` code is contained in the `clsPropName.cls` file in the `UCPerson.vbp` project. The purpose of this method is to update information from the data store, while ensuring that the data in the object has not become stale. The `ObjectDelete` method for the *Person* PropName is identical to its Level I counterpart. This code was discussed in Chapter 7.

The user centric `ObjectDelete` code accomplishes four things:

❑ Checks the object to see if it is emancipated
❑ It instantiates the data centric object
❑ It calls the `ObjectDelete` method of the Data Centric object
❑ It informs the user of any collisions or other errors

The Data Centric Object Code

The `ObjectDelete` procedure of the Data Centric object carries out the data centric portion of the *Delete* process. Surprisingly, it is a little more complex than the `ObjectInsert` method. That is because we must perform collision checking before we update or delete a record from the data store. What this means in real terms is that this method requires two trips to SQL Server.

The data centric `ObjectDelete` code accomplishes six things:

❑ It opens a connection to the data store
❑ It requests the current state for the target object from the data store including the Concurrency ID
❑ It performs a macro data collision test on a field-by-field basis comparing the parameter starting values with the current information in the data store
❑ It creates a delete stored procedure call using the information passed into the routine via the parameters
❑ It executes the stored procedure call, which handles a micro data collision test using the Concurrency ID as its criterion for collisions
❑ It returns the results of that stored procedure to the User Centric object

Note that we use two Concurrency IDs in this routine, just like we did in the `ObjectUpdate` routine above:

```
Public Sub ObjectDelete(lngStampID As Long, lngSaveStampID As Long, lngID As _
                  Long, lngSaveID As Long, lngControllingTypeID As _
                  Long, lngSaveControllingTypeID As Long, _
                  lngDataTypeID As Long, lngSaveDataTypeID As Long, _
                  lngSecurityLevel As Long, lngSaveSecurityLevel As _
                  Long, lngDisplayOrder As Long, lngSaveDisplayOrder _
                  As Long, lngTypeID As Long, lngSaveTypeID As Long, _
                  dtmStampDateTime As Variant, dtmSaveStampDateTime As_
                  Variant, intDataLocking, blnChangeAll As Boolean, _
                  blnSaveChangeAll As Boolean, strStampUser As String, _
                  strSaveStampUser As String, strStampAction As String, _
                  strSaveStampAction As String, strDataMessage, _
                  strPropertyName As String, strSavePropertyName As _
                  String, strDataTypeName As String, strSaveDataTypeName _
                  As String, strAccessLevel As String, _
                  strSaveAccessLevel As String, strListAvailable As _
                  String, strSaveListAvailable As String)

    Dim strSQL As String
    Dim lngRows As Long
    Dim strCollision As String

    Dim lngConcurrencyID1 As Long
    Dim lngConcurrencyID2 As Long
```

```
Dim ctxObject As ObjectContext
Set ctxObject = GetObjectContext()

On Error GoTo ObjectDeleteError

Dim ThisConnection As ADODB.Connection
Dim ThisRecordset As ADODB.Recordset

Set ThisConnection = New ADODB.Connection
Set ThisRecordset = New ADODB.Recordset

strCollision = ""

ThisConnection.Open mstrConnect, GetLogon(mstrConnect), GetPassword(mstrConnect)

strSQL = "spPersonPropNameGet " & lngID & jamComma & lngTypeID

On Error Resume Next

ThisRecordset.Open strSQL, ThisConnection

If DataLocking > 0 Then
   If Not ThisRecordset.EOF Then
      lngConcurrencyID1 = ThisRecordset.Fields("ConcurrencyID1").Value
      lngConcurrencyID2 = ThisRecordset.Fields("ConcurrencyID2").Value
      CurrentID = ThisRecordset.Fields("ID").Value
      CurrentControllingTypeID = ThisRecordset.Fields("ControllingTypeID").Value
      CurrentDataTypeID = ThisRecordset.Fields("DataTypeID").Value
      CurrentSecurityLevel = ThisRecordset.Fields("SecurityLevel").Value
      CurrentDisplayOrder = ThisRecordset.Fields("DisplayOrder").Value
      CurrentTypeID = ThisRecordset.Fields("TypeID").Value
      CurrentPropertyName = FixNulls(ThisRecordset.Fields("PropertyName").Value)
      CurrentDataTypeName = FixNulls(ThisRecordset.Fields("DataTypeName").Value)
      CurrentAccessLevel = FixNulls(ThisRecordset.Fields("AccessLevel").Value)
      CurrentListAvailable = FixNulls(ThisRecordset.Fields("ListAvailable").Value)
      ThisRecordset.Close
   Else
      strDataMessage = "The requested delete did not occur, the record " & _
                    "was not found."
    'Free up the object in MTS and set the Transaction Aborted flag
      ctxObject.SetAbort
      ThisConnection.Close
      Set ThisConnection = Nothing
      Set ctxObject = Nothing
      Exit Sub
   End If

   If NzString(CurrentPropertyName) <> NzString(strSavePropertyName) Then
      If Len(strCollision) > 0 Then
         strCollision = strCollision & "*" & PropertyName & "|" & _
                    CurrentPropertyName
      Else
         strCollision = PropertyName & "|" & CurrentPropertyName
      End If
   End If

End If

  If Len(strCollision) > 0 Then
     If DataLocking = 1 Then
```

```
          strDataMessage = "Unable to Delete the record because it was being " & _
                          "edited by another user."
        'Free up the object in MTS and set the Transaction Aborted flag
        ctxObject.SetAbort
        ThisConnection.Close
        Set ThisConnection = Nothing
        Set ctxObject = Nothing
        Exit Sub
      ElseIf DataLocking = 2 Then
          strDataMessage = "The Following Collisions have occured * " & _
                          strCollision
        'Free up the object in MTS and set the Transaction Aborted flag
        ctxObject.SetAbort
        ThisConnection.Close
        Set ThisConnection = Nothing
        Set ctxObject = Nothing
        Exit Sub
      Else
          strDataMessage = ""
      End If
  End If

  strSQL = "spPersonPropNameDelete " & _
          jamQuote & strStampUser & jamQuote & jamComma & _
          lngID & jamComma & _
          lngTypeID & jamComma & _
          lngConcurrencyID1 & jamComma & _
          lngConcurrencyID2

  On Error Resume Next

  ThisRecordset.Open strSQL, ThisConnection

  If ThisConnection.Errors.Count > 0 Then
      strDataMessage = ThisConnection.Errors(0).Description
      ' Roll Back the Transaction
      ctxObject.SetAbort
  Else
      If ThisRecordset.Fields(0).Name = "ErrorCondition" Then
          strDataMessage = ThisRecordset.Fields(0).Value
          'Free up the object in MTS and set the Aborted flag
          ctxObejct.SetAbort
      Else
          strDataMessage = ""
          'Free up the object in MTS and set the Transaction Completed flag
          ctxObject.SetComplete
      End If
  End If

  ThisConnection.Close
  Set ThisConneciton= Nothing
  Set ctxObject = Nothing

  Exit Sub

ObjectDeleteError:

  HandleError

End Sub
```

The Stored Procedure

The `spPersonPropNameDelete` stored procedure deletes a record from the Object table, adds a history record to the Audit table, and returns either an error message or a count of 1 which indicates success.

The order of the main objectives for this stored procedure is as follows:

- ❑ Add an audit record to mark the deletion.
- ❑ Delete the assignment record from the Bridge table.
- ❑ Test to find out whether or not another PSD is also using this Property Definition.
  If not then delete the Property Definition.
  If so, then set the `ControllingTypeID` if required.
- ❑ Mirror the results of the procedure back to the user.

```
CREATE PROCEDURE spPersonPropNameDelete
@StampUser varchar(10), @ID int, @TypeID int, @Concurrency1 int,
@Concurrency2 int

AS

DECLARE @trncnt int, @ErrorNumber int, @rows int, @err int,
        @PropertyConcurrency int, @BridgeConcurrency int,
        @ControllingType int, @ControllingTypeUnknown char(1)

SELECT @ErrorNumber = -1
SELECT @PropertyConcurrency = @Concurrency1
SELECT @BridgeConcurrency = @Concurrency2
```

Standard transaction handling:

```
SELECT @trncnt = @@trancount
/* issue begin or save transaction based on transaction count */
IF @trncnt = 0
   BEGIN TRANSACTION T1
ELSE
   SAVE TRANSACTION T1
```

Add an audit record to fix the state of the object:

```
INSERT PersonPropNameAudit
       (StampUser, StampAction, StampDateTime, StampID, ControllingTypeID,
       TypeID, PropertyName, DataTypeID, DataTypeName, ListAvailable,
       DisplayOrder, AccessLevel, SecurityLevel)

SELECT @StampUser, 'D', GetDate(), PersonPropName.ID,
       PersonPropName.ControllingTypeID, PersonTypePropertyBridge.TypeID,
       PersonPropName.PropertyName, PersonPropName.DataTypeID,
       Common..DataTypeObject.DataTypeName, PersonPropName.ListAvailable,
       PersonTypePropertyBridge.DisplayOrder,
       PersonTypePropertyBridge.AccessLevel,
       PersonTypePropertyBridge.SecurityLevel

FROM          PersonTypePropertyBridge
```

```
INNER JOIN      PersonPropName ON
                PersonTypePropertyBridge.PropertyID = PersonPropName.ID

INNER JOIN      Common..DataTypeObject ON
                PersonPropName.DataTypeID = Common..DataTypeObject.ID

WHERE           PersonTypePropertyBridge.PropertyID = @ID AND
                PersonTypePropertyBridge.TypeID = @TypeID

IF @@error <> 0 GOTO ErrorHandler
```

Delete the Property Definition to PSD assignment:

```
DELETE PersonTypePropertyBridge

WHERE     PropertyID = @ID AND TypeID = @TypeID AND
          ConcurrencyID = @BridgeConcurrency

SELECT @err = @@error, @rows = @@RowCount

IF @err <> 0 GOTO ErrorHandler
```

Standard concurrency error handling:

```
IF @rows = 0
   BEGIN
       SELECT @ErrorNumber = 100
       GOTO ErrorHandler
   END
```

Standard test to determine whether or not this object (in this case the object is a Property Definition, not a *Person* object) has been assigned to another PSD:

```
IF (SELECT COUNT(*) FROM PersonTypePropertyBridge WHERE PropertyID = @ID) = 0
```

If this Property Definition is not being used by any other PSDs then, in addition to deleting the record in the Bridge table, we can also delete the actual Property Definition:

```
BEGIN
    DELETE PersonPropName
    WHERE ID = @ID AND ConcurrencyID = @PropertyConcurrency
    SELECT @err = @@error, @rows = @@RowCount
    IF @err <> 0 GOTO ErrorHandler
```

Standard concurrency error handling:

```
    IF @rows = 0
        BEGIN
            SELECT @ErrorNumber = 100
            GOTO ErrorHandler
        END
    END
ELSE
```

This is an important section of the stored procedure. It works like this. If more than one PSD is sharing the same Property Definition, then we need to find out which PSD originally created the Property Definition. If it is the PSD that is controlling this delete, then we set the controlling PSD value to none (-1). This allows all of the remaining PSDs that are using the Property Definition to continue sharing the Property Definition. The only real difference is that now no one PSD can claim ownership of the Property Definition:

```
    BEGIN
       SELECT @ControllingType =
         (SELECT ControllingTypeID FROM PersonPropName WHERE  ID = @ID)
       IF @ControllingType = @TypeID
         BEGIN
             UPDATE PersonPropName SET ControllingTypeID = -1
             WHERE ID = @ID
             SELECT @ControllingType = -1
         END
    END
END
```

Standard commit transaction handling:

```
  IF @trncnt = 0 COMMIT TRANSACTION T1
```

Mirror the results to the user. In this case, the user is the programmer, so we craft a single row return that indicates:

- Whether or not the delete was successful
- Whether or not the controlling type is known

```
IF @ControllingType = -1
   SELECT @ControllingTypeUnknown = 'Y'
ELSE
   SELECT @ControllingTypeUnknown = 'N'
SELECT 'RowCount' = @rows, 'ControllingTypeUnknown'= @ControllingTypeUnknown

RETURN (0)
```

Standard error handling:

```
ErrorHandler:
   ROLLBACK TRANSACTION T1
   SELECT   ErrorCondition
   FROM     Common..ErrorMessage
   WHERE    ErrorNumber = @ErrorNumber
   RETURN   (100)
```

The Show Deleted Process

The *Show Deleted* process returns a collection of objects that are currently deleted to the user centric object. This process is virtually identical to the *Load* process below. In fact, the VB code for both processes is almost 100% interchangeable.

The User Centric Object Code

The user centric `ShowDeleted` code is contained in the `colPropName.cls` file in the `UCPerson.vbp` project. The main purpose of this method is to retrieve a collection of deleted objects from the data store. The `ShowDeleted` method for the *Person* PropName is identical to its Level I counterpart. This code was discussed in Chapter 7.

The user centric `ShowDeleted` code accomplishes six things:

- ❏ Collects selection information in its parameters
- ❏ It instantiates the Data Centric object
- ❏ It calls the `FetchDeleted` method of the Data Centric object using the selection information provided
- ❏ It unpacks the information about each object from a single variant array that holds all of the deleted objects
- ❏ It re-creates the individual objects from the data above
- ❏ It adds each object to the deleted objects collection.

The Data Centric Object Code

The data centric `FetchDeleted` code is contained in the `colPropNameData.cls` file in the `DCPerson.vbp` project. The main purpose of this method is to call a stored procedure from the database and return the results to the User Centric object in a variant array. The `FetchDeleted` method for the *Person* PropName is identical to its Level I counterpart. This code was discussed in Chapter 7.

The data centric `FetchDeleted` code accomplishes four things:

- ❏ It opens a connection to the data store
- ❏ It creates a stored procedure call
- ❏ It executes the stored procedure call
- ❏ It packages the results from the stored procedure into a recordset which is passed to the User Centric object

The Stored Procedure

The `spPersonPropNameAuditDeletes` stored procedure calculates the number of rows it will return and then returns a list of objects that are currently deleted from the Audit table to the Data Centric object.

The main objective for this stored procedure is that the results are mirrored to the user:

```
CREATE PROCEDURE spPersonPropNameAuditDeletes
@TypeID int

AS
```

Mirror the results to the user:

```
SELECT PersonPropNameAudit.ID, PersonPropNameAudit.StampUser,
       PersonPropNameAudit.StampDateTime, PersonPropNameAudit.StampAction,
```

```
                PersonPropNameAudit.StampID, PersonPropNameAudit.ControllingTypeID,
                PersonPropNameAudit.TypeID, PersonPropNameAudit.PropertyName,
                PersonPropNameAudit.DataTypeID, PersonPropNameAudit.DataTypeName,
                PersonPropNameAudit.ListAvailable, PersonPropNameAudit.DisplayOrder,
                PersonPropNameAudit.AccessLevel, PersonPropNameAudit.SecurityLevel

FROM            PersonPropNameAudit

INNER JOIN      vPersonPropNameDelete ON
                PersonPropNameAudit.ID = vPersonPropNameDelete.ID

LEFT OUTER JOIN PersonTypePropertyBridge ON
                PersonPropNameAudit.StampID =
                PersonTypePropertyBridge.PropertyID AND
                PersonPropNameAudit.TypeID = PersonTypePropertyBridge.TypeID

WHERE           PersonPropNameAudit.StampAction = 'D' AND
                PersonPropNameAudit.TypeID = @TypeID AND
                PersonTypePropertyBridge.PropertyID IS NULL

ORDER BY StampDateTime DESC

RETURN (0)
```

The Restore From Deleted Process

The purpose of the *Restore From Deleted* process is to restore an object from a deleted state back to its state at the time of its deletion. During this process, a record is added to an Audit table that indicates that the restoration took place. The end result of this process is that the User Centric object is populated with the most current information concerning this object that exists in the data store.

The User Centric Object Code

The user centric code for the ObjectRestoreFromDeleted method is found it the clsPropName.cls file in the UCPerson.vbp project. Its main purpose is to command the data centric object to restore an object from a deleted state and to present the most current information about that object to the user interface programmer.

The ObjectRestoreFromDeleted method for the *Person* PropName is identical to its Level I counterpart. This code was discussed in Chapter 7.

The user centric ObjectRestoreFromDeleted code accomplishes three things:

- ❑ It instantiates the Data Centric object
- ❑ It calls the ObjectRestoreFromDeleted method of the Data Centric object
- ❑ It resets the object's local state

The Data Centric Object Code

The data centric ObjectRestoreFromDeleted code is found in the clsPropNameData.cls file in the DCPerson.vbp project. The purpose of this method is to update the data in the data store with changed information. It is also responsible for managing data collisions and ensuring that the updates are only performed on fresh data.

Administrating Properties

The `ObjectRestoreFromDeleted` process for the *Person* PropName is identical to its Level I counterpart. This code was discussed in Chapter 7.

The data centric `ObjectRestoreFromDeleted` code accomplishes four things:

- ❑ It opens a connection to the data store
- ❑ It creates a stored procedure call using information passed into the routine in the parameters
- ❑ It executes the stored procedure
- ❑ It returns the results of that stored procedure to the User Centric object

The Stored Procedure

The `spPersonPropNameRestore` stored procedure copies a record from the Audit table to the Object table, adds a history record to the Audit table, and returns the current representation of the object from the data store to the Data Centric object.

The order of the main objectives for this stored procedure is as follows:

- ❑ Select the record to restore from the Audit table.
- ❑ Test to find out whether or not another PSD is also using this Property Definition.
    If not then, re-insert the Property Definition and the bridge.
    If so, just insert the bridge record.
- ❑ Add an audit record to mark the restoration.
- ❑ Mirror the results of the procedure back to the user.

```
CREATE PROCEDURE spPersonPropNameRestore
@StampUser varchar(10), @RestoreID int

AS

DECLARE @trncnt int, @ErrorNumber int, @ID int, @TypeID int,
        @PropertyName varchar(60), @DataTypeID int, @ListAvailable char(1),
        @DisplayOrder int, @AccessLevel char(1), @SecurityLevel int

SELECT  @ErrorNumber = -1
```

Standard transaction handling:

```
SELECT @trncnt = @@trancount
/* issue begin or save transaction based on transaction count */
IF @trncnt = 0
   BEGIN TRANSACTION T1
ELSE
   SAVE TRANSACTION T1
```

Select the record that needs to be restored from the Audit table:

```
SELECT @ID = StampID, @TypeID = TypeID, @PropertyName = PropertyName,
       @DataTypeID = DataTypeID, @ListAvailable = ListAvailable,
       @DisplayOrder = DisplayOrder, @AccessLevel = AccessLevel,
       @SecurityLevel = SecurityLevel
```

475

```
FROM     PersonPropNameAudit

WHERE    ID = @RestoreID
```

Standard test to determine whether or not another PSD is currently using this Property Definition:

```
IF (SELECT COUNT(*) FROM PersonPropName WHERE ID = @ID) = 0
```

If no other PSDs are currently using this Property Definition, then re-insert the record with the original ID by setting the autonumbering feature of SQL Server off while inserting the record:

```
BEGIN
  SET Identity_Insert PersonPropName ON

  INSERT  PersonPropName
          (ID, ControllingTypeID, PropertyName, DataTypeID,
           ListAvailable, ConcurrencyID)

  VALUES (@ID, @TypeID, @PropertyName, @DataTypeID, @ListAvailable, 1)

  IF @@error <> 0 GOTO ErrorHandler

  SET Identity_Insert PersonPropName OFF

END
```

Insert a record into the Bridge table to re-assign this Property Definition to the PSD:

```
INSERT  PersonTypePropertyBridge
        (TypeID, PropertyID, DisplayOrder, AccessLevel,
         SecurityLevel,  ConcurrencyID)

VALUES (@TypeID, @ID, @DisplayOrder, @AccessLevel, @SecurityLevel,  1)

IF @@error <> 0 GOTO ErrorHandler
```

Add an audit record that marks the restoration:

```
INSERT PersonPropNameAudit
      (StampUser, StampAction, StampDateTime, StampID, ControllingTypeID,
       TypeID, PropertyName, DataTypeID, DataTypeName, ListAvailable,
       DisplayOrder, AccessLevel, SecurityLevel)

SELECT @StampUser, 'R', GetDate(), PersonPropName.ID,
       PersonPropName.ControllingTypeID, PersonTypePropertyBridge.TypeID,
       PersonPropName.PropertyName, PersonPropName.DataTypeID,
       Common..DataTypeObject.DataTypeName, PersonPropName.ListAvailable,
       PersonTypePropertyBridge.DisplayOrder,
       PersonTypePropertyBridge.AccessLevel,
       PersonTypePropertyBridge.SecurityLevel

FROM           PersonTypePropertyBridge

INNER JOIN     PersonPropName ON
```

```
                        PersonTypePropertyBridge.PropertyID = PersonPropName.ID

INNER JOIN              Common..DataTypeObject ON
                        PersonPropName.DataTypeID = Common..DataTypeObject.ID

WHERE                   PersonTypePropertyBridge.PropertyID = @ID AND
                        PersonTypePropertyBridge.TypeID = @TypeID

IF @@error <> 0 GOTO ErrorHandler
```

Standard commit transaction handling:

```
IF @trncnt = 0 COMMIT TRANSACTION T1
```

Mirror the results of the procedure to the user:

```
SELECT      PersonPropName.ID, PersonPropName.ControllingTypeID,
            PersonTypePropertyBridge.TypeID, PersonPropName.PropertyName,
            PersonPropName.DataTypeID, Common..DataTypeObject.DataTypeName,
            PersonPropName.ListAvailable,
            PersonTypePropertyBridge.DisplayOrder,
            PersonTypePropertyBridge.AccessLevel,
            PersonTypePropertyBridge.SecurityLevel,
            PersonPropName.ConcurrencyID AS ConcurrencyID1,
            PersonTypePropertyBridge.ConcurrencyID AS ConcurrencyID2

FROM        PersonTypePropertyBridge

INNER JOIN PersonPropName ON
            PersonTypePropertyBridge.PropertyID = PersonPropName.ID

INNER JOIN Common..DataTypeObject ON
            PersonPropName.DataTypeID = Common..DataTypeObject.ID

WHERE       PersonTypePropertyBridge.PropertyID = @ID AND
            PersonTypePropertyBridge.TypeID = @TypeID

RETURN (0)
```

Standard error handling:

```
ErrorHandler:
    ROLLBACK TRANSACTION T1
    SELECT   ErrorCondition
    FROM     Common..ErrorMessage
    WHERE    ErrorNumber = @ErrorNumber
    RETURN   (100)
```

The Audit History Process

The *Audit History* process provides the user interface programmer with a collection of objects that represent the history of a single object over some period of time.

The User Centric Object Code

The user centric `ObjectAuditHistory` code is contained in the `clsPropName.cls` file in the `UCPerson.vbp` project. The purpose of this method is to retrieve a collection that consists of all of the previous states for a particular object. Although this routine is an object rather than a collection level routine it does return a collection, so the code is really quite similar to the `Load` or `ShowDeleted` methods. The `ObjectAuditHistory` routine for the *Person* PropName is identical to its Level I counterpart. This code was discussed in Chapter 7.

The user centric `ObjectAuditHistory` code accomplishes six things:

- ❑ Collects selection information in its parameters
- ❑ It instantiates the Data Centric object
- ❑ It calls the `ObjectHistory` method of the Data Centric object using the selection information provided
- ❑ It unpacks the information about each object from a single variant array that holds all of the deleted objects
- ❑ It re-creates the individual objects from the data above
- ❑ It adds each object to the deleted objects collection.

Data Centric Code – colPropNameData.cls

The data centric `ObjectHistory` code is contained in the `colPropNameData.cls` file in the `DCPerson.vbp` project. This method is virtually the same as the `ShowDeleted` method we looked at earlier. The `ObjectHistory` routine for the *Person* PropName is identical to its Level I counterpart. This code was discussed in Chapter 7.

The data centric `ObjectHistory` code accomplishes four things:

- ❑ It opens a connection to the data store
- ❑ It creates a stored procedure call
- ❑ It executes the stored procedure call
- ❑ It packages the results from the stored procedure into a recordset which is passed to the User Centric object

The Stored Procedure

The `spPersonPropNameAuditList` stored procedure returns a list of objects from the Audit table that represent snapshots of the target object's states in time past.

The main objective for this stored procedure is to mirror the results of the stored procedure to the user:

```
CREATE PROCEDURE spPersonPropNameAuditList
@ID int, @TypeID int

AS
```

Mirror the results of this stored procedure to the user:

```
SELECT    ID, StampUser, StampDateTime, StampAction, StampID,
          ControllingTypeID, TypeID, PropertyName, DataTypeID, DataTypeName,
          ListAvailable, DisplayOrder, AccessLevel, SecurityLevel

FROM      PersonPropNameAudit

WHERE     StampID = @ID AND TypeID = @TypeID

ORDER BY StampDateTime DESC

RETURN (0)
```

The Load Process

The *Load* process returns a collection of objects that meet some criteria. For higher-level objects, the criteria may be one or several of the objects' Property Values. This method also accepts a SQL string as a parameter. We use this parameter in conjunction with Connector objects. We will go over this in great detail in Chapter 13. The *Load* process provides the user interface programmer with a collection of objects that meet some specific selection criteria.

The User Centric Obejct Code

The user centric `Load` code is contained in the `colPropName.cls` file in the `UCPerson.vbp` project. The purpose of this method is to retrieve a collection that consists of all of the previous states for a particular object. The `Load` method for the *Person* PropName is identical to its Level I counterpart. This code was discussed in Chapter 6.

The user centric `Load` code accomplishes six things:

- ❑ Collects selection information in its parameters
- ❑ It instantiates the Data Centric object
- ❑ It calls the `Fetch` method of the Data Centric object using the selection information provided
- ❑ It unpacks the information about each object from a single variant array that holds all of the objects
- ❑ It re-creates the individual objects from the data above
- ❑ It adds each object to the object collection.

The Data Centric Object Code

The data centric `Fetch` code is contained in the `colPersonData.cls` file in the `DCPerson.vbp` project. This method is virtually the same as the `FetchDeleted` method we looked at earlier. The `Fetch` method for the *Person* PropName is identical to its Level I counterpart. This code was discussed in Chapter 6.

The data centric `Fetch` code accomplishes four things:

- ❑ It opens a connection to the data store
- ❑ It creates a stored procedure call
- ❑ It executes the stored procedure call
- ❑ It packages the results from the stored procedure into a recordset which is passed to the User Centric object

479

The Stored Procedure

The main objective for this stored procedure is to mirror the results of the stored procedure to the user:

```
CREATE PROCEDURE spPersonPropNameList
@TypeID int

AS
```

Mirror the results of the stored procedure to the user:

```
SELECT  PersonPropName.ID, PersonPropName.ControllingTypeID,
        PersonTypePropertyBridge.TypeID, PersonPropName.PropertyName,
        PersonPropName.DataTypeID, Common..DataTypeObject.DataTypeName,
        PersonPropName.ListAvailable, PersonTypePropertyBridge.DisplayOrder,
        PersonTypePropertyBridge.AccessLevel,
        PersonTypePropertyBridge.SecurityLevel,
        PersonPropName.ConcurrencyID AS ConcurrencyID1,
        PersonTypePropertyBridge.ConcurrencyID AS ConcurrencyID2

FROM        PersonTypePropertyBridge

INNER JOIN PersonPropName ON
        PersonTypePropertyBridge.PropertyID = PersonPropName.ID

INNER JOIN Common..DataTypeObject ON
        PersonPropName.DataTypeID = Common..DataTypeObject.ID

WHERE       PersonTypePropertyBridge.TypeID = @TypeID

RETURN (0)
```

The Property Item Object (PropItem)

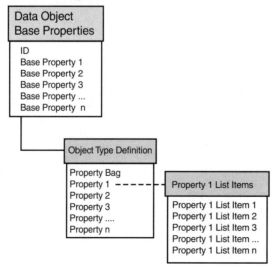

As the name suggests, the PropItem object manages the list of valid items available for a particular property. Let's take a look at how to use the PropItem object. Once we have created a property name and have set the flag indicating that a list of valid responses is available, we can assign any number of items to that property. Each item represents a valid response for the property. In the *Media* example earlier, we created an Object Type Definition named Audio. Its Property Set Definition contained two Property Names that had the ListAvailable flag set to true. The first name was Audio Media Type and it offered 8 Track, Cassette, and Reel as valid responses. The second Property Name with a list was Music Type. It offered Rock, Blues, Jazz, and Alternative as valid responses.

The PropItem object is really a specialized Level I object. It has exactly the same functionality as any other Level I object. That means that it offers a complete history, the ability to perform unlimited undo's, and the ability to restore an object from deleted. It also means that you already know how to code the PropItem object.

The Tables and Views

The PropItem object just uses the standard pair of tables we have come to expect for a Level I ECDO. By design, the PropItem object is very simple. Take a look at the PersonPropItem table. It has a field called ID; by now we know that this field is common to every other ECDO. It also has something called a PropertyID; this field is used to define a relationship between the Property Definition and the individual property items. The fact that this field is in this table means that we are defining a one-to-many relationship between the Property Definition and the property items. This is not as complicated as it sounds, all it means is that we can use the PropertyID as the selection criterion to return the correct list of items. The next field is called DisplayValue, as you might expect, this field holds the value that the user sees when they see a list of items in a combo box or something. We have taken just about the same approach with the PropItem object as we did with the PropName object earlier. In other words, all of the relationships in the data store are based upon the numeric ID values for each PropItem object – not the text values. This means that if somebody decides to change these things, we don't care in the least. As far as the database is concerned the item lists that we deliver to the users are merely additional information attached to the ID for each object. The next field, DisplayOrder, was originally supplied to allow administrators to define a particular sort order for the combo boxes. I say originally because as you might remember when we developed the Administrative User Interface, I never got around to providing this functionality at the user interface. You should really give this a shot. The objects already have the necessary plumbing and the ability to sort a pick list is something worth working for. The Audit table and the views for this object are old hat.

PersonPropItem

```
CREATE TABLE dbo.PersonPropItem
(
    ID int IDENTITY (1, 1) NOT NULL ,
    PropertyID int NOT NULL ,
    DisplayValue varchar (255) NOT NULL ,
    DisplayOrder int NOT NULL ,
    ConcurrencyID int NOT NULL
)
```

PersonPropItemAudit

```
CREATE TABLE dbo.PersonPropItemAudit
(
```

```
       ID int IDENTITY (1, 1) NOT NULL ,
       StampUser char (15) NOT NULL ,
       StampDateTime datetime NOT NULL ,
       StampAction char (1) NOT NULL ,
       StampID int NOT NULL ,
       PropertyID int NOT NULL ,
       DisplayValue varchar (255) NOT NULL ,
       DisplayOrder int NOT NULL
       )
```

vPersonPropItemDelete

```
CREATE VIEW vPersonPropItemDelete AS

SELECT StampID, 'ID'=Max(ID)

FROM    PersonPropItemAudit

WHERE   StampAction = 'D'

GROUP   BY StampID
```

The Eight Data Handling Processes

We've been through these processes many times already. By now you should have gotten the hang of it, and there's nothing new to see in the VB code for this object. Therefore, I'm just going to quickly run through the stored procedures for each process.

> *These stored procedures work in* exactly *the same way as those we discussed in Chapters 6 and 7, but I have given them here just so you can be sure what's going on at the Data sphere from the perspective of the Property Bag. Feel free to skip them if you are already comfortable with what's going on.*

The Fetch Process Stored Procedure

The spPersonPropItemGet stored procedure selects a single object from the database and sends the results to the Data Centric object.

The order of the main objectives for this stored procedure is as follows:

❑   Select the record from the data store
❑   Mirror the results to the user

```
CREATE PROCEDURE spPersonPropItemGet
@ID int

AS

SELECT ID, PropertyID, DisplayValue, DisplayOrder, ConcurrencyID AS ConcurrencyID1

FROM    PersonPropItem

WHERE   ID = @ID
```

The Insert Process Stored Procedure

The `spPersonPropItemInsert` stored procedure adds a new record to the object table, adds a history record to the Audit table, and returns the current representation of the object from the data store to the data centric object.

The order of the main objectives for this stored procedure is as follows:

- ❑ Insert a new property record if this one is new and not shared
- ❑ Assign this Property Definition to the PSD indicated by the TypeID
- ❑ Insert an audit record that marks the insertion
- ❑ Mirror the results of the procedure back to the user

```
CREATE PROCEDURE spPersonPropItemInsert
@StampUser varchar(10), @PropertyID int, @DisplayValue varchar (255),
@DisplayOrder int

AS

DECLARE @trncnt int, @ErrorNumber int, @ID int

SELECT @ErrorNumber = -1
```

Standard transaction handling:

```
SELECT @trncnt = @@trancount
/* issue begin or save transaction based on transaction count */
IF @trncnt = 0
    BEGIN TRANSACTION T1
ELSE
    SAVE TRANSACTION T1
```

Insert a new record into the Object table:

```
INSERT PersonPropItem
       (PropertyID, DisplayValue, DisplayOrder, ConcurrencyID)

VALUES (@PropertyID, @DisplayValue, @DisplayOrder, 1)

IF @@Error <> 0 GOTO ErrorHandler

SELECT @ID = @@Identity
```

Add a record to the Audit table to mark the insertion:

```
INSERT PersonPropItemAudit
       (StampUser, StampDateTime, StampAction, StampID, PropertyID,
       DisplayValue, DisplayOrder)

SELECT @StampUser, GetDate(), 'I', ID, PropertyID, DisplayValue, DisplayOrder

FROM   PersonPropItem

WHERE  ID = @ID

IF @@Error <> 0 GOTO ErrorHandler
```

Standard commit transaction handling:

```
IF @trncnt = 0 COMMIT TRANSACTION T1
```

Mirror the results of this stored procedure to the user:

```
SELECT   ID, PropertyID, DisplayValue, DisplayOrder, ConcurrencyID AS
         ConcurrencyID1

FROM     PersonPropItem

WHERE    ID = @ID

RETURN (0)
```

Standard error handling:

```
ErrorHandler:
    ROLLBACK TRANSACTION T1
    SELECT    ErrorCondition
    FROM      Common..ErrorMessage
    WHERE     ErrorNumber = @ErrorNumber
    RETURN    (100)
```

The Update Process Stored Procedure

The `spPersonPropItemUpdate` stored procedure changes a record in the Object table, adds a history record to the Audit table, and returns the current representation of the object from the data store to the data centric object.

The order of the main objectives for this stored procedure is as follows:

❑   Add an audit record to mark the update
❑   Update the Property Definition
❑   Update the PSD assignment which is stored in the Bridge table
❑   Mirror the results of the procedure back to the user

```
CREATE PROCEDURE spPersonPropItemUpdate
@StampUser varchar(10), @ID int, @PropertyID int, @DisplayValue varchar (255),
@DisplayOrder int, @ConcurrencyID1 int

AS

DECLARE @trncnt int, @ErrorNumber int, @rows int, @ConcurrencyID int, @err int

SELECT @ErrorNumber = -1
SELECT @ConcurrencyID = @ConcurrencyID1
```

Standard transaction handling:

```
SELECT @trncnt = @@trancount
/* issue begin or save transaction based on transaction count */
IF @trncnt = 0
```

```
    BEGIN TRANSACTION T1
ELSE
    SAVE TRANSACTION T1
```

Add an audit record to mark the data change before updating the data:

```
INSERT PersonPropItemAudit
     (StampUser, StampDateTime, StampAction, StampID, PropertyID, DisplayValue,
     DisplayOrder)

SELECT @StampUser, GetDate(), 'U', ID, PropertyID, DisplayValue, DisplayOrder

FROM   PersonPropItem

WHERE  ID = @ID

IF @@Error <> 0 GOTO ErrorHandler
```

Update the record in the Object table:

```
UPDATE PersonPropItem

SET PropertyID = @PropertyID, DisplayValue = @DisplayValue,
    DisplayOrder = @DisplayOrder, ConcurrencyID = ConcurrencyID +1

WHERE  ID = @ID AND ConcurrencyID = @ConcurrencyID

SELECT @err = @@error, @rows = @@RowCount

IF @err <> 0 GOTO ErrorHandler
```

Standard concurrency error handling:

```
IF @rows = 0
  BEGIN
      SELECT @ErrorNumber = 100
      GOTO ErrorHandler
  END
```

Standard commit transaction handling:

```
IF @trncnt = 0 COMMIT TRANSACTION t1
```

Mirror the results from this stored procedure back to the user:

```
SELECT ID, PropertyID, DisplayValue, DisplayOrder, ConcurrencyID AS ConcurrencyID1

FROM PersonPropItem

WHERE  ID = @ID

RETURN (0)
```

Standard error handling:

```
ErrorHandler:
    ROLLBACK TRANSACTION T1
    SELECT    ErrorCondition
    FROM      Common..ErrorMessage
    WHERE     ErrorNumber = @ErrorNumber
    RETURN    (100)
```

The Delete Process Stored Procedure

The `spPersonPropItemDelete` stored procedure deletes a record from the Object table, adds a history record to the Audit table, and returns either an error message or a count of 1 which indicates success.

The order of the main objectives for this stored procedure is as follows:

❑ Add an audit record to mark the deletion.

❑ Delete the assignment record from the Bridge table.

❑ Test to find out whether or not another PSD is also using this Property Definition.
   If not, then delete the Property Definition.
   If so, then set the controlling TypeID if required.

❑ Mirror the results of the procedure back to the user.

```
CREATE PROCEDURE spPersonPropItemDelete
@StampUser varchar(10), @ID int, @ConcurrencyID1 int

AS

DECLARE @trncnt int, @ErrorNumber int, @rows int, @err int, @ConcurrencyID int

SELECT @ErrorNumber = -1
SELECT @ConcurrencyID = @ConcurrencyID1
```

Standard transaction handling:

```
SELECT @trncnt = @@trancount
/* issue begin or save transaction based on transaction count */
IF @trncnt = 0
   BEGIN TRANSACTION T1
ELSE
   SAVE TRANSACTION T1
```

Add an audit record that marks the deletion before we delete the record:

```
INSERT PersonPropItemAudit
       (StampUser, StampDateTime, StampAction, StampID, PropertyID,
       DisplayValue, DisplayOrder)
SELECT @StampUser, GetDate(), 'D', ID, PropertyID, DisplayValue, DisplayOrder

FROM   PersonPropItem
```

Retrieve audit record to be restored:

```
SELECT @ID = StampID, @PropertyID = PropertyID,
       @DisplayValue = DisplayValue, @DisplayOrder = DisplayOrder

FROM PersonPropItemAudit

WHERE ID = @RestoreID
```

Re-add the PersonPropItem record:

```
SET Identity_Insert PersonPropItem ON
INSERT PersonPropItem
       (ID, PropertyID, DisplayValue, DisplayOrder, ConcurrencyID)
VALUES (@ID, @PropertyID, @DisplayValue, @DisplayOrder, 1)

IF @@Error <> 0 GOTO ErrorHandler

SET Identity_Insert PersonPropItem OFF
```

Add audit record:

```
INSERT PersonPropItemAudit
       (StampUser, StampDateTime, StampAction, StampID, PropertyID,
        DisplayValue, DisplayOrder)

SELECT @StampUser, GetDate(), 'R', ID, PropertyID, DisplayValue,
       DisplayOrder

FROM    PersonPropItem

WHERE   ID = @ID

IF @@Error <> 0 GOTO ErrorHandler
```

Standard commit transaction handling:

```
IF @trncnt = 0 COMMIT TRANSACTION t1
```

Return restored record for verification:

```
SELECT ID, PropertyID, DisplayValue, DisplayOrder,
       ConcurrencyID As ConcurrencyID1

FROM    PersonPropItem

WHERE   ID = @ID

RETURN(0)
```

Standard Error Handling:

```
ErrorHandler:
    ROLLBACK TRANSACTION t1
    SELECT   ErrorCondition
    FROM     Common..ErrorMessage
    WHERE    ErrorNumber = @ErrorNumber
    RETURN   (100)
```

The Show Deleted Process Stored Procedure

The `spPersonPropItemAuditDeletes` stored procedure returns a list of objects that are currently deleted from the Audit table to the Data Centric object.

```
CREATE PROCEDURE spPersonPropItemAuditDeletes
@PropertyID int

AS

SELECT   PersonPropItemAudit.StampID,
         PersonPropItemAudit.StampUser, PersonPropItemAudit.StampDateTime,
```

```
         PersonPropItemAudit.StampAction, PersonPropItemAudit.ID,
         PersonPropItemAudit.PropertyID, PersonPropItemAudit.DisplayValue,
         PersonPropItemAudit.DisplayOrder

FROM            PersonPropItemAudit

INNER JOIN      vPersonPropItemDelete ON
                PersonPropItemAudit.ID = vPersonPropItemDelete.ID

LEFT OUTER JOIN PersonPropItem ON
                PersonPropItemAudit.StampID = PersonPropItem.ID

WHERE           PersonPropItemAudit.StampAction = 'D' AND
                PersonPropItem.ID IS NULL AND
                PersonPropItemAudit.PropertyID=@PropertyID

ORDER BY StampDateTime DESC

RETURN (0)
```

The Restore From Deleted Process Stored Process

The `spPersonPropItemRestore` stored procedure copies a record from the Audit table to the Object table, adds a history record to the Audit table, and returns the current representation of the object from the data store to the data centric object.

```
CREATE PROCEDURE spPersonPropItemRestore
@StampUser varchar(10), @RestoreID int

AS

DECLARE @trncnt int, @ErrorNumber int, @ID int, @PropertyID int,
        @DisplayValue varchar (255), @DisplayOrder int

SELECT  @ErrorNumber = -1
```

Standard transaction handling:

```
SELECT @trncnt = @@trancount

IF @trncnt = 0
   BEGIN TRANSACTION T1
ELSE
   SAVE TRANSACTION T1
```

Select the record to restore from the Audit table:

```
SELECT @ID = StampID, @PropertyID = PropertyID, @DisplayValue = DisplayValue,
    @DisplayOrder = DisplayOrder

FROM    PersonPropItemAudit

WHERE   ID = @RestoreID
```

Add the item record:

```
SET Identity_Insert PersonPropItem ON

INSERT PersonPropItem
    (ID, PropertyID, DisplayValue, DisplayOrder, ConcurrencyID)

VALUES
    (@ID, @PropertyID, @DisplayValue, @DisplayOrder, 1)

IF @@Error <> 0 GOTO ErrorHandler

SET Identity_Insert PersonPropItem OFF
```

Add the audit record:

```
INSERT PersonPropItemAudit
    (StampUser, StampDateTime, StampAction, StampID, PropertyID,
    DisplayValue, DisplayOrder)

SELECT @StampUser, GetDate(), 'R', ID, PropertyID, DisplayValue, DisplayOrder

FROM PersonPropItem

WHERE   ID = @ID

IF @@Error <> 0 GOTO ErrorHandler
```

Standard commit transaction handling:

```
IF @trncnt = 0 COMMIT TRANSACTION T1
```

Mirror the results from this stored procedure to the user:

```
SELECT ID, PropertyID, DisplayValue, DisplayOrder, ConcurrencyID AS ConcurrencyID1

FROM    PersonPropItem

WHERE   ID = @ID

RETURN(0)
```

Standard error handling:

```
ErrorHandler:
    ROLLBACK TRANSACTION T1
```

```
SELECT    ErrorCondition
FROM      Common..ErrorMessage
WHERE     ErrorNumber = @ErrorNumber
RETURN    (100)
```

The Audit History Process Stored Procedure

The spPersonPropItemAuditList stored procedure calculates the number of rows it will return and then returns a list of objects from the Audit table that represent snapshots of the target object's states in time past.

The main objective is simply to mirror the results of the stored procedure to the user:

```
CREATE PROCEDURE spPersonPropItemAuditList
@StampID int

AS

SELECT    StampID, StampUser, StampDateTime, StampAction,
          ID, PropertyID, DisplayValue, DisplayOrder

FROM      PersonPropItemAudit

WHERE     StampID = @StampID

ORDER BY StampDateTime DESC

RETURN (0)
```

The Load Process Stored Procedure

The spPersonPropItemList stored procedure calculates the number of rows it will return and then returns a list of objects from the Object table.

The order of the main objectives for this stored procedure is as follows:

- ❑ Determine how many rows this stored procedure will return
- ❑ Mirror the results of the stored procedure to the user

```
CREATE PROCEDURE spPersonPropItemList
@PropertyID int

AS

DECLARE @CountOfRows int
```

Determine how many rows this stored procedure will return:

```
SELECT @CountOfRows =
       (SELECT Count(*)
        FROM   PersonPropItem
        WHERE  PropertyID = @PropertyID)

SELECT 'RowCount' = @CountOfRows, ID, PropertyID, DisplayValue, DisplayOrder
```

```
FROM      PersonPropItem

WHERE     PropertyID = @PropertyID

RETURN    (0)
```

Summary

The code in this chapter along with the code in the previous chapter provides us with all of the tools we need to create an Administrative Interface for our Property Bag. Combining this programmable interface with the user interface in Chapter 9 creates a management system that can be used for any higher-level object. This Administrative Interface is independent of any particular user interface. The sample application in Chapter 16 shows how to use this programmable interface with a DHTML web-based interface. This is the user interface we use for our enterprise. It gives a high level of control from literally anywhere in the world.

So far, we've only really covered half the functionality of the Property Bag. In the next chapter, we'll move onto the remaining half - the Production User Interface.

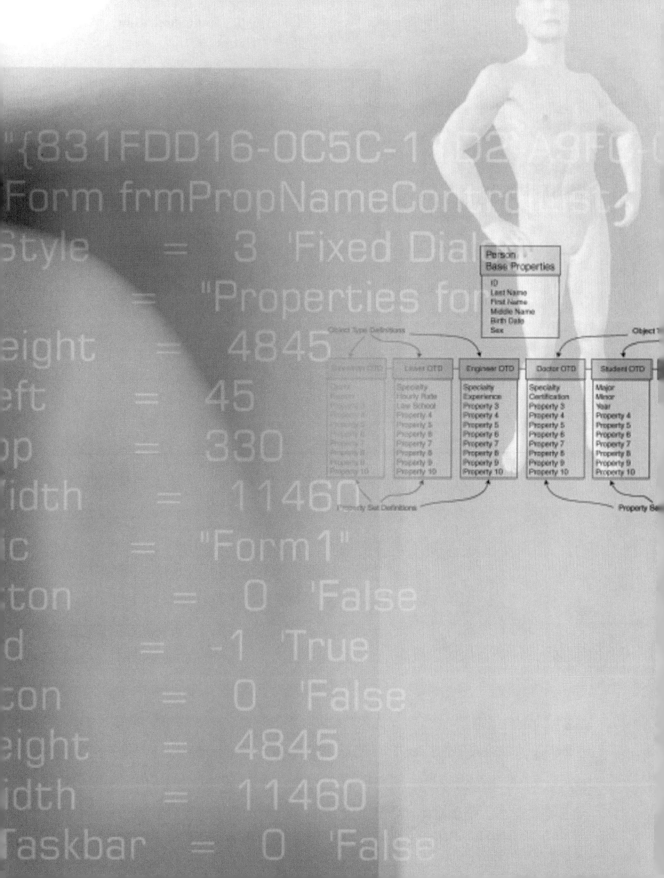

12

Working with the Property Bag

In the last chapter, we learned that we can work with the Property Bag in two very different ways. We saw that in order to define the Property Bag for a particular Property Set Definition, all we really need is the *concept* of the Property Bag. What we actually work with is individual Property Definitions. We learned that when we are defining Property Definitions we are working with the Property Bag's programmable Administrative Interface.

We also briefly saw that there is another way to work with the Property Bag. That way is to use the Property Bag directly to set the values of the various properties defined by the Property Bag. In order to do this we need to use the Property Bag's programmable Production Interface. This is what we'll learn to build in this chapter.

Technically, this may be the most important chapter in this whole book. The Property Bag's programmable Production Interface is the mechanism that makes 4-Dimensional Data Objects possible. It gives us a simple, reproducible way to add extended properties to any Level II object. The Property Bag is what can transform a simple *Person* object into anything from an Astronaut to a Zoologist. And, best of all, the programmable Production Interface exposes a simple tool located on the User Centric sphere that can be mastered by even junior programmers.

The Property Bag's Programmable Production Interface

The Property Bag handles the complex logic that is necessary to store and retrieve Property Name/Value pairs from the data store. Each time a new object (or new type for an existing object) is created, the Property Bag constructs a complete, but empty, set of extended properties for that object. If an object is deleted, the Property Bag handles the deletion of the extended property set. If an object is restored from a deleted state, the Property Bag handles the restoration of *each* and *every* extended property without intervention. However, from the perspective of the casual developer or user interface programmer, the Property Bag's programmable Production Interface simply exposes all of that functionality as a single object, the **PropBag object**.

Of course, the PropBag object is anything but simple. It relies upon some fairly sophisticated coding at both the Data sphere and the Data Centric sphere. In fact, the PropBag object can probably be best viewed more as a proxy for a number of related sub-objects rather than as the PropBag object itself. Let me explain what it does.

The PropBag object instantiates and controls the actions of several sub-objects. Through these objects, it requests related information from different tables in the data store, pieces together all of those bits of information, and delivers them as single object that is exposed to the User Centric sphere as the PropBag object. Remember when we learned about views? We found that we could join two or more tables with a SELECT statement and have the results from that join appear as single table. Well, that is kind of what we are doing with the Property Bag. The Property Bag gives us the illusion that we are working with a single object, like the view gives us the illusion that we are working with a single table. So, when the user updates a Property Value, the PropBag object appears to accept the changes and manage the transaction. But behind the scenes, it really instantiates each of the necessary sub-objects and updates the information in the data store using each sub-object's data handling processes.

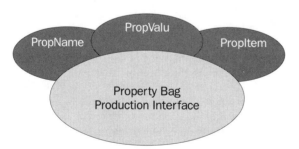

Whenever a new object of a particular type is added to the data store, the PropBag object builds an appropriate property set which prepares the object to store the extended information it was designed to manage. In many ways, the Production Interface of the PropBag object is like a funnel. It provides a single point of exit and entry for an object's Property Values. But behind the scenes, it widens its scope to encompass the many portions of the data store that can be affected when a Property Value is added, deleted, or changed.

Due to the complex nature of the Property Bag, some of the functionality is hidden from the user interface programmer and the end user. For instance while it is possible to delete a Property Definition using the programmable Administrative Interface, it is not possible to delete a Property Definition using the programmable Production Interface. Think about it, to ensure data integrity, we need to make sure that all objects that have a particular OTD have the full compliment of the Property Definitions given by the PSD. It wouldn't do to have Property Definitions deleted from some objects and not others. To ensure that we maintain this integrity, we don't even give the user interface programmer the ability delete a Property Definition from within the Production Interface. This makes it impossible for the user interface programmer to accidentally give the casual end users this functionality. Of course, the user interface programmer always has the option of using the programmable Administrative Interface to accomplish deleting a Property Definition.

In order for the PropBag object to function, it requires that several sub-objects be available to it. These are:

- ❑ The Property Definition object (PropName)
- ❑ The Property Item object (PropItem)
- ❑ The Property Value object (PropValu)

We saw how to build the PropName and PropItem objects in the previous chapter, so let's move on to considering the PropValu object.

The Property Value (PropValu) Object

The Property Value, or PropValu, object is used to manage the *values* within a particular property. This as you may recall, is the main purpose of the Production Interface. However, we don't use this object as you might expect. Instead of exposing it directly as part of the programmable Production Interface we hide it behind the PropBag object. This is because in order to manage Property Values we also need to work with the PropName and PropItem objects. By only exposing the PropBag object to the Production user we can hide all the complexity of the object interactions behind a simple programmable interface.

In terms of coding the PropValu object, we need to mutate our Enterprise Caliber Data Object a bit, for although the PropValu object exhibits many behaviors common to EDCOs, it is at the same time used in a very unique way.

It never gets instantiated at any sphere other than the Data Centric sphere. And it is never instantiated as a stand-alone object. It is designed to be controlled by the PropBag object. This means that although we will find most of the code for the 8 basic data handling processes on the Data Centric sphere we will find none for the User Centric sphere.

The Tables

Although the PropValu object doesn't really expose a User Centric half, at its core it is still an Enterprise Caliber Data Object. That means that we still need to provide it with the standard Object and Audit tables it needs to manage a temporal relationship.

The PersonPropValu Table

The Property Value table is used to store the particular Property Values for a given Property Definition – owner combination. Look at the fields in this table. You will see that there is an ID field. This gives each Property Value a unique identifier in the data store. We use this field exactly the same way that we have used the ID field in all other data objects. The next field, ObjectID, is used to relate this particular set of Property Values back to some base object. In other words, if have a base person named *John* and he has six extended Property Values in the data store, we would be able to retrieve all six of those values by matching up *John*'s ID with the ObjectIDs in this table. The next field, PropertyID, is used to pair up this Property Value with a particular Property Name. Let's go back to *John* again. Let's say that one of the extended properties for *John* was something we called Mother's Maiden Name. The PropertyID field in this table, contains the ID that points back to the Property Name, in this case, Mother's Maiden Name. The next field is why we are here in the first place. It contains the value that we want to associate with the Property Name. So, if *John*'s mother's maiden name was *Smith*, we would find the Property Value "Smith" in this field.

```
CREATE TABLE dbo.PersonPropValu
  (
  ID int IDENTITY (1, 1) NOT NULL ,
  ObjectID int NOT NULL ,
  PropertyID int NOT NULL ,
  PropertyValue varchar (255) NULL ,
  ConcurrencyID int NOT NULL
  )
```

The PersonPropValuAudit Table

The Property Value Audit table is used to store a complete history for each individual Property Value. This gives 4-Dimensional Data Objects the ability to track a history for each Property Value. Of course, as you know by now, this is the table we use to be able to restore an object from a deleted state and offer the user the ability to perform unlimited undo's.

```
CREATE TABLE dbo.PersonPropValuAudit
  (
  ID int IDENTITY (1, 1) NOT NULL ,
  StampUser char (15) NOT NULL ,
  StampDateTime datetime NOT NULL ,
  StampAction char (1) NOT NULL ,
  StampID int NOT NULL ,
  OwnerID int NOT NULL ,
  PropertyID int NOT NULL ,
  Value varchar (255) NULL ,
  Name varchar (60) NOT NULL
  )
```

The Eight Data Handling Processes

As I said before, the PropValu object is an Enterprise Caliber Data Object. That means that it has the ability to handle each of the eight data handling processes that we have been working with throughout this book. But as we go through this section, it is important to remember that we are using the PropValu object as something that is controlled by the PropBag object. We will make some small, but important, changes to the way we expose these processes due to the PropValue object's subordinate nature. Although it is a challenge to write the code for this object, I have some very good news for you. It is possible to write this code once and reuse it as a portion of a generic PropBag object. This code does not need to change from object-to-object other than in the minor ways indicated. Of course, although you can reuse the VB portion of the Property Bag for every object, you do still need to create the necessary tables, views, and stored procedures in the data store. It is an excellent exercise. My teams have created a single Property Bag object that accepts the name of the object as a parameter. I would like to suggest that you make the same changes to this code. Although our sample here is for a specific object, the *Person* object, you will find that I have shown you the changes you might make to generalize the PropBag object.

We need to extend our `PersonObjectPropBag` group file some more to include the additional code modules we need for this chapter. Using the table below, add the following files to `PersonObjectPropBag.vbg`:

System Sphere	Directory	Source File Name
User Centric	\..\Ch12\UCObject\	clsPropBag.cls
(UCPerson.vbp)	\..\Ch12\UCObject\	colPropBags.cls
Data Centric	\..\Ch12\DCObject\	clsPropBagData.cls
(DCPerson.vbp)	\..\Ch12\DCObject\	colPropBagData.cls
	\..\Ch12\DCObject\	clsPropValuData.cls
	\..\Ch12\DCObject\	colPropValuData.cls
	\..\Ch12\DCObject\	clsPropBagMgr.cls
	\..\Ch12\DCObject\	colPropBagMgr.cls
	\..\Ch12\DCObject\	clsPropValueMgr
	\..\Ch12\DCObject\	colPropValueMgr.cls

The Fetch Process

The Property Bag object's Production Interface does not offer the ability to fetch a *single* object since the PropValu object always returns the *entire* collection of properties for a given extended object. However, we still need to write an `spPersonPropValuGet` stored procedure. Remember that this is also used by the *Update* and *Delete* processes to test the freshness of the data.

The Stored Procedure

This stored procedure can be used for any object that you build. The only thing that has to be changed is the base name for the target object as shown in the example below:

Change all references to `Person`:

```
CREATE PROCEDURE spPersonPropValuGet
```

To read the name of the target object:

```
CREATE PROCEDURE spObjectNamePropValuGet
```

The stored procedure is quite straight forward except that it contains a new piece of SQL syntax that we haven't encountered before. We'll discuss it below:

```
CREATE PROCEDURE spPersonPropValuGet
@ID int

AS

SELECT PersonPropValu.ID, PersonPropValu.ObjectID As OwnerID,
       PersonPropValu.PropertyID, PersonPropName.PropertyName As Name,

       (CASE PersonPropName.ListAvailable
           WHEN 'Y' THEN (
               SELECT  DisplayValue
               FROM    PersonPropItem
               WHERE   CONVERT(char(10),ID) = PersonPropValu.PropertyValue)
           ELSE
               PersonPropValu.PropertyValue
           END) AS Value, PersonPropValu.ConcurrencyID AS ConcurrencyID1

FROM          PersonPropName

INNER JOIN    PersonPropValu ON
              PersonPropName.ID = PersonPropValu.PropertyID

WHERE         PersonPropValu.ID = @ID

RETURN (0)
```

The new syntax is for the CASE statement. The syntax for the SQL CASE statement is as follows:

```
CASE expression
    WHEN expression1 THEN expression1
    [[WHEN expression2 THEN expression2] [...]]
    [ELSE expressionN]
END
```

The syntax is similar to the VB Case statement except for the THEN keyword. Here is the same Case statement using SQL and VB for comparison:

```
CASE intTestValue
     WHEN 1 THEN intReturnValue = 2
     WHEN 2 THEN intReturnValue = 3
     ELSE intReturnValue = 0
END

Select Case intTestValue
     Case 1
          IntReturnValue = 2
     Case 2
          IntReturnValue = 3
     Case Else
          IntReturnValue = 0
End Select
```

Note that in our code we have enclosed the entire CASE statement in parenthesis and set our column named Value equal to the result of the parenthetical statement. This has the effect of returning the value that results from the CASE statement as a value in the column specified.

The Insert Process

The Property Bag's Production Interface does not allow the casual user to insert a value into the data store. Think about this. Property Values mean nothing at all unless they can be related back to a Property Name. Remember we talked about a guy named *John* earlier and we said that in the data store we had a Property Value assigned to him that contained his Mother's Maiden Name. We also said that the value in this field was "Smith". Suppose that rather than using the Property Bag to manage the transaction we just inserted the Property Value "Smith" into the data store and related it back to *John* but we forgot to include or incorrectly identified the relationship between the Property Value and the Property Name. What we would end up with was a value assigned to *John* that contained the word "Smith", but we wouldn't know what this value meant. The word "Smith" might mean that John crafts horseshoes for a living for all we know.

> **Property Values are *worthless* without their related Property Names.**

This relationship between the Property Value, the Property Name, and the property's Owner is critical. It must be handled perfectly each and every time. So, rather than taking the chance that someone might define this relationship for an object incorrectly, we encapsulate this definition in the Property Bag.

What this means for the PropValu *Insert* Process is that it is *only* controlled from within the Property Bag. The code we need to write for the Data Centric PropValu's object Insert subroutine is really the same as the routine wrote way back in Chapter 6.

The Data Centric Object Code – clsPropValuData.cls

```
Public Sub ObjectInsert(lngStampID As Long, lngID As Long, lngOwnerID As Long, _
              lngPropertyID As Long, lngOwnerTypeID As Long, _
              dtmStampDateTime As Variant, intDataLocking As Integer, _
              blnChangeAll As Boolean, strStampUser As String, _
              strStampAction As String, strDataMessage As String, _
              strValue As String, strName As String)
```

```
Dim strSQL As String

Dim ctxObject As ObjectContext
Set ctxObject = GetObjectContext()


On Error Goto ObjectInsertError

Dim ThisConnection As ADODB.Connection
Dim ThisRecordset As ADODB.Recordset

Set ThisConnection = New ADODB.Connection
Set ThisRecordset = New ADODB.Recordset

ThisConnection.Open mstrConnect, GetLogon(mstrConnect), GetPassword(mstrConnect)

strSQL = "spPersonPropValuInsert " & _
         jamQuote & strStampUser & jamQuote & jamComma & _
         lngOwnerID & jamComma & _
         lngPropertyID & jamComma & _
         jamQuote & strValue & jamQuote

On Error Resume Next

ThisRecordset.Open strSQL, ThisConnection

If ThisConnection.Errors.Count > 0 Then
   strDataMessage = ThisConnection.Errors(0).Description
  'Free up the object in MTS and set the Transaction Aborted flag
   ctxObject.SetAbort
Else

   If Not ThisRecordset.EOF Then

      If ThisRecordset.Fields(0).Name = "ErrorCondition" Then
         strDataMessage = ThisRecordset.Fields(0).Value
        ' Free up the object in MTS and set the Transaction Aborted flag
         ctxObject.SetAbort
      Else
        ' This Resets the Starting Values with the current values in the UC
        ' Object
         lngID = ThisRecordset.Fields("ID").Value
         lngOwnerID = ThisRecordset.Fields("OwnerID").Value
         lngPropertyID = ThisRecordset.Fields("PropertyID").Value
         lngOwnerTypeID = ThisRecordset.Fields("OwnerTypeID").Value
         strDataMessage = ""
         strValue = FixNulls(ThisRecordset.Fields("Value").Value)
         strName = FixNulls(ThisRecordset.Fields("Name").Value)
        ' Free up the object in MTS and set the Transaction Completed flag
         ctxObject.SetComplete
      End If

   Else
      strDataMessage = "Unable to Insert Record"
     ' Free up the object in MTS and set the Transaction Aborted flag
      ctxObject.SetAbort
   End If

End If
```

```
    Exit Sub

    ThisConnection.Close
    Set ThisConnection = Nothing
    Set ctxObject = Nothing

ObjectInsertError:

    Error Handler

End Sub
```

The Stored Procedure

This stored procedure can be used for any object that you build. The fields for the Property Bag table are always the same for every object. The only thing that changes from one object to another is that each object has its own table; all of the tables have an identical structure. This means that the only thing that has to be changed in this stored procedure is the base name for the target object.

The first portion of the stored procedure handles those topics we discussed in earlier chapters, like transaction handling, error handling, etc. so we won't go over those topics again. Instead I would like to direct your attention to the next section of the stored procedure:

```
CREATE PROCEDURE spPersonPropValuInsert
@StampUser varchar(10), @OwnerID int, @PropertyID int, @Value varchar(255)

AS

DECLARE @trncnt int, @ID int, @ErrorNumber int, @retValue int,
        @ListAvailable  char(1), @StoreValue varchar(255)

SELECT @ErrorNumber = -1
```

Standard transaction handling:

```
SELECT @trncnt = @@trancount
/* issue begin or save transaction based on transaction count */
IF @trncnt = 0
    BEGIN TRANSACTION T1
ELSE
    SAVE TRANSACTION T1
```

Remember that it is possible for us to define a list of valid responses for a property. This portion of the stored procedure is used to test for the existence of a list of items. All it does is to return the value we entered when we defined this particular property. Remember that we used a combo box to indicate whether or not a list was available. If there was, we chose "Y" from the combo box if not, we chose "N". Well all this select statement is doing is finding out whether we picked "Y" or "N". The variable @ListAvailable will contain either "Y" or "N" after this line executes:

```
SELECT @ListAvailable = (SELECT ListAvailable
                         FROM   PersonPropName
                         WHERE  ID = @PropertyID)
```

The next line may seem a little curious. It speaks to an issue we haven't really talked about just yet. It is possible to restore a Property Definition and all of its related values. Think about it. Suppose we deleted *John* from the data store. Now, *John*'s base object is an ECDO - That means that we can restore *John* if we want to. Of course, not only will we need to restore *John*, but we will also need to restore each and every property that was related to *John* at the same time. Remember from the previous chapters that when we restore anything from a deleted state we are really re-inserting that thing back into the Object table. It works the same way for Property Name/Value pairs. The next SELECT statement is used to determine whether this particular insert is really a restore in disguise. All it does is to attempt to retrieve a record from the Audit table. If it is found, then the @ID variable will not be equal to zero:

```
SELECT @ID =
    (SELECT       PersonPropValuAudit.ID
     FROM         vPersonPropValuDelete
     INNER JOIN PersonPropValuAudit ON
                  vPersonPropValuDelete.ID = PersonPropValuAudit.ID
     WHERE        PersonPropValuAudit.PropertyID = @PropertyID AND
                  PersonPropValuAudit.OwnerID = @OwnerID)
```

If the @ID variable is other than zero, then perform a restoration rather than an insertion:

```
IF @ID <> 0
   BEGIN
       EXEC @retValue = spPersonPropValuRestore @StampUser, @ID
       IF @retValue <> 0 GOTO ErrorHandler
   END
```

Otherwise just insert the record:

```
ELSE
   BEGIN
      IF @ListAvailable = 'Y' AND @Value <> ''
          BEGIN
```

This SELECT statement is just used to perform the translation between the display value sent into the stored procedure and the ID of the item which is the value we really want to store. At the present time, we are working to find another way to handle this particular piece of code. The CONVERT function is a dead giveaway that there is a better way to handle this block of code. One of the things we are looking at is adding another field to the Property Value table that would allow us to store both the ID and the Display values for an object with an Item list. Anyway...

```
          SELECT @StoreValue = (SELECT  CONVERT(Char(10),ID)
                                FROM    PersonPropItem(Updlock)
                                WHERE   DisplayValue = @Value AND
                                        PropertyID = @PropertyID)
          IF IsNull(@StoreValue,'') = ''
```

If this Property Definition indicated that this property should use a list and we don't find a value, then that means that something is wrong. This should never happen as long as all database updates are handled through the data objects, but this little error handler is designed to trap the error in case someone deleted an item from the database without going through the object:

```
              BEGIN
                SELECT @ErrorNumber = 103
                GOTO ErrorHandler
              END
          END
        ELSE
```

If a list is not indicated, then we set the `@StoreValue` variable equal to the parameter that was passed into the routine. Just in case this is getting a little difficult to follow, remember that the next statement is really the second leg of the `IF` statement that checked for the existence of a list of items earlier:

```
      SELECT @StoreValue = @Value
```

So, at this point, the `@StoreValue` variable either has the value that was passed into the procedure or a translated Item ID. In either case we can finally perform the insert:

```
INSERT PersonPropValu
    (ObjectID, PropertyID, PropertyValue, ConcurrencyID)

VALUES
    (@OwnerID, @PropertyID, @StoreValue, 1)
      IF @@error <> 0 GOTO ErrorHandler

SELECT @ID = @@Identity
```

As always, we add a record to the Audit table to mark the insertion

```
INSERT PersonPropValuAudit
  (StampUser, StampAction, StampDateTime, StampID, OwnerID, PropertyID, Name,
  Value)

SELECT @StampUser, 'I', GetDate(), PersonPropValu.ID, PersonPropValu.ObjectID,
       PersonPropValu.PropertyID, PersonPropName.PropertyName

       (CASE PersonPropName.ListAvailable
           WHEN 'Y' THEN (
               SELECT  DisplayValue
               FROM    PersonPropItem
               WHERE   CONVERT(char(10),ID) = PersonPropValu.PropertyValue)
           ELSE
               PersonPropValu.PropertyValue
       END) AS Value

FROM            PersonPropName

INNER JOIN      PersonPropValu ON
                PersonPropName.ID = PersonPropValu.PropertyID

LEFT OUTER JOIN PersonPropItem ON
                PersonPropValu.PropertyID = PersonPropItem.PropertyID AND
                PersonPropValu.PropertyValue =
                         CONVERT(Char(10),PersonPropItem.ID)

WHERE           PersonPropValu.ID = @ID
      IF @@error <> 0 GOTO ErrorHandler
```

Then we mirror the results from this stored procedure back to the user:

```
SELECT PersonPropValu.ID, PersonPropValu.ObjectID As OwnerID,
       PersonPropValu.PropertyID, PersonPropName.PropertyName AS Name,

       (CASE PersonPropName.ListAvailable
           WHEN 'Y' THEN (
               SELECT  DisplayValue
               FROM    PersonPropItem
               WHERE   CONVERT(char(10),ID) = PersonPropValu.PropertyValue)
           ELSE
               PersonPropValu.PropertyValue
           END) AS Value, PersonPropValu.ConcurrencyID AS ConcurrencyID1

FROM            PersonPropName

INNER JOIN      PersonPropValu ON
                PersonPropName.ID = PersonPropValu.PropertyID

WHERE           PersonPropValu.ID = @ID

END
```

Standard commit transaction handling:

```
IF @trncnt = 0 COMMIT TRANSACTION T1
```

Standard error handling:

```
ErrorHandler:
    ROLLBACK TRANSACTION T1
    SELECT    ErrorCondition
    FROM      Common..ErrorMessage
    WHERE     ErrorNumber = @ErrorNumber
    RETURN    (100)
```

The Update Process

Under all circumstances the PropValu *Update* process is really what we expose to the casual user. Recall that we always build a set of Property Name/Value pairs for each object when the object is first instantiated. What this means is that the casual user is always presented with a list of values that exist in the data store – even when the base object is brand new. What we do when an object is first instantiated is to insert a zero length string as, let's call it, a *placeholder* for each Property Value. So when the user first inserts a new object, we mirror back to the user a set of Property Name/Value pairs that have a zero length string as their value. What this means is that the user *always* performs an update to a Property Value.

> There is no way for a casual user to insert new properties or delete existing properties. casual users *always* perform updates.

Let's think about *John* again. Say that some casual user decided that *John* shouldn't have the property Mother's Maiden Name for one reason or another. If we allowed this user to delete the entire Property Name/Value pair, then *John*'s "record" would be incomplete. In that case, deleting the Mother's Maiden Name property is really more like removing a column from a table than it is like deleting a value in a column in a table. That type of activity – restructuring tables or Property Set Definitions – is an Administrative function. So, what we really need to give the casual user the ability to do is remove the value from the Property Name/Value pair. In other words, what we need the user to do here is to select the value for *John*'s Mother's Maiden name, "Smith" and remove the value or the word "Smith", and press Save or Update. This effectively 'deletes' the value from *John*'s "record" while it still allows the columns in *John*'s "table" or Property Set Definition to remain intact.

Again, the code we are using here is really pretty much what we have come to expect. The biggest difference with this code is that we don't call the Data Centric Object from its User Centric counterpart. Instead, we call it from the UCPropBag object. Other than that, you already know how to write this data centric code. It is also important for you to realize that the code here given here can be used to as the PropValu `ObjectUpdate` code for any object. I have pointed out the very minor differences in the code sections that follow:

The Data Centric Object Code – clsPropValuData.cls

To re-use this code for another object, replace the two lines of code as indicated.

Change this line:

```
strSQL = "spPersonPropValuGet " & lngID
```

To read:

```
strSQL = "sp" & ObjectName & "PropValuGet " & lngID
```

Change this line:

```
strSQL = "spPersonPropValuUpdate " & _
```

To read:

```
strSQL = "sp" & ObjectName & "PropValuUpdate " & _
```

Otherwise, use the code exactly as it is printed.

```
Public Sub ObjectUpdate(lngStampID As Long, lngSaveStampID As Long, _
                lngID As Long, lngSaveID As Long, lngOwnerID As Long, _
                lngSaveOwnerID As Long, lngPropertyID As Long, _
                lngSavePropertyID As Long, lngOwnerTypeID As Long, _
                lngSaveOwnerTypeID As Long, dtmStampDateTime As Variant, _
                dtmSaveStampDateTime As Variant, _
                intDataLocking As Integer, blnChangeAll As Boolean, _
                blnSaveChangeAll As Boolean, strStampUser As String, _
                strSaveStampUser As String, strStampAction As String, _
                strSaveStampAction As String, strDataMessage As String, _
                strValue As String, strSaveValue As String, _
                strName As String, strSaveName As String)
```

```
    Dim strSQL As String
    Dim lngConcurrencyID1 As Long

    Dim ctxObject As ObjectContext
    Set ctxObject = GetObjectContext()

    On Error Goto ObjectUpdateError

    Dim ThisConnection As ADODB.Connection
    Dim ThisRecordset As ADODB.Recordset

    Set ThisConnection = New ADODB.Connection
    Set ThisRecordset = New ADODB.Recordset

    Dim strCollision As String
    strCollision = ""

    ThisConnection.Open mstrConnect, GetLogon(mstrConnect), GetPassword(mstrConnect)

    On Error Resume Next

    If DataLocking > 0 Then
      'Select the record to update using the fetch stored procedure
      strSQL = "spPersonPropValuGet " & lngID
      ThisRecordset.Open strSQL, ThisConnection

      If Not ThisRecordset.EOF Then
        lngConcurrencyID1 = ThisRecordset.Fields("ConcurrencyID1").Value
        CurrentID = ThisRecordset.Fields("ID").Value
        CurrentOwnerID = ThisRecordset.Fields("OwnerID").Value
        CurrentPropertyID = ThisRecordset.Fields("PropertyID").Value
        CurrentValue = FixNulls(ThisRecordset.Fields("Value").Value)
        CurrentName = FixNulls(ThisRecordset.Fields("Name").Value)
        ThisRecordset.Close
      Else
        strDataMessage = "Unable to find the record to update in the datastore"
        'Free up the object in MTS and set the Transaction Aborted flag
        ctxObject.SetAbort
        ThisConnection.Close
        Set ThisConnection = Nothing
        Set ctxObject = Nothing
        Exit Sub
      End If
    End If
```

In this case, the only field-level data collision we have to be on the lookout for is the actual Property Value itself:

```
    If NzString(CurrentValue) <> NzString(strSaveValue) Then
      If Len(strCollision) > 0 Then
        strCollision = strCollision & "*" & Value & "|" & CurrentValue
      Else
        strCollision = Value & "|" & CurrentValue
      End If
    End If
```

```
End If

If Len(strCollision) > 0 Then
  If DataLocking = 1 Then
```

```
            strDataMessage = "Unable to save changes, the record was being " & _
                        "edited by another user."
          'Free up the object in MTS and set the Transaction Aborted flag
          ctxObject.SetAbort
          ThisConnection.Close
          Set ThisConnection = Nothing
          Set ctxObject = Nothing
          Exit Sub
      ElseIf DataLocking = 2 Then
          strDataMessage = "The Following Collisions have occured * " & strCollision
          'Free up the object in MTS and set the Transaction Aborted flag
          ctxObject.SetAbort
          ThisConnection.Close
          Set ThisConnection = Nothing
          Set ctxObject = Nothing
          Exit Sub
      Else
          strDataMessage = ""
      End If

End If

strSQL = "spPersonPropValuUpdate " & _
        jamQuote & strStampUser & jamQuote & jamComma & _
        lngID & jamComma & _
        lngOwnerTypeID & jamComma & _
        jamQuote & strValue & jamQuote & jamComma & _
        lngConcurrencyID1

ThisRecordset.Open strSQL, ThisConnection

If ThisConnection.Errors.Count > 0 Then
   strDataMessage = ThisConnection.Errors(0).Description
   'Roll back the transaction
   ctxObject.SetAbort
Else
    If ThisRecordset.Fields(0).Name = "ErrorCondition" Then
        strDataMessage = ThisRecordset.Fields(0).Value
        'Free up the object in MTS and set the Transaction Aborted flag
        ctxObject.SetAbort
    Else
      ' This Resets the Starting Values with the current values in the Database
        lngID = ThisRecordset.Fields("ID").Value
        lngSaveID = ThisRecordset.Fields("ID").Value
        lngOwnerID = ThisRecordset.Fields("OwnerID").Value
        lngSaveOwnerID = ThisRecordset.Fields("OwnerID").Value
        lngPropertyID = ThisRecordset.Fields("PropertyID").Value
        lngSavePropertyID = ThisRecordset.Fields("PropertyID").Value
        lngOwnerTypeID = ThisRecordset.Fields("OwnerTypeID").Value
        lngSaveOwnerTypeID = ThisRecordset.Fields("OwnerTypeID").Value
        strDataMessage = ""
        strValue = FixNulls(ThisRecordset.Fields("Value").Value)
        strSaveValue = Value = FixNulls(ThisRecordset.Fields("Value").Value)
        strName = FixNulls(ThisRecordset.Fields("Name").Value)
        strSaveName = Name = FixNulls(ThisRecordset.Fields("Name").Value)
        'Free up the object in MTS and set the Transaction Completed flag
        ctxObject.SetComplete
    End If
End If
```

```
    ThisConnection.Close
    Set ThisConnection = Nothing
    Set ctxObject = Nothing

    Exit Sub

ObjectUpdateError:

    ErrorHandler

End Sub
```

The Stored Procedure

The code for this stored procedure deserves a little extra comment. Remember from our earlier discussions that properties can have lists of valid items, e.g. the Cover Material property could be only Hard or Paperback. These valid items are the subject of our PropItem object. You should remember from the last chapter that our PropItem object has a property called ID and another property called DisplayValue. As with all normalized databases, we prefer to store the ID value rather than the DisplayValue as redundant information. The reasons for this are obvious. It is less expensive to store 100 integers than it is to store 100 eighty-character text fields. It is also easier to change a single field that describes all Property Values with an given ID than it is to change all of the fields individually.

What this means is that when we use a property that has a list available, the value we store in the database is really a numeric value rather than the (probably) text value that the user is expecting. We could have chosen to handle the required translation at any level in the system, but one of our guiding design principles is that we should always execute any processing closest to the machine responsible for that processing. Therefore, we have taken the approach of handling the translation at its source - the database.

What this means is that our Update stored procedure must do the following:

❑   Always accept the displayed value as a parameter
❑   Determine the access level for the property
❑   Determine whether or not a list is available for this Property Value
❑   If a list does exist, then the stored procedure must perform a translation from the display value to the numeric value and store the numeric value
❑   If a list does not exist, then the stored procedure must store the display value
❑   Update the Audit table to record the action
❑   Mirror the results of the transaction back to the user

The first portion of the stored procedure handles those topics we discussed in earlier chapters, like transaction handling, error handling, etc. so we won't go over those topics again. Instead I would like to direct your attention to the next section of the stored procedure.

```
CREATE PROCEDURE spPersonPropValuUpdate
@StampUser varchar(10), @ID int, @TypeID int, @Value varchar(255),
@Concurrency1 int
```

```
AS

DECLARE @trncnt int, @ConcurrencyID int, @ErrorNumber int, @rows int, @err int,
        @AccessLevel char(1), @ShareCount int, @ListAvailable char(1),
        @StoreValue varchar(255), @PropertyID int

SELECT @ConcurrencyID = @Concurrency1
SELECT @ErrorNumber = -1

SELECT @trncnt = @@trancount

/* issue begin or save transaction based on transaction count */
IF @trncnt = 0
   BEGIN TRANSACTION T1
ELSE
   SAVE TRANSACTION T1
```

Now we must test for the access level and the existence of a list of items. To do this, we just execute a simple `SELECT` statement that fills our local variables with the results. The syntax is the same as we used in the insert stored procedure to select a single value, for the `@ListAvailable` variable, except for in this case our stored procedure returns three values instead of one. The remainder of the `SELECT` statement should be self-explanatory. Notice that we must join `PersonPropName` and `PersonTypePropertyBridge` tables to get the information we need:

```
SELECT      @AccessLevel = PersonTypePropertyBridge.AccessLevel,
            @ListAvailable = PersonPropName.ListAvailable,
            @PropertyID = PersonPropName.ID

FROM        PersonPropValu

INNER JOIN PersonPropName On
            PersonPropValu.PropertyID = PersonPropName.ID

INNER JOIN PersonTypePropertyBridge ON
            PersonPropName.ID = PersonTypePropertyBridge.PropertyID

WHERE       PersonPropValu.ID = @ID AND
            PersonTypePropertyBridge.TypeID = @TypeID
```

The next thing we do is perform a test to determine the number of types that are currently sharing this property. We do that by selecting the `COUNT(*)` of references to this particular `PropertyID`. This statement will return a row for each reference to the same `PropertyID`:

```
SELECT @ShareCount =
   (SELECT COUNT(*)

      FROM PersonTypeBridge

      INNER JOIN PersonPropValu ON
              PersonTypeBridge.ObjectID = PersonPropValu.ObjectID

      INNER JOIN PersonTypePropertyBridge ON
              PersonPropValu.PropertyID = PersonTypePropertyBridge.PropertyID
AND
              PersonTypeBridge.TypeID = PersonTypePropertyBridge.TypeID
   WHERE       PersonPropValu.ID = @ID)
```

If the property is shared among different Object Type Definitions, then we must check to see whether this property is a read only property. If it is a read only property, then we set an error number that indicates that this property is read only and exit the stored procedure by branching to the ErrorHandler routine. The 101 error will return a message indicating that this property is read only for this user.

```
IF @AccessLevel <> 'W' AND @ShareCount > 1
   BEGIN
      SELECT @ErrorNumber = 101
      GOTO ErrorHandler
   END
```

The next section of code in the stored procedure should look familiar; all we are doing here is adding a record to the Audit table that marks the update:

```
INSERT PersonPropValuAudit
   (StampUser, StampAction, StampDateTime, StampID, OwnerID, PropertyID,
    Name, Value)

SELECT @StampUser, 'U', GetDate(), PersonPropValu.ID, PersonPropValu.ObjectID,
   PersonPropValu.PropertyID, PersonPropName.PropertyName,
   (CASE PersonPropName.ListAvailable

         WHEN 'Y' THEN (Select  DisplayValue
            FROM     PersonPropItem
            WHERE    CONVERT(char(10),ID) = PersonPropValu.PropertyValue)
         ELSE
            PersonPropValu.PropertyValue
         END) AS Value

   FROM            PersonPropName

   INNER JOIN      PersonPropValu ON
                   PersonPropName.ID = PersonPropValu.PropertyID

   LEFT OUTER JOIN PersonPropItem ON
                   PersonPropValu.PropertyID = PersonPropItem.PropertyID And
                   PersonPropValu.PropertyValue =
                   CONVERT(Char(10), PersonPropItem.ID)

   WHERE           PersonPropValu.ID = @ID

IF @@error <> 0 GOTO ErrorHandler
```

Next we test whether this Property Value should draw its value from a list and whether or not the value passed into the stored procedure @Value is not a zero length string. This is just like the Insert stored procedure above, but it bears repeating. If the @Value has been provided and there is not list of valid responses, then that means that the value in the @Value variable is the one we need to store in the database. So, in that case, we just stuff the value into the @StoreValue variable and allow the stored procedure to continue executing:

```
IF @ListAvailable = 'Y' AND @Value <> ''
   BEGIN
```

If the previous statement returns true, then that means that there is a list available and that the user has specified a value for that list. If a list is available and the current value of the variable @Value is not equal to a zero length string, then our variable @Value will contain a numeric value that is the ID of the Property Value we need to update.

So, at this time, what we need to do is to perform the translation and select the descriptive value that is paired with our numeric value. Then we stuff the descriptive value into another variable called @StoreValue. This is the value we will place into the PropValu table.

```
SELECT @StoreValue = (SELECT  CONVERT(Char(10),ID)
                      FROM    PersonPropItem(Updlock)
                      WHERE   DisplayValue = @Value AND
                              PropertyID = @PropertyID)
```

If we are executing this branch of the IF statement and our translation does not return a value, then that means there is no paired value for our ID. This is an error condition that can only occur if someone made changes to the database without using the objects. In this case we set the @ErrorNumber value equal to a number that indicates the cause of the problem and branch to the error handler:

```
        IF IsNull(@StoreValue,'') = ''
          /* Property Value not in list */
          BEGIN
            SELECT @ErrorNumber = 103
            GOTO ErrorHandler
          END

    END

ELSE
    SELECT @StoreValue = @Value
```

As with the Insert stored procedure we saw earlier most of the work we need to do is preparation and housekeeping. The following line is the one that actually performs the update. It is self-explanatory:

```
UPDATE PersonPropValu

SET    PropertyValue = @StoreValue,
       ConcurrencyID = ConcurrencyID + 1

WHERE  ID = @ID AND
       ConcurrencyID = @ConcurrencyID

SELECT @err = @@error, @rows = @@RowCount

IF @err <> 0 GOTO ErrorHandler
```

Standard concurrency error handling:

```
IF @rows = 0
    BEGIN
        SELECT @ErrorNumber = 100
        GOTO ErrorHandler
    END
```

Standard commit transaction handling:

```
IF @trncnt = 0 COMMIT TRANSACTION T1
```

Mirror results of this stored procedure back to the user:

```
SELECT PersonPropValu.ID, PersonPropValu.ObjectID As OwnerID,
       PersonPropValu.PropertyID, PersonPropName.PropertyName AS Name,

              (CASE PersonPropName.ListAvailable
                  WHEN 'Y' THEN
                     (SELECT   DisplayValue
                      FROM     PersonPropItem
                      WHERE    CONVERT(char(10),ID) = PersonPropValu.PropertyValue)
                  ELSE
                  PersonPropValu.PropertyValue
                  END) AS Value,
                  PersonPropValu.ConcurrencyID AS ConcurrencyID1

FROM            PersonPropName

INNER JOIN      PersonPropValu ON
                PersonPropName.ID = PersonPropValu.PropertyID

WHERE           PersonPropValu.ID = @ID

RETURN (0)
```

Standard error handler:

```
ErrorHandler:
    ROLLBACK TRANSACTION T1
    SELECT   ErrorCondition
    FROM     Common..ErrorMessage
    WHERE    ErrorNumber = @ErrorNumber
    RETURN   (100)
```

The Delete Process

As we said earlier, *we don't let casual users delete Property Values.* That does not mean that we never delete Property Values. Of course if an administrator decides that Mother's Maiden Name is no longer something our company cares about, then the administrator can decide to remove that Property Definition from the Property Set Definition for that particular Object Type Definition. In this case, not only do we need to remove the Property Name, but we also need to remove the Property Values. We also need to delete Property Values when the user deletes a base object. Although we don't let the casual user decide which properties should be in *John*'s Property Bag, we do allow the user to delete *John* if that is what the casual user needs to do. When the user deletes *John*, we need to be sure and delete all of *John*'s extended properties as well.

As an aside, realize that this means that when a user restores a base object we also need to be able to restore the extended properties – both names and values back to their state at the time the base object was deleted. We are building ECDOs here, so that means that we should also restore the extended properties' audit trails as well. This task may sound daunting, but we have handled it the way we do everything else around here – "One Step at a Time." All we really need to do to be able to ensure this functionality is to ensure that each of our sub-objects conforms to the rigorous set of standards we have placed upon all ECDOs. As long as we are careful to give each sub-object its full compliment of eight data handling processes, we can always use them when we need to at a later time. You may not remember this, but I said something way back in Chapter 4 with respect to our original over capable object design. I said that:

- ❏ Make each block of code, even the simple ones, perfect
- ❏ Never skimp on the foundation

I hope that now you are beginning to see what I meant way back then. In this chapter, we can almost take for granted things like audit trails, the ability to perform unlimited undo's, and the ability to restore objects (in this case Property Value objects) from a deleted state. The reason we have this luxury at this minute is because we have paid our dues. Even when it was hard, we followed those two guiding principles. We learned to make each sub-object, even the simple ones, **perfect**. Those sub-objects are the foundation for everything we need to do. When one of your friends or co-workers marvels at your ability to restore a deleted object, all of its properties, and complete audit trails for both of those things. Shrug it off, and tell them it was easy. Tell them that all they have to do is to follow two simple guiding principles…

Because we don't expose the PropValud *Delete* process to the casual user directly, there is no reason to provide any user centric code for this process. That portion of the process is handled by the UCPropBag Object. You should find that you already know the code we need to write for the Data Centric PropValu `ObjectDelete`. Here is the listing:

The Data Centric Object Code – clsPropValuData.cls

```
Public Sub ObjectDelete(lngID As Long, strStampUser As String, _
                        strDataMessage As String)

    Dim strSQL As String
    Dim lngConcurrencyID1 As Long
    Dim strCollision As String

    Dim ctxObject As ObjectContext
    Set ctxObject = GetObjectContext()

    On Error GoTo ObjectDeleteError

    Dim ThisConnection As ADODB.Connection
    Dim ThisRecordset As ADODB.Recordset

    Set ThisConnection = New ADODB.Connection
    Set ThisRecordset = New ADODB.Recordset

    ThisConnection.Open mstrConnect, GetLogon(mstrConnect), GetPassword(mstrConnect)

    On Error Resume Next
```

```
' Select the Record to be deleted
  strSQL = "spPersonPropValuGet " & lngID
  ThisRecordset.Open strSQL, ThisConnection

  If DataLocking > 0 Then

     If Not ThisRecordset.EOF Then
        lngConcurrencyID1 = ThisRecordset.Fields("ConcurrencyID1").Value
        CurrentID = ThisRecordset.Fields("ID").Value
        CurrentOwnerID = ThisRecordset.Fields("OwnerID").Value
        CurrentPropertyID = ThisRecordset.Fields("PropertyID").Value
        CurrentValue = FixNulls(ThisRecordset.Fields("Value").Value)
        CurrentName = FixNulls(ThisRecordset.Fields("Name").Value)
        ThisRecordset.Close

     Else
        strDataMessage = "The Requested Delete did not occur because " & _
                         "the Record was not found."
        ctxObject.SetAbort
        ThisConnection.Close
        Set ThisConnection = Nothing
        Set ctxObject = Nothing
        Exit Sub

     End If

  End If

' This Code checks the values of each field and builds a collision string which
' is passed to the user centric object for further processing

  If NzString(CurrentValue) <> NzString(strSaveValue) Then
     If Len(strCollision) > 0 Then
        strCollision = strCollision & "*" & Value & "|" & CurrentValue
     Else
        strCollision = Value & "|" & CurrentValue
     End If
  End If

  If Len(strCollision) > 0 Then

     If DataLocking = 1 Then
        strDataMessage = "Unable to Delete the record because it was being " & _
                         "edited by another user."
        'Free up the object in MTS and set the Transaction Aborted flag
        ctxObject.SetAbort
        ThisConnection.Close
        Set ThisConnection = Nothing
        Set ctxObject = Nothing
        Exit Sub
     ElseIf DataLocking = 2 Then
        strDataMessage = "The Following Collisions have occured * " & strCollision
        'Free up the object in MTS and set the Transaction Aborted flag
        ctxObject.SetAbort
        ThisConnection.Close
        Set ThisConnection = Nothing
        Set ctxObject = Nothing
        Exit Sub
     Else
        strDataMessage = ""
     End If
```

```
   End If

   strSQL = "spPersonPropValuDelete " & _
            jamQuote & strStampUser & jamQuote & jamComma & _
            lngID & jamComma & _
            lngConcurrencyID1

ThisRecordset.Open strSQL, ThisConnection

If ThisConnection.Errors.Count > 0 Then
   strDataMessage = ThisConnection.Errors(0).Description
 ' Roll Back the Transaction
   ctxObject.SetAbort

Else

   If ThisRecordset.Fields(0).Name = "ErrorCondition" Then
      strDataMessage = ThisRecordset.Fields(0).Value
    'Free up the object in MTS and set the Transaction Aborted flag
      ctxObject.SetAbort
   Else
      strDataMessage = ""
    'Free up the object in MTS and set the Transaction Completed flag
      ctxObject.SetComplete
   End If

End If

ThisConnection.Close
Set ThisConnection = Nothing
Set ctxObject = Nothing

Exit Sub

ObjectDeleteError:

ErrorHandler

End Sub
```

The Stored Procedure

There are a couple of unexpected twists and turns in this stored procedure, but if you have worked through the earlier ones in this chapter, I think that you will find that this one is really just more of the same. As with everything else in this book, we learn to do something simple very well and then we use it for all it is worth. I will point out more interesting things about this stored procedure as we work our way through it. Remember that this stored procedure, like all of the ones we have seen in this chapter can be used for any object that you build. The only thing that has to be changed is the base name for the target object.

The first portion of the stored procedure handles those topics we discussed in earlier chapters, like transaction handling, error handling, etc. so we won't go over those topics again. Instead I would like to direct your attention to the next section of the stored procedure.

```
CREATE PROCEDURE spPersonPropValuDelete
@StampUser varchar(10), @ID int, @ConcurrencyID1 int

AS

DECLARE @trncnt int, @ErrorNumber int, @rows int, @err int, @ConcurrencyID int,
        @ShareCount int

SELECT @ErrorNumber = -1
SELECT @ConcurrencyID = @ConcurrencyID1
SELECT @rows = 0
```

Standard transaction handling:

```
SELECT @trncnt = @@trancount
/* issue begin or save transaction based on transaction count */
IF @trncnt = 0
    BEGIN TRANSACTION T1
ELSE
    SAVE TRANSACTION T1
```

I said something about twists and turns earlier, so that I could warn you to brace yourself and hold on for this one. Remember that we can share properties between different Property Set Definitions. I think we share the UseLogonID property between the IT Resource and the IT Customer PSDs. Well that little extra something wasn't free. When we delete Property Values we have to remember that we can share them. That means that before we delete a value, we need to check to see whether or not anyone else is using the value. If someone else is using it, then we what we really need to delete is our *relationship* to the value. If someone else is using it, we cannot delete the value. OK, now that I have prepared you for the worst, I hope it you are pleasantly surprised to learn that this really very easy to do. All we need to do is perform our standard shared value test:

```
SELECT @ShareCount =
    (SELECT     COUNT(*)

    FROM        PersonTypeBridge

    INNER JOIN PersonPropValu ON
                PersonTypeBridge.ObjectID = PersonPropValu.ObjectID

    INNER JOIN PersonTypePropertyBridge ON
                PersonPropValu.PropertyID = PersonTypePropertyBridge.PropertyID AND
                PersonTypeBridge.TypeID = PersonTypePropertyBridge.TypeID

    WHERE       PersonPropValu.ID = @ID)
```

If there is only a single entry in the Bridge table, then that means that we are the only one using this property at this minute. If this value is greater than one, that means that someone else is using it. Notice that it doesn't matter to us who else is using the property of for that matter how many others are using the property. This is a binary problem. Either it is shared and we can't delete it, or it is not shared and we can delete it. The two legs of this IF statement handle the possibilities:

```
IF @ShareCount = 1
    BEGIN
```

This might be in the middle of that IF statement, but it is the same old stuff we have been doing all along. Add a record to the Audit table to fix the object's state in the Audit table before deleting the object:

```
INSERT PersonPropValuAudit
    (StampUser, StampAction, StampDateTime, StampID, OwnerID, PropertyID, Name,
    Value)

SELECT
    @StampUser, 'D', GetDate(), PersonPropValu.ID, PersonPropValu.ObjectID,
    PersonPropValu.PropertyID, PersonPropName.PropertyName,

    (CASE PersonPropName.ListAvailable
        WHEN 'Y' THEN (
            SELECT  DisplayValue
            FROM    PersonPropItem
            WHERE   CONVERT(char(10),ID) = PersonPropValu.PropertyValue)
        ELSE
            PersonPropValu.PropertyValue
        End) AS Value

FROM            PersonPropName

INNER JOIN      PersonPropValu ON
                PersonPropName.ID = PersonPropValu.PropertyID

LEFT OUTER JOIN PersonPropItem ON
                PersonPropValu.PropertyID = PersonPropItem.PropertyID AND
                PersonPropValu.PropertyValue =
                                    CONVERT(Char(10),PersonPropItem.ID)

WHERE           PersonPropValu.ID = @ID

IF @@error <> 0 GOTO ErrorHandler
```

As with the other stored procedures, it is almost anti-climatic when we actually perform the action given in the name of the stored procedure. The delete in this stored procedure is handled by a single line of code. Everything else is either preparation or housecleaning:

```
DELETE PersonPropValu Where ID = @ID AND ConcurrencyID = @ConcurrencyID
    SELECT @err = @@error, @rows = @@RowCount
    IF @err <> 0 GOTO ErrorHandler

Standard concurrency error handling:

    IF @rows = 0
        BEGIN
            SELECT @ErrorNumber = 100
            GOTO ErrorHandler
        END
    END
```

Standard commit transaction handling:

```
IF @trncnt = 0 COMMIT TRANSACTION T1
```

Mirror the results of this stored procedure back to the user.

```
IF @ShareCount = 1
    SELECT 'RowCount' = @rows
ELSE
```

If the number of PSDs, sharing this particular property definition was greater than one, then we build just build a recordset that returns the number or other PSDs also using the same Property Definition. This is really of little practical use to the end user. It is intended as an aid to administrators. This will prevent them from accidentally deleting Property Values that may be in use by another PSD. The addition of the OTD names can also be useful to give the administrator a trail to follow if he or she is determined to remove this Property Definition and its associated values from this data store, this list will be quite helpful:

```
    SELECT      'RowCount' = @rows,
                'ShareCount' =@ShareCount,
                PersonObjType.Name

    FROM        PersonTypeBridge

    INNER JOIN PersonPropValu On
                PersonTypeBridge.ObjectID = PersonPropValu.ObjectID

    INNER JOIN PersonTypePropertyBridge ON
                PersonPropValu.PropertyID = PersonTypePropertyBridge.PropertyID AND
                PersonTypeBridge.TypeID = PersonTypePropertyBridge.TypeID

    INNER JOIN PersonObjType ON
                PersonTypeBridge.TypeID = PersonObjType.ID

    WHERE       PersonPropValu.ID = @ID

RETURN (0)
```

Standard error handling:

```
ErrorHandler:
   ROLLBACK TRANSACTION T1
   SELECT   ErrorCondition
   FROM     Common..ErrorMessage
   WHERE    ErrorNumber = @ErrorNumber
   RETURN   (100)
```

The Show Deleted Process

If you think about it, the *Show Deleted* process we have been using all along is really just a simple SELECT statement that is run against the Audit table. The only thing that differentiates this process from the standard *Audit History* is that we filter out everything except for the last deletion for each object's ID. This is designed to make it easier for the user to select the deleted object from the list. We really don't need this functionality, we could teach the users to look through the Audit table and find the entry that is there to mark the last deletion for an object. Of course, this would also mean that they would pick the wrong entry from time-to-time, so instead we use this process. It filters out the Audit table and only gives the users the option of restoring the last deletion for an object. Because it is *not possible for a casual user to delete a property value*, we do not need to show them a list of deleted values available for restoration.

That doesn't mean that they don't have access to this functionality. It only means that we expose the functionality in a different manner. Remember that a user can effectively 'delete' a value by removing the value from the text box and performing a standard Save or Update. This deletes the value by saving a zero length string in its place. It also means that the audit history will reflect each change. If the current value for a property shows up on the user's screen as a blank text box, the user can press the Show History button for that property and return a list of previous values. In other words, the user can 'restore' a 'deleted' value by performing an undo.

The Restore From Deleted Process

OK now that I just got finished telling you that a casual user cannot delete a Property Value and therefore cannot perform the traditional restore from deleted process, I am about to give you a stored procedure that we use to perform a restore from deleted! No, I haven't lost my mind. Remember that although we don't allow the casual user to perform deletions or traditional restorations against Property Values, we do allow the user to delete and restore the base object. When the user restores the base object, we restore the properties, both names and values, for the user via the Property Bag.

If you think back a few pages to the ObjectInsert we looked at earlier, you may remember that we called this stored procedure from within that stored procedure. This makes a lot of sense. When you think about it, this Restore stored procedure is really the same as an insert. The only difference between a restore and an insert is where the values come from. In an insert, we pass the values into the procedure, in a restore, we select the values from the Audit table.

Once again, you know everything you need to know to write this stored procedure. I have provided some comments to make it easier for you to get through it, but I am sure that you can probably do just fine without me now.

The Stored Procedure

```
CREATE PROCEDURE spPersonPropValuRestore
@StampUser varchar(10), @RestoreID int

AS

DECLARE @trncnt int, @ErrorNumber int, @ID int, @OwnerID int, @PropertyID int,
        @Value varchar(255), @ListAvailable char(1), @StoreValue varchar(255)

SELECT @ErrorNumber = -1
```

Standard transaction handling:

```
SELECT @trncnt = @@trancount
/* issue begin or save transaction based on transaction count */
IF @trncnt = 0
   BEGIN TRANSACTION T1
ELSE
   SAVE TRANSACTION T1
```

Select the object to be restored from the Audit table:

```
SELECT @ID = StampID, @OwnerID = OwnerID, @PropertyID = PropertyID, @Value = Value

FROM    PersonPropValuAudit

WHERE   ID = @RestoreID
```

Test for the existence of a list for this Property Definition:

```
SELECT @ListAvailable = (SELECT ListAvailable
                         FROM PersonPropName
                         WHERE  ID = @PropertyID)
```

If there is a list, then perform the translation:

```
IF @ListAvailable = 'Y' AND @Value <> ''
  BEGIN
    SELECT @StoreValue = (SELECT  CONVERT(Char(10),ID)
                          FROM    PersonPropItem(Updlock)
                          WHERE   DisplayValue = @Value AND
                                  PropertyID = @PropertyID)
  END
ELSE
```

Otherwise, set the @StoreValue variable equal to the value we found from the Audit table search:

```
    SELECT @StoreValue = @Value
```

Re-insert the Property Value. Remember that this requires managing the autonumbering function:

```
SET Identity_Insert PersonPropValu ON

   INSERT PersonPropValu
      (ID, ObjectID, PropertyID, PropertyValue, ConcurrencyID)

   VALUES  (@ID, @OwnerID, @PropertyID, @StoreValue, 1)

SET Identity_Insert PersonPropValu OFF

IF @@error <> 0 GOTO ErrorHandler
```

Add a record to the Audit table to mark the insertion:

```
INSERT PersonPropValuAudit
     (StampUser, StampAction, StampDateTime, StampID, OwnerID, PropertyID,
     Name, Value)

  SELECT @StampUser, 'R', GetDate(), PersonPropValu.ID, PersonPropValu.ObjectID,
        PersonPropValu.PropertyID, PersonPropName.PropertyName,

        (CASE PersonPropName.ListAvailable
            WHEN 'Y' THEN (
               SELECT  DisplayValue
               FROM    PersonPropItem
               WHERE   CONVERT(char(10),ID) = PersonPropValu.PropertyValue)
            ELSE
               PersonPropValu.PropertyValue
            END) AS Value

  FROM            PersonPropName

  INNER JOIN      PersonPropValu ON
                  PersonPropName.ID = PersonPropValu.PropertyID

  LEFT OUTER JOIN PersonPropItem ON
                  PersonPropValu.PropertyID = PersonPropItem.PropertyID AND
                  PersonPropValu.PropertyValue =
                           CONVERT(Char(10),PersonPropItem.ID)

  WHERE           PersonPropValu.ID = @ID

IF @@error <> 0 GOTO ErrorHandler
```

Standard commit transaction handling:

```
IF @trncnt = 0 COMMIT TRANSACTION T1
```

Mirror the results of the stored procedure to back to the user:

```
SELECT PersonPropValu.ID, PersonPropValu.ObjectID As OwnerID,
       PersonPropValu.PropertyID, PersonPropName.PropertyName AS Name,

       (CASE PersonPropName.ListAvailable
           WHEN 'Y' THEN (
              SELECT DisplayValue
              FROM   PersonPropItem
              WHERE  CONVERT(char(10),ID) = PersonPropValu.PropertyValue)
           ELSE
              PersonPropValu.PropertyValue
           END) AS Value, PersonPropValu.ConcurrencyID AS ConcurrencyID1

FROM            PersonPropName

INNER JOIN      PersonPropValu ON
                PersonPropName.ID = PersonPropValu.PropertyID

WHERE           PersonPropValu.ID = @ID

RETURN (0)
```

Standard error handling:

```
ErrorHandler:
   ROLLBACK TRANSACTION T1
   SELECT    ErrorCondition
   FROM      Common..ErrorMessage
   WHERE     ErrorNumber = @ErrorNumber
   RETURN    (100)
```

The Audit History Process

We have really talked about the how's and why's concerning this process when we looked at the non-existent *Show Deleted* process above. This process takes on a little additional responsibility when we are talking about Property Values, because it is also used to give the user the ability to 'restore' a value from a 'deleted' state within the confines we talked about earlier. This code and the stored procedure it calls are really nothing new. I have provided them here mostly because except for the name of the object, you can use this code for a generic Property Bag object.

The Data Centric Object Code – colPropValuData.cls

```
Public Function ObjectHistory(lngID As Long) As Recordset

  Dim strSQL As String

  Dim ctxObject As ObjectContext
  Set ctxObject = GetObjectContext()

  On Error GoTo ObjectHistoryError

  Set ThisConnection = New ADODB.Connection
  Set ThisRecordset = New ADODB.Recordset

  Dim ThisRecordset As ADODB.Recordset
  Dim ThisConnection As ADODB.Connection

  ThisConnection.Open mstrConnect, GetLogon(mstrConnect), GetPassword(mstrConnect)

  If Len(strSelectStatement) = 0 Then
     strSQL = " spPropValuObjectAuditList " & lngID
  Else
     strSQL = strSelectStatement
  End If

  On Error Resume Next

  ThisRecordset.Open strSQL, ThisConnection

  If ThisConnection.Errors.Count > 0 Then
     Set ThisRecordset = New ADODB.Recordset
     ThisRecordset.Fields.Append "DataMessage", adChar, 255
     ThisRecordset.Open
     ThisRecordset.AddNew
     ThisRecordset.Fields(0).Value = ThisConnection.Errors(0).Description
     ThisRecordset.Update
     'Free up the object in MTS and set the Transaction Aborted flag
     ctxObject.SetAbort
     Set ObjectHistory = ThisRecordset
  Else
```

```
        'Free up the object in MTS and set the Transaction Completed flag
        ctxObject.SetComplete
        Set ObjectHistory = ThisRecordset
    End If

    ThisConnection.Close
    Set ThisConnection = Nothing
    Set ctxObject = Nothing

    Exit Function

ObejctHistoryError:

    ErrorHandler

End Function
```

The Stored Procedure

All we need to do here is to select the correct list of snapshots for the Property Value indicated by the ID. This code is elementary, but take a minute or two to think about the power we have built into the system to make it this capable. Perhaps the unique ID field we placed into the PropValu and PropValueAudit tables makes a little more sense when we look at it from this perspective. Imagine how difficult it would be to locate this history if we didn't give each Property Value a unique ID:

```
CREATE PROCEDURE spPersonPropValuAuditList
@ID int

AS

SELECT StampUser, StampDateTime, StampAction, StampID,
       ID, OwnerID, PropertyID, Name, Value

FROM         PersonPropValuAudit

WHERE        StampID = @ID

ORDER BY     StampDateTime DESC

Return (0)
```

The Load Process

Once again this process is not at all exceptional. It relies upon the same tried and true techniques we have been using all along. As with the other functionality of the PropValu object, we handle the developer's interaction with this process using the PropBag as an intermediary. The one thing that I do need to bring to your attention is the TypeID parameter. A base object can have several OTDs defined for it. This means that in order to return the correct set of properties, we need to know what OTD is being used. This parameter is what allows us to select the correct set of Property Name/Value pairs for a particular extension of a base object.

The Data Centric Object Code –colPropValuData.cls

```
Public Function Fetch(Optional strSelectStatement As String, _
                      Optional lngOwnerID, Optional lngTypeID) As Recordset

  Dim strSQL As String

  Dim ctxObject As ObjectContext
  Set ctxObject = GetObjectContext()

  On Error GoTo FetchErrorOut

  Dim ThisConnection As ADODB.Connection
  Dim ThisRecordset As ADODB.Recordset

  Set ThisConnection = New ADODB.Connection
  Set ThisRecordset = New ADODB.Recordset

  ThisConnection.Open mstrConnect, GetLogon(mstrConnect), GetPassword(mstrConnect)

  If Len(strSelectStatement) = 0 Then
     strSQL = " spPersonPropValuList " & lngOwnerID & ", "  lngTypeID
  Else
     strSQL = strSelectStatement
  End If

  On Error Resume Next

  ThisRecordset.Open strSQL, ThisConnection

  If ThisConnection.Errors.Count > 0 Then
     Set ThisRecordset = New ADODB.Recordset
     ThisRecordset.Fields.Append "DataMessage", adChar, 255
     ThisRecordset.Open
     ThisRecordset.AddNew
     ThisRecordset.Fields(0).Value = ThisConnection.Errors(0).Description
     ThisRecordset.Update
     'Free up the object in MTS and set the Transaction Aborted flag
     ctxObject.SetAbort
  Else
     Set Fetch = ThisRecordset
     'Free up the object in MTS and set the Transaction Completed flag
     ctxObject.SetComplete
  End If

  ThisConnection.Close
  Set ThisConnection = Nothing
  Set ctxObject = Nothing

  Exit Function

FetchErrorOut:

  ErrorHandler

End Function
```

The Stored Procedure

The purpose here is simply to mirror the results back to the user. The only remarkable thing to notice here is that we need to pass in two parameters in order to be able to return the correct list of properties. Think about this. We can have a single person who is both a doctor and patient, a student and a teacher, an employee and a customer, or some combination of any of those things. This means that in order to return the correct set of properties for the base object, we need to pass the ID that identifies the OTD that the base object is using. This value is passed in the `@OwnerTypeID` parameter:

```
CREATE PROCEDURE spPersonPropValuList
@OwnerID int, @OwnerTypeID int

AS

SELECT    PersonPropValu.ID,PersonPropValu.ObjectID As OwnerID,
          PersonPropValu.PropertyID, PersonPropName.PropertyName AS Name,

          (CASE Personpropname.ListAvailable
              WHEN 'Y' THEN (
                 SELECT    DisplayValue
                 FROM      PersonPropItem
                 WHERE     CONVERT(char(10),ID) = PersonPropValu.PropertyValue)
              ELSE
                 PersonPropValu.PropertyValue
          END) AS Value, PersonPropValu.ConcurrencyID As ConcurrencyID1

FROM             PersonTypePropertyBridge

INNER JOIN       PersonPropValu ON
                 PersonTypePropertyBridge.PropertyID = PersonPropValu.PropertyID

INNER JOIN       PersonPropName ON
                 PersonPropValu.PropertyID = PersonPropName.ID

WHERE            PersonTypePropertyBridge.TypeID = @OwnerTypeID AND
                 PersonPropValu.ObjectID = @OwnerID

RETURN (0)
```

The Property Bag (PropBag) Object

As we discussed earlier in the chapter, we can think of the PropBag object much the same way we think about a view in the database. The PropBag Object manages the complex relationships that exist between the PropName, PropItem and PropValu objects. Let's explore this relationship in a bit more detail.

How the Objects in the Property Bag Relate

Let's go back to the library example we discussed in the previous chapter to understand how the PropBag object needs to function. Let's say we've just received a new shipment of books and we want to enter them into the library system. From the casual user's perspective, this means that the user needs to bring up something like an Add New Book screen. Behind the scenes, what we do is to create a new *Media* object, with OTD *Book*. As we learned earlier in this chapter, whenever we instantiate a new object, we immediately create a new set of Property Name/Value pairs based upon the instructions given by the Property Set Definition.

If the whole concept of the Property Set Definition has been giving you some trouble up to this point, I think that this section will help to make it clear. In order to know what se t of properties we needed to create for this OTD, we look that information up by loading the set of Property Names that are related to this OTD. What that means, in this case, is that we would pass the ID that indicates the OTD we are using, the OTD for a book, into the stored procedure that fetches a list of Property Names.

Using our library example, when we passed in the OTD for Book, the PropName `Load` function would return three Property Names:

❑ Number of Pages

❑ Number of Chapter

❑ Cover Material - which can be either Hard or Paperback

The next thing we would do is to check to see whether there were any values for these names already in the data store. We would do that by passing the ID of the object and the ID of the OTD into the PropValu *Load* process. We covered that process earlier in the chapter. All it does is to return a set of Property Values for a particular Object Type Definition for a Particular Base Object. Of course, in this example we are adding a *new* book to the data store, so we this list would come back empty.

As we said in the discussion above, it is not reasonable to have a Property Name without a related Property Value. *The two things depend upon each other.* So, we would take this opportunity to create an empty Property Value for each Property Name and select these empty values.

At this point, we essentially have two collections of items:

❑ On the one hand, we have a collection of Property Names; Number of Pages, Number of Chapters, and Cover Material.

❑ On the other hand we have a collection of Property Values; in this case they are all empty.

Both collections have one thing in common. They both have a PropertyID value. This means that we can iterate through the collections and pair up the Property Names with the Property Values. When we find a matching pair, we merge their properties into a single object and add that object to a third collection. This collection is what we call the Property Bag. It contains pairs of Property Names that come from the PropName objects and their related Property Values that come from the PropValue object.

When we return the PropBag to the user so that they can add information about the book, they actually add this information into the third object that we created above – The PropBag object. After the user has entered the values into this third collection and presses Save, we perform the same process as above in reverse. Rather than combining each Name/Value pair into the PropBag object we disassemble the PropBag into its constituent components, discard the Name information except for its ID and perform an update using the PropValu object.

In our library example, that would mean that we would do the following, if we have a book with 700 pages, 16 chapters and a Hardback cover. To enter these values the Property Bag would do the following:

1. Save a new base *Media* object and associate that object to the OTD *Book*

2. Instantiate an instance of the PropBag object

3. The Property Bag would retrieve a list of Property Names for the OTD *Book*

4. The Property Bag would attempt to retrieve a list of Property Values. To do this it would pass the following parameters into the PropValu *Load* process:

    ❑   The base *Media* object's ID

    ❑   The OTD that indicates this *Media* object is being used as a book

5. Depending upon the results of this load, the Property Bag will do one of two things:

    ❑   If a set of values were found that were related to the *Media* object given by the ID, then the Property Bag would pair those values with the names retrieved in Step 3. While it does this, it would also resolve any discrepancies between the list of Property Names and the list of Property Values. In other words, if it finds a value without a related name, it will delete this value. If it finds a Property Name without a related value, it will insert a new blank value into the data store for this Property Name/Value pair. This ensures that every object of a particular type always exposes the same complete set of Property Name/Value pairs that describe the OTD.

    ❑   If no values are found, then the Property Bag iterates through the list of Property Names it found for this particular OTD. For each Property Name it finds, it inserts an empty Property Value into the data store. This ensures that we always have a mated Name/Value pair for each property defined by the Property Set Definition.

6. Next the Property Bag, which now consists of a collection of Property Name/Value pairs, is delivered to the user. The user provides information for each of the Property Values using whatever user interface has been provided to handle this data collection task. In this case that would mean that the user would enter:

    ❑   700 into the Property Value identified by the Number of Pages name

    ❑   16 into the Property Value identified by the Number of Chapters name

    ❑   The user would select Hardcover from the dropdown list for the Cover Material Property Name

7. When the user presses the Save button, the object's base properties are saved in a conventional manner. The extended properties are saved using the mechanism provided by the Property Bag. That mechanism is given as follows:

    ❑   From the Production Interface, there is no way to change a Property Name. This is an Administrative function, so we can really ignore this information. Instead, we just take the information from the Property Bag that we need to perform an PropValu ObjectUpdate – ObjectID, PropertyID, and Property Value - along with the typical information like StampUser, DataSourceName etc. Then we instantiate a Data Centric PropValu object and pass this information to it using its `ObjectUpdate` method. In this case, we would do that three times once for each Property Name/Value pair in the PropBag collection.

    ❑   The next time the user retrieves the extended object, it will be return with the Property Name/Value pairs that belong to this particular instance of the object.

I think you should be beginning to get an idea of the complexity of the object interactions going on here. I think it's a bit easier to understand if we go back to our analogy that each of the objects really represent tables in a database. Relating tables is something we're a bit more familiar with. Let's therefore examine how the tables of a Person Property Bag inter-relate. Here's a quick recap of the tables:

❑ The PersonObject Table - used to store the base set of Person properties. Also has a corresponding Audit table.

❑ The PersonObjType Table - used to store the data that is used for each 4- Dimensional Data Object's Object Type Definitions. Also has a corresponding Audit table.

❑ The PersonPropItem Table - used to store information about the property items that are assigned to each Property Definition that has a list of valid items. Also has a corresponding Audit table.

❑ The PersonPropName Table - used to store the information about each Property Definition. The information in this table manages Property Set Definitions via its OwnerTypeID property. Also has a corresponding Audit table.

❑ The PersonTypeBridge Table - used to connect a particular object to its Object Type Definition(s).

❑ The PersonTypePropertyBridge Table - used to manage Property Set Definitions and to relate those PSDs to a particular Object Type Definition.

We can now see how these tables all fit together to form the Property Bag:

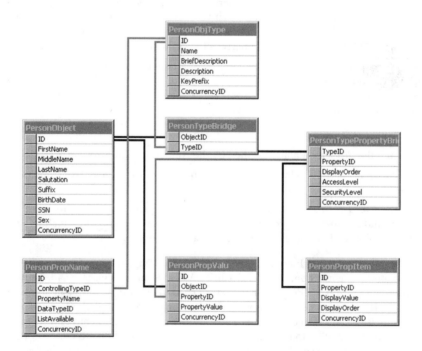

So we could think of using the PropBag object in the Production Interface like so:

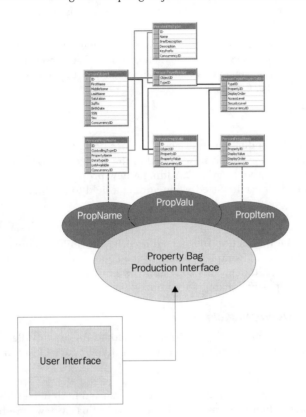

Coding the PropBag Object

The following section describes how the Property Bag Production Interface exposes or hides each of the eight basic capabilities we expect from an Enterprise Caliber Data Object.

The Fetch Process

The Property Bag's programmable Production Interface does not offer the ability to fetch a *single* object via the PropBag object. Rather the PropBag object always returns the *entire* collection of properties for a given extended object. This is a decision I made for my treatment of the Property Bag. As I have described, I use the Data Centric Load routine of the PropBag object to ensure that every object's current Property Bag has been synchronized with the PSD for the particular OTD. If you choose to handle this synchronization in another manner, then there is no reason why you couldn't choose to expose this process if you wanted to. You would have to do the following:

❑ Use the PropertyID to locate the correct PropName object.

❑ Use the PropertyID and the ID of the base object to locate the correct PropValu object.

- ❏ If the PropValu exists, then you can just return them. If it doesn't exist, then you need to insert an empty PropValu as a place holder.

- ❏ The last step in this process is really trivial. When you are working with two collections of related Property Name/Value pairs you need to find the mating Name/Value and place those values into the PropBag object. In this case, you have a mated pair already, so all you have to do is to place that information into a PropBag Object.

The Insert Process

The Property Bag's programmable Production Interface also does not offer the ability to insert a new property via the PropBag object. Properties must be added to the *Property Set Definition* for an Object Type Definition using the Administrative Interface. Adding a new property to an extended object should be treated with the same deliberation used when adding a field to a table.

The Update Process

The Property Bag's programmable Production Interface does offer the ability to update a property's value via the PropBag object. Below is a complete listing of the code that performs the Property Value update. Please be aware that, although this code appears similar to standard Level I object code, it is not. Some subtle but important changes are utilized.

The User Centric Object Code – clsPropBag.cls

At first glance, the code for the user centric ObjectUpdate method for the PropBag object appears nearly identical to every other set of ObjectUpdate code. But if you take a closer look you will notice a subtle difference.

In all of the code we have worked with until now, we have always used both halves (the user and data centric halves) of the same object when working with that object. In this case, we are breaking tradition. When we perform an object update from the PropBag object, we are actually instantiating a different Data Centric object half – the PropValu object.

If you think about it for a minute, this does make sense. When we update a property, we are really only changing the property's *value*. We have chosen to control all of the objects that make up the PropBag from within a single object. We could, of course, teach every developer about all of the different pieces that make up the PropBag object, but this would really serve no purpose. Our object is more usable if our object insulates the developer and user interface programmers from unnecessary complexity. We call this practice **encapsulation**.

Other than the fact that we are creating a different Data Centric component than normal, the code is pretty much the same as we have come to expect from Enterprise Caliber Data Objects:

```
Public Sub ObjectUpdate()

  If IsChild Then Err.Raise 445

' Instantiate the remote object
  Dim ThisDataObject As DCPerson.clsPropValuData
  Set ThisDataObject = CreateObject("DCPerson.clsPropValuData")

' Update the Data In the Remote Object
  With ThisDataObject
    .SetDataSource mstrConnect
```

```
        .ObjectUpdate mlngStampID, mlngSaveStampID, mlngID, mlngSaveID, _
                mlngOwnerID, mlngSaveOwnerID, mlngPropertyID, _
                mlngSavePropertyID, mlngTypeID, mlngSaveTypeID, _
                mdtmStampDateTime, mdtmSaveStampDateTime, mintDataLocking, _
                mblnChangeAll, mblnSaveChangeAll, mstrStampUser, _
                mstrSaveStampUser, mstrStampAction, mstrSaveStampAction, _
                mstrDataMessage, mstrValue, mstrSaveValue, mstrPropertyName, _
                mstrSavePropertyName
    End With

    If Len(Trim(strDataMessage)) > 0 Then
        'Some Data Centric Problem Has Occurred
        If InStr(strDataMessage, "The Following Collisions have occured *") > 0 Then
            CollisionMessages = ParseCollisions(Trim(strDataMessage))
            Err.Raise vbObjectError + 1111, "PropValu Update", _
                    "Data Collisions have occured "
        Else
            ' An Data Error Other than a collision has occured.
            Err.Raise vbObjectError + 1234, "PropValu", strDataMessage
        End If
    Else
        ' Reset the local object's State
        ObjectIsDirty False
        ObjectIsNew False
    End If

    Set ThisDataObject = Nothing

End Sub
```

The Data Centric Object Code – clsPropBagData.cls
We already covered this code when we looked at the PropValu object earlier in the chapter.

The Stored Procedure
We also took a good look at this stored procedure earlier.

The Delete Process
Properties must be deleted from a Property Set Definition for an Object Type Definition using the programmable Administrative Interface. This functionality is not available from the programmable Production Interface. Although 4-Dimensional Data Objects make it easy to delete a property from an object, this functionality should not be exposed to the casual user. Deleting a property from an object should be treated with the same deliberation that is used when deleting a column or field from a table. It is important to note that while users cannot delete properties, they can 'delete' the value by removing the data from the field.

The Show Deleted Process
We've just said that properties can't be deleted from the programmable Production Interface so there is no reason to expose the *Show Deleted* functionality to the casual user. Instead, they can perform a functionally equivilent action by using the Audit History Process. This process is treated below.

The Restore From Deleted Process

By the same reasoning, there is no reason to expose the *Restore From Deleted* functionality to the casual user. As far as the user is concerned, deleting a Property Value means removing the data from the field. That means that the user can undo a deleted Property Value using the *Audit History* process.

The Audit History Process

The *Audit History* functionality is available from within the PropBag object. This allows users to view a history of previous values for any given property. It offers the casual user the ability to undo any action that was taken at any time against a particular property. Remember that we discussed that this also allows users to "restore" a Property Value that has been deleted within the confines available to the users for deleting values – essentially blanking out the field.

The way I did this may seem kind of tricky, but all we are really doing here is taking advantage of the fact that the information we need to retrieve for this routine is the same information that would be returned if we made the same call to the PropValu's *Audit History* process. In other words, all we really need to do here is to call the stored procedure we would expect to call from the PropValu Data Centric object from within the Data Centric PropBag object. Let's take a look at how this works.

The User Centric Object Code – colPropBag.cls

The code at this point is exactly the way we might imagine. No changes are made to the User Centric `clsPropBag` code. The only thing of any note here is that we declare and instantiate `objData` as `colPropBagData`:

```
Dim objData As DCPerson.colProgBagData
Set objData = CreateObject("DCPerson.colPropBagData")
```

The Data Centric Object Code – colPropBagData.cls

The really unexpected part of this routine occurs in the data centric code. Based upon our previous treatments, we would expect this routine to call the `spPersonPropBagAuditList` stored procedure. But in this case we are calling the `spPersonPropValuAuditList`. The reason we can do this is that we designed the `spPersonPropValuAuditList` to return the values the PropBag object expects:

```
strSQL = "spPersonPropValuAuditList " & lngID
```

The Stored Procedure

We've already covered the stored procedure for the PropValu object.

The Load Process

This process is the most important one in the whole book. The beauty and power of 4-Dimensional Data Objects is that you can define the properties for any extended object on the fly. If the accounting department decides that you need to track some additional information for customers, for employees, or for both, all you need to do is to add a new property definition to the PSD. The *Load* process is what makes this level of flexibility possible.

As we talked about when we looked at the Production User Interface, for 4-Dimensional Data Objects, we can always present the additional properties for any extended object using a listview or maybe some other user creative interface techniques (any ideas?). As long as we take that step at the user interface, we can change the information that we are collecting or managing for any 4-Dimensional Data Object object in **real-time** using a simple data entry routine we provided in the Administrative interface. And, maybe more importantly, even if we didn't make our user interface dynamic enough to handle something as flexible as a Property Bag, thanks to the Property Bag, the only code that we need to address when we add a property now is the code in the interface.

The *Load* process is what makes the Property Bag work.

The *Load* process performs several tasks:

❑   Determines whether or not a local Property Set Definition exists for the object indicated by `lngOwnerID` and `lngTypeID` variables.

❑   If a local Property Set Definition does exist, then the `Load` routine returns the Property Names and the Property Values as the PropBag object. At this time the PropBag `Load` routine also performs some other housekeeping chores:

❑   If a new Property Name has been added to the Property Set Definition for this type of extended object, then a new Property Value is added to the current set of Property Name/Value pairs for this particular object. This is repeated as many times as necessary to ensure that the current property set for this object is synchronized with the PSD defined by the Object Type Definition.

❑   If a property was deleted from the Property Set Definition for this type of extended object, then the corresponding Property Value is deleted from this object's PSD. This is also repeated as many times as necessary to ensure that the PSD for this object is synchronized with the PSD defined by the Object Type Definition.

❑   If a previously deleted property was restored to the global Property Set Definition, then the corresponding Property Name and value is restored in this object's current property set. This is repeated as many times as necessary to ensure that the PSD for this object is synchronized with the global PSD.

❑   If an individual Property Set doesn't already exist for the object then, the data centric portion of the `Load` routine creates a new set of mated Property Name/Value pairs for the object with all of the values set to their defaults *(In this book we will view defaults as a zero length string. Again, any ideas?).*

Once again, as a tribute to our push towards modularization, we have been able to confine all of the complexity of this process in a single place. As you look through the user centric code for this process, you should be struck by its simplicity. It is the same as any other User Centric `Load` routine. It doesn't do any thing remarkable or different. You will find the differences localized in the Data Centric `Fetch` process.

The User Centric Object Code – colPropBag.cls

```
Public Sub Load(lngOwnerID As Long, lngTypeID As Long, strStampUser As String)

    Dim objData As DCPerson.colPropBagData
    Set objData = CreateObject("DCPerson.colPropBagData")
```

```
        Dim TheAnswer As ADODB.Recordset

    With objData
      .SetDataSource mstrConnect
        Set TheAnswer = .Fetch(lngOwnerID, lngTypeID, strStampUser)

    If TheAnswer.RecordCount = 1 Then
        If Len(TheAnswer.Fields("DataMessage").Value) > 0 Then
            Err.Raise vbObjectError, "PropBag Load", _
                    TheAnswer.Fields("DataMessage").Value
        Else
            With TheAnswer
                Add !StampID, !ID, !OwnerID, !PropertyID, !TypeID, _
                    !DataTypeID, !SecutityLevel, !DisplayOrder, _
                    "", 2, "", !StampUser, "", "", !Value, _
                    !PropertyName, !DataTypeName, !ListAvailable, _
                    !AccessLevel, !UpdateInstruction
            End With
        End If

    Else

        Do While Not TheAnswer.EOF

            With TheAnswer
                Add !StampID, !ID, !OwnerID, !PropertyID, !TypeID, _
                    !DataTypeID, !SecutityLevel, !DisplayOrder, _
                    "", 2, "", !StampUser, "", "", !Value, _
                    !PropertyName, !DataTypeName, !ListAvailable, _
                    !AccessLevel, !UpdateInstruction
                .MoveNext
            End With

        Loop

    End If

    End With

    Set objData = Nothing
    Set TheAnswer = Nothing

End Sub
```

The Data Centric Object Code – colPropBagData

This is where all of the work for this process really takes place. If the *Load* process for the PropBag is the most important process in this book, then this block of code is the most important code in this book. As we work through the code, you will notice that it is quite different than any previous Data Centric `Fetch` routines we have looked at earlier. But you should also notice a similarity. Even though there is a lot of code in this routine, the code that is there is mostly used to control Data Centric objects. We have been doing this all along. The only difference here is that we are doing it from within another Data Centric object rather than from within a User Centric object as we have in the past.

The data centric portion of the *Load* process uses a subroutine called the `Fetch` subroutine. This routine requires 4 special helper objects:

❑   `clsPropBagMgr` - used to provide a convenient way to handle the PropBag data. All it contains is property handlers for the PropBag object.

❑   `colPropBagMgr` - used to manage a collection of `clsPropBagMgr` objects. It is a standard collection object with `Add`, `Remove`, `Count` etc. methods.

❑   `clsPropValueMgr` used to manages the information about the Property Values. Like the PropBagMgr object it just contains property handlers.

❑   `colPropValueMgr` - used to manage a collection of `clsPropValueMgr` objects. It is also a standard collection object.

The code for these helper classes can be found in Appendix C. You can also use the ones that have been provided with the sample code. There is no reason to ever change a single line of code in these four class files.

There is no reason to ever have to change a single line of code in these objects.

Now, we can begin to look at the code in the data centric `Fetch` subroutine:

```
Public Function Fetch(lngOwnerID As Long, lngTypeID As Long, _
                    strStampUser As String) As Recordset

    Dim strSQL As String
    Dim strValue As String
    Dim strValue As String
    Dim strData Message As String

    Dim ctxObject As ObjectContext
    Set ctxObject = GetObjectContext()

    On Error Goto FetchErrorOut
```

The first part of the code just creates the helper objects and other Data Centric objects we will control from within this procedure.

There is no reason to use the `CreateObject` command when we instantiate the helper classes. We only use these classes to help us to manage the data within this subroutine. These helper objects do not and will never participate in a transaction that will be controlled by MTS. What this means in real terms is that it is OK to use the New keyword when instantiating these helper objects. You might also notice that the Instancing property of these classes has been set accordingly.

```
' Create the local PropNames Collection and Object  ** HELPER CLASSES
    Dim PropNames As colPropBagMgr
    Set PropNames = New colPropBagMgr

    Dim ThisPropDef As clsPropBagMgr

' Create the local Property Values Collection  ** HELPER CLASSES
    Dim PropValues As colPropValueMgr
    Set PropValues = New colPropValueMgr

    Dim ThisPropValue As clsPropValueMgr
```

Dimension and create all of the data objects and collections we will need for this procedure:

```
' This is the Data Handler For Property Names
Dim PropertyDefs As DCPerson.colPropNameData
Set PropertyDefs = CreateObject("DCPerson.colPropNameData")

Dim rcdPropertyData As Recordset

Dim PropertyDef As DCPerson.clsPropNameData
Set PropertyDef = CreateObject("DCPerson.clsPropNameData")

' This is the Data Handler For Property Valu
Dim PropertyValues As DCPerson.colPropValuData
Set PropertyValues = CreateObject("DCPerson.colPropValuData")

Dim ThisPropertyValue As clsPropValuData
Set ThisPropertyValue = CreateObject("DCPerson.clsPropValuData")
```

Once the required objects have been instantiated, the next step is to load the `PropertyNames` collection for this particular Object Type Definition. This is handled in the following block of code. Let's step through it.

First, we tell the object where to get the data by passing the value of the `colPropBagData.GetDataSource` function into the `SetDataSource` method:

```
With PropertyDefs
   .SetDataSource GetDataSource
```

Then we load a local recordset with the Property Names for this Object Type Definition. Once we have filled the recordset, we simply move the values from the recordset into our helper collection of `PropBags` objects.

> *When I first wrote this routine, I used the helper classes to make it easier for me to keep track of where everything was going. At that time, I was also using variant arrays rather than the recordset we are using here. I haven't done it yet. But I think that it would be worth the time and effort to test the effects of using the recordsets directly without the aid of the helper classes. This would mean that we might need to hold onto the database connection a little longer, but it may provide an overall increase in efficiency and performance:*

```
Set rcdPropertyData = .Fetch(lngTypeID)

Do While Not rcdPropertyData.EOF

    With rcdPropertyData
        Set ThisPropName = New clsPropBagMgr
        ThisPropName.StampID = !StampID
        ThisPropName.ID = !ID
        ThisPropName.ControllingTypeID = !ControllingTypeID
        ThisPropName.DataTypeID = ! DataTypeID
        ThisPropName.SecurityLevel = !SecurityLevel
        ThisPropName.DisplayOrder = !DisplayOrder
        ThisPropName.TypeID = !TypeID
        ThisPropName.StampDateTime = FixNulls(!StampDateTime)
        ThisPropName.DataLocking = 2
```

```
                ThisPropName.ChangeAll = FixNulls(!ChangeAll)
                ThisPropName.StampUser = FixNulls(!StampUser)
                ThisPropName.StampAction = FixNulls(!StampAction)
                ThisPropName.DataMessage = ""
                ThisPropName.PropertyName = FixNulls(!PropertyName)
                ThisPropName.DataTypeName = FixNulls(!DataTypeName)
                ThisPropName.AccessLevel = FixNulls(!AccessLevel)
                ThisPropName.ListAvailable = FixNulls(!ListAvailable)
                PropNames.Add 0, 0, ThisPropName.ID, "", "I", ThisPropName.TypeID, _
                        ThisPropName.PropertyName, ThisPropName.DataTypeID, _
                        ThisPropName.DataTypeName, ThisPropName.ListAvailable, _
                        ThisPropName.DisplayOrder, ThisPropName.AccessLevel, _
                        ThisPropName.SecurityLevel, ""

            End With

        Loop

    End With Set
```

So far, this process has provided us with a lot of information. Now we know each of the Property Names that the Property Set Definition currently contains, and we also know some detailed information about each property definition:

- ❑ The Data Type – This property tells us what type of information each property was designed to hold, Integer, String, Long, etc.

- ❑ The Security Level – This property contains a number that we use to determine the security level required to access this property. It works like this: Say a User A has security level 5 and that User B has security level 7. If the property in question has a security level of 6, User A will be able to access the property, while User B will not even be aware that the property exists.

- ❑ The Access Level – This property indicates whether Object Type Definitions that share this property can change its value or only view the existing value

- ❑ The Display Order – This property is used to sort a list of properties into a meaningful order that does not necessarily have to be alphabetic or numeric.

- ❑ The List Available - Whether or not a List is available for this property

At this point, we have a helper class that is full of Property Definition information called PropNames. Next we need to retrieve the Property Values from the data store.

The next section of code performs essentially the same task as the last section of code performed. Except that in this case we are concerned with the actual Property Values for the target object. The one thing to note, here is that we set the UpdateInstruction parameter, the third parameter in the call to the Add function, to the value "I". This stands for insert. What we have done here is to set the default Update instruction for every Property Value to insert. We also set the Delete parameter value, the fifth parameter in the call to the Add function, to True. We will use these values later:

```
    With PropertyValues
        .SetDataSource mstrConnect
        Set rcdPropertyData = Fetch(lngOwnerID, lngTypeID)

        Do While Not rcdPropertyData.EOF
            With rcdPropertyData
```

```
            Set ThisPropValue = New clsPropValueMgr
            ThisPropValue.StampID = !StampID
            ThisPropValue.ID = !ID
            ThisPropValue.OwnerID = !OwnerID
            ThisPropValue.PropertyID = !PropertyID
            ThisPropValue.OwnerTypeID = !OwnerTypeID
            ThisPropValue.StampDateTime = FixNulls(!StampDateTime)
            ThisPropValue.DataLocking = 2
            ThisPropValue.ChangeAll = FixNulls(!ChangeAll)
            ThisPropValue.StampUser = FixNulls(!StampUser)
            ThisPropValue.StampAction = FixNulls(!StampAction)
            ThisPropValue.DataMessage = ""
            ThisPropValue.Value = FixNulls(!Value)
            ThisPropValue.Name = FixNulls(!Name)

            PropValues.Add ThisPropValue.ID, ThisPropValue.PropertyID, _
                        "I", ThisPropValue.OwnerID, True, _
                        ThisPropValue.Value
        End With

    Loop

End With
rcdPropertyData = Nothing
Set ThisConnection = Nothing
```

The two blocks of code above have given us all of the information we need from the data store. Now we can free up the database connection so that another object can use it.

At this time we have two different helper object collections. One contains information that defines properties we call this collection the `PropNames` collection. The other collection, `PropValues`, contains information that amounts to the set of Property Values that should be paired to the Property Names in the first collection. Our job here is simply to pair up the Names with the Values. To do that, we iterate through the `PropNames` collection and attempt to find its mate in the `PropValues` collection.

Remember that the objects in both helper class collections have a PropertyID value and that we set this value with the information we found in the data store. This means that we will know if we found a match if the Property Name and the Property Value both have the same value for PropertyID.

For example, if we were working with *John*'s information from above, we would find the words Mother's Maiden Name in the `PropNames` collection maybe it has the PropertyID value set to 7. This means that when we iterate through the `PropValues` collection we are looking for the Property Value that also has its PropertyID set to 7. When we find this PropertyID, it will have the word "Smith" stored in its `Value` property. Every time we find a match, we copy the necessary information from the PropValu object into the mating PropName object which has a property set up to handle it.

At this time, we also set a couple of flags for the object. We set the `UpdateInstruction` property to U and the `Delete` property to False:

```
For Each ThisPropName In PropNames

    For Each ThisPropValue In PropValues
```

```
        If ThisPropValue.PropertyID = ThisValue.PropertyID Then
            ThisPropValue.Value = ThisValue.Value
            ThisPropValue.UpdateInstruction = "U"
            ThisPropValue.ID = ThisValue.ID
            ThisPropValue.OwnerID = ThisValue.OwnerID
            ThisPropValue.Delete = False
            Exit For
        End If

    Next ThisPropValue
Next ThisPropName
```

Once we have iterated through all of the properties in the PropNames, the following changes will have taken place:

❑ If a Property Value was found, we change UpdateInstruction to U otherwise it is still set to I. The U means that we found a Property Value, so the user will be able to Update the Property Value. The I means that we didn't find an associated Property Value for this Property Name, so need to insert a new default value for this property.

❑ If a Property Value was found, we set its Delete property to False, otherwise it is still set to True. This flag is used to tell us whether or not the Property Name has been deleted. If we find a Property Value that for some reason is not related to a Property Name, then we will need to delete the Property Value. We will do that a little later.

❑ The Property Definitions and their corresponding values are now paired.

The next section of code tests the Delete property to determine whether or not to delete this Property Value from the data store. I think the code is self-explanatory:

```
For Each ThisPropValue In PropValues

    If ThisPropValue.Delete Then
        Set ThisPropertyValue = New clsPropValuData
        ThisPropertyValue.ObjectDelete ThisValue.ID, strStampUser, strDataMessage
    End If

Next ThisPropValue
```

This little block of code is used to delete any values that do not have a mate at the end of the pairing process. This code is responsible for.

❑ Deleting Property Values if their mating Property Definition no longer exists

The last section of code in this block tests the UpdateInstruction to determine whether or not to insert a new, blank, Property Value into the data store for this object:

```
For Each ThisPropName In PropNames

    If ThisPropName.UpdateInstruction = "I" Then
        Set ThisPropertyValue = New clsPropValuData
        lngPropertyID = ThisPropName.PropertyID
        lngOwnerTypeID = ThisPropName.TypeID
        strName = ThisPropName.Name
```

```
        strValue = "" 'initialize to empty string
        ThisPropertyValue.SetDataSource mstrConnect
        ThisPropertyValue.ObjectInsert 0, lngID, lngOwnerID, _
                                    lngPropertyID, lngOwnerTypeID, _
                                    "", 2, _
                                    "", strStampUser, "", _
                                    "", strValue, strName
      ThisPropName.ID = lngID
      ThisPropName.Value = strValue
    End If

  Next ThisProp
```

The block of code above is primarily concerned with ensuring that each Property Name currently in the Property Set Definition has an associated Property Value with a default value (in this case a zero length string).

❑ Inserting empty Property Values to match new properties that have been added since last time this property set was accessed

After all this work, what we have now is a valid collection of Property Name/Value pairs for that can be attached to the base object according to the Object Type Definition ID that was passed into the Fetch routine at the beginning.

All that's left to do is create the recordset and feed in the Property Values to be returned to the Load routine:

```
Dim TheAnswer as ADODB.Recordset
Set TheAnswer = New ADODB.Recordset

With TheAnswer.Fields
  .Append "StampID", adInteger
  .Append "ID", adInteger
  .Append "OwnerID", adInteger
  .Append "PropertyID", adInteger
  .Append "TypeID", adInteger
  .Append "DataTypeID", adInteger
  .Append "SecutityLevel", adInteger
  .Append "DisplayOrder", adInteger
  .Append "StampDateTime", adDate
  .Append "DataLocking", adInteger
  .Append "ChangeAll", adChar, 255
  .Append "StampUser", adChar, 15
  .Append "StampAction", adChar, 60
  .Append "DataMessage", adChar, 255
  .Append "Value", adChar, 255
  .Append "PropertyName", adChar, 80
  .Append "DataTypeName", adChar, 80
  .Append "ListAvailable", adChar, 1
  .Append "AccessLevel", adChar, 1
  .Append "UpdateInstruction", adChar, 1
End With

TheAnswer.Open

For Each ThisPropName In PropNames
```

```
        With TheAnswer
          .AddNew
          .Fields("StampID") = ThisPropName.ID
          .Fields("ID") = ThisPropName.ID
          .Fields("OwnerID") = ThisPropName.OwnerID
          .Fields("PropertyID") = ThisPropName.PropertyID
          .Fields("TypeID") = ThisPropName.TypeID
          .Fields("DataTypeID") = ThisPropName.DataTypeID
          .Fields("SecurityLevel") = ThisPropName.SecurityLevel
          .Fields("DisplayOrder") = ThisPropName.DisplayOrder
          .Fields("StampDateTime") = ""
          .Fields("DataLocking") = 2
          .Fields("ChangeAll") = ""
          .Fields("StampUser") = strStampUser
          .Fields("StampAction") = ""
          .Fields("DataMessage") = ""
          .Fields("Value") = ThisPropName.Value
          .Fields("PropertyName") = ThisPropName.PropertyName
          .Fields("DataTypeName") = ThisPropName.DataTypeName
          .Fields("ListAvailable") = ThisPropName.ListAvailable
          .Fields("AccessLevel") = ThisPropName.AccessLevel
          .Fields("UpdateInstruction") = ThisPropName.UpdateInstruction
          .Update
        End With

    Next ThisPropName

    Set Fetch = TheAnswer

    ctxObject.SetComplete

    Set TheAnswer = Nothing
    Set ThisPropName = Nothing
    Set PropName = Nothing
    Set PropValues = Nothing
    Set ThisPropValue = Nothing
    Set ctxObject = Nothing

    Exit Function

FetchErrorOut:

    ErrorHandler

End Function
```

The Call to PropItem Load

There is one other thing we should do if we want the developers who use our objects to be able to work with the entirety of the Property Bag's programmable Production Interface from a single place. We should give the developer the ability to load a list of valid responses or PropItems for a particular property. This is not as difficult as it sounds. All we need to do to be able to provide this capability is to add a one line of code to the declaration section of our `UCPropBag.colPropBags` module and add a one simple function that manages the PropItem `Load` call:

```
Private mobjPropItems as UCPerson.colPropItems
```

Notice that we don't use a property handler to manage this local variable. Instead, we use a single function call that will manage the process of loading the list of items for a particular property. This function requires a single parameter, the ID of the property we need to retrieve the list for:

```
Public Function GetItemsForProperty(lngPropertyID As Long) As
UCPerson.colPropItems

  On Error Resume Next

  Set mobjPropItems = Nothing
  Set mobjPropItems = CreateObject("UCPerson.colPropItems")
  mobjPropItems.SetDataSource mstrConnect
  mobjPropItems.Load lngPropertyID
  Set GetItemsForProperty = mobjPropItems

End Function
```

Notice that before we attempt to load the list of items that we take the time to destroy and recreate the local variable. This is an easy way to ensure that the developer is always getting a fresh list of items each time this function is called.

Summary

Over the last few chapters, we have gone through all of the code that we use for a 4-Dimensional Data Object. Now we have an understanding of a few very important concepts:

❑   An Object Type Definition (OTD) allows us to specify a category for an extension for a base object

❑   A Property Set Definition (PSD) allows us to specify what set of properties are required for a particular OTD.

❑   A Property Definition allows us to manage data using a Name/Value property pair.

❑   The Property Bag PropBag object allows us to manage the PSD for a particular OTD.

Now that we've covered these concepts we understand the hows and whys and of 4-Dimensional Enterprise Caliber Data Objects. We can now move onto thinking about how to combine numerous objects together to create applications.

In the next chapter, we'll look at how to actually connect various ECDOs together and then in Chapter 14, we'll see how we can apply business rules to our data objects, in the form of a veneer, to create business objects.

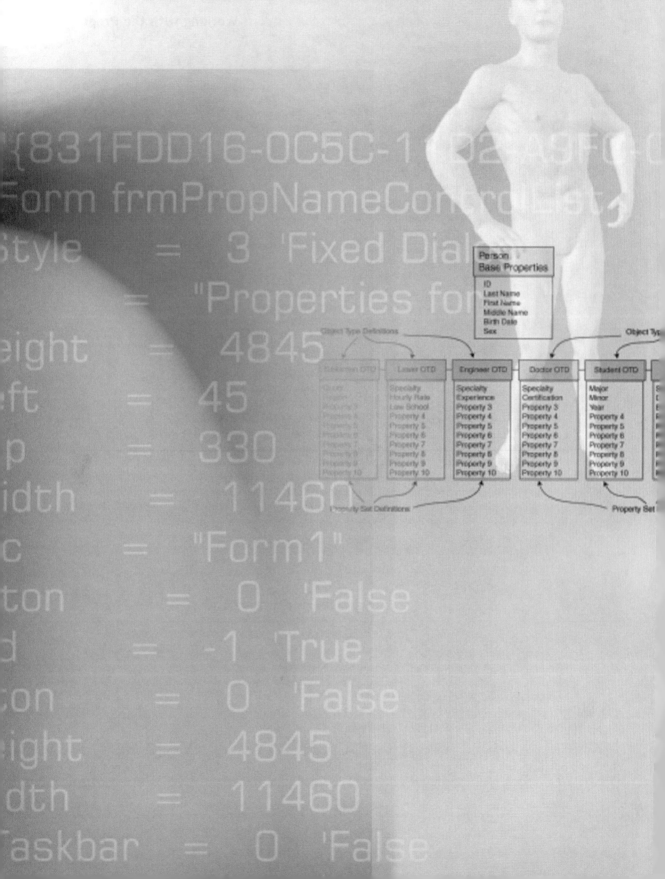

```
{831FDD16-0C5C-1              2   A9F
Form frmPropNameContr  List
Style        =    3  'Fixed Dial
             =    "Properties for
eight        =    4845
ft           =    45
p            =    330
idth         =    11460
c            =    "Form1"
ton          =    0   'False
d            =    -1  'True
con          =    0   'False
eight        =    4845
dth          =    11460
askbar       =    0   'False
```

13

Connecting Objects

Over the last seven chapters we learned to build some very capable data objects. While we did this, I was very careful not to allow us to become sidetracked into thinking too much about things like how does one object relate to another object. You may not have noticed, but I was also very careful to ensure that we only included base properties that directly described the object that we were designing. For instance over the last few chapters we have been busy building something we called the *Person* object. If you look back at what we did, you will find that the only information (properties) that we allowed to become part of the *Person* object was just the information that helped us to describe an actual person. Nowhere in the *Person* object do we consider things that are merely related to an actual person, like addresses or telephone numbers etc. We didn't really talk about it at the time, but this design approach – limiting an object's base properties to include only that information that directly describes the object – is one of the fundamental tenets of good data object design. This purity of content is *the* thing that makes it possible to reuse data objects. To help to ensure this purity of content, I always try to design objects using the following two principles:

- ❑ Include *only* those base properties that directly define a single real-world entity
- ❑ Try not to use base properties that serve only to define relationships to other objects

If you are like most people I have talked with, you are probably nodding your head in agreement with the first principle. You are also probably quietly wondering to yourself, "how the heck are we going to get any real work done if we can't define relationships within the data objects. Surely this guy is talking about that second *principle* in purely theoretical terms. I don't care how good we make these objects they won't do us any good if they aren't designed to work with other objects." I agree. Even the best data objects can't exist in a vacuum. In order for us to take advantage of the real power of Enterprise Caliber Data Objects, we are going to need a way to be able to manage the relationships that exist between objects. Those relationships, or connections, between objects are what this chapter is all about. What we are going to do in this chapter is develop a technique that allows us to manage the relationships between data objects from outside of the data objects.

As with every other programming problem we have faced in this book, we will solve this one by employing an Enterprise Caliber Data Object. In this case, we will use a special kind of ECDO that we will call a **Connector object**. As the name implies, we use a Connector object to manage the relationship or connection between two other ECDOs.

You might think that writing the code for an object that is used to manage potentially complex relationships between other data objects would be difficult. I am happy to say that this is not the case. You will find that you already know just about everything you need to know to be able to build a Connector object. At their core, these objects are really just special cases of an ordinary Level I Data Object. This is really good news, because it means that we won't have to spend too much time learning how to code these things. This means that we will be able to spend more time thinking about ways that we might use Connector objects. But, I think that before we begin to think about ways that we can use these new objects, it might be a good idea for us to stop an go over what we know about the objects we already have.

Data Objects - A Review

We divided the task of learning how to code Enterprise Caliber Data Objects into three sections. First we learned how to code a Level I Data Object. We found that we could think of Level I Data Objects as something of a model for an ordinary database table. Once we felt comfortable with the code we needed to write to build a Level I Data Object, we took on the task of building something we called a Level II Data Object. We designed this object to be very much like a Level I Data Object that also had the ability to categorize things using something we called an Object Type Definition. In our example, we built a Level II *Person* object and used it to create OTDs like Salesman, Lawyer, Engineer, etc. Unfortunately, we soon discovered that while this ability to categorize things was a good quality, if we wanted to design an object that could truly model a real-world entity we would need the ability to be able to carry around some additional information for each OTD. We rose to this challenge by designing something called a Level III or 4-Dimensional Data Object. The 4-Dimensional Data Object we conjured up was really just a Level II Object that had something called a Property Bag attached to it. This Property Bag gave our new object the ability to be extended by carrying around a different set of information for each OTD.

IDs and TypeIDs

One other way that we can describe the different levels of objects is by looking at the information (Key) that we use to uniquely identify each level of object. All ECDOs have a unique ID that is assigned by the data store when the object is first inserted into the data store. We can always use an object's ID to uniquely identify a base object. This is an important thing to remember when we are developing a technique to manage a relationship between objects. In order to be able to define a relationship between two objects we need a reliable way to be able to identify each object in the relationship.

> **We can always uniquely identify an ECDO's base Property Set by its ID.**

As long as we are talking about Level I Objects, we don't really need to think about more than the objects' IDs to uniquely identify each object. However, as soon as we move into the Level II Objects or higher (i.e. objects with an OTD), we have something else to consider. Remember that we can use an OTD to categorize an object.

We can use an OTD to categorize the *Person* object into Salespeople, Lawyers, Engineers, etc. What actually happens at the database when we categorize an object is that in addition to the object's unique ID value we also insert a second kind of ID. This second ID uniquely identifies the particular category or OTD for the person. Because this ID is used to uniquely identify a type of object, we call this second ID a TypeID. What this means is that, for a Level II or Level III Object, we might need to specify two ID values to uniquely identify a specific instance of an object.

Let me give you an example.

The information in the following view shows that Joan is a Salesperson, a Lawyer, and an Engineer. It also shows the Henry is an Engineer:

ID	TypeID	PersonName	TypeName
1	1	Joan	Salesperson
1	2	Joan	Lawyer
2	3	Henry	Engineer
1	3	Joan	Engineer

Think about what this means. If I need to get information about Joan as a Salesperson, I need to know two things. I need to know that Joan's ID is 1 and I need to know that the Salesperson ID is 1. It takes both of these pieces of information to uniquely identify Joan within the Salesperson OTD. If all I knew was Joan's ID, then the best I could do is to retrieve 3 records from this view. There are times when we might want to do this, but right now we are trying to learn how to develop relationships.

We have already said that in order to develop relationships we need to be able to uniquely identify each base object. I think that now we can safely say that we also need to be able to uniquely identify categorized or extended instances of objects as well. In other words, if I wanted to get information about Joan as a Lawyer, then I would need to provide two bits of information – ID = 1 and TypeID = 2. If I wanted to find out whether or not Henry was also a Lawyer, I could get the answer to that question by using Henry's ID (2) paired with the TypeID for a Lawyer (2). What I would find is that we don't have Henry listed as a Lawyer.

> We can always identify a unique instance of an extended ECDO by using the object's ID along with a TypeID.

The following table summarizes the options we have available to us for identifying the different levels of objects in our data store:

Object Level	ID	TypeID
Level I	Yes	No
Level II	Yes	Yes
Level III (4-D DO)	Yes	Yes

The table shows that when we are working with a Level I Object, we can only identify that object using its ID. But when we are using Level II or Level III Objects, we can further refine our selection criteria by using a TypeID.

Relationships

OK, now that we know that we can uniquely identify each object by using either its ID or a combination of ID and TypeID, we can take some time to see how we can apply this to the task of managing relationships between objects. Let's take on the simplest case first. Let's suppose that we have two Level I Objects.

- ❑ A Level I Object that contains a list of products
- ❑ A Level I Object that contains a list of sizes

Let's suppose that the tables for these objects looked like the following:

PRODUCT	
ID	**Name**
1	Top-notch perfume
2	Second-notch perfume
3	Top-notch men's cologne
4	Second-notch men's cologne

SIZE	
ID	**Size**
1	1 ounce
2	2 ounce
3	3 ounce
4	4 ounce

If we needed to show that we have each product available in all four sizes, we would need to add a third table to this data store. We would add a table that we can call a **Bridge table**. We would call the columns in that table ProductID and SizeID:

PRODUCTSIZEBRIDGE	
ProductID	**SizeID**
1	1
1	2

PRODUCTSIZEBRIDGE	
ProductID	**SizeID**
1	3
1	4
2	1
2	2
2	3
2	4
3	1
3	2
3	3
3	4
4	1
4	2
4	3
4	4

Notice that the names we have chosen give us a great deal of information about the relationship that the Bridge table contains. The first portion of the name specifies the table name and the second portion of the name specifies the column name in that table.

- ❏   ProductID – ID column in the Product table
- ❏   SizeID – ID column in the Size table

We said that all of the products in this example were available in all four sizes. In this case, that means that our Bridge table would have sixteen rows. We can look at each row in this Bridge table and find the unique pairing of records it represents in the other two tables. For instance, the highlighted row in the Bridge table reads ProductID = 2 and SizeID = 3. If we look up these ID numbers in the two tables above we find that they point to a 3 ounce bottle of second-notch perfume.

From this example, we should realize:

- ❏   A Level I Object is a proxy for a single table in the data store
- ❏   We can manage relationships by using a single table in the data store

> **This means that we can manage relationships between two Level I Objects by using another Level I Object.**

Let's take a look at a slightly more complex example. In this case we will say that our products are available in two categories. That means that our Product object has an OTD. As we covered earlier, this means that we will have a third table to manage the OTD information.

Let's suppose that the third table containing the Product OTD information looked like the following (the other two tables remain the same so we won't show them here):

PRODUCTTYPE	
ID	**Name**
1	Bottle
2	Atomizer

In this case, we also want to show that we have all of the products available in all four sizes, but our Product is a Level II or Level III Object. This means that any of the Product objects could exist in one or more OTD categories. Using the ProductType table, we find that this means that we might have product in regular bottles or in atomizer containers.

This means that in order to show this relationship in the Bridge table, we need to add a third field to the Bridge table. We use the same naming convention for the third field in the table. That means we name this field ProductTypeID because it points to the ID column in the ProductType table. The other two fields remain the same:

PRODUCTSIZEBRIDGE		
ProductID	**ProductTypeID**	**SizeID**
1	1	1
1	2	1
1	1	2
1	2	2
1	1	3
1	2	3
1	1	4
1	2	4
2	1	1
2	2	1
etc	etc	etc

Just like the previous example, we can look at each row in this Bridge table and find the unique pairing of records it represents in the other three tables. For instance, the highlighted row in the Bridge table reads ProductID = 1, ProductTypeID = 2, and SizeID = 4. If we look up these ID numbers in the two tables above we find that they point to a 4 ounce atomizer of top-notch perfume.

From this example, we should realize:

- ❑   A Level I Object is a proxy for a single table in the data store
- ❑   We can manage relationships between a Level I and a Level II or III Object with a single table in the data store

> **This means that we can manage the relationships between Level I and Level II or III Objects using a Level I Object.**

Let's take a look at a slightly more complex example. In this case, we will say that our sizes are available in two categories. That means that our Size object has an OTD. As we covered earlier, this means that we will have a fourth table to manage the Size OTD information. Therefore, we have:

- ❑   A Level II or Level III Object that contains a list of Products
- ❑   A Level II or Level III Object that contains a list of Sizes

Let's suppose that the table for the Size OTD information looked like the following (again, the other three tables are the same as those shown previously, so we won't show them again):

SIZETYPE	
ID	**Name**
1	Normal
2	50% free

In this case, we also want to show that we have all of the products available in all four sizes. Our product is a Level II or Level III Object and our size is also a Level II or Level III Object. This means that any of the Product objects could exist in one or more OTD categories, and that any of our Sizes could exist in one or more OTD categories. Using the tables, we find that this means that we might have product in regular bottles or in atomizer containers and that we have two sizes available - the normal size and the 50% free size. (I know this is getting ridiculous, but we are worried about the relationships here.) This means that in order to show this relationship in the Bridge table, we need to add a fourth field to this table. We use the same naming convention for this field. That means we name this field SizeTypeID because it points to the ID column in the SizeType table. The other three fields remain the same.

PRODUCTSIZEBRIDGE			
ProductID	**ProductTypeID**	**SizeID**	**SizeTypeID**
1	1	1	1
1	1	1	2
1	2	1	1
1	2	1	2
etc	etc	etc	etc

Now, the highlighted row in the Bridge table reads ProductID = 1, ProductTypeID = 2, SizeID = 1, and SizeTypeID = 2. If we look up these ID numbers in the tables above, we find that they point to a 1 ounce atomizer of top-notch perfume that offers half an ounce for free.

From this example, we should realize:

- ❏ A Level I Object is a proxy for a table in the data store
- ❏ We can manage relationships between two Level II or III Objects with a single table in the data store

> **This means that we can manage the relationships between two Level II or III Objects using a Level I Object.**

We can summarize the information we just went over by defining the following three types of Connector objects:

- ❏ ID to ID Connector object
- ❏ ID to ID + TypeID Connector object
- ❏ ID + TypeID to ID + TypeID Connector object

The following three tables give us the base set of properties for the three general cases for Connector objects.

ID to ID Connector Object

Properties for an ID to ID Connector Object			
ID	**Data Type**	**Size**	**Brief Description**
ObjectOneID	Long	4	Contains Object One's ID
ObjectTwoID	Long	4	Contains Object Two's ID

ID to ID + TypeID Connector Object

Properties for an ID to ID + TypeID Connector Object			
ID	**Data Type**	**Size**	**Brief Description**
ObjectOneID	Long	4	Contains Object One's ID
ObjectTwoID	Long	4	Contains Object Two's ID
ObjectTwoTypeID	Long	4	Contains Object Two's TypeID

ID + TypeID to ID + TypeID Connector Object

Properties for an ID + TypeID to ID + TypeID Connector Object			
ID	Data Type	Size	Brief Description
ObjectOneID	Long	4	Contains Object One's ID
ObjectOneTypeID	Long	4	Contains Object One's TypeID
ObjectTwoID	Long	4	Contains Object Two's ID
ObjectTwoTypeID	Long	4	Contains Object Two's TypeID

At this point, we should realize mathematically that we have three options available to us for connecting one object to another and that we can do that using a Level I Object we will call a Connector object. Let's take a few minutes to understand this Connector from another perspective.

Connector Objects

In all honesty, Connector objects are really a something of a throwback to my childhood. You may be surprised to learn, as my new employers usually are, that I always walk into a new assignment with a very large canister of TinkerToys® under my arm. I use the TinkerToys to model information systems in much the same way that I learned to model complex organic molecules using molecular models.

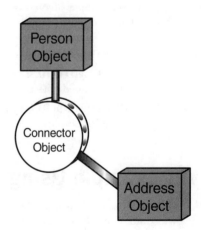

Just in case you are not familiar with TinkerToys, look at the image on the right. It shows the relationship between a *Person* object and an *Address* object using a Connector object (which looks remarkably like a TinkerToy). Remember from our discussion above that we said that one of our guiding principles is that we should always strive to design data objects without using properties that define a relationship to other objects. Connector objects allow us to do that, because they manage the relationship between two objects from outside of either object.

Connector objects are what enable us to create data objects without having to consider the countless relationships that an object may have to manage during its lifetime.

> **We can say that just like a Level I object is really a proxy for a single table in the data store, the Connector object is a proxy for a single Bridge table in the data store.**

Connector objects are easy to build. As we said earlier, they are really just a special case of a Level I object with a few extra stored procedures. In many ways, they are actually easier to build than a Level I object because there are only three possible sets of properties for a Connector object. Building applications with Connector objects is also quite easy. You use Connector objects in almost *exactly* the way you use any other Level I data object.

Because Connector objects are really Level I objects, they have the same eight data handling processes that we have come to expect from an Enterprise Caliber Data Object. In other words, when you need to create a new relationship between two objects, you just use the Connector object's `ObjectInsert` method. When you need to remove a relationship between any two objects, you just use the Connector object's `ObjectDelete` method. Of course we can also learn about previous relationships between objects using either the `ObjectAuditHistory` or `ShowDeleted` methods of the Connector object.

> **Connector objects give us an easily reproducible technique that we can use to manage relationships between objects.**

All Connector objects have essentially the same set of properties. As we found from our discussion above, there are really only three different possible configurations for Connector objects:

- ❑   **ID to ID.** These objects are used to manage a relationship between two base objects.
- ❑   **ID + TypeID to ID.** These objects are used to manage a relationship between one base object and one extended object.
- ❑   **ID + TypeID to ID + TypeID.** These objects are used to manage a relationship between two extended objects.

An Example Using Connector Objects

Data objects allow us to design and construct applications in a very natural way. In this chapter, we will think about Connector objects by looking at how we might use them to handle a task that we have all probably had to do at one time or another – manage a list of names and addresses. We will use the *Person* object we built earlier along with a couple of other objects you will find in the sample code for this chapter to develop a small application that has the functionality of an address book. Our primary purpose here is to learn to use Connector objects to create and manage relationships between objects.

As far as we are concerned right now, think of this example application as a big filing cabinet that keeps track of individuals and their contact information. You can imagine that there are folders in the cabinet and that each folder is designed to hold all of the contact information for a particular individual. In other words, if I were to open up a folder for John Smith, that folder would contain base information about John as well as a list of the addresses related to him – home, summer home, business, temporary address, etc. This folder would also contain all of the telephone numbers and email addresses that are related to John as well.

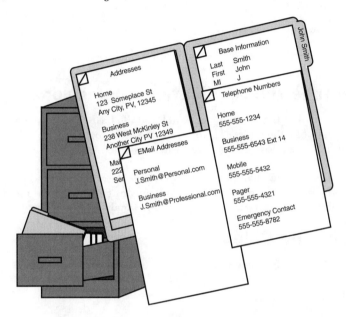

If we were to think about designing this application in a conventional manner, we would have to carefully plan for all of the possible relationships that could occur before we could really begin to develop the application. We would have to think in terms of database tables and relationships. This can get complex quickly. Just consider for example that, in addition to John, there might also be a Mrs. Smith who should really share a great deal of the contact information with her husband. How would you express those relationships? Would you keep two copies of a single home telephone number in the data store – one for John and another for his wife Sally? What about their children, the elderly parent they care for, or their live-in housekeeper who all share the same home telephone number? What do you do when the telephone company issues a new area code or prefix for the phone number? What do you do when the eldest child goes off to college and moves into the dormitory? I think you can see my point about the potential complexity. Notice, that we haven't even begun to consider the database issues that are related to audit trails, unlimited undos, restoring data from deleted state, etc. It is no wonder that most applications have difficultly expressing the time dimension.

Fortunately for us, we don't need to think about all of those things right now. We are working with Enterprise Caliber Data Objects! That means that we can model this application in terms of the real world entities that are contained (or managed) in the example rather than thinking about the database tables and their complex relationships. We can think about and model the functionality we need in terms of people, addresses, telephone numbers, and email addresses.

The job of delivering applications using 4-Dimensional Data Objects requires 6 steps:

1. Determine the application's functionality
2. Acquire the base objects necessary to deliver that functionality
3. Extend the base objects with type definitions if necessary
4. Connect the objects
5. Add the business rules
6. Build a user interface and deploy the application

Step 1 - Determine the Application's Functionality

We have already spent a lot of time learning how to build the base objects. We can write them from scratch, we can use a tool like the Object Factory to write them for us, or we can use the pre-existing objects that came with the sample code delivered with this book.

For this example, we have already handled step 1. We have described our basic functionality as something we can compare to an address book. So that means that we should move onto the next step - acquiring the base objects necessary to deliver that functionality.

Step 2 - Acquire the Objects

For this example, we will need four main objects:

- ❏ A *Person* object
- ❏ An *Address* object
- ❏ A Telephone Number object
- ❏ An Email Address object

Person Object

If you have worked through the code in the last few chapters, you should now have a working model for a *Person* object. In this exercise, we will work with the *Person* object without really considering the extension of the base person – engineer, employee, customer, etc.

> *You can find the Address, Telephone Number, and Email Address ECDOs in the sample code for this chapter. If you haven't taken the time to download the sample code, now would be a good time to do that.*

Address Object

As the name implies, the *Address* object is used to manage standard postal addresses. OK, now I have a confession to make. Although I said we never build Level II objects, I have provided you with an *Address* object that is essentially a Level II object. It has a type, but it doesn't have a Property Bag. You will also find that the same is true for the *Telephone Number* object and the *Email Address* object. I have done this for the following reason.

I want you to focus on the connections between the objects. The Property Bag that comes with a Level III object doesn't help us to think about connections. It just gives us a way to carry around extra properties – to understand connections, we need to think about the things like base objects and OTDs. Level II objects, by definition, are base objects with an OTD.

> *Of course, now that I have given you a couple of Level II objects, you will probably rattle off a list of properties that you could have added to these objects. If so, that just goes to prove my point. Whenever you find an object that you think can be modeled as a Level II object, treat it as a Level III object anyway.*

For our purposes here, Level II objects are ideal. They have enough complexity to allow us to examine all of the possible connections without being burdened with the additional complexity of the Property Bag.

We can describe the *Address* object with the following table:

Property Name	Data Type	Size	Brief Description
ID	Long	4	Uniquely identifies each *Address* object – NOT NULL
StreetLine1	String	60	Contains line 1 of the street address – NOT NULL
StreetLine1	String	60	Contains line 2 of the street address – NULL OK
City	String	60	Contains the name of city – NOT NULL
State	String	2	Contains 2 character state code – NOT NULL
ZipCode5	String	5	Contains 5 digit zip code string – NOT NULL
ZipCode4	String	4	Contains 4 digit zip code extension – NULL OK
TypeID	Long	4	Contains unique ID for Object Type Definition – NOT NULL
TypeName	String	80	Contains text description for OTD – NOT NULL
KeyPrefix	String	10	Contains KeyPrefix for OTD – NOT NULL

Take a minute here to make sure that you have registered the `UCAddress` and `DCAddress` DLLs. You can do this using the same technique we have been using throughout this book. Enter the `regsver32` command followed by the path name of the DLL into the Run dialog.

Telephone Number Object

As the name implies, the *Telephone Number* object is used to manage standard telephone numbers. Once again, I have provided you with a Level II object to model the telephone numbers in this example. We have already gone over the reasons for this when we talked about the *Address* object above.

We can describe the *Telephone Number* object with the following table:

Property Name	Data Type	Size	Brief Description
ID	Long	4	Uniquely identifies each *Telephone Number* object – NOT NULL
CountryCode	String	4	Contains the country code – NOT NULL
AreaCode	String	3	Contains the area code – NOT NULL
Number	String	7	Contains the telephone number – NOT NULL
TypeID	Long	4	Contains unique ID for Object Type Definition – NOT NULL
TypeName	String	80	Contains text description for OTD – NOT NULL
KeyPrefix	String	10	Contains KeyPrefix for OTD – NOT NULL

Take a minute here to make sure that you have registered the UCPhone and DCPhone DLLs. You can do this using the same technique we have been using throughout this book. Enter the regsvr32 command followed by the pathname of the DLL into the Run dialog.

Email Address Object

As the name implies, the *Email Address* object is used to manage email addresses. Once again, I have provided you with a Level II object to model the email addresses in this example. We have already gone over the reasons for this when we talked about the *Address* object above.

We can describe the *Email Address* object with the following table:

Property Name	Data Type	Size	Brief Description
ID	Long	4	Uniquely identifies each *Email Address* object – NOT NULL
Address	String	255	Contains the email address – NOT NULL
TypeID	Long	4	Contains unique ID for Object Type Definition – NOT NULL
TypeName	String	80	Contains text description for OTD – NOT NULL
KeyPrefix	String	10	Contains KeyPrefix for OTD – NOT NULL

Take a minute here to make sure that you have registered the UCEMail and DCEMail DLLs.

Step 3 - Extend the Base Objects

If you have worked through the examples in the previous chapters, you should already have several different OTDs defined for the *Person* object. The focus of this chapter is really not concerned with the task of creating and maintaining OTDs and PSDs. We have already covered that material over the last few chapters.

We will need to take a minute and create the OTDs for the three new objects that we will be using in this chapter. Take a minute and do that now using the individual interfaces provided with each object. The technique you use to create these OTDs is exactly the same as the technique we used to create the *Person* OTDs back in Chapters 9 and 10. For this example, you should create the OTDs for each object as given in the following tables.

Address Object Type Definitions

ID	Name
1	Home Address
2	Business Address
3	Mailing Address

Telephone Number Object Type Definitions

ID	Name
1	Home Telephone Number
2	Business Telephone Number
3	Mobile Telephone Number
4	Pager Number

Email Address Object Type Definitions

ID	Name
1	Business Email Address
2	Personal Email Address

Step 4 - Connect the Objects

> This step is what this chapter is really all about.

We are going to take some time to go over the different options available to us for connecting the *Person* object to the other three objects we will be using in this example.

Take a look at the image on the right. It is supposed to depict a base *Person* object and three different extensions of that base *Person* object. It also shows images that are supposed to represent the other objects we have been talking about in this chapter, *Address, Telephone Number,* and *Email Address*:

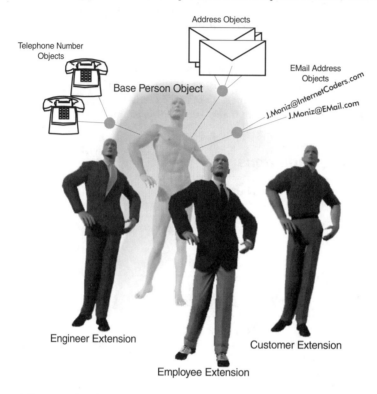

If you look carefully, you should notice that I have drawn some lines connecting the *Address, Telephone Number,* and *Email Address* objects to the base *Person* object. This is a subtle thing, but it is also a very powerful notion.

These lines indicate that our connections between our *Address, Telephone Number,* and *Email Address* objects and our *Person* object have been created as ID to ID + TypeID connections.

I am guessing that this might be a source of confusion for you right now. Good! I wanted to take a minute or two to work through why I have chosen to use this particular kind of connection in this instance. In this case we are connecting a Level III *Person* object to one of three Level II objects, *Address, Telephone Number, Email Address,* but we have *not* chosen to use the ID + TypeID to ID + TypeID connection. From the information we covered earlier in this chapter, it may have been reasonable for you to assume that we would always connect two Level II or higher objects using an ID + TypeID to ID + TypeID connection. That is what we did in our example. But as you can see here, that is not the case. That is because the examples we looked at earlier were designed to show you the most specific connection we could use between two particular object levels. This concept of specificity is really another way of describing relationships between objects in terms of the one-to-one or one-to-many relationship models.

Remember our brief discussion of the relational model for OTDs, back in Chapter 10. We talked very briefly about things like the one-to-one, one-to-many, and many-to-many relationships that we could form between objects. If you are like most people in the universe, you probably glazed over while reading that section of the chapter. Don't feel bad. I was probably getting a little glazed over myself. It is really hard to think about these relationships.

Fortunately for us, we are using a structured thing called a Connector object to manage relationships between objects rather than the more amorphous options available to us at the database. In other words, we now have this curious choice of relationships between objects down to a science. We have a single table to describe the entire universe of relationship possibilities available to us with Connector objects.

Take a look at the following table:

Option	Objects being Connected	Connection Options Available	Object Specificity
1	Level I to Level I	ID to ID	One base to one base
2	Level I to Level II or higher	ID to ID	One base to one base
3	Level I to Level II or higher	ID + TypeID to ID	One base to many extensions
4	Two Level IIs or higher	ID to ID	One base to one base
5	Two Level IIs or higher	ID + TypeID to ID	One base to many extensions
6	Two Level IIs or higher	ID + TypeID to ID + TypeID	Many extensions to many extensions

I have chosen to use option 5 in this case. In other words, we are connecting two Level II or higher objects together using a one base to many extensions relationship. It may be a little difficult to decipher what this means to us in terms of our overall enterprise model without taking some time to think about it.

Take another look at the image relating the base *Person* to the *Address*, *Telephone Number*, and *Email Address* objects. Remember that we depicted the connections between the *Person* and the *Address*, *Telephone Number*, and *Email Address* objects as existing between the base *Person* object rather than the extended *Person* object. In other words we can say that we are connecting the *Person*'s ID to the *Address*' ID + TypeID combination, or the *Person*'s ID to the *Telephone Number*'s ID + TypeID combination, or the *Person*'s ID to the *Email Address*'s ID + TypeID combination.

This means that if we look at any of the extended *Person* objects, we have all of the information (the *Person* ID) that we need to be able to connect that particular extension of the *Person* with the same *Address*, *Telephone Number*, and *Email Address* that is assigned to the base *Person*.

What this means to an enterprise is that it is very easy to share common information between different applications. In practice it means that if someone in sales learns that a customer's address has changed, then the billing department will also be notified of the change immediately. It means that if someone in accounting learns that John Smith's home telephone number has been changed, that everyone else in the organization will know about the change in real time. I know that this sounds a little scary – having a common source of information throughout an enterprise or organization, but remember that we are using ECDOs here. We might make it easy for people to change information, but we have also taken great pains to ensure that we track each and every change using our audit trails. We always know who changed the data, when it was changed, and what it was before it was changed. ECDOs also give us the ability to undo any change, including deletions that have been made to the data our objects manage.

Now that we know that we are going to use the ID + TypeID to ID Connector object to connect each of the three objects to our base *Person* object, we can define the Connector objects we will need for this task. We will need three connectors:

- ❑ A connector to manage the relationship between the *Address* and the *Person* objects
- ❑ A connector to manage the relationship between the *Telephone Number* and the *Person* objects
- ❑ A connector to manage the relationship between the *Email Address* and the *Person* objects

We have already said that we would be using the ID + TypeID to ID Connector object. What this means is that we will be able to manage relationships between one base *Person* and many different extensions of the *Address, Telephone Number*, or *Email Address* objects. In other words we will be able to know that John Smith has both a home and business address in the data store, and we will be able to identify each type of address specifically. Of course, the same holds true for the *Telephone Number* and *Email Address* objects as well.

You might have noticed that we have used rigorous naming conventions throughout this book. This helps us to live up to our Enterprise Caliber Design Objectives from Chapter 4, that stated that we should be creating maintainable, reusable code. Well, we are not going to break tradition now. Connector objects also follow a strict naming convention. We always prefix the base name of a Connector object with the letters cn – short for connector. We always (well almost always) make the base name of the Connector object by combining the first three letters of each of the two objects that we are going to connect. In other words if we were going to connect a *Person* object to an *Address* object, we would have a base object name of *PerAdd*. Notice that I hinted that this might not always be the case. Although we always try to follow this naming convention it is not always possible. Sometimes the first three letters of two base objects have already been used, etc. In those cases, we do the best we can to identify each base object in three letters.

> *Please note that although we might specify one object before the other in the name, this in no way changes the functionality of the Connector object. By nature Connector objects are bi-directional. In other words, we use the same object to connect a Person to an Address that we use to connect an Address to a Person.*

The following three tables define the properties that we need for each of our three Connector objects. Notice that in addition to the properties our objects use to manage the relationship between the other objects, we also have included a unique ID for each Connector object as well. That is because Connector objects are ECDOs and they must work the same way as every other ECDO – expose eight data handling processes, maintain audit histories, etc.

cnPerAdd Property Set

Property Name	Data Type
ID	Long
PersonID	Long
AddressID	Long
AddressTypeID	Long

cnPerPho Property Set

Property Name	Data Type
ID	Long
PersonID	Long
PhoneID	Long
PhoneTypeID	Long

cnPerEma Property Set

Property Name	Data Type
ID	Long
PersonID	Long
EmailID	Long
EmailTypeID	Long

How to Write the Code and Use a Connector Object

As I said earlier, Connector objects are really just special versions of standard Level I objects. That means that you really know almost everything you need to know to be able to create a Connector object. In the remainder of this chapter, I will present and comment on the required code for the Connector object that we will use to connect the *Person* and *Address* objects. Some of this information is virtually identical to the information presented in Chapters 5 through 7 - so I haven't presented it again here. I have not shortened the SQL in this chapter, however, because I wanted to make it as easy to read as possible.

Connector Object Special Capabilities

The power of Connector objects is really wrapped up in a few special capabilities. Some of these special capabilities provide us with a way to manage an extra set of stored procedures and to instantiate the Connected objects.

> One of the main thrusts of this methodology is to eliminate all SQL from the
> object or user interface code.

Without Connector objects this would be difficult, because there is no way to know, when you make a data object, what other objects it might need to connect to in the future. Connector objects give us a way to provide access to all of the extra SQL we might ever need, without adding any actual SQL code in our applications. This allows us to use all of the functionality that we have come to expect from a relational database, while we still get all of the benefits inherent in working with data objects. This technique gives the person who develops each Connector object the ability to give that object all of the capabilities that might be required for that object. This offers several advantages:

❑ The person who is creating the Connector object is able to package some of his or her knowledge about the data store into the object. This means that the developers that use the object don't need to have the same level of understanding of the actual database structure to be able to achieve the same level of functionality.

❑ This technique only places the names and parameter lists for the stored procedures in the Connector object. That means that the person who originally developed the Connector object (or anyone else authorized to do so for that matter) can always change the structure of the database, the code in the stored procedures, or any of the views in the database without requiring a change to the Connector object's code.

❑ If special requirements arise that call for additional stored procedure calls etc., it is possible to add this functionality to a Connector object without breaking the applications that may be using the Connector object. In these cases, we just need to be sure to follow the basic rules concerning binary compatibility of objects in general. We can summarize these rules for our purposes as follows:

❑ We can always add properties, methods, or events to an object without breaking the other objects or applications that are using that object.

❑ We **cannot remove** any properties, methods, or events from an object without breaking the objects or applications that are using that object.

❑ We **cannot remove or change** the data type of any parameters in any property handler or other method without breaking the objects or applications that are using the object.

❑ The developer of an object must take steps to ensure that the GUID for an object that is being used by another object or application does not change. If the GUID changes it will break all objects and or applications that are accessing that object using early binding techniques. This GUID problem is not an issue for those objects and or applications that use late binding techniques.

So, I guess that we can characterize Connector objects by saying that:

> Connector objects are a proxy for a single Bridge table in the data store
> that also contains a list of valid commands (stored procedure names), that
> allow us to exercise additional controls over the objects we select when we
> use the *Load* process of any object.

Let me give you an example of how this can work. Let's say that we want to load a collection with all of the *Person* objects that are related to a particular *Address*. If we wanted to do this without connectors, we would have to understand the structure of the database, write the special SQL statement that would return this information, and then add that special SQL statement into our application's code. When we do this with connectors, we rely upon the Connector object to "know" how to ask the correct question to retrieve the information that we need. As one of the reviewers of this book thoughtfully pointed out to me, this really means that, "in essence that the connector code is used to perform the joins in the database."

Let's take a minute or two to see what it takes to do this in code. We will use the Connector object that we will build below for this example.

First we dimension both objects, in this case we want to return a list of *Persons* that are connected to a unique *Address* and type of *Address*. Now our standard *Person* `Load` method doesn't know how to do this, but if you remember way back in Chapter 6, we were careful to give that method an optional parameter called `strSelectStatement`. At the time we covered this, I said that we would go over the reason why we added this optional parameter when we got to Chapter 13. Here is the reason. Now that we have Connector objects, we can "ask" the Connector object to give us the correct SQL command to execute against the data store to retrieve a filtered list of *Person* objects. Here is a general example of how to do that.

First, create the *Person* object (or any other object that you create) and the Connector object that knows how to ask the question you want to pose to the database. In this case that means that we have to write the following two lines of code:

```
Dim colPersons as UCPerson .colPersons
Dim objcnPerAdd As UCcnPerAdd.clsPerAdd
```

Of course we also have to instantiate the objects, so we would also write the following two lines of code as well:

```
Set colPersons = CreateObject("UCPerson .colPersons")
Set objcnPerAdd = CreateObject("UCcnPerAdd.clsPerAdd")
```

Now if we want to place a filtered `Load` call to the data store, we can supply the name of the stored procedure that knows how to carry out the joins by using something like the following line of code:

```
colPersons.Load(objcnPerAdd.SQLListPersonsForAddress(12,1,2))
```

What this code will do is to fill the optional `strSelectStatement` parameter with the correct stored procedure call, which will return a list of *Persons* for a particular *Address*. When this line executes, the `colPersons` collection will be filled with a collection of objects that meet the selection criteria given by the stored procedure. Yes! The Connector object just has a simple function that returns a string. That string is always the name and correct parameter list for the stored procedure that will perform the filtering indicated by the name of the function. If you are thinking that this is too easy, GOOD! That is exactly why I designed it to work this way. Remember way back in Chapter 1 that I said that we would build an enterprise using classic engineering principles. One of those principles is that **simple is good**!

I bet that the last few paragraphs answered quite a few questions that were probably on your mind about techniques you might use to do things like return a filtered collection. As you can see Connector objects make this very easy because they are proxy for a Bridge table and they can have as many extra stored procedures as required to allow us to use this Bridge table to return just about any filtered collection of objects. Of course, before we can retrieve a filtered collection using the Bridge table we need to develop a technique for placing that information into the Bridge table in the first place.

There are essentially three different tasks that we employ Connector objects to perform. We use them to:

❑ Insert a connection between two objects that have not been connected previously

❑ Restore a connection between two objects that were connected but are presently unconnected

❑ Disconnect two objects

We perform these three tasks by using some combination of the eight data handling processes we have come to expect from any ECDO. So, when we write the code for a Connector object, we actually do provide all eight data handling processes. In a way I guess I do this to be thorough, but I don't actually use the *Update* process in production. It may be a theoretical argument, maybe it is just common sense, but it seems wrong to perform an update against a Bridge table.

Think about it. When we connect two objects, we insert a record into the Bridge table. If we disconnect two objects we remove that record from the Bridge table. Updates don't seem to work here. If we perform an update on a Bridge table what we are saying is, "this object used to be connected to that object and now it is connected to another object." I know that physically an update will show this, but I don't employ this practice. Instead, whenever I need to perform an update against a Bridge table, I remove the existing connection and insert a new one. Logically this makes more sense to me. I think that it also gives the Audit tables a truer picture of exactly what went on in the physical world.

The next few sections go over the general set of steps that you need to follow to accomplish the three tasks of connecting, disconnecting, and reconnecting objects. I have provided some code snippets using the *Person* and *Address* objects to give you a sense of how to accomplish these tasks. The Object Factory will write five functions for you that encapsulate these three processes, but I think that in this case a general sense of what you need to do here is a lot more valuable than code that has been designed to handle the connection between two particular objects.

Once we understand the techniques we need to use to manage data in the Bridge table, we will take a look at the techniques we can use to employ the Bridge table along with some stored procedures to provide filtered collections to our users.

Connecting Objects

When we are connecting two objects we should follow these steps:

❑ Ensure that both objects are currently available in the data store in an undeleted state. This means that you might need to insert or restore one or both objects that you are planning to connect.

❑ Use the *Insert* process of the Connector object to insert a record marking the connection into the data store.

The following function offers an example of one way that you could perform this task within a Connector object. The programmer passes both objects to be connected into the routine along with the logon name of the person requesting the connection and the name of the data store we should perform the insert against. The code should look quite familiar, it is really like something we might expect to write in a user interface. This function is designed to return the ID number that was returned for this connection from the data store. The calling routine can test the return value of this function to determine whether it failed or succeeded. If the insertion was successful, then this function will return the ID of the new connection. If not the function will return a -1 to indicate failure.

Create this function in UCcnPerAdd.clscnPerAdd:

```
Public Function ConnectObjects(objPerson As UCPerson.clsPerson, _
                                objAddress As UCAddress.clsAddress, _
                                strUserLogon As String, _
                                strConnect As String) As Long
    SetDataSource strConnect
    mstrStampUser = strStampUser
    mlngPersonID = objPerson.ID
    mlngAddressID = objAddress.ID
    mlngAddressTypeID = objAddress.TypeID

    ObjectInsert

    If mlngID > 0 Then
        ConnectObjects = mlngID
    Else
        ConnectObjects = -1
    End if

End Function
```

Reconnecting Objects

When we are reconnecting two objects we should follow these steps:

❑   Ensure that both objects are currently available in the data store in an undeleted state. This means that you might need to insert or restore one or both objects that you are planning to connect.

❑   Use the *Restore From Deleted* process of the Connector object to reinsert the currently deleted record back into the Bridge table.

The following function offers an example of a function that can be used to reconnect the link between two objects that have been disconnected. This function call can be made after retrieving the Connection object that needs restoration via a call to the *Show Deleted* process. The code should look quite familiar; it is really very much like something we might expect to write in a user interface. This function is designed to return the ID number of the connection that was restored from the data store. The calling routine can test the return value of this function to determine whether it failed or succeeded. If the restoration was successful, then this function will return the ID of the new connection. If not the function will return a -1 to indicate failure.

Create this function in UCcnPerAdd.colcnPerAdd:

```
Public Function ReConnectObjects(objcnPerAdd as UCcnPerAdd.clscnPerAdd,
                                 strUserLogon As String,
                                 strConnect As Stirng) As Long
```

```
        objcnPerAdd.SetDataSource strConnect
        objcnPerAdd.StampUser = strUserLogon
        objcnPerAdd.RestoreFromDeleted
        If objcnPerAdd.ID > 0 Then
            ReConnectObjects = mlngID
        Else
            ReConnectObjects = -1
        End if

    End Function
```

Disconnecting Objects

When we need to disconnect two objects we should use the *Delete* process of the Connector object.

This function must be written in `UCcnPerAdd.clscnPerAdd`. It offers an example of a function that can be used to disconnect the link between two objects that are connected. Again, the code should look quite familiar, it is really like something we might expect to write in a user interface. Notice that all we are doing is using one of the eight data handling processes, *Delete* in this case, that we have seen so many times before. This function is designed to return a +1 to indicate success and a -1 if it fails for any reason:

```
    Public Function DisConnectObjects(objPerson As UCPerson.clsPerson, _
                                  objAddress As UCAddress.clsAddress, _
                                  strUserLogon As String, _
                                  strConnect As String) As Long

        SetDataSource strConnect
        mstrStampUser = strStampUser
        mlngPersonID = objPerson.ID
        mlngAddressID = objAddress.ID
        mlngAddressTypeID = objAddress.TypeID

        ObjectDelete

        If mlngID > 0 Then
            ReConnectObjects = 1
        Else
            ReConnectObjects = -1
        End if

    End Function
```

The following list methods (functions that return strings) provide the standard functionality we require from any Connector object. The Object Factory will add these methods to a Connector object by default. Of course, you can add as many additional ones as you need for your purposes.

SQLListPersonsForAddress

This method returns the stored procedure call that will return a list of *Persons* of a specific type for a particular *Address*. The string that this method returns is simply passed into the `strSelectStatement` parameter of the *Person* object's `Load` method. We would use this function to call the stored procedure below. This stored procedure returns a list of *Person* objects filtered by the *Address* object.

```
Public Function SQLListPersonsForAddress(lngAddressID As Long, _
           lngAddressTypeID As Long, lngPersonTypeID As Long) _
           As String

    'the stored procedure assigned to the SQL string below will
    'return a list of persons for an address
    SQLListPersonsForAddress = "spcnPerAddObjectLstObjPerson" & _
                               lngAddressID & ", " & _
                               lngAddressTypeID & ", " & _
                               lngPersonTypeID

End Function
```

The Stored Procedure

This is the stored procedure that is invoked by the call above. Notice that the only real difference between this stored procedure and the standard stored procedure we use to return a list of persons, spPersonObjectList, is found in the additional criteria in the WHERE clause:

```
CREATE PROCEDURE spcnPerAddObjectLstObjPerson
@AddressID int, @AddressTypeID int, @PersonTypeID int

AS

SELECT     PersonObjType.ID As TypeID,
           PersonObjType.Name As TypeName,
           PersonObjType.KeyPrefix As KeyPrefix,
           PersonObject.ID,
           PersonObject.LastName,
           PersonObject.FirstName,
           PersonObject.MiddleName,
           PersonObject.Salutation,
           PersonObject.Suffix,
           PersonObject.SSN,
           PersonObject.ConcurrencyID AS ConcurrencyID1
FROM       PersonObject
INNER JOIN cnPerAddObject ON
           PersonObject.ID = cnPerAddObject.PersonID
INNER JOIN PersonObjType ON
           cnPerAddObject.PersonTypeID = PersonObjType.ID
WHERE      cnPerAddObject.AddressID = @AddressID AND
           cnPerAddObject.AddressTypeID = @AddressTypeID AND
           cnPerAddObject.PersonTypeID = @PersonTypeID
RETURN (0)
```

SQLListAddresssForPerson

This method returns the stored procedure call, which will itself return a list of *Addresses* of a specific type for a particular base *Person*. The string that this method returns is simply passed into the strSelectStatement parameter of the *Address* object's Load method.

```
Public Function SQLListAddresssForPerson(lngPersonID As Long, _
           lngPersonTypeID As Long, lngAddressTypeID As Long) _
           As String

    'the stored procedure assigned to the SQL string below will
    'return a list of addresses for a person
```

```
        SQLListAddresssForPerson = "spcnPerAddObjectLstObjAddress" & _
                                   lngPersonID & ", " & _
                                   lngPersonTypeID & ", " & _
                                   lngAddressTypeID
   End Function
```

The Stored Procedure

This is the stored procedure that is invoked by the call above. Notice that the only real difference between this stored procedure and the standard stored procedure we use to return a list of *Addresses*, spAddressObjectList, is found in the additional criteria in the WHERE clause:

```
CREATE PROCEDURE spcnPerAddObjectLstObjAddress
@PersonID int, @PersonTypeID int, @AddressTypeID int

AS
SELECT      AddressObject.ID,
            AddressObject.StreetLine1,
            AddressObject.StreetLine2,
            AddressObject.City,
            AddressObject.State,
            AddressObject.ZipCode5,
            AddressObject.ZipCode4,
            AddressObjType.ID AS TypeID,
            AddressObjType.Name AS TypeName,
            AddressObjType.KeyPrefix AS KeyPrefix,
            AddressObject.ConcurrencyID AS ConcurrencyID1
FROM        AddressObject
INNER JOIN  cnPerAddObject ON
            AddressObject.ID = cnPerAddObject.AddressID
INNER JOIN  AddressObjType ON
            cnPerAddObject.AddressTypeID = AddressObjType.ID
WHERE       cnPerAddObject.PersonID = @PersonID AND
            cnPerAddObject.PersonTypeID = @PersonTypeID AND
            cnPerAddObject.AddressTypeID = @AddressTypeID
RETURN (0)
```

SQLListUnLinkedPersonsForAddress

This method returns a collection of *Person* objects that were previously linked to an *Address* of a given type. The string that this method returns is simply passed into the strSelectStatement parameter of the *Person* object's ShowDeleted method. We handle this **exactly** the same way that we handled the Load example we looked at earlier:

```
Public Function SQLListUnLinkedPersonsForAddress _
              (lngAddressID As Long, lngAddressTypeID As Long, _
            lngPersonTypeID As Long) As String

   'the stored procedure assigned to the sql string below will
   'return a list of Persons previously linked to a Address
   SQLListUnLinkedPersonsForAddress = "spcnPerAddObjectDelObjPerson" & _
                                      lngAddressID & ", " & _
                                      lngAddressTypeID & ", " & _
                                      lngPersonTypeID

End Function
```

The Stored Procedure

This stored procedure is a little more challenging. It also introduces a major new concept in SQL – the **temporary table**. The first portion of the stored procedure is not really any different from the stored procedures that we have used before. It just sets up the parameters:

```
CREATE PROCEDURE spcnPerAddObjectDelObjPerson

@AddressID int,
@AddressTypeID int,
@PersonTypeID int
AS
```

The first unusual thing we find in this stored procedure is the temporary table. A temporary table is just what it sounds like. This command instructs SQL Server to create a table in memory.

> *Of course, SQL Server can decide to write the data out to the disk if it needs to, but that is SQL Server's problem – not ours.*

Notice that the syntax to create a temporary table is identical to the syntax we use to create an ordinary table. The only difference is that we prefix the name of the table with the number sign - #. This character tells SQL Server that we are building a temporary table with a scope that is local to this stored procedure.

> *We can also create temporary tables that have a "global" scope by preceding the name of the table with two number signs - ##. I still haven't found too many tasks that might benefit from a globally scoped temporary table, but I thought I would tell you how to do it just in case you thought of a reason to use one.*

Anyway, once we have created this local temporary table, we can use it throughout the remainder of this stored procedure in exactly the same way that we would use any other table. Notice that with the temporary table, we have allowed all the fields to contain null values. This is fine because we control the contents of the fields in other places.

```
/* create temporary table for holding results */
CREATE TABLE #tmpPersons (
    StampUser char(15) NULL,
    StampDateTime datetime NULL,
    StampAction varchar(60),
    StampID int NULL,
    LastName char(50) NULL,
    FirstName char(50) NULL,
    MiddleName char(50) NULL,
    Salutation char(5) NULL,
    Suffix char(10) NULL,
    SSN char(9) NULL,
    TypeID int NULL
    TypeName varchar(80) NULL
    KeyPrefix char(10) NULL
    ID int NULL
```

Now that we have a place to put them, we can select the list of *Person* objects from the Object table, which represents the *Persons* that are not deleted, but whose connection to an *Address* object has been deleted. We have covered the INSERT statement before. The only difference here is that we are inserting into a temporary table rather than into a physical table:

```
INSERT #tmpPersons (
    StampUser,
    StampDateTime,
    StampAction,
    StampID,
    LastName,
    FirstName,
    MiddleName,
    Salutation,
    Suffix,
    SSN,
    TypeID,
    TypeName,
    KeyPrefix,
    ID)
SELECT      vcnPerAddObjectAuditDeletes.StampUser,
            vcnPerAddObjectAuditDeletes.StampDateTime,
            vcnPerAddObjectAuditDeletes.StampAction,
            vcnPerAddObjectAuditDeletes.ID,
            PersonObject.LastName,
            PersonObject.FirstName,
            PersonObject.MiddleName,
            PersonObject.Salutation,
            PersonObject.Suffix,
            PersonObject.SSN,
            PersonTypeBridge.TypeID,
            PersonObjType.Name AS TypeName,
            PersonObjType.KeyPrefix,
            PersonObject.ID
```

The real trick here is the Select statement that we use to get the list to insert. That statement uses a view to return a list of existing *Persons* who have a currently deleted link to an *Address* object. Although this relationship looks a little daunting, don't let it throw you. This kind of relationship is always expressed in exactly the same way for every Connector object.

```
FROM        vcnPerAddObjectAuditDeletes
INNER JOIN  PersonTypeBridge ON
            vcnPerAddObjectAuditDeletes.PersonID = PersonTypeBridge.ObjectID AND
            vcnPerAddObjectAuditDeletes.PersonTypeID = PersonTypeBridge.TypeID
INNER JOIN  PersonObject ON
            PersonTypeBridge.ObjectID = Person Object.ID
INNER JOIN  PersonObjType ON
            PersonTypeBridge.TypeID = PersonObjType.ID
WHERE       vcnPerAddObjectAuditDeletes.AddressID = @AddressID AND
            vcnPerAddObjectAuditDeletes.AddressTypeID = @AddressTypeID AND
            vcnPerAddObjectAuditDeletes.Person TypeID = @PersonTypeID
```

In this next section of the stored procedure, we are really performing nearly the same task we performed above. The only difference here is that we are returning a list of *Person* objects that have deleted *Address* links and the *Person* objects have also been deleted. The cool thing, and the reason we used a temporary table, is that we can just insert this second set of *Person* objects into the same temporary table. That means that we now have a single source for *Person* objects that represents the results from two distinct SELECT statements:

```
INSERT #tmpPersons (
    StampUser,
    StampDateTime,
    StampAction,
    StampID,
    LastName,
    FirstName,
    MiddleName,
    Salutation,
    Suffix,
    SSN,
    TypeID,
    TypeName,
    KeyPrefix,
    ID)

SELECT      PersonObjectAudit.StampID,
            vcnPerAddObjectAuditDeletes.StampUser,
            vcnPerAddObjectAuditDeletes.StampDateTime,
            vcnPerAddObjectAuditDeletes.StampAction,
            vcnPerAddObjectAuditDeletes.ID,
            PersonObjectAudit.LastName,
            PersonObjectAudit.FirstName,
            PersonObjectAudit.MiddleName,
            PersonObjectAudit.Salutation,
            PersonObjectAudit.Suffix,
            PersonObjectAudit.SSN,
            PersonObjectAudit.TypeID,
            PersonObjectAudit.TypeName,
            PersonObjectAudit.KeyPrefix,
            PersonObjectAudit.ID
FROM        vcnPerAddObjectAuditDeletes
INNER JOIN  vPersonObjectDelete ON
            vcnPerAddObjectAuditDeletes.PersonID = vPersonObjectDelete.StampID
            AND vcnPerAddObjectAuditDeletes.PersonTypeID =
            PersonObjectDelete.TypeID
INNER JOIN  PersonObjectAudit ON
            vPersonObjectDelete.ID = PersonObjectAudit.ID
LEFT OUTER JOIN PersonTypeBridge ON
            PersonObjectAudit.StampID = PersonTypeBridge.ObjectID AND
            PersonObjectAudit.TypeID = PersonTypeBridge.TypeID
WHERE       PersonTypeBridge.ObjectID IS NULL AND
            vcnPerAddObjectAuditDeletes.AddressID = @AddressID AND
            vcnPerAddObjectAuditDeletes.AddressTypeID = @AddressTypeID AND
            vcnPerAddObjectAuditDeletes.Person TypeID = @PersonTypeID
```

Of course the last step in this process is just to return the contents of the temporary table to the calling method. There is nothing unusual about this section except that we are selecting the data from a temporary table rather than a physical table. It is also important to remember to add the little housekeeping task at the end. We must instruct SQL Server to delete the temporary table from memory. I would like to think that SQL Server is smart enough to do this without any instructions from me – we did tell it that the temporary table's scope was local, but it is a good idea to spell it out just in case:

```
SELECT StampUser,
       StampDateTime,
       StampAction,
       StampID,
```

```
            LastName,
            FirstName,
            MiddleName,
            Salutation,
            Suffix,
            SSN,
            TypeID,
            TypeName,
            KeyPrefix,
            ID
    FROM    #tmpPersons
    ORDER BY StampDateTime DESC


    /* delete temporary table */
    DROP TABLE #tmpPersons
```

SQLListUnLinkedAddresssForPerson

This method returns a collection of *Address* objects that were previously linked to a *Person* of a given type. The string that this method returns is simply passed into the `strSelectStatement` parameter of the *Address* object's `ShowDeleted` method. We handle this in **exactly** the same way that we handled the `Load` example we looked at earlier:

```
Public Function SQLListUnLinkedAddresssForPerson _
                (lngPersonID As Long, lngPersonTypeID As Long, _
                lngAddressTypeID As Long) As String

    'the stored procedure assigned to the SQL string below will
    'return a list of addresses previously linked to a person
    SQLListUnLinkedAddresssForPerson = "spcnPerAddObjectDelObjAddress" & _
                                lngPersonID & ", " & _
                                lngPersonTypeID & ", " & _
                                lngAddressTypeID

End Function
```

The Stored Procedure

I am not going to walk through this stored procedure. It is identical to the one above in all respects save one. In this case we are returning a list of *Addresses* rather than a list of *Persons*. I have highlighted the important aspects of this routine so that they would be easy to find.

```
CREATE PROCEDURE spcnPerAddObjectDelObjAddress
@PersonID int, @PersonTypeID int, @AddressTypeID int
AS

/* create temporary table for holding results */
CREATE TABLE #tmpAddresss (
    StampUser char(15) NULL,
    StampDateTime datetime NULL,
    StampAction varchar(60),
    StampID int NULL,
    StreetLine1 varchar(60) NULL,
    StreetLine2 varchar(60) NULL,
    City varchar(60) NULL,
    State char(2) NULL,
```

```
      ZipCode5 char(5) NULL,
      ZipCode4 char(4) NULL,
      TypeID int NULL
      TypeName varchar(80) NULL
      KeyPrefix char(10) NULL
      ID int NULL        /* id of connection audit record */

  /* add rows to result table for deleted connections for which
     the Address is still active */

  INSERT #tmpAddresss (
          StreetLine1,
          StreetLine2,
          City,
          State,
          ZipCode5,
          ZipCode4,
          ID)
  SELECT  StampUser,
          StampDateTime,
          StampAction,
          StampID,
          vcnPerAddObjectAuditDeletes.StampAction,
          vcnPerAddObjectAuditDeletes.StampDateTime,
          vcnPerAddObjectAuditDeletes.StampUser,
          AddressTypeBridge.TypeID,
          AddressObjType.Name As TypeName,
          AddressObjType.KeyPrefix,
          vcnPerAddObjectAuditDeletes.ID,
          AddressObject.StreetLine1,
          AddressObject.StreetLine2,
          AddressObject.City,
          AddressObject.State,
          AddressObject.ZipCode5,
          AddressObject.ZipCode4,
          TypeID,
          TypeName,
          KeyPrefix,
          ID
  FROM       vcnPerAddObjectAuditDeletes
  INNER JOIN AddressTypeBridge ON
             vcnPerAddObjectAuditDeletes.AddressID = AddressTypeBridge.ObjectID
             AND vcnPerAddObjectAuditDeletes.AddressTypeID =
             AddressTypeBridge.TypeID
  INNER JOIN AddressObject ON
             AddressTypeBridge.ObjectID = AddressObject.ID
  INNER JOIN AddressObjType ON
             AddressTypeBridge.TypeID = AddressObjType.ID
  WHERE      vcnPerAddObjectAuditDeletes.PersonID = @PersonID AND
             vcnPerAddObjectAuditDeletes.PersonTypeID = @PersonTypeID AND
             vcnPerAddObjectAuditDeletes.AddressTypeID = @AddressTypeID

  /* add rows to result table for deleted connections for which
     the Address has also been deleted */
  INSERT #tmpAddresss (
          StampUser,
          StampDateTime,
          StampAction,
          StampID,
```

```
            StreetLine1,
            StreetLine2,
            State,
            City,
            ZipCode5
            ZipCode4,
            TypeID,
            TypeName,
            KeyPrefix,
            ID)
SELECT    vcnPerAddObjectAuditDeletes.StampUser,
          vcnPerAddObjectAuditDeletes.StampDateTime,
          vcnPerAddObjectAuditDeletes.StampAction,
          AddressObjectAudit.StampID,
          AddressObjectAudit.StreetLine1,
          AddressObjectAudit.StreetLine2,
          AddressObjectAudit.City,
          AddressObjectAudit.State,
          AddressObjectAudit.ZipCode5,
          AddressObjectAudit.ZipCode4,
          AddressObjectAudit.TypeID,
          AddressObjectAudit.TypeName,
          AddressObjectAudit.KeyPrefix,
          vcnPerAddObjectAuditDeletes.ID,
FROM        vcnPerAddObjectAuditDeletes
INNER JOIN  vAddressObjectDelete ON
            vcnPerAddObjectAuditDeletes.AddressID = vAddressObjectDelete.StampID
            AND vcnPerAddObjectAuditDeletes.AddressTypeID =
            vAddressObjectDelete.TypeID
INNER JOIN  AddressObjectAudit ON
            vAddressObjectDelete.ID = AddressObjectAudit.ID
LEFT OUTER JOIN AddressTypeBridge ON
            AddressObjectAudit.StampID = AddressTypeBridge.ObjectID AND
            AddressObjectAudit.TypeID = AddressTypeBridge.TypeID
WHERE       AddressTypeBridge.ObjectID IS NULL AND
            vcnPerAddObjectAuditDeletes.PersonID = @PersonID AND
            vcnPerAddObjectAuditDeletes.PersonTypeID = @PersonTypeID AND
            vcnPerAddObjectAuditDeletes.AddressTypeID = @AddressTypeID

SELECT  StampUser,
        StampDateTime,
        StampAction,
        StampID,
        Street1,
        City,
        PostalCode5,
        Street2,
        StateCode,
        PostalCode4,
        TypeID,
        TypeName,
        KeyPrefix,
        ID
FROM    #tmpAddresss
ORDER BY StampDateTime DESC
/* delete temporary table */
DROP TABLE #tmpAddresss

Return (0)
```

The remainder of the functionality that we need from an object designed as a proxy for a Bridge table in the data store is given by our old faithful eight data handling processes. Rather than go through the same old code over and over again, I have written a brief description of each of the data handling processes. In these descriptions I have tried to give you a sense of how we use each one of these processes to build and manage relationships between the other objects that a Connector object is charged with managing.

The Eight Data Handling Processes

We don't need to go through all of the code for the eight data handling processes for the Connector object. You already know how to write this code. It is almost identical, to the code you created in the earlier chapters. The only difference between this code and that code is the names of the properties. That means that you can either use the sample code or follow the code found in the sections indicated under each of the eight data handling processes.

Fetch

The purpose of the *Fetch* process is to return a single object from the data store. The *Fetch* process for the Connector object is identical to its Level I counterpart. Because all ECDOs, including Connector objects, use a unique ID, it is possible to use the *Fetch* process to return a single object that represents a connection between two other objects. I haven't found too many uses for this process with respect to Connector objects, but that doesn't mean that other people might not find this capability useful. The *Fetch* process is designed to accept a single long parameter, the Connector object's ID. This code was discussed in Chapter 7.

Insert

The purpose of the *Insert* process is to add a new object's data to the data store, make a record that indicates that the new data was inserted, and to return the most current information about the target object back to the user. The *Insert* process for the Connector object is identical to its Level I counterpart. The thing that we need to consider when we work with *Insert* process of the Connector object is that it is a good practice to search for a pre-existing but deleted relationship before we insert a new one. This code was discussed in Chapter 6.

Update

The purpose of the *Update* process is to change the information in the data store, make a record that indicates the update took place, and to return the most current information about the target object in the data store back to the user. As I said earlier, I have included this routine for the sake of completeness. And, just because I think that performing an update against a Bridge table is logically incorrect doesn't mean that you should be prohibited from doing this if you want to. The *Update* process for the Connector object is identical to its Level I counterpart. This code was discussed in Chapter 7.

Delete

The purpose of the *Delete* process is to delete the information for a particular object from the data store, make a record that indicates that the deletion took place, and to return the most current information about the target object in the data store back to the user. With Connector objects, the *Delete* process performs the task of disconnecting two objects from one another. The *Delete* process for the Connector object is identical to its Level I counterpart. This code was discussed in Chapter 7.

Audit History

The purpose of the *Audit History* process is to return a complete history for a particular object. This history is in essence a series of snapshots of the object taken every time the data in the data store was changed for any reason. This may be tricky. It might almost seem as though I wouldn't use the *Audit History* process for Connector objects because I don't perform updates against a Bridge table. While it is true that I don't perform updates against Bridge tables, we need to remember that the *Audit History* also stores information about all previous deletions and reconnections. This means that it contains a wealth of information and we can use it to learn about the connection history for any object. The *Audit History* process for the Connector object is identical to its Level I counterpart. This code was discussed in Chapter 7.

Restore From Deleted

The purpose of the *Restore From Deleted* process is to restore an object from a deleted state back to its state at the time of its deletion, make a record that indicates that the restoration took place, and to return the most current information about the target object in the data store back to the user. This process is used directly in Connector objects. It is the preferred way to reconnect two objects that have been disconnected. If we use this process in conjunction with the *Audit History* process above we will always be able to know "where an object has been". The *Restore From Deleted* process for the Connector object is identical to its Level I counterpart. This code was discussed in Chapter 7.

Show Deleted

The purpose of the *Show Deleted* process is to return to the user a list of the deleted objects that are available for restoration from the data store. This process is used in conjunction with the *Delete*, *Restore From Deleted*, and *Audit History* processes to provide us with knowledge about the history of connections between objects. The *Show Deleted* process for the Connector object is identical to its Level I counterpart. This code is discussed in Chapter 7.

Load

The purpose of the *Load* process is to return a collection of objects that meet some criteria. This process also accepts a SQL string as a parameter. We use this parameter in conjunction with Connector objects. The *Load* process for the Connector object is identical to its Level I counterpart. This code is discussed in Chapter 6.

Summary

In this chapter, we learned that we have a special kind of ECDO called a Connector object that is essentially a proxy for a Bridge table in the data store. In addition to managing the Bridge table we need to depict a relationship between objects, it also offers several functions and stored procedures that we can use to retrieve filtered collections of objects from the data store. It offers us a single "place" within our enterprise to manage any additional stored procedures or SQL that our applications may require.

During the course of this chapter, we considered some of the steps that we need to take to build an application using the ECDO methodology. We learned that this methodology requires us to take 6 distinct steps to deliver an application. In this chapter we covered four of those steps:

1. Determine the application's functionality
2. Acquire the base objects necessary to deliver that functionality
3. Extend the base objects with type definitions if necessary
4. Connect the objects

In the next three chapters, we will cover the remaining two:

5. Add the business rules – Veneers
6. Build a user interface and deploy the application – Active Server Pages

14

Veneers, Components, and Applications

This chapter is designed to allow you to shine. We spent the last eight chapters trudging through every last detail of Enterprise Caliber Data Objects, and by now you must be wondering if it was all worth it. Well you can rest easy now, because it's all downhill from here.

In this chapter we will put the purely mechanical objects we have created to work. What's more, we'll do that without changing a single line of code in those objects. Remember that the data objects are *mechanical* in nature, that we made them *over-capable*, and we that can trust that they will perform their assigned tasks. We can treat them, to use an engineering term, as *black boxes*. If you are still reading this book, that means that you paid your dues while I dragged you through the quagmire of purely mechanical tasks we are obliged to perform on a daily basis. Well I think that means that I owe you something. I like to think that this chapter is that something.

But if all these black boxes can do is manage data, how do we create functional applications. The answer lies in the business rules and how we put all the different bits and pieces together. You might not be able to see it yet, but we've done all the hard work, so now we're going to enjoy ourselves.

Business Rules

I am sure that some of you have noticed that we are nearly at the end of the book, but I still haven't written anything about business rules. That was intentional.

> One of the driving forces of multi-sphere development is the segregation of business rules from the purely mechanical aspects of development.

Mechanics vs. Art

Let me clarify what I mean by the purely mechanical aspects. I really hate to admit this, but if you think about it, most of the things that we do during the development process are really not subject to interpretation or could be considered *art*. Let's imagine that we have a table with a single field. For the sake of argument, let's also say that this field has been designed to store a Long value. The decision to have this field contain a Long value *fixes* a portion of any application that uses that field. For instance, to manage the information in that field we need to dimension Long variables in VB. Of course, I know that we could make due with variants, singles, or doubles etc. But I am not talking about *making due* here. I am saying that we can prove *mathematically* that the optimal datatype that we need to manage a numeric value between -2,147,483,648 and +2,147,483,647 in Visual Basic is a Long datatype. In other words, the choice of what datatype we can use for a variable intended to manage the information stored in this field is a purely *mechanical* choice. And it doesn't end there. Let's try to approach the same example from the perspective of the user interface.

A text box, combo box, or other input control intended to manage the data for our single field must also have certain characteristics. For instance, this control should not accept keystrokes that contain alphabetic characters. It should not accept dollar signs. It should not accept periods. It should accept keystrokes that result in numeric characters, a single negative sign, and perhaps a comma (or other thousands separator). Yeah I know; this is just common sense. You're absolutely right; it is not rocket science. It is also *not* a business rule. *It is not subject to interpretation.*

> *A control designed to manage a Long value should only accept keystrokes that will result in a Long value.*

This is just a very small portion of the purely mechanical tasks we perform when we are working with a field designed to store Long values.

If you would like some more examples of the purely mechanical tasks that we must perform once we have decided to store a particular type of information in a field, go back and re-read all of the code in this book up to this chapter. By the way, you can even go forward to the chapter on Active Server Pages. Every last bit of code in this book, including the ASP, was written by a computer program. What does that tell you? It says that a lot of the work that we have to do everyday is purely *mechanical* in nature. Think about it. If we can teach a computer to perform a task, then that task bends to the rules of logic and is really no more than a glorified equation or, maybe, a set of equations.

> *What I can do is to show you how to segregate the purely mechanical tasks from the creative tasks.*

Make no mistake about it; what we have covered until this point was purely mechanical in nature. There was not a lot of room for creativity. This is not the same as saying that there is no room for improvement. The code in this book was intended to provide you with a working model that can and should be improved upon.

Enter The Veneer

4-Dimensional Data Objects – spheres – and now Veneers, right about now you must be thinking to yourself that this guy is probably just making this stuff up. And you are soOOOO right!!! I am exercising my ability to be *creative*. I designed this system because I knew that I didn't want to spend my life chained to the menial tasks of managing a set of pre-defined data rules. So, in order to free myself from this drudgery I designed 4-Dimensional Data Objects to handle the ho-hum tasks of managing the mechanical rules for me. Of course, this meant that I created a new problem for myself. Where the heck do I put the business rules? To be honest, I really didn't know when I first started. I think I just assumed that I would get around to putting the business rules in the data objects when the time came, but then it struck me. As soon as I add a single business rule to a data object, that object will no longer be completely reusable.

> **It will take on the personality of a particular business problem, and it will no longer be a purely mechanical device.**

This meant that every time some bean-counter decided that a business rule needed to change I would have to operate on one of my faithful servants. Now, I shouldn't have to tell you that data objects, like all other programs, are susceptible to a myriad of complications and bugs as soon as they go under the knife. If at all possible we should avoid performing surgery on our dependable minions.

What I needed was a universal gadget that could provide a malleable face to a set of data objects and their associated Connector objects without needing to change the underlying objects. This gadget had to be a lightweight device that could be torn down and rebuilt under battlefield conditions if necessary. And most of all, this gadget had to be able to house the plethora of constantly changing business rules and also have the ability to enforce those rules. The device I dreamt up to handle this task is something I named a **Veneer**. I call it a Veneer because it is really just a thin coating of business rules that surround a collection of related data objects and their associated Connector objects.

I would like you to think about the work we did in the last chapter with Connector objects. It doesn't matter whether you wrote the code for those objects by hand, used the Object Factory to write the code for you, or if you just downloaded the completed DLLs, all you had when you finished with the last chapter was a bunch of data objects. Sure, some of those objects were Connector objects, and we know that you can use a Connector objects to, say, relate a person to an address, phone number, etc. But even with the Connector objects you still just have a bunch of data objects – something was still missing. That something was the set of business rules that "knows" *why* we should connect this person to this address or that phone number.

Take a look at this next image. It looks a lot like the image we used in the last chapter to work through the concept of Connector objects. Notice that we only see a single extension of the *Person* object. That is where we are going with Veneers. We are going to learn to take some very generic data objects apply some business rules to them, and build some very specific business objects in the process.

Notice also, that in this image there is a ring surrounding the data objects, the Connector objects, and the business rules. This ring or coating is one way that you can envision the Veneer – very much like the candy-coating on the outside of an M&M®.

With M&Ms, the candy-coat Veneer is designed to keep the chocolate localized in one protected place so that it doesn't melt in your hands. With ECDOs, our Veneer is designed to do just about the same thing. It gives us a way to package the data objects, connectors, and business rules into a single business object or component so that the business rules don't… I want to say melt in your hands, but you know what I mean.

> **Veneers give us a way to package a number of different things into a single easy to manage business object or component so that our business rules, like the chocolate in the M&M, stay localized in one protected place.**

Take a minute to think about the example we worked with in the last chapter to learn about Connector objects. Imagine what would happen if we could take the relationships that we created in that chapter and package them into a single business object. If we could do that, then we would only have to do that job *once*. You would no longer have to spend the precious minutes of your day continually defining and redefining the same set of relationships over and over again. Instead, you could take this big M&M of a business object and drop it into any application that might be able to make use of a *Person* object that comes complete with contact information. Can you think of any applications you have developed that could have used a Person and also may have needed to access other information like say, Addresses, Telephone numbers, and Email addresses?

Working with Veneers

Veneers give us a *single* place to put the business rules that represent our organization's skill and talent while still allowing us to create **pure** data objects unfettered by the constantly changing landscape that permeates the world of business rules. The Veneer is the place where we can put a rule that knows how to *decide* that a particular person should be *related* to a particular address or phone number. Notice that I said, "knows how to decide" not "knows how to insert" the connection. The physical act we need to perform in order to define this relationship is a purely mechanical device or call to an object method.

Veneers also allow our ECDOs to have their own lifecycles separate from the applications that use them. In other words, as long as we follow the rules set out by the principles of binary compatibility we outlined in the last chapter, our ECDOs can be changed and improved without placing the other objects, components, or applications that use them in jeopardy.

Boy, you would think that something that can do so much for us would be a hard thing to build. But as far as the basic Veneer goes, they are really very easy to build. All they do is expose the underlying functionality of our ECDOs using very simple mapping techniques.

> **The real trick with building Veneers is knowing what business rules to apply for your organization, and you are the only one that can know or implement the business rules for your enterprise.**

We'll be seeing how exactly we create the Veneer for our data objects later in the chapter.

Components

I usually reserve the phrase business object for the type of Veneer that is very specific – solves a specific business problem – usually for a single customer. I also have another word that I apply when working with Veneers and that word is **component**.

I use the word component to refer to a set of one or more ECDOs that work together to perform some common task that is more general in nature. I have provided an example component - the Person–Contact Information component - in the sample code, which I think provides a very good example of a general-purpose component.

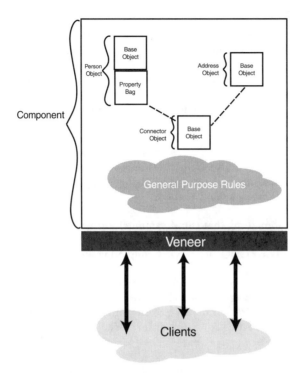

A component exposes a set of methods that allow the developer to decide which connections to create. That means that this particular Veneer is not very 'smart' with respect to business rules. This is not necessarily a bad thing. I think that there is a lot of room for developing this type of general-purpose component. When it comes to components, we can say that:

❑ Components are used to encapsulate several ECDOs and their associated Connector objects into a single package bound by a common set of general rules. Components use general rather than business rules to decide upon how to handle a particular chore, this type of Veneer is designed to expose its functionality to the developer.

❑ Components like the Person–Contact Information component can be used as the building blocks for more sophisticated components or applications. Although there are really no business rules in this type of Veneer, the processes that need to occur to ensure data integrity have been exposed as a set of methods.

As you might imagine, we can combine data objects, components, and connectors into another Veneer that we can call an **application**.

A New Breed of Application

What all of this means is that we have designed a methodology for developing applications that truly separate the data from the business in the enterprise. We have a new tool set to work with that consists of:

- ❑ Enterprise Caliber Data Objects
- ❑ Connector data objects
- ❑ Veneers – Business objects/components
- ❑ Applications – A single DLL that contains ECDOs, business objects/components, Connector objects and manages their interaction with business rules without relying upon any particular user interface for its operation.
- ❑ User Interfaces – Display-only devices that do not contain business rules. These interfaces can be VB Client Applications, Web Applications, MS Office Applications, or any other interface that can make use of ActiveX components.

This methodology is designed to free up the developer from the tedium and redundant actions that must be performed every time we develop an application. Once we have acquired the data objects we need for an application – remember this is a purely mechanical task - we can focus all of our energies on the task of merging the business rules with the data and developing world class user interfaces for the application.

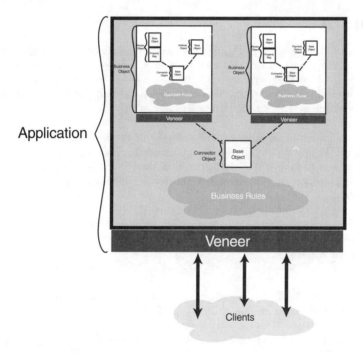

The image is designed to give you a sense of how we can these tools as the building blocks for our applications. I hope that this vision helps to take some of the sting out of all of the work we did in order to learn how to design and build such capable data objects. Notice that nothing has gone to waste here. Every last bit of functionality that we thought to incorporate into our ECDOs is here waiting to be used.

All of a sudden we find that we don't have to work very hard to give our users world-class applications.

❏   Every application we design will be able to offer a high level of internal security because we built that security into our data objects.

❏   Every application we design will be able to offer a complete audit history of every action that was ever taken against the data in the data store because we built that audit trail capability into our data objects.

❏   Every application we design will be able to offer the users the ability to perform unlimited undos including restoring deleted information because we built that capability into our data objects.

Way back in Chapter 1, I said that it was a worthwhile endeavor to build **high quality data components**. I am sure that during some of the tougher portions of this book that you wondered whether that statement was entirely true. Thanks for sticking it out. Work with me through the last step in the process here. Let's learn how to cover the *Computer* ECDO with a Veneer so that you will be finished with these mundane mechanics. Once you have learnt this last bit you can get on to the creative pursuits that await.

Building a Veneer

In the last chapter we found that we had the ability to connect two data objects using something we called a Connector object. We spent most of that chapter thinking more about the concept of connecting objects than we did working with the code that we needed to write to make the physical connections occur. Of course the reason for that was because you already know all of the code you need to know in order to build any ECDO, including Connector objects.

And, now that you have mastered the minutia of writing the code required to build ECDOs, I want you to forget it. That's right. Put all the detail out of your mind this instant. When someone says the words Database, Table, or Stored Procedure I want you to respond with an anguished, querying, "duh?" and mean it. If someone mentions the words Data Centric sphere or Data sphere, I want you to look at them with disdain and disbelief.

> **From this moment on, we are leaving the world of details and drudgery to the computer where it belongs.**

From now on when we talk about ECDOs, we are going to talk in terms of Employees, Patients, Corporations, Partnerships, Addresses, Phone Numbers, and so on…

All of the work you did over the last 8 chapters was designed to give you an insight to the inner workings of the Enterprise Caliber Data Object. You learned how to write each and every line of Visual Basic code you needed so that, now, you can build any variation of the beast. I am confident you know how to design data structures and create stored procedures with the best of them. I hope this brought you some satisfaction. But as I said earlier, that work is really mechanical in nature. Go back over the last eight chapters again with a fresh perspective and you will see that a system – a highly structured, reproducible, technique was used to create each data object. For instance, each data object has eight data handling processes. I bet you can recite them from memory by now: *Fetch, Insert, Update, Delete, Audit History, Show Deleted, Restore From Deleted*, and *Load*.

We went through each of the steps required to perform these data handling processes over and over again until I bet you thought your head was going to explode. The work was repetitive. We used nearly the same code, with a few subtle but important exceptions, in every chapter. *What came before was my duty.* I was honor bound to deliver to you every last tidbit of information in my head concerning ECDOs.

What follows is my pleasure. From now on, we are going to spend our time and talent developing techniques for delivering style and creativity to our deserving users. We are going to, in engineering-speak, **black box** the data objects. From this moment on, we won't concern ourselves with the mere mechanics in our data objects. We have paid our dues. We have spent 8 chapters learning how to build data objects, in this chapter we are going to put our little black boxes to work doing our bidding.

The Computer Object Veneer

I suppose that we could take on the task of developing a Veneer that we could use to manage the relationships between a person, and some addresses, phone numbers, and email addresses. But I am afraid that the complexity involved in doing this might cause the truly simple concepts you need to understand to build Veneers to become quite lost in the confusion.

Rather than taking on this huge challenge with so few pages of this book remaining, I have chosen to introduce you to the coding techniques you need to know to be able to create a Veneer using a simpler subject. We will learn about Veneers by using them to cover the *Computer* object you built way back in Chapter 7. I think that this simple ECDO will give us an excellent opportunity to both learn the mechanical task of coding Veneers and more importantly, I think that it will give us an opportunity to develop an intuitive understanding of the important difference between **content** and **extended functionality**.

> *That doesn't mean that I forgot about all of the work that you did to develop the Person, Address, Phone, Email ECDOs and their Connectors. I have included a well-commented project in the sample code that you can use at your leisure to build a Person–Contact Information component. In fact, by the time you finish this chapter, you will be able to "read" the code in that component project without any trouble.*

Way back in Chapter 7 you might have though that it was curious that all we did was to give this object the ability to manage information in the data store. You probably thought that something called a *Computer* object should have the ability to somehow interact with a computer, maybe even ask the computer a question or two. You know, "Hey how much memory do you have?" "How much space is left on your C drive?" "Hey look Mr. Computer I have all these properties that need to be filled. Why don't you tell me a thing or two about yourself?" Now that is what I would call a *Computer* object.

I have to agree. I think that we could have done a much better job on the *Computer* object, but if you remember Chapter 7, you may also remember that you were pretty busy way back then. I believe that during that chapter you learned to how to write the code for 6 of the 8 data handling processes that are the foundation of all ECDOs. You will have to forgive me, if I thought that it might not be a good idea to pile yet another major concept on you during that chapter. Especially since I knew that we were going to have to work through this whole Veneer concept anyway. As I said earlier in this chapter, the code we need to write to create a Veneer really just consists of some fairly trivial mapping techniques.

That means that while we are learning to write this mapping code we will be able to spend some extra time working through a pretty interesting set of business rules for our *Computer* object. We are going to use this *Computer* Veneer as an excuse to play around with the Windows API. In other words we are going to cover our ECDO with a Veneer that can really do things like ask the computer a couple of questions. Sound like fun? I thought it would. But before we can get our hands into the API, we should take a couple of minutes and get ourselves set up with a Veneer project.

The Veneer Project

OK, now that you have a sense of what constitutes a Veneer, let's get on with the writing the code for one. Up until this point, we have used a naming convention for our VB modules that was kind of technical. For example, we used the prefix `cls` to indicate that we were working with a class module the defined a single object and the prefix `col` to indicate that we were working with a class module that defined a collection of objects. We also used the suffix `Data` on most of our modules to differentiate between the User and Data Centric data objects in our system. We also use a naming convention for Veneers, but it is really very un-technical:

❑   Veneers that represent single objects are given a descriptive name for the object, for example: Employee, Doctor, Dog, Computer, etc.

❑   Veneers that represent a collection of objects are given the same descriptive name with the addition of a suffix that indicates the plurality, for example, Employees, Doctors, Dogs, Computers, etc.

Open a new ActiveX DLL project in VB. Remove the default class and add the two class files you can find in the source code for this chapter - they are called `Computer.cls` and `Computers.cls`.

This application is going to use the *Computer* object we created earlier in this book, so we will need to make a reference to that object. Think about this for a minute. Even though the *Computer* object consists of two halves, we only need to reference the user centric half of the object from our Veneer project.

When you get finished setting up the `ComputerVeneer` project the window in your Project Explorer should look like the one here:

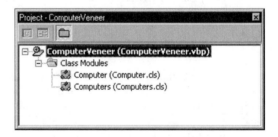

At this point, it may seem a little ironic, that we are about to approach the construction of a distributed application using a single project when we used three projects to create a single data object. But, this is by design. We did the lion's share of the work during the design and construction of the Enterprise Caliber Data Objects. And, if we have done our jobs well up until this point, we have created a set of reusable building blocks that are *easy* to use.

> **Veneers are the place where we consider the business WHYs; we have already taken care of the technical HOWs with the ECDO.**

Veneers allow us to physically separate the data objects from the business rules. Our ECDOs are DLLs. There is no way for, even well-intentioned, developers to accidentally type a line of code representing a business rule into an ECDO DLL without going to a *lot* of trouble. This means that when we open up a business application for modifications, we are only exposing the business rules' portion of that single application to infections or bugs. Just like we don't worry about breaking a text box when we open a user interface application for modifications, we don't need to worry about breaking our ECDO. If it worked when we started, it will work when we are finished. If the business application we are modifying doesn't work when we are done with the modifications, we have made a mistake in implementing the business rules. Notice how much easier this makes diagnosing problems in applications.

The idea is that as lead programmers, or as an object development team, we have really encapsulated our talent. We can distribute ECDOs to the other members of our development team, or to other development teams who can count on our data objects to build data stores, ensure integrity, and manage Audit tables without each developer needing to understand every bit of code or database design it takes to make these things possible.

> *Most developers will come to know ECDOs the way we see them (or don't see them here) as references in projects that enable them to work with the data the ECDO manages.*

Now that we have the project set up, we can get on with writing the code. As we are doing this remember that a Veneer is a *proxy* for an underlying data object. This means that we need to address *each* property, method, and event in the underlying object that we want our Veneer to expose. It also means that we need to go through essentially the same steps we used to write every other object so far in this book. We need to write code for a declaration section, property handlers, methods, and events. Veneers just like the data objects they cover have both an object class and a collection class.

One of the reason that the core code for a Veneer is so easy to write is that there are a number of properties, methods and events that are common – word-for-word – to every Veneer you will ever write. I want to make this clear. It doesn't matter whether you are making a Veneer for a Dog, or a Person, or an Airplane, some of the code you need to write will not need to be changed. This is *not* the same as saying that you might not treat the code differently than I have here. You might decide for security or some other reason not to expose some of these properties or methods. In that case, you can replace the code that I have given you here with something else that does the same job in a different way. But no matter how you do it, that job does need to be done. Say for instance that you decide that the user interface programmer doesn't really need access to things like `StampUser` or `StampDateTime`. You can choose not to expose those things to the UI programmer, but you still need to address them in the covered ECDO in the code you provide.

Our Veneer is designed to cover an ECDO, which means that we will need to write a Veneer that exposes both a single object and a collection of objects. Let's look at the object class first.

The Core Code For a Single Veneer Object

The code for a Veneer is really quite simple. If you have ever used the ActiveX Control Interface Wizard in VB, then you already know how a Veneer works. It is really just a very thin piece of code that maps a set of events, methods, and properties to a set of underlying DLL or ActiveX control.

The Declarations Section

Open up the `Computer.cls` module for editing. Building a Veneer is very much like building any other type of object, the first thing we need to do is to create some local storage variables. This Veneer is designed to cover a *Computer* object, so we need to create a local object for this Veneer. We make it a practice to declare the underlying variable as `mobjUCObject` in every Veneer. This helps to make it clear to the developer that we are working with a User Centric object. Anyway, remember to declare this object variable `WithEvents`. This will allow us to take advantage of the object's ability to know when all of the required information has been collected. The following block of code is the same in every Veneer designed to cover a single object. The only thing that changes is the name of the covered object. In other words if this Veneer was designed to cover an *Airplane* object the line would read `mobjUCObject As UCAirplane.clsAirplane`.

```
Option Explicit

Private WithEvents mobjUCObject As UCComputer.clsComputer
```

In addition to declaring the `mobjUCObject` private storage variable `WithEvents`, we also want to add an event to the `Computer` Veneer that we can map to the underlying object's event. In order to do that, we need to declare the event as follows:

```
Event Valid(blnIsValid As Boolean)
```

The Initialize and Terminate Subroutines

The following block of code is the same in every Veneer designed to cover a single object. The only thing that changes is the name of the covered ECDO. In other words if this Veneer was designed to cover a *Dog* ECDO the line would read `Set mobjUCObject As UCDog.clsDog`.

```
Private Sub Class_Initialize()

   Set mobjUCObject = CreateObject("UCComputer.clsComputer")

End Sub
```

There is another side to this instantiation problem. We also need to remember to set any of the local object variables to `Nothing` whenever we are done with them. We do that in a Veneer in the `Class_Terminate` subroutine:

```
Private Sub Class_Terminate()

' Note!! Remember to set all of the local object variables to nothing
  On Error Resume Next
  Set mobjUCObject = Nothing

End Sub
```

Event Bubbling

The next thing we need to do is to make use of the Valid event we created in the declaration section above. We used the broken rules class to determine whether or not each of the data rules we defined for an object was satisfied. It works like this. Every time a monitored property changes, the data object tests the data to ensure that it meets the specified criterion. If the data doesn't pass the test, its name is added to a collection of broken rules. If the data meets the test, its name is removed from the collection of broken rules. Every time a monitored property changes, the object counts the number of names in the broken rules collection. If the number of broken rules in the collection is greater than zero, then the Valid event is fired off with the value of False stuffed into its blnIsValid parameter. If the number of broken rules is zero, then that means that the object has satisfied all of the rules we defined and the Valid event if fired off with the value of True stuffed into its blnIsValid parameter.

You might remember how we used this event when we constructed the Visual Basic interfaces in the previous chapters. We tied the enable property of the Save command button to the event using the mobjUCObject_Valid subroutine. This routine is executed every time the Valid event of the mobjUCOBject is fired:

```
Private Sub mobjUCObject_Valid(blnIsValid As Boolean)

  cmdSave.Enabled = blnIsValid

End Sub
```

This simple one line subroutine causes the Save button to remain disabled until the data object becomes valid. And, because it is fired off every time a monitored property changes, it also disables the command button if the object becomes invalid for any reason. When we construct a Veneer, we want to pass the information about the validity of the underlying data object to the user interface programmer that is using the Veneer in place of the underlying data object. In order to do this, we have declared a separate Valid event in the Veneer. Then we tie that event to the event in the underlying object using essentially the same technique we used with the command button above. The only difference here is that instead of responding to the event in the underlying data object by changing the enabled property of a command button, we respond to the event in the underlying data object by raising an identical event in the Veneer. We can say that we are enabling the event in the underlying data object to *bubble up* to and through the Veneer.

This means that our Veneer object will have a `Valid` event that will behave exactly like the underlying data object's `Valid` event. The image shows that the *Computer* ECDO in the center of the Veneer is broadcasting its current valid condition. It also shows that the Veneer surrounding the ECDO is sending out an identical `Valid` event. In this image, the OK button on the Form is tied to the Veneer's `Valid` event rather than to the underlying `UCComputer` object's `Valid` event. What this means is that a user interface programmer can write exactly the same code that we used to control the OK button above whether the reference the user interface programmer is using is the Veneer or the underlying object.

Although I have seen people make working with events quite difficult, it really only requires a single step in addition to the declaration. That step is the line that causes the event to be fired off. The syntax couldn't be simpler:

```
Private Sub mobjUCObject_Valid(blnIsValid As Boolean)

  RaiseEvent Valid(blnIsValid)

End Sub
```

Think about what we did here. We responded to an event in the underlying data object by raising an event in the Veneer. We can call this technique **mapping**. Events are not the only thing that we can map. We can map properties, functions, and subroutines as well. Keep this in mind as we go through this chapter.

About Scope and Business Rules

When we considered the `Valid` event, we realized immediately that this was something that we wanted the user interface programmer to have access to. So in that case, we just mapped the event as if it existed in the underlying data object directly. We didn't do anything to control the user interface programmer's access to the information nor did we modify the information in any way. That doesn't always have to be the case. There may be events, methods, or properties that we want to *hide* from the UI programmer completely. There are a couple of ways we can accomplish this. The first is to manage the scope of the item we wish to hide. We can define the scope of a method or property as `Private`, but most of the time this practice limits the amount of real use that we can expect from the item. Fortunately, VB also gives us the option of declaring methods or properties as `Friend`.

We have used the `Friend` scope declaration before without comment, but I think that it really deserves our attention when we are talking about Veneers. When we build an application using Enterprise Caliber Data Objects, we are really pulling together the Veneers for each of the data objects we need to define the application. We can then take those Veneers and place all of them into a single ActiveX DLL. Think about this. While we might wish to hide some of the functionality from the user interface programmer, we probably really want the full compliment of functionality of each Veneer available to us from within the application. The `Friend` scope offers exactly that capability. When we declare a method or property as `Friend`, that method or property is available to the rest of the modules in the application but not to the UI programmer. As long as we are working in the same project where the module(s) with the methods or properties scoped as `Friend` reside, we can use those methods or properties as though they were declared as `Public`:

```
Friend Sub MarkObjectAsDeleted()

  mobjUCObject.MarkObjectAsDeleted
```

```
    End Sub

    Friend Sub MarkObjectAsUNDeleted()

      mobjUCObject.MarkObjectAsUNDeleted

    End Sub
```

However, if anything from outside of the same project attempts to access the methods or properties we have scoped as `Friend`, they will not be allowed to access those methods or properties. This means that we can hide methods or properties from user interface programmer and still have full access to their functionality by declaring those methods and properties with the `Friend` scope. That is not the only way that we can hide or otherwise control the user interface programmer's access to the Veneer's functionality.

If you're reading this book, then I am going to bet that you might be like me and therefore have been told more than once that everything in the world is not black and white. I hear this all the time, and to be perfectly honest I am really still not convinced. The way I figure it, if you take anything down to a low enough level of detail, you will eventually be able to find a series of on/off switches. I only mention this because I cannot believe what I am about to say. Although the `Friend` scope gives us the ability to switch a method or property off as far as the user interface programmer is concerned, everything is not always black and white. Ouch! Sometimes we do need to give the user interface programmers access, but we also need to control exactly how they get to use the underlying data. In other words, sometimes we expose a method or property but we intervene between the UI programmer and the UC object with some kind of business rule. Let's consider an example.

Say that we are designing a Veneer to cover an underlying *Cash* object that we are using in a banking application. At the level of the *Cash* object, all we can really do is to perform one of the eight data handling processes that Enterprise Caliber Data Objects offer. We can insert, update, delete, etc, but we don't really have a method for a deposit. Of course that is not a problem, we all know that at some level, a deposit is just a record added to the proper table in the data store. So I guess we can say that a deposit is really nothing more than an `ObjectInsert` for a *Cash* object. But if you think about it, it is actually a little more complicated. With a typical `ObjectInsert`, we don't do things like test to see whether we are inserting a positive amount or a negative amount. We just ensure that the data exists in the proper format for the data store and perform the insert. I suppose we could build data objects that expose multiple `ObjectInserts` and call them Deposit, Withdrawal, etc., but then we might also have to expose the same `ObjectInserts` as Payment, Refund, and so on... This takes away the simplicity of the underlying data object, and it causes business rules to migrate into the objects. That is not the extent of the problem, it might also mean that the underlying data object needs to be *aware of* and *rely upon* other data objects. *That type of thinking is the path to a monolithic application.* A better way to accomplish the same task is to use a Veneer that exposes the method in the underlying data object in a controlled fashion.

This means that we might choose to expose the `ObjectInsert` method of the *Cash* object to the user interface programmer several times. We might expose it as a deposit in one case and as a withdrawal in another. The code might look something like the following:

```
Public Function Deposit(curDeposit As Currency) As String

  If Account.IsOpen Then ' Where Account is another Veneer in the Application
```

```
      If curDeposit > 0 Then
        mobjUCObject.setDataStore mstrConnect
        mobjUCObject.Amount = curDeposit
        mobjUCObject.AccountID = Account.ID
        mobjUCObject.StampUser = UserLogon
        mobjUCObject.ObjectInsert
        Deposit = "Your Current Balance is now " & mobjUCObject.Balance
      Else
        Deposit = "You cannot deposit a negative amount of cash"
      End If

    Else
      Err.Raise vbObjectError, "Deposit", _
                "No Account has been opened to receive the deposit"
    End If

  End Function
```

My algebra teacher would be so proud. A withdrawal is simply an insertion of a negative value:

```
  Public Function Withdrawal(curDeposit As Currency) As String

    If Account.IsOpen Then ' Where Account is another Veneer in the Application

      If curDeposit > 0 Then
        curDeposit = curDeposit * -1
        mobjUCObject.setDataStore mstrConnect
        mobjUCObject.Amount = curDeposit
        mobjUCObject.AccountID = Account.ID
        mobjUCObject.StampUser = UserLogon
        mobjUCObject.ObjectInsert
        Withdrawal = "Your Current Balance is now " & mobjUCObject.Balance
      Else
        Withdrawal = "You cannot withdraw a negative amount of cash"
      End If

    Else
      Err.Raise vbObjectError, "Withdrawal", _
                "No Account has been opened from which to withdraw"
    End If

  End Function
```

The previous example was designed to illustrate the fact that you can use data objects covered by Veneers to accomplish anything that you could achieve by just modifying the underlying data objects. What we did above was really just an example of a method that applies a business rule between the Veneer and the UC object. The particulars of the business rule we used in this case are not important. The important thing to realize is that it is always possible to intervene in this manner.

> **In a well designed system, the act of moving data into and out of some storage area does not have anything to do with the business rules that we apply to the data.**

And, as I have already said, you are the only one who can figure out the best way to handle your organization's business rules. That will take a greater understanding of the problem and more creativity in that area than I can muster. This business rule type of routine is really more about creative problem solving and excellence in VB programming than it is about working with Enterprise Caliber Data Objects or distributed architecture design.

What I will do in this chapter is to point out those events, methods, and properties that *must* be included in an object's Veneer. During that process, I will work through any special techniques that you might need to master in order to design your own business objects.

The Core Subroutines

The following basic routines are supplied in the Veneer code that is generated by the Object Factory. They are not required, but they are used so commonly, that I have included the code. If nothing else, they should serve as good example of how to work with the underlying data object from within the Veneer. The following blocks of code are the same in every Veneer designed to cover a single object. The only thing that changes is the name of the covered ECDO. In other words if this Veneer was designed to cover an *Airplane* object the line would read `mobjUCObject As UCAirplane.clsAirplane`.

The Save Method

This routine is designed to free the user interface programmer from the task of determining whether an object needs to be inserted or updated. With this routine, all the user interface programmer needs to do to either insert or update an object is to call the `Save` method:

```
Public Sub Save(DSN As String, UserLogon As String)

    StampUser = UserLogon
    SetDataSource DSN

    If IsNew Then
        mobjUCObject.ObjectInsert
    Else
        mobjUCObject.ObjectUpdate
    End If

End Sub
```

Notice that we have forced the user interface programmer to supply the data source name and the user logon as parameters of the subroutine. This means that the user interface programmer will be prompted via IntelliSense to supply the, possibly unexpected, information that the Enterprise Caliber Data Object requires to function. This way we don't need to worry about the UI programmer forgetting to pass in the necessary information, which they might not know is required.

The Delete Method

This routine exposes the underlying data object's `ObjectDelete` method. Notice that, once again, we have forced the user interface programmer to supply the data source name and the user logon as parameters of the subroutine:

```
Public Sub Delete(DSN As String, UserLogon As String)

    StampUser = UserLogon
    SetDataSource DSN

    mobjUCObject.ObjectDelete

End Sub
```

This `Delete` routine is very simple; the only thing that we are doing for the user interface
programmer here is ensuring that the data source name and the identity of the currently logged on
user have been passed into the covered data object. I know that these tasks are not difficult and that
any programmer would learn to do them quickly, but I firmly believe that anything we can do to
make the job of programming easier is a good thing.

The History Method

This routine exposes the underlying data object's `ObjectAuditHistory` method. This is a good
example of how we can use Veneers to make the user interface programmer's job so much easier. All
the UI programmer needs to do to retrieve a complete audit history for an object is to pass the data
source name while calling the Veneer's `History` function:

```
Public Function History(DSN As String) As UCComputer.Computers

    Dim objUC As UCComputer.clsComputer
    Dim objVeneer As UCComputer.Comptuer

    SetDataSource DSN
    Set History = CreateObject("UCComputer.Computers")

' Load underlying collection with object history
    History.UCCollection = UCObject.ObjectAuditHistory()

' Add object to Veneer collection for each object
' in underlying collection
    For Each objUC In History.UCCollection
        Set objVeneer = CreateObject("UCPerson.Person")
        objVeneer.UCObject = objUC
        History.AddObject objVeneer
    Next objUC

End Function
```

The GetObject Method

This routine exposes the underlying data object's `ObjectFetch` method. The following block of
code is the same in every Veneer designed to cover a single object:

```
Public Sub GetObject(DSN As String, ID As Long)

    SetDataSource DSN
    mobjUCObject.ObjectFetch ID

End Sub
```

You may want to change the name of the routine to something more meaningful to the user interface programmer. I've used `GetObject` because it is more generic and can be used in all Veneers, however, you might prefer to expose a method called `GetComputer` or `GetAirplane` to elucidate the method's function better.

The Restore Method

This routine exposes the underlying data object's `ObjectRestoreFromDeleted` method. This allows the user interface programmer to restore an object from a deleted state:

```
Public Sub Restore(DSN As String, UserLogon As String)

  StampUser = UserLogon
  SetDataSource DSN

  mobjUCObject.ObjectRestoreFromDeleted

' Load properties for restored Person since the underlying
' Load method restores the property values
' If this were a 4DDO we would need to add the TypeID parameter and
' uncomment this line.
' Properties.Load DSN, UserLogon, ID, TypeID

End Sub
```

Note that the call to `PropertiesLoad` is commented out. I showed it here because when we are using an object with a Property Bag, we also need to call the `PropertiesLoad` method to ensure that the Property Bag has been loaded when the object is restored. I'll discuss how to create Veneers for Property Bags later.

The Required Veneer Methods

The following methods must be included or managed internally by the Veneer. Notice that the `SetDataSource` method has been declared with the `Friend` scope. This may seem rather unusual. But if take another look at the methods above, you should notice that the user interface programmer is always required to pass the name of the data source as a parameter of each function or subroutine. This is another example of how we can use Veneers to insulate the user interface programmer from some of the technical requirements of using Enterprise Caliber Data Objects. The remainder of the required functions simply map the underlying data object to the Veneer. The following blocks of code are the same in every Veneer designed to cover a single object. Notice that we don't even need to consider the name of the covered ECDO with these methods:

```
Friend Function SetDataSource(strConnect)

  mobjUCObject.SetDataSource strConnect

End Function

Public Function IsChild() As Boolean

  IsChild = mobjUCObject.IsChild

End Function
```

```
Public Function IsNew() As Boolean

   IsNew = mobjUCObject.IsNew

End Function
```

```
Public Function IsDirty() As Boolean

   IsDirty = mobjUCObject.IsNew

End Function
```

```
Public Function IsDeleted() As Boolean

   IsDeleted = mobjUCObject.IsDeleted

End Function
```

```
Public Function IsBeingEdited() As Boolean

   IsBeingEdited = mobjUCObject.IsBeingEdited

End Function
```

```
Public Sub CancelEdit()

   mobjUCObject.CancelEdit

End Sub
```

The Local Object Property Handlers

As always, in addition to the private storage variables, we also need a pair of object property handlers to manage the object storage variables. These are not very much different than the object property handlers we have been constructing all along. The Get simply returns the object stored in the private storage variable, and the Set stuffs a data object into the private storage variable. The following block of code is the same in every Veneer designed to cover a single object. The only thing that changes is the name of the covered ECDO. In other words if this Veneer was designed to cover an *Airplane* object the Get declaration line would read: As UCAirplane.clsAirplane:

```
Friend Property Get UCObject() As UCComputer.clsComputer

   Set UCObject = mobjUCObject

End Property
```

```
Friend Property Set UCObject(objUCObject As UCComputer.clsComputer)

   Set mobjUCObject = objUCObject

End Property
```

Notice that I haven't included the property handlers that map to the underlying data object in this section. That was intentional. There is a real conceptual difference between the two. In this case our property handlers are managing a local variable that actually exists in our Veneer class. This same set of property handlers exists in *every* Veneer. The other property handlers we will look at below do not manage information that is contained in this Veneer. Instead, they manage information that is in the covered data object.

The Required Veneer Property Handlers

The following property handlers must be exposed to the UI programmer or be managed internally by the Veneer. Remember that when we are designing Veneers we always have the option of hiding some of the functionality from the UI programmer. We also have the option of exposing some of the functionality in a controlled fashion. It is important to realize that we must address each of these properties to use an ECDO. That means that if we choose to insulate the UI programmer from the following property handlers we must ensure that we are doing something else to make sure that they are addressed. Once again, all we need to do here is to map the Veneer's properties to the underlying data object. And once again, notice that we don't need to change any of this code, not even the name of the covered ECDO. I know it may be a little boring to read this kind of code, but I think that this similarity speaks well for Veneers in general:

```
Public Property Let StampID(lngStampID As Long)

  mobjUCObject.StampID = lngStampID

End Property

Public Property Get StampID() As Long

  mobjStampID = UCObject.StampID

End Property

Public Property Let StampDateTime(dtmStampDateTime As Variant)

  mobjUCObject.StampDateTime = dtmStampDateTime

End Property

Public Property Get StampDateTime() As Variant

  mobjStampDateTime = UCObject.StampDateTime

End Property

Public Property Let DataLocking(intDataLocking As Integer)

  mobjUCObject.DataLocking = intDataLocking

End Property

Public Property Get DataLocking() As Integer

  mobjDataLocking = UCObject.DataLocking

End Property

Public Property Let StampUser(strStampUser As String)

  mobjUCObject.StampUser = strStampUser

End Property
```

```
Public Property Get StampUser() As String

    mobjStampUser = UCObject.StampUser

End Property
```

```
Public Property Let StampAction(strStampAction As String)

    mobjUCObject.StampAction = strStampAction

End Property
```

```
Public Property Get StampAction() As String

    mobjStampAction = UCObject.StampAction

End Property
```

```
Public Property Let DataMessage(strDataMessage As String)

    mobjUCObject.DataMessage = strDataMessage

End Property
```

```
Public Property Get DataMessage() As String

    mobjDataMessage = UCObject.DataMessage

End Property
```

```
Public Property Let ChangeAll(strChangeAll As String)

    mobjUCObject.ChangeAll = strChangeAll

End Property
```

```
Public Property Get ChangeAll() As String

    mobjChangeAll = UCObject.ChangeAll

End Property
```

```
Public Property Get Key() As String

    mobjKey = UCObject.Key

End PropertyPublic
```

```
Public Property Let ID(lngID As Long)

    mobjUCObject.ID = lngID

End Property
```

```
Public Property Get ID() As Long

    mobjID = UCObject.ID

End Property
```

The Additional Properties for a Veneer

In addition to the required properties, the Veneer should also manage or expose the base properties for the underlying data object. Once again, all we need to do to with these properties is to map them to the underlying data object. In the case of the *Computer* object we would need a property handler for all the base properties of a computer. For the *Computer* object we'll need the following properties:

- ❑ Name
- ❑ OperatingSystem
- ❑ ProcessorType
- ❑ TotalPhysMemory
- ❑ AvailPhysMemory
- ❑ TotalVirtualMemory
- ❑ AvailVirtualMemory
- ❑ DriveCSizeMeg
- ❑ DriveCSpaceMeg

The following property handlers are given as an example:

```
Public Property Let Name(strName As String)

  mobjUCObject.Name = strName

End Property
```

```
Public Property Get Name() As String

  Name = mobjUCObject.Name

End Property
```

The Core Code for a Collection Veneer

While the job of coding an object Veneer may change considerably depending upon the base properties of the underlying data object, the collection Veneer code does not really change unless the business rules require special events, methods, or properties.

The Declarations Section

The declaration section requires the following private storage variables:

```
Option Explicit
```

```
Private mCol As Collection
Private mintCurrentIndex As Integer y
Private mstrConnect As String

Private mcolUCCollection As UCPerson.colPersons
```

The Initialize and Terminate Subroutines

As with the single object Veneer, the collections are instantiated as soon as the Veneer is instantiated:

```
Private Sub Class_Initialize()

' Creates the collection when this class is created
    Set mCol = New Collection
    Set mcolUCCollection = CreateObject("UCComputer.colComputers")

End Sub
```

As with the single object Veneer above, we use the `Class_Terminate` routine to ensure that we have removed all of the objects from memory:

```
Private Sub Class_Terminate()

    On Error Resume Next
    Set mCol = Nothing
    Set mcolUCCollection = Nothing

End Sub
```

The Required Veneer Methods

The following methods must be included or managed internally by the Veneer. Notice that the `SetDataSource` method has been declared with the `Friend` scope. Once again the methods that are exposed to the user interface programmer have been designed to require a data source name. This means that the user interface programmer does not need to access the `SetDataSource` method:

```
Friend Function SetDataSource(strConnect As String)

    UCCollection.SetDataSource strConnect
    mstrConnect = strConnect

End Function
```

The following two methods allow the user interface programmer to work with a collection, mark the objects that should be deleted, and then use the batch save method rather than saving each object individually. These methods are direct maps to the underlying data object:

```
Public Sub MarkAsDeleted(lngID As Long)

    mobjUCCollection.MarkAsDeleted lngID

End Sub
```

```
Public Sub MarkAsUNDeleted(lngID As Long)

    mobjUCCollection.MarkAsUNDeleted lngID

End Sub
```

The CheckOutObject and CheckInObject Functions

The `CheckOutObject` and `CheckInObject` function are used to manage the parent-child relationship between a collection and the objects contained in that collection. Though these methods are a little more complex than the ones we have used before, at some level they simply provide a map to the underlying data objects.

```
Public Function CheckOutObject(lngID As Long) As UCComputer.Computer

  Dim objUC As UCComputer.clsComputer
  Dim objVeneer As UCComputer.Computer

  Set objUC = UCCollection.CheckOutObject(lngID)
  Set objVeneer = CreateObject("UCComputer.Computer")

  For Each objVeneer In mCol
    If objVeneer.ID = objUC.ID Then
      Set CheckOutObject = objVeneer
      Exit Function
    End If
  Next objVeneer

  Set CheckOutObject = CreateObject("UCComputer.Computer")
  CheckOutObject.UCObject = objUC

End Function
```

```
Public Sub CheckInObject(objThis As UCComputer.Computer)

  Dim objVeneer As UCComputer.Computer
  Dim objUC As UCComputer.clsComputer
  Dim blnFound As Boolean

  UCCollection.CheckInObject objThis.UCObject
  Set objVeneer = CreateObject("UCComputer.Computer")

  For Each objVeneer In mCol
    If objVeneer.ID = objThis.ID Then
      blnFound = True
      Exit For
    End If
  Next objVeneer

  If Not blnFound Then
    'New object, so locate in underlying collection and add
    'to Veneer collection
    For Each objUC In UCCollection
      If objUC.ID = objThis.ID Then
        objThis.UCObject = objUC
        AddObject objThis
        Exit For
      End If
    Next objUC

  End If

End Sub
```

I think that it is really a much better idea to hide these two methods from the UI programmer. Not because they are dangerous or anything, but just because they are so important. Think about the different ways that you could decide to provide this functionality.

The Load Subroutine

The `Load` method is mapped directly to the *Load* process in the underlying data object. Notice that this code is really just like the code we have been writing into the VB user interfaces. This is an important concept. Every line of code that we place into the Veneer is another line we don't have to consider at the user interface. This is especially important when we are using interfaces like ASP.

```
Public Sub Load(DSN As String, TypeID As Long, Optional Name as String, _
            Optional SQLString as String)

   Dim ThisObject As UCComputer.clsComputer
   Dim ThisVeneer As UCComputer.Computer

   Set mCol = New Collection

   SetDataSource DSN

   UCCollection.ClearCollection

   If Len(SQLString) > 0 Then
      UCCollection.Load SQLString
   Else
      UCCollection.Load
   End If

   For Each ThisObject In UCCollection
      Set ThisVeneer = CreateObject("UCComputer.Computer")
      ThisVeneer.UCObject = ThisObject
      AddObject ThisVeneer
   Next ThisObject

End Sub
```

The LoadDeleted Subroutine

The `LoadDeleted` method is mapped directly to the *Show Deleted* process in the underlying data object. Again, notice that this code is really just like the code we have been writing into the VB user interfaces.

```
Public Sub LoadDeleted(DSN As String, TypeID As Long, Optional SQLString As
String)

   Dim ThisObject As UCComputer.clsComputer
   Dim ThisVeneer As UCComputer.Computer

   Set mCol = New Collection

   SetDataSource DSN

   UCCollection.ClearCollection
```

```
      If Len(SQLString) > 0 Then
         UCCollection.ShowDeleted SQLString
      Else
         UCCollection.ShowDeleted TypeID
      End If

      Set ThisObject = CreateObject("UCComputer.clsComputer")

      For Each ThisObject In UCCollection
        Set ThisVeneer = CreateObject("UCconComputer.Computer")
        ThisVeneer.UCObject = ThisObject
        AddObject ThisVeneer
      Next ThisObject

   End Sub
```

The AddObject Subroutine

The AddObject method is used to manage the local collection. This method does *not* map to the underlying data object, instead it calls the Add method of the collection object:

```
   Friend Sub AddObject(objPerson As UCconPerson.Person)

      mCol.Add objPerson, objPerson.Key

   End Sub
```

The Required Veneer Property Handlers

The following property handlers must be exposed to the UI programmer or be managed internally by the Veneer. Most of them are the standard properties that we expect when working with a collection.

The NewEnum Property

This NewEnum property is required to allow the user interface programmer to loop through the collection using the For Each syntax:

```
   Public Property Get NewEnum() As IUnknown

   ' This property allows you to enumerate
   ' this collection with the For...Each syntax
     Set NewEnum = mCol.[_NewEnum]

   End Property
```

In order for this property to work we need to make some changes to the procedure's attributes. Open the Procedure Attributes dialog (it's located on the Tools menu) and select the NewEnum routine in the Name combo box. Use the Advanced >> button to change the Procedure ID to -4 and check the Hide this member box:

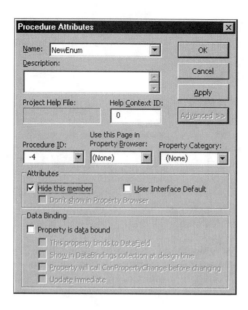

The Count Property

The Count property simply provides a direct mapping to the underlying data object's count property:

```
Public Property Get Count() As Long

' Used when retrieving the number of elements in the collection.
Count = UCCollection.Count

End Property
```

The Item Property

This property does not map to the underlying data object. It is used to retrieve objects that are stored in the local collection:

```
Public Property Get Item(vntIndexKey As Variant) As UCComputer.Computer

' Used when referencing an element in the collection
' vntIndexKey contains either the Index or Key to the collection,
' this is why it is declared as a Variant
Set Item = mCol(vntIndexKey)

End Property
```

We also want to set this property as the Default procedure using the Procedure Attributes dialog.

The CurrentIndex Property

The CurrentIndex property is also used with the local collection rather than the underlying data object:

```
Private Property Get CurrentIndex() As Integer

  CurrentIndex = mintCurrentIndex

End Property
```

```
Private Property Let CurrentIndex(intCurrentIndex As Integer)

  mintCurrentIndex = intCurrentIndex

End Property
```

The UCCollection Property

The `UCCollection` property is used internally in the Veneer. It does map directly to the underlying data object:

```
Friend Property Get UCCollection() As UCComputer.colComputers

  Set UCCollection = mcolUCCollection

End Property
```

```
Friend Property Set UCCollection(colUCCollection As UCComputer.colComputers)

  Set mcolUCCollection = colUCCollection

End Property
```

About the Property Bag Veneer Code

At first, I included all of the code that you needed to write a Veneer for a Property Bag in this chapter, but I decided to move it into Appendix C. The nature of the code is the same as the code we just looked at. All it does is to map the properties, methods, and events from the covered Property Bag to the Veneer. The sample code for the Person–Contact Information component also provides you with a good working example of the code that you need to write to cover a Property Bag with a Veneer. I want to get onto the real reason that we use Veneers in the first place – the business rules.

The Computer Object's Business Rules

The ECDO we built way back in Chapter 7 was a capable device, but it was merely a data object. It was designed to manage data. It doesn't really care where the data comes from or where it is going. All the ECDO does is ensure that data meets the set of mechanical requirements we talked about at the beginning of this chapter. Well, that is all well and good, but our job is so much more than shuffling data around from point A to point B. We need to design innovative ways to collect and distribute that data.

The job of the *Computer* object is to query its host computer for configuration information like, processor type, amount of physical memory, size of local disks, operating system, etc. and store that information in the **common system data store**. If we take this information and pair it with the information we collect with the *ErrCond* and *EntApp* objects we have already discussed, we can begin to discover information in our enterprise that may have been difficult or impossible to determine otherwise. Let's consider an example.

Say that, as a test, we have the *Computer* object installed on 50 different client machines throughout our enterprise, and that we have 5 in-house applications deployed on some of those machines. Assume that each in-house application is using the *ErrCond* object.

All of a sudden, the help desk starts getting a few calls. Strange, everything was working fine yesterday. We look at the information stored in the *ErrCond* data store and find that the errors are being generated from several different code blocks in several different modules. There doesn't appear to be any rhyme or reason to the errors and we can't reproduce them on the development machines. For a while, we are stymied. Then all of a sudden a junior programmer realizes that all of the errors are being generated on only 9 of the 50 computers. Of course, something *must* be wrong with the computers, but what? Enter the *Computer* object. It has been out on the client machines doing its job – collecting information and notifying the data store of any changes in its host computer's configuration. And, because this business object is based on an Enterprise Caliber Data Object, it will have been busy maintaining an audit history that recorded every change about the computers in the data store. So, thanks to our *Computer* object, we are able to take a closer look at each of the suspect computers and learn exactly what has changed on those 9 computers.

The *Computer* object Veneer uses a series of Windows API calls to query its host computer. Once it has filled its local properties with the information from its host computer, it attempts to fetch any pre-existing configuration information from the common system data store. If it doesn't find any pre-existing information, it adds its local property values to the data store. If it does find pre-existing information, it compares that information to current configuration for the computer. If any differences exist, the object updates the data store.

API Calls

The day Microsoft included the native compiler in Visual Basic 5.0 even the most adamant critics had to admit that Visual Basic was all grown up. It had become a real programming language. Personally, I was glad to see the converts, but truthfully, many of us had been doing *real* programming with Visual Basic for years. We knew we could do almost anything a C programmer could do as long as we harnessed one of the same tools they used – the Windows API.

Many VB programmers shy away from using API calls, and it is easy to understand why. The documentation is sparse at best, and when you are lucky enough to find a scrap of documentation, you can be sure it was written by a C programmer for other C programmers. I don't think they want us VB guys to find out how easy it actually is to use the API. Well I am sorry to blow the whistle, but...

The API Text Viewer

If you installed Visual Basic 5.0 or 6.0 on your computer, you should find that an unassuming menu entry – API text viewer – has been added to your Visual Studio 6 menu options under Tools | API Text Viewer.

This little utility is the Rosetta stone that makes the Windows API decipherable. To be honest, it is still difficult to find out exactly which function to use for a specific task. MSDN does make this easier, but it still takes a bit of research and often some trial and error to find the right call to get the job done. But when you do figure it out, this handy little utility does everything short of typing the function calls into your procedures for you.

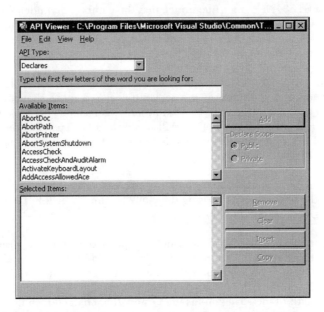

There are really only three things you need to do to access the API:

❑ First, declare the API function call and its parameters somewhere in your application
❑ Second, prepare the necessary constants and types
❑ Third, call the function exactly the way you would call a native Visual Basic function

That's it! The next few paragraphs show you how to use the API text viewer to declare functions, search out constant information, and locate type structure information.

For our first example, we are going to teach our *Computer* object to find out its host computer's name. In order to do this, we will make a call to the API using the, what else, `GetComputerName` function. And you thought this was going to be hard:

```
Private Declare Function GetComputerName Lib "kernel32" Alias "GetComputerNameA" _
                    (ByVal lpBuffer As String, nSize As Long) As Long
```

Once you know what function to call, the only really hard thing is finding out what dynamic link library the function lives in and what parameters it requires. That is where the API text viewer comes in. To use it, load the Windows API text file into the viewer by selecting File | Load Text File... from the main menu. In this case you load the `Win32API.txt` file. I used the default Visual Studio 6.0 installation parameters and I found this file located in `\Program Files\Microsoft Visual Studio\Common\Tools\WinApi\` subdirectory.

This is a little off the subject, but while I am talking about installing Visual Studio I should mention one other thing. Visual Studio comes with a wide assortment of tools that are supposed to be installed when you perform the default installation. Well, I guess someone at Microsoft goofed. Most of the extra tools that come with Visual Studio do not actually get installed. You can find them on one of the other CDs in the installation set. Just do a file search for `Tools` *on the CDs and you will find a directory chock full of goodies. I hope I didn't give you whiplash with that little diversion, anyway back to the task at hand.*

Once you have loaded the `Win32API.txt` file, notice that the combo box under the words API Type offers three choices: Constants, Declares, and Types. Select Declares. The list box below the combo box will be filled with the names of all the API function calls in the text file. Browse down through the list and locate the GetComputerName entry.

If you double-click on the GetComputerName entry the selected items list box will display the entire declaration statement for you. If you do not see the declaration statement as shown above, then select View from the main menu and make sure the Full Text option is selected. There is one other small thing to note. For our purposes, we will declare the API functions as `Private`. You can tell the API text viewer that you would like to declare the functions as `Private` by selecting the Private option in the Declare Scope frame.

Once the declaration statement in the Selected Items list box looks like the one in the code snippet above, you can copy it to the clipboard by pressing the Copy button. After it has been copied, you simply paste it into the correct location in your code.

As soon as the API function has been declared, we can use it just like any native Visual Basic function. We dimension the parameters the function requires and call the function as shown below. The only curious thing you need to be aware of is that the API returns strings terminated with the ASCII character 0 (this is the norm in the C world and we just have to live with it). In this case, the function also returns the length of the string minus the terminating character, so there is really no problem. In other cases, we need to determine the position of the terminating character ourselves. It is really that simple.

```
Dim strComputerName As String
Dim strBuffer As String
Dim lngSize As Long

strBuffer = Space(255)
lngSize = Len(strBuffer)

Call GetComputerName(strBuffer, lngSize)

If lngSize > 0 Then
    strComputerName = Trim(Left$(strBuffer, lngSize))
Else
    strComputerName = vbNullString
End If
```

OK, now that you have got your feet wet, let's take on a little more complex example. In this case, the API function we want to use requires a data structure as one of its parameters. This function returns memory information from the host computer. It is called, as you might have guessed, `GlobalMemoryStatus`. As I said before, finding out which functions exist and learning which one to call is the real art in this simple task. Anyway, once you know what function to call you can get the declaration statement by using the API text viewer.

Select Declares from the API Type combo box and double-click on the GlobalMemoryStatus entry. It should look exactly like this:

```
Private Declare Sub GlobalMemoryStatus Lib "kernel32" Alias _
            "GlobalMemoryStatus" (lpBuffer As MEMORYSTATUS)
```

That was simple, but we are faced with another problem. What the heck is a MEMORYSTATUS variable? Well, really it is a data structure, but in VB we cast this character as a **Type**. That sounds reasonable, but you must be wondering exactly how you are supposed find out what elements exist in this type? Again the API text viewer has the answer. Go back to the API Type combo box and select Types. The Available Items list box will be filled up with all of the types in the Win32API.txt file. Scroll down through the list and find the MEMORYSTATUS item. Double-click on the entry. The Selected Items list box will be filled with the entire MEMORYSTATUS type declaration statement. Easy! It should look exactly like the one below:

```
Private Type MEMORYSTATUS
        dwLength As Long
        dwMemoryLoad As Long
        dwTotalPhys As Long
        dwAvailPhys As Long
        dwTotalPageFile As Long
        dwAvailPageFile As Long
        dwTotalVirtual As Long
        dwAvailVirtual As Long
End Type
```

Now the GlobalMemoryStatus function is available for us to use just as though Microsoft had placed it into the Visual Basic Box at the factory. Below is a snippet of code that uses this function:

```
Dim ThisMemory As MEMORYSTATUS
Dim Memory As String
Dim VirtualMemory As String

GlobalMemoryStatus ThisMemory

Memory = "Physical Total: " & CLng(ThisMemory.dwTotalPhys / 1048576) & " megs, " _
         & "Physical Available: " & CLng(ThisMemory.dwAvailPhys / 1048576) _
         & " megs "

VirtualMemory = "Virtual Total: " & CLng(ThisMemory.dwTotalVirtual / 1048576) & _
                " megs, Virtual Available: " & _
                CLng(ThisMemory.dwAvailVirtual / 1048576) & " megs"
```

We just call the GlobalMemoryStatus function, passing it a variable typed as a MEMORYSTATUS type. The call fills the elements of the type with the requested information and we use the elements to build two strings that tell us about the Memory and Virtual Memory characteristics of the host machine. How simple is this?

By now you have probably figured out that the Constants choice from the API Type combo box will fill up the Available Items list box with a list of all of the constants in the Win32API.txt file. You are right! Let's look at an example that uses a constant to signal what type of processor is in the host computer. This is the most complex example we have looked at so far. The name of the function we need to declare is GetSystemInfo. It requires both a type definition and a set of constants used to interpret the long values it returns. Of course we can find both of these things by using the API text viewer. First we find the function declaration as shown below:

```
Private Declare Sub GetSystemInfo Lib "kernel32" (lpSystemInfo As SYSTEM_INFO)
```

Now that we know the name of the data structure the call requires, SYSTEM_INFO, we can find that by using the API text viewer. The SYSTEM_INFO data structure is as follows:

```
Private Type SYSTEM_INFO
    dwOemID As Long
    dwPageSize As Long
    lpMinimumApplicationAddress As Long
    lpMaximumApplicationAddress As Long
    dwActiveProcessorMask As Long
    dwNumberOfProcessors As Long
    dwProcessorType As Long
    dwAllocationGranularity As Long
    wProcessorLevel As Integer
    wProcessorRevision As Integer
End Type
```

This function returns a lot of information, but for now we are only interested in the dwProcessorType element. It returns a long value that we can translate into a particular type of processor. We do that by using a series of constants found in the Win32API.txt file. Sorry, but there is no really direct way to find out what constants are paired with what function or type element using the API text viewer. Too bad! But with a little research in MSDN and some common sense, we can learn that the constants we need to use are those constants whose names begin with the word PROCESSOR. We use them exactly the way we would use any other VB constant. The code snippet below builds a brief description of the host computer's processor based upon the evaluation of a simple Case statement. It should be self-explanatory:

```
Dim ThisSystem as SYSTEM_INFO

GetSystemInfo ThisSystem

Select Case ThisSystem.dwProcessorType

    Case PROCESSOR_ARCHITECTURE_INTEL = 0
      BriefDescription = "386 - Level: " & ThisSystem.wProcessorLevel _
                         & " Revision: " & ThisSystem.wProcessorRevision

    Case PROCESSOR_INTEL_486 = 486
      BriefDescription = "486 - Level: " & ThisSystem.wProcessorLevel & _
                         " Revision: " & ThisSystem.wProcessorRevision

    Case PROCESSOR_INTEL_PENTIUM = 586
      BriefDescription = "Pentium - Level: " & _
                         ThisSystem.wProcessorLevel & " Revision: " _
                         & ThisSystem.wProcessorRevision

End Select
```

I hope this little detour cleared up some of the mystery surrounding API calls. I will use them again as needed, without further comment, throughout the remainder of this book. If you want to know more about API calls you can find quite a few really good books on this subject, including *VB6 Win32 API Tutorial* published by Wrox Press. All I am trying to do here is to kind of smash the aura of mystery that surrounds this subject. Have some fun with these guys. They are a powerful addition to any programmer's toolbox.

The Computer Veneer's API calls

For our Computer object we needed to declare the following:

Declares

```
Private Declare Function GetUserName Lib "advapi32.dll" Alias "GetUserNameA" _
                (ByVal lpBuffer As String, nSize As Long) As Long

Private Declare Function GetComputerName Lib "kernel32" Alias "GetComputerNameA" _
                (ByVal lpBuffer As String, nSize As Long) As Long

Private Declare Function GetDiskFreeSpace Lib "kernel32" Alias _
                "GetDiskFreeSpaceA" (ByVal lpRootPathName As String, _
                lpSectorsPerCluster As Long, _
                lpBytesPerSector As Long, _
                lpNumberOfFreeClusters As Long, _
                lpTotalNumberOfClusters As Long) As Long

Private Declare Function GetVersionEx Lib "kernel32" Alias "GetVersionExA" _
                (lpVersionInformation As OSVERSIONINFO) As Long

Private Declare Sub GetSystemInfo Lib "kernel32" (lpSystemInfo As SYSTEM_INFO)

Private Declare Sub GlobalMemoryStatus Lib "kernel32" (lpBuffer As MEMORYSTATUS)
```

Constants

```
Private Const VER_PLATFORM_WIN32_NT = 2
Private Const VER_PLATFORM_WIN32_WINDOWS = 1
Private Const VER_PLATFORM_WIN32s = 0

Private Const PROCESSOR_ARCHITECTURE_INTEL = 0
Private Const PROCESSOR_INTEL_486 = 486
Private Const PROCESSOR_INTEL_PENTIUM = 586
```

Types

```
Private Type OSVERSIONINFO
   dwOSVersionInfoSize As Long
   dwMajorVersion As Long
   dwMinorVersion As Long
   dwBuildNumber As Long
   dwPlatformID As Long
   szCSDVersion As String * 128
End Type

Private Type SYSTEM_INFO
   dwOemID As Long
   dwPageSize As Long
   lpMinimumApplicationAddress As Long
   lpMiximumApplicationAddress As Long
   dwActiveProcessorMask As Long
   dwNumberOfProcessors As Long
   dwProcessorType As Long
   dwAllocationGranularity As Long
   wProcessorLevel As Integer
   wProcessorRevision As Integer
End Type
```

```
Private Type MEMORYSTATUS
        dwLength As Long
        dwMemoryLoad As Long
        dwTotalPhys As Long
        dwAvailPhys As Long
        dwTotalPageFile As Long
        dwAvailPageFile As Long
        dwTotalVirtual As Long
        dwAvailVirtual As Long
End Type
```

The QueryComputer Method

The `QueryComputer` method uses a series of API calls to find out information about the host computer. The code that follows is a toned downed version of the `QueryComputer` method we use in our enterprise. You can use it as shown or add as many additional calls as your application requires. We have already gone over the information you need to know to write this method, so I will not take up space with another explanation about how to make API calls. This code should be self-explanatory:

```
Public Sub QueryComputer()

    Dim strBuffer As String
    Dim lngSize As Long
    Dim VersionInformation As OSVERSIONINFO
    Dim ThisSystem As SYSTEM_INFO
    Dim ThisMemory As MEMORYSTATUS
    Dim intPosition As Integer
    Dim strDriveLetter As String
    Dim lngHold As Long
    Dim SectorsPerCluster As Long
    Dim BytesPerSector As Long
    Dim NumberofFreeClusters As Long
    Dim TotalNumberOfClusters As Long

    strDriveLetter = "C:\"

    Dim str As String, ln As Integer

    str = VersionInformation.szCSDVersion
    ln = InStr(str, vbNullChar)
    If ln > 0 Then
        str = Left(str, ln - 1)
    Else
        str = ""
    End If

    strBuffer = Space$(255)
    lngSize = Len(strBuffer)
    Call GetUserName(strBuffer, lngSize)
    If lngSize > 0 Then
        StampUser = Left$(strBuffer, lngSize)
    Else
        StampUser = vbNullString
    End If
```

```
strBuffer = Space$(255)
lngSize = Len(strBuffer)
Call GetComputerName(strBuffer, lngSize)
If lngSize > 0 Then
   Name = Left(strBuffer, lngSize)
Else
   Name = vbNullString
End If

VersionInformation.dwOSVersionInfoSize = 148

Call GetVersionEx(VersionInformation)

Select Case VersionInformation.dwPlatformID

  Case VER_PLATFORM_WIN32_NT
    OperatingSystem = "Windows NT Major: " & _
                      VersionInformation.dwMajorVersion & "." & _
                      VersionInformation.dwMinorVersion & "  Build " & _
                      VersionInformation.dwBuildNumber

  Case VER_PLATFORM_WIN32_WINDOWS
    OperatingSystem = "Windows 95 Major: " & _
                      VersionInformation.dwMajorVersion & "." & _
                      VersionInformation.dwMinorVersion & "  Build " & _
                      VersionInformation.dwBuildNumber

  Case VER_PLATFORM_WIN32s
    OperatingSystem = "Windows 3.11 Major: " & _
                      VersionInformation.dwMajorVersion & "." & _
                      VersionInformation.dwMinorVersion & "  Build " & _
                      VersionInformation.dwBuildNumber

End Select

str = VersionInformation.szCSDVersion
ln = InStr(str, vbNullChar)
If ln > 0 Then
  str = Left(str, ln - 1)
Else
  str = ""
End If
OperatingSystem = OperatingSystem & " " & str

lngHold = GetDiskFreeSpace(strDriveLetter, SectorsPerCluster, BytesPerSector, _
                        NumberOfFreeClusters, TotalNumberOfClusters)

DriveCSizeMeg = ((TotalNumberOfClusters / 1000) * SectorsPerCluster * _
               BytesPerSector)

DriveCSpaceMeg = ((NumberOfFreeClusters / 1000) * SectorsPerCluster * _
               BytesPerSector)

GetSystemInfo ThisSystem

Select Case ThisSystem.dwProcessorType

  Case PROCESSOR_ARCHITECTURE_INTEL = 0
    ProcessorType = "386 - Level: " & ThisSystem.wProcessorLevel & _
                " Revision: " & ThisSystem.wProcessorRevision
```

```
      Case PROCESSOR_INTEL_486 = 486
          ProcessorType = "486 - Level: " & ThisSystem.wProcessorLevel & _
                          " Revision: " & ThisSystem.wProcessorRevision

      Case PROCESSOR_INTEL_PENTIUM = 586
          ProcessorType = "Pentium - Level: " & ThisSystem.wProcessorLevel & _
                          " Revision: " & ThisSystem.wProcessorRevision

   End Select

   GlobalMemoryStatus ThisMemory

   TotalPhysMemory = CLng(ThisMemory.dwTotalPhys / 1048576

   AvilPhysMemory = CLng(ThisMemory.dwAvailPhys / 1048576)

   TotalVirtualMemory = CLng(ThisMemory.dwTotalVirtual / 1048576)

   AvailVirtualMemory = CLng(ThisMemory.dwAvailVirtual / 1048576)

End Sub
```

Summary

I hope that you can now understand why we took so much care over the coding of our Enterprise Caliber Data objects. Because of the time and effort we put in before, we can now easily and quickly slap together different data objects, connectors and business rules to create applications in next to no time at all. But we also gained something equally, if not more, important.

By using these building blocks to construct our applications we are able to effectively and efficiently separate our business rules from our data. This is one of the key goals of Enterprise Architecture and we've finally achieved it. This allows us to keep our data objects pure, which ultimately means they can be easily reused in many different applications without having to change a single line of code in them.

With business objects out the way, all we need to do now is deploy our applications, which is what we'll do over the final two chapters.

Person
Base Properties

ID
Last Name
First Name
Middle Name
Birth Date
Sex

Object Type Definitions

Object T...

... OTD	Lawyer OTD	Engineer OTD	Doctor OTD	Student OTD
Date	Specialty	Specialty	Specialty	Major
	Hourly Rate	Experience	Certification	Minor
Property 3	Law School	Property 3	Property 3	Year
Property 4	Property 4	Property 4	Property 4	Property 4
Property 5	Property 5	Property 5	Property 5	Property 5
Property 6	Property 6	Property 6	Property 6	Property 6
Property 7	Property 7	Property 7	Property 7	Property 7
Property 8	Property 8	Property 8	Property 8	Property 8
Property 9	Property 9	Property 9	Property 9	Property 9
Property 10	Property 10	Property 10	Property 10	Property 10

Property Set Definitions

Property Se...

15

Deploying Across an Enterprise

We have covered a lot of material in this book, so in this chapter I will try to pull all of the different topics we have discussed into a single vision of the overall system. We'll start by taking another look at the physical architecture that will host our applications. Now that you have actually worked through the coding of some objects with both data centric and user centric halves, I think that the server farm designs we looked at earlier may make a little more sense. While we look at the physical architecture, we will view the computers in the server farm more as software elements, SQL Server, MTS, IIS, rather than as hardware elements CPUs, disks, and memory.

What we'll do in this chapter is walk through each step that must be taken to deploy an application across our enterprise. Before we begin, let's take a minute to define the outcome we expect to achieve with this deployment. We need to consider several issues before we can develop and deliver an application to our users. Of course the first thing we need to do is to handle the development of the application itself. What that means to us, using ECDOs, is that we need to:

- ❏ Determine the application's functionality
- ❏ Acquire the base objects necessary to deliver that functionality
- ❏ Extend the base objects with type definitions if necessary
- ❏ Connect the objects
- ❏ Add the business rules
- ❏ Handle deployment issues

I guess if you think about it, this list shows that we have really taken the huge leap into the world of distributed architecture development. Most of this book, until now, has really been about handling steps 2 through 5 in a professional manner. I guess I always took it for granted that if you picked up a book on Enterprise Application Architecture that you are probably a master at determining the functionality for an application. Anyway, what we have to do now is to take a look at exactly what it means to deploy a distributed application across our architecture.

The Application Methodology

Before we go on to talk about deployment specifics I want to take the time to outline the life-cycle of developing applications for our enterprise.

Development

Developing applications with data objects is really a lot of fun when you get used to it. Of course as you have seen, the actual code we need to write when we build an ECDO is challenging to say the least. But, once you have built one, you can use it again and again. During the development stages, we spend a good amount of time searching through the ECDOs that we have already built. Most applications really seem to make use of the same set of base ECDOs:

- ❑ The *Person* object extended into one or more different types of people; Doctor, Patient, Employee, Engineer, etc.

- ❑ The *Organization* object. Extensions for the object include things like Company, Incorporation, and Government Agencies. As a hint about how you might think of an *Organization* object, I've found that I could use the *Organization* object to represent a family or a collection of *Person* objects.

- ❑ The *Address* object – Obvious

- ❑ The *Telephone Number* object – Obvious

- ❑ The *Email Address* object – Obvious

Of course there are other ones that we use quite frequently like the *Cash* and *Time* objects, but you get the idea. The first thing we do is to actively look for ways that we can *reuse* the objects we have already built. The key here is to be *creative*. You need to learn to think about, say, the *Person* object as a *real* person. Remember that you can always add an OTD and a Property Bag to the base object and turn the object into anything that a real person can be. The same goes for the *Organization* or any other 4-Dimensional Data Object that you have taken the time to build.

Only after we have exhausted the reuse possibilities do we even think about creating any new ECDOs. Usually we find that we do need to make a few new ones to handle some special kind of information for an application. At this point, we STOP. We take time to THINK about the FUTURE, and we work hard to design the base property set for any new ECDOs - so that we might be able to reuse them in the future.

The next step in this process is to work through the relationships between the objects. When we are working with ECDOs that means that we need to think about Connector objects. In just about every application, we do need to build at least a few Connector objects. But as we saw in the chapters on Connectors and Veneers it is possible to package common relationships like Person – Address – Telephone Number – Email Address into something we call a component. This frees us up from having to develop the same kind of Connector objects over and over again. Think about how you might design an *Organization* object. You know, one that manages things like companies, agencies, and even families. Now try to think about even one organization you know that doesn't have at least one person associated with it.

Anyway, organizations tend to have people. They also usually have contact information like Address – Telephone Number – and maybe even an Email Address. This means that we need to think about these things and consider the possibility that we might design something like an *Organization* component. Again, this frees us up from having to work through the relationship problem over and over again.

Notice what you just did! You were thinking about different kinds of organizations and their relationships to people.

> **You did not think about a table in the database.**

That is what we do during development:

- ❑ We think about real things.
- ❑ Then we build objects to model those things.
- ❑ Once we have the objects, we think about the real world connections between those things.
- ❑ Then we build objects to model those connections.
- ❑ The last step in this process is to work through the business rules that our organization uses to manage the connections we have made possible with our data objects and their associated connectors.
- ❑ We take these rules and package them into something we call a Veneer.

This is where we do most of the work in application development. We write specialized business rules into a tiny bit of VB project that we call a Veneer.

The Location of Development

During development, we usually copy all of the DLLs for the objects we need onto a local workstation. During very early development phases, we might even use a local SQL Server rather than our common development box. We don't normally use MTS at this time. We try to keep things as *simple* as possible. This allows us to focus on the *real* problem we are left with when we are developing an application using ECDOs - the business rules in the veneer.

Notice that I said that we might use a local SQL Server rather than the our common development box. I want you to think about all of the work we did passing Connect strings between all of the different spheres in our system. You didn't write one piece of code that didn't require a Connect string. I am sorry if this was troubling at the time, but let's think about what it means to us now. We have objects that are capable of creating their own tables, views, and stored procedures. This means that we can drop a few of these guys on our desktop, create a disposable local database, and hack away at the business problems. This gives us the same kind of interactive development process at the application level that makes VB so powerful at the user interface level.

Once a developer has finished, I am going to call it understanding the problem (hacking away), then we generally take the small step of pointing the ECDOs at the common development SQL Server box. We also take any new ECDOs or Connectors that the developer has created and perform a standard set of tests against them. We use the Object Factory to make the ECDOs so we don't normally have problems in this area, but these objects are reusable so we do test them before we move them into the common development MTS/IIS servers. Once the objects are in the common development area, they become a part of the process we talked about earlier. In other words, we try to find reuse possibilities for all of the ECDOs.

After we have moved the data store and the objects to the common development platform, the developer continues to work through the business rules. This step also gives the developer the opportunity to see exactly how the ECDOs are performing across the common development platform, which is really just three machines that we use to model a server farm. This allows us to catch any problems that might occur in this area before we get into the staging platform.

Staging

By the time an application has moved into staging, most of the bugs, including any that might arise from operating across a distributed platform, have been worked out. Our staging platform is a perfect, but scaled down replica of our production system. You can think of it as a 'piece of pie' rather than as the whole pie using the vision of the concentric ring server farm from Chapter 3.

Normally, the move of an 'application' from development into the staging arena is not all that difficult. That is because we *reuse* ECDOs. This means that often most of the data objects we need for an application have already been installed on the staging platform. This is a blessing. It means that at least a portion of each application has been tested under staging conditions. The things we do have to install on the staging machines for new applications are usually just a few Connector objects across the three inner spheres, a Veneer that only exists on the User Centric sphere, and the Interface on the IIS servers on the Presentation Sphere.

The next thing we do may seem a little strange, but immediately after we deploy the ASP interface on the staging IIS machines and perform some basic tests, we bring the customers into the development process. We usually give one developer authority for an application at this point and that developer works with the users in real time. This means that every day we ask the users to "play" with the application deployed across the staging platform. During this time, we impress upon the users that this application is theirs, and that now is the time for them to suggest any changes, modifications, or point out any problems. Thanks to our web-based deployment technique, we have the ability to make changes to the interface and have those changes on the users' desks in minutes. Of course, I like things to be consistent, so we don't actually update the staging system in real time. Instead, we try to get a list of comments from the user test base each day. Then we take that list, and work out the issues on that list on the development platform. Each night, we take any changes we have made and tested on the development platform and implement those changes on the staging platform.

As I said earlier, our staging platform has been purposefully designed to model the production system. In other words, it has the full set of capabilities of the production system including the correct positioning of the Cluster Servers. This gives us an opportunity to do things that we can't do in the development system, like perform fail-over test scenarios.

In many ways, I consider our staging system a **choke point** for our development process. Although our core object team is purposefully small, the objects are made available to a wide range of developers with a wide range of talents. The staging platform gives everyone of those developers a model to follow and a set of standards to meet. If the application they developed cannot exist on the staging platform, then it will *not* be moved into production until it can. This is not as ominous as it sounds, in actual practice, the move from development to staging is one place where all the developers get to "meet" and a lot of learning takes place here.

The staging system is not just a one-way street from development to production. We also perform a nightly replication of data from the production system back to the staging system. This keeps the staging servers synchronized a day behind the production system in terms of the data stored in the system. That allows us to work with not only the type of information stored in the production system but also to work with about the same volume of information. This gives us the opportunity to do things like test the effects of adding indexes to the database, etc. It also gives us a safe place we can use to replicate any problems that the users of the production systems may have been experiencing. If we are experiencing a problem in production, we replicate the problem on the staging machines and "have a conversation" with the users using the staging machines as our medium. Once we have nailed down the bug, we hack away at the bug on the development system, fix it. Then we move it back to staging and test it. Only when we, and the users, have signed off on the problem does the fix get placed into production.

You should notice that the rollout process from development towards staging may be a long and drawn out, but that is by design. The staging step in process is intended to provide a tough hurdle on the way to deployment on the production system.

Production

The deployment of an application on the production system really doesn't involve anything more than installing each of the new pieces required on the proper servers and making sure that the correct connect strings are being passed to the correct data objects. By this time, the tables, views, and stored procedures that the new data objects will create in the system have been tested at least twice. The new data objects, the Connector objects, the business rules in the Veneer, and the user interface have undergone a thorough testing on the staging platform. Once the pieces have been installed on the correct servers, all we need to do to deploy an application is to give the correct user base the permission to access the application using the *EntApp* object and the *Person* object extended as an IT Customer.

Dividing the Enterprise

In order to deploy our objects across our enterprise we need to examine the infrastructure that we have designed for our enterprise system. What follows is a quick review of how we divided the system up in the earlier chapters.

Processing Divisions

One of the very first things we talked about in this book was how to divide the system by isolating particular processes that are going on. We further saw how we could sub-divide the processing into major and minor processes.

Major Processing Divisions

In Chapter 2, we determined that there were two types of major process isolation:

OLTP - On Line Transaction Processing

OLTP is designed for real-time transaction processing. We expect the OLTP portion of the system to respond immediately to all requests, updates, etc. This system is optimized (at the database level) for speed first and then ease of use when dealing with single items (one employee, one customer, one purchase etc.). Over time, we have gradually reached the point where we have driven most of the redundancy out of our well-designed database systems. As an industry we have learned to design and optimize our systems around a unit of work we call a transaction. The most optimal transaction uses the smallest possible data set that will get a particular task accomplished. The Data objects we learned to design and build in this book are optimized for OLTP.

OLAP - On Line Analytical Processing

The OLAP or DSS system is not designed for real-time transaction processing; it is really something of a data warehouse. It is optimized in a manner that makes it easy to get answers to, even complex-enterprise-wide, questions in a very short time. We expect the OLAP portion of the system to provide us with easy access to answers for difficult (maybe formerly impossible) questions that span multiple (enterprise wide, all the employees, all the customers in France, etc.) items. Although we took the time to realize that we do need to separate the OLAP data storage activities from the OLTP data storage activities, we did not get a chance to learn to code the special Data objects that handle the OLAP portion of our system.

Minor Processing Divisions

The next thing we discovered was that in addition to the two major processing divisions in every system, we could also identify four minor processing divisions.

Data Storage Processes

These processes are responsible for the physical storage and retrieval of data from some persistent source. If we design our system correctly, this may be one of the few places where the system is actually performing reads and writes to an actual physical disk.

Data Manipulation Processes

Data Manipulation Processes are designed to know where an organization's data is stored and know the steps that must be taken to retrieve, remove, or change that data. These processes do not typically perform tasks like disk I/O themselves. They usually invoke other processes, most of them on another physical machine, to handle the physical writes and reads. The Data Manipulation processes are designed to wrap around the core of data available to our organization and give the programmers, and the users, access to the entirety of that data as though the data existed on a single machine. In reality, that data may exist on a centralized SQL Server machine, but it may also exist in legacy machines like mainframes, tired old UNIX systems, in flat files, and maybe even somewhere out on the Internet.

Data/Business Rule Integration Processes

While Data Manipulation processes know about the organization's data, the Data/Business Rule Integration processes know about the organization's talent. Their job is to pull together data and business rules and by combining the two increase the value of both.

Presentation Processes

The Presentation processes' job is to present or receive data to or from the end user. We found that these processes are really most like the Data Storage processes we looked at above. The real difference between the Data Storage and Presentation set of processes is where we write the end result of the process. While the Data Storage processes primarily write to the system's disks, the Presentation processes primarily write to the end users workstations' screens, files, and printers. But, both sets of process are concerned with changing fleeting binary data transmissions into something of a more *persistent* nature.

So splitting the enterprise according to processing resulted in this:

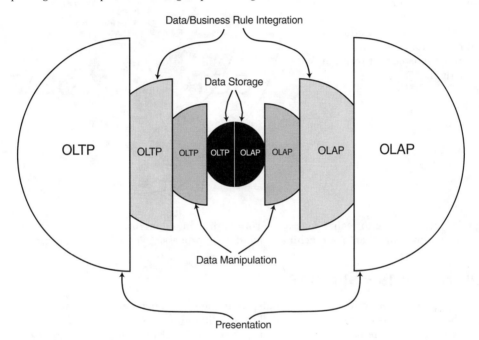

Physical Divisions - Tiers

We found that it was possible to deploy the available physical resources in a manner that mirrored the processing divisions. We split the servers into the following physical tiers:

- ❑ The Data tier - Handles the Data Storage processes
- ❑ The Data Centric tier - Handles the Data Manipulation processes
- ❑ The User Centric tier - Handles the Data/Business Rule Integration processes
- ❑ The Presentation tier - Handles the Presentation processes

Although tier divisions is not a new concept in distributed architecture, we found that when we combined this divisional strategy to our processing divisions, we could focus the processing power of a large number of presentation, object broker/transaction processing servers, towards a very much smaller number of database servers at the center of our system. In other words, it made more sense to imagine that the servers existed as a series of concentric rings:

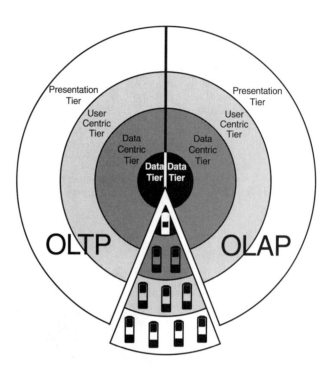

During this time, we came to realize that at the core of distributed architecture is the very simple idea that we can employ more than one machine to handle the processing load for our enterprise.

Logical Divisions - Spheres

At this time, we also realized that in order to distribute the processing load across more than one machine, the applications we developed needed to be a little different from what we might have grown accustomed to in the past. We found that we needed to learn to think of our applications as the set of related processes we talked about earlier rather than as a single monolithic block of code. The reasoning for this was simple. It doesn't matter if we have 10, or 100, or even 1000 servers available to execute our code. If that code exists as a monolith, then we can only run that block of code on one server at a time. On the other hand, if we break the monolith down into several sets of complimentary logical processes, we can run each of the different processes on different machines simultaneously.

This meant that it was possible to have both our physical and logical system set up in a complimentary manner. When we paired this idea with the server farm designs we looked at earlier a new vision of our enterprise emerged. This combining of physical and logical assets in a parallel fashion had the curious effect of allowing us to envision our system a series of spheres. Where each one of the spheres represented a minor processing division:

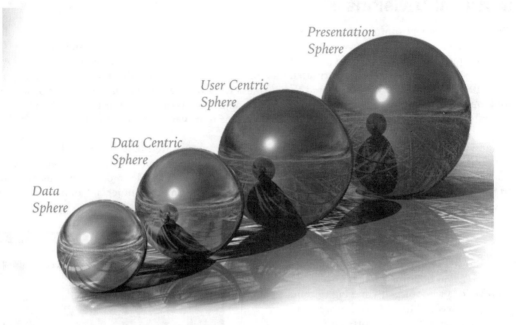

Just like we did with the servers in the physical system above we placed the smallest sphere, the Data sphere, in our logical system at the center of the enterprise. The reason we did this was because knew that the power of distributed architecture lay in its ability to share the processing load across as many machines as possible. We intuitively understood that the distribution of the processing load across a system did not mean that we had to distribute the data we stored in that system. We learned to position our available resources, both hardware and software, in a fashion that focused the energy of the system towards the core of data at the center of the system.

Once we had positioned our Data sphere at the center of our enterprise, we set out to construct a system that would allow us to share the smallest possible number of database servers at the core of our enterprise to the largest number of users. We found that we could envision the different spheres, Data sphere, Data Centric sphere, User Centric sphere, and Presentation sphere as a series of nested spheres. Although I didn't take time to make it too clear as we were working through the chapters, we started solving our programming problems at the center of this system, at the Data sphere.

During the time that we were learning to develop ECDOs, we were very careful to craft each data object as a set of three distinct sets of processes. We designed one set of processes, the stored procedures, to be executed on the Data sphere. We crafted another set of processes, those in the DC Object, to be executed on the Data Centric sphere. And a third set of processes, given by the UC Object that were destined to be executed on the User Centric sphere. The end result of this careful design and execution is that we have, in a very real way, moved the data store out to the third sphere in our system. Remember that while we were learning to build these data objects, we often called them something like a 'proxy for a table' or a 'proxy for a view'.

ECDOs are distributed data objects that inherently spread out the load normally forced upon the database servers across as many servers as we have available in the Data Centric and User Centric spheres.

Functional Divisions

Although the physical processing improvements our distributed object enable are great, we did something far more important with the ECDO when we effectively moved the database to the User Centric sphere in the system. We purified our application design and development practices. While we were learning how to build distributed data objects, we didn't allow business rules to creep into our data object designs. We eliminated the business rules from all of our data handling processes. We took on the elimination of business rules from our objects with such a fervor that we didn't even begin to consider the business rules in our applications until very late in our journey.

When we did finally begin to think about business rules, we ensured that they wouldn't infiltrate our data objects by designing a couple of special objects to handle business rules. We called these special objects Connector objects and Veneers. We learned that it was possible to distill the business rules from a set of requirements and handle all of these rules just using data objects, Connector objects, and Veneers.

This showed us that it was entirely possible to think about building *database* applications without really having to think about databases. This means that we can divide our development efforts into two separate challenges. The first is to create reusable data objects that can be shared amongst different applications. The second is to take the reusable data objects and to incorporate them into unique applications using Connector objects and Veneers:

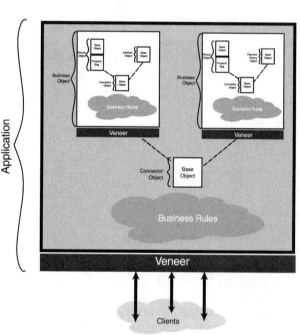

What we can garner from the last paragraph is that when we start to think about deployment issues for our enterprise, we really need to think about deployment in two phases:

- ❑ The first phase is the deployment of involves distributing the reusable data objects across the spheres in our system.
- ❑ Once these data objects are available throughout the enterprise, then we can begin to think about the deployment issues on the level of the individual applications.

In the next section of this chapter, we are going to consider the deployment of data objects across the spheres of the system. In order to handle these deployment issues, we need to think about SQL Server at the Data sphere, Microsoft Transaction Server managing transactions at the Data Centric sphere, Microsoft Transaction Server operating as an object broker at the User Centric sphere, and then Internet Information Server on the Presentation sphere.

Distributing Data Objects

This book is about Enterprise Architecture. We are using a 4 Sphere Architectural Model; that means that we should be able to define the tasks required to meet our objective in terms of a series of sub tasks that must be handled on each sphere. Over the next few pages, we will cover the things that must be accomplished on each sphere in order to deploy an application. In this chapter, we will be more concerned with the operational tasks rather than the programming tasks. I am sure that by now, you either know how to handle the programming or know where to look up the information you need. What we need to cover is the actual hands on activity that needs to take place on each sphere in order to deploy an application.

I would like to approach the deployment issue the same way we worked through the development issues we talked about throughout this book. In other words, I would like to start at the inner most sphere of the system and work out from the database to the user. This will allow us to work through deployment issues for each sphere so we will arrive at the last chapter of this book at the Presentation sphere with only some ASP concepts to finish.

The Data Sphere - SQL Server

All of the objects we have worked with in this book rely upon a relational database data core.

In our installation, we use SQL Server 7.0, but anything we have done in this book could be accomplished using SQL Server 6.5.

> *Of course, it is also possible to use exactly the same techniques with other relational databases, Oracle, Informix, etc. If you use one of the other databases, you might have to make some minor changes to some of the stored procedures. Microsoft's Transact SQL is not universal by any means, but any changes that you do need to make are likely to be rather trivial syntax changes rather than major conceptual overhauls.*

As a suggestion, if you are currently using SQL 6.5 and you have the option of migrating to SQL 7.0, by all means do it. I am not going to go through a feature-by-feature comparison, you can do that for yourself. But I will tell you that SQL Server 7.0 has `varchar` fields that can hold 8,000 characters compared to the 255 character `varchars` that SQL Server 6.5 offers. This means that in all but the rarest cases, we can virtually eliminate the handling of binary large objects, BLOBs, and text fields from our list of programming chores. This in and of itself may be enough to cause most shops to switch from 6.5 to 7.0, but there are other, performance based, reasons to make the switch. During our switch from 6.5 to 7.0, I took the time to run some simple comparison tests between the two versions. The outcome of the test was that, out of the box, SQL 7.0 showed about a 300% improvement in throughput.

Comparing SQL Server 6.5 and 7.0

The tests consisted of a simple driver application that ran a series of database actions against the server. To remove any client or networking bottlenecks, I used multiple client machines to drive the tests against both SQL Server versions. When I ran the tests against the 6.5 version using the default configuration, I was limited to approximately 125,000 database actions per hour. It didn't seem to matter how many client machines I used to drive the test, the 125,000 number stood. Curiously, this limitation was not due to the CPUs or I/O capabilities of the machine. The resource monitor showed the CPU utilization steady at around 10%. The limitation seemed to be due to some internal SQL Server factors. Anyway, I ran the same test against the SQL 7.0 version, again using the default configuration. The results were impressive. The 7.0 version allowed 400,000 database actions per hour. The 7.0 version also made better use of the available resources. I didn't need to use any additional client machines because the CPU utilization with 7.0 was around 60%. This test was performed using objects that hit SQL Server directly without any of the pooling capabilities of MTS.

After I performed this test, I devised another test that was designed to measure the effect MTS had on the overall system. I added another machine to the mix. This machine only had MTS installed on it. Next I moved the DLLs from the client machines to the MTS machine. Then I created a package for the DLLs and informed the client applications that they were to use the DLLs in MTS instead of a local copy of the DLL. Finally, I ran exactly the same test as above against the MTS/SQL pair. The results were astounding! First, the number of database actions that were completed per hour went from 400,000 to 500,000. This alone would have been significant, but it was not what surprised me. The amazing thing was that the CPU utilization for the machine that hosted SQL Server 7.0 went down to 12% for 500,000 actions compared to 60% for 400,000 actions. Of course, the processing power had to come from somewhere. It did. The MTS machine's CPU utilization was between 40 and 50%! This was a tribute to Microsoft's tight integration between MTS and SQL. It also confirmed the ability of the connection pooling resources of MTS.

The Data sphere of our system consists of three types of database objects – tables, views, and stored procedures. Of course our objects are designed with the capability of constructing all of the database objects that they need to function, so by deploying our data objects on the Data Centric sphere, provided we have set up a database for them, we can leave the handling of the Data sphere to our objects. Once again, the time and effort we put into building high quality data objects has paid off.

The Data Centric Sphere - MTS

Microsoft Transaction Server (MTS) handles the middle spheres of our system. Although Microsoft named this application Transaction Server, this name really doesn't convey all of the things that we can do with it.

> *I'm only going to give a brief overview of MTS here. If you want to learn more, and I recommend that you do, I suggest you try Professional MTS and MSMQ with VB and ASP, also published by Wrox Press.*

MTS provides a stable run time environment for our objects. It serves as an object broker and can manage a number of instances of a particular object. Unfortunately, the current version of MTS doesn't offer us the level of administrative control that some other middle-ware managers like TOP END® does. We cannot, for instance, tell MTS to keep X number of objects of a particular type in a pool instantiated and available for service. As I understand it, this type of functionality will be available in the next release of MTS. But, as far as I am concerned, this lack of administrative tuning capabilities is not that much of a disadvantage.

It has been my experience that MTS really does a good job of managing the number of available objects without any interference from the likes of me. In other words, while other products like TOP END® do give the administrator a higher level of control, MTS uses a sophisticated optimization algorithm to perform that task without any intervention. Although I cannot prove it, I suspect that the algorithm may be more capable than most administrators would be under the same circumstances.

As we learned by examining the results of the testing above, one of the other things MTS offers is superb resource pooling capabilities. The increase in performance we saw was completely due to MTS's ability to manage several pools of resources including database connections, processes, and threads. Again, MTS doesn't offer as rich an administrative interface as some other middle-ware applications do in this regard. We cannot really do much to tune or otherwise effect the pooling of available resources. MTS does this without interference via some internal logic. And once again, I really think that this may be a good thing. The things that people tend to view as complicated like real-time optimization of resources are tasks that are often better handled by automation.

If you remember the fairly complicated server farm designs we looked at way back in Chapter 3, you may have thought that it would be incredibly difficult to manage objects spread out over all of those machines. Well MTS makes it very easy to deploy, test, and re-deploy objects across a multiple machine platform. MTS can be easily programmed to replicate components across a battery of machines. It has been my experience that this administrative facility may be more important to overall system performance than the ability to manage the number of instances of an object on a particular machine. The way we administer MTS is to **macro manage** the system. In other words, if we need more processing power, we add another machine or two to the pool of available servers. Then as we covered above we can allow MTS to **micro manage** the pool of resources (and object instances) on each server.

Another advantage MTS offers is the ability to provide two additional levels of security to our system. We can write code in the objects that allow just certain groups of users to gain access to certain properties and methods. This security scheme is called **programmatic security**. This allows us to create objects that can actually transform their interface to bend to meet security concerns. In other words, we may need everyone in the company to be able to gain access to some *Cash* object. But through programmatic security we can ensure that only persons in group X can void a cash transaction. There is another type of security we can employ with MTS. It is called **declarative security**. This type of security really allows (or denies) certain individuals access to a particular object under the control of MTS.

Last but not least, we can use MTS to, surprise surprise, manage transactions. This is one of the most important functions of this server.

MTS and Transactions

You should remember that in all our Data Centric object's processes' code we used a Context object variable to manage transactions. The calls to `SetComplete` and `SetAbort` informed the MTS environment whether our transaction was successful or not and allowed MTS to deactivate the object. At this point I'd briefly like to draw your attention to an property of our objects which you may not have noticed.

Visual Basic 6.0 introduced a new class property that you could set in the Properties dialog, just like any other property. This new property was MTSTranasctionMode:

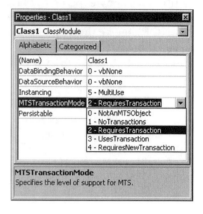

As you can see there are five potential settings for this property, which determines how MTS handles an instance of this class.

NotAnMTSObject

Specifies that the object will not be involved with MTS. This is the default option.

NoTransactions

The class will not support transactions. An object context will still be created, but it will not participate in any transactions. This value is useful for when you are just using MTS as a central repository for a component class. With this value, there will not be a transaction as part of the class.

RequiresTransactions

This value mandates that the object must run within a transaction. When a new instance of the object is created, if the client has a transaction already running then the object's context will inherit the existing transaction. If that client does not have a transaction associated with it, MTS will automatically create a new transaction for the object.

UsesTransactions

This choice indicates that should a transaction be available when the object is created then it will use the existing transaction. If no transaction exists then it will also run but without any transactional support.

RequiresNewTransaction

This indicates that the object will execute within its own transaction. When a new object is created with this setting, a new transaction is created regardless of whether the client already has a transaction.

> *If you look at the source code you will see that for all our classes in the DCPerson.dll that the MTSTransactionMode property has been set to 2-RequiresTransaction.*

In the section that follows we will work through a procedure you can use to create MTS Packages for the Data Centric objects.

Data Centric Package Creation on MTS

The steps that we must perform to create the MTS packages for the Data Centric objects and the installation procedures we must follow do not change even if you need to install both the Data Centric and User Centric halves of the objects on the same machine. Over the next few pages, we will work through the steps that are required to create a Data Centric MTS package for the *Person* object. You can repeat exactly the same process for any other Data Centric objects.

1. Copy the `DCPerson.dll` to a directory on the Data Centric MTS machine. We use a directory called `Components` on each MTS machine to hold the DLLs for the objects that are installed on that machine. It makes it easier to find and work with the components as the need arises. In addition, we also use a simple directory structure under the `Components` directory that separates each object:

2. Start Microsoft Transaction Server Explorer. This MTS administrative application is delivered as a snap-in for Microsoft Management Console (MMC).

This set of steps assumes that you have accepted the default setup parameters for NT Option Pack 4. They also assume that you are working directly on the target machine that hosts the Data Centric objects.

3. Navigate through the Console tree view to the Packages Installed node under the My Computer node. As long as you are working on the target machine, you can always use the My Computer node to perform any administrative functions that need to be performed. The MTS snap-in is just like any standard Explorer interface:

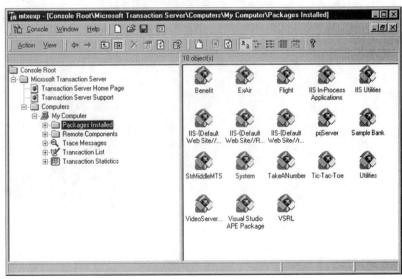

4. Select the Packages Installed node on the treeview. Then right-click your mouse. You should see a pop-up menu. Select New and then click on the Package option. This will start MTS's Package Wizard. The wizard will walk you through the steps that are necessary to create a new MTS package:

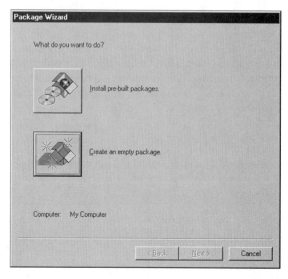

5. In this case, we do not have a pre-built package for you Data Centric *Person* object, so we are going to create an empty package. All you need to do is click on the Create an empty package button on the form. That will bring up the next step of the Package Wizard:

6. Type in the name for the new empty package. In this case we would type in the word DCPerson. Once you have typed in the name for the package, press the Next button:

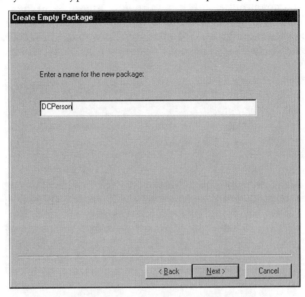

7. The next screen is used to set the package identity. In my enterprise, I have a single MTS account that we use. This allows me to control the permissions using a single account. You probably don't have a particular MTS account set up in your domain, so for the time being, just accept the Interactive user – the current logged on user option and press the Finish button. At this point we have successfully created an empty MTS package named DCPerson.

8. Now that we have the package, we need to add at least one component to the object. In our installation, we use a single package for each data object half. We have found that this offers us the greatest amount of flexibility and promotes the reuse of the data objects. What this means in real terms is that we only need to add one DLL to the newly created DCPerson package. In order to do that, highlight the Components node under the DCPerson node as shown in the image below. Right-click your mouse and select the New | Component option from the pop-up menu:

9. At this point, the MTS explorer invokes a new wizard – the Components Wizard. As it is likely that this machine won't be the one we developed the object on, we need to select the Install new component(s) button.

10. This brings up the Install Components screen of the wizard. Here we need to press the Add files button and navigate to the Person directory under the Components directory on the machine. Once we have located the DCPerson.dll file, all we need to do is to press the Open button on the open file dialog box:

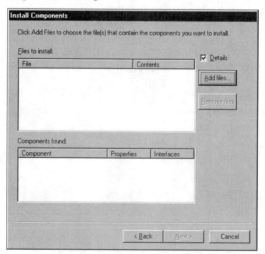

11. After you have selected the `DCPerson.dll` you will be returned to the same screen as above, but now it will display each of the class files that make up the person component as shown. Notice that MTS considers each class under the main object as a separate component:

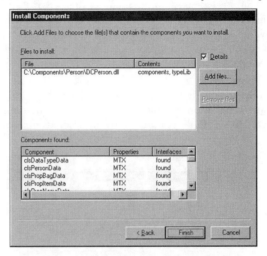

Another thing to notice is that MTS goes through the trouble of testing the object to determine what interfaces it exposes that MTS can tie into. In this case you will notice that MTS found the MTX (Context) object that we implemented when we developed the Data Centric halves of our objects. Press the Finish button, and the MTS explorer should look something like the image below:

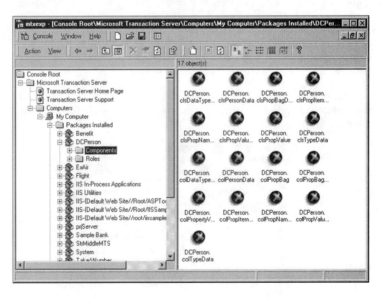

The User Centric Sphere - MTS

If you are installing the User Centric objects on the same machine as the Data Centric objects, then just follow the same set of instructions that we covered earlier for the User Centric components. Of course in this case we would create a second package called UCPerson in addition to the DCPerson package, but everything else is exactly the same. If you are using a different machine for the User Centric sphere, then we need to add a couple of extra steps. As you might imagine, we need to instruct the User Centric MTS as to the location of the Data Centric objects. We do this by installing them as remote components.

1. The first step we need to do in order to create a remote component package on the User Centric MTS machine is to introduce the User Centric machine to the Data Centric machines. We do that by adding remote computers to the User Centric computer's Computers folder. To do this, just right-click on the Computers node and select the New | Computer option from the pop-up menu:

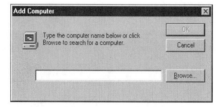

2. This will bring up the Add Computer dialog box. Navigate over to the computer that contains the Data Centric objects and press OK. The other Data Centric computer will be added to the list of remote computers to this machine and then we can browse the packages available on that computer and install them as remote components on this computer.

3. Once the computers have been introduced, you can search through the available components on the remote computer and add those to the remote computer folder of the machine you are presently working on. In our case, we need to add the DC *Person* object as a remote component on our User Centric MTS machine.

4. Right-click on the Remote Components folder under My Computer and select New | Remote Components. In the dialog box that appears, select the remote computer and package that contain the components you want to invoke remotely:

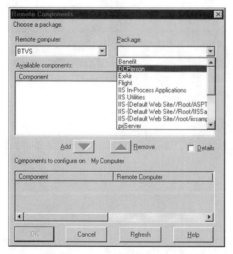

5. From the Available Components list, select the component that you want to invoke remotely, and click the down arrow (Add). This adds the component and the computer on which it resides to the Components to configure on box. If you click the Details checkbox, the Remote Computer, Package, and Path for DLLs are displayed. Add all the DC *Person* components:

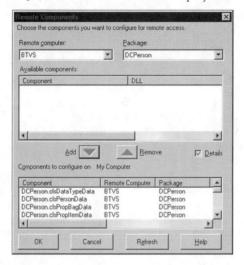

When this process is finished, you will find that you have a new directory on the User Centric MTS machine. The DCPerson directory will be added to the Program Files\MTS\Install\Remote\DCPerson. This is where the User Centric machine stores all of the information it needs to communicate with the data centric machine:

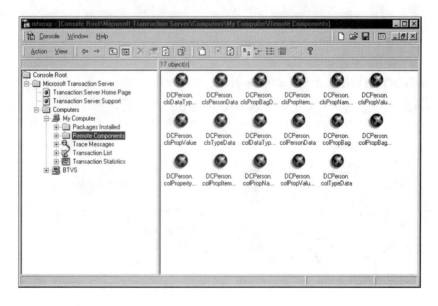

The Veneer

Now that we have installed the local components and instructed the User Centric computer about where to find the remote components, we can install our Veneer component. Remember that this is where all of the business rules for our application are stored. To do this, simply follow the same instructions we used for the Data Centric component above. The only difference is that in this case, is that we add the Veneer DLL to a Veneer package rather than a data object. Otherwise, the procedure is exactly the same. Although it isn't necessary, I usually take the approach of adding all of the data objects a Veneer requires before I add the Veneer.

At this minute, you should have something similar to this image. It doesn't matter that right now you may have SQL Server and MTS running on a single server. Even if you had to install the data store, DC objects, UC objects, and the Veneer on a single machine, you can always separate them later. Right now you should have, at least logically, a system that looks something like this:

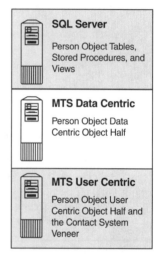

The next sphere we need to consider is the Presentation sphere. For our purposes, we will consider the Presentation sphere the machine, or machines, that are hosting IIS. We will take a look at what we need to do for the client machines a little bit later.

The Presentation Sphere - IIS

As important as SQL Server and MTS servers are to the enterprise, the star of the system may very well be Internet Information Server (IIS). It serves as a bastion host in the Demilitarized zone:

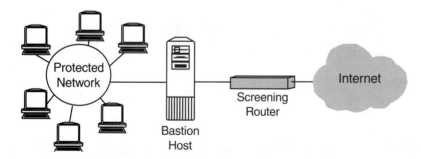

It can deliver files, web pages, and entire applications with a high level of security and speed. It is also possible, although I wouldn't recommend it, to use IIS as the primary dispatcher in a software-based load-balancing scheme. (I covered all these details in Chapter 2 so you may want to quickly flip back for a refresher.)

IIS is capable of performing the duties of a bastion host because it can make use of the full range of security facilities available to Windows NT. Remember from Chapter 2 that a bastion host stands guard over the second screening router in a belt and suspenders system. This type of security is used to keep intruders outside of the protected network area. IIS also offers the ability to protect information that is being transmitted outside of the protected network area. It does this by rendering the information unusable via an encryption scheme called **Secured Socket Layer** (**SSL**). The newest version of SSL (3.0), allows IIS to verify any user *before* the user is allowed to log onto the server.

Using ASP, IIS is also responsible for dynamically creating the application interface that an enterprise delivers to its clients. IIS can also be used to provide a level of transaction control to our applications.

> *In an Enterprise Caliber installation we use a combination of MTS and SQL to handle this function.*

In my enterprise, I use a directory structure like the one shown here to house our web-based applications. This structure allows us to use IIS in combination with our user object (*Person* object) to provide our first and second levels of security:

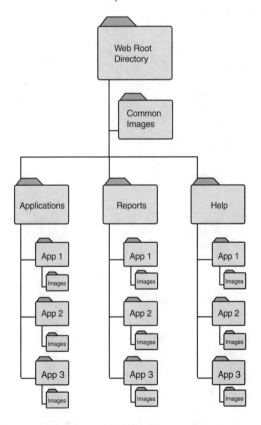

It works as follows. Each user in the domain(s) is given permission to access the IIS Root Directory – remember that IIS is really just using standard NT security. So, if an individual that is not an authorized user attempts to gain access to this directory, Windows NT will not grant that person access to the objects (files) in that directory.

This means that only persons with a valid account on the domain(s) will be allowed to begin the next step of the security process. For the purposes of this discussion, consider that there is only one file, *active server page*, in this directory. This page provides the second level of security by determining the authorized user's Logon ID. Once it has this information it retrieves a list of applications that this authorized user is allowed to access.

It uses this list of applications to dynamically construct a menu of applications that the particular user has permission to access. If the user is requesting information from a browser, then the user is presented with a single "menu" page that contains links for the applications that user is allowed to access. If the user is accessing the enterprise through the client-side Launch Pad application (we will learn how to build this application later), the page is formatted in a manner that can be used by Launch Pad to dynamically construct its pull down menus.

In either case, the end result of these first two levels of security is a list of applications and their associated HTML addresses. The following section will give you step-by-step instructions for creating an application directory under IIS, providing permissions to that directory, and installing an application (a group of Active Server Pages stored in a single directory intended to perform a particular purpose).

Setting up the Presentation Sphere

1. Create a directory to contain the Contact-Information Application. It doesn't really matter where you place this directory. It can be on the same machine as IIS, a good idea for performance reasons, or it can be on another machine if you like. It is also not a requirement that the directory exist under the virtual root directory for the IIS server. In fact, for security reasons, it may be better to create this directory in a different location – perhaps even on another drive. I wanted to make those things clear to avoid any misconceptions before we began, but for this example we will create the Contact-Information Application directory on the IIS machine under the virtual root directory:

2. Start the Internet Service Manager. This IIS administrative application is delivered as a snap-in for Microsoft Management Console (MMC).

Selecting this option will bring up the Microsoft Management Console just like the MTS option did earlier. This time, the MMC will transform itself into an administrative tool for IIS instead of an administrative tool for MTS. Keep this functionality in mind. It will come in handy when we take a look at the Launch Pad application below.

Notice that when we open up MMC to use IIS, it contains the MTS snap-in as well. Anyway, from this point, navigate through the treeview until you find the Default Web Site node on the Internet Information Server branch of the tree. It should look something like the image below:

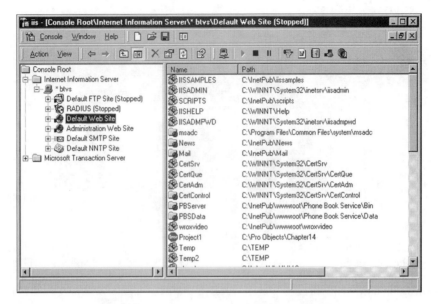

3. Create a new Virtual Directory. Right-click on the Default Web Site node and select the New | Virtual Directory option from the pop-up menu. This will invoke the New Virtual Directory Wizard. Enter the name for the virtual directory in the text box as shown:

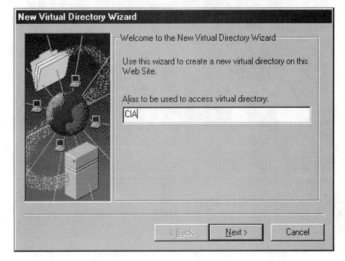

4. Map the virtual directory to the physical directory we created earlier. You can either type in the path of the directory or press the Browse button to navigate over to the actual physical directory:

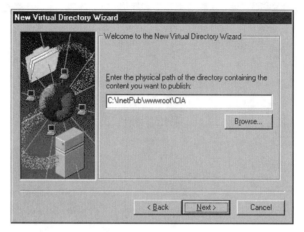

5. Set the Permissions for the Virtual Directory. The wizard will display another dialog box that will allow us to specify the permissions for the directory. Select the options as shown here and press Finish to continue:

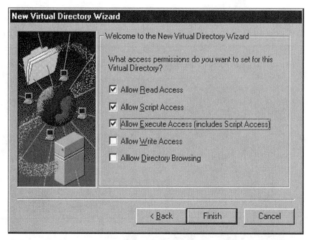

Once you have pressed, the Finish button, you will be returned to the Management Console for IIS. Notice that there is a new node under the Default Web Site. This node is where we will install our application. The next major phase in our installation concerns setting the IIS security for the Virtual Directory.

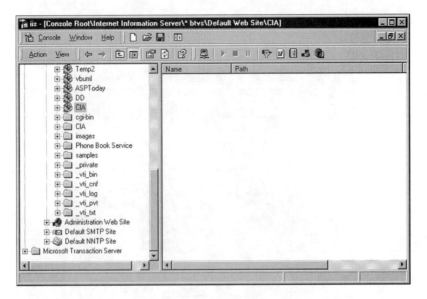

6. Configure the IIS settings for the Virtual Directory. Navigate through the treeview shown above and highlight the CIA node, or Virtual Directory. Once this directory has been selected, right-click your mouse and select Properties from the pop-up menu. From the Properties dialog box, select the options for the Virtual Directory as shown in the image. Then switch to the Directory Security tab:

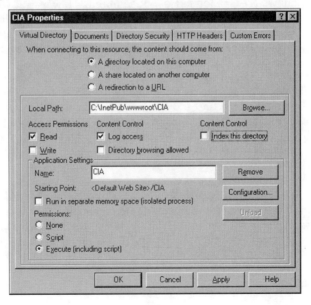

7. Setting the Directory Security. From the Directory Security tab, press the Edit button in the Anonymous Access and Authentication Control frame set. This will bring up another modal dialog:

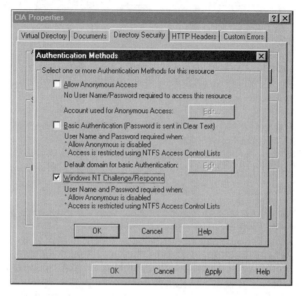

We use this box to set the authentication methods. The best way to handle authentication is to select only the Windows NT Challenge/Response option. However, if you need to use outside Internet Service Providers (ISP) you might have to select Basic Authentication as well. If you do this, you will also need to use Secured Sockets Layer to encrypt the data if you want to ensure a high degree of system security. Under no circumstances should you check the Allow Anonymous Access option for a directory that contains a web-based application:

This completes the work we need to do to configure the IIS security. Notice that IIS Virtual Directory security is not really a fine-grained mesh the way that Windows NT security is. This is not a problem because IIS conforms to the Windows NT security model. That means that in addition to the broad security swath that we can control with IIS, we can provide additional security by utilizing the NT model to control the objects (files) in the physical directory that this Virtual Directory maps to.

8. Setting up a group of authorized users to manage permissions for the physical directory using Windows NT. NT security gives us the ability to create groups of users that have access to a particular resource or set of resources. This eases our administrative tasks. In this case we will create a local user's group on the IIS machine that contains a list of users that have permission to use the CIA application. Then when we need to work with the permissions for the physical directory we can work with a single group of users at one time rather than working with the individual users.

Select the New Local Group option from the User Manager for Domains console:

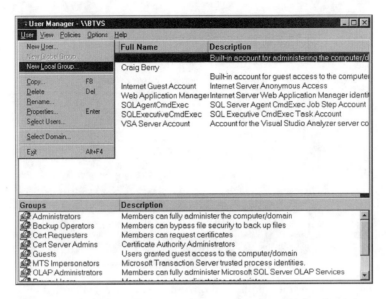

This will bring up a dialog box that we can use to create a new local user's group. All we need to do here is to type in a group name (and optionally a description). In this case, we are creating a group named CIA. The sole purpose for this grouping of users is to identify those individuals that will have permission to access the Contact-Information Application:

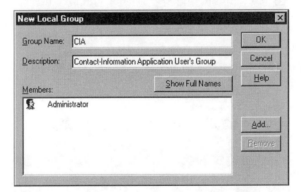

Next, we need to add the users to this group. We can specify which users to add as individuals or as other groups that contain individuals. For instance, maybe you have a group called Accounting that contains all of the users in your organization that work in the accounting department. You can choose to add all the users in Accounting to the CIA group as individuals or you could also just add the entire Accounting Group.

The next image shows the Add Users and Groups dialog that is presented when you press the Add button on the New Local Group dialog. Our only goal here is to identify all of the users that we want to access our CIA application and make sure those users end up in the lower listview on the Add Users And Groups dialog. Don't worry too much about getting this exactly right the first time. You can always go back and modify the list of users as the need arises:

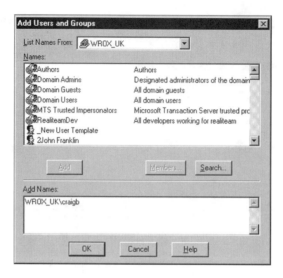

9. Setting the permissions on the physical directory – this task is handled outside of the MMC. All we need to use to set the permissions on the directory is Windows Explorer. You are probably familiar with this technique, but just to be thorough navigate to the physical CIA directory and right click your mouse. Select Properties from the pop-up menu.

Select the Security tab from the Properties dialog and then press the Permissions command button. This will bring up the next dialog, which will let us set permissions for the directory using standard NT security:

This will be an easy job for us because we have taken the time to set up a user's group for our application. All we will need to do in the Directory Permissions dialog is to specify which user group we want to give access to. From this point on, we can control user access to the application via access to that group. Press the Add button to add users or groups.

The next dialog should look familiar. It is the same one we used earlier to add the members to the CIA user's group. In this case, we will use the Add Users and Groups dialog to give the CIA group Full Control over the physical directory:

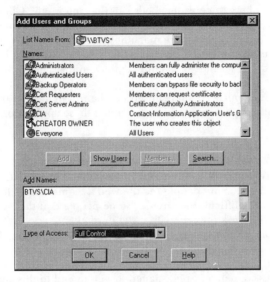

We could specify less control over the directory to be safer, but for our purposes here Full Control is appropriate. Make sure that you also give Full Control to the system administrator and to the developers that are responsible for this directory. If not, they will not be able to place the ASP files in the directory etc.

That is really all there is to it. To recap, now we have a physical directory that can only be accessed by the members of a single users group CIA. We have given this group full control over the CIA directory.

I would recommend that you give your users the lowest possible access level. This example is designed so that the developers are also in the CIA user's group. In real life I would have created two groups CIA Users and CIA Developers or Administrators with different permissions.

That physical directory is mapped to an IIS Virtual Directory. We used the IIS administrative tool to set the security on this directory to require Challenge Response Authorization (and possibly Basic Authentication if all else fails) and have set the broad swathe of security around that directory to allow the users to execute scripts in the directory. All we have to do now is to copy our ASP files that make up the application into the physical CIA directory on the IIS machine.

At this point, we have really handled all the 4 Spheres we have talked about throughout this book. We have the tables, views, and stored procedures on the Data sphere, the Data Centric objects on the Data Centric sphere, the User Centric objects and Veneers on the User Centric sphere, and we have created a location on the Presentation sphere to hold the user interface files. Now I want to introduce you to a new sphere - the **Client sphere**.

The Clients

We still have one other of sphere to consider. Let's call that sphere the Client sphere. If you go back to Chapter 3 where we talked about the server farm you will see that as we moved away from the database we were able to add more and more machines to each sphere. Well, the Client sphere is no different. Depending upon the number of machines that you have used to create your server farm, you should be able to handle thousands of client machines in the Client sphere.

As I hinted to earlier although our web applications can be run in an IE 4.0 or higher browser, there are quite a few reasons for using another vehicle to launch these applications

Perceptions

Even though the web really just gives another way to handle our job of safeguarding and managing our user's information for them, many people see the web as something inherently evil and untrustworthy. It is still a little difficult to convince some people that the work we do with a web application is the same as the work they do with a standard client-server interface. I think they have the perception that all of our customers are out having a good time surfing the web rather than doing any serious work.

The web-based applications we deliver are designed to put an end to this silliness. We understand that we still need to battle a lot of misconceptions, so we make an all out effort to remove as much webbiness from our applications as possible. We build interfaces that resemble standard client-server applications in every way. Other than a couple of quirky HTML leftovers like the ability to select everything on a page, it is nearly impossible to tell the difference between our web-based applications and a similarly designed VB interface. The only thing that resembles a web page in our applications is the browser. And, because we are nothing if not thorough, we even found a way to hide that from the naysayers. We use a wrapper for the IE browser that allows us to use its functionality without having to deal with all-of-its standard user interface capabilities. This wrapper is called the Launch Pad application, and we'll see how to build it shortly.

Corral the User

There are really a couple of very sound reasons to direct our users to our applications through a specialized browser besides the sentiments of the anti-web group. The most important is that standard browsers give the users a little too much control over their next action. Let me explain – while it is fine for Wally the Web Surfer to change his mind in mid-stream and go to another web site, this kind of indecisiveness is not alright for Eddie the Employee. In a web-based application, it is important for the user to control the direction of the application from within the page. If we expect the user to press one of two or three command buttons and the user decides to type in the address of the sports page instead or to press the back button 6 or 7 times, we have no way of stopping him. Of course everything in our installation is designed to ensure that our data retains all of its integrity and that it is safe, but we have failed to create an application that helps (guides) the user through the process he is trying to accomplish.

This means we build a client-side application that is really nothing more than a wrapper for Microsoft Internet Explorer. Of course it is not necessary to use this application to deploy web-based applications, but it does offer several advantages. It allows us to remove all external browser-based controls from the user. This means that we can force the user to use the controls provided on the page to work with the information in the application. This gives us a tighter reign on the user's activities while they are working within the application. This makes it easier for us to control the processing order within an application. It also allows us to remove the address text box from the user's view. This measure gives an additional layer of security. It means that rather than allowing the user to navigate at will throughout our application server (IIS), we can use Launch Pad to provide them with a standard pull-down menu of options that appears identical to any standard VB application.

Security

The pull-down menu that is used in Launch Pad is populated at run time. In other words, as soon as a user opens up the Launch Pad application, we perform a query that returns a collection of applications that this particular user is allowed to access. The first level of security begins here. If the user is not an authorized user for the domain or a trusted domain, the query will not be executed. Assuming that the user is authorized and the query does execute, we take the resulting collection and use it to populate the pull-down menus in Launch Pad. That means that we can control user access to each application from a centrally managed database application that works exactly the same way all of the other security measures in Windows NT are managed.

We treat each application as an object and then we either allow or deny access on a user-by-user basis. This is the second stage of security. Notice that the levels of security tighten rather than lessen as the user is allowed in closer to the enterprise's data. Remember that we learned techniques earlier that allowed us to exercise a control at the user/property – user/method level. Remember too, that this control is handled in exactly the same way that all other Windows NT security is handled. In other words, we treat the properties and methods as objects and then grant control of those objects on a user-by-user basis.

The Launch Pad Application

Launch Pad gives us a framework upon which to deliver a top-notch help system. In my installations, Launch Pad is the preferred medium for delivering applications. It provides structure and helps the users to learn to work with the application from within the page. However, if the user base is sophisticated enough – or have had enough time with the application – we also offer the option of accessing the application directly through the browser. This is a boon for those individuals that are on the road and do not have their own computers with them.

Building The Launch Pad Application

The Launch Pad application that we'll be building here is really a cut down version of the one I usually distribute. This version has all the core functionality but I normally offer some additional tricks such as Help and Reporting features.

For the most part, this application is very simple. The only real trick is the coding – or maybe I should say the *concept* – required to communicate from within an ASP and a host application written in VB.

Open up a new Standard EXE project in VB. Add one MDI Form, 2 standard forms, and one module to the project. Name the project `LaunchPad.vbp` and rename the forms and module as indicated. Set `frmBrowser` as an MDIChild. When you get finished the Project Explorer in the VB IDE should look something like this:

Let's work through the code we need to add to the General module.

General Module Code

This code is really quite simple. All we are doing is creating 4 `Public` variables that will be used throughout the life of the application. The `UserLogon` variable is self-explanatory. `strDispatcher` is used to hold the address for the ASP files on the IIS server so that we don't need to hard code this into our application. We'll be using the registry to set this variable in the Splash form. The additional variables are string arrays that will be used to dynamically create the pull-down menus for the application:

```
Option Explicit
```

```
Public strDispatcher As String
Public UserLogon As String
Public ApplicationAddresses() As String
Public CurrentApplication() As String
```

The only other thing in this module is the `Sub Main` routine. It is self-explanatory, but what it does is very important. As we will learn in the next section, we use the Splash form to initialize this application.

```
Sub Main()

    frmSplash.Show

End Sub
```

You'll also need to specify Sub Main as the Start Up object in the Project Properties dialog.

The Splash Form

As I said earlier, the Splash form is really responsible for initializing the Launch Pad Application. The way it does this is probably the most important concept in this section of the book. The Splash form contains a web browser that sends a single parameter and retrieves a single page from the IIS machine. The parameter it passes is the user's NT Logon ID and the page that is returned contains a list of applications that user has permission to access.

All you need to do to create a browser is to draw a browser control on any form. How easy is that? The control you need to add to your project in order to perform this miracle is called Microsoft Internet Controls. Microsoft has changed the name of this control several times, but so far the `SHDOCVW.dll` has remained more or less constant:

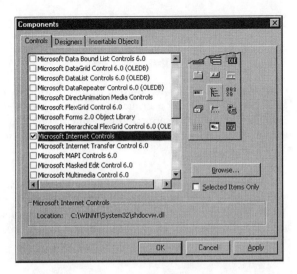

Add a timer control, a web browser control, and a picture box to the form:

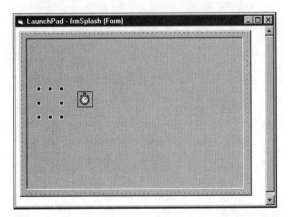

The timer is called `tmrTimer` and has an Interval of 5; the browser is called `brwWebBrowser` and the picture box `picSplash`.

> *The picture box has been added to give you a place to put something nice for the user to look at while the application is configured. Of course it is also possible, and maybe preferable, to eliminate this picture box control and allow the web browser to be visible. Then you could specify what the splash screen would look like from the server by changing the looks of the ASP page that is used for the splash screen. We use a picture box because it is immediate and as an organization we have decided upon a specific look for all our applications.*

Remember that this screen calls an ASP page with a single parameter – the currently logged in user's NT Logon ID. In order to accomplish this task, the Splash form must learn the name of the authorized user. It does that by using a single API call `GetUserName`. We covered techniques you can use to make API calls in Chapter 14. Remember that the first step was to create a declaration statement:

```
Option Explicit
```

```
Private Declare Function GetUserName Lib "advapi32.dll" Alias "GetUserNameA" _
                         (ByVal lpbuffer As String, nSize As Long) As Long
```

The next bit of code we have to write is the `Form_Load` routine. In this routine we determine the name of the user using our API call. If we find a valid user name then we proceed, if not we just end the application. If we have found a user Logon ID we append that value to the address of the page designed to return a list of applications for this user. Then we load that page into the browser by using the `brwWebBrowser.Navigate strAddress` line.

> *Notice that we have used a registry entry to store the name of the IIS dispatcher machine. This is to allow us to change the name or IP address of the dispatcher server if the need ever arises. Of course, if we followed the principles laid out in Chapter 3, our dispatcher will be a redundant machine that will never go down.*

```
Private Sub Form_Load()

  Dim strAddress As String
  Dim i As Long
  Dim strBuffer As String
  Dim lngSize As Long

  strDispatcher = GetSetting(App.Title, "Settings", "Dispatcher", "BTVS")
  strBuffer = Space$(255)
  lngSize = Len(strBuffer)

  Call GetUserName(strBuffer, lngSize)

  If lngSize > 0 Then
  ' Place the user's logon into the local memory variable
    UserLogon = Left$(strBuffer, lngSize - 1)
  Else
  ' Every User must have and use a valid Windows NT User Logon
  ' If not, give 'em the boot
    End
  End If

  strAddress = "http://" & strDispatcher  & "/UserLogonScreen.asp?UserLogon=" _
               & UserLogon

  On Error Resume Next

  If Len(strAddress) > 0 Then
    tmrTimer.Enabled = True
    brwWebBrowser.Navigate strAddress
  Else
    End
  End If

End Sub
```

You should notice that before we called for the page using the `brwWebBrowser.Navigate strAddress` line we enabled the timer we drew on the form earlier. Let's take a look at the code in the tick event of the timer to see why. This is the code that really does all of the work. As usual, read through the code, we will go over it in detail below:

```
Private Sub tmrTimer_Timer()

    Dim i As Integer
    Dim lngCount As Long
    Dim ThisObject As Object
    Dim strMenu As String
    Dim aryMenu() As String

    On Error Resume Next

    If brwWebBrowser.Busy = False Then
        tmrTimer.Enabled = False
        Me.Caption = brwWebBrowser.LocationName

        For Each ThisObject In brwWebBrowser.Document.All
            If Left(ThisObject.id, 1) = "A" Then
                lngCount = lngCount + 1
                ReDim Preserve aryMenu(lngCount)
                strMenu = Right(ThisObject.id, Len(ThisObject.id) - 4)
                aryMenu(lngCount - 1) = strMenu
            End If
        Next ThisObject

        ReDim ApplicationAddresses(lngCount)
        ReDim CurrentApplication(lngCount)

        With frmMain
            For i = 0 To lngCount - 1
                If i = .mnuApplicationOption.Count Then
                    Load .mnuApplicationOption(i)
                End If

                .mnuApplicationOption(i).Caption = aryMenu(i)
                ApplicationAddresses(i) = "Http:// " & strDispatcher & _
                                          "//Applications/" & aryMenu(i) & _
                                          "/MainMenu.asp"
                CurrentApplication(i) = aryMenu(i)
            Next
            .Show
        End With

        Unload Me

    Else
        Me.Caption = "Performing Security Check for ..."

    End If

End Sub
```

The first real work in this procedure is done in the following block of code:

```
For Each ThisObject In brwWebBrowser.Document.All
    If Left(ThisObject.id, 1) = "A" Then
        lngCount = lngCount + 1
        ReDim Preserve aryMenu(lngCount)
        strMenu = Right(ThisObject.id, Len(ThisObject.id) - 7)
        aryMenu(lngCount - 1) = strMenu
    End If
Next ThisObject
```

657

Chapter 15

What is happening here is that we are examining the ASP file that has been delivered in response to the request we made during the `Form_Load`. Remember we asked for a list of applications that the authorized user has permission to access. The way it works is as follows: Every tag in a HTML document is considered an object. All of those objects are stored in the `Document.All` collection. That means that we can iterate through each object in the document in just the same way we would iterate through any other collection. We have formatted the ASP Response page by creating a text box for each application. This text box is named by combining the name of the application with the prefix "Address". That means that as we iterate through the collection we can identify the objects that contain the name of applications that the authorized user has permission to access. As we iterate through the collection, we increase the size of the `aryMenu` string array each time we find a new application. Then we extract the name of the application from the name of the text box and add it to the array.

After we have finished iterating through the document's `All` collection we re-dimension each of the four arrays we declared earlier so that they can hold the necessary information for each application:

```
ReDim ApplicationAddresses(lngCount)
ReDim CurrentApplication(lngCount)
```

The next block of code uses the information we collected from the document to build the menu options for the user. In case you are unfamiliar with the VB `Load` method, the `Load` method is used to add new controls to a control array at run-time. In this case, we are adding a menu option to the Application menu for each application that the authorized user has permission to access:

```
With frmMain
    For i = 0 To lngCount - 1
        If i = .mnuApplicationOption.Count Then
            Load .mnuApplicationOption(i)
        End If
```

In addition to adding the menu option, we also build a string that represents a valid address for each menu option. Then we stuff that string into the appropriate array. This has the effect of synchronizing the menu option indexes with the indexes of the array containing the addresses. In other words, if I select the menu option with the Index 3 from the Application menu, the address for the application I selected would be stored as the fourth element of the `ApplicationAddresses` array – the arrays are zero based so the 4th element has the Index 3. The same thing holds true for the Current Application array.

```
        .mnuApplicationOption(i).Caption = aryMenu(i)
        ApplicationAddresses(i) = "Http:// " & strDispatcher & _
                            "//Applications/" & aryMenu(i) & _
                            "/MainMenu.asp"
        CurrentApplication(i) = aryMenu(i)
    Next
    .Show
End With
```

We'll take a look at what the ASP will be doing in the next chapter.

The only other routine in this form is a tiny block of code that just responds to the `NavigateComplete` event for the browser control. When the navigation is complete, it simply sets the caption on the form equal to the name of the ASP document.

658

```
Private Sub brwWebBrowser_NavigateComplete2(ByVal pDisp As Object, URL As Variant)

  On Error Resume Next
  Me.Caption = brwWebBrowser.LocationName

End Sub
```

At this point in time, we have configured the Launch Pad application for an individual authorized user. It has the menu options that can point this user to the applications that the user has permission to access. That means that all the user has to do to work with a web application is to select it from the Applications menu option in Launch Pad. Let's take a look at the code in the MDI form that causes this to happen.

The Main MDI Form

The MDI form for Launch Pad is really quite simple. It has three main menu options:

- ❑ File – This is really just used to give us a place to put the exit command
- ❑ Applications – This option is used to allow the user to navigate to a particular application.
- ❑ Window – This just contains all of the standard Window Management commands. It is especially useful because it allows users to flip between different applications, reports, etc.

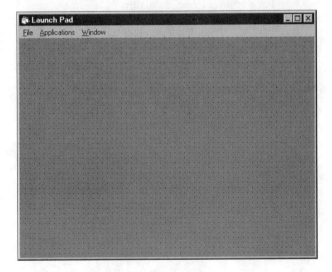

These three menus also contain the following sub-items:

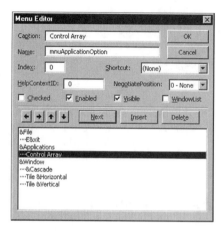

As you can see the Applications menu contains one sub-menu that is a control array. This is the array that we loaded from the Splash form.

The first real work gets done in the Form_Load routine. All that we are doing here is retrieving the settings for the size of the MDI form exactly as the user left them when they closed the application the last time. Just in case this is the first time the program was run and there are no last known values stored in the registry, we provide some reasonable defaults as the last parameter:

```
Private Sub MDIForm_Load()

    Me.Left = GetSetting(App.Title, "Settings", "MainLeft", 1000)
    Me.Top = GetSetting(App.Title, "Settings", "MainTop", 1000)
    Me.Width = GetSetting(App.Title, "Settings", "MainWidth", 6500)
    Me.Height = GetSetting(App.Title, "Settings", "MainHeight", 6500)

End Sub
```

The flip side of the Form_Load is the Form_Unload subroutine. What we are doing here is either creating or updating the registry values that represent the size state of the application when the user shuts down the application:

```
Private Sub MDIForm_Unload(Cancel As Integer)

    If Me.WindowState <> vbMinimized Then
        SaveSetting App.Title, "Settings", "MainLeft", Me.Left
        SaveSetting App.Title, "Settings", "MainTop", Me.Top
        SaveSetting App.Title, "Settings", "MainWidth", Me.Width
        SaveSetting App.Title, "Settings", "MainHeight", Me.Height
    End If

End Sub
```

Most of the work we need to do in this application is handled in the menu event handlers.

In the `ApplicationOption` menu item control array, we accept an `Index` that tells us what option the user selected. Then we use that value to retrieve an appropriate address from the `ApplicationAddresses` array. For housekeeping purposes, we set the value of the browser's `CurrentApplication` property to the value of the current application as indicated by the index. The last thing we do before we show the display this instance of the Browser form is to navigate to the address that the user selected:

```
Private Sub mnuApplicationOption_Click(Index As Integer)

  Dim frmAppBrowser As New frmBrowser

  With frmAppBrowser
     .CurrentApplication = CurrentApplication(Index)
     .DocumentAddress = ApplicationAddresses (Index)
     .brwWebBrowser.Navigate .DocumentAddress
     .Show
  End With

End Sub
```

The following Window handling subroutines are self-explanatory:

```
Private Sub mnuWindowTileVertical_Click()

  Me.Arrange vbTileVertical

End Sub
```

```
Private Sub mnuWindowTileHorizontal_Click()

  Me.Arrange vbTileHorizontal

End Sub
```

```
Private Sub mnuWindowCascade_Click()

  Me.Arrange vbCascade

End Sub
```

Finally, this is used to close the Launch Pad Application:

```
Private Sub mnuFileExit_Click()

' Unload the form
  Unload Me

End Sub
```

The Browser Form

This next form we will look at is the `frmBrowser` form. This form is incredibly simple. It is really not much more than a MDI child form with a browser control placed upon it.

We've already added the browser control component to the project so just draw a browser on the form. It doesn't matter what it looks like. We have to handle the sizing of this control in a dynamic fashion:

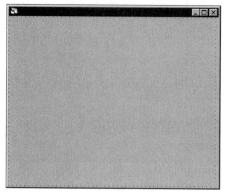

As always, we use the declaration section of any module to declare the private variables that we will use to store the property values. In this case we need two property storage variables. One for the `DocumentAddress` property another for the `CurrentApplication` property. I have also added another variable `mblnDontNavigateNow` that is used to indicate that the browser control is currently busy:

```
Option Explicit

Private mblnDontNavigateNow As Boolean
Private mstrDocumentAddress As String
Private mstrCurrentApplication As String
```

As usual after the declaration section, we need to provide the necessary property handlers. In this case that is given by the following code:

```
Public Property Get DocumentAddress() As String

   DocumentAddress = mstrDocumentAddress

End Property
```

```
Public Property Let DocumentAddress(strDocumentAddress As String)

   mstrDocumentAddress = Trim(strDocumentAddress)

End Property
```

```
Public Property Get CurrentApplication() As String

   CurrentApplication = mstrCurrentApplication

End Property
```

```
Public Property Let CurrentApplication(strCurrentApplication As String)

   mstrCurrentApplication = strCurrentApplication

End Property
```

The `Form_Load` for this form is simple, all we do is to show the form and call the `Form_Resize` routine:

```
Private Sub Form_Load()

  On Error Resume Next
  Me.Show
  Form_Resize

End Sub
```

This subroutine just updates the caption of the form to reflect its contents:

```
Private Sub brwWebBrowser_DownloadComplete()

  On Error Resume Next
  Me.Caption = brwWebBrowser.Document.All("Title")

End Sub
```

The `Form_Resize` routine is also amazingly simple. All we need to do here is to make sure that the browser is essentially the same size as the form it rests on:

```
Private Sub Form_Resize()

  On Error Resume Next
  brwWebBrowser.Width = Me.ScaleWidth - 100
  brwWebBrowser.Height = Me.ScaleHeight

End Sub
```

That is really all of the work we have to do in order to create an application that provides a controlled environment for our applications' ASPs.

Summary

All we have really achieved in this chapter is to stand back a little and take a look at all the pieces from a different perspective. We started the book off by examining the intrastructure that we would be using to house our data objects and then we spend a long time focussing in on the particulars of how to build the objects. Finally, in this chapter we have been able to combine the two and look at how we can deploy our carefully constructed data objects across the enterprise's arhcitecture.

We looked at our physical architeture from a more software oriented approach, so that we saw the the Data sphere as SQL Server, the Data and User Centric spheres as MTS and the Presentation sphere as IIS. Finally, we talked about limiting the client's actions by constructing a typical desktop interface but with embedded components. There's only one thing left to do now and that's take a look at the ASP going on behind the scenese.

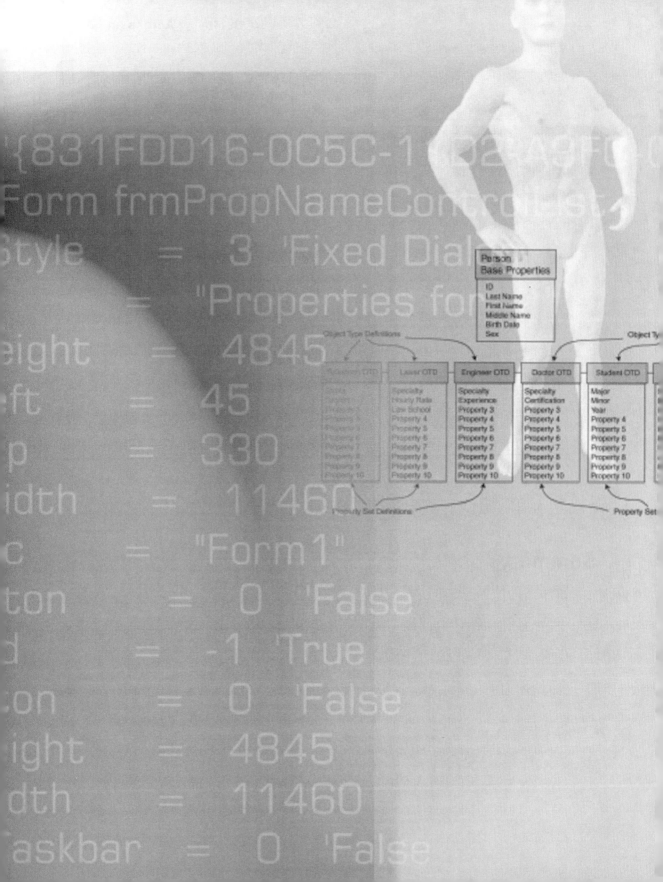

Active Server Pages

Active Server Pages offer one of the richest development environments available. Do you remember way back in Chapter 5 when you constructed the VB interface without ever having met an Enterprise Caliber Data Object? For many of you, I am fairly certain that was the first time you had built an application with real data objects, data objects that could actually insulate the user interface developer from the database while simultaneously increasing that developer's effectiveness. Maybe way back then the exercise seemed unnecessary or even foolish. In this chapter, after you have come to understand the inner workings of Enterprise Caliber Data Objects, you have earned the freedom to take on the task of designing and developing world-class ASP interfaces without having to deal with the trivialities those objects encapsulate.

As I have said many times before, let me warn you that you are in for quite a challenge. We are going to attack the problem of learning ASP, DHTML, VBScript and web-based application development in general, with unprecedented fervor. This chapter is an exercise in acceleration. It will begin with a snail's pace while we work to build a common bag of simple tools that will give you yet another set of building blocks. Once we have gotten a handle on those tools, we will work at light speed through enough examples of solid ASP design and construction to give you a sense of mastery over the topic.

By the time you finish this chapter you will understand the following:

- ❑ Some basic HTML coding techniques
- ❑ The difference between dynamically created HTML and Dynamic HTML
- ❑ How to code the five major sections for any interactive, data-enabled, Active Server Page
- ❑ How to write server-side script using VBScript
- ❑ How to write client-side script using VBScript
- ❑ How to use ASP to develop a multi page interface for any Enterprise Caliber Data Object

Overview

Think about the work you need to do to deploy a typical executable-on-the-desktop application. First, you need to build the application, then you need build an installation program for the application, and then you need to go to each and every client machine and install the application on that client. This may not sound like too much trouble if you are talking about 5 or even 25 clients. But when you start getting up into the hundreds of clients, it is a real pain to put it mildly. Now think about the work that is involved with maintaining the same application. Every time you need to make a change for any reason you must go through several steps. First you need to modify the source code, maybe you also need to create a new installation program, and then you need to deliver the changes to each and every client machine that uses the application. This process can take days or weeks. OK, now multiply that effort by the number of applications running on your enterprise.

I know that Microsoft has given us tools like System Management Server (SMS), which allows us to automate the mechanical process of installing applications on each client machine. Like a faithful servant, SMS can go out to each client, perform installations, and synchronize the files across an enterprise. This is a great tool, we use it everyday, but all SMS is really doing is automating a mechanical process – it doesn't change the process. ASP is a quantum leap in deployment methodology, it doesn't automate a bad process – it changes the process. It ignores the traditional boundaries and gives us a completely new way to deliver applications. The best way I can describe the difference conceptually is to have you imagine a powerful sports car – a car with maybe 300 horsepower. Now I want you to imagine the same car being pulled by three hundred horses... Theoretically, the two vehicles have exactly the same horsepower, but that is where the similarity ends. How would you like to be responsible for the care and feeding of 300 horses? ASP (and internet technologies in general) allows us to construct and **deploy** high-powered applications without all of the care and feeding required by their execute-on-the-desktop ancestors. Of course ASP is not perfect, but it is the direction. If you know VB, this chapter will give you all of the tools you need to be able to take advantage of this quantum leap in deployment methodology.

The Basics

In the beginning there was HTML. In order to display a page in a web browser, a developer had to write something we could loosely call code. In reality, all the developer was doing was surrounding blocks of text with markup tags that could be interpreted by the browser so that it knew how to display the text or image. For example, if the browser read the following:

```
<STRONG>Hello World</STRONG>
```

It would display the words Hello World in strong (bold) letters. This simple markup language ushered in the single greatest change in information technology. It is the Rosetta Stone. It gave all computers a common language to be able to display information that humans could also understand. Its simplicity was its greatest asset.

In the early days, every page was a unique expression of its author – every line of markup code was hand-crafted. Of course, this was time consuming and completely unnecessary. The individuals that used HTML were, generally, a very bright lot and they soon developed techniques that allowed the computer to generate the HTML pages dynamically. In other words, whenever someone requested a page, that page was "written" based upon the results of a query against a data store. Of course at first, the fairly complex techniques that powered these dynamic pages were essentially one-up designs, generally CGI scripts, developed and maintained by their creators.

CGI (Common Gateway Interface) enables the contents of a page to be generated dynamically by a program (typically written in C) or scripting language (such as Perl), allowing pages to be constructed from information held in a database. Each CGI request creates a process which is terminated after the request has been handled. Unfortunately, because of the repeated process creation and database opening, heavily hit sites suffer an excessive overhead on system resources.

If this new technology was to going to amount to anything, someone had to develop a standard technique for the dynamic creation of HTML pages. Microsoft took a great step towards this standardization when it introduced the Internet Database Connector (IDC) concept a few years back. This simple tool gave developers a consistent reproducible way to perform low-level database access and port the results of that access into a dynamically created HTML page. The developers were free to concentrate on the data and its expression without the overhead of writing complex CGI scripts to manage the database interaction. ASP takes the IDC concept forward a couple of generations. It encapsulates a lot of the drudgery that dynamic web page generation requires without the benefit of ASP.

In many ways, ASP is a throwback to an earlier time. Most of us have either embraced event-driven programming or are young enough to have known nothing else. ASP is not event-driven. ASP is procedural in nature; for the most part, the code on the page executes sequentially from the top down. So that is the way we will learn to write Active Server Pages, from the top down. We will divide the tasks required to write an Active Server Page into five sections starting at the top. We will briefly cover each of those sections. Once you understand what needs to happen in each section, we will work through some of the sample code that is included with this book. The sample code in this chapter will give you the information you need to begin constructing Enterprise Caliber Applications with ASP and 4-Dimensional Data Objects. The code in this chapter was created with the Object Factory; it is intended to provide the developer with a solid starting point for further development. This chapter is not intended to be the ultimate guide to ASP or DHTML. There are plenty of books written on ASP and DHTML. I would suggest two Wrox titles – *Instant IE4 Dynamic HTML* (ISBN 1-861000-68-5) and *Professional Active Server Pages 2.0* (ISBN 1-861001-26-6). *Instant IE4 Dynamic HTML* has a wonderful appendix and is an invaluable resource for the ASP developer. I have a copy of this book on my desk at all times. So does every member of my development teams.

Those of you developing for the IE5 web-browser might be interested in taking a look at the IE5 Dynamic HTML Programmer's Reference (ISBN 1-861001-74-6).

Before we begin the work of dissecting some Active Server Pages, I would like to take some time to acquaint you with some very fundamental concepts in web development. Although we will approach this section from a very simple perspective, don't be misled, the information presented here is invaluable. It really provides the foundation for the remainder of the code in this chapter.

You will need to have IIS 4.0 installed to work through the samples in this section. In this chapter, I will assume that you have accepted the default settings and that the root directory for your server is `C://inetpub/wwwroot`.

Hello World from an Active Server Page

Believe it or not, the following code is an ASP page. It doesn't do anything more than we could do with standard HTML, but it is an Active Server Page because it has the extension `asp`.

> **An Active Server Page can contain both HTML and server-side code.**

That means that IIS will "read" this file and perform any tasks the server-side code on the page directs it to perform before it delivers the page to the user.

Write the code exactly as shown using Notepad, save it using `HelloWorld.asp` as the filename, and place it in the root directory for your web server (usually `wwwroot`):

```
<HTML>
    <HEAD>
    </HEAD>

        <BODY>
         Hello World from ASP
        </BODY>

</HTML>
```

You can "execute" this page by using your browser and typing in `http://YourServerName/HelloWorld.asp` as the address. Of course, you will have to replace `YourServerName` with the name of your IIS server:

Server-Side Code

OK that was too easy; IIS didn't have to do any work. Let's add a few lines of server-side code and put the server to work. Modify your `HelloWorld.asp` file as follows and save it again without changing the name or location of the file. Execute the changed page the same way you did earlier.

```
<%@ Language=VBScript %>
<HTML>
<%
    strUserName = "Joseph"
    strMessage="Hello " & strUserName
%>

<HEAD>
</HEAD>
    <BODY>
        <% = strMessage %>
    </BODY>
</HTML>
```

When you execute the page, your browser should display a page something like the one above. We will go over the syntax we used to make this happen in a minute. First, I would like you to view the source code the browser used to display this page. We really need to compare it with the `HelloWorld.asp` file from above. In order to view the source code, place your cursor somewhere on the page, right-click the mouse and select the View Source option from the menu:

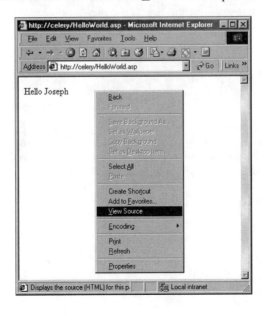

Your browser will open up Notepad and you will see something like the following:

```
<HTML>

<HEAD>
</HEAD>
    <BODY>
        Hello Joseph
    </BODY>

</HTML>
```

What Notepad is displaying is the file that the server delivered to the browser (client). Notice that it is quite different than the file that we just saved and asked the server to deliver. In the original file we had two variables and we performed a concatenation. None of this shows up on the client. That is because the server executed the code that we enclosed between the <% and %> characters before it delivered the page. As far as the browser was concerned, it just displayed the file exactly as it received it from the server. IIS actively read and executed the instructions in the page before it served the page to the client – hence the name Active Server Pages. This is a simple example of HTML that was dynamically created by the server.

This is not an example of Dynamic HTML, we will get to that in a moment.

The code is really quite simple. Notice that we didn't declare the variables before we used them. As far as we are concerned, in ASP all variables are treated as variants. We don't need to use the `Dim` statement unless we are creating an array. Other than the missing `Dim` statements and the curious <% and %> characters, this code looks just like regular VB. That is because this code is really just another flavor of VB – **VBScript**. That means that except for a few minor exceptions, if you got this far in this book, you already know enough VBScript to begin creating world class Active Server Pages.

Notice that in the only line of code between the BODY tags, that we make strange use of an ill-placed equal sign. This is not a typo, the equal sign directs the server to write the results of the statement on the page. In this case, the server wrote the words "Hello Joseph" in place of the original line in the file:

```
<BODY>
    <% = strMessage %>.
</BODY>
```

Although this example was incredibly simple, it illustrates the primary purpose of ASP. Active Server Pages write HTML code. We use a server-side scripting language, in this case VBScript, to instruct the server exactly how to create each line of HTML code. Let's take a look at another simple example. Change the `HelloWorld.asp` file to look like the following:

```
<%@ Language=VBScript %>
<HTML>
    <HEAD>
    </HEAD>

        <BODY>
            <% For i = 1 to 10 %>
                The Value of i = <% = i %><BR>
            <% Next %>
        </BODY>
</HTML>
```

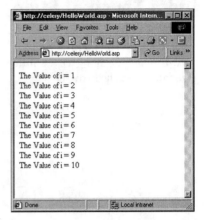

It should come as no surprise that when you request this file, your browser displays something like the following image:

Notice that this time we instructed the server to write a line of code in a For...Next loop. The <% Next %> line disturbs a lot of VB programmers. It is a common but unnecessary practice in VB to write something more akin to Next i where we identify the control variable i. You may be surprised to learn that this practice is optional in standard VB, and that the code actually executes a little faster if we omit the reference to the control variable in the Next line. Anyway, with VBScript, we **cannot** use the name of the control variable in the Next line. Sadly, this practice causes an error in VBScript. Let's take a look at the source code for this page.

```
<HTML>
<HEAD>
</HEAD>
<BODY>
     The Value of i = 1<BR>
     The Value of i = 2<BR>
     The Value of i = 3<BR>
     The Value of i = 4<BR>
     The Value of i = 5<BR>
     The Value of i = 6<BR>
     The Value of i = 7<BR>
     The Value of i = 8<BR>
     The Value of i = 9<BR>
     The Value of i = 10<BR>
</BODY>
</HTML>
```

Notice that the server did exactly what we told it to do. It wrote a line for each iteration in the For...Next loop, and placed the value of the control variable i in each line. The <BR> tag is standard HTML, it instructs the browser that this line is finished and tells it to start a new line. If we omit the <BR> we will get something like the following:

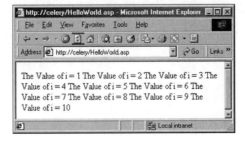

Add a Touch of Style

The information we have just gone over concerns server-side code. This is truly the essence of ASP, but web development in general offers a lot more. Let's go back to our original "Hello World from ASP" example and give it a little style. Take a look at the code below and the resulting page that is displayed in the browser:

```
<HTML>
<HEAD>
    <STYLE>
        .HelloDisplayClass
        {
        position:absolute;
        top:100;
        left:100;
        font-size:25pt;
        }
    </STYLE>
</HEAD>
    <BODY>
        <DIV CLASS=HelloDisplayClass>
            Hello World from ASP
        </DIV>
    </BODY>
</HTML>
```

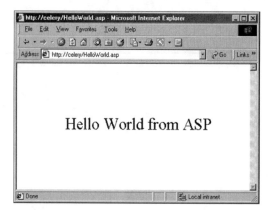

Notice that in this example, the words "Hello World from ASP" are larger and are positioned differently than they were above. This was accomplished by employing something we can call a **display class**. Just think of it as an object that contains display properties. There are three steps we must perform to use a display class:

1. Create a style section in the ASP page. This is done by adding two tags, an opening tag `<STYLE>` and a closing tag `</STYLE>` in the `<HEAD>` section of the page. The data enclosed between the two `<STYLE>` tags is known as a **style sheet**.

2. Next we create the actual class definition by giving it a name preceded by a period. Once we have named the class, we can define its properties by providing the name and value for each display property we need to use. The syntax calls for a colon (:) between the name and the value, and a semi-colon (;) between the different property pairs. I make it a practice of typing the class definitions as shown above to make them easier to read, but white space is ignored, so you can write all of the property pairs on a single line if you like. All the property pairs are enclosed in curly braces {}. The most difficult thing to learn about defining styles is the names of all of the properties and their associated values. If you work through all of the sample code in this chapter you will be introduced to the most common property names and values. But, there are a lot more possibilities. Get Instant IE4 Dynamic HTML from Wrox and use the appendix. It is great.

3. The last thing we need to do to work with the style is to tell the browser which class to apply to which blocks of text (or images, etc.) in the file. In the example above I have used a <DIV> tag. Notice that in that tag I wrote CLASS=HelloDisplayClass. If we'd named the display class something else, OurClass for instance, we would have written CLASS=OurClass. We might have defined 6 or 20 different classes in the style section and we could use the CLASS= line to instruct the browser about which class to apply to the text (or image, etc).

If you view the source code for this page you'll see that the code Notepad displays is identical to the code we entered into HelloWorld.asp. All of the code in this example was executed on the client-side.

We can do a lot with style sheets and display classes. We will examine some of the possibilities throughout the remainder of this chapter. For now, I would like to move onto another basic concept we need for developing web applications - **Dynamic HTML**.

Dynamic HTML

I hope you noticed that I was careful to draw the distinction between dynamically generated HTML and Dynamic HTML (DHTML) above. Most people get this very confused.

> **DHTML is a special kind of HTML that allows the code on the page to be executed on the client, by the (client) browser. It employs client-side scripting and can include style sheets.**

Let's look at an example of a very simple DHTML page:

```
<HTML>
<HEAD>
<STYLE>
      .SilverBox
           {
              position:absolute;
              top:100;
              left:100;
              height:100;
              width:100;
```

```
            background-color:silver;
        }
</STYLE>
<SCRIPT LANGUAGE = VBScript>
    Sub ClickThis_OnClick()
        msgbox "Hello World"
    End Sub
</SCRIPT>
</HEAD>
    <BODY>
        <DIV CLASS=SilverBox ID=ClickThis>
            Click This
        </DIV>
</BODY>
</HTML>
```

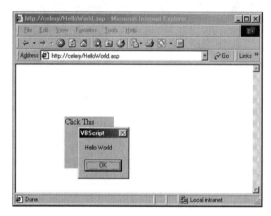

In the example above, we used a display class called SilverBox. This display class described a silver box with the dimensions, height=100 and width=100, and the attributes, top=100 and left=100.

The style definition is useless unless we put it to work in the BODY section of the page. We used the class to define the display properties for the <DIV> (or division) tag just like we did earlier:

```
<DIV CLASS=SilverBox ID=ClickThis>
```

This <DIV> tag always represents a rectangular space on our page. In this case, we used the class to define the limits and the color of that space. So far this is identical to what we did earlier, but if you look at this treatment you will notice one additional thing. We have added an ID property for this tag in the opening line of the description.

This ID gives us something very much like a handle for a window. We can use it in code to refer to the particular object it is assigned to. In this case the ID called ClickThis is assigned to a division object. Now that we have a way to identify this division object, we can control this object at the browser (client) via a client-side scripting language. In this book we are using VBScript as that language. However, if you are unsure of which browser will be used on the client machines (for example, if you are intending to put this client-side code on the Internet) you should always use JavaScript instead. JavaScript is a univeral scripting language, while VBScript is incompatible with Netscape Navigator.

> Note that the client-side VBScript is enclosed between the `<SCRIPT LANGUAGE = VBScript>` and `</SCRIPT>` tags, whereas the server-side VBScript that we looked at previously was enclosed between `<%` and `%>` and VBScript had been declared as the scripting language with the line, `<%@ Language=VBScript %>`. This is a subtle point, but one that is important to mention.

The following block of code represents a client-side script:

```
<SCRIPT LANGUAGE = VBScript>

    Sub ClickThis_OnClick()
        msgbox "Hello World"
    End Sub

</SCRIPT>
```

Again, if you know VB, this code should look quite familiar. In this case we are trapping an event on the client – a mouse click on the `ClickThis` division - and responding to that event by raising a message box with the words **Hello World**. The only thing that is difficult about this is that when we are writing VB in ASP pages instead of in VB forms, we have to write our own procedure stubs. In other words, we need to know that the division can respond to an `OnClick` event and we have to write the words:

```
    Sub ClickThis_OnClick()

    End Sub
```

Simple Huh? Good, let's try another example. In this case we will use the VBScript `OnClick` event to change the display class the `ClickThis` division is using. This means that we need to create another display class. Let's create a class called `BlackBox` to complement the `SilverBox` class we already have. Notice that this class is really the same as the `SilverBox` class except that rather than displaying black text against a silver background, it will display white text against a black background. There are many ways to accomplish this type of display change on the client, but I have found that the code is a lot more readable if I change the entire class rather than the individual properties for a class. Let's take a look at some code that we can use to accomplish just that:

```
<HTML>
<HEAD>
<STYLE>
    .SilverBox
        {
        position:absolute;
        top:100;
        left:100;
        height:100;
        width:100;
        background-color:silver;
        color:black;
        }
    .BlackBox
        {
```

```
                position:absolute;
                top:100;
                left:100;
                height:100;
                width:100;
                background-color:black;
                color:white;
                }
    </STYLE>


    <SCRIPT LANGUAGE = VBScript>

        Sub ClickThis_OnClick()
            If ClickThis.className= "SilverBox" Then
                ClickThis.className = "BlackBox"
            Else
                ClickThis.className = "SilverBox"
            End If
            msgbox "Hello World From a " & ClickThis.className
        End Sub

    </SCRIPT>

    </HEAD>

        <BODY>
            <DIV CLASS=SilverBox ID=ClickThis>
                Click This
            </DIV>
        </BODY>

    </HTML>
```

Other than the addition of the second display class, the only code that has changed is the ClickThis_OnClick() subroutine. Let's take a closer look at it.

```
        Sub ClickThis_OnClick()
            If ClickThis.className= "SilverBox" Then
                ClickThis.className = "BlackBox"
            Else
                ClickThis.className = "SilverBox"
            End If
            msgbox "Hello World From a " & ClickThis.className
        End Sub
```

This subroutine tests the division to learn what display class it is currently using. Then it changes the name of the display class. Once it has finished, a message box is raised that includes the current class name for the division.

This example just used plain DHTML, if we had saved this code as `HelloWorld.html` instead it would have worked exactly the same - the code in this example was executed only on the client-side. However, just like we can use ASP to dynamically generate HTML pages, we can also use ASP to generate DHTML pages and that's what we'll do next.

Believe it or not, you have already learned a lot about developing ASP. It is time to consider another very basic point that often confuses newcomers to Web development – passing parameters.

Passing Parameters Between ASP Pages

Passing parameters between any HTML-based application is really something of an art. Microsoft has given us a lot of tools that we can use in addition to the standard `QueryString` technique I will cover in this chapter. If you download the sample code from Wrox's web site, you will find sample code that shows how to pass parameters using forms and server-side storage techniques. The reason I have chosen to use `QueryString` exclusively in this chapter is really to make it easier to digest the overall concept of passing parameters. We are going to cover a lot of material in this chapter and I don't want to add to any confusion. Once you feel comfortable with this technique, I encourage you to examine other techniques and find the one that suits your style. Let's get on to the code.

Type the code below into Notepad. Save the code in the root directory of your web server with the name `PageOne.asp`:

```
<%@ Language=VBScript %>
<HTML>
<HEAD>
<STYLE>
    .SilverBox
        {
            position:absolute;
            top:100;
            left:100;
            height:100;
            width:100;
            background-color:silver;
        }
    .BlackBox
        {
            position:absolute;
            top:100;
            left:250;
            height:100;
            width:100;
            background-color:black;
            color:white;
        }
</STYLE>
```

```
<SCRIPT LANGUAGE = VBScript>
   Sub Document_OnClick()
      strWord = window.event.srcElement.id
      strAddress = "PageTwo.asp?Parameter1=" & strWord
      window.navigate strAddress
   End Sub
</SCRIPT>

</HEAD>
   <BODY>
      <DIV CLASS=SilverBox ID=Silver>CLICK ME</DIV>
      <DIV CLASS=BlackBox ID=Black>CLICK ME</DIV>
   </BODY>
</HTML>
```

When you view this page in your browser you should see this:

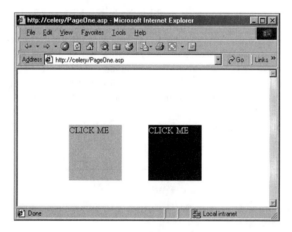

We have really gone over everything on this page except for the small block of client-side VBScript. Let's take a closer look at that block of code. The first thing you should notice about this code is that we are not specifying what element or object on the page should fire off this event. Instead, I have used a very generic subroutine named `Document_OnClick()`. This event handler will fire off whenever any element on the page is clicked including any of the whitespace around the boxes. This is a bug, but for demonstration purposes it's not worth addressing. This allows us to build generic event handlers that can respond to any event. In this case, no matter which division receives the click, this single routine will handle it the same way. Sometimes less code is better code!

```
   Sub Document_OnClick()
      strWord = window.event.srcElement.id
      strAddress = "PageTwo.asp?Parameter1=" & strWord
      window.navigate strAddress
   End Sub
```

This small block of code introduces one of the main characters in client-side coding – the `window` object. This object allows us to interface with the client's operating system. Let's see how it works.

```
   strWord = window.event.srcElement.id
```

The `window` object exposes an `event` object. When the operating system passes information about an event, say a mouse click to the browser, we can use this object to trap that event so that we can respond to it. In this case, we are responding to the event by asking the object what element caused the event, and storing the ID of that object in a variable. In the next line of code, we build an address string by concatenating the ID of the object that caused the event onto a string that contains the name of the page we need to call next:

```
strAddress = "PageTwo.asp?Parameter1=" & strWord
```

Notice the construction of the address variable. It contains the name of a page `PageTwo.asp`. This is followed directly by a question mark and the parameter name `Parameter1`. The question mark is a signal to the receiving page that the requesting page is passing some additional information in the form of a query string. The `Parameter1=` section of the address provides the property name half of a property pair. The second part of this property pair, the value, is given by the variable we are concatenating to the base address string. In other words, if the `strWord` variable contained the value "Black", then `strAddress` would contain the value "PageTwo.asp?Parameter1=Black".

The last line of code in this subroutine uses the `window` object again. This time it directs the host browser to replace the page currently in the browser with the page given in its address parameter:

```
window.navigate strAddress
```

The effect of this line of code is exactly the same as if the user had typed `PageTwo.asp?Parameter1=Black` into the address textbox of the browser and pressed *Enter*.

So, let's review what this page does. First, it presents two divisions on the screen for the user to click. Then it responds to a click of either of those boxes by calling another ASP page, `PageTwo.asp` and it passes that page a parameter that indicates what box the user pressed.

Let's take a look at `PageTwo.asp` and see how we can receive and use that parameter's value:

```
<%@ Language=VBScript %>
<HTML>
<% strWord = Request.QueryString("Parameter1") %>
    <HEAD>

      <STYLE>
        .ClickMeBox
            {
                position:absolute;
                top:100;
                left:100;
                height:100;
                width:100;
                background-color:<% = strWord %>;
    <% If strWord="Black" Then %>
                color:white;
    <% Else %>
                color:black;
    <% End If %>
            }
        </STYLE>
```

```
        <SCRIPT LANGUAGE=VBScript>
          Sub <% = strWord %>_OnCLick()
            msgBox "You clicked the <% = strWord %> box on Page One"
          End Sub
        </SCRIPT>

    </HEAD>

    <BODY>
        <DIV CLASS=ClickMeBox ID=<% = strWord %> >Click on me too!</DIV>
    </BODY>
</HTML>
```

The first thing to notice about this ASP page is the line that receives the parameter from the requesting page:

```
    <% strWord = Request.QueryString("Parameter1") %>
```

Microsoft has graciously given us some server-side objects to complement the client-side `window` object. In this case, we are using the `Request` object. The `Request` object contains information about the request that the client has made for the second page.

The `Request` object is quite powerful. In this case we are using the `Request` object to retrieve the value of a parameter that was passed in the `QueryString`. `QueryString` is actually a collection, which we can use to retrieve the values of query strings - the parameters tagged onto the end of a requested URL. This means that by specifying a parameter name (in this case `Parameter1`), we can retrieve that parameter's value (either `Black` or `White` here). It wasn't that long ago when we used to have to parse that stuff out by hand. I must be getting old.

Although we only passed one parameter into this page, the `QueryString` will handle multiple parameter pairs. The proper syntax for multiple parameter pairs is as follows:

```
    ?Parameter1=P1Value&Paramter2=P2Value& … ParameterN=PNValue
```

All you need to do to pass multiple parameters is to separate the parameter pairs with an ampersand. The `Request` object will handle the parsing. The `Request` object can do more than work with parameters. It contains a complete list of information about the requesting page, its client, and the host server. We will examine some of these other features in the sample code that follows.

The next thing to notice on this page is some of the things that we can do with dynamically generated HTML pages. In this case we are creating a conditional display object in our `<STYLE>` section:

```
            background-color:<% = strWord %>;
        <% If strWord="Black" Then %>
            color:white;
        <% Else %>
            color:black;
        <% End If %>
```

Of course, the result of this section of code will be to specify a background color and foreground color based upon what value is passed into the page. If the user clicked the silver box on the first page, then `background-color:<% = strWord %>;` will be equivalent to `background-color:Silver;` and the box on the second page, `PageTwo.asp`, will also be silver.

Notice the structure of the `If` statement. This has the effect of choosing between the two possible lines of code. If the value of `strWord` is "Black", then the page shown on the client will contain the line:

```
color:white;
```

Otherwise, the client page will contain the line:

```
color:black;
```

Note that all of this activity is taking place on the server. If you view the source for this ASP page you won't see any of the `If...Then...Else` statements - just a line specifying that the `color` is either `black` or `white`. Remember that you can always tell server-side code because it is surrounded with the `<% %>` tags.

The next thing we are doing with the parameter that was passed into the page is rather curious. We are using the parameter to help us to write client-side VBScript. Yeah that's right. This stuff is powerful!

```
Sub <% = strWord %>_OnClick()
    msgBox "You clicked the <% = strWord %> box on Page One"
End Sub
```

Look at the tiny block of code above. We are using the parameter that was passed into the page to name the subroutine. If the user clicked the silver box on `PageOne.asp`, then this subroutine will be named `Silver_OnClick()`. If the user clicked the black box on `PageOne.asp` then this routine will be named `Black_OnClick()`. Of course as we learned earlier, there are other ways to build event handlers that will respond to any element, but I just want you to consider some of the possibilities. This means that we can create custom client-side script every time the page is accessed. I am afraid that it is almost anti-climatic, but notice that we are also using the parameter to build a message string that will be displayed when the user clicks the box on `PageTwo.asp`.

The last thing we are going to do with this parameter is to use it to name the division on our page. That is done with the following line of code:

```
<DIV CLASS=ClickMeBox ID=<% = strWord %> >Click on me too!</DIV>
```

The end result of all of this is that no matter what box the user clicked, we will create a custom page to respond to that click. If the user clicked the silver box, they would be presented with the page below on the left. If they clicked the black box, the user would be presented with the page below on the right.

Let's recap what we've just done:

- ❑ On PageOne.asp, we used client-side script to respond to an event on the client.
- ❑ We used the window.event.srcElement object to determine which element received the mouseclick.
- ❑ Then we passed the ID of that element using a QueryString to a second ASP page, PageTwo.asp using the navigate method of the window object.
- ❑ In PageTwo.asp, we used the parameter passed into the page to dynamically fill the properties of a display class.
- ❑ Then we used the parameter to help us to custom craft some client-side script - the OnClick event of our boxes.
- ❑ Finally, we used the parameter passed into the page to write some HTML code. It provided the ID for our single element on the page.

That is a lot of work so I would suggest that you run the samples in this section and try to do a little experimentation on your own before you continue. The next thing we will do in this chapter is to develop a system for writing ASP pages. You might want to take a break before we begin.

Note that for the sake of clarity, these pages run only in Internet Explorer. Navigator users should bear in mind that client-side VBScript doesn't work in their browser and that it deals with style classes in a different fashion to IE.

The Five Major Sections of an Active Server Page

As far as we are concerned in this book, an Active Server Page consists of five main sections. Each one of these sections has a characteristic purpose. More than that, some of the sections are primarily designed to be executed on the server, while other sections are primarily designed to be executed on the client. This server-side/client-side code is probably the most confusing aspect to beginning ASP developers.

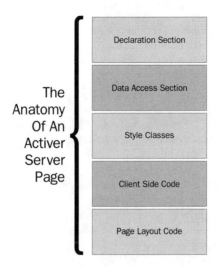

The
Anatomy
Of An
Activer
Server
Page

Declaration Section

Data Access Section

Style Classes

Client Side Code

Page Layout Code

As we work through each of the five main sections, I will make a special effort to point out what code will execute on the server and what code will execute on the client. Although it can be confusing, by the time we finish this overview we will have developed a general set of rules that will guide you through all of your development efforts. If you worked through the earlier exercises then you know this. But for the rest of you it is important to realize that although we will develop some general rules about what kind of code executes where, it is important to remember that server-side code can exist anywhere on an Active Server Page. As we learned above, we can even use server-side script to write client-side script.

Declaration

The section of code that I call the **Declaration section** exists at the beginning of each ASP page. It is the place where we write the code that extracts parameters passed into our page and stuffs those parameters into variables that we use throughout the remainder of the page. ASP is really a free format medium. In other words, there are no rules that state that we have to have a Declaration section at the beginning of a page. We could really wait until we need the parameter and use it directly. For example, in the last treatment of `PageTwo.asp` we stuffed the value of `Parameter1` into a variable at the beginning of the page. That meant that when we used the value to determine the `background-color` for the box we could write the code as:

```
background-color:<% = strWord %>;
```

It would have been just as valid for us to create this line of code using the following:

```
background-color:<% = Request.QueryString("Parameter1") %>;
```

In fact if we only use the variable once in the page, the second treatment will be more efficient. But we are developing code that will be used across an enterprise. There is a lot of value in creating code that is predictable and easy to read. Towards that end, all my teams use the concept of a Declaration section at the beginning of each page. It gives the code a consistency and makes it easier to find errors. As we touched on earlier, one of the main "characters" in the Declaration section of an ASP is the `Request` object.

The Request Object

The `Request` object is a server-side object that contains information about the calling page. It stores this information in several collections, namely `ClientCertificate`, `Cookies`, `QueryString`, `Form`, `ServerVariables`, and in the `TotalBytes` property. In this book, we will only be using two or three of these sources of information.

QueryString

As we saw earlier, we can consider `QueryString` to be like a method that accepts a parameter name as an argument and returns the correct value for that parameter. If we were to call a page using the following address with a `QueryString`:

```
PageTwo.asp?Parameter1=Hello&Parameter2=World&Parameter3=9
```

We could extract the values out of `QueryString` using `Request.QueryString` as follows:

```
<%
    vntParameter1 = Request.QueryString("Parameter1")
    vntParameter2 = Request.QueryString("Parameter2")
    vntParameter3 = Request.QueryString("Parameter3")
%>
```

Of course, QueryString is actually a collection with an item method rather than a method in itself, but that is the beauty of encapsulation. As long as it works, it really doesn't matter how the functionality is handled internally.

Form

`QueryString` is not the only, nor is it the best, way to pass parameters between Active Server Pages. The `Request` object also exposes another collection, `Form`. As far as we are concerned, `Form` works almost exactly like `QueryString`. The only difference is that instead of giving it the name of a parameter as an argument, we give it the name of an input control on the form of the calling page. Boy, that was a mouthful. Let me give you an example.

In a very simplified view, a form is a logical construct on an HTML page that contains a collection of input objects enclosed between <FORM> tags. A form has an `ACTION` attribute that specifies which URL should recieve the data passed by the form. We can create a form on a page by writing code like the following:

```
<HTML>
<HEAD>
</HEAD>
<BODY>
<FORM ACTION="PageResponse.asp">
    <INPUT TYPE=TEXT ID=text1 NAME=txtOne VALUE=One><BR>
    <INPUT TYPE=TEXT ID=text2 NAME=txtTwo VALUE=2><BR>
    <INPUT TYPE=TEXT ID=text3 NAME=txtThree VALUE=Three><BR>
    <INPUT TYPE=TEXT ID=text4 NAME=txtFour VALUE=4><BR>
    <INPUT TYPE=RESET VALUE=Reset ID=reset1 NAME=reset1>
    <INPUT TYPE=SUBMIT VALUE=Submit ID=submit1 NAME=submit1>
</FORM>
</BODY>
</HTML>
```

This code results in the following form:

If the user clicked the **Submit** button, this page would call the next page, `PageResponse.asp`, as directed in the form's `ACTION` attribute. In the Declaration section of the `PageResponse.asp` page, we could extract the values from the requesting page's form by using the `Form` collection of the `Request` object. We would do that by writing the following lines of code in the Declaration section of the ASP page:

```
<%
    vntOne = Request.Form("txtOne")
    vntTwo = Request.Form("txtTwo")
    vntThree = Request.Form("txtThree")
    vntFour = Request.Form("txtFour")
%>
```

This would give us four variables that represented the values the user had typed into the textboxes on the requesting page. Of course, we can use these values in a myriad of ways. All we are concerned with in this section is extracting the information from the requesting page and placing it into variables.

ServerVariables

The last of the `Request` object's collections that we will look at in this section is `ServerVariables`. We can use this collection to give us information that the host server, the server executing the page we are working with, has available. This is a rich source of information for developers. Among other things, it contains the name and IP address of the server. Right now, it may seem ridiculous to be interested in this information. You would expect that a developer would be smart enough to know what server his Active Server Pages would be executing on. But if you think about it, when we are writing a page, we really don't know what the future holds. Our pages may end up on a server that doesn't even exist today. We can use the `Server_Name` variable to learn what server our page exists on when it is actually called. This allows us to create portable code using a technique as follows:

```
<% strServerName = Request.ServerVariables("Server_Name") %>
```

... lines of code

```
strAddress= "http://" & <%  = strServerName %> & "/PageName.asp"
```

It also allows us to extract the name of the authorized user that has requested the page as follows:

```
<% strAuthorizedUser = Request.ServerVariables("Auth_User") %>
```

... lines of code

```
<% If strAuthorizedUser = "Guest" Then
    Response.Redirect "http://www.yahoo.com"
   End If %>
```

Of course we have other security methods available to us, this example was just designed to give you something to think about. In actual practice, we use the name of the authorized user first to give us the StampUser value for our data objects.

The Response Object

In addition to the Request object, Microsoft has also provided us with another server-based object. This one is called the Response object. Where the Request object represented the page that called the page we are working on, the Response object represents the page we are working on.

Buffer

The first use you will find for the Response object in the Declaration section of an ASP page is the following two lines, which should always be placed close to the top:

```
<%
    Response.Buffer = True
    Response.Expires = 0
%>
```

These two lines of code ensure that our user always receives a fresh page every time the user asks the server for this page.

Setting the Buffer to True means that the user will see none of the page until it has all been sent to the browser. Expires represents the time in minutes before the page expires. Setting Expires to 0 means that as soon as the page is delivered from the server it has expired. If the browser recieves a page that has already expired it will not storeit in the client's cache.

Retrieving a page from the local cache is OK for some web sites and saves precious bandwidth, but it is devastating for a real application that needs to deliver data in real time to users. We need to be sure that every time a user requests an ASP page from our server that the user gets a fresh copy of the data. These two lines accomplish that.

> Although, Response.Expires = 0 should, theoretically, make the page expire the instant it is recieved by the browser and so prevent caching; you may need to declare Response.Expires = -1441 instead. Let's say a server delivers a page at 10.00am, then the page will expire on the client at 10.00am. If the internal clock of the client is running behind that of the server you won't get immediate expiry of the page. If you set the Expires value to 24 hours and 1 minute (1441) ago on the server, you will almost certainly always get immediate expiry.

Redirect

The other thing we will use the Response object for in this chapter is to redirect the user from the current page to another page. We saw an example of this above when we looked at the ServerVariables collection of the Request object. In that case we tested the name of the authorized user. If that name was Guest, then we used the Response object to redirect that user to Yahoo.com:

```
<% If strAuthorizedUser = "Guest" Then
      Response.Redirect "http://www.yahoo.com"
   End If %>
```

This is one of the most commonly used methods of the `Response` object.

The next major section of code we need to consider follows the Declaration section. We can call it the **Data Access section**. In this block of code, we transfer information into and out of the data store using the VB objects that we learned to create earlier in this book.

Data Access Section

This is the section within the Active Server Page that we reserve for all data access activities. The main "character" in this section of the page is the actually the `Server` object. We use it to instantiate all of the data objects that we use in the page.

CreateObject

The `Server` object uses a method called `CreateObject` to instantiate an object within a process space created by IIS. The syntax is nearly identical to the standard VB `CreateObject` method:

```
Set colTypes = Server.CreateObject("UCPerson.colTypes")
```

Remember that we don't actually dimension variables, other than arrays, in VBScript. If we need to use a data object, all we need to do is to use a line similar to the one above to create the object. Once we have the object, we can use it in almost exactly the same way that we would use it in standard Visual Basic. Our data objects will have the same properties and methods that we used when we created VB interfaces. In fact, if you use Visual Interdev 6.0 as your development environment, then you will also have the added feature of IntelliSense to aid you in using the data objects in this book for development purposes.

The following block of code is used to load a collection named `colTypes` with all of the possible Property Set Definitions for the *Person* object. As you can see, the code is not much different than it would be if we were to write it in standard VB. The only unusual things here are the references to the `Server` object. Other than that, it is virtually identical to the standard VB treatment:

```
<%
   strConnect = "Common"
   Set colTypes = Server.CreateObject("UCPerson.colTypes")
   colTypes.SetDataSource strConnect
   colTypes.Load
   Set objType = Server.CreateObject("UCPerson.clsType")
%>
```

Most of the time, you will find that the data access techniques we use in an ASP are the same as the VB techniques we learned earlier. There are a couple of exceptions. The first one has to do with the fact that VBScript treats all variables as variants. Remember that our data objects are typed strongly. In other words, we always expect a particular type of variable. When we pass parameters into our objects from an ASP page, we need to ensure that we convert the variable from a variant into the required type as follows:

```
<% objType.ObjectFetch, Clng(lngID) %>
```

In most pages, the data access requirements are really quite simple. The only real difficult programming task occurs in the data access section of the Detail page. This page is designed to handle many different data access scenarios. For instance, we use the same page to add a new object, edit an object, or to control the deletion of an object. This can get pretty complex. To make it a little easier, we employ a consistent `Select Case` statement in the data access section of any Detail page. When we enter a page, we pass a parameter into a variable named `strAction` that describes what type of data access we will perform in the page. The structure of that `Select Case` statement is always as follows:

```
<%
Select Case strAction

  Case "N"
     strAction = "A"

  Case "A"
     Set objType = Server.CreateObject("UCPerson.clsType")
     objType.SetDataSource strConnect
     ' set the object's properties
     ' EXAMPLE:
     ' objType.ID = Clng(lngID)
     objType.ObjectInsert
     Set objType = Nothing
     Response.Redirect "PersonTypeList.asp?StampUser=" & strStampUser

  Case "E"
     strAction = "U"
     Set objType = Server.CreateObject("UCPerson.clsType")
     objType.SetDataSource strConnect
     objType.ObjectFetch, Clng(lngID)

  Case "U"
     Set objType = Server.CreateObject("UCPerson.clsType")
     objType.SetDataSource strConnect
     ' set the object's properties
     ' EXAMPLE:
     ' objType.ID = Clng(lngID)
     objType.ObjectUpdate
     Response.Redirect "PersonTypeList.asp?StampUser=" & strStampUser

  Case "D"
     Set objType = Server.CreateObject("UCPerson.clsType")
     objType.SetDataSource strConnect
     ' set the object's properties
     ' EXAMPLE:
     ' objType.ID = Clng(lngID)
     objType.ObjectFetch, Clng(lngID)
     objType.ObjectDelete
     Response.Redirect "PersonTypeList.asp?StampUser=" & strStampUser

  Case "R"
     Set objType = Server.CreateObject("UCPerson.clsType")
     Set objThis = Server.CreateObject("UCPerson.clsType")
     objType.SetDataSource strConnect
     objType.ID = Clng(lngOriginalID)
     Set colTypes = objType.ObjectAuditHistory
```

```
        For Each objThis In colTypes
            If objThis.ID = Clng(lngAuditID) Then
                Set objType = objThis
                Exit For
            End If
        Next

        strAction = "U"
        blnRestored = True

    End Select
%>
```

As you can see there are six possible data access activities that we might need to perform on a Detail page. Let's work through them one at a time:

- The first possibility is that the object is brand new and the user should be presented with an empty page so that he or she can supply the values. In this case, strAction will contain the value "N" for new. All we need to do here is to set strAction to "A" for add and continue to process the page with an empty object.

- The second possibility is that the user has supplied all of the necessary values for a new object and now wants to insert that object into the data store. In this case, strAction will contain the value "A". What we do in this case is to create a new object, fill its properties with the parameters passed into the page, and then call the object's ObjectInsert method just as we would in VB. Once the insertion has been completed, we use the Response object's Redirect method to send the user back to the List page. Of course, the List page will be refreshed in the process and the user will see that the new object is now contained in the list.

- The third possibility is that the user wants to edit an existing object. In this case, the strAction variable will contain the value "E" for edit. What we do in this case is fetch the current values for the object that the user specified and present the page to the user for further inspection/editing. We also use this time to prepare the page for the user's most likely next step. In other words, after the user is presented with an object for editing, the user will probably want to update the values for the object. To facilitate this, we change the strAction variable to read "U" for update.

- The fourth possibility is that the user has edited an object and now wants to save the new values that he or she has typed into the Detail page. In this case, we first fetch a new copy of the object from the data store. Then we fill the object with the edited values. Once we have supplied all of the new values, we save the object using its ObjectUpdate method. After an update, we always redirect the user back to the List form. In addition, as with the object insertion, the List page is refreshed in the process and displays the changed values to the user.

- The fifth possibility is that the user wants to delete an object. In that case, the strAction variable contains the value "D" for delete. As you may have come to expect, what we do here is to fetch the correct object from the data store using the ID the user passed into the page. Once we have the object, we simply use its ObjectDelete method. Lastly, just like with the insert and update methods, when the deletion is completed, we redirect the user back to the List form. The List form is refreshed in the process and displays the most current list from the data store. In this case, the list should have one less entry because the user just deleted an object.

❑   The sixth and last case is that the user may want to restore an object to a previous state. In this case, the strAction variable will contain the value "R" for restore. This is by far the most complex of the data access activities. In order to restore an object we first fill a collection with the history for that object. Then we iterate through the collection until we find the object ID in that collection that points to the previous state that the user selected for restoration. Once we have found the correct object, we change the strAction value to "U" for update and allow the page to continue executing. This has the effect of displaying the restored information to the user. The user must press Save to complete the restoration. When this happens, the same page executes and the restored information is simply saved as an update.

Style Sheets

The next section of code in our 5-section treatment is always the **Style Sheet section**. It is possible and really quite efficient to use a single style sheet for all of your Active Server Pages. We can do this by linking to the style sheet rather than typing the actual style class descriptions into the current page.

I think that this is one of those rare cases where less is not more. In other words, my teams prefer to work with the class descriptions in the same page. It makes it a lot easier to design a page if you can scroll up and look at the display class definition. I realize that we could save quite a few kilobytes a year if we abandoned this practice and linked a few style sheets. Generally, though, I think the savings in network traffic would be overshadowed by the additional development costs this practice would cause.

Classes

We have already covered the basic concept of the display class above, but I will give you a couple of additional samples in this section. You can always use them as a reference.

This design class describes a blue box:

```
.BlueBox
    {
    position:absolute;
    top:100;
    left:100;
    height:100;
    width:100;
    background-color:blue;
    }
```

This design class describes a particular style of text that will display big, bright red letters:

```
.BigBrightRedLetters
    {
    position:absolute;
    font-family:times;
    font-size:32pt;
    color:red;
    }
```

While we are talking about style sheet display classes, let me mention that all of the properties for any class can be overridden after they have been defined. We will cover this later, but if we needed bigger `BigBrightRedLetters` we could do something like the following in the `BODY` section of our ASP page:

```
<DIV CLASS=BigBrightRedLetters STYLE="font-size:54pt;"> Hello World</DIV>
```

This would cause the words "Hello World" to be displayed with the properties of the `BigBrightRedLetters` class, but the `font-size` property would be overridden by the in-line style. When this page showed up on the client's screen, the red letters would be displayed using 54 point type rather than the 32 point specified in the class. All of the properties for a design class can be overridden in a similar manner.

Absolute Positioning

In this book I only use absolute positioning. That is because I use ASP to create applications, not the typical web pages most people are used to working with. When I develop an interface with ASP, I need to be sure that each textbox, combobox, and command button, etc is placed exactly where I need it on a particular screen. We use ASP to create very VB-like pages.

Client Side Code

Perhaps the richest development environment for an ASP page is the **Client Side Code section**. We can use VBScript to perform almost any task that we could perform with standard VB. I would like to express a word of caution here. It is important to remember that one of our enterprise design goals was to create interfaces that did not contain business rules. This is important. We covered some very sophisticated business rule handling techniques when we looked at application veneers. It would not do our enterprise any good if we went through all of the trouble to build great objects and then placed all of the business rules in our ASP files.

The Window Object

We have already looked at some of the things we can accomplish on the server-side using the `window` object. Again, I must caution you that this book is not intended to be a reference for working with DHTML. That said, I will cover some of the basics of the `window` object again so that you will have them available as a reference.

Event

The `window` object exposes an `event` object that contains a slew of properties. It is possible to use this object to learn what button was pressed using its `keyCode` property. It is also possible to determine which mouse button a user clicked as well the x and y coordinates that define where it was clicked.

Navigate

The easiest way to think about the `navigate` method is to realize that it amounts to exactly the same thing you do when you type an address into the address combo box in IE or Netscape and press *Enter*. The `navigate` method allows the programmer to perform this task for the user. This offers a couple of advantages. First, it can give us a high degree of control over the user's action and second, it allows us to focus the user's attention on the page within the browser rather than on the browser.

Page Layout Code

The last one of the five major sections for any ASP page is the **Page Layout section**. While the other four major sections are fairly well defined, the page layout code is where it all comes together. I mean that literally, not figuratively. In this section of code we combine server-side code, client-side code, data elements, style sheets, and run of the mill HTML. Rather than trying to describe exactly how all of this stuff fits together I am simply going to move on to the next section of this chapter where this topic will be illustrated properly - the *Person* object pages.

The Person Object Pages

As you already know, the *Person* object is a true 4-Dimensional Data Object. That means that it has the following characteristics that we need to expose to the user:

- ❑ A set of base properties
- ❑ A set of extended properties
- ❑ The ability to display an object's audit history
- ❑ The ability to restore an object to a previous state
- ❑ The ability to display a list of deleted objects
- ❑ The ability to restore an object from a deleted state

Heavy Active Server Pages

When I developed the first set of Active Server Page templates for the Object Factory, I made myself follow one very stringent rule. That rule was that I would not allow the pages to contain any ActiveX controls, Java Beans or the like so that the pages were compatible with all web browsers. The results were pretty impressive. I ended up with a set of pages that offered just about all the functionality anyone might expect. And that wasn't the good part. The good part was that the pages were the ultimate expression of a thin client interface. You will find those original templates included with the sample code in this book. They are also created by default whenever you create a new object using the Object Factory.

There was only one thing missing from those ultra-thin client interfaces. I really missed the listview control that was available to me as a VB developer. You can do wondrous things with the HTML <TABLE> tag, but they still don't measure up to the functionality available in Microsoft's listview control. Alas, I caved and designed a second set of page templates that make use of this one control. I didn't think that it was fair to call these pages a true thin-client interface anymore seeing that I had broken my own rule about not using any ActiveX controls, so I changed the name of the pages we are about to learn about to **Heavy Active Server Pages**. I reasoned that although these pages were no longer my ultimate expression of a thin-client interface, they also were not fat client interfaces by any stretch of the imagination. Since the pages fell somewhere between a thin client and fat client interface I called them Heavy Active Server Pages.

The Person List Page

The Person List page performs nearly the same tasks as the Visual Basic Person List form that we used in some previous chapters. It is designed to present the user with something of a pick list. It is also something of a starting point for the other pages we will create. From this page, the user can raise the Person Detail page to add or edit a new *Person* object. The user can also delete an existing *Person* from this page. This page is not an exact duplicate of the Visual Basic expression. Although the user can retrieve a list of deleted objects from this page, the page itself does not morph into a page that contains a second listview like the VB form. (It could, but I didn't like the way it looked.) Instead, when the user asks to view a list of deleted objects, this page raises a second modal page that displays the list.

Before we begin to work through the *Person* object Active Server Pages, you should create a directory under the wwwroot directory of your IIS server. Just so that we are all using the same directory structure, call this directory Person. After you have created the directory, copy the HelloWorld.asp file you created earlier into this directory and open it up in your browser. Type the URL http://YourServerName/Person/HelloWorld.asp in the address combo box of your browser and press *Enter*. If all is well, you should see the same results you got earlier when you opened up this page. The easiest way to work with the code in this section is to extract the code from the zip file and copy all of the files located in the Person\UInterface\HeavyASP directory into the Person directory you just created under the wwwroot directory.

Of course, you will also need to have the UCPerson and DCPerson DLLs registered on the IIS machine. If that is not already the case, you will need to copy the DLLs you created in one of the last chapters over to the IIS machine. (If you haven't compiled the DLLs yet, you can use the ones provided in the sample code.)

> *I make it a habit of storing all of the DLLs on our machines in a single directory called* components. *Then I create a directory under the* components *directory for each object that is registered on that machine. In this case that would mean that you could create a* components *directory on one of the local drives of the IIS machine. Under that directory create a sub-directory called* Person *and copy the two DLLs into that sub-directory.*

The only other thing you need to do is to make sure that you have a valid ODBC connection on the IIS machine for the SQL Server database that you want to use. To keep it simple, I suggest that you use the same one we have been using all along – `Common`.

That should be about it. Let's get on to the work of creating the pages. If you have a copy of Interdev 6.0, by all means use it to work with the sample code. Interdev is an excellent ASP editor. Among other things it provides the IntelliSense feature. If you don't have a copy of Interdev, don't worry! You can always use the best HTML editor ever invented – the venerable Notepad.

Using whatever editor you have at your disposal, open up the `PersonList.asp` file from the `\wwwroot\Person` directory on the IIS machine. As I said earlier, we will work through the task of learning ASP by learning how to write each of the five sections that make up an Active Server Page. The first section is the Declaration section.

The Declaration Section

The first line of the `PersonList.asp` informs the IIS machine that we will be using VBScript as the server-side scripting language. We could also use Java script and I suppose other scripting languages, but in this book we will use VBScript:

```
<%@ LANGUAGE="VBSCRIPT" %>
```

The next few lines of code are very important. We've seen these before, they just to instruct the browser never to cache this page:

```
<%
    Response.Buffer = True
    Response.Expires = 0
%>
```

The next few lines just tell us about the type of page to expect, `<HTML>`, and identify the program that created the ASP template:

```
<HTML>
<HEAD>
    <META NAME="GENERATOR" CONTENT="N-Sphere Object Factory 6.0">
    <META HTTP-EQUIV="Content-Type" CONTENT="text/html; charset=iso-8859-1">
```

As we learned above in the section on passing parameters, this page is expecting the calling page to provide two values – one to identify the person requesting the page, `StampUser`, and another to identify the type of *Person* that should be included in this list, `TypeID`. We also take a line here to provide the name of the ODBC connection we will use for this page. Of course, we don't need to use a variable to contain this value in this page, but it is a good practice that will come in handy when we write some more complex pages:

```
<%
  strConnect = "Common"
  strStampUser = Request.QueryString("StampUser")
  lngTypeID = Request.QueryString("TypeID")
%>
```

The fact that this page is expecting some parameters means that we have an obligation to provide them. In this case we can do that by typing a valid address into the address combo box in IE. A valid address string that can be used to call this page would look something like the following:

```
http://celery/Person/PersonList.asp?StampUser=Joe&TypeID=1
```

The Data Access Section

The code in this section should look kind of familiar. There are a few differences from standard VB, but the similarities are really something. The first thing you might notice is that we didn't dimension the object variables before we used them. Remember from above that we don't use the `Dim` statement in VBSript except when we are dimensioning an array. The second thing you should notice is that we have prefixed the `CreateObject` command with the word `Server`. This command just instructs IIS to do whatever is necessary to create the object we need to use:

```
<%
  Set colPersons = Server.CreateObject("UCPerson.colPersons")
  Set objPerson = Server.CreateObject("UCPerson.clsPerson")
```

Now that IIS has instantiated the objects we requested, we can use the objects in nearly the same fashion we would use them in standard VB. In this case, we want to retrieve a list of *Persons* of a particular type, so we just use the `Load` method of the `colPerson` object. Because we are using Enterprise Caliber Data Objects, that is really all there is to it as far as data access goes – a simple two step process:

- ❑ Point the object at the correct data store
- ❑ Invoke the `Load` method

```
  colPersons.SetDataSource Cstr(strConnect)
  colPersons.Load Clng(lngTypeID)
%>

      <TITLE>Person List</TITLE>
```

After these two lines have executed, what we have is an Enterprise Caliber Data Object – in this case a collection – filled with the data we need to present to the user.

The Style Sheet Section

The style sheet for the List page is the ultimate in simplicity. The only thing we need to do is to set the background color. We didn't even have to use a style sheet to do this. It may have made more sense to set this style using an in-line technique, but I wanted to show you a couple of things. First, notice that immediately following the `<STYLE>` tag that I have typed in a curious set of characters `<!--`. When a browser that doesn't understand style sheets sees these characters, it ignores whatever is typed until it sees this tag's closing tag, `-->`. These tags are used as comment delimiters in HTML. The second thing that I wanted to show you is a special class definition. Notice that the word BODY is not preceded by a period. We learned above that we should prefix style class definitions with a period. What gives? Well, the reason we didn't proceed this class definition with a period is because it is a kind of like a pre-defined class. BODY is an intrinsic class of every HTML document. So, we don't need to define it. It already exists. This is the same with all of the standard HTML tags. When we use these in the style sheet section of our ASP, we do not need to create the display class, we just set its properties:

```
<STYLE>
<!--
BODY
      {
      background-color:silver;
      }
-->
</STYLE>
```

The Client-Side Code Section

Ahh, now we get to the interesting part. In this section of the ASP, we are writing the code that will execute on the client's machine. This never ceases to amaze me. I started working with the Web in a time when it was great just to deliver plain text with a few lightweight images strewn around for effect. It has evolved into one heck of a development environment.

Anyway, in a minute or two you may think I am crazy to call this section the client-side code section. You don't have to look too far into this section to see the now familiar <% %> tags that indicate that this code should be executed on the server.

> **The cool thing is that the code that is executing on the server is actually writing the client-side code for us.**

I am not kidding! We will go over how this works in a minute or two. I want to be sure that I don't skip over the first few lines so let's step through them.

First, we need to be sure to tell the browser that it should expect to find VB Script as the scripting language. If you are thinking that we already did this earlier, then you are probably not alone. We have to remember that when we create an ASP page, we are really writing a piece of code that is designed to be executed in two different environments. Once on the server – that was the purpose of the first tag <% @LANGUAGE = VBSCRIPT %> we saw earlier. And once on the browser – that is the purpose of this <SCRIPT LANGUAGE = VBScript> line:

```
<SCRIPT LANGUAGE=VBScript>
```

We are using a listview to contain the collection of persons on this ASP page. That means that we need to prepare the listview to accept and display the list to the user. Remember that we performed this task in the Form_Load subroutine in the VB forms we worked with before. Well, ASP doesn't have a Form_Load, so we need to build one. We do that by creating a subroutine that will execute as soon as the page loads. This is really a two step process. I have used the name Page_Initialize for the subroutine, but this name is not magic by any means. This routine will not execute when the page loads unless we instruct it to do so. The way we do that is by changing the BODY tag in the page layout section below to read as follows:

```
<BODY ONLOAD="Page_Initialize">
```

What we are doing here is instructing the page to run the following subroutine when the page loads – `ONLOAD = "Page_Initialize"`. That means that we could have called this routine `Tom` or `Jill` and we still could have made it execute when the page loaded. All we would have needed to do to make that happen is to change the opening `BODY` tag to read `ONLOAD="Tom"` or `ONLOAD="Jill"`. I don't mean to make a big thing out of this, but more than one of the people I have shown this code to seemed to think that the somehow the `Page_Initialize` routine might work like the `Form_Load` subroutine without any additional coaxing. I really think it was a pretty logical assumption on their paert, so I thought I should make this clear.

```
Sub Page_Initialize()
```

The listview setup code is identical to standard VB syntax. In this case, we are using a 5.0 service pack 2 listview (from `COMCTL32.OCX`). For some curious reason, the 6.0 listview (in `MSCOMCTL.OCX`)acts quite flaky in an ASP environment. From time to time, the 6.0 listview will simply decide on its own to display white letters against a white background. There doesn't seem to be any rhyme or reason about why it does this, so I have stopped using it for now. There have already been two service packs sent out for Visual Studio 6.0 as I write this, so maybe the problem has been addressed. I really hope so, the 6.0 listview is so much better than the 5.0. It offers movable columns and full row selects among other things. Oh… sorry about that, let's get back to the code.

All we are doing here is just adding the column headers for the listview:

```
lvwPersons.ColumnHeaders.Add , ,"BirthDate",100
lvwPersons.ColumnHeaders.Add , ,"FirstName",100
lvwPersons.ColumnHeaders.Add , ,"MiddleName",100
lvwPersons.ColumnHeaders.Add , ,"LastName",100
lvwPersons.ColumnHeaders.Add , ,"Salutation",100
lvwPersons.ColumnHeaders.Add , ,"Suffix",100
lvwPersons.ColumnHeaders.Add , ,"SSN",100
lvwPersons.ColumnHeaders.Add , ,"Sex",100
lvwPersons.ColumnHeaders.Add , ,"TypeName",100
lvwPersons.ColumnHeaders.Add , ,"KeyPrefix",100
```

In an Active Server Page, we need to translate some of the constants for the listview. I suppose we could have linked to a file that carried all of the constants, but we only use one constant and here it is:

```
lvwPersons.View = 3 'lvwReport
```

Once the listview has been setup, we iterate through the collection we loaded above and write code on the server that will be executed on the client to load the listview there. What this means is that once this server-side code has finished executing, it will have written a client-side statement to load each *Person* object's information into the listview:

```
<% For each objPerson in colPersons %>
  Set objItem = lvwPersons.ListItems. _
    Add(,"<% = objPerson.Key %>","<% = objPerson.BirthDate %>")
  objItem.SubItems(1) = "<% = objPerson.FirstName %>"
  objItem.SubItems(2) = "<% = objPerson.MiddleName %>"
  objItem.SubItems(3) = "<% = objPerson.LastName %>"
  objItem.SubItems(4) = "<% = objPerson.Salutation %>"
  objItem.SubItems(5) = "<% = objPerson.Suffix %>"
  objItem.SubItems(6) = "<% = objPerson.SSN %>"
```

```
      objItem.SubItems(7) = "<% = objPerson.Sex %>"
      objItem.SubItems(8) = "<% = objPerson.TypeName %>"
      objItem.SubItems(9) = "<% = objPerson.KeyPrefix %>"
   <% Next %>

End Sub
```

The next subroutine is very straightforward. It is just like the VB one we created way back in Chapter 5. It allows the user to sort the contents of the listview by any column simply by clicking on the column header:

```
Sub lvwPersons_ColumnClick(ColumnHeader)
   lvwPersons.SortKey = ColumnHeader.Index - 1
   lvwPersons.Sorted = True
   If lvwPersons.SortOrder = 1 Then
      lvwPersons.SortOrder = 0
   Else
      lvwPersons.SortOrder = 1
   End If
   lvwPersons.Refresh
End Sub
```

The next subroutine is exactly like the VB one you wrote in Chapter 5. It just invokes the Edit button click:

```
Sub lvwPersons_DblClick()
   cmdEdit_Click
End Sub
```

The next subroutine is fired off when the user clicks the Add button. It is similar to the one we used earlier to move from `PageOne.asp` to `PageTwo.asp` in the sample code above. All we do here is to create an address string that is used to load the Person Detail page into the browser. Notice that we are supplying three parameters:

❑   An `Action`, that instructs the Detail page about what we want to do – in this case `N` (for new)

❑   The name of the user that may perform an action – `StampUser`

❑   The type of person we want to add – `TypeID`

After we have built the address string, all we need to do to call the `navigate` method of the `window` object to call the next page. This gives us a way to direct the user through a process without requiring the user to type complex addresses into the address combo box:

```
Sub cmdAdd_Click()
   strAddress = "Person.asp?Action=N&StampUser=" & _
      "<% = strStampUser %>&TypeID=<% = lngTypeID %>"
   window.navigate strAddress
End Sub
```

The work we are doing with the `cmdEdit_Click` routine is quite similar to the work we did above in the `cmdAdd_Click` event handler. In both cases we build an address string and call the next page. The difference here is that we need to edit an existing object, so we need to pass the ID of that object in the parameters of the address. We also need to send the Detail page a value for the action parameter. In this case, we pass the Detail page an `E` for edit. Notice that we use the same technique to extract the ID from the listview here as we used in the VB forms back in Chapter 5. Then we just append that information to the address string and call the next ASP page using the `navigate` method of the `window` object:

```
Sub cmdEdit_Click()
    strAddress = "Person.asp?Action=E&ID=" & _
      Right(lvwPersons.SelectedItem.Key, _
      Len(lvwPersons.SelectedItem.Key) - 3) & _
      "&StampUser=<% = strStampUser %>&TypeID=<% = lngTypeID %>"
    window.navigate strAddress
End Sub
```

The `cmdDelete_Click` routine is identical to the `cmdEdit_Click` event except for one thing. In this case, the `Action` parameter value we are passing in this case is `D` for delete

```
Sub cmdDelete_Click()
    strAddress = "Person.asp?Action=D&ID=" & _
      Right(lvwPersons.SelectedItem.Key, _
      Len(lvwPersons.SelectedItem.Key) - 3) & _
      "&StampUser=<% = strStampUser %>&TypeID=<% = lngTypeID %>"
    window.navigate strAddress
End Sub
```

Although at first glance the `ShowDeleted_Click` code may not look too much different than the code above, it is really quite different. It uses a modal dialog box to display a page of deleted objects for the user to browse. It accepts a return value from the modal dialog box. We will go over it below, but if any value was returned from the modal dialog, that means that an object was restored. If no value is returned from the modal dialog box, then that means that no object was restored. This routine tests the return value from the modal dialog box. If an object was restored, then it refreshes the `PersonList.asp` by navigating to the same page again. Remember that we instructed the browser (the client) that the page would expire at the moment that it was created on the server, with the `Response.Expires = 0` statement above. This means that the restored object will be displayed in the list at the end of this subroutine. If no object was restored, then nothing is done.

```
    Sub cmdShowDeleted_Click()
        strAddress = "PersonShowDeleted.asp?Action=L&StampUser=" & _
          "<% = strStampUser %>&TypeID=<% = lngTypeID %>"
        strResponse = window.showModalDialog(strAddress, ShowDeleted)
        If Len(Trim(strResponse)) > 0 Then
          window.navigate "PersonList.asp?StampUser=" & _
            "<% = strStampUser %>&TypeID=<% = lngTypeID %>"
        End If
      End Sub
    </SCRIPT>
    </HEAD>
```

The Page Layout Section

This section of the ASP page may look confusing, but that is mostly because we are using the listview control. Other , than that, this particular page layout section is really quite simple. In other words, don't let the complex looking code between the object tags throw you. All that code does is to identify the listview control and specify its size, etc.

You should remember the `<BODY>` tag line discussion from above:

```
<BODY LANGUAGE = VBScript ONLOAD="Page_Initialize">
```

The next few lines of code are just used to create a title for the body of the page:

```
<SPAN STYLE="position:absolute;top:2;left:2;font-size:14pt;color:#6B6B6B;">
    Person List
</SPAN>
<SPAN STYLE="position:absolute;top:0;left:0;font-size:14pt;color:white;">
    Person List
</SPAN>
```

Notice that in this case we aren't using a style sheet to define the way the title should look. This technique is called an **in-line style**. I referred to this earlier without additional comment. I hope it makes a little more sense now that you have seen how to write the in-line style code. The combined effect of the two SPAN tags is to provide a 3D title. The first tag represents a shadow and is 2 pixels lower and further to the right than the white letters. We used to have to resort to bitmaps for even simple effects like this. Compare the file size of even a tiny bitmap with the few characters we used to achieve this effect and you will start to get a sense of just how powerful a medium this is.

Another thing that throws many developers when they see it is the #6B6B6B color references. Don't be intimidated, no one can possibly know what color all of these numbers equates to. You can use just about any decent paint program, or FrontPage, or Interdev to provide the translation for you. In most cases, all you need to do is to pick out a color with your mouse and the program will give you the hex code that equates to the color you selected. For those of you that just have to know, the first two characters represent the amount of red in the color, the second two represent the amount of green in the color and the last two characters represent the amount of blue in the color.

This means that #FFFFFF is all of the colors or white, #000000 is no color at all or black, #FF0000 is 100% red, #00FF00 is 100% green, and #0000FF is 100% blue. Everything else is some combination of those basic colors. IE can also translate between the English names of the colors as shown in the second SPAN tag.

As I said earlier, pay no attention to the code between the `<OBJECT>` tags. The total effect of all this code is simply to draw the listview control in the body of the ASP page. This code is not something you have to know how to write by hand. You can copy and paste this into notepad if you have to or you can use a tool like Interdev to write this kind of object code for you. All you need to do to write this object code with Interdev 6.0 is to drag the listview control onto the page and resize it the way you would in VB:

```
<OBJECT classid="clsid:58DA8D8A-9D6A-101B-AFC0-4210102A8DA7" id=lvwPersons
  style="HEIGHT: 445px; LEFT: 0px; TOP: 25px; WIDTH: 600px; POSITION:
  ABSOLUTE;"  width=600>
<PARAM NAME="_ExtentX" VALUE="15875">
<PARAM NAME="_ExtentY" VALUE="11774">
<PARAM NAME="SortKey" VALUE="0">
<PARAM NAME="View" VALUE="3">
<PARAM NAME="Arrange" VALUE="0">
<PARAM NAME="LabelEdit" VALUE="1">
<PARAM NAME="SortOrder" VALUE="0">
<PARAM NAME="Sorted" VALUE="0">
<PARAM NAME="MultiSelect" VALUE="0">
<PARAM NAME="LabelWrap" VALUE="-1">
<PARAM NAME="HideSelection" VALUE="-1">
<PARAM NAME="HideColumnHeaders" VALUE="0">
<PARAM NAME="OLEDragMode" VALUE="0">
<PARAM NAME="OLEDropMode" VALUE="0">
<PARAM NAME="_Version" VALUE="327682">
<PARAM NAME="ForeColor" VALUE="-2147483640">
<PARAM NAME="BackColor" VALUE="-2147483643">
<PARAM NAME="BorderStyle" VALUE="1">
<PARAM NAME="Appearance" VALUE="1">
<PARAM NAME="MousePointer" VALUE="0">
<PARAM NAME="Enabled" VALUE="1">
<PARAM NAME="NumItems" VALUE="0"></OBJECT>
```

In the last portion of this page layout section all we are doing is defining the command buttons we referred to earlier in the client-side code section. I know that it seems a little strange for us VB programmers to write the code before we draw the command buttons, but other than that everything here works pretty much the same way it does in VB:

```
<INPUT TYPE=Button VALUE="Show Deleted" ID=cmdDeleted NAME=cmdDeleted
  ONCLICK="cmdShowDeleted_Click"
  STYLE="position:absolute; height: 25px; left: 0px; top: 485px; width:100px">
</INPUT>
```

The ONCLICK = "cmdShowDeleted_Click" is really redundant. The way we have written the client-side code, we really do not need to instruct this control about what it should do when it is clicked. Other than that, the rest of the code in this section is really self-explanatory:

```
<INPUT TYPE=Button VALUE="Add" ID=cmdAdd NAME=cmdAdd
  ONCLICK="cmdAdd_Click"
  STYLE=
  "position:absolute; height: 25px; left: 105px; top: 485px; width:100px">
</INPUT>

<INPUT TYPE=Button VALUE="Edit" ID=cmdEdit NAME=cmdEdit
  ONCLICK="cmdEdit_Click"
  STYLE=
  "position:absolute; height: 25px; left: 210px; top: 485px; width: 100px">
</INPUT>
```

```
<INPUT TYPE=Button VALUE="Delete" ID=cmdDelete NAME=cmdDelete
  ONCLICK="cmdDelete_Click"
  STYLE=
  "position:absolute; height: 25px; left: 315px; top: 485px; width: 100px">
</INPUT>

<INPUT TYPE=Button VALUE="OK" ID=cmdOK NAME=cmdOK
  ONCLICK="cmdOK_Click"
  STYLE=
  "position:absolute; height: 25px; left: 500px; top: 485px; width: 100px">
</INPUT>

</BODY>
</HTML>
```

The Person Show Deleted Page

This page is really almost the same as the List page. There are really only a couple of differences. The first is that this page is designed to be called into a modal window. The second is more of logical issue. This listview will contain a list of deleted *Person* objects rather than a list of active *Person* objects.

The Declaration Section

The declaration section is almost identical to the PersonList.asp page we looked at earlier. The only difference is the addition of the blnRestore flag as shown by the highlighted line below:

```
<%@ LANGUAGE="VBSCRIPT" %>
<%  Response.Buffer = True
    Response.Expires = 0 %>

<HTML>
<HEAD>
<META NAME="GENERATOR" CONTENT="N-Tier Object Factory 6.0">
<META HTTP-EQUIV="Content-Type" CONTENT="text/html; charset=iso-8859-1">
```

```
<% strConnect = "Common"
   strStampUser = Request.QueryString("StampUser")
   strAction = Request.QueryString("Action")
   lngID = Request.QueryString("ID")
   lngTypeID = Request.QueryString("TypeID")
   blnRestore = False %>
```

This flag is used to determine whether or not an object was restored.

The Data Access Section

The data section is almost exactly the same as the `PersonList.asp` code above. We ask the server to create an object and a collection for us:

```
<%
   Set colPersons = Server.CreateObject("UCPerson.colPersons")
   Set objPerson = Server.CreateObject("UCPerson.clsPerson")
```

What is different about this code is that we are testing the `Action` parameter that was passed into the page. This parameter can have two values – an `L` which indicates that we should show a list of deleted *Persons*, and an `R` – which indicates that we should restore a *Person* from a deleted state.

If we need to display a list of deleted objects, all we need to do is to point the object at a data store, and call the `ShowDeleted` method of the *Persons* collection. In this case, we pass it a `TypeID` because we want to filter the list that is returned so that it only contains one type of deleted *Persons*:

```
Select Case strAction
   Case "L"
      colPersons.SetDataSource strConnect
      colPersons.ShowDeleted Clng(lngTypeID)
```

If we need to restore a person from a deleted state, we have to perform four steps:

- ❏ Point the object at the correct data store
- ❏ Provide the `ID` of the object that we need restored
- ❏ Call the `ObjectRestoreFromDeleted` method of the *Person* object
- ❏ Change the value of the `blnRestore` flag to true to mark the restoration

```
   Case "R"
      objPersons.SetDataSource strConnect
      objPerson.ID = lngID
      objPerson.StampUser = strStampUser
      objPerson.ObjectRestoreFromDeleted
      blnRestore = "True"
End Select
%>
```

The Style Section

This style section is identical to the one above:

```
<STYLE>
<!--

    BODY
          {
           background-color:silver;
          }
</STYLE>
```

The Client-Side Code Section

This page can perform two main functions. It can be used to display a list of deleted objects, and it can be used to handle the restoration of an object from a deleted state. The way we handle the two possibilities is apparent in the `Page_Initialize` routine. When we are going to display a list of deleted objects, the `Page_Initialize` routine is nearly identical to the standard List page above. But, if what we are doing in this page is restoring an object, we change the `Page_Initialize` routine completely.

Remember that if this page was called to restore an object, that restoration has already taken place in the server-side sction above. That means that as soon as this page has been delivered to the user we want to close the page. We do that by calling the `window.close` method in the `Page_Initialize` routine. This has the effect of closing the window as soon as the page is loaded:

```
<SCRIPT LANGUAGE=VBScript>

Sub Page_Initialize()
    <% If blnRestore = "True" Then %>
       window.close
    <% Else %>
```

If the task of this page is to display a list of deleted objects to the user, we perform essentially the same task as we did in the `PersonList.asp` file above. The only difference here is that the source of the objects is the list of deleted objects rather than the list of active object, and we add those extra columns that we normally associate with a list of deleted objects:

```
    lvwPersonsDeleted.ColumnHeaders.Add ,,"BirthDate",100
    lvwPersonsDeleted.ColumnHeaders.Add ,,"StampAction",100
    lvwPersonsDeleted.ColumnHeaders.Add ,,"FirstName",100
    lvwPersonsDeleted.ColumnHeaders.Add ,,"MiddleName",100
    lvwPersonsDeleted.ColumnHeaders.Add ,,"LastName",100
    lvwPersonsDeleted.ColumnHeaders.Add ,,"Salutation",100
    lvwPersonsDeleted.ColumnHeaders.Add ,,"Suffix",100
    lvwPersonsDeleted.ColumnHeaders.Add ,,"SSN",100
    lvwPersonsDeleted.ColumnHeaders.Add ,,"Sex",100
    lvwPersonsDeleted.ColumnHeaders.Add ,,"TypeName",100
    lvwPersonsDeleted.ColumnHeaders.Add ,,"Date Deleted",100
    lvwPersonsDeleted.ColumnHeaders.Add ,,"Deleted By User",100
    lvwPersonsDeleted.ColumnHeaders.Add ,,"Original ID",100
    lvwPersonsDeleted.ColumnHeaders.Add ,,"Audit ID",100
    lvwPersonsDeleted.View = 3 'lvwReport
```

```
       <% For each objPerson in colPersons %>
           Set objItem = lvwPersonsDeleted.ListItems.Add _
             (,"<% = objPerson.Key %>","<% = objPerson.BirthDate %>")
           objItem.SubItems(1) = "<% = objPerson.StampAction %>"
           objItem.SubItems(2) = "<% = objPerson.FirstName %>"
           objItem.SubItems(3) = "<% = objPerson.MiddleName %>"
           objItem.SubItems(4) = "<% = objPerson.LastName %>"
           objItem.SubItems(5) = "<% = objPerson.Salutation %>"
           objItem.SubItems(6) = "<% = objPerson.Suffix %>"
           objItem.SubItems(7) = "<% = objPerson.SSN %>"
           objItem.SubItems(8) = "<% = objPerson.Sex %>"
           objItem.SubItems(9) = "<% = objPerson.TypeName %>"
           objItem.SubItems(10) = "<% = objPerson.StampDateTime %>"
           objItem.SubItems(11) = "<% = objPerson.StampUser %>"
           objItem.SubItems(12) = "<% = objPerson.StampID %>"
           objItem.SubItems(13) = "<% = objPerson.ID %>"
       <% Next %>
       <% End If %>
    End Sub
```

The `lvwPersonsDeleted_ColumnClick` is practically identical to the `lvwPersons_ColumnClick` above:

```
    Sub lvwPersonsDeleted_ColumnClick(ColumnHeader)

        lvwPersonsDeleted.SortKey = ColumnHeader.Index - 1
        lvwPersonsDeleted.Sorted = True
        If lvwPersonsDeleted.SortOrder = 1 Then
          lvwPersonsDeleted.SortOrder = 0
        Else
          lvwPersonsDeleted.SortOrder = 1
        End If
        lvwPersonsDeleted.Refresh

    End Sub
```

If the user clicks the **Close** button, we just call the `window.close` method. We don't return any value, so the calling page will not be reloaded:

```
    Sub cmdClose_Click()
        window.close
    End Sub
```

If the user clicks the **Restore** button, then we call the page we are on, but we pass it an `Action` parameter value of R for restore. This causes the `PersonShowDeleted.asp` page to be executed, the selected object to be restored, and the window for the second version of the page to close as soon as it opens. This returns control to this original page, which also closes but only after it has sent the value `"Restored"` back to the calling `PersonList.asp` page above. Remember that if the length of the return value is greater than zero, then the `PersonList.asp` page will refresh itself:

```
Sub cmdRestore_Click()

    strAddress = "PersonShowDeleted.asp?Action=R&ID=" & _
      Right(lvwPersonsDeleted.SelectedItem.Key, _
      Len(lvwPersonsDeleted.SelectedItem.Key) - 3) & _
      "&StampUser=<% = strStampUser %>&TypeID=<% = lngTypeID %>"
    strReturn=window.showModalDialog(strAddress)
    window.returnValue = "Restored"
    window.close

End Sub
```

The lvwPersonsDeleted_DblClick just gives the users another way to invoke the *Restore From Deleted* process:

```
Sub lvwPersonsDeleted_DblClick()
    cmdRestore_Click
End Sub
```

```
</SCRIPT>
</HEAD>
```

The Page Layout Section

This portion of the page is nearly identical to the PersonList.asp treatment above:

```
<BODY LANGUAGE = VBScript ONLOAD="Page_Initialize">

<OBJECT classid="clsid:58DA8D8A-9D6A-101B-AFC0-4210102A8DA7"
    height=440 id=lvwPersonsDeleted
    style="HEIGHT: 392px; LEFT: 0px; TOP: 0px; WIDTH: 498px" width=498>
 <PARAM NAME="_ExtentX" VALUE="13176">
 <PARAM NAME="_ExtentY" VALUE="11642">
 <PARAM NAME="SortKey" VALUE="0">
 <PARAM NAME="View" VALUE="3">
 <PARAM NAME="Arrange" VALUE="0">
 <PARAM NAME="LabelEdit" VALUE="1">
 <PARAM NAME="SortOrder" VALUE="0">
 <PARAM NAME="Sorted" VALUE="0">
 <PARAM NAME="MultiSelect" VALUE="0">
 <PARAM NAME="LabelWrap" VALUE="-1">
 <PARAM NAME="HideSelection" VALUE="-1">
 <PARAM NAME="HideColumnHeaders" VALUE="0">
 <PARAM NAME="OLEDragMode" VALUE="0">
 <PARAM NAME="OLEDropMode" VALUE="0">
 <PARAM NAME="_Version" VALUE="327682">
 <PARAM NAME="ForeColor" VALUE="-2147483640">
 <PARAM NAME="BackColor" VALUE="-2147483643">
 <PARAM NAME="BorderStyle" VALUE="1">
 <PARAM NAME="Appearance" VALUE="1">
 <PARAM NAME="MousePointer" VALUE="0">
 <PARAM NAME="Enabled" VALUE="1">
 <PARAM NAME="NumItems" VALUE="0"></OBJECT>
```

```
<INPUT TYPE=Button VALUE="Restore" ID=cmdRestore NAME=cmdRestore
    ONCLICK="cmdRestore_Click"
    STYLE=
    "position:absolute; height: 25px; left: 20px; top: 420px; width: 100px">
</INPUT>
<INPUT TYPE=Button VALUE="Close" ID=cmdClose NAME=cmdClose
    ONCLICK="cmdClose_Click"
    STYLE=
    "position:absolute; height: 25px; left: 378px; top: 420px; width: 100px">
</INPUT>

</BODY>
</HTML>
```

The Person Detail Page

The Person Detail page is virtually identical to the VB Person Detail form. The only difference is that, like with the `PersonList.asp` page above - rather than morphing the page to display an audit history for an object - a second, modal dialog page is used to display this information.

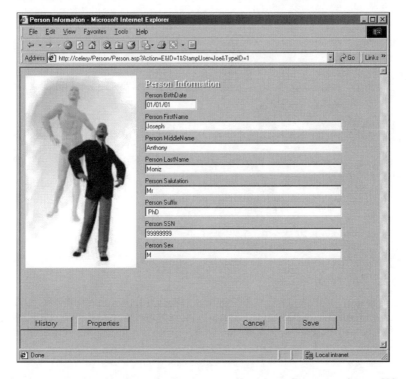

Open up the `Person.asp` file from the `\wwwroot\Person` directory of your IIS machine. You will notice right away that this file is quite a bit longer than the other two files we looked at earlier. That is, in part, because this same page is used to carry out just about every method that can be performed with an individual Enterprise Caliber Data Object.

The Declaration Section

The first few lines of the declaration section are the same as the other ASP files we have looked at earlier:

```
<%@ LANGUAGE="VBSCRIPT" %>
<%
    Response.Buffer = True
    Response.Expires = 0
%>

<HTML>
<HEAD>
<META NAME="GENERATOR" CONTENT="N-Tier Object Factory 6.0">
<META HTTP-EQUIV="Content-Type" CONTENT="text/html; charset=iso-8859-1">
```

The only real difference in the Declaration section is the shear number of parameters that have been or can be passed into the page. Notice that this page also has a flag that indicates whether or not the page will be used to restore an object:

```
<% On Error Resume Next
    strConnect = "Common"
    strStampUser =  Request.QueryString("StampUser")
    blnRestored = False
    strAction = Request.QueryString("Action")
    lngAuditID = Request.QueryString("AuditID")
    lngOriginalID = Request.QueryString("OriginalID")
    lngID = Request.QueryString("ID")
    lngTypeID = Request.QueryString("TypeID")
    dtmBirthDate = Request.QueryString("BirthDate")
    strDataMessage = Request.QueryString("DataMessage")
    strFirstName = Request.QueryString("FirstName")
    strMiddleName = Request.QueryString("MiddleName")
    strLastName = Request.QueryString("LastName")
    strSalutation = Request.QueryString("Salutation")
    strSuffix = Request.QueryString("Suffix")
    strSSN = Request.QueryString("SSN")
    strSex = Request.QueryString("Sex")
    strTypeName = Request.QueryString("TypeName")
%>
```

The Data Access Section

The most complex portion of this page may be the data access section that follows. As we covered much earlier in this chapter, we use a single Select Case statement here to handle quite a few different processes. The key that we use to decide which process to execute is found in the Action parameter that is passed into the page in the QueryString:

```
<%
Select Case strAction
```

The first possibility that is handled is that this object may be a completely new object. In that case, we just ask the server to create a new empty *Person* object. Then we change the value of the `Action` parameter to `"A"` so that if the user fills in the values and calls this page again with the new values, we will execute the code in the second branch of this `Case` statement. Also note that we are setting the `strNew` variable's value to `"Y"`. Remember from the Person Detail VB form that we need to make sure that the object's base properties have been saved before we can allow a user to supply value for the extended properties. This `strNew` variable is the flag that tells us not to let the user save extended properties for this unsaved object:

```
Case "N" ' new
    strAction = "A"
    Set objPerson = Server.CreateObject("UCPerson.clsPerson")
    strNew = "Y"
```

In this next branch, we are actually adding a new object's data to the data store. This is nearly identical the standard VB treatment. All we really need to do is to create a new object, point the object to a particular data store, provide values for all of the properties, and call the `ObjectInsert` method:

```
Case "A" ' add
    Set objPerson = Server.CreateObject("UCPerson.clsPerson")
    objPerson.SetDataSource strConnect
    objPerson.StampUser = strStampuser
    objPerson.ID = lngID
    objPerson.TypeID = lngTypeID
    objPerson.BirthDate = dtmBirthDate
    objPerson.DataMessage = strDataMessage
    objPerson.FirstName = strFirstName
    objPerson.MiddleName = strMiddleName
    objPerson.LastName = strLastName
    objPerson.Salutation = strSalutation
    objPerson.Suffix = strSuffix
    objPerson.SSN = strSSN
    objPerson.Sex = strSex
    objPerson.TypeName = strTypeName
    objPerson.ObjectInsert
```

Once that has been done, we set the object to `Nothing`. This allows the same object to be recycled sooner:

```
set objPerson = Nothing
```

The next step illustrates a new concept. We have already used the `Response` object several times before. In the previous cases, we used it to change the information in the header of the page (response) that we were sending back to the user. Specifically, we placed information into the header that instructed the browser not to cache the page, but to download a new copy each time the user requested the page. This time we are going to let our response to the user's request be an entirely different page. We are going to redirect the user to another page instead of delivering the page the user requested. We do that by employing the `Redirect` method of the `Response` object as shown below:

```
Response.Redirect "PersonList.asp?StampUser=" & _
    strStampUser & "&TypeID=" &lngTypeID
```

If `strAction` contained the value `"E"` then this means that the user has asked us to retrieve an object so that the user can view and potentially change that object. In this case, all we need to do is to invoke the `ObjectFetch` routine of the *Person* object. We also take the time to change the value of the `strAction` variable to `"U"`. This will enable us to execute the code in the update branch if the user changes and then saves this object:

```
Case "E" 'edit
    strAction = "U"
    Set objPerson = Server.CreateObject("UCPerson.clsPerson")
    objPerson.SetDataSource strConnect
    objPerson.ObjectFetch, Clng(lngID), Clng(lngTypeID)
```

This is a third level object, so in addition to loading the base set of properties with the `ObjectFetch` routine, we also need to load the additional properties for this *Person*. In order to do that, all we do is point the object at a particular data store, and call the `PropBag`'s `Load` method:

```
    Set objProp = Server.CreateObject("UCPerson.clsPropBag")
    Set PropBag = Server.CreateObject("UCPerson.colPropBags")
    PropBag.SetDataSource strConnect
    PropBag.Load Clng(lngID), Clng(lngTypeID), Cstr(strStampUser)
```

If the `strAction` parameter contained the value `"U"` for update, then this means the user has changed the object's values and that we should perform an update. In order to do this, we create a new empty object, fetch the object the user wants to change, update the object's values with the changed values, and then call the object's `ObjectUpdate` method:

```
Case "U" 'Update
    Set objPerson = Server.CreateObject("UCPerson.clsPerson")
    objPerson.SetDataSource strConnect
    objPerson.ObjectFetch, Clng(lngID), Clng(lngTypeID)
    objPerson.SaveID = objPerson.ID
    objPerson.ID = lngID
    objPerson.SaveTypeID = objPerson.TypeID
    objPerson.TypeID = lngTypeID
    objPerson.SaveBirthDate = objPerson.BirthDate
    objPerson.BirthDate = dtmBirthDate
    objPerson.SaveFirstName = objPerson.FirstName
    objPerson.FirstName = strFirstName
    objPerson.SaveMiddleName = objPerson.MiddleName
    objPerson.MiddleName = strMiddleName
    objPerson.SaveLastName = objPerson.LastName
    objPerson.LastName = strLastName
    objPerson.SaveSalutation = objPerson.Salutation
    objPerson.Salutation = strSalutation
    objPerson.SaveSuffix = objPerson.Suffix
    objPerson.Suffix = strSuffix
    objPerson.SaveSSN = objPerson.SSN
    objPerson.SSN = strSSN
    objPerson.SaveSex = objPerson.Sex
    objPerson.Sex = strSex
    objPerson.SaveTypeName = objPerson.TypeName
    objPerson.TypeName = strTypeName
    objPerson.StampUser = strStampUser
    objPerson.ObjectUpdate
```

Notice that when after we have performed an `ObjectUpdate` that we redirect the user back to the List page. This will have the effect of refreshing the List page. The updated values in the data store will then be visible on the user's screen:

```
Response.Redirect "PersonList.asp?StampUser=" & _
    strStampUser & "&TypeID=" & lngTypeID
```

If the `strAction` parameter contains the value `"D"` for delete then we create a new object, point it at a particular data store and fetch the object that user wants to delete. Then we tell the object who wants to delete it, and we call the `ObjectDelete` method:

```
Case "D" ' delete
    Set objPerson = Server.CreateObject("UCPerson.clsPerson")
    objPerson.SetDataSource strConnect
    objPerson.ID = lngID
    objPerson.ObjectFetch, Clng(lngID), Clng(lngTypeID)
    objPerson.StampUser = strStampUser
    objPerson.ObjectDelete
```

Notice that when we delete an object that we redirect the user to back to the List page. This has the effect of refreshing the List page. The updated values in the data store will then be visible to the user. The deleted object will not be visible unless the user presses the Show Deleted button.

```
Response.Redirect "PersonList.asp?StampUser=" & _
    strStampUser & "&TypeID=" & lngTypeID
```

If the `strAction` parameter contains the value `"R"` for restore, then we ask the server to create two new *Person* objects. Then we fetch the *Person* object from the data store that represents the current object. Once we have that object, we use it to retrieve a complete history for that object. We iterate through that history until we find the snapshot that the user selected. When we find it, we replace the current object with the snapshot object. Finally, we set the `strAction` parameter value to `"U"` so that the user can save the changes:

```
Case "R" 'restore
    Set objPerson = Server.CreateObject("UCPerson.clsPerson")
    Set objThis = Server.CreateObject("UCPerson.clsPerson")
    objPerson.SetDataSource strConnect
    objPerson.ObjectFetch, Clng(lngOriginalID), Clng(lngTypeID)
    Set colPersons = objPerson.ObjectAuditHistory
    For each objThis in colPersons
        If objThis.ID = Clng(lngAuditID) Then
            Set objPerson = objThis
            Exit For
        End If
    Next
    strAction = "U"
    blnRestored = True
End Select
%>
```

The Style Section

The Style section for the Detail page is really quite rich when we compare it to the other pages we have worked with so far. In particular, it has four new display classes that are used to give us functionality similar to the tab control in VB. Those classes are PropertySetVisible, PropertySetNotVisible, GeneralVisible, and GeneralNotVisible.

```
<TITLE>Person Information</TITLE>
<STYLE>
<!--

    BODY
         {
          background-color:silver;
         }
    .Label
         {
          font-family:MS Sans Serif;
          font-size:9pt;
         }
    .InputBox
         {
          font-family:MS Sans Serif;
          font-size:9pt;
         }
```

Notice that the only difference between PropertySetVisible and PropertySetNotVisible is the visibility property. Thanks to these two classes, we can toggle between a visible and invisible property set by just changing the class's name:

```
.PropertySetVisible
     {
      position:absolute;
      top:20;
      left:240;
      height:400;
      width:380;
      background-color:silver;
      visibility:visible;
     }

.PropertySetNotVisible
     {
      position:absolute;
      top:20;
      left:240;
      height:400;
      width:380;
      background-color:silver;
      visibility:hidden;
     }
```

Take the time to notice the similarity between GeneralVisible and GeneralNotVisible and the PropertySetVisible and PropertySetNotVisible. Once again, the only differrence between the two is the visibility property. Thanks to these two classes, we can toggle between a visible and invisible General Property Set by just changing the class's name:

```
.GeneralVisible
    {
    position:absolute;
    top:20;
    left:240;
    height:400;
    width:380;
    background-color:silver;
    visibility:visible;
    }

.GeneralNotVisible
    {
    position:absolute;
    top:20;
    left:240;
    height:400;
    width:380;
    background-color:silver;
    visibility:hidden;
    }
-->
</STYLE>
```

The Client-Side Code Section

Again, as with the server-side data access section above, the client-side code for the Detail form is far more complex than the other client side code we have used previously:

This subroutine is a general routine that is not connected to any particular control. It is used, as the name suggests, to parse the string that is returned from the modal dialog window. The code is self-explanatory. It is no different than code we might write in a standard VB code module:

```
<SCRIPT LANGUAGE=VBScript>

Sub ParseReturnString(strIn, strOut, lngPosition)
    strParseReturnString = ""
    For i = lngPosition To Len(strIn)
      strChar = mid(strIn, i, 1)
      If strChar <> "|" Then
        strParseReturnString = strParseReturnString & strChar
      Else
        Exit For
      End If
    Next
    strOut = strParseReturnString
    lngPosition = i
End Sub
```

The code that is executed when the cmdHistory button is clicked is kind of like the cmdShowDeleted subroutine we looked at earlier. We are using a modal dialog window in this case to retrieve a list of snapshots of an object instead of retrieving a list of deleted objects. Besides the different list of objects, we also do something a little different with the string that the modal dialog presents us after it has completed its task:

```
Sub cmdHistory_Click()
    lngID = document.all("txtPersonID").Value
    strAddress = "PersonObjectHistory.asp?ID=" & lngID & _
        "&StampUser=<% = strStampUser %>&TypeID=<% = lngTypeID %>"
    strReturn = window.ShowModalDialog(strAddress, MyDialog, "")
```

If the length of the string is greater than zero, then we use call the `ParseReturnString` routine from above to extract the values from the return string. In this case we are expecting two values, so we call the `ParseReturnString` twice. This gives us the two values we were expecting:

```
If Len(strReturn) <> 0 Then
    lngStartValue = 2
    ParseReturnString strReturn, strValue, lngStartValue
    lngStartValue = lngStartValue + 1
    lngAuditID = strValue
    strValue = ""

    ParseReturnString strReturn, strValue, lngStartValue
    lngStartValue = lngStartValue + 1
    lngOriginalID = strValue
    strValue = ""
```

Once we have those values (`lngAuditID` and `lngOriginalValue`), we can call this same page with these values. We also need to set the value of the `Action` parameter to `"R"` for restore:

```
strAddress = "Person.Asp?Action=R&AuditID=" & lngAuditID & _
    "&OriginalID=" & lngOriginalID & _
    "&StampUser=<% = strStampUser %>&TypeID= <% = lngTypeID %>"
```

After we have built the address string, all we need to do is to call the `window.navigate` method to call this page recursively:

```
    window.navigate strAddress
    End if
End Sub
```

If the user clicks the Cancel button, then we just replace this page with the `PersonList.asp` page, refreshing that page in the process:

```
Sub cmdCancel_Click()
    strAddress = "PersonList.asp?StampUser=<% = strStampUser %>&TypeID=" & _
        "<% = lngTypeID %>"
    window.navigate strAddress
End Sub
```

This is the section of code that we use to emulate the VB tab control. When the user clicks on the `cmdProperties` button, we either make the Properties or General tab visible and make the remaining one invisible. We also take this time to change the name on the button to reflect the current state:

```
Sub cmdProperties_Click()
   If document.all("Properties").ClassName = "PropertySetVisible" Then
      document.all("Properties").ClassName = "PropertySetNotVisible"
      document.all("General").ClassName = "GeneralVisible"
      document.all("cmdProperties").Value = "Properties"
      document.all("cmdHistory").Style.Visibility = "visible"
      document.all("cmdSave").Style.Visibility = "visible"
   Else
      document.all("Properties").ClassName = "PropertySetVisible"
      document.all("General").ClassName = "GeneralNotVisible"
      document.all("cmdProperties").Value = "General Info"
      document.all("cmdHistory").Style.Visibility = "hidden"
      document.all("cmdSave").Style.Visibility = "hidden"
   End If
End Sub
```

When the user clicks the cmdSave button, we take the values from the input controls on the form and place them into variables. Then we use those variables to create an address string:

```
Sub cmdSave_Click()
   lngID = document.all("txtPersonID").Value
   dtmBirthDate = Trim(document.all("txtBirthDate").Value)
   strFirstName = Trim(document.all("txtFirstName").Value)
   strMiddleName = Trim(document.all("txtMiddleName").Value)
   strLastName = Trim(document.all("txtLastName").Value)
   strSalutation = Trim(document.all("txtSalutation").Value)
   strSuffix = Trim(document.all("txtSuffix").Value)
   strSSN = Trim(document.all("txtSSN").Value)
   strSex = Trim(document.all("txtSex").Value)
   strAddress = "Person.ASP?Action=<% = strAction %>" & _
      "&ID=" & lngID & _
      "&BirthDate=" & dtmBirthDate & _
      "&StampAction=" & strStampAction & _
      "&FirstName=" & strFirstName & _
      "&MiddleName=" & strMiddleName & _
      "&LastName=" & strLastName & _
      "&Salutation=" & strSalutation & _
      "&Suffix=" & strSuffix & _
      "&SSN=" & strSSN & _
      "&Sex=" & strSex & _
      "&TypeID=<% = lngTypeID %>" & _
      "&TypeName=<% = strTypeName %>" & _
      "&StampUser=<% = strStampUser %>"
```

Once the address string has been constructed, we just call this same page with the new values:

```
   window.navigate strAddress
End Sub
```

The Page_Initialize routine for this page is really very much like the ones we looked at earlier. The only difference here is that we execute another subroutine, the TestExistance subroutine, at the end of the Page_Initialize routine:

```
Sub Page_Initialize()
    lvwProperties.ColumnHeaders.Add ,,"Property Name",100
    lvwProperties.ColumnHeaders.Add ,,"Property Value",220
    lvwProperties.ColumnHeaders.Add , ,"ID", 20
    lvwProperties.View = 3 ' lvwReport
    <% For Each objProp in PropBag %>
            Set objListItem = lvwProperties.ListItems.Add _
            (,"<% = objProp.Key %>", "<% = objProp.PropertyName %>")
            objListItem.Subitems(1) = "<% = objProp.Value %>"
            objListItem.SubItems(2) = "<% = objProp.ID %>"
    <% Next %>
    TestExistance
End Sub
```

If the user double-clicks on the Property listview, we need to give the user a way to edit the property that he or she has selected. This means that we need to raise a modal dialog box just like we did with the standard VB treatment:

```
Sub lvwProperties_DblClick()
    txtPropertyName.value = lvwProperties.SelectedItem.Text
    lngPropertyID = Right(lvwProperties.SelectedItem.Key, _
                Len(lvwProperties.SelectedItem.Key) - 3)
    If Clng(lngPropertyID) > 0 Then
        strAddress = "PersonPropertyValue.asp?PropertyID=" & lngPropertyID & _
                "&ID=<% = lngID %>" & _
                "&TypeID=<% = lngTypeID %>" & _
                "&StampUser=<% = strStampUser %>"
        strFeatures = "dialogWidth=500px;dialogHeight=300px;"
        strResponse =  window.showModalDialog(strAddress,"ModalDialog", _
                "dialogWidth=500px;dialogHeight=300px;")
```

Once we recover strResponse from the modal dialog box, then we need to extract the value (if one exists) from this string and update the current value in the listview:

```
        If Left(strResponse,3) = "OK~" Then
            strResponse = Right(strResponse, Len(strResponse) - 3)
            For Each objItem In lvwProperties.ListItems
              If objItem.Key = "Key" & lngPropertyID Then
                  objItem.SubItems(1) = strResponse
              End If
            Next
        End If
    End If
End Sub
```

The following is just the standard sort routine that allows the user to sort a listview by the clicking on the columnheader:

```
Sub lvwProperties_ColumnClick(ColumnHeader)
    lvwProperties.SortKey = ColumnHeader.Index - 1
    lvwProperties.Sorted = True
    If lvwProperties.SortOrder = 1 Then
        lvwProperties.SortOrder = 0
    Else
        lvwProperties.SortOrder = 1
    End If
        lvwProperties.Refresh
End Sub
```

The following is an example of using the `window.event.keyCode` property to limit the keystrokes that can be entered into a text box:

```
Sub txtBirthDate_OnKeyPress()
    intKeyAscii=window.event.keyCode
    Select Case CLng(intKeyAscii)
        Case 48, 49, 50, 51, 52, 53, 54, 55, 56, 57 ' Numbers 0 - 9
        Case 47 ' Forward Slash "/"
        Case Else
            window.event.keyCode=0
    End Select
End Sub
```

This is an example of using the `OnBlur` event (this equates to the VB `LostFocus` event) to perform some rudimentary data validation:

```
Sub txtBirthDate_OnBlur()
    strTextBoxValue=document.all("txtBirthDate").value
    If IsDate(strTextBoxValue) Then
        document.all("txtBirthDate").value=CDate _
            (document.all("txtBirthDate").value)
        TestExistance
    ElseIf Len(strTextBoxValue)=0 Then
    Else
        MsgBox document.all("txtBirthDate").value & " is not a valid date."
        document.all("txtBirthDate").focus
    End If
End Sub
```

The following subroutine is used to perform some rudimentary data validation on the client. It just checks to make sure that each of the required inputs has been given a value. If we couple this routine with the keypress and `onBlur` routines from above, we can quite a powerful data validation machine right at the user interface. This should not be used to enforce business rules, but it is a lot more efficient to perform these simple data validation tests at the client. The effect of this subroutine is to enable or disable the save, history and property buttons:

```
Sub TestExistance()
    If _
      Len(Trim(document.all("txtBirthDate").Value)) = 0 Or _
      Len(Trim(document.all("txtFirstName").Value)) = 0 Or _
      Len(Trim(document.all("txtMiddleName").Value)) = 0 Or _
      Len(Trim(document.all("txtLastName").Value)) = 0 Or _
      Len(Trim(document.all("txtSalutation").Value)) = 0 Or _
      Len(Trim(document.all("txtSuffix").Value)) = 0 Or _
      Len(Trim(document.all("txtSSN").Value)) = 0 Or _
      Len(Trim(document.all("txtSex").Value)) = 0 Or Then
        cmdSave.disabled = True
        cmdHistory.disabled = True
        cmdProperties.disabled = True
    ElseIf UCase(Trim("<% = strAction %>")) = "A" Then
        cmdSave.disabled = False
        cmdHistory.disabled = True
        cmdProperties.disabled = True
    Else
```

```
            cmdSave.disabled = False
            cmdHistory.disabled = False
            cmdProperties.disabled = False
        End If
End Sub
```

```
</SCRIPT>
```

The Page Layout Section

As usual, we begin the Page Layout section with the following line:

```
<BODY LANGUAGE = "VBScript" ONLOAD = "Page_Initialize">
```

This is used to display a simple image to the left of the textboxes as shown in the image above:

```
        <IMG Src = "../Images/SilverProject1.jpg">
```

The following is used to create a division to hold the Property listview. Notice that at first the Property listview is hidden. It will only be displayed if the user clicks on the **Properties** button.

```
<DIV CLASS=PropertySetNotVisible ID=Properties>

  <SPAN STYLE="position:absolute;top:2;left:2;font-size:14pt;color:#6B6B6B;">
    Person Property Information
  </SPAN>

  <SPAN STYLE="position:absolute;top:0;left:0;font-size:14pt;color:white;">
    Person Property Information
  </SPAN>
```

This is the Property listview. I have eliminated some of the parameters for the sake of brevity. They are identical to the ones we saw above:

```
<OBJECT classid=clsid:58DA8D8A-9D6A-101B-AFC0-4210102A8DA7 height=400
  id=lvwProperties
  style="position:absolute; HEIGHT: 350px; LEFT: 0px; TOP: 25px;" & _
        "WIDTH: 400px" width=428 VIEWASTEXT>
  <PARAM NAME="NumItems" VALUE="0">
  .... Other Parameters
  <PARAM NAME="NumItems" VALUE="0">
</OBJECT>
</DIV>
```

If this object is in the process of being restored, then we need to keep track of the object's original ID. If not, then we need to keep track of the object's current ID. This `If` block creates the correct input control:

```
      <% If blnRestored Then %>
        <INPUT TYPE = Hidden ID=txtPersonID VALUE=<% = lngOriginalID %> ></INPUT>
      <% Else %>
        <INPUT TYPE = Hidden ID=txtPersonID VALUE=<% = objPerson.ID %> ></INPUT>
      <% End If %>

      <INPUT TYPE = Hidden ID=txtPropertyName VALUE = ""></INPUT>
      <INPUT Type = Hidden ID=txtPropertyValue VALUE = ""></INPUT>
```

The following division is used to contain the base set of properties for the *Person* object. This division, in conjunction with the property listview division above, enables the user to switch between the base and extended properties with the click of a single button. This action emulates the VB tab control without the additional overhead. Notice that the General or base property division has been set to visible:

```
<DIV CLASS=GeneralVisible ID=General>
    <SPAN STYLE="position:absolute;top:2;left:2;font-size:14pt;color:#6B6B6B;">
        Person Information
    </SPAN>
    <SPAN STYLE="position:absolute;top:0;left:0;font-size:14pt;color:white;">
        Person Information
    </SPAN>
```

I prefer to use a variable to set the relative heights of each input control. What I do is to use the i variable to position the labels for each control and the j variable to position the textboxes (or combo boxes etc). At first this practice may seem rather bizarre, but it does make it very easy to reposition a lot of controls in a very short period of time. For example if we wanted to move everything down 10 pixels, all we would have to do is to add change the two lines below that are used to initialize the i and j variables:

```
<% i = 25 %>
<% j = 40 %>
```

The <SPAN> tags that are used in this section provide labels for the input controls:

```
<SPAN CLASS=Label STYLE="position:absolute;top:<% = i %>;left:0;">
    Person BirthDate
</SPAN>
```

The first input control in each section contains the value of the current object:

```
<INPUT CLASS=InputBox ID=txtBirthDate TYPE=Text
    STYLE="position:absolute;top:<% = j %>;left:0;width:100;"
    VALUE = "<% = objPerson.BirthDate %>" >
</INPUT>
```

The second input control in each section is used to store the save values for collision handling purposes:

```
<INPUT TYPE = Hidden ID=txtSaveBirthDate VALUE="<% = objPerson.BirthDate %>" >
</INPUT>
```

The remainder of the code in this section is used to place the rest of the textboxes on the screen. It is handled exactly the same way as those sections we looked at above:

```
<% i = i + 40 %>
<% j = j + 40 %>
<SPAN CLASS=Label STYLE="position:absolute;top:<% = i %>;left:0;">
    Person FirstName
</SPAN>
<INPUT CLASS=InputBox ID=txtFirstName TYPE=Text
```

```
          STYLE="position:absolute;top:<% = j %>;left:0;width:380;"
          VALUE = "<% = objPerson.FirstName %>" >
</INPUT>
<INPUT TYPE = Hidden ID=txtSaveFirstName
      VALUE="<% = objPerson.FirstName %>" >
</INPUT>
<% i = i + 40 %>
<% j = j + 40 %>
<SPAN CLASS=Label STYLE="position:absolute;top:<% = i %>;left:0;">
      Person MiddleName
</SPAN>
<INPUT CLASS=InputBox ID=txtMiddleName TYPE=Text
      STYLE="position:absolute;top:<% = j %>;left:0;width:380;"
      VALUE = "<% = objPerson.MiddleName %>" >
</INPUT>
<INPUT TYPE = Hidden ID=txtSaveMiddleName
      VALUE="<% = objPerson.MiddleName %>" >
</INPUT>
<% i = i + 40 %>
<% j = j + 40 %>
<SPAN CLASS=Label STYLE="position:absolute;top:<% = i %>;left:0;">
      Person LastName
</SPAN>
<INPUT CLASS=InputBox ID=txtLastName TYPE=Text
      STYLE="position:absolute;top:<% = j %>;left:0;width:380;"
      VALUE = "<% = objPerson.LastName %>" >
</INPUT>
<INPUT TYPE = Hidden ID=txtSaveLastName VALUE="<% = objPerson.LastName %>" >
</INPUT>
<% i = i + 40 %>
<% j = j + 40 %>
<SPAN CLASS=Label STYLE="position:absolute;top:<% = i %>;left:0;">
      Person Salutation
</SPAN>
<INPUT CLASS=InputBox ID=txtSalutation TYPE=Text
      STYLE="position:absolute;top:<% = j %>;left:0;width:380;"
      VALUE = "<% = objPerson.Salutation %>" >
</INPUT>
<INPUT TYPE = Hidden ID=txtSaveSalutation
      VALUE="<% = objPerson.Salutation %>" >
</INPUT>
<% i = i + 40 %>
<% j = j + 40 %>
<SPAN CLASS=Label STYLE="position:absolute;top:<% = i %>;left:0;">
      Person Suffix
</SPAN>
<INPUT CLASS=InputBox ID=txtSuffix TYPE=Text
      STYLE="position:absolute;top:<% = j %>;left:0;width:380;"
      VALUE = "<% = objPerson.Suffix %>" >
</INPUT>
<INPUT Type = Hidden ID=txtSaveSuffix Value="<% = objPerson.Suffix %>" >
</INPUT>
<% i = i + 40 %>
<% j = j + 40 %>
<SPAN CLASS=Label STYLE="position:absolute;top:<% = i %>;left:0;">
      Person SSN
</SPAN>
<INPUT CLASS=InputBox ID=txtSSN TYPE=Text
      STYLE="position:absolute;top:<% = j %>;left:0;width:380;"
      VALUE = "<% = objPerson.SSN %>" >
```

```
</INPUT>
<INPUT TYPE = Hidden ID=txtSaveSSN VALUE="<% = objPerson.SSN %>" >
</INPUT>
<% i = i + 40 %>
<% j = j + 40 %>
<SPAN CLASS=Label STYLE="position:absolute;top:<% = i %>;left:0;">
    Person Sex
</SPAN>
<INPUT CLASS=InputBox ID=txtSex TYPE=Text
    STYLE="position:absolute;top:<% = j %>;left:0;width:380;"
    VALUE = "<% = objPerson.Sex %>" >
</INPUT>
<INPUT TYPE = Hidden ID=txtSaveSex VALUE="<% = objPerson.Sex %>" >
</INPUT>
<% i = i + 40 %>
<% j = j + 40 %>
</DIV>

<INPUT TYPE=Button VALUE="Save" ID=cmdSave NAME=cmdSave
  ONCLICK="cmdSave_Click"
  STYLE=
  "position:absolute; height: 25px; left: 510px; top: 465px; width:100px">
</INPUT>
<INPUT TYPE=Button VALUE="Cancel" ID=cmdCancel NAME=cmdCancel
  ONCLICK="cmdCancel_Click"
  STYLE=
  "position:absolute; height: 25px; left: 400px; top: 465px; width: 100px">
</INPUT>
<INPUT TYPE=Button VALUE="Properties" ID=cmdProperties NAME=cmdProperties
  ONCLICK="cmdProperties_Click"
  STYLE=
  "position:absolute; height: 25px; left: 110px; top: 465px; width: 100px">
</INPUT>
<INPUT TYPE=Button VALUE="History" ID=cmdHistory NAME=cmdHistory
  ONCLICK="cmdHistory_Click"
  STYLE=
  "position:absolute; height: 25px; left: 0px; top: 465px; width: 100px">
</INPUT>

</BODY>
<% set objPerson = Nothing %>
</HTML>
```

Summary

In this chapter we worked our way through an awful lot of ASP code. Specifically, we looked at:

- ❑ Dynamically created HTML
- ❑ Dynamic HTML
- ❑ Style sheets
- ❑ The `Request` object
- ❑ The `Response` object
- ❑ The `window` object

Finally, we saw how to combine all these elements into a fully functional ASP version of our VB forms.

I wish I had more space to give this subject the treatment it deserves, but there is enough information in this chapter to allow you work with the ASP code that the Object Factory creates for each data object.

And that's it. It's taken some time and we've come a long, long way from Chapter 1. I hope you didn't get lost, at least not too many times, along the way. I know we covered some pretty treacherous ground at times but I think you'll agree the end result was worth it. At the moment you may not realize what we have actually managed to achieve. It will probably take a bit of time to sink in. I think once you've had a bit of time to play around with the code and the sample applications you will be begin to get a better idea of the potential of what you've just learnt.

At this point, I think this is the best thing that I can recommend you do. It's only by experimenting with different techniques that you can actually learn how to do things. Way back at the beginning of the book, I talked about not knowing anything until you try it, well I hope now you'll be able to adopt the same philosophy. Remember if you believe it can be done then anything's possible.

Good Luck!

{831FDD16-0C5C-1...

Form frmPropNameControlList

Style = 3 'Fixed Dial...

= "Properties for...

eight = 4845

eft = 45

p = 330

idth = 11460

c = "Form1"

ton = 0 'False

d = -1 'True

con = 0 'False

eight = 4845

dth = 11460

askbar = 0 'False

Person
Base Properties

- ID
- Last Name
- First Name
- Middle Name
- Birth Date
- Sex

Object Type Definitions

Lawyer OTD	Lawyer OTD	Engineer OTD	Doctor OTD	Student OTD
	Specialty	Specialty	Specialty	Major
	Hourly Rate	Experience	Certification	Minor
	Law School	Property 3	Property 3	Year
	Property 4	Property 4	Property 4	Property 4
	Property 5	Property 5	Property 5	Property 5
	Property 6	Property 6	Property 6	Property 6
	Property 7	Property 7	Property 7	Property 7
	Property 8	Property 8	Property 8	Property 8
	Property 9	Property 9	Property 9	Property 9
	Property 10	Property 10	Property 10	Property 10

Property Set Definitions

The Code in this Book

The Downloadable Source Code

All the code in this book, including some extra goodies can be found for download at the Wrox web site: www.wrox.com. You will find several options for file downloads. You can download:

❑ All the sample code found in the chapters of this book
❑ Additional sample code for things like the Contact-Information Application
❑ The Object Factory

There will be more precise instructions for running the various code samples and applications with the downloads but here's some general information you need to get started.

Setting up the Code

The sample code in this book, and the Object Factory below both assume that you have either SQL Server 6.5 or 7.0 installed somewhere on your site. Further, both also assume that you have a database available on that server named **Common**.

Here are the steps you need to follow to create this database in SQL Server 6.5:

1. Open SQL Enterprise Manager.

2. Right-click on the Database Devices node in the treeview in Enterprise Manager. Select the New Device... option from the pop-up menu.

3. Create a New Database Device – I use the name CommonData for mine. Specify the amount of space you will require. I would make this at least 10 megs for the samples in this book.

4. Optionally, you can also create another Database Device to contain the Log files if you want to. If you do, a good name for this Device might be CommonLog. This Device can be smaller than the Data Device.

5. Right-click on the Database node in the treeview in Enteprise Manager. Select the New Database... option from the pop-up menu

6. Type in the name Common for the Database

7. Select the Data Device, CommonData, you created in the step above to house the Data portion of the data store.

8. Optionally you can also specify that you would like to use the CommonLogs to house the transaction logs from this screen.

9. Press Create Now

Here are the steps you need to follow to create this database in SQL Server 7.0:

1. Open Enterprise Manager

2. Assuming you already have a server registered, expand the server to you can see the array of folders

3. Right-click in the Databases folder and select New Database...

4. This dialog allows you to set up the databases properties. Enter a name of Common, and set the Initial size to 10 MB. This also sets up a Log database automatically for you; flip to the Transaction Log tab to see it

5. Click OK

6. SQL Server 7.0 goes away and creates your database for you

Finally, here are the steps you need to follow to create an ODBC connection on your workstation to point to that database:

1. Open the Control Panel

2. Double-click the ODBC Data Sources (32 bit) icon

3. Select the tab that says System DSN

4. Press the Add button this will bring up a dialog box with list of possible drivers

5. Select SQL Server from the list of drivers

6. Press Finish

7. Another dialog will be presented, enter a Name for the Data Source: "Common"

8. Enter a Description for the Data Source: "Common ODBC Connection"

9. Select the appropriate SQL Server from the list of Servers. If you are using a SQL Server installed on your workstation, select [local]

10. Provide a Valid User Account and password. For the examples in this book, I assume that you are using the system administrator, "sa", account with no password.

11. Specify the Default Database for this connection as Common

12. Test the connection

The Object Factory

The Object Factory is one of my great joys, and I am both happy and proud to be able to share it with you. In case I didn't make it clear throughout the chapters of this book I love the ideas, concepts, and challenges that we get to work with as developers, but I really hate mundane tasks like typing code into the IDE. The Object Factory is a code generator that I have been working on for, well, it seems like forever. It is *not* perfect, I don't think it ever will be, but it can create all of the files that you would normally need to type to create an ECDO.

The version of the Object Factory that you can download from Wrox is designed to be used with SQL Server 6.5. It will also work on SQL Server 7.0 without modification. I usually use the Common database to house the tables, views, and stored procedures that the Object Factory requires, so this application is expecting the same DSN that we have been using throughout this book. Make sure that you have this ODBC connection available before you start up the application. The first time you run the Object Factory, it will build the tables, views, and stored procedures that it requires for operation.

All you really need to do to use the Object Factory is to select the Create New Object Option from the Main menu. This brings up the Object Wizard. All you really need to do is to follow the steps the Wizard makes available to you:

1. Provide a name for the object you want to build. You do this by typing the name of the object into the text box provided. The Object Wizard will check the name you provided against the existing objects in its data store. For obvious reasons, it will not allow you to have two objects with the same name.

2. Tell the wizard where to put the code. You do this by pointing at a particular directory on your hard drive. The wizard will create the necessary directory structure below this directory.

3. Tell the wizard what kind of object you want to make. Of course the options are Level I, Level II, and 4-Dimensional Data Object.

4. Based upon which kind of object you selected the Object Factory will fill in some required property definitions, e.g. ID, StampID, StampDateTime, etc.

5. Then you define each of the base properties for the data object. This requires that you type a name for each property, select a datatype, and if appropriate provide a value for this property's length or size.

6. Repeat Step 5 for each of the properties your base object requires. If you spend enough time designing your objects, this list should be fairly small. It should represent only those things that are common to all extensions of the base object.

7. When you have entered all your base properties, you will be presented with a list that displays each of the properties you have selected. Make sure that this list is complete. Then press Finish.

8. The Object Factory will create all of the code that you need to build the object you described. This code includes:

   ❑ The Visual Basic code for the User Centric half of the object.

   ❑ The Visual Basic code for the Data Centric half of the object – remember that the DC Object also has the `EstablishDataStore` routine that includes the table definitions, the views, and the stored procedures.

   ❑ At this time, the Object Factory will also provide you with the portion of the Veneer code that handles the mapping between the Veneer and the covered UC Object. By default, I just map all of the properties, methods, and events directly. You can remove or modify these as necessary.

   ❑ This step is to remind you to make a copy of the Veneer before you make any changes to it. Remember from Chapter 14, that you can expose a Veneer for each different extension of a 4-Dimensional Data objects. Sorry but I had to stop short of supplying the business rules in the Veneers.

      ❑ The Object Factory will make write the code for 3 different types of User Interfaces:

      ❑ The Standard Visual Basic interface

      ❑ An ASP over DHTML interface

      ❑ The Heavy Interface code we looked at in Chapter 16.

Once you have created at least two base objects, you can also use the Object Factory to write the code for the Connector objects you will need manage the relationships between the objects. To do that, select the **Create Connector Object** option from the **Main** menu. This will bring up, you guessed it, the **Connector Object Wizard**. To create a Connector Object, follow these steps:

1. Select a location for the code

2. Select the first object you need to connect from the list of available objects

3. Select the second object you need to connect from the list of available objects

4. The Object Factory will create a name for the Connector object based upon the names of the two objects you selected earlier

5. Press **Finish**

6. The Object Factory will create all of the code that you need to build the Connector object you described. This code includes:

   ❑ The Visual Basic code for the User Centric half of the object

   ❑ The Visual Basic code for the Data Centric half of the object – remember that the DC Object also has the `EstablishDataStore` routine that includes the table definitions, the views, and the stored procedures.

   ❑ At this time, the Object Factory will also provide you with the portion of the Veneer code that handles the mapping between the Veneer and the covered UC Object. By default, I just map all of the properties, methods, and events directly. You can remove or modify these as necessary.

   ❑ This step is to remind you to make a copy of the Veneer before you make any changes to it. Remember from Chapter 14, that you can expose a veneer for each different extension of a 4 Dimensional Data objects. Sorry but I had to stop short of supplying the business rules in the Veneers.

     ❑ The Object Factory will make write the code for 3 different types of User Interfaces

     ❑ The Standard Visual Basic interface

     ❑ An ASP over DHTML interface

     ❑ The Heavy Interface code we looked at in Chapter 16.

I know that we didn't talk about building interfaces for Connector objects. That is because we don't normally use them for production purposes. Generally, we use these interfaces to test the underlying Connector object. As an aside, the raw code in them also comes in handy for making a special kind of interface I call an Assignment interface. You can think about this kind of interface as something similar to the Property Control Set Form we used in the Property Bag Administrative User Interface. Remember that we had one list of available properties in a list box on the left and a list view on the right that we could use to assign the property definitions to the list box items. If you think about it, the act of dragging something from an available list box to a listview container is an excellent metaphor for inserting a relationship into the database. Of course, removing an object from the list view and having that object return to the list box is comparable to deleting a relationship from the database.

There are a few other options available on the menu. You can

- ❑ Modify an existing object definition
- ❑ Create new object code for an existing definition
- ❑ Create a new set of Veneer code for an existing object definition
- ❑ Create a new set of Visual Basic interface code for an existing object definition
- ❑ Create a new set of Heavy ASP for an existing object.

> **BE WARNED!** If you create new code for an object that already has code, the Object Factory will write over the existing code in the directory. If you have modified the code and you wish to preserve those modifications, you will need to move the code to a save place before you use the **Create New Object** code option. You should only choose this option if you don't need to preserve your changes or if you want to start over.

B

Some Additional Considerations

OLAP

When I created the original outline for this book, I set aside one-third of the book to discuss the concepts concerning the OLTP half of the architecture; one-third to discuss the concepts concerning the OLAP half of the architecture; and one-third to consider the deployment of applications, which bridged the other halves. As you can see, we were really only able to really consider the OLTP half of the system in any level of detail.

We were able to get some sense about some of the deployment options available to us using distributed architecture, but we really only scratched the surface of this topic. My biggest disappointment is that we didn't have time or space to consider the OLAP half of our Distributed Application Architecture. At this minute, the only thing we really know about OLAP or DSS is that it is important, is has something to do with the concept of a Data Warehouse, and that it is one of the two major processing divisions.

As far as my own personal interests go, I think that the OLAP half of the system is by far the more interesting half. It houses a summary of all of the data our OLTP system has collected over the course of doing business. While it is true that the OLTP view of the data in our system is a rich store of information, this information is stored in a manner that makes it difficult for anyone, even those individuals that claim to understand the entirety of an enterprise's data store, to be able to get a global view of the enterprise's data. The OLAP system on the other hand is designed with this as its primary purpose. If I were to compare the two, I think that I might have to say that OLTP is like knowing how to write a couple of functions, while OLAP is more like understanding the reasons behind why we might need to write a couple of functions. While I was writing this book, I almost considered adding a chapter or at least some examples of OLAP objects to the book. At this minute I am glad that I didn't. The topic is far too important to be treated so lightly.

At the present time, it appears that Microsoft has finally decided that OLAP is as important as OLTP. SQL Server 7.0 has been given a host of new capabilities that are designed to address issues directly related to OLAP. In practice, I have addressed the OLAP half of Enterprise Architecture with the same attention to detail that we gave to the OLTP half in this book. This treatment has evolved into complimentary set of objects that are designed to handle the OLAP half of the system. As you might expect, the OLAP objects have essentially the same distributed design that utilizes the three center spheres of the enterprise. If you liked what we did in this book, keep an eye out for my next one. I didn't forget the OLAP, I just want to give it the attention it deserves.

Organizational Overview

I have saved the organizational overview for last on purpose. The physical and the programming design really just spoke about the same thing from two different perspectives. In fact, the final system design that came about in each section really mirrored the other design perfectly. This is important. In order for an overall system to work well, each of the pieces in that system must be constructed solidly and be designed to compliment the system as a whole. It is easy to design systems with things like hardware and software, but unfortunately that is really only a part of the problem. Organizations also need to know how to line up their resources (talented people) in a manner that makes it easy for them to build and manage a distributed system. That is what this section is about.

Management 101 – Let's Apprise the Current Situation

I hate to oversimplify our jobs but if you cut away all of the bologna, basically what we do is to accept some information from some users and safeguard that information until the users need it again. Sure there are an infinite number of ways that we can approach this problem and we might perform a few calculations here and there, but if you really think about it, our customers want to be able to trust us to safeguard their data. Keep this in mind.

Over about the past 15 or so years, PC development started as something of a sideline for most good-sized organizations. Over time, management learned that they could count on these energetic groups of developers to construct decent solutions to complex problems in a relatively short period of time. Of course, due to the limitations of their equipment (*both hardware and operating system*), these solutions were typically targeted at small user groups. In most organizations, this (*equipment forced*) fragmentation lead to the development of an organizational structure that consisted of a large number of small development teams with each team responsible to some small number of users. This organizational structure held some promise. It was reasonable to think that if we had many small teams of developers, that these teams could mobilize and act quickly to serve the needs of the IT department's customers.

This part of the theory is wonderful. The ability to mobilize quickly and stretch to meet the customer's wants and needs should be the badge of a good development team. However as the demands placed upon PC based development teams increase, this organizational structure makes the original promise more and more difficult to fulfill. It is quite a different thing to develop an application intended for 2, 3 or 10 users than it is to develop an Enterprise Caliber application that can be used throughout an organization by thousands of users. To give you a sense of the problem, consider this book. It probably has something like seven or eight hundred pages of fairly complex information. Yet this book represents only about a third of the elements that must be considered when delivering an enterprise caliber installation – the decision support service (DSS) and overall deployment issues could easily consume two more books of at least the same size and depth.

What that means is that the small teams at the extremities of an organization that should be responding to the customer's every whim are instead treading water to keep up with the swiftly changing currents in the information technology industry. As a tribute to their ingenuity and capability, most of the teams still manage to get something out the door and on to the customers' desks more or less on schedule. The trouble is that in order to do that each team, or more than likely one or two individuals within a team, has probably concocted some brilliant, but virtually irreproducible technique to satisfy the demands made upon the team. These guys get their juice as gurus and miracle workers of the team. Unfortunately, they are performing these *miracles* in a vacuum. Sadly, there is probably a better than average chance that some team down the hall or in a different building has already solved the same problem before using a completely different technique.

> *I don't want you to miss this point. This means that there two, or more, different copies of code that must be understood and maintained separately.*

Unfortunately, in most organizations the teams operate almost ignorant of the other teams' existence, there is no way for these guys to know that the problem has been solved. So they just tough it out, take whatever joy they can in recreating the wheel, and roll a product out the door. This is not a manageable process, and it doesn't have to be like this.

Let me give you a thought problem to bring this conversation down to earth. How long do you think a company like McDonalds® would remain in business if every restaurant had their own *unique* recipe cooking and selling hamburgers?

Imagine it, instead of the golden arches, I guess that some restaurant might be sporting silver Ws. I'm sure that each restaurant would have its own special menu. Maybe some of the restaurant wouldn't even sell hamburgers. And of course, each store would set its own prices. I can see it now, designer gourmet hamburgers from renegade McDonalds franchises selling at ten times the going price for a Big Mac. If this discourse sounds ridiculous, GOOD! It is intended to make a point.

> **We are in the business of building information systems – systems that impact lives and drive the economy – but we attempt to perform that monumental task with an organizational structure that a smart company like McDonalds wouldn't apply to the task of making a hamburger.**

What McDonalds has learned, or maybe has accepted, is that it is possible to create a methodical system for the delivery of hamburgers. I don't mean to single out McDonalds; Wal★Mart® has arrived at essentially the same conclusion for the retail industry and I am sure you can think of plenty of your own high-quality company examples as well.

> **What these companies have in common is that they have a standardized technique for everything right up to the point of contact with the customer.**

They have created an environment, which allows the individuals that do contact the customer to be able to focus all of their energies *on that customer*. The point is that the guy or girl at the McDonalds' delivery counter probably doesn't need to think about things like the average weight of cattle on the hoof in Texas in during the month of June. And, one of the reasons the person in the CD department in Wal★Mart can give you all of her attention is because she isn't currently involved with negotiating the purchase of 1,000,000 cases of Lucky Charms or Corn Flakes with a major breakfast food distributor.

These successful companies execute so well at the extremities because they operate from a central core of quality that radiates outward. They do not count on, or demand that a customer service specialist understand every facet of the organization. Rather than the organization depending upon the individual at the customer interface for all of its needs, the organization is poised to support that individual.

Once again, we are creating information systems, not making hamburgers. So we can never expect that our teams, exposed to the customers, will ever be able to just follow a 95% pre-defined set of rules, but we can make their jobs a little easier by creating a central core of quality that they can count on for support. Just imagine how much happier your customers would be if you could take the gurus or wizards that you do have and allow them to devote 50% more of their time to the customer's real concerns. This is possible. It requires that your organization build a core of quality in its IT department.

Management 101 – Quality Core Solution

The key to building a quality core for an IT department is simple to state:

> **Write fewer lines of higher quality code.**

Of course this is a lot easier to say than it is to execute. This is especially true if we have an organizational structure that demands that each team make the long journey all the way from the user's screens to the database alone each and every time. What we need is an organizational structure that makes possible to write fewer lines of higher quality code.

This type of organizational structure still has teams dedicated to the users needs, but, in this case, instead of each of the teams making redundant journeys from the user's screen all the way to database each of the teams meet a core team someplace between the clients machines and the database. This technical / organizational structure allows the teams to operate more like participants in a relay race rather than like sprinters or marathon runners.

Think about the difference. I know that it's subtle, but try to imagine what real effect a sprinter's manager has on the events that occur during the actual race. Now imagine how much effect the same manager might have on the results of a relay race. With the sprint, once the race is on, all the manager can do is to hope and have faith. Everything depends upon the legs of the runner. Contrast this with a relay race, the end result of this race is not dependent upon any single sprinter. The end result is a true team effort that depends not only upon the strength and endurance of the athletes but also bends to meet efforts to manage or allocate resources.

This organizational structure will not be too unusual to most IT departments. I think that most of them actually believe that they have accomplished essentially the same thing when they divided the development and database administration DBA teams. Nothing could be further from the truth. But, once again the difference is a subtle one. Good DBAs believe that they are doing their job if they hold the third-normal-form (3NF) line. Typically, the relationship between developers and DBAs is that the DBAs build the database structures according to solid design (3NF) principles. Then they leave it to the developers to make some sense out of the resulting knot of tables. In this organizational structure, the core object team actually consists of both DBAs and developers who work together to create data objects, ECDOs, that can both meet the 3NF requirements while simultaneously freeing the developers from the requirement to understand the reasoning behind the DBAs devotion to 3NF.

Generally, the organizational structure calls for the creation of one core team that we call the Core Object Team. This team handles the flow of information into and out of the data store(s). It does the by creating the Data Object "programs" that we learnt about in this book. In order to create a data object, the members of this team must posses a command of both database design principles and solid programming skills. Ideally, this team should consist of both developers and DBAs.

If the organization is large enough, it is probably an excellent idea to create another team(s) that is responsible for turning the data objects into applications by creating veneers that contain the indispensable business rules. This team does need to possess excellent programming skills, but it is not necessary for this team to be proficient in database design or database management.

The last set of teams that we need to consider are the user interface teams. These teams require individuals that are capable of delivering good solid user interfaces. They should have excellent communication skills and really should act as project managers or analysts. They should be able to understand the user's needs and pass that information onto the application development or object development teams as required. They should be able to count on the application development or object development teams to provide them with the rock solid building blocks they need to address the customers' needs.

{831FDD16-0C5C-1...

Form frmPropNameControl...

Style = 3 'Fixed Dial...

= "Properties for...

eight = 4845

ft = 45

p = 330

dth = 11460

c = "Form1"

ton = 0 'False

d = -1 'True

on = 0 'False

ight = 4845

dth = 11460

askbar = 0 'False

Person
Base Properties

ID
Last Name
First Name
Middle Name
Birth Date
Sex

Object Type Definitions

Employee OTD	Lawyer OTD	Engineer OTD	Doctor OTD	Student OTD
Salary	Specialty	Specialty	Specialty	Major
Project	Hourly Rate	Experience	Certification	Minor
Property 3	Law School	Property 3	Property 3	Year
Property 4	Property 4	Property 4	Property 4	Property 4
Property 5	Property 5	Property 5	Property 5	Property 5
Property 6	Property 6	Property 6	Property 6	Property 6
Property 7	Property 7	Property 7	Property 7	Property 7
Property 8	Property 8	Property 8	Property 8	Property 8
Property 9	Property 9	Property 9	Property 9	Property 9
Property 10	Property 10	Property 10	Property 10	Property 10

Object Ty...

Property Set Definitions

Property Se...

Additional Code

The ErrorHandler Routine

The error handling routine we use in ECDOs actually makes use of the *ErrCond* ECDO you built way back in Chapter 6. Here are the two blocks of code that you need to write to use the *ErrCond* object as an error-recording device.

The first block of code is placed within the routine that might cause the error. In the example below, we are calling the ErrorHandler from the PersonListForm's Form_Load routine. Notice that we pass the enough information into the ErrorHandler so that we can identify the cause of the error right to the individual routine. I guess we could have taken this a step further and tried to determine the line that each error occurred on, but most of the routines we use are so short that this gives us a good indication of the source of the error:

```
PersonListForm_LoadError:

    ErrorHandler lngAppID, Err.Number, "Presentation", Err.Description, _
            "frmPersonList.frm", "Form_Load", UserLogon
End Sub
```

The call above invokes this routine which instantiates an *ErrCond* object, fills its properties, and inserts that information about the error into the data store:

```
Public Sub ErrorHandler(lngApplicationID As Long, lngErrorNumber As Long, _
                    strSystemTier As String, strErrorDescription As _
                    String, strCodeModuleName As String, _
                    strCodeBlockName As String, strUserLogon As String)

    On Error Resume Next

    Dim ThisError As UCErrCond.clsErrCond
```

```
Set ThisError = New UCErrCond.clsErrCond

ThisError.SetDataSource "Common"
ThisError.ApplicationID = lngApplicationID
ThisError.ErrorID = lngErrorNumber
ThisError.SystemTier = strSystemTier
ThisError.ErrorDescription = strErrorDescription
ThisError.CodeModuleName = strCodeModuleName '
ThisError.CodeBlockName = strCodeBlockName
ThisError.AvailableDiskSpace = ThisError.GetAvailableDiskSpace
ThisError.AvailableMemory = ThisError.GetAvailableMemory

If Len(strUserLogon) > 0 Then
    ThisError.UserID = strUserLogon
Else
    strUserLogon = ThisError.GetThisUserName
    ThisError.UserID = strUserLogon
End If

ThisError.ComputerID = ThisError.GetThisComputerName
ThisError.StampUser = strUserLogon
ThisError.ErrorTime = Now()
ThisError.ObjectInsert

Set ThisError = Nothing

End Sub
```

The PropBag Helper Object's Code

In Chapter 12, we mentioned that the PropBag object has 4 helper manager classes. The code for them is very straightforward:

clsPropBagMgr

```
Option Explicit
```

```
'local variable(s) to hold property value(s)
Private mvarID As Long, mvarOwnerID As Long, mvarPropertyID As Long
Private mvarValue As String, mvarUpdateInstruction As String, mvarTypeID As Long
Private mvarPropertyName As String, mvarDataTypeID As Long
Private mvarDataTypeName As String, mvarListAvailable As String
Private mvarDisplayOrder As Long, mvarAccessLevel As String
Private mvarSecurityLevel As Long
```

```
Public Property Let SecurityLevel(ByVal vData As Long)
    mvarSecurityLevel = vData
End Property
```

```
Public Property Get SecurityLevel() As Long
    SecurityLevel = mvarSecurityLevel
End Property
```

```
Public Property Let AccessLevel(ByVal vData As String)
  mvarAccessLevel = vData
End Property

Public Property Get AccessLevel() As String
  AccessLevel = mvarAccessLevel
End Property

Public Property Let DisplayOrder(ByVal vData As Long)
  mvarDisplayOrder = vData
End Property

Public Property Get DisplayOrder() As Long
  DisplayOrder = mvarDisplayOrder
End Property

Public Property Let ListAvailable(ByVal vData As String)
  mvarListAvailable = vData
End Property

Public Property Get ListAvailable() As String
  ListAvailable = mvarListAvailable
End Property

Public Property Let DataTypeName(ByVal vData As String)
  mvarDataTypeName = vData
End Property

Public Property Get DataTypeName() As String
  DataTypeName = mvarDataTypeName
End Property

Public Property Let DataTypeID(ByVal vData As Long)
  mvarDataTypeID = vData
End Property

Public Property Get DataTypeID() As Long
  DataTypeID = mvarDataTypeID
End Property

Public Property Let PropertyName(ByVal vData As String)
  mvarPropertyName = vData
End Property

Public Property Get PropertyName() As String
  PropertyName = mvarPropertyName
End Property

Public Property Let TypeID(ByVal vData As Long)
  mvarTypeID = vData
End Property

Public Property Get TypeID() As Long
    TypeID = mvarTypeID
End Property

Public Property Let UpdateInstruction(ByVal vData As String)
    mvarUpdateInstruction = vData
End Property
```

```vb
Public Property Get UpdateInstruction() As String
  UpdateInstruction = mvarUpdateInstruction
End Property


Public Property Let Value(ByVal vData As String)
  mvarValue = vData
End Property


Public Property Get Value() As String
  Value = mvarValue
End Property


Public Property Let PropertyID(ByVal vData As Long)
  mvarPropertyID = vData
End Property


Public Property Get PropertyID() As Long
  PropertyID = mvarPropertyID
End Property


Public Property Let OwnerID(ByVal vData As Long)
  mvarOwnerID = vData
End Property


Public Property Get OwnerID() As Long
  OwnerID = mvarOwnerID
End Property


Public Property Let ID(ByVal vData As Long)
  mvarID = vData
End Property


Public Property Get ID() As Long
  ID = mvarID
End Property
```

colPropBagMgr

```vb
Option Explicit


Private mCol As Collection


Public Function Add(ID As Long, OwnerID As Long, PropertyID As Long, _
              Value As String, UpdateInstruction As String, _
              TypeID As Long, PropertyName As String, _
              DataTypeID As Long, DataTypeName As String, _
              ListAvailable As String, DisplayOrder As Long, _
              AccessLevel As String, SecurityLevel As Long, _
              Optional sKey As String) As clsPropBag

' Create a new object
  Dim objNewMember As clsPropBag
  Set objNewMember = New clsPropBag
```

```vb
    ' Set the properties passed into the method
    objNewMember.ID = ID
    objNewMember.OwnerID = OwnerID
    objNewMember.PropertyID = PropertyID
    objNewMember.Value = Value
    objNewMember.UpdateInstruction = UpdateInstruction
    objNewMember.TypeID = TypeID
    objNewMember.PropertyName = PropertyName
    objNewMember.DataTypeID = DataTypeID
    objNewMember.DataTypeName = DataTypeName
    objNewMember.ListAvailable = ListAvailable
    objNewMember.DisplayOrder = DisplayOrder
    objNewMember.AccessLevel = AccessLevel
    objNewMember.SecurityLevel = SecurityLevel

    If Len(sKey) = 0 Then
       mCol.Add objNewMember
    Else
       mCol.Add objNewMember, sKey
    End If

    ' Return the object created
    Set Add = objNewMember
    Set objNewMember = Nothing

End Function
```

```vb
Public Property Get Item(vntIndexKey As Variant) As clsPropBag
    Set Item = mCol(vntIndexKey)
End Property
```

```vb
Public Property Get Count() As Long
    Count = mCol.Count
End Property
```

```vb
Public Sub Remove(vntIndexKey As Variant)
    mCol.Remove vntIndexKey
End Sub
```

```vb
Public Property Get NewEnum() As IUnknown
    Set NewEnum = mCol.[_NewEnum]
End Property
```

```vb
Private Sub Class_Initialize()
    Set mCol = New Collection
End Sub
```

```vb
Private Sub Class_Terminate()
    Set mCol = Nothing
End Sub
```

clsPropValueMgr

```
Option Explicit

Private mvarID As Long, mvarPropertyID As Long, mvarUpdateInstruction As String
Private mvarOwnerID As Long, mvarDelete As Boolean, mvarValue As String

Public Property Let Value(ByVal vData As String)
  mvarValue = vData
End Property

Public Property Get Value() As String
  Value = mvarValue
End Property

Public Property Let Delete(ByVal vData As Boolean)
  mvarDelete = vData
End Property

Public Property Get Delete() As Boolean
  Delete = mvarDelete
End Property

Public Property Let OwnerID(ByVal vData As Long)
  mvarOwnerID = vData
End Property

Public Property Get OwnerID() As Long
  OwnerID = mvarOwnerID
End Property

Public Property Let UpdateInstruction(ByVal vData As String)
  mvarUpdateInstruction = vData
End Property

Public Property Get UpdateInstruction() As String
  UpdateInstruction = mvarUpdateInstruction
End Property

Public Property Let PropertyID(ByVal vData As Long)
  mvarPropertyID = vData
End Property

Public Property Get PropertyID() As Long
  PropertyID = mvarPropertyID
End Property

Public Property Let ID(ByVal vData As Long)
  mvarID = vData
End Property

Public Property Get ID() As Long
  ID = mvarID
End Property
```

colPropValueMgr

```
Option Explicit

Private mCol As Collection

Public Function Add(ID As Long, PropertyID As Long, _
                    UpdateInstruction As String, OwnerID As Long, _
                    Delete As Boolean, Value As String, _
                    Optional sKey As String) As clsPropValue

' Create a new object
  Dim objNewMember As clsPropValue
  Set objNewMember = New clsPropValue

' Set the properties passed into the method
  objNewMember.ID = ID
  objNewMember.PropertyID = PropertyID
  objNewMember.UpdateInstruction = UpdateInstruction
  objNewMember.OwnerID = OwnerID
  objNewMember.Delete = Delete
  objNewMember.Value = Value

  If Len(sKey) = 0 Then
     mCol.Add objNewMember
  Else
     mCol.Add objNewMember, sKey
  End If

  Set Add = objNewMember
  Set objNewMember = Nothing

End Function

Public Property Get Item(vntIndexKey As Variant) As clsPropValue
  Set Item = mCol(vntIndexKey)
End Property

Public Property Get Count() As Long
  Count = mCol.Count
End Property

Public Sub Remove(vntIndexKey As Variant)
  mCol.Remove vntIndexKey
End Sub

Public Property Get NewEnum() As IUnknown
  Set NewEnum = mCol.[_NewEnum]
End Property

Private Sub Class_Initialize()
  Set mCol = New Collection
End Sub

Private Sub Class_Terminate()
' Destroys collection when this class is terminated
  Set mCol = Nothing
End Sub
```

The Property Bag Veneer Code

The following code is needed to create a Veneer for 4-Dimensional Data Objects. The Object Factory will cut this code for you if you specify that you are developing a 4DDO.

Required for a Level III ECDO

The Properties Function

This routine exposes the underlying data object's Property Bag:

```
Public Property Get Properties() As UCPerson.PersonProperties

   If mobjProperties Is Nothing Then
      Set mobjProperties = CreateObject("UCPerson.PersonProperties")
   End If

   Set Properties = mobjProperties

End Property
```

The TypeName Function

This routine exposes the underlying data object's Type Name. It allows the user interface programmer to determine the Type Name for a Level II or 4DDO object. This routine handles the iteration through the collection of Type Names and returns the correct Type Name as a string:

```
Public Function PersonTypeName(DSN As String, TypeID As Long) As String

   Dim objTypes As UCPerson.colTypes
   Dim objType As UCPerson.clsType

   Set objTypes = CreateObject("UCPerson.colTypes")

   PersonTypeName = ""

   objTypes.SetDataSource DSN
   objTypes.Load

   For Each objType In objTypes
      If objType.ID = TypeID Then
         PersonTypeName = objType.Name
         Exit For
      End If
   Next objType

   Set objType = Nothing
   Set objTypes = Nothing

End Function
```

The LoadProperties Subroutine

This routine is used to load the Property Bag for an object. The only parameters that must be passed
are the data source name and the user logon parameters. The remaining parameters are optional
because we can retrieve this information from the object's local properties. The reason we have
supplied these optional parameters is so that we can use a shortcut when necessary. In other words, if
we already had a person's ID and TypeID, we could load the properties for that person without
having to load the *Person* object as well. We don't use this functionality too often when we are
creating user interfaces with tools like VB, but we use this technique frequently when we are
developing ASP applications. Notice that this routine uses the `Properties` property we created
earlier rather than directly referencing the underlying data object:

```
Public Sub LoadProperties(DSN As String, UserLogon As String, Optional PersonID _
                       As Variant, Optional PersonTypeID As Variant)

   Dim lngPersonID As Long
   Dim lngPersonTypeID As Long

   If Not IsMissing(PersonID) And Not IsMissing(PersonTypeID) Then
      lngPersonID = Clng(PersonID)
      lngPersonTypeID = Clng(PersonTypeID)
      Properties.Load DSN, UserLogon, lngPersonID, lngPersonTypeID
   Else
      Properties.Load DSN, UserLogon, ID, TypeID
   End If

End Sub
```

The PropertyNames Subroutine

This routine is used to load the Property Names for an object. This function has been provided to
give the user interface programmer the ability to retrieve a list of names for a particular object type in
a dynamic fashion. It helps the user interface programmer to design interfaces that are flexible by
nature.

```
Public Function PropertyNames(DSN As String, TypeID As Long) As _
       UCPerson.PropertyNames

   Dim colPropNames As UCPerson.colPropNames
   Dim objPropName As UCPerson.clsPropName
   Dim objPropertyName As UCPerson.PropertyName

   Set colPropNames = CreateObject("UCPerson.colPropNames")
   Set PropertyNames = CreateObject("UCPerson.PropertyNames")

   colPropNames.SetDataSource DSN
   colPropNames.Load TypeID

   For Each objPropName In colPropNames
      PropertyNames.Add objPropName.ID, objPropName.PropertyName
   Next objPropName

End Function
```

Additional Required Properties for all Level II or Level III ECDOs

These properties must be managed internally by the Veneer or exposed to the user interface programmer when the underlying ECDO uses an Object Type Definition:

```
Public Property Let TypeID(lngTypeID As Long)

  mobjUCObject.TypeID = lngTypeID

End Property
```

```
Public Property Get TypeID() As Long

  mobjTypeID = UCObject.TypeID

End Property
```

```
Public Property Let TypeName(strTypeName As String)

  mobjUCObject.TypeName = strTypeName

End Property
```

```
Public Property Get TypeName() As String

  mobjTypeName = UCObject.TypeName

End Property
```

```
Public Property Let KeyPrefix(strKeyPrefix As String)

  mobjUCObject.KeyPrefix = strKeyPrefix

End Property
```

```
Public Property Get KeyPrefix() As String

  mobjKeyPrefix = UCObject.KeyPrefix

End Property
```

{831FDD16-0C5C-1...2-A3...

Form frmPropNameCon...

Style   =   3 'Fixed Dial...

              =   "Properties for...

...eight   =   4845

...eft   =   45

...p   =   330

...dth   =   11460

...c   =   "Form1"

...ton   =   0   'False

...d   =   -1 'True

...con   =   0   'False

...eight   =   4845

...dth   =   11460

...askbar   =   0   'False

Person
Base Properties

ID
Last Name
First Name
Middle Name
Birth Date
Sex

Student Type Definitions

Object

Salesman OTD	Lower OTD	Engineer OTD	Doctor OTD	Student OTD
Quota	Specialty	Specialty	Specialty	Major
Region	Hourly Rate	Experience	Certification	Minor
Territory	Law School	Property 3	Property 3	Year
Property 4	Property 4	Property 4	Property 4	Property 4
Property 5	Property 5	Property 5	Property 5	Property 5
Property 6	Property 6	Property 6	Property 6	Property 6
Property 7	Property 7	Property 7	Property 7	Property 7
Property 8	Property 8	Property 8	Property 8	Property 8
Property 9	Property 9	Property 9	Property 9	Property 9
Property 10	Property 10	Property 10	Property 10	Property 10

Property Set Definitions

Property 8...

Index

Index

Index

Index

Index

Index

Index

Index

Index

Index

Index

Index

Index

Index

Index

Index

Index

Index

Index

Index

Index

Index

Index

Index

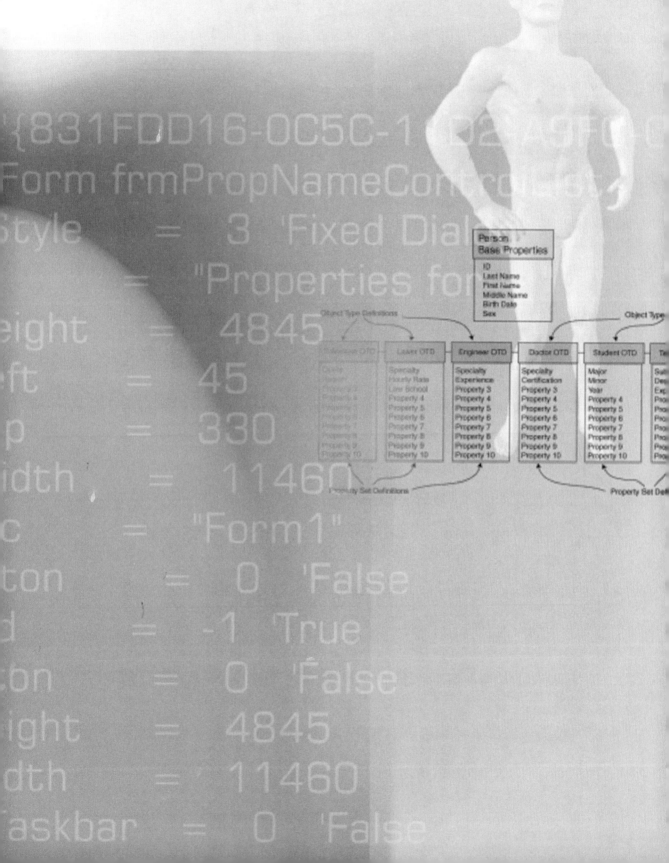

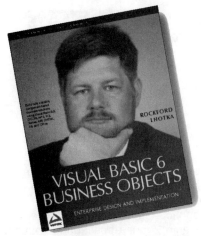

Visual Basic 6 Business Objects

Authors: Rockford Lhotka
ISBN: 186100107X
Price: $59.99 C$89.95 £55.99

This book is about the design of business software with Visual Basic 6.0, following my object-oriented philosophy and incorporating DCOM and MTS. I demonstrate my component-based, scalable logical architecture that allows business code to be reused. My architecture allows different UIs and back-end databases to be added as circumstances dictate, with minimum disruption to your core business code. Over the course of the book, we'll create and implement a fully-worked example to demonstrate my architecture in a solid object model. Along the way, I'll cover the specific techniques that make this whole concept work efficiently in the Visual Basic environment. In addition, I'll demonstrate how my general architectural techniques can apply equally well to all development - whether it be for single-tier, multi-tier or Internet-based applications.

This book is aimed at experienced Windows application developers. It assumes you know how to program with Visual Basic, but takes the time to cover version 6.0 innovations and issues. I also provide coverage of the server technologies DCOM, MTS, IIS, DHTML, and ASP.

What does this book cover?
- Defining and using business objects
- Designing business objects using Visual Basic
- Creating component-based applications in Visual Basic 6
- How business objects can make UI design more flexible
- Using scalable database access - ADO and OLE DB
- How to use DCOM to full advantage in a client-server connection
- Adding transaction support with MTS and SQL Server
- Packaging up code for client distribution
- Building the 'VideoStore' example to illustrate my theory in action

UML (Unified Modeling Language) provides a powerful and comprehensive way for us to design and develop our Visual Basic projects. In this book, I'll show you how you can use UML to make well-designed, successful Visual Basic applications. This book covers much more than just designing your applications though: it goes on to show you how to directly implement UML designs in Visual Basic. A comprehensive VB to UML mapping is supplied at the end of the book.

We'll build a functional three-tier distributed application in Visual Basic. By the time you get to the last chapter, you'll have the foundation of a working, re-usable Visual Basic Enterprise framework. I will not only show you how to design this framework using UML, but also how to turn your UML design into Visual Basic code. You'll also see how you can build VB projects using patterns. With this practical example, we'll see the enormous benefits of taking the time to design our projects with UML.

Who is this book for?
This book is aimed at Visual Basic 6 developers who want to learn how to use UML. It assumes that you know how to program in Visual Basic, and provides a working overview of ADO, RDS and MTS.

What does this book cover?
• All the stages of the UML design and development process
• How UML applies to Visual Basic programming
• A comprehensive mapping of UML to VB code
• A guide to building three-tier DNA applications
• Uses ADO, RDS and MTS with Visual Basic
• How to determine your user requirements
• Use Cases, Interaction diagrams and Class diagrams
• Activity diagrams: defining your system processes
• A fully working DNA application written in VB

ASP Today

www.**asp**today.com

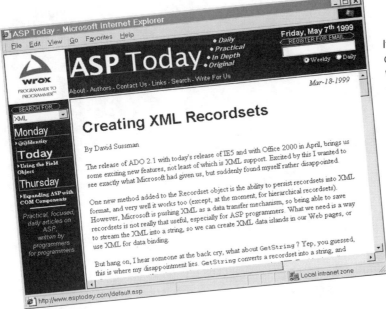

It's not easy keeping up to date with what's hot and what's not in the ever-changing world of internet development. Even if you confine yourself to one topic like ASP, trawling through the mailing lists each day to find new and better code is still a full time job. Expand your focus to include ASP's related server-side technologies and certain bionic qualities are required. And so to us...

You may already be familiar with Wrox Press from its series of books on ASP and other web development technologies. Despite this coverage we recognize that books alone cannot chart the changes inherent in this industry; ASP Today seeks to remedy this situation. Simply pop in for a look at www.asptoday.com and every weekday you'll find brand new tips, tricks and techniques for you to try and test out in your development. Whether you want to develop components, pull images from a database or find out more about ADO, RDS, Web Security, Site Server or XML to name but a few things, just log in each day to learn something new.

We hope that you won't be shy in telling us what you think of the site and the content we've put on it either. Our archive of material is fully searchable, but if you think we're missing something, then we'll address it accordingly. If you've got something to write, then do so and we'll include it. We want our site to be a global effort by and for the entire ASP community and it would seem 5,000 people a day support the idea.

See you online,
Dan Maharry, ASPToday.com

wrox

PROGRAMMER TO PROGRAMMER™

Wrox writes books for you. Any suggestions, or ideas about how you want information given in your ideal book will be studied by our team. Your comments are always valued at Wrox.

Free phone in USA 800-USE-WROX
Fax (312) 397 8990

UK Tel. (0121) 687 4100   Fax (0121) 687 4101

Enterprise Application Architecture - Registration Card

Name _____

Address _____

_____

_____

_____

City _____ State/Region _____

Country _____ Postcode/Zip _____

E-mail _____

Occupation _____

How did you hear about this book? _____

☐ Book review (name) _____

☐ Advertisement (name) _____

☐ Recommendation _____

☐ Catalog _____

☐ Other _____

Where did you buy this book? _____

☐ Bookstore (name) _____ City _____

☐ Computer Store (name) _____

☐ Mail Order _____

☐ Other _____

What influenced you in the purchase of this book?

☐ Cover Design
☐ Contents
☐ Other (please specify) _____

How did you rate the overall contents of this book?

☐ Excellent   ☐ Good
☐ Average   ☐ Poor

What did you find most useful about this book? _____

What did you find least useful about this book? _____

Please add any additional comments. _____

What other subjects will you buy a computer book on soon? _____

What is the best computer book you have used this year? _____

Note: This information will only be used to keep you updated about new Wrox Press titles and will not be used for any other purpose or passed to any other third party.

Check here if you DO NOT want to receive support for this book ☐

wrox

PROGRAMMER TO PROGRAMMER™

NB. If you post the bounce back card below in the UK, please send it to:

Wrox Press Ltd., Arden House, 1102 Warwick Road,
Acocks Green, Birmingham B27 6BH. UK.

——— *Computer Book Publishers* ———

ASP Today

www.**asp**today.com

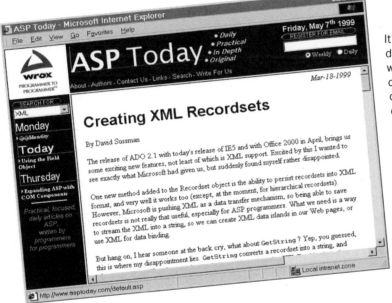

It's not easy keeping up to date with what's hot and what's not in the ever-changing world of internet development. Even if you confine yourself to one topic like ASP, trawling through the mailing lists each day to find new and better code is still a full time job. Expand your focus to include ASP's related server-side technologies and certain bionic qualities are required. And so to us...

You may already be familiar with Wrox Press from its series of books on ASP and other web development technologies. Despite this coverage we recognize that books alone cannot chart the changes inherent in this industry; ASP Today seeks to remedy this situation. Simply pop in for a look at www.asptoday.com and every weekday you'll find brand new tips, tricks and techniques for you to try and test out in your development. Whether you want to develop components, pull images from a database or find out more about ADO, RDS, Web Security, Site Server or XML to name but a few things, just log in each day to learn something new.

We hope that you won't be shy in telling us what you think of the site and the content we've put on it either. Our archive of material is fully searchable, but if you think we're missing something, then we'll address it accordingly. If you've got something to write, then do so and we'll include it. We want our site to be a global effort by and for the entire ASP community and it would seem 5,000 people a day support the idea.

See you online,
Dan Maharry, ASPToday.com